Executive Functions in Health and Disease

Executive Functions in Health and Disease

Edited by

Elkhonon Goldberg
New York University School of Medicine
New York, NY, United States

ACADEMIC PRESS
An imprint of Elsevier

Academic Press is an imprint of Elsevier
125 London Wall, London EC2Y 5AS, United Kingdom
525 B Street, Suite 1800, San Diego, CA 92101-4495, United States
50 Hampshire Street, 5th Floor, Cambridge, MA 02139, United States
The Boulevard, Langford Lane, Kidlington, Oxford OX5 1GB, United Kingdom

Notices
Knowledge and best practice in this field are constantly changing. As new research and experience broaden
our understanding, changes in research methods, professional practices, or medical treatment may become
necessary.

Practitioners and researchers must always rely on their own experience and knowledge in evaluating and
using any information, methods, compounds, or experiments described herein. In using such information or
methods they should be mindful of their own safety and the safety of others, including parties for whom they
have a professional responsibility.

To the fullest extent of the law, neither the Publisher nor the authors, contributors, or editors, assume any
liability for any injury and/or damage to persons or property as a matter of products liability, negligence or
otherwise, or from any use or operation of any methods, products, instructions, or ideas contained in the
material herein.

British Library Cataloguing-in-Publication Data
A catalogue record for this book is available from the British Library

Library of Congress Cataloging-in-Publication Data
A catalog record for this book is available from the Library of Congress

ISBN: 978-0-12-803676-1

For Information on all Academic Press publications
visit our website at https://www.elsevier.com/books-and-journals

Working together
to grow libraries in
developing countries

www.elsevier.com • www.bookaid.org

Publisher: Nikki Levy
Acquisition Editor: Nikki Levy
Editorial Project Manager: Barbara Makinster
Production Project Manager: Caroline Johnson
Cover Designer: Matthew Limbert

Typeset by MPS Limited, Chennai, India

Contents

List of Contributors   xv
Preface   xix

Part I
Executive Functions in Health

1. Prefrontal Executive Functions Predict and Preadapt
    Joaquín M. Fuster

    Introduction   3
    The PA Cycle   4
    Executive Attention   7
    Working Memory   10
    Decision-Making   12
    References   15

2. The Cellular Mechanisms of Executive Functions and
    Working Memory: Relevance to Mental Disorders
    Taber C. Lightbourne and Amy F.T. Arnsten

    Introduction   21
    Topography of PFC and Its Relevance to Neuropsychiatric
        Pathology   22
    Dorsolateral Prefrontal Cortex   25
    Physiology and Microcircuitry of Working Memory   26
    Molecular Regulation of dlPFC Representational Circuits   28
    Mechanisms That Weaken dlPFC Network Connections   29
    Mechanisms That Strengthen dlPFC Network Connections   31
    Catecholamine Modulation of Mechanisms That Weaken PFC
        Activity During Uncontrollable Stress   32
    Alpha-2A Noradrenergic Influence: Successful Translation
        Modulation of Mechanisms That Both Weaken and
        Strengthen Firing   33
    Conclusion   34
    Acknowledgments   35
    References   35

3.   Gene Expression in the Frontal Lobe

Željka Krsnik and Goran Sedmak

Introduction	41
Development of Cerebral Neocortex and Circuitry in the Human Fetal Brain	42
Methodological Limitations of Human Transcriptomic Studies	48
Gene Expression in the Cerebral Cortex of the Human Brain	50
Global Gene Expression Patterns in the Cerebral Cortex	50
Specificities of the Human Neocortical Transcriptome During Prenatal Period	52
Specificities of the Human Brain Transcriptome During Postnatal Period	55
Sex-Biased Gene Expression Patterns and Laterality of the Human Brain Transcriptome	57
Noncoding RNAs as a Posttranscriptional Regulators of Gene Expression	58
Transcriptomic Studies as a Tool to Study Evolution of the Human Cerebral Cortex	59
Conclusion	61
The Transcriptome Is Important But Just One Piece in the Puzzle of the Development and Function of Human Frontal Cortex	61
References	62

4.   A Functional Network Perspective on the Role of the Frontal Lobes in Executive Cognition

Adam Hampshire

The Classic Approach to Functional Brain Mapping	71
Probing the Functional Heterogeneity of the Human PFC Using an FMRI Optimized Intradimensional–Extradimensional Switching Paradigm	72
Limitations of Modular Perspectives	75
Response Inhibition and the Inferior Frontal Gyrus	76
A Broader Role for the RIFG in Cognition?	78
Voodoo Neuroimaging Validations of Cognitive Constructs	82
A General Intelligence System Within the Frontal and Parietal Cortices?	84
A Network-Based Fractionation of Human Intelligence	85
Network-Oriented Cognitive Constructs	88
Network Dynamics During Relational Integration	91
Combining Modular and Network Perspectives	94
Functional Network Markers of Neuropathology in Retired NFL Players	96
Conclusion	97
References	100

5.   Neural Network Models of Human Executive Function
      and Decision Making
      Daniel S. Levine

      Introduction: What Are Neural Networks?   105
      Models of Decision Making   107
      Models of the IGT   109
      Models of Other Decision Data and Phenomena   111
      Models of Sequence Learning and Working Memory   113
      Models of Overcoming Habitual Responses   116
      Models of the WCST   116
      Models of the Stroop Test   119
      Models of General Cognitive Control   120
      General Discussion   122
      References   124

6.   Crucial Role of the Prefrontal Cortex in Conscious
      Perception
      Seth Lew and Hakwan Lau

      Early Neuroimaging Evidence of Prefrontal Cortex's Involvement
          in Conscious Perception   129
      The "No-Report" Argument Against PFC's Role in
          Consciousness   129
      Responses to the No-Report Argument   132
      The Argument Based on Lesion Studies   133
      Responses to the "Lesion" Argument   134
      Why Do PFC Lesions Produce Such Subtle Effects?   136
      Implications for Theories of Consciousness   138
      References   139

7.   Neurodevelopment of the Executive Functions
      Layne Kalbfleisch

      Introduction   143
      Defining and Locating Executive Functions   144
      Gray Matter, White Matter, and Executive Function   147
      Influence and Interplay of Internal and External Environmental
          Factors   149
      Understanding How Executive Function Training May Affect
          Learning   151
      References   157
      Further Reading   167

8. **Executive Functions and Neurocognitive Aging**
    R. Nathan Spreng, Leena Shoemaker and Gary R. Turner

    Introduction   169
    Functional Brain Changes and Executive Functioning:
        A Metaanalytic Review   170
    Executive Functions, Brain Activity, and Aging:
        An Updated Metaanalytic Review   172
    Metaanalysis Methods   172
    Creation of Activation Likelihood Estimation (ALE) Maps   173
    Metaanalysis Results   177
    Brain Networks and Executive Functions in Older Adulthood   182
    Aging, Brain Function, and Executive Control: Conclusions
        and Future Directions   187
    References   189

9. **Assessment of Executive Functions in Research**
    Yana Suchy, Madison A. Niermeyer and Rosemary E. Ziemnik

    Conceptualizing Executive Functions in the Research Context   197
    Tools Available for Executive Functions Assessment   199
    Clinical Measures of Executive Functioning   199
    Experimental Measures of Executive Functioning   200
    Self- and Informant-Reports   201
    Challenges and Considerations in Test Selection   202
    Matching the Method to the Population(s) and Research Question(s)   202
    Considering the Appropriateness of Test Norms   204
    Considering Test Reliability   205
    Including Measures of Component Processes and Intelligence   205
    Interpretive Considerations   206
    Impairments Versus Group Differences   206
    Interpretation of Repeat Assessments   207
    Limitations in Interpreting Factor Structures   208
    Recognizing the Difference between Self-report and
        Performance-based Measures   209
    Conclusions   210
    References   210

Part II
Executive Functions in Disease

10. **Cognitive, Emotional, and Behavioral Inflexibility and
    Perseveration in Neuropsychiatric Illness**
    *Daniel S. Weisholtz, John F. Sullivan, Aaron P. Nelson,
    Kirk R. Daffner and David A. Silbersweig*

    Perseveration as a Manifestation of Frontal Lobe Impairment   223

Frontal Lobe Lesions   223
Schizophrenia   225
Perseveration as a Form of Habitual Behavior and
    Frontal–Subcortical Dysfunction   229
Addiction   231
Obsessive Compulsive Disorder and Tourette Syndrome   232
Emotional and Cognitive Perseveration in Disorders
    of Mood and Anxiety With Frontolimbic
    Dysfunction   234
Impaired Fear Extinction in Posttraumatic Stress Disorder   234
Rumination in Generalized Anxiety Disorder   236
Perseveration of Mood and Rumination in Depression   237
Conclusion   240
References   241

11. Functional Neuroimaging of Deficits in Cognitive Control

Melissa-Ann Mackie and Jin Fan

Definition of Cognitive Control   249
Information Theory Approach to Cognitive Control   250
The Cognitive Control Network   252
Cognitive Control Network Deficits in Patient Populations   254
Autism Spectrum Disorder   255
Schizophrenia   262
Depression   267
Common Deficits in the Cognitive Control Network Deficits
    Across the Three Disorders   272
Discussion   273
Appendix A Supplemental Method   279
References   279
Further Reading   294

12. Executive Function in Striatal Disorders

João J. Cerqueira and Nuno Sousa

Anatomical and Functional Organization of the Striatum   301
Executive Dysfunction in Parkinson's Disease   303
Executive Dysfunction in Huntington's Disease   308
Executive Dysfunction in Chronic Stress   309
Final Words   312
References   312

13. **Neurodevelopmental Disorders and the Frontal Lobes**
    Masao Aihara

Introduction	319
Response/Behavior Inhibition	321
Subjects and Methods	321
Differences Between ADHD and Controls	322
Decision-Making	323
Subjects and Methods	323
Differences Between the Frontal Lesion Group and Controls	325
Temporal Integration (An Ability to Organize Reasoning)	326
Subjects and Methods	326
Developmental Changes in Cognitive Reasoning	327
Lesion Study	328
Conclusion	329
Acknowledgments	329
Conflict of Interest	329
References	329

14. **Executive Control and Emerging Behavior in Youth With Tourette's Syndrome**
    Kjell Tore Hovik

Introduction	333
Tourette's Syndrome in Brief	334
Executive Functions in Tourette's Syndrome	335
A Critical Period of Development	336
Many Factors Influence Tic Expression	340
Brain Adaptation and Compensatory Behavior	342
Findings From Research Project Investigating EF and Cognitive Control in TS	343
A Daunting Disorder	348
Clinical Implications	351
Future Research	352
Conclusion	352
References	352

15. **Inside the Triple-Decker: Tourette's Syndrome and Cerebral Hemispheres**
    Kjell Tore Hovik, Merete Øie and Elkhonon Goldberg

The Triple-Decker	363
Subtyping Tourette's Syndrome	365
Methods	366
Participants	366
Ethics Statement	368

Procedure   368
Clinical Questionnaires and Scales   368
Neurocognitive Assessment   368
Test of Fine Motor Dexterity   369
Data Analyses   369
Results   369
TS Versus TDC Sample Comparison   369
TS Subtype Comparison   373
Clinical Diagnosis and Left Versus Right "Hemi-TS"   379
Discussion   379
TS Subtypes and Lateralized Frontostriatal Involvement   379
"Hemi-TS" and Clinical Diagnosis   382
Exploratory Behavior Versus Hyperactivity   383
Cutting Across Taxonomic Boundaries and Redefining TS   384
Acknowledgments   385
References   385
Disclosure   389
Appendix Description of the Diagnostic Instruments
    Used in the Study   389
Neurocognitive Assessment   389
Clinical Questionnaires and Scales   391

16. Executive Dysfunction in Addiction

Antonio Verdejo-Garcia

Introduction   395
Cannabis   396
Cocaine   396
Methamphetamine   397
Opioids   398
Discussion and Future Directions   399
References   400

17. Seizures of the Frontal Lobes: Clinical Presentations and Diagnostic Considerations

Sara Wildstein and Silvana Riggio

Introduction   405
The Frontal Lobe and Its Anatomy   405
Etiology and Genetics   407
Clinical Presentations of Frontal Lobe Epilepsy   408
Differentiating FLE From Psychiatric Disorders and Parasomnias   410
Diagnostic Evaluation   412
Conclusion   416
References   417

18. **Executive Functions After Traumatic Brain Injury: From Deficit to Recovery**
Irene Cristofori and Jordan Grafman

Traumatic Brain Injury	421
Executive Function Deficits After Traumatic Brain Injury	423
Working Memory	423
Inhibition	424
Cognitive Flexibility	424
Planning	425
Location of Brain Lesions Associated With EF Deficits	425
Neuropsychological Testing to Assess EF in TBI	426
Standard Tests of Executive Functions	426
Ecological Tests for Evaluating Executive Functions	426
Executive Function Neuroplasticity and Traumatic Brain Injury	427
Attempts to Remediate EF After TBI	428
Recovery of EF After TBI	429
Cognitive Rehabilitation of Executive Functions	429
From Executive Function Rehabilitation to Social Reintegration	431
Noninvasive Brain Stimulation: TMS and TDCS Studies in TBI	432
Genetic Predisposition, Executive Functions, and Traumatic Brain Injury	433
Catechol-O-Methyltransferase	433
Brain-derived Neurotrophic Factor	434
Apolipoprotein E	434
Future Directions	435
References	436

19. **Dementias and the Frontal Lobes**
Michał Harciarek, Emilia J. Sitek and Anna Barczak

Introduction	445
Alzheimer's Disease	446
Frontal Variant of Alzheimer's Disease	447
Vascular Dementia	449
Subtypes of Vascular Dementia and Their Relationship to Frontal Lobe Function	450
Frontotemporal Dementia	452
Behavioral Variant Frontotemporal Dementia	453
Language Variant Frontotemporal Dementia (Primary Progressive Aphasia)	456
Progressive Supranuclear Palsy and Corticobasal Syndrome	457
Executive Functions	457
Behavior and Affect	460
Motor Neuron Disease	461
Executive Functions	461
Behavior and Affect	462
Parkinson's Disease	462
Executive Functions	462

Behavior and Affect   463
Dementia With Lewy Bodies   464
Executive Functions   464
Behavior and Affect   464
Huntington's Disease   465
Executive Functions   466
Behavior and Affect   467
Assessment of Executive Function in Dementia   467
Summary   470
References   470

20. Executive Function in Posttraumatic Stress Disorder

Jennifer Newman and Charles Marmar

Chapter Overview   487
Diagnosis and Prevalence of Posttraumatic Stress Disorder   488
Cognitive Functioning in Posttraumatic Stress Disorder   489
Executive Function   491
Working Memory   492
Brain Imaging Research   493
Functional Neuroimaging   493
Structural Neuroimaging   494
Developmental Factors   495
Childhood Trauma and Executive Function   495
Aging   497
Possible Confounding Factors   498
Premorbid Functioning   499
Traumatic Brain Injury   500
Depression   503
Substance Use   504
Other Comorbidities   505
**Executive Function and Treatment for Posttraumatic Stress
    Disorder**   507
Conclusions   509
Acknowledgments   511
References   511

21. Executive Dysfunction in Medical Conditions

Michał Harciarek and Aleksandra Wojtowicz

Introduction   525
Hypertension   526
Diabetes Mellitus   527

Chronic Kidney Disease   530
Executive Function in Patients With End-stage Renal Disease
    Treated With Dialysis   530
Executive Function in Patients With End-stage Renal Disease
    Following a Successful Kidney Transplant   532
Human Immunodeficiency Virus   533
Hepatic Encephalopathy   534
Thyroid Disease   536
Rheumatoid Arthritis   538
Conclusions   540
Acknowledgments   541
References   541
Further Reading   550

22. Assessment of Executive Functions in Clinical Settings

Yana Suchy, Rosemary E. Ziemnik and Madison A. Niermeyer

Assessment of Executive Functions in Clinical Settings   551
Clinically Useful Definition of Executive Functioning   551
Assessment Considerations and Challenges in Relation to
    Assessment Purposes   553
Assessment Methods: Gathering Background Information   558
Assessment Methods: Patient's Presentation During Assessment   560
Conclusions   563
References   564

Index   571

List of Contributors

Masao Aihara Graduate Faculty of Interdisciplinary Research, University of Yamanashi, Yamanashi, Japan

Amy F.T. Arnsten Department of Neuroscience, Yale University School of Medicine, New Haven, CT, United States

Anna Barczak Neurodegenerative Department, Neurology Clinic, MSW Hospital, Warsaw, Poland

João J. Cerqueira Neuroscience Domain, University of Minho and ICVS/3B's - PT Government Associate Laboratory, Braga/Guimarães, Portugal

Irene Cristofori Cognitive Neuroscience Laboratory, Rehabilitation Institute of Chicago, Chicago, IL, United States; Department of Physical Medicine and Rehabilitation, Feinberg School of Medicine, Northwestern University, Chicago, IL, United States

Kirk R. Daffner Department of Neurology, Brigham & Women's Hospital, Harvard Medical School, Boston, MA, United States

Jin Fan The Graduate Center, The City University of New York, New York, NY, United States; Department of Psychology, Queens College, The City University of New York, Queens, NY, United States; Department of Psychiatry, Icahn School of Medicine at Mount Sinai, New York, NY, United States; Department of Neuroscience, Icahn School of Medicine at Mount Sinai, New York, NY, United States

Joaquín M. Fuster Semel Institute, School of Medicine, University of California Los Angeles, Los Angeles, CA, United States

Elkhonon Goldberg Luria Neuroscience Institute, New York, NY, United States; New York University School of Medicine, New York, NY, United States

Jordan Grafman Cognitive Neuroscience Laboratory, Rehabilitation Institute of Chicago, Chicago, IL, United States; Department of Physical Medicine and Rehabilitation, Feinberg School of Medicine, Northwestern University, Chicago, IL, United States; Department of Neurology, Feinberg School of Medicine, Northwestern University, Chicago, IL, United States

Adam Hampshire The Computational Cognitive and Clinical Neuroimaging Laboratory (C^3NL), The Division of Brain Sciences, Imperial College London, London, United Kingdom

Michał Harciarek Department of Clinical Psychology and Neuropsychology, Institute of Psychology, University of Gdańsk, Gdańsk, Poland; Department of Social Sciences, University of Gdańsk, Gdańsk, Poland

Kjell Tore Hovik Division of Mental Health Care, Innlandet Hospital Trust, Sanderud, Norway; Department of Neurology, Innlandet Hospital Trust, Elverum, Norway

Layne Kalbfleisch Department of Pediatrics, The George Washington School of Medicine and Health Sciences, Washington, DC, United States

Željka Krsnik Laboratory for Digitalization of Zagreb Brain Collection, Croatian Institute for Brain Research, University of Zagreb School of Medicine, Salata, Zagreb, Croatia; Laboratory for Neurogenomics and InSitu Hybridization, Croatian Institute for Brain Research, University of Zagreb School of Medicine, Salata, Zagreb, Croatia

Hakwan Lau Psychology Department, University of California Los Angeles, Los Angeles, CA, United States; Brain Research Institute, University of California Los Angeles, Los Angeles, CA, United States

Daniel S. Levine Department of Psychology, University of Texas at Arlington, Arlington, TX, United States

Seth Lew Psychology Department, University of California Los Angeles, Los Angeles, CA, United States

Taber C. Lightbourne Department of Neuroscience, Yale University School of Medicine, New Haven, CT, United States

Melissa-Ann Mackie The Graduate Center, The City University of New York, New York, NY, United States; Department of Psychology, Queens College, The City University of New York, Queens, NY, United States

Charles Marmar Department of Psychiatry, New York University Langone Medical Center, New York, NY, United States

Aaron P. Nelson Department of Psychiatry, Brigham & Women's Hospital, Harvard Medical School, Boston, MA, United States

Jennifer Newman Department of Psychiatry, New York University Langone Medical Center, New York, NY, United States

Madison A. Niermeyer Department of Psychology, University of Utah, Salt Lake City, UT, United States

Merete Øie Research Department, Innlandet Hospital Trust, Lillehammer, Norway; Department of Psychology, University of Oslo, Oslo, Norway

Silvana Riggio Department of Psychiatry, Icahn School of Medicine at Mount Sinai, New York, NY, United States; Department of Neurology, Icahn School of Medicine at Mount Sinai, New York, NY, United States; Psychosomatic Medicine, Consultation Liaison Psychiatry Service, James Peters Bronx Veterans Administration Hospital, Bronx, NY, United States

Goran Sedmak Division of Developmental Neuroscience, Croatian Institute for Brain Research, University of Zagreb School of Medicine, Salata, Zagreb, Croatia

Leena Shoemaker Department of Psychology, York University, Toronto, ON, Canada

David A. Silbersweig Department of Neurology, Brigham & Women's Hospital, Harvard Medical School, Boston, MA, United States; Department of Psychiatry, Brigham & Women's Hospital, Harvard Medical School, Boston, MA, United States

Emilia J. Sitek Department of Neurology, St. Adalbert Hospital, Gdańsk, Poland; Department of Neurological and Psychiatric Nursing, Medical University of Gdańsk, Gdańsk, Poland

Nuno Sousa Neuroscience Domain, University of Minho and ICVS/3B's - PT Government Associate Laboratory, Braga/Guimarães, Portugal

R. Nathan Spreng Department of Human Development, Cornell University, Ithaca, NY, United States; Human Neuroscience Institute, Cornell University, Ithaca, NY, United States

Yana Suchy Department of Psychology, University of Utah, Salt Lake City, UT, United States

John F. Sullivan Department of Neurology, Brigham & Women's Hospital, Harvard Medical School, Boston, MA, United States; Department of Psychiatry, Brigham & Women's Hospital, Harvard Medical School, Boston, MA, United States

Gary R. Turner Department of Psychology, York University, Toronto, ON, Canada

Antonio Verdejo-Garcia School of Psychological Sciences and Monash Institute of Cognitive and Clinical Neurosciences (MICCN), Melbourne, VIC, Australia

Daniel S. Weisholtz Department of Neurology, Brigham & Women's Hospital, Harvard Medical School, Boston, MA, United States

Sara Wildstein Department of Psychiatry, Icahn School of Medicine at Mount Sinai, New York, NY, United States

Aleksandra Wojtowicz Department of Social Sciences, University of Gdańsk, Gdańsk, Poland

Rosemary E. Ziemnik Department of Psychology, University of Utah, Salt Lake City, UT, United States

Preface

Neuroscience used to be the monopoly of a few elite universities located in a handful of countries. Neuropsychology used to be a quaint niche discipline relatively unconnected to the larger world of neuroscience and content in its methods with paper-and-pencil tests. Neuroscience itself was relatively unconcerned with higher-order cognition, and the very term "cognitive neuroscience" was often met with rolled eyes by scientists working in more established areas of brain research (a personal observation made in the 1980s and even 1990s on more than one occasion). And the interest in executive functions was shared by a very small club of neuropsychologists and neuroscientists, a fact often noted in their times by the pioneers of "frontal-lobe" research Alexander Luria and a generation later Patricia Goldman-Rakic.

None of this is true today. Important neuroscience research is conducted at numerous academic and biomedical centers worldwide. We are witnessing a substantial fusion, or at least blending, of cognitive neuroscience and neuropsychology. The terms "executive functions" and "frontal-lobe functions" are no longer used interchangeably, and a more refined understanding of both has emerged. Executive functions in health and disease have become the target of intense investigation by scores of researchers, arguably one of the most heavily populated territories of cognitive and clinical neuroscience (I recall a slide used in her lectures by the late Goldman-Rakic, with the number of stick-men drawn in each lobe reflecting the relative level of research interest in its functions. The slide, with its conspicuous near-absence of stick-men in the frontal lobe, would have to be re-drawn today). The range of research tools deployed for the understanding of executive function and dysfunction has also grown and continues to grow. Today it includes animal models, genetic studies, biochemical approaches, various forms of structural and functional neuroimaging, computational modeling involving neural nets and other methods, lesion and specific disorder studies, as well as a constantly expanding arsenal of sophisticated cognitive probes. In its clinical applications, the research into the nature of executive dysfunction is no longer limited to the traditional neuropsychological territory of focal lesions directly contained within the frontal lobes, and has expanded into a wide range of both focal and non-focal disorders whose impact is not restricted to the prefrontal cortex.

The vast expansion of interest in both healthy and impaired executive functions is reflected in the chapter composition of this book. Among the contributors are recognized authorities who played a pivotal role in shaping the modern understanding of executive functions, as well as young neuroscientists who joined the field relatively recently. The contributors employ a wide range of technologies and tools and conduct their research at universities in North America; Western, Central, and Eastern Europe; Asia; and Australia. Capturing the generational, geographic, and methodological expanse of the interest in executive functions has been the editor's intent and is a distinguishing feature of the volume.

The book is divided into two sections: Executive Functions in Health and Executive Functions in Disease. In the first section, various aspects of healthy executive functions are examined. The topics include a broad general conceptualization of executive functions by a preeminent pioneer of the field (Joaquin Fuster); cellular mechanisms of executive functions and working memory (Taber Lightbourne and Amy Arnsten); gene expression in the frontal lobes (Zeljka Krznik and Goran Sedmak); large-scale networks and the frontal lobes (Adam Hampshire); computational neural net modeling of executive functions and decision making (Daniel Levine); frontal lobes and consciousness (Seth Lew and Hakwan Lau); neurodevelopmental aspects of executive functions (Layne Kalbfleisch); changes affecting executive functions in aging (Nathan Spreng, Leena Shoemaker, and Gary Turner); and a broad survey of neuropsychological assessment methods used in the neuropsychological research into executive functions (Yana Suchi, Rosemary Ziemnik, and Madison Niermeyer).

In the second sections, multiple forms of executive dysfunction are examined across a wide range of neurological, psychiatric, and medical conditions. Both broad categories of disorders and specific disorders are examined. The broad clinical categories examined include the mechanisms of cognitive, behavioral and emotional inflexibility, and perseveration across a number of neuropsychiatric disorders (Daniel Weisholtz, John Sullivan, Aaron Nelson, Kirk Daffner, and David Silbersweig); large-scale cognitive control network alteration in neuropsychiatric disorders, including autism, schizophrenia, and depression (Melissa-Ann Makie and Jin Fan); executive functions in neurodevelopmental disorders, including ADHD, focal frontal lesions, and epileptic foci (Masao Aihara); executive dysfunction in striatal disorders, including Parkinson's disease, Huntington's disease, and chronic stress (Joao Cergueira and Nuno Sousa); executive dysfunction in dementias, including Alzheimer's disease, vascular dementia, frontotemporal dementia, progressive supranuclear palsy and corticobasal syndrome, motor neuron disease, Parkinson's disease, Lewy body dementia, and Huntington's disease (Michal Harciarek, Emilia Sitek, and Anna Barczak); executive dysfunction in medical conditions, including hypertension, diabetes mellitus, chronic kidney disease, HIV encephalopathy, hepatic encephalopathy, thyroid disease, and rheumatoid arthritis (Michal Harciarek and Aleksandra Wojtowicz); addictions to a number of substances, including cannabis, cocaine, methamphetamine, and opioids (Antonio Verdejo-Garcia); examination of the parallels between the effects of lateralized frontal lesions, hemiparkinsonian syndromes, and variants of Tourette's syndrome (Kjell Hovik, Merete Oie, and Elkhonon Goldberg); as well as a broad survey of neuropsychological assessment methods used for the clinical assessment of executive functions (Yana Suchi). The specific disorders examined include executive dysfunction and efforts to rehabilitate it in traumatic brain injury (Irene Christofori and Jordan Grafman); frontal-lobe seizures (Sara Wildstein and Silvana Riggio); executive deficit in post-traumatic stress disorder (Jennifer Newman and Charles Marmar); and executive dysfunction in Tourette's syndrome (Kjell Hovik).

From being a niche research enterprise, executive functions research has burgeoned into a vast area of neuroscience with its own niches and sub-niches, often with relatively little interaction between them. While probably unavoidable, such "Balkanization" of the field is unfortunate and self-defeating. Hopefully, combining in one volume chapters on basic and clinical executive functions research employing a variety of approaches and methodologies will help update the readers' knowledge of the advances in their own niches as well as help familiarize them with the state of affairs in others; both update the readers about the more recent work by acknowledged leaders in the field, and introduce him to the new generation of neuroscientists advancing our understanding of executive function and dysfunction and representing the future of the field.

Elkhonon Goldberg
December 2016
New York City

Part I

Executive Functions in Health

Chapter 1

Prefrontal Executive Functions Predict and Preadapt

Joaquín M. Fuster
Semel Institute, School of Medicine, University of California Los Angeles, Los Angeles, CA, United States

INTRODUCTION

Based on the theory of evolution and his experience with the effects of brain lesions, Jackson, the father of neurology, was the first to postulate the hierarchical organization of the nervous system, which he considered both a representational and a coordinating system at all levels, from top to bottom (Jackson, 1882). To exemplify the identity of representational and executive neural substrates, he used the motor cortex. Here, the same assemblies of cells that represent a movement are in charge of its execution. By "representation" in this cortex he meant, of course, the executive memory of skeletal movement, which we may call "phyletic memory" because it is genetically inherited and common to all members of the species. In the frontal lobe, at the top of the executive motor hierarchy, Jackson placed the "highest centers" for the representation and execution of complex movement, the highest nerve agencies for the memory and coordination of the actions of the "whole organism." He was obviously referring to premotor and prefrontal areas. Thus, extending his hierarchical principle to those cortical regions, he attributed the representation and coordination of purposeful and goal-directed actions. Language was one among them, which he called more specifically as the "capacity to propositionise" (Jackson, 1915). Luria, later (1966), would not only make that capacity a fundamental fontal function but also extend it to the coordination of all forms of complex action, in other words, to what Lashley (1951) had termed the "syntax of action."

To "propositionise" is to make propositions, which for Jackson meant the commonly accepted ability to construct grammatical sentences with words and ideas. In modern times, however, based on a large body of clinical evidence, it can be confidently asserted that the propositions that higher frontal cortex makes include also *proposals*, in other words, schemes or plans of

Executive Functions in Health and Disease. DOI: http://dx.doi.org/10.1016/B978-0-12-803676-1.00001-5

action, transcending language, to be executed in the more or less distant future. Luria (1966), probably more clearly than anybody else, attributed to higher frontal cortex the capacity to implement those proposals by organizing complex and purposeful goal-directed behavior in the temporal domain. As a logical consequence, the incapacity to formulate and carry out plans is now universally recognized as a pathognomonic symptom of substantial prefrontal damage (Fuster, 2015). From this, incapacity derives the general notion that as part of its role in the temporal organization of behavior, the normal prefrontal cortex opens the organism to its future, by predicting events, including its own actions, and by *preadapting* the organism to those events before they happen.

The central topic of this chapter is the future perspective of the three major executive functions of the prefrontal cortex: (1) executive attention, (2) working memory, and (3) decision-making. All three are functionally intertwined and share common biological objectives or *teleonomic* goals (Monod, 1971), which include the adaptation of the organism to predictable changes in its internal or external environment. Accordingly, in this chapter, I will outline and support the prospective aspects of each of those functions. I will preface the discussion of the three functions with a brief presentation of the general biological principle they obey. That principle is the perception—action (PA) cycle, which is the circular cybernetic processing of information that regulates the relationships between nervous system and environment in goal-directed behavior and language.

THE PA CYCLE

Biologist Uexküll (1926) remarked that living organisms adapt to their environment by a circular flow of information that runs through the environment and the brain, with a structural sensing interface ("mark organ") and an effector interface ("action organ"). The sea anemone senses the chemistry of the water for nutrients, which reflexively mobilize their "action organ" toward them for their ingestion. It is a simple feed-forward reflex arc (Fig. 1.1). However, in the brain of higher organisms, Uexküll noted that there is internal feedback that bypasses the environment through the brain and from the "action organ" that flows back into the "mark organ." That internal feedback provides the brain with a measure of additional supraordinate control of the cycle.

In the primate brain, that adaptation cycle, with its internal feedback countercycle, evolves into a hierarchy of concentric cycles of cerebral structures and processes that adjust the animal to its external environment while satisfying immediate and future biological needs. At the highest level of that hierarchy, the cycle involves the cerebral cortex, which harbors networks for processing information from sensory to motor areas through associative cortex. The cycle has received various names from neurologists and

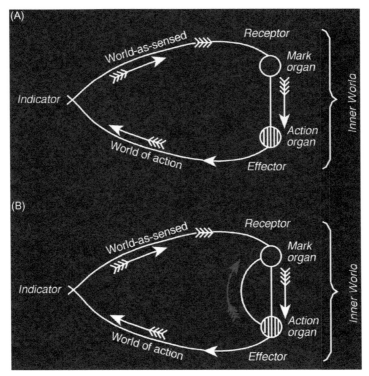

FIGURE 1.1 Uexküll's diagram of the adaptation of the organism to its environment. He writes (A) "The inner world is divided into two parts; one, that receives the impressions, faces the world-as-sensed, and the other, that distributes the effects, faces the world of action." (B) "In the highest animals, however, the creature's own action-rule penetrates further into the world-as-sensed, and *there, assumes direction and control* (my italics) ... A new circle *(red arrow)* is introduced within the animal's own central organ for the support of the external function-circle, and this connects the action organ with the mark-organ." *From Uexküll (1926). Theoretical Biology. New York: Harcourt, Brace & Co, 155–157.*

neuroscientists; I favor the *PA cycle* denomination to emphasize the cognitive, memory-related, aspect of sensation in its higher circuits. Essentially, in the integration of complex goal-directed behavior, the PA cycle functions as follows (Fig. 1.2). Inputs from the environment or the internal milieu are processed through cognitive networks or *cognits* (Fuster, 2009) of posterior cortex (parietal—temporal—occipital, PTO). The output from that processing flows into the prefrontal cortex, where, through executive cognitive networks, it informs consequent action upon the environment; that action is effected through the premotor cortex, the basal ganglia, and the pyramidal system. The action produces changes in the environment, which are processed through the senses and fed back into posterior cortex toward further action. Thus, the entire cycle works as a self-correcting and guiding cybernetic system that regulates behavior and language toward their goals. It is

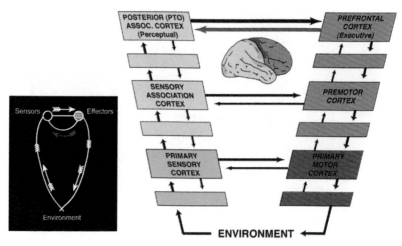

FIGURE 1.2 Circuitry of the PA cycle through cortex and environment. A perceptual hierarchy of cognits (cognitive neuronal networks) is depicted on the left and an executive one on the right (The top-left compartment, PTO, includes both unimodal and multimodal association cortex). Major feed-forward connectivity runs through thick arrows. Thin arrows mark intracortical feedback connections that play important roles in cognitive control. *PA*, perception−action; *PTO*, parietal−temporal−occipital. *Bottom left*: Uexkull's internal feedback in lower animals (red arrow), which in the human cycle at right is represented by the red arrow from prefrontal to PTO cortex. That arrow symbolizes schematically essential components of the three executive functions subsumed by cognitive control (executive attention, working memory, and decision-making).

important to note that the cycle can be set in motion by events anywhere within it, in the cortex or in the environment (external or internal milieu), obviating the need for a "center of will" or "central executive."

As in lower organisms, however, there is internal countercyclical feedback from effectors to receptors in the primate brain. That internal feedback, I argue in this chapter, has future-oriented functions that modulate the PA cycle in anticipation of predicted percepts, actions, and rewards. In both the human and nonhuman primate, those are the executive functions of the prefrontal cortex to be discussed below. Their essential infrastructural support is made of corticocortical connections from that cortex upon posterior perceptual cortex and the cognitive networks of this cortex. In the aggregate, those functions constitute what has been termed "cognitive control" (Miller & Cohen, 2001) argued at the service of the temporal organization of goal-directed behavior (Fuster, 2001).

Based on their work on insects and fish, von Holst and Mittelsteadt (1950) were the first to postulate the predictive properties of the internal feedback from executive to sensing sectors of the brain (red arrow in Figs. 1.1 and 1.2). They called that internal feedback "reafference." According to them, it consisted of signals from the motor system, which, immediately *before* the execution of a reflex motor response to sensory stimulation, flowed back into the sensory system to refine that response and to integrate it with the responses of other parts of the organism. That anticipated feedback, which internally bypassed the environment and overrode the reflex act, had the fundamental property of preparing the organism for better adaptation on the basis of what those authors called the "plasticity" of both systems, sensory and motor, to memory or experience. The feedback itself contained a neural replicate of the forthcoming movement, named by others the "efferent copy" or "corollary discharge" (McCloskey, 1981); the first term reflects its duplicative character and the second its consequential functional implications for the nervous system in the process of integrating impending behavior. Theoretically and partly based on psychophysical and electrophysiological evidence from primates, Teuber (1972) made corollary discharge a fundamental function of the prefrontal cortex. He said that by that function, "the organism presets its sensory systems for the anticipated consequences of its own action."

Now we have abundant evidence that Teuber's prefrontal "corollary discharge," mutatis mutandis for complex behavior and language, incorporates the three executive cognitive functions that are the subject of this chapter. All three have a fundamental future dimension to accommodate PA cycles that in the human extend to months and years. The failure of one or more of those functions is at the root of the frontal lobe, patient's inability to form and execute plans of goal-directed action. However, it should be noted before their discussion that all three are physiologically and psychologically intertwined. Therefore, it is difficult and to a large degree unjustified to allocate any of them to a well-defined anatomical domain of the frontal cortex.

EXECUTIVE ATTENTION

Attention is the optimal and selective allocation of limited resources to information processing in the central nervous system. It operates in the two major sectors of neurocognitive function: perceptual and executive. In both sectors, attention operates by the tandem use of two simultaneous and reciprocal mechanisms: the excitation of cognitive networks with presently relevant content and the inhibition of those with irrelevant or interfering content. The first mechanism constitutes the inclusive aspect of attention; it serves to focus neural resources on the currently applicable portion of a cognitive sector toward a goal. The second, exclusionary aspect of attention, serves to suppress, block, or inhibit irrelevant or interfering information, whether that comes from the organism itself or from the environment. It protects the organism from distraction. Arguably, this function of inhibitory control is an executive function in its own right (Fuster, 2015), but it does not have the marked prospective properties that characterize the three discussed functions in this chapter.

Executive attention is identical to what we elsewhere have called "attentive set" (Fuster & Bressler, 2015). In general terms, it consists in the preparation or priming of sensory and motor systems for an expected and predictable adaptive response of the organism to a stimulus or environmental event. In the cortical PA cycle, the carriers of executive attention are connections and signals flowing mainly from prefrontal cortex upon posterior association cortex (perceptual cortex, PTO) and lower stages of the executive hierarchy, such as the premotor cortex and the basal ganglia. In the monkey, those signals seem to originate in the dorsolateral prefrontal cortex. Some of the most direct evidence for the role of that cortex in the attentive set for selective motor action come from studies of monkeys performing delay tasks, where a motor choice is contingent on a stimulus presented a few seconds earlier (Fig. 1.3).

In the human, the best electrophysiological evidence of cortical involvement in executive attention consists in the slow potentials that develop on the surface of the scalp between a sensory stimulus and a motor response contingent on it after a period of delay. Those potentials are commonly designated the "expectancy wave," the "readiness potential," and the "contingency negative variation" (Brunia, Haagh, & Scheirs, 1985; Deecke, Kornhuber, Lang, Lang, & Schreiber, 1985; Fuster, 2015). Although they have different morphology, polarity, and time course, all of them originate in the dorsal prefrontal cortex and are clearly correlated in amplitude and duration with the attention to, and preparation of, the motor response to the stimulus.

Imaging studies have implicated frontoparietal networks in the executive attentive processes. These networks would be activated and engage in those processes, whereas the "default mode network," which is normally active at rest, becomes deactivated (Hellyer et al., 2014; Raichle et al., 2001; Sadaghiani & D'Esposito, 2015). Neuroimaging also provides evidence of specific correlations between prefrontal activation and attentive motor set. Scheidt, Lillis, and Emerson (2010), by using a sensorimotor task, adjusted the direction of manual movements to a predicted motor "load," that is, the rectilinearity of the hand path that the subject anticipated would be necessary to execute the motor reaction. In a similar manner as in the monkey experiment described earlier (Fig. 1.3; Quintana & Fuster, 1999), prefrontal activation correlated with a parameter of the expected motor act, in this case the rectilinearity of movement.

Both electrophysiological and neuroimaging signals (Diekhof, Kaps, Falkai, & Gruber, 2012; Kable & Glimcher, 2007; Potts, Martin, Kamp, & Donchin, 2011; Rutledge, Dean, Caplin, & Glimcher, 2010) predict by their magnitude the expected reward and value in the outcome of a prospective action. However, particularly strong signals can be recorded from the anterior cingulate cortex (medial prefrontal cortex) after error or failure of predicted reward (prediction error).

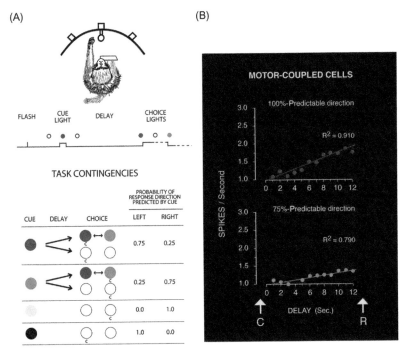

FIGURE 1.3 Prefrontal neurons attuned to motor response set. (A) Delay task with temporal and spatial separation between color cues and motor responses (*below left*, contingencies between cue and response). The animal faces three stimulus-response buttons over a pedal on which the operant hand rests at all times except to respond to stimuli. A trial starts with the cue, a brief color illumination on the central button. The cue is followed by a delay of some 10 s, after which the two lateral buttons light up simultaneously, either one red and the other green or both white. If they turn red and green, the animal must choose the color of the cue (red or green). If both turn white, it must choose left for red cue, right for green cue, right for yellow cue, or left for blue cue. Consequently, if the cue has been yellow or blue, during the delay the animal can predict with certainty the response direction (right or left, respectively). If the cue has been red or green, the correct response side can be predicted with only 75% probability (left if red, right if green). Cue color and position of correct choice change at random from trial to trial. *c*, correct choice. (B) Accelerating activation of motor-coupled neurons during a 12-s delay. These cells are presumably responsible for the priming of the motor system in anticipation of the motor response. The slope of the ramp of their accelerated firing accorded with the predictability of that response: the steepness of the firing ramp was greater when that predictability was 100% than when it was only 75%. C, cue; R, response; R^2, square of correlation coefficient. *From Quintana & Fuster (1999). From perception to action: Temporal integrative functions of prefrontal and parietal neurons. Cerebral Cortex, 9, 213–221; with permission.*

Both the inclusionary and exclusionary aspects of top–down predictive cognitive control are revealed by neuroimaging. In accordance with neuropsychological evidence, imaging methodology suggests a double dissociation of prefrontal cortex regarding the two fundamental mechanisms of attentive set, inclusionary and exclusionary. Whereas the former seems mainly under the control of the dorsolateral cortex (Chadick & Gazzaley, 2011), the exclusionary or inhibitory one seems under the control of the ventrolateral cortex (Bari & Robbins, 2013). These two mechanisms evidently work in tandem, top—down, on the neural substrates of perception and action as part of the cognitive control of so-called "biased competition" (Desimone & Duncan, 1995) of attentive set. It is obviously essential that in the attentive set, the excitatory component of attention be complemented by the inhibitory component. There are two main reasons for it: (1) attention is selective by definition because it is served by limited neural resources and (2) the inhibition of memory representations of irrelevant or interfering motor acts would detract from the accuracy and contrast of the acts currently in the focus of those resources.

WORKING MEMORY

Working memory is by definition a prospective, future-oriented, function. It is the temporary retention of information for performing a task or solving a problem in the near future (Baddeley, 1983). The purpose and intentionality in the definition differentiate working memory from other states and forms of short-term memory.

The first step in the elucidation of the brain mechanisms of working memory was the discovery of "memory cells" in the prefrontal cortex of monkeys (Funahashi, Bruce, & Goldman-Rakic, 1989; Fuster, 1973; Niki, 1974; Romo, Brody, Hernández, & Lemus, 1999). These are cells that show persistent elevated firing during the retention of a sensory stimulus for a prospective action. The conventional behavioral paradigm to reveal them is the performance of so-called "delay tasks," notably delayed response and delayed matching-to-sample.

Although the first memory cells were discovered in the prefrontal cortex, subsequently they were also found in other cortical areas. They were demonstrated in inferotemporal cortex when the working memory memorandum was visual (Fuster & Jervey, 1982; Miller, Li, & Desimone, 1993; Miyashita & Chang, 1988), in anterior parietal cortex when it was tactile or haptic (Koch & Fuster, 1989; Zhou & Fuster, 1996) and in posterior parietal cortex when it was visuospatial (Andersen, Bracewell, Barash, Gnadt, & Fogassi, 1990). Furthermore, cross-modal (auditory—visual or visual—haptic) memory cells have been found in prefrontal cortex (Fuster, Bodner, & Kroger, 2000) and also in inferotemporal cortex (Gibson & Maunsell, 1997) and parietal cortex (Zhou & Fuster, 2000).

In monkeys performing working memory tasks, the cooling of lateral prefrontal cortex—which causes its reversible inactivation—together with the concomitant recording of single units in posterior cortex, or vice versa, indicate that the retention of working memory depends on functional interactions between those cortices (Chafee & Goldman-Rakic, 2000; Fuster, Bauer, &

Jervey, 1985; Quintana, Fuster, & Yajeya, 1989); presumably, the interactions take place through anatomically well-demonstrated corticocortical connections (reviewed in Fuster, 2015). Those results are fully consistent with two key conclusions: (1) working memory is maintained by persistent reentrant, recurrent, or reverberating activity in cortical circuits and (2) working memory mediates cross-temporal contingencies in the PA cycle (Fig. 1.4). Both conclusions are supported by empirical computational modeling and by functional neuroimaging.

On the basis of a large body of neurobiological and behavioral data, it has become an established principle that the fundamental mechanism of working memory consists of reverberating excitation within the cortex or between the latter and subcortical structures such as the thalamus. This has led to numerous computational models that have substantiated the plausibility of that principle (Compte, Brunel, Goldman-Rakic, & Wang, 2000; Durstewitz, 2009; Liang, Wang, & Zhang, 2010; Tang, Li, & Yan, 2010; Verduzco-Flores, Bodner, Ermentrout, Fuster, & Zhou, 2009; Wang et al., 2013; Zipser, Kehoe, Littlewort, & Fuster, 1993). Most of these models have a reentrant functional architecture and are trained or instructed by the modeler to reproduce the persistent activity that characterizes memory cells in working memory. In the real brain, it is almost certain that the reentrant

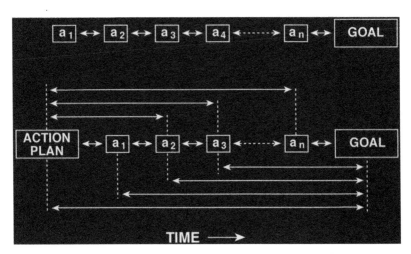

FIGURE 1.4   Succession of acts (a_1-a_n) in a plan of action toward its goal. Two-way arrows represent contingencies between acts across time (each contingency is double: if now this then later that, if earlier that then now this). Some contingencies link individual acts to each other, whereas others link individual acts to the plan or goal of the action, and still others the plan to each goal. *Top*: A chain of well-learned or instinctual acts, where one act is only contingent on the immediately previous and succeeding acts without cross-temporal contingencies. The three executive functions discussed in this chapter, especially working memory, serve the mediation of contingencies in the lower sequence.

activity that supports working memory makes use of reciprocal corticocortical connections that, anatomically and functionally, link executive frontal cortex with perceptual posterior cortex.

Functional imaging, especially functional magnetic resonance imaging, evinces the reentrant functional connectivity between frontal and posterior cortex in working memory. Whereas some imaging studies focus on temporal correlations of activation between prefrontal and posterior association cortices, other studies, by changing the features of the memory tests administered to the experimental subjects, attempt to define the precise aspect of working memory in which the prefrontal cortex is involved. Explicitly or implicitly, all studies assume a prospective role for that cortex in working memory, and their results are compatible with the reentry principle.

An extensive graphic meta-analysis of numerous imaging studies (Fuster, 2015) reinforces that principle. The analysis showed that in the maintenance of working memory there is a concomitant activation of a prefrontal region together with that of one or several posterior regions, which vary depending on the modality of the memorandum. Those posterior areas are supposed to harbor perceptual memory networks (cognits) updated by the memorandum. In all cases, it appears that a reentrant loop of excitation ties the prefrontal cortex with those posterior areas. That reentrant loop would bridge the memory period—i.e., the cross-temporal contingency—of the working memory task or test. Both prefrontal and posterior cortices would thus engage in reentrant loops leading the PA cycle to its goal or goals. Fig. 1.5, derived from the mentioned meta-analysis, illustrates the activation of the cortical components of that cycle during a working memory test with visual memorandum.

The role of corticocortical reentry is further supported by imaging and electrophysiological studies that reveal the coupling between frontal and posterior sensory areas in the course of working memory (Ardestani, Shen, Darvas, Toga, & Fuster, 2016; Baldauf & Desimone, 2014; Lowe, Dzemidzic, Lurito, Mathews, & Phillips, 2000). Reentry is also indicated by a study of effective corticocortical connectivity in verbal working memory (Honey et al., 2002). In conclusion, the imaging and electrical evidence point to a role of the lateral prefrontal cortex, in coordination with posterior associative cortical areas and in the maintenance of working memory. That role follows a time course that reflects the gradual transition of activation of perceptual networks to that of prefrontal executive cognits, all within the PA cycle.

DECISION-MAKING

Making decisions is the third major executive function of the prefrontal cortex. Similar to the other two discussed earlier, this function is prospective and embedded in the workings of the PA cycle. A decision that is a deliberate choice of prospective action among alternatives is determined by

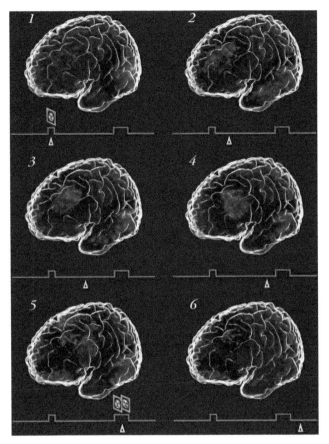

FIGURE 1.5   Cortical activation at six moments in time (yellow triangles) in the course of a visual memory task (delayed matching-to-sample with a face as the memorandum): *1*, sample presentation; *2*, beginning of the delay; *3*, middle of the delay; *4*, end of the delay; *5*, matching choice; *6*, posttrial. Note the concomitant (reentrant?) activation of inferotemporal and prefrontal cortex during the delay (memory period), also the progression of activation from the former to the latter, presumably the mediation of the cross-temporal contingency between sample and choice in the PA cycle. *From a metaanalysis of imaging studies of working memory in Fuster (2015).* The prefrontal *cortex (5th ed.). London: Academic Press.*

numerous factors. Fig. 1.6 offers a broad schematic view of those factors influencing the prefrontal cortex of the human in making a decision, whether the decided action is to take place in the short term or the long term. Those factors can be grouped into two basic categories. One consists of the influences from memory and prior learning, coming to prefrontal cortex from perceptual and executive cognitive networks in posterior and frontal associative cortex, the latter the prefrontal cortex itself. Those networks contain information in long-term memory as well as high-level values and ethical norms of

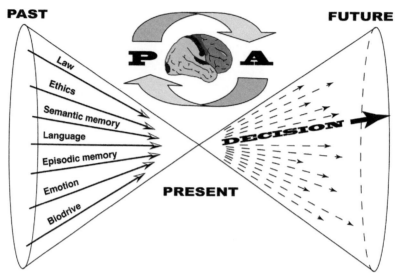

FIGURE 1.6 Schematic representation of neural influences converging on the present for the integration of a decision.

behavior. Their influences on the lateral prefrontal cortex, where complex decisions are converted into action, come to this cortex via corticocortical connections.

The second category of factors impinging on decision consists of influences from the neural substrates of emotion and biological drives, including the expectation of reward. Those influences come, through inputs to the orbital prefrontal cortex, from the thalamus, the hypothalamus, and limbic structures (Asaad & Eskandar, 2011; Diekhof et al., 2012; Kable & Glimcher, 2007; Kennerley, Behrens, & Wallis, 2011; Rolls & Grabenhorst, 2008; Rushworth & Behrens, 2008; Schultz, 2006; Wunderlich, Dayan, & Dolan, 2012).

Within the broad dynamics of the PA cycle, the two categories of cerebral influences on the decision process, that is, the cortical cognitive and the internal emotional, are susceptible to being triggered or modulated by environmental and internal inputs in the form of sensory or visceral stimuli. In some situations, one such stimulus, after processing through posterior or limbic cortex, may unleash a goal-directed series of actions, the stimulus thus serving as a single determinant of decision (Bunge, 2004; Buschman, Denovellis, Diogo, Bullock, & Miller, 2012; Durstewitz, Vittoz, Floresco, & Seamans, 2010; Eiselt & Nieder, 2013; Montojo & Courtney, 2008; Nee et al., 2013; Reverberi, Gorgen, & Haynes, 2012).

In most situations, however, a decision and the involvement of the prefrontal cortex in it are multifactorial, the result of the confluence of several signals. The signals may be simple and discrete, such as those consisting in a simple sensory stimulus, or complex, such as those dependent on its associated context. Such complex signals may be mixed, encoding what Rigotti et al. (2013), based on primate data, call "mixed selectivity."

To sum up in conclusion, decisions processed through the prefrontal cortex may be (1) determined by only one factor, such as a critical internal or external stimulus; (2) "vectorial," that is, the result of the interplay of several synergistic factors with different "weights" (e.g., degree of salience or motivational significance); (3) "winner-takes-all," where one factor decisively outweighs the others relevant at that time; or (4) Bayesian, that is, probabilistically grounded on the updating of hypotheses or expectations. Before all decisions, an executive network or cognit is activated in prefrontal cortex by prediction based on experience. It is reasonable to conclude that the prefrontal cortex, informed by posterior cortex, by limbic structures, and by high-level cognits within itself (e.g., rules), leads to decisions and their implementation by the orderly activation of lower stages of the executive hierarchy within the framework of the PA cycle. Functional imaging substantiates that downward trend or cascade of the processing of decided goal-directed actions (Azuar et al., 2014; Badre, Hoffman, Cooney, & D'Esposito, 2009; Charron & Koechlin, 2010; Koechlin & Hyafil, 2007).

It goes without saying that, within the PA cycle, and taking into account the multifactorial character of most decisions, the concept of a single supreme agent, such as the prefrontal cortex itself, loses its meaning. Indeed, the concept of a supraordinate neural entity, such as the prefrontal cortex, leads to an unresolvable infinite regress. To put it simply, postulating that entity unavoidably begs the question of what other entity commands it, and then that one, and so on at infinitum. In the PA cycle, where an action can start anywhere within it and is executed under continuous regulation by the prefrontal cortex through its executive functions, those questions become moot.

REFERENCES

Andersen, R. A., Bracewell, R. M., Barash, S., Gnadt, J. W., & Fogassi, L. (1990). Eye position effects on visual, memory, and saccade-related activity in areas LIP and 7a of macaque. *Journal of Neuroscience, 10,* 1176–1196.

Ardestani, A., Shen, W., Darvas, F., Toga, A. W., & Fuster, J. M. (2016). Modulation of fronto-parietal neurovascular dynamics in working memory. *Journal of Cognitive Neuroscience, 28,* 379–401.

Asaad, W. F., & Eskandar, E. N. (2011). Encoding of both positive and negative reward prediction errors by neurons of the primate lateral prefrontal cortex and caudate nucleus. *Journal of Neuroscience, 31,* 17772–17787.

Azuar, C., Reyes, P., Slachevsky, A., Volle, E., Kinkingnehun, S., Kouneiher, F., et al. (2014). Testing the model of caudo-rostral organization of cognitive control in the human with frontal lesions. *NeuroImage, 84,* 1053–1060.

Baddeley, A. (1983). Working memory. *Philosophical Transactions of the Royal Society, London, B302,* 311–324.

Badre, D., Hoffman, J., Cooney, J. W., & D'Esposito, M. (2009). Hierarchical cognitive control deficits following damage to the human frontal lobe. *Nature Neuroscience, 12*, 515−522.

Baldauf, D., & Desimone, R. (2014). Neural mechanisms of object-based attention. *Science, 344*, 424−427.

Bari, A., & Robbins, T. W. (2013). Inhibition and impulsivity: behavioral and neural basis of response control. *Progress in Neurobiology, 108*, 44−79.

Brunia, C. H. M., Haagh, S. A. V. M., & Scheirs, J. G. M. (1985). Waiting to respond: Electrophysiological measurements in man during preparation for a voluntary movement. In H. Heuer, U. Kleinbeck, & K.-H. Schmidt (Eds.), *Motor behavior* (pp. 35−78). New York: Springer.

Bunge, S. A. (2004). How we use rules to select actions: A review of evidence from cognitive neuroscience. *Cognitive Affective & Behavioral Neuroscience, 4*, 564−579.

Buschman, T. J., Denovellis, E. L., Diogo, C., Bullock, D., & Miller, E. K. (2012). Synchronous oscillatory neural ensembles for rules in the prefrontal cortex. *Neuron, 76*, 838−846.

Chadick, J. Z., & Gazzaley, A. (2011). Differential coupling of visual cortex with default or frontal-parietal network based on goals. *Nature Neuroscience, 14*, 830−832.

Chafee, M. V., & Goldman-Rakic, P. S. (2000). Inactivation of parietal and prefrontal cortex reveals interdependence of neural activity during memory-guided saccades. *Journal of Neurophysiology, 83*, 1550−1566.

Charron, S., & Koechlin, E. (2010). Divided representation of concurrent goals in the human frontal lobes. *Science, 328*, 360−363.

Compte, A., Brunel, N., Goldman-Rakic, P. S., & Wang, X. J. (2000). Synaptic mechanisms and network dynamics underlying spatial working memory in a cortical network model. *Cerebral Cortex, 10*, 910−923.

Deecke, L., Kornhuber, H. H., Lang, W., Lang, M., & Schreiber, H. (1985). Timing function of the frontal cortex in sequential motor and learning tasks. *Human Neurobiology, 4*, 143−154.

Desimone, R., & Duncan, J. (1995). Neural mechanisms of selective visual attention. *Annual Review of Neuroscience, 18*, 193−222.

Diekhof, E. K., Kaps, L., Falkai, P., & Gruber, O. (2012). The role of the human ventral striatum and the medial orbitofrontal cortex in the representation of reward magnitude—An activation likelihood estimation meta-analysis of neuroimaging studies of passive reward expectancy and outcome processing. *Neuropsychologia, 50*, 1252−1266.

Durstewitz, D. (2009). Implications of synaptic biophysics for recurrent network dynamics and active memory. *Neural Networks, 22*, 1189−1200.

Durstewitz, D., Vittoz, N. M., Floresco, S. B., & Seamans, J. K. (2010). Abrupt transitions between prefrontal neural ensemble states accompany behavioral transitions during rule learning. *Neuron, 66*, 438−448.

Eiselt, A. K., & Nieder, A. (2013). Representation of abstract quantitative rules applied to spatial and numerical magnitudes in primate prefrontal cortex. *Journal of Neuroscience, 33*, 7526−7534.

Funahashi, S., Bruce, C. J., & Goldman-Rakic, P. S. (1989). Mnemonic coding of visual space in the monkey's dorsolateral prefrontal cortex. *Journal of Neurophysiology, 61*, 331−349.

Fuster, J. M. (1973). Unit activity in prefrontal cortex during delayed-response performance: Neuronal correlates of transient memory. *Journal of Neurophysiology, 36*, 61−78.

Fuster, J. M. (2001). The prefrontal cortex—An update: Time is of the essence. *Neuron, 30*, 319−333.

Fuster, J. M. (2009). Cortex and memory: Emergence of a new paradigm. *Journal of Cognitive Neuroscience, 21*, 2047−2072.

Fuster, J. M. (2015). *The prefrontal cortex* (5th. Edition). London: Academic Press.

Fuster, J. M., Bauer, R. H., & Jervey, J. P. (1985). Functional interactions between inferotemporal and prefrontal cortex in a cognitive task. *Brain Research, 330*, 299−307.

Fuster, J. M., Bodner, M., & Kroger, J. K. (2000). Cross-modal and cross-temporal association in neurons of frontal cortex. *Nature, 405*, 347−351.

Fuster, J. M., & Bressler, S. L. (2015). Past makes future: Role of pFC in prediction. *Trends of Cognitive Science, 27*, 639−654.

Fuster, J. M., & Jervey, J. P. (1982). Neuronal firing in the inferotemporal cortex of the monkey in a visual memory task. *Journal of Neuroscience, 2*, 361−375.

Gibson, J. R., & Maunsell, J. H. R. (1997). Sensory modality specificity of neural activity related to memory in visual cortex. *Journal of Neurophysiology, 78*, 1263−1275.

Hellyer, P. J., Shanahan, M., Scott, G., Wise, R. J., Sharp, D. J., & Leech, R. (2014). The control of global brain dynamics: opposing actions of frontoparietal control and default mode networks on attention. *Journal of Neuroscience, 34*, 451−461.

Honey, G. D., Fu, C., Kim, J., Brammer, M. J., Croudace, T., Suckling, J., et al. (2002). Effects of verbal working memory load on cortical connectivity modeled by path analysis of functional magnetic resonance imaging data. *NeuroImage, 17*, 573−582.

Jackson, J. H. (1882). On some implications of dissolution of the nervous system. *Medical Press and Circular, ii*, 411−426.

Jackson, J. H. (1915). On affections of speech from disease of the brain. *Brain, 38*, 107−174.

Kable, J. W., & Glimcher, P. W. (2007). The neural correlates of subjective value during intertemporal choice. *Nature Neuroscience, 10*, 1625−1633.

Kennerley, S. W., Behrens, T. E., & Wallis, J. D. (2011). Double dissociation of value computations in orbitofrontal and anterior cingulate neurons. *Nature Neuroscience, 14*, 1581−1589.

Koch, K. W., & Fuster, J. M. (1989). Unit activity in monkey parietal cortex related to haptic perception and temporary memory. *Experimental Brain Research Journal, 76*, 292−306.

Koechlin, E., & Hyafil, A. (2007). Anterior prefrontal function and the limits of human decision-making. *Science, 318*, 594−598.

Liang, L., Wang, R., & Zhang, Z. (2010). The modeling and simulation of visuospatial working memory. *Cognitive Neurodynamics, 4*, 359−366.

Lowe, M. J., Dzemidzic, M., Lurito, J. T., Mathews, V. P., & Phillips, M. D. (2000). Correlations in low-frequency BOLD fluctuations reflect cortico-cortical connections. *NeuroImage, 12*, 582−587.

Luria, A. R. (1966). *Higher cortical functions in man*. New York: Basic Books.

McCloskey, D. I. (1981). Corollary discharges: motor commands and perception. In V. B. Brooks (Ed.), *Handbook of physiology: nervous system* (2nd ed., pp. 1415−1447). Bethesda: *American Physiology Society*.

Miller, E. K., & Cohen, J. D. (2001). An integrative theory of prefrontal cortex function. *Annual Review of Neuroscience, 24*, 167−202.

Miller, E. K., Li, L., & Desimone, R. (1993). Activity of neurons in anterior inferior temporal cortex during a short-term memory task. *Journal of Neuroscience, 13*, 1460−1478.

Miyashita, Y., & Chang, H. S. (1988). Neuronal correlate of pictorial short-term memory in the primate temporal cortex. *Nature, 331*, 68−70.

Monod, J. (1971). *Chance and necessity*. New York: Knopf.

Montojo, C. A., & Courtney, S. M. (2008). Differential neural activation for updating rule versus stimulus information in working memory. *Neuron, 59*, 173−182.

Nee, D. E., Brown, J. W., Askren, M. K., Berman, M. G., Demiralp, E., Krawitz, A., et al. (2013). A meta-analysis of executive components of working memory. *Cerebral Cortex, 23*, 264−282.

Niki, H. (1974). Differential activity of prefrontal units during right and left delayed response trials. *Brain Research*, *70*, 346–349.

Potts, G. F., Martin, L. E., Kamp, S. M., & Donchin, E. (2011). Neural response to action and reward prediction errors: Comparing the error-related negativity to behavioral errors and the feedback-related negativity to reward prediction violations. *Psychophysiology*, *48*, 218–228.

Quintana, J., & Fuster, J. M. (1999). From perception to action: Temporal integrative functions of prefrontal and parietal neurons. *Cerebral Cortex*, *9*, 213–221.

Quintana, J., Fuster, J. M., & Yajeya, J. (1989). Effects of cooling parietal cortex on prefrontal units in delay tasks. *Brain Research*, *503*, 100–110.

Raichle, M. E., MacLeod, A. M., Snyder, A. Z., Powers, W. J., Gusnard, D. A., & Shulman, G. L. (2001). A default mode of brain function. *Proceedings of the National Academy of Sciences of the United States of America*, *98*, 676–682.

Reverberi, C., Gorgen, K., & Haynes, J. D. (2012). Distributed representations of rule identity and rule order in human frontal cortex and striatum. *Journal of Neuroscience*, *32*, 17420–17430.

Rigotti, M., Barak, O., Warden, M. R., Wang, X. J., Daw, N. D., Miller, E. K., et al. (2013). The importance of mixed selectivity in complex cognitive tasks. *Nature*, *497*, 585–590.

Rolls, E. T., & Grabenhorst, F. (2008). The orbitofrontal cortex and beyond: from affect to decision-making. *Progress in Neurobiology*, *86*, 216–244.

Romo, R., Brody, C. D., Hernández, A., & Lemus, L. (1999). Neuronal correlates of parametric working memory in the prefrontal cortex. *Nature*, *399*, 470–473.

Rushworth, M. F., & Behrens, T. E. (2008). Choice, uncertainty and value in prefrontal and cingulate cortex. *Nature Neuroscience*, *11*, 389–397.

Rutledge, R. B., Dean, M., Caplin, A., & Glimcher, P. W. (2010). Testing the reward prediction error hypothesis with an axiomatic model. *Journal of Neuroscience*, *30*, 13525–13536.

Sadaghiani, S., & D'Esposito, M. (2015). Functional characterization of the cingulo-opercular network in the maintenance of tonic alertness. *Cerebral Cortex*, *25*, 2763–2773.

Scheidt, R. A., Lillis, K. P., & Emerson, S. J. (2010). Visual, motor and attentional influences on proprioceptive contributions to perception of hand path rectilinearity during reaching. *Experimental Brain Research Journal*, *204*, 239–254.

Schultz, W. (2006). Behavioral theories and the neurophysiology of reward. *Annual Review of Neuroscience*, *57*, 87–115.

Tang, H., Li, H., & Yan, R. (2010). Memory dynamics in attractor networks with saliency weights. *Neural Computation*, *22*, 1899–1926.

Teuber, H.-L. (1972). Unity and diversity of frontal lobe functions. *Acta Neurobiologiae Experimentalis*, *32*, 625–656.

Uexküll, J. V. (1926). *Theoretical Biology*. New York: Harcourt, Brace & Co.

Verduzco-Flores, S., Bodner, M., Ermentrout, B., Fuster, J. M., & Zhou, Y. (2009). Working memory cell's behavior may be explained by cross-regional networks with synaptic facilitation. *PLoS One*, *4*, e6499.

von Holst, E., & Mittelstaedt, H. (1950). Das Reafferenzprinzip. *Naturwissenschaften*, *20*, 464–476.

Wang, M., Yang, Y., Wang, C. J., Gamo, N. J., Jin, L. E., Mazer, J. A., et al. (2013). NMDA receptors subserve persistent neuronal firing during working memory in dorsolateral prefrontal cortex. *Neuron*, *77*, 736–749.

Wunderlich, K., Dayan, P., & Dolan, R. J. (2012). Mapping value based planning and extensively trained choice in the human brain. *Nature Neuroscience*, *15*, 786–791.

Zhou, Y., & Fuster, J. M. (1996). Mnemonic neuronal activity in somatosensory cortex. *Proceedings of the National Academy of Sciences of the United States of America, 93,* 10533–10537.

Zhou, Y.-D., & Fuster, J. M. (2000). Visuo-tactile cross-modal associations in cortical somatosensory cells. *Proceedings of the National Academy of Sciences of the United States of America, 97,* 9777–9782.

Zipser, D., Kehoe, B., Littlewort, G., & Fuster, J. (1993). A spiking network model of short-term active memory. *Journal of Neuroscience, 13,* 3406–3420.

Chapter 2

The Cellular Mechanisms of Executive Functions and Working Memory: Relevance to Mental Disorders

Taber C. Lightbourne and Amy F.T. Arnsten

Department of Neuroscience, Yale University School of Medicine, New Haven, CT, United States

INTRODUCTION

The prefrontal cortex (PFC) constitutes one-third of the human cerebral cortex; it plays a central role in high-order cognition and dysfunctions in many neuropsychiatric disorders (Fuster, 2001). The PFC guides our thoughts, emotions, and actions by representing relevant knowledge. The ability to generate mental representations in the absence of sensory stimulation is the foundation of abstract thought and executive functions (Arnsten, 2011). Through these mental representations, the PFC allows us to hold information in mind to inform future action. We are thus able to plan for both the long-term (careers and complex projects) and short-term (connecting the beginning and end of a sentence), so that we can act deliberately and live purposefully (Goldman-Rakic, 1991). The PFC also protects purposeful behavior from distractions and compulsions, underscoring its critical role in self-control and inhibition that is necessary for refined behavior (Aron, Robbins, & Poldrack, 2004). Finally it is key for high-order decision-making (Seo & Lee, 2007) and meta-cognition (i.e., thinking about thinking), which facilitates awareness of self (Jurado et al., 1998), other people's thoughts (Gilbert et al., 2007), and moral conscience (Anderson et al., 1999). The unique representational abilities of the PFC facilitates its involvement in advanced cognition from working memory and reason to executive functions such as attention regulation and planning for the future (Fuster, 2008; Robbins, 1996; Thompson-Schill et al., 2002). This fundamental property of the PFC is often captured on working memory tasks.

Executive Functions in Health and Disease. DOI: http://dx.doi.org/10.1016/B978-0-12-803676-1.00002-7

TOPOGRAPHY OF PFC AND ITS RELEVANCE TO NEUROPSYCHIATRIC PATHOLOGY

The PFC exerts top-down guidance of our thoughts, actions, and emotions in a topographically organized manner (Fig. 2.1). One such organizational schema can be found in the distinction between functions of the lateral versus medial areas of the PFC. The lateral surface represents the external world, whereas the medial and ventral PFC represent our internal, visceral world and emotion (Goldman-Rakic, 1987; Ongur & Price, 2000). For instance, there are circuits in the dorsolateral PFC that represent visual space (Funahashi, Bruce, & Goldman-Rakic, 1989) and circuits in the dorsomedial PFC that represent punishment (Seo & Lee, 2009). This organization arises from the connections of these areas. The lateral surface has reciprocal connections with the visual, auditory, and association cortices (Fig. 2.2; Goldman-Rakic, 1987), the ventral regions receive inputs from olfactory—gustatory circuits, insular cortex, and limbic structures (Fig. 2.3; Ongur & Price, 2000), whereas the medial surface serves as a visceromotor center and projects to limbic structures (e.g., hypothalamus) and brainstem (Fig. 2.3; Ongur & Price, 2000). The same topography extends to the basal ganglia where the

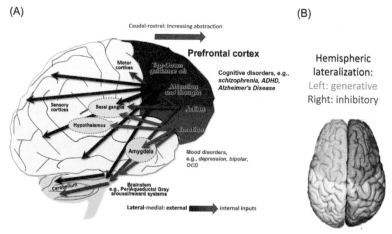

FIGURE 2.1   Topographic organization of PFC in primates. (A) The PFC provides top-down guidance of attention and thought (blue), action (purple), and emotion (red) through extensive neural projections. PFC is topographically organized and major patterns discussed in the text are highlighted here. First is caudal—rostral, denoted by maroon arrow, where the PFC manages increasingly abstract information the further rostral you go. Second is lateral—medial, where lateral PFC processes information from our external world, while ventral and medial regions represent our internal world, e.g., emotions and visceral sensation. This organization is reflected in PFC projection to basal ganglia via dorsal and ventral striatum. (B) Last topographical pattern is hemispheric lateralization where the left hemisphere is associated with generative processes, while the right is involved in inhibition and impulse control. *PFC*, prefrontal cortex; *ADHD*, attention-deficit hyperactivity disorder; *ODR*, oculomotor delayed response.

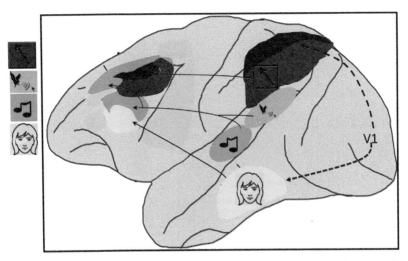

FIGURE 2.2 **Visual and auditory processing streams in PFC (spatial and feature nuclei).** Parallel visual pathways for the processing of visual space and features begin in the primary visual cortex (V1). Pathways remain in parallel as they project into the PFC. Similar distinctions can be found in the auditory processing stream, where parallel pathways exist for auditory space versus feature information. Visuospatial circuit is shown in shades of purple; auditory spatial is shown in orange; visual feature is shown in blue; auditory feature is shown in green. *PFC,* prefrontal cortex. *Adapted from a Goldman-Rakic neuroscience lecture at Yale and Amy Arnsten's review paper on the history and neurobiology of thought.*

dorsolateral PFC projects to the dorsal striatum (caudate) and the ventromedial PFC projects to the ventral striatum.

The PFC can also be thought of as having a rostral-caudal organization (Fig. 2.1), where the more rostral areas are involved in processing abstract information (Badre & D'Esposito, 2007). For instance, the most rostral areas are involved in metacognition, the act of thinking about thinking (Fleming, Huijgen, & Dolan, 2012). Rostral and dorsomedial areas of the PFC are involved in social cognition, including Theory of Mind, the ability to consider what another person might be thinking (Amodio & Frith, 2006). Finally, the PFC in humans exhibits hemispheric lateralization, where the left hemisphere is specialized in generative processes (Robinson et al., 1985), while the right hemisphere drives the inhibition of inappropriate thoughts, actions, and emotions (Aron, 2011).

This topographical organization is reflected in the pattern of PFC dysfunction in clinical disorders (Fig. 2.1). It thus follows that cognitive disorders such as Alzheimer's disease (AD) and schizophrenia involve dysfunction of the dorsolateral prefrontal cortex (dlPFC). Postmortem studies of patients with schizophrenia have demonstrated reduced density of neuropil, dendrites, and spines from pyramidal cells in deep layer III and possibly layer V (Black et al., 2004; Glantz & Lewis, 2000; Selemon & Goldman-Rakic, 1999). While previous

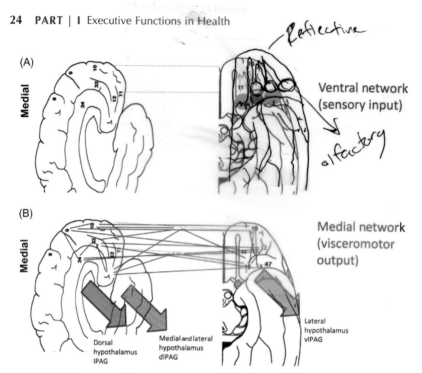

FIGURE 2.3   Summary of cortical connections within the ventral and medial prefrontal cortex. (A) The orbital network receives sensory inputs and integrates information from three major modalities: olfaction (green), visceral (red), and gustatory (blue). (B) In contrast the medial network, serves as a visceromotor output system for the interconnected processing streams in the orbitomedial prefrontal cortex with projections to nuclei in the hypothalamus and periaqueductal gray. *Adapted from summary of orbital and medial networks presented in review paper on orbital and medial PFC networks, Ongur, D., & Price, J. L. (2000). The organization of networks within the orbital and medial prefrontal cortex of rats, monkeys and humans. Cerebral Cortex, 10(3), 206–219.*

findings from rodent studies using N-methyl-D-aspartate receptor (NMDAR) antagonism as a model for schizophrenia have suggested that pathology might be due to excessive glutamate signaling, recent studies in postmortem tissue of patients with schizophrenia have implied the opposite (Napolitano et al., 2014). Recent transcriptome analyses on pyramidal cells of layer III and V in patients with schizophrenia have suggested an under-active state as evinced by mitochondrial markers (Arion et al., 2015). In addition, neuropathology studies in patients with schizophrenia have demonstrated compensatory GABA interneuron underactivity (Curley et al., 2013; Lewis, 2014).

In contrast to schizophrenia where extensive neuronal connections are lost while cell bodies survive, in AD, layers III and V dlPFC pyramidal cells are engulfed by neurofibrillary tangles and degenerate (Bussiere et al., 2003). Tau pathology afflicts the pyramidal cells in the association cortices with the most cortical–cortical connections (Bussiere et al., 2003).

Interestingly, primary sensory cortices are spared in this AD pathology, highlighting a key difference in the vulnerability of these tissues (Lewis et al., 1987; Pearson et al., 1985).

Pathology of the ventromedial cortex, responsible for representation of our internal world, has been implicated in mood disorders, such as depression (Fig. 2.1; Drevets et al., 1997; Mayberg et al., 2005). Imaging studies have revealed the subgenual cingulate (also known as BA 25) to be active when healthy subjects think of sad events and overactive in patients with depression (Mayberg et al., 1999; Mayberg, 2009). However, effective treatment of depression has been shown to reduce activity in BA 25 (Mayberg et al., 2005). Based on this evidence, deep brain stimulation (DBS) has been used to reduce activity in BA 25 and associated white matter tracts in patients with treatment resistant depression. Some patients have reported rapid and profound relief (Mayberg, 2009). Additionally, regions of the ventromedial cortex have also been implicated in obsessive compulsive disorder (OCD) (Insel, 1992). Neuroimaging studies have revealed increased activity in several brain regions of patients with OCD relative to healthy controls: orbital PFC, anterior cingulate, and head of the caudate. This hyperactivity has been shown to be decreased with successful treatment of OCD (Maia, Cooney, & Peterson, 2008).

Finally, the laterality distinctions mentioned earlier are also reflected in certain disease states. For instance, the right PFC has been implicated in disorders marked by impaired impulse control such as attention-deficit hyperactivity disorder (ADHD) and the manic phase of bipolar disorder (Aron, Robbins, & Poldrack, 2014; Blumberg et al., 1999; Shaw et al., 2009). A longitudinal neuroimaging study by Shaw et al. (2009) revealed abnormal development of the right inferior PFC in children with ADHD with respect to healthy controls. The same area was also shown to be underactive in bipolar patients during mania in a positron emission tomographic study (Blumberg et al., 1999). Blumberg and colleagues replicated these findings in an fMRI study in which subjects performed a Stroop task requiring suppression of certain responses. They found that bipolar patients in a manic state showed blunted right PFC activation during the task when compared to healthy controls or patients in a depressed state (Blumberg et al., 2003).

In sum, the PFC has been implicated in many neuropsychiatric disorders; thus, understanding the cellular basis of the PFC may help in uncovering the etiology and treatment of psychiatric disease.

DORSOLATERAL PREFRONTAL CORTEX

A remarkable amount of work has been done to elucidate the cellular mechanisms by which dlPFC circuits generate persistent representations in the absence of external stimuli. As stated above, this is the foundation of higher order processes, in particular working memory. The central role of the dlPFC in working memory was first revealed by Jacobsen who noted that monkeys with bilateral dlPFC lesions could not retain information for even a short amount of time. Monkeys in his study could solve difficult puzzles if the information was present during the task; however, their performance was reduced to chance on tasks that required even minimal recall of information (Arnsten, 2013; Jacobsen, 1936). Goldman-Rakic (1995) paved the way for more detailed knowledge of the mechanisms of working memory through studies of spatial working memory in rhesus monkeys. She delineated a subregion of the dlPFC around the caudal two-thirds of the principal sulcus (walker area 46) that is critical for visuospatial working memory (Goldman & Rosvold, 1970). As shown in Fig. 2.2, this region shares reciprocal connections with the parietal association cortices specialized for visual spatial processing (Cavada & Goldman-Rakic, 1989; Goldman-Rakic, Selemon, & Schwartz, 1984; Selemon & Goldman-Rakic, 1988). She also showed that more ventral areas on the lateral surface receive visual feature information (Fig. 2.2), serving as a parallel visual processing stream (Goldman-Rakic, 1987; Haxby et al., 1991). A few years later, analogous pathways devoted to auditory information were found, with separate networks specialized for the receipt of auditory spatial and auditory feature information (Fig. 2.2; Romanski et al., 1999). These data revealed topography for high-order cognitive processing of sensory stimuli where spatial information resided more dorsally within the cortex and feature information ventrally (Goldman-Rakic, 1987).

PHYSIOLOGY AND MICROCIRCUITRY OF WORKING MEMORY

The cellular basis of visuospatial working memory was uncovered through electrophysiology studies in monkeys (Goldman-Rakic, 1995). Goldman-Rakic's group adapted an earlier task (Hikosaka & Wurtz, 1983) to explore the cellular underpinnings of visuospatial working memory (Funahashi et al., 1989). They recorded neuronal activity in area 46, as monkeys performed an oculomotor delayed response (ODR) task (Fig. 2.4A). The task consists of briefly presenting the subject with a spatial cue. The subject must remember the position of the cue after a delay period of several seconds. After the delay period, the monkey can make a hand or eye movement (saccade) to the remembered location. Correct responses are rewarded.

Neuronal recordings from area 46 have revealed several cell types with task-related firing, as summarized in Fig. 2.4B. Some neurons seem to convey simple sensory or motor information, e.g., cue cells that fire in response to the spatial cue, presaccadic response cells activated in anticipation of a motor response (in this case a saccade or hand movement), and postsaccadic response cells are thought to convey feedback about the motor response, a process referred to as corollary discharge (Wang, Vijayraghavan, &

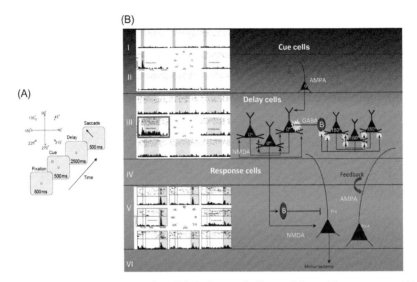

FIGURE 2.4 Neural circuits in dlPFC that underlie spatial working memory. (A) Schematic illustration of the oculomotor delayed response task, in which a cue briefly (0.5 s) appears at one of eight locations (e.g., 135 degrees), while the monkey fixates on a central spot. The location must be remembered over a delay period of several seconds until the fixation spot disappears, and the monkey can move its eyes to the remembered location for a juice reward. The cued location changes over many trials, requiring constant updating of working memory. (B) Cue, delay, and response cells recorded from area 46 of the monkey dlPFC as a monkey performs ODR task and the corresponding microcircuitry thought to underlie working memory. Cue cells fire when the cue is presented but stop firing during the delay period. Delay cells often fire to the cue (and/or to saccadic response) but are remarkable for their ability to maintain persistent firing across the delay period for the neuron's preferred direction. Usually, delay cells are spatially tuned such that they fire across the delay period for the neuron's preferred direction (e.g., 180 degrees as depicted here) while decreasing firing for all other nonpreferred directions. Increased activity observed in the preferred direction is outlined by a red box. Microcircuits underlying delay cell activity reside in layer III (and also possibly layer V) and are described in the text. In contrast to delay cells, response cells are thought to reside in layer V. Response cells are often inhibited during the delay period and fire leading up to, during, and/or after the motor response, either initiating action or conveying feedback. *DlPFC*, dorsolateral prefrontal cortex; *ODR*, oculomotor delayed response.

Goldman-Rakic, 2004). However, there is a large population of cells referred to as delay cells that demonstrate spatially tuned, persistent firing throughout the delay period when position of the cue must be maintained through working memory (Funahashi et al., 1989). In other words, the continuous firing of these cells allows the animal to hold information about the spatial location of that cue over a short amount of time to guide a subsequent response.

The microcircuits that generate spatially tuned persistent firing reside predominantly in deep layer III (Kritzer & Goldman-Rakic, 1995) and are summarized in Fig. 2.4B. Pyramidal cells with similar preferred directions excite each other through glutamate receptor synapses on long, thin spines to maintain firing across the delay period. Conversely, spatial tuning is refined by lateral inhibition from GABAergic interneurons (Goldman-Rakic, 1995). This marks a diversion from more classic circuits, e.g., in V1, where feedforward rather than lateral inhibition serves this purpose (Gabernet et al., 2005). Interestingly, dlPFC layer III enlarges in primate evolution, with increased dendritic complexity and the number of spines. Importantly, these microcircuits are a focus of pathology in schizophrenia (Glantz & Lewis, 2000; Glausier & Lewis, 2013) and aging (Morrison & Baxter, 2012).

MOLECULAR REGULATION OF dlPFC REPRESENTATIONAL CIRCUITS

Layer III pyramidal cell networks in the dlPFC interconnect on dendritic spines and excite each other through NMDAR synapses (Fig. 2.5; Wang et al., 2013). The NMDAR pore is blocked by Mg^{2+} in a hyperpolarized membrane but is able to transmit both sodium and calcium when sitting in a depolarized membrane. Delay cell firing depends on NMDAR stimulation, including NMDAR with NR2B subunits (Wang et al., 2013). Electron microscopy demonstrated that NMDAR-NR2B are localized exclusively in the postsynaptic density and are not extrasynaptic as they are in many classic synapses (Wang et al., 2013). Iontophoresis of an NMDAR-NR2B antagonist markedly reduced delay cell firing (Wang et al., 2013). In contrast,

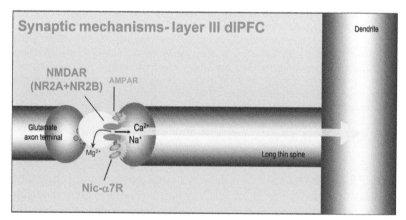

FIGURE 2.5 Mechanisms underlying synaptic transmission in thin spines of the dlPFC. This is a schematic illustration of mechanisms underlying synaptic transmission of excitatory impulses between spines in layer III dlPFC. In contrast to "traditional" synapses (dark green), NMDAR-NR2Bs are exclusively localized in the postsynaptic density and are not extrasynaptic. These synapses have only a subtle AMPAR component, and the permissive excitation needed for NMDAR opening is mediated, in large part, by cholinergic stimulation of nic-α7R (light green). *DlPFC*, dorsolateral prefrontal cortex; *NMDAR*, N-methyl-D-aspartate receptor; *AMPAR*, α-amino-3-hydroxy-5-methyl-4-isoxazolepropionic acid receptor.

iontophoresis of α-amino-3-hydroxy-5-methyl-4-isoxazolepropionic acid receptor (AMPAR) antagonists had a significantly smaller influence on neuronal firing than NMDA blockade (Fig. 2.5; Wang et al., 2013). This was surprising, as AMPARs have been shown to be essential for depolarizing the membrane and permitting NMDAR opening in the sensory cortices or subcortical structures such as the hippocampus. However, AMPARs do not appear to play a large permissive role in the NMDAR-mediated firing of dlPFC delay cells (Wang et al., 2013).

Recent research has shown that this key permissive role is instead mediated by cholinergic stimulation of nicotinic alpha-7 receptors (nic-α7R) in the dlPFC (Yang et al., 2013). Nic-α7Rs are localized within glutamate synapses on layer III spines, positioned to depolarize the synaptic membrane (Fig. 2.5; Yang et al., 2013). Stimulation of nic-α7R enhanced delay cell firing in monkeys performing a working memory task, and most importantly, NMDA was not able to excite delay cells if nic-α7R were blocked. As acetylcholine is released during wakefulness but not in deep sleep (Hobson, 1992); conscious thought during wakefulness may arise from nic-α7R stimulation permitting dlPFC network connections (Yang et al., 2013). These data have also prompted an exploration of other cholinergic receptors, i.e., the muscarinic-1-receptor, which are also localized in layer III glutamate synapses on spines (Mrzljak, Levey, & Goldman-Rakic, 1993). α7-nAchR agonists are being developed as potential cognitive enhancers (Hajos & Rogers, 2010; Yang et al., 2013).

These data suggest that arousal state has a profound influence on the strength of dlPFC network connections. In addition to cholinergic mechanisms, recent research has revealed a new form of plasticity in the PFC, whereby the strength of PFC network connections can be rapidly and powerfully altered in a dynamic manner by the arousal systems, a process termed dynamic network connectivity (Arnsten et al., 2010; Arnsten, Wang, & Paspalas, 2012). Thus, modulators such as dopamine (DA), norepinephrine, and glutamate itself can alter the strength of dlPFC layer III synapses by opening or closing potassium channels on long, thin spines (Arnsten et al., 2012). The following describes the mechanisms that rapidly reduce activity in dlPFC networks, e.g., weaken connectivity under conditions of stress.

MECHANISMS THAT WEAKEN dlPFC NETWORK CONNECTIONS

DlPFC network connections are rapidly weakened by feedforward cyclic AMP (cAMP)-calcium signaling opening of potassium channels, e.g., HCN (hyperpolarization-activated cyclic nucleotide gated) channels in dendritic spines (Fig. 2.6). Layer III thin spines commonly contain a calcium-storing spine apparatus, the extension of the smooth endoplasmic reticulum into the spine (Paspalas, Wang, & Arnsten, 2013). cAMP-related signaling proteins, HCN and KCNQ potassium channels cluster near the spine apparatus in layer

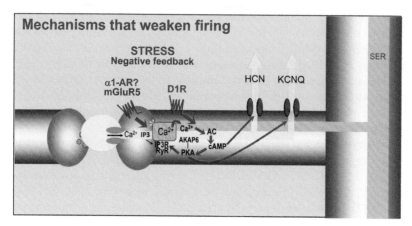

FIGURE 2.6   Dynamic network connectivity: mechanisms of negative feedback and weakened connectivity. Mechanisms that increase feedforward calcium-cAMP-PKA signaling (shown in red, many engaged by stress) *weaken* synaptic connections by opening nearby K$^+$ channels (HCN, KCNQ) on the spine head and/or neck. However this system is also engaged by glutamatergic receptors such as mGluR5 (depicted in maroon) to provide *negative feedback* on excitatory activity when there is an excess of glutamate in the synapse. *PKA*, protein kinase-A; *cAMP*, cyclic AMP; *HCN*, hyperpolarization-activated cyclic nucleotide.

III spines, positioned to allow a positive feedback loop whereby Ca^{2+} release from the spine apparatus can drive the production of cAMP, and cAMP-Protein Kinase A (PKA) signaling can enhance IP3 receptor and ryanodine receptor−mediated Ca^{2+} release from the spine apparatus (Soulsby & Wojcikiewicz, 2005). These feedforward actions would promote a rapid increase in cAMP-PKA signaling. cAMP increases the open state of HCN channels, whereas PKA increases the open state of KCNQ channels (Delmas & Brown, 2005; Paspalas et al., 2013). Thus, feedforward Ca^{2+}-cAMP-PKA signaling can induce a rapid opening of HCN and KCNQ channels and reduce delay cell persistent neuronal firing (Arnsten, 2015). This process may be further propagated by calcium activation of protein kinase C (PKC) by a variety of mechanisms, e.g., facilitating adenylyl cyclase activity and/or uncoupling alpha-2 adrenergic receptors that normally inhibit cAMP signaling. Metabotropic glutamate receptors mGluR1α and mGluR5 are localized near the synapse in layer III spines (Muly, Maddox, & Smith, 2003) and may drive Ca^{2+} release from the spine apparatus through Gq/IP3 signaling. This may provide important negative feedback in a recurrent excitatory network, preventing excessive neuronal firing in response to high levels of glutamate release. This mechanism also appears to contribute to the "sculpting" of network inputs, weakening nonpreferred inputs to the neuron. Thus, low levels of DA stimulation of D1 receptors (D1R) can sculpt neuronal activity to remove "noise" by increasing cAMP signaling, sharpening the tuning of the delay cell for its preferred direction (Vijayraghavan et al., 2007).

The finding that Ca^{2+}-cAMP signaling *reduces* delay cell firing in the dlPFC marks another divergence from mechanisms elucidated in earlier work on circuits in the hippocampus and sensory cortices, where cAMP-PKA and PKC signaling enhance synaptic transmission via long-term potentiation (LTP) (Abel et al., 1997; Hongpaisan & Alkon, 2007). These transient mechanisms that weaken the circuitry at precise locations allow for sculpting of information held in working memory, or the ability to take dlPFC "off-line" during fatigue when there is insufficient energy to maintain persistent firing or during stress exposure to switch the brain to a more reflexive state, as described later in the chapter.

MECHANISMS THAT STRENGTHEN dlPFC NETWORK CONNECTIONS

In contrast, there are a variety of cellular processes that strengthen PFC network connections, including a number of mechanisms that reduce cAMP signaling in layer III dlPFC spines (Fig. 2.7). The phosphodiesterase 4A (PDE4A) is concentrated in layer III spines near the spine apparatus (Paspalas et al., 2013), positioned to catabolize cAMP and reduce feedforward cAMP-Ca^{2+} signaling. Importantly, PDE4A is anchored near the spine apparatus by DISC1 (disrupted in schizophrenia). Thus loss of DISC1, e.g., in families with a translocation in the DISC1 gene would likely lead to

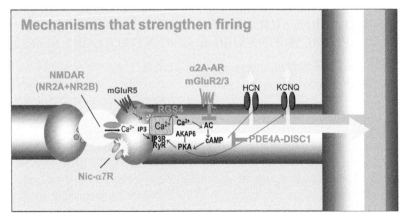

FIGURE 2.7 Dynamic network connectivity: mechanisms that enhance connectivity in dlPFC. Dynamic network connectivity also includes mechanisms that strengthen synaptic transmission by inhibiting feedforward calcium-cAMP-PKA signaling (green), enhancing delay cell firing. Loss of inhibition, e.g., through genetic insults to DISC1, may contribute to spine loss and impaired dlPFC function. The unique modulation of layer III dlPFC pyramidal cell synapses provides strategies for therapeutic targets in the treatment of cognitive disorders (e.g., stimulation of alpha2A-AR with agents like guanfacine). *DlPFC*, dorsolateral prefrontal cortex; *PKA*, protein kinase-A; *cAMP*, cyclic AMP; *HCN*, hyperpolarization-activated cyclic nucleotide.

dysregulated cAMP signaling in spines and weakening of dlPFC network connections. This may contribute to the dlPFC gray matter loss observed in patients with schizophrenia (Cannon et al., 2005; Szeszko et al., 2008).

There are also a number of receptors that inhibit cAMP signaling concentrated on dlPFC layer III spines. As described in more detail below, noradrenergic (NE) α2A-AR are localized on spines next to HCN channels, and stimulation of α2A-AR increases delay cell firing by inhibiting cAMP production and improves working memory (Wang et al., 2007). Conversely, blockade of these receptors produces a rapid loss of firing that can be rescued by blocking HCN channels (Wang et al., 2007). More recent, unpublished data find similar effects with mGluR2/3, receptors that also inhibit cAMP production (Jin and Arnsten, unpublished).

It is also possible, although currently untested, that layer III microcircuits are strengthened by the actions of RGS4 (regulator of G protein signaling 4). RGS4 can inhibit Gq/IP3/PKC signaling and thus may reduce Ca^{2+} release from the spine apparatus. ImmunoEM shows that RGS4 is positioned to perform this function in dlPFC spines (Paspalas, Selemon, & Arnsten, 2009), but its physiology remains untested. This issue is of special interest because RGS4 levels are markedly reduced in the dlPFC of individuals with schizophrenia (Mirnics et al., 2001), and a polymorphism in the gene encoding for RGS4 is associated with PFC gray matter loss, reduced connectivity, and reduced BOLD signals in patients with schizophrenia, a population know to have working memory deficits (Buckholtz et al., 2007; Prasad et al., 2005).

CATECHOLAMINE MODULATION OF MECHANISMS THAT WEAKEN PFC ACTIVITY DURING UNCONTROLLABLE STRESS

Exposure to uncontrollable stress, acute or chronic, causes loss of PFC cognitive function in rodents, monkeys, and humans and exacerbates most mental illness (Arnsten et al., 2015). Thus it is of great interest to understand the neurobiological mechanisms underlying these impairments. Even mild, acute uncontrollable stress induces high levels of catecholamine release in the medial PFC in rodents (Finlay, Zigmond, & Abercrombie, 1995; Murphy et al., 1996) and in the dlPFC in monkeys (Kodama et al., 2014). As illustrated in Fig. 2.6, high levels of catecholamine release during stress reduce dlPFC delay cell firing and impair working memory by increasing feedforward cAMP-Ca^{2+}-K^+ channel signaling.

ImmunoEM studies in monkeys revealed that DA D1R are localized in the synapse of layer III spines next to HCN channels (Arnsten, Wang, Paspalas, 2015). Electrophysiological studies revealed that D1R stimulation reduces delay cell firing through cAMP opening of HCN channels (Gamo et al., 2015; Vijayraghavan et al., 2007). High levels of NE α1-adrenoreceptor stimulation also markedly reduce delay cell firing via increased Ca^{2+}-PKC signaling (Birnbaum et al., 2004). In the presence of danger, this rapid loss of PFC function could confer a survival advantage, allowing more primitive, reflexive circuitry to guide behavior (Birnbaum et al., 2004).

Studies in rats have shown that chronic stress exposure leads to architectural changes in PFC, with atrophy of layer III dendrites and loss of dendritic spines that correlate with impaired cognitive performance (Hains et al., 2009; Liston et al., 2006). Dendritic spine density and working memory performance are both protected from chronic stress exposure by daily treatment with agents that inhibit Ca^{2+}-PKC signaling (chelerythrine) or cAMP-PKA signaling (guanfacine) (Arnsten & Jin, 2012).

The α1-AR antagonist, prazosin, and guanfacine are now in use for the treatment of PTSD based in part on this research in animals (Arnsten et al., 2015). As the PFC plays a large role in human behavior, restoring PFC function during stress is of particular importance to therapeutics.

ALPHA-2A NORADRENERGIC INFLUENCE: SUCCESSFUL TRANSLATION MODULATION OF MECHANISMS THAT BOTH WEAKEN AND STRENGTHEN FIRING

In contrast to high levels of NE release during stress, low to moderate levels of NE exert essential beneficial effects on PFC function via α2A-adrenoreceptors (α2A-AR), which have high affinity for NE. α2A-AR agonists have been shown to improve PFC function in mice (Franowicz et al., 2002), rats (Tanila, Rama, & Carlson, 1996), monkeys (Arnsten, Cai, & Goldman-Rakic, 1988; Rama et al., 1996), and humans (Jakala et al., 1999). The enhancing effects of these agents on PFC function can be dissociated from the sedating properties of these compounds at higher doses (Arnsten et al., 1988). The beneficial effects of α2A-AR stimulation on working memory are largely due to drug actions at postsynaptic receptors in dlPFC (Arnsten 1985). In monkey dlPFC, α2A-ARs are colocalized with HCN channels on layer III spines near the synapse and in the spine neck (Wang et al., 2007). α2A receptors are coupled to Gi proteins that inhibit cAMP signaling. Stimulation of α2A-ARs with guanfacine increases delay cell firing by inhibiting cAMP-HCN channel signaling in spines, preferentially increasing the neuron's response to the preferred direction (Wang et al., 2007). Conversely, blockade of α2A-AR with yohimbine reduces delay cell firing, and neuronal activity is rescued by blocking HCN channels (ibid).

Behavioral studies in animal models revealed a myriad of beneficial effects with special relevance for ADHD. Research has revealed that α2A-AR stimulation with guanfacine not only improves working memory (Wang et al., 2007) but also improves attention regulation (Arnsten & Contant, 1992; O'Neill et al., 2000) and behavioral inhibition (Steere & Arnsten, 1997). In addition, a study in monkeys revealed that guanfacine was able to improve impulse control in monkeys performing delayed discounting tasks

(Kim et al., 2012). Delayed discounting tasks involve offering subjects the choice of smaller immediate rewards versus larger delayed rewards (Lempert et al., 2012). In the aforementioned study, Kim et al. (2012) showed that guanfacine-treated monkeys demonstrated increased ability to resist immediate small reward and wait for a larger reward. Conversely, blockade of α2A-AR in the dlPFC impairs working memory, induces locomotor hyperactivity, and impairs impulse control (Li & Mei, 1994; Ma, Arnsten, & Li, 2005; Ma et al., 2003).

As described above, systemic administration of guanfacine can protect PFC layer II/III dendritic spine loss and working memory from the deleterious effects of chronic stress (Hains, Yabe, & Arnsten, 2015). Rodent studies have also shown that it can protect PFC spines from oxygen deprivation (Kauser et al., 2013) and can enhance spine maturation in vitro in cultured PFC neurons (Ren, Liu, & Li, 2012). Thus, guanfacine appears to have architectural and physiological actions in PFC.

Given the robustness of these data, across species and domains of cognition, guanfacine is now being used to treat a variety of PFC disorders. An extended release formulation was approved for the treatment of pediatric ADHD. Weaker PFC function is a key feature of ADHD, particularly in the right inferior PFC that is important for inhibiting inappropriate actions (Kauser et al., 2013). This PFC subregion normally enlarges as a child's brain matures but fails to follow that trajectory in children with ADHD (Shaw et al., 2009). Guanfacine helps ADHD patients to better self-regulate their behavior by inhibiting inappropriate distractions and impulses (Biederman et al., 2008; Scahill et al., 2001). Finally, guanfacine also diminishes inappropriate aggressive impulses (Connor et al., 2013; McCracken et al., 2010), perhaps through enhancing activity in the ventral PFC.

CONCLUSION

In sum, the PFC is a unique and complex region of the brain shaped by numerous, intricate mechanisms that allow for the variety of functions it subserves. The ability to transiently adjust connectivity of circuits in the PFC allows our cognitive state to be tailored to an ever changing environment and demands at hand. While this confers great flexibility, it also allows for vulnerability in these higher order circuits. In addition, the PFC provides top-down guidance to other CNS structures to drive our thoughts, emotions, and actions. Thus deficits in subregions of the PFC can have devastating effects on neurological function and result in disease. It is therefore imperative to continue exploring the unique features of the PFC to more fully understand neuropsychiatric disease and develop effective treatment for patients.

ACKNOWLEDGMENTS

Much of the work discussed was executed by Drs. Arnsten's lab group at Yale, funded by PHS Pioneer Award DP1AG047744, R01AG043430, RO1 MH100064, and R01 MH 093354.

REFERENCES

Abel, T., et al. (1997). Genetic demonstration of a role for PKA in the late phase of LTP and in hippocampus-based long-term memory. *Cell*, *88*(5), 615–626.

Amodio, D. M., & Frith, C. D. (2006). Meeting of minds: The medial frontal cortex and social cognition. *Nature Reviews Neuroscience*, *7*(4), 268–277.

Anderson, S. W., et al. (1999). Impairment of social and moral behavior related to early damage in human prefrontal cortex. *Nature Neuroscience*, *2*(11), 1032–1037.

Arion, D., et al. (2015). Distinctive transcriptome alterations of prefrontal pyramidal neurons in schizophrenia and schizoaffective disorder. *Molecular Psychiatry*, *20*(11), 1397–1405.

Arnsten, A. F. (2011). Prefrontal cortical network connections: Key site of vulnerability in stress and schizophrenia. *International Journal of Developmental Neuroscience*, *29*(3), 215–223.

Arnsten, A. F. (2013). The neurobiology of thought: The groundbreaking discoveries of Patricia Goldman-Rakic 1937-2003. *Cerebral Cortex*, *23*(10), 2269–2281.

Arnsten, A. F. (2015). Stress weakens prefrontal networks: Molecular insults to higher cognition. *Nature Neuroscience*, *18*(10), 1376–1385.

Arnsten, A. F., & Contant, T. A. (1992). Alpha-2 adrenergic agonists decrease distractibility in aged monkeys performing the delayed response task. *Psychopharmacology (Berl)*, *108* (1–2), 159–169.

Arnsten, A. F., Cai, J. X., & Goldman-Rakic, P. S. (1988). The alpha-2 adrenergic agonist guanfacine improves memory in aged monkeys without sedative or hypotensive side effects: Evidence for alpha-2 receptor subtypes. *Journal of Neuroscience*, *8*(11), 4287–4298.

Arnsten, A. F., & Jin, L. E. (2012). Guanfacine for the treatment of cognitive disorders: A century of discoveries at Yale. *Yale Journal of Biology and Medicine*, *85*(1), 45–58.

Arnsten, A. F., Wang, M. J., & Paspalas, C. D. (2012). Neuromodulation of thought: Flexibilities and vulnerabilities in prefrontal cortical network synapses. *Neuron*, *76*(1), 223–239.

Arnsten, A. F., Wang, M., & Paspalas, C. D. (2015a). Dopamine's actions in primate prefrontal cortex: Challenges for treating cognitive disorders. *Pharmacological Reviews*, *67*(3), 681–696.

Arnsten, A. F., et al. (2010). Dynamic network connectivity: a new form of neuroplasticity. *Trends in Cognitive Sciences*, *14*(8), 365–375.

Arnsten, A. F. T., et al. (2015). The effects of stress exposure on prefrontal cortex: Translating basic research into successful treatments for post-traumatic stress disorder. *Neurobiology of Stress*, *1*, 89–99.

Aron, A. R. (2011). From reactive to proactive and selective control: Developing a richer model for stopping inappropriate responses. *Biological Psychiatry*, *69*(12), e55–e68.

Aron, A. R., Robbins, T. W., & Poldrack, R. A. (2004). Inhibition and the right inferior frontal cortex. *Trends in Cognitive Sciences*, *8*(4), 170–177.

Aron, A. R., Robbins, T. W., & Poldrack, R. A. (2014). Inhibition and the right inferior frontal cortex: One decade on. *Trends in Cognitive Sciences*, *18*(4), 177–185.

Badre, D., & D'Esposito, M. (2007). Functional magnetic resonance imaging evidence for a hierarchical organization of the prefrontal cortex. *Journal of Cognitive Neuroscience*, *19*(12), 2082–2099.

Biederman, J., et al. (2008). A randomized, double-blind, placebo-controlled study of guanfacine extended release in children and adolescents with attention-deficit/hyperactivity disorder. *Pediatrics, 121*(1), e73−e84.

Birnbaum, S. G., et al. (2004). Protein kinase C overactivity impairs prefrontal cortical regulation of working memory. *Science, 306*(5697), 882−884.

Black, J. E., et al. (2004). Pathology of layer V pyramidal neurons in the prefrontal cortex of patients with schizophrenia. *American Journal of Psychiatry, 161*(4), 742−744.

Blumberg, H. P., et al. (1999). Rostral and orbital prefrontal cortex dysfunction in the manic state of bipolar disorder. *American Journal of Psychiatry, 156*(12), 1986−1988.

Blumberg, H. P., et al. (2003). A functional magnetic resonance imaging study of bipolar disorder: State- and trait-related dysfunction in ventral prefrontal cortices. *Archives General Psychiatry, 60*(6), 601−609.

Buckholtz, J. W., et al. (2007). Allelic variation in RGS4 impacts functional and structural connectivity in the human brain. *Journal of Neuroscience, 27*(7), 1584−1593.

Bussiere, T., et al. (2003). Progressive degeneration of nonphosphorylated neurofilament protein-enriched pyramidal neurons predicts cognitive impairment in Alzheimer's disease: Stereologic analysis of prefrontal cortex area 9. *Journal of Comparative Neurology, 463*(3), 281−302.

Cannon, T. D., et al. (2005). Association of DISC1/TRAX haplotypes with schizophrenia, reduced prefrontal gray matter, and impaired short- and long-term memory. *Archives General Psychiatry, 62*(11), 1205−1213.

Cavada, C., & Goldman-Rakic, P. S. (1989). Posterior parietal cortex in rhesus monkey: II. Evidence for segregated corticocortical networks linking sensory and limbic areas with the frontal lobe. *Journal of Comparative Neurology, 287*(4), 422−445.

Connor, D. F., et al. (2013). An open-label study of guanfacine extended release for traumatic stress related symptoms in children and adolescents. *Journal of Child and Adolescent Psychopharmacology, 23*(4), 244−251.

Curley, A. A., et al. (2013). Role of glutamic acid decarboxylase 67 in regulating cortical parvalbumin and GABA membrane transporter 1 expression: Implications for schizophrenia. *Neurobiology Disease, 50*, 179−186.

Delmas, P., & Brown, D. A. (2005). Pathways modulating neural KCNQ/M (Kv7) potassium channels. *Nature Reviews Neuroscience, 6*(11), 850−862.

Drevets, W. C., et al. (1997). Subgenual prefrontal cortex abnormalities in mood disorders. *Nature, 386*(6627), 824−827.

Finlay, J. M., Zigmond, M. J., & Abercrombie, E. D. (1995). Increased dopamine and norepinephrine release in medial prefrontal cortex induced by acute and chronic stress: Effects of diazepam. *Neuroscience, 64*(3), 619−628.

Fleming, S. M., Huijgen, J., & Dolan, R. J. (2012). Prefrontal contributions to metacognition in perceptual decision making. *Journal of Neuroscience, 32*(18), 6117−6125.

Franowicz, J. S., et al. (2002). Mutation of the alpha2A-adrenoceptor impairs working memory performance and annuls cognitive enhancement by guanfacine. *Journal of Neuroscience, 22*(19), 8771−8777.

Funahashi, S., Bruce, C. J., & Goldman-Rakic, P. S. (1989). Mnemonic coding of visual space in the monkey's dorsolateral prefrontal cortex. *Journal of Neurophysiology, 61*(2), 331−349.

Fuster, J. M. (2001). The prefrontal cortex—An update: Time is of the essence. *Neuron, 30*(2), 319−333.

Fuster, J. M. (2008). *The prefrontal cortex* (4th Edition). San Diego, CA: Academic Press.

Gabernet, L., et al. (2005). Somatosensory integration controlled by dynamic thalamocortical feed-forward inhibition. *Neuron, 48*(2), 315−327.

Gamo, N. J., et al. (2015). Stress impairs prefrontal cortical function via d1 dopamine receptor interactions with hyperpolarization-activated cyclic nucleotide-gated channels. *Biological Psychiatry, 78*(12), 860−870.

Gilbert, S. J., et al. (2007). Distinct regions of medial rostral prefrontal cortex supporting social and nonsocial functions. *Social Cognitive and Affective Neuroscience, 2*(3), 217−226.

Glantz, L. A., & Lewis, D. A. (2000). Decreased dendritic spine density on prefrontal cortical pyramidal neurons in schizophrenia. *Archives General Psychiatry, 57*(1), 65−73.

Glausier, J. R., & Lewis, D. A. (2013). Dendritic spine pathology in schizophrenia. *Neuroscience, 251*, 90−107.

Goldman, P. S., & Rosvold, H. E. (1970). Localization of function within the dorsolateral prefrontal cortex of the rhesus monkey. *Experimental Neurology, 27*(2), 291−304.

Goldman-Rakic, P. S. (1991). Prefrontal cortical dysfunction in schizophrenia (relevance of working memory). In J. E. Barett, & B. J. Carroll (Eds.), *Psychopathology and the brain*. New York: Raven Press.

Goldman-Rakic, P. S. (1995). Cellular basis of working memory. *Neuron, 14*(3), 477−485.

Goldman-Rakic, P.S. (1987). Circuitry of primate prefrontal cortex and regulation of behavior by representational memory. In: Comprehensive physiology, Supplement 5: Handbook of physiology, the nervous system, higher functions of the brain. John Wiley & Sons, Inc., Hoboken, N.J.; 373−417.

Goldman-Rakic, P. S., Selemon, L. D., & Schwartz, M. L. (1984). Dual pathways connecting the dorsolateral prefrontal cortex with the hippocampal formation and parahippocampal cortex in the rhesus monkey. *Neuroscience, 12*(3), 719−743.

Hains, A. B., Yabe, Y., & Arnsten, A. F. (2015). Chronic stimulation of alpha-2a-adrenoceptors with guanfacine protects rodent prefrontal cortex dendritic spines and cognition from the effects of chronic stress. *Neurobiology Stress, 2*, 1−9.

Hains, A. B., et al. (2009). Inhibition of protein kinase C signaling protects prefrontal cortex dendritic spines and cognition from the effects of chronic stress. *Proceedings of the National Academy of Sciences of the United States of America, 106*(42), 17957−17962.

Hajos, M., & Rogers, B. N. (2010). Targeting alpha7 nicotinic acetylcholine receptors in the treatment of schizophrenia. *Current Pharmaceutical Design, 16*(5), 538−554.

Haxby, J. V., et al. (1991). Dissociation of object and spatial visual processing pathways in human extrastriate cortex. *Proceedings of the National Academy of Sciences of the United States of America, 88*(5), 1621−1625.

Hikosaka, O., & Wurtz, R. H. (1983). Visual and oculomotor functions of monkey substantia nigra pars reticulata. III. Memory-contingent visual and saccade responses. *Journal of Neurophysiology, 49*(5), 1268−1284.

Hobson, J. A. (1992). Sleep and dreaming: induction and mediation of REM sleep by cholinergic mechanisms. *Current Opinion in Neurobiology, 2*(6), 759−763.

Hongpaisan, J., & Alkon, D. L. (2007). A structural basis for enhancement of long-term associative memory in single dendritic spines regulated by PKC. *Proceedings of the National Academy of Sciences of the United States of America, 104*(49), 19571−19576.

Insel, T. R. (1992). Neurobiology of obsessive compulsive disorder: A review. *International Clinical Psychopharmacology, 7*(Suppl 1), 31−33.

Jacobsen, C. (1936). Studies of cerebral function in primates. *Comparative Psychology Monographs, 13*, 1−68.

Jakala, P., et al. (1999). Guanfacine, but not clonidine, improves planning and working memory performance in humans. *Neuropsychopharmacology, 20*(5), 460–470.

Jurado, M. A., et al. (1998). Overestimation and unreliability in "feeling-of-doing" judgements about temporal ordering performance: Impaired self-awareness following frontal lobe damage. *Journal of Clinical and Experimental Neuropsychology, 20*(3), 353–364.

Kauser, H., et al. (2013). Guanfacine is an effective countermeasure for hypobaric hypoxia-induced cognitive decline. *Neuroscience, 254,* 110–119.

Kim, S., et al. (2012). Effects of α-2A adrenergic receptor agonist on time and risk preference in primates. *Psychopharmacology (Berl), 219*(2), 363–375.

Kodama, T., et al. (2014). Higher dopamine release induced by less rather than more preferred reward during a working memory task in the primate prefrontal cortex. *Behavioural Brain Research, 266,* 104–107.

Kritzer, M. F., & Goldman-Rakic, P. S. (1995). Intrinsic circuit organization of the major layers and sublayers of the dorsolateral prefrontal cortex in the rhesus monkey. *Journal of Comparative Neurology, 359*(1), 131–143.

Lempert, K. M., et al. (2012). Individual differences in delay discounting under acute stress: The role of trait perceived stress. *Frontiers in Psychology, 3,* 251.

Lewis, D. A. (2014). Inhibitory neurons in human cortical circuits: Substrate for cognitive dysfunction in schizophrenia. *Current Opinion in Neurobiology, 26,* 22–26.

Lewis, D. A., et al. (1987). Laminar and regional distributions of neurofibrillary tangles and neuritic plaques in Alzheimer's disease: A quantitative study of visual and auditory cortices. *Journal of Neuroscience, 7*(6), 1799–1808.

Li, B. M., & Mei, Z. T. (1994). Delayed-response deficit induced by local injection of the alpha 2-adrenergic antagonist yohimbine into the dorsolateral prefrontal cortex in young adult monkeys. *Behavioral and Neural Biology, 62*(2), 134–139.

Liston, C., et al. (2006). Stress-induced alterations in prefrontal cortical dendritic morphology predict selective impairments in perceptual attentional set-shifting. *Journal of Neuroscience, 26*(30), 7870–7874.

Ma, C.-L., Arnsten, A. F. T., & Li, B.-M. (2005). Locomotor hyperactivity induced by blockade of prefrontal cortical α2-adrenoceptors in monkeys. *Biological Psychiatry, 57*(2), 192–195.

Ma, C.-L., et al. (2003). Selective deficit in no-go performance induced by blockade of prefrontal cortical α2-adrenoceptors in monkeys. *Neuroreport, 14*(7), 1013–1016.

Maia, T. V., Cooney, R. E., & Peterson, B. S. (2008). The neural bases of obsessive-compulsive disorder in children and adults. *Development and Psychopathology, 20*(4), 1251–1283.

Mayberg, H. S. (2009). Targeted electrode-based modulation of neural circuits for depression. *J Clinical Investigation, 119*(4), 717–725.

Mayberg, H. S., et al. (1999). Reciprocal limbic-cortical function and negative mood: Converging PET findings in depression and normal sadness. *The American Journal of Psychiatry, 156*(5), 675–682.

Mayberg, H. S., et al. (2005). Deep brain stimulation for treatment-resistant depression. *Neuron, 45*(5), 651–660.

McCracken, J. T., et al. (2010). Possible influence of variant of the P-glycoprotein gene (MDR1/ABCB1) on clinical response to guanfacine in children with pervasive developmental disorders and hyperactivity. *Journal of Child and Adolescent Psychopharmacology, 20*(1), 1–5.

Mirnics, K., et al. (2001). Disease-specific changes in regulator of G-protein signaling 4 (RGS4) expression in schizophrenia. *Molecular Psychiatry, 6*(3), 293–301.

Morrison, J. H., & Baxter, M. G. (2012). The aging cortical synapse: Hallmarks and implications for cognitive decline. *Nature Reviews Neuroscience, 13*(4), 240–250.

Mrzljak, L., Levey, A. I., & Goldman-Rakic, P. S. (1993). Association of m1 and m2 muscarinic receptor proteins with asymmetric synapses in the primate cerebral cortex: Morphological evidence for cholinergic modulation of excitatory neurotransmission. *Proceedings of the National Academy of Sciences of the United States of America, 90*(11), 5194−5198.

Muly, E. C., Maddox, M., & Smith, Y. (2003). Distribution of mGluR1alpha and mGluR5 immuno-labeling in primate prefrontal cortex. *Journal of Comparative Neurology, 467*(4), 521−535.

Murphy, B. L., et al. (1996). Increased dopamine turnover in the prefrontal cortex impairs spatial working memory performance in rats and monkeys. *Proceedings of the National Academy of Sciences of the United States of America, 93*(3), 1325−1329.

Napolitano, A., et al. (2014). In vivo neurometabolic profiling to characterize the effects of social isolation and ketamine-induced NMDA antagonism: A rodent study at 7.0 T. *Schizophrenia Bulletin, 40*(3), 566−574.

O'Neill, J., et al. (2000). Effects of guanfacine on three forms of distraction in the aging macaque. *Life Sciences, 67*(8), 877−885.

Ongur, D., & Price, J. L. (2000). The organization of networks within the orbital and medial pre-frontal cortex of rats, monkeys and humans. *Cerebral Cortex, 10*(3), 206−219.

Paspalas, C. D., Selemon, L. D., & Arnsten, A. F. (2009). Mapping the regulator of G protein signaling 4 (RGS4): Presynaptic and postsynaptic substrates for neuroregulation in prefrontal cortex. *Cerebral Cortex, 19*(9), 2145−2155.

Paspalas, C. D., Wang, M., & Arnsten, A. F. (2013). Constellation of HCN channels and cAMP regulating proteins in dendritic spines of the primate prefrontal cortex: Potential substrate for working memory deficits in schizophrenia. *Cerebral Cortex, 23*(7), 1643−1654.

Pearson, R. C., et al. (1985). Anatomical correlates of the distribution of the pathological changes in the neocortex in Alzheimer disease. *Proceedings of the National Academy of Sciences of the United States of America, 82*(13), 4531−4534.

Prasad, K. M., et al. (2005). Genetic polymorphisms of the RGS4 and dorsolateral prefrontal cor-tex morphometry among first episode schizophrenia patients. *Molecular Psychiatry, 10*(2), 213−219.

Rama, P., et al. (1996). Medetomidine, atipamezole, and guanfacine in delayed response perfor-mance of aged monkeys. *Pharmacology Biochemistry and Behavior, 55*(3), 415−422.

Ren, W. W., Liu, Y., & Li, B. M. (2012). Stimulation of alpha(2A)-adrenoceptors promotes the maturation of dendritic spines in cultured neurons of the medial prefrontal cortex. *Molecular and Cellular Neuroscience, 49*(2), 205−216.

Robbins, T. W. (1996). Dissociating executive functions of the prefrontal cortex. *Philosophical transactions of the Royal Society of London, 351*(1346), 1463−1470 , discussion 1470-1

Robinson, R. G., et al. (1985). Mood disorders in left-handed stroke patients. *American Journal of Psychiatry, 142*(12), 1424−1429.

Romanski, L. M., et al. (1999). Dual streams of auditory afferents target multiple domains in the primate prefrontal cortex. *Nature Neuroscience, 2*(12), 1131−1136.

Scahill, L., et al. (2001). A placebo-controlled study of guanfacine in the treatment of children with tic disorders and attention deficit hyperactivity disorder. *American Journal of Psychiatry, 158*(7), 1067−1074.

Selemon, L. D., & Goldman-Rakic, P. S. (1988). Common cortical and subcortical targets of the dorsolateral prefrontal and posterior parietal cortices in the rhesus monkey: evidence for a distributed neural network subserving spatially guided behavior. *Journal of Neuroscience, 8*(11), 4049−4068.

Selemon, L. D., & Goldman-Rakic, P. S. (1999). The reduced neuropil hypothesis: A circuit based model of schizophrenia. *Biological Psychiatry, 45*(1), 17−25.

Seo, H., & Lee, D. (2007). Temporal filtering of reward signals in the dorsal anterior cingulate cortex during a mixed-strategy game. *Journal of Neuroscience, 27*(31), 8366–8377.

Seo, H., & Lee, D. (2009). Behavioral and neural changes after gains and losses of conditioned reinforcers. *Journal of Neuroscience, 29*(11), 3627–3641.

Shaw, P., et al. (2009). Development of cortical asymmetry in typically developing children and its disruption in attention-deficit/hyperactivity disorder. *Archives General Psychiatry, 66*(8), 888–896.

Soulsby, M. D., & Wojcikiewicz, R. J. H. (2005). The type III inositol 1,4,5-trisphosphate receptor is phosphorylated by cAMP-dependent protein kinase at three sites. *Biochemical Journal, 392*(3), 493–497.

Steere, J. C., & Arnsten, A. F. (1997). The alpha-2A noradrenergic receptor agonist guanfacine improves visual object discrimination reversal performance in aged rhesus monkeys. *Behavioral Neuroscience, 111*(5), 883–891.

Szeszko, P. R., et al. (2008). DISC1 is associated with prefrontal cortical gray matter and positive symptoms in schizophrenia. *Biological Psychology, 79*(1), 103–110.

Tanila, H., Rama, P., & Carlson, S. (1996). The effects of prefrontal intracortical microinjections of an alpha-2 agonist, alpha-2 antagonist and lidocaine on the delayed alternation performance of aged rats. *Brain Research Bulletin, 40*(2), 117–119.

Thompson-Schill, S. L., et al. (2002). Effects of frontal lobe damage on interference effects in working memory. *Cognitive, Affective, & Behavioral Neuroscience, 2*(2), 109–120.

Vijayraghavan, S., et al. (2007). Inverted-U dopamine D1 receptor actions on prefrontal neurons engaged in working memory. *Nature Neuroscience, 10*(3), 376–384.

Wang, M., Vijayraghavan, S., & Goldman-Rakic, P. S. (2004). Selective D2 receptor actions on the functional circuitry of working memory. *Science, 303*(5659), 853–856.

Wang, M., et al. (2007). Alpha2A-adrenoceptors strengthen working memory networks by inhibiting cAMP-HCN channel signaling in prefrontal cortex. *Cell, 129*(2), 397–410.

Wang, M., et al. (2013). NMDA receptors subserve persistent neuronal firing during working memory in dorsolateral prefrontal cortex. *Neuron, 77*(4), 736–749.

Yang, Y., et al. (2013). Nicotinic alpha7 receptors enhance NMDA cognitive circuits in dorsolateral prefrontal cortex. *Proceedings of the National Academy of Sciences of the United States of America, 110*(29), 12078–12083.

Chapter 3

Gene Expression in the Frontal Lobe

Željka Krsnik[1,2] and Goran Sedmak[3]
[1]*Laboratory for Digitalization of Zagreb Brain Collection, Croatian Institute for Brain Research, University of Zagreb School of Medicine, Salata, Zagreb, Croatia, [2]Laboratory for Neurogenomics and InSitu Hybridization, Croatian Institute for Brain Research, University of Zagreb School of Medicine, Salata, Zagreb, Croatia, [3]Division of Developmental Neuroscience, Croatian Institute for Brain Research, University of Zagreb School of Medicine, Salata, Zagreb, Croatia*

INTRODUCTION

Understanding the neurobiological basis of human cognitive functions and behavior (social and emotional) is one of the most intriguing challenges in contemporary neuroscience. Frontal lobe of the human brain is a seat of various higher cognitive abilities such as planning, goal-directed behavior, decision-making, working memory, attention, language, and personality expression. One of the biological prerequisites for the proper cortical functional organization is precise regulation of spatiotemporal gene expression from early development throughout whole life span.

Despite recent impressive advancement in reveling genetic blueprint of the human neocortex, our knowledge on real operation of neural assemblies during cognitive, social, and emotional frontal lobe functions is rather limited. More specifically, application of microarrays and RNA sequencing (RNA-seq) techniques in the last decade has broadened our knowledge about the gene expression in different regions of the human brain throughout whole life span. However, understanding of the higher cognitive functions requires not only genetic approach but also analysis of interaction between genes and environment in shaping neuronal circuitry and modulation of neural assemblies.

Knowing complexity of connectivity and functions of frontal lobe in humans, Petanjek, Judaš, et al. (2011) said that it is not surprising that its development is prolonged, beginning in fetal life in different transient forms and lasting throughout the life (life-long maturation). The question still remains what is the role of the transient prefrontal cortical circuitry that develops in utero before its executive functions are needed?

Executive Functions in Health and Disease. DOI: http://dx.doi.org/10.1016/B978-0-12-803676-1.00003-9

Although neuronal circuitry involved in spontaneous endogenous (not dependent on sensory input) activity in the human prefrontal cortex (PFC) started to develop at early fetal period, initial "cognitive" circuitry required for goal-directed behavior does not reach proper maturation level until infancy (Diamond & Goldman-Rakic, 1989, Kostović, Judaš, Petanjek, & Šimić, 1995). It is not known whether all components of the circuitry, namely long associative pathways, short corticocortical pathways, local circuitry, and subcortical input participate equally in early cognitive functions. In that respect, data analysis of spatiotemporal gene expression pattern needs to be complemented with the effects of environmental influence on neuronal circuit development. Due to uniqueness of human cognitive potential, integrated data on regulation of these complex molecular and cellular neurodevelopmental processes over prolonged period of time may eventually lead us to closer understanding of the developmental background of disorders of higher brain functions, such as ASD (autism spectrum disorder) and schizophrenia.

In this chapter, we give an overview of the current knowledge on the gene expression in the cerebral cortex of the human brain during prenatal, perinatal, and postnatal period with the special emphasis on the PFC. We start with the human neocortical development with the focus on circuitry development in PFC that serves as a neurobiological substrate for cognitive functions.

DEVELOPMENT OF CEREBRAL NEOCORTEX AND CIRCUITRY IN THE HUMAN FETAL BRAIN

Adult six-layered cerebral neocortex is a result of highly orchestrated series of morphogenetic events regulated by differential gene expression, such as proliferation, migration, molecular specification, aggregation, neuronal differentiation, axonal outgrowth and ingrowth, and synaptogenesis. Sequence and timing of these prenatal neurogenetic events during corticogenesis in humans is well established (Fig. 3.1) (for review, see Silbereis, Pochareddy, Zhu, Li, & Sestan, 2016).

There is a close correlation between cellular neurogenetic events and transient cortical lamination that is the major feature of embryonic and fetal telencephalic wall (Boulder Committee, 1970; Bystron, Blakemore, & Rakic, 2008) (Fig. 3.2). Ventricular zone and subventricular zone are transient fetal proliferative zones where progenitor cells for all future cortical neurons and macroglia reside and exponentially expand progenitor population by symmetric cell division. It is considered that increase in surface area in PFC during human evolution is mainly due to the increased number of mitotic cycles in the proliferative zones (Rakic, 1995). By contrast, asymmetric progenitor division does not amplify the stem cell population but generates a postmitotic neuron and a glial cell. Newly born neurons migrate through the intermediate zone along the radial glial cells and settle down in the cortical plate (CP). Appearance of the CP in cortical anlage at 8 PCW (postconceptional weeks) together with the marginal zone (MZ) and presubplate marks the beginning of

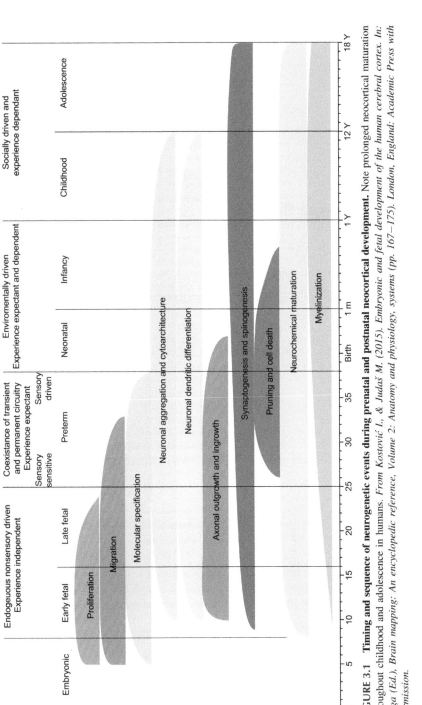

FIGURE 3.1 Timing and sequence of neurogenetic events during prenatal and postnatal neocortical development. Note prolonged neocortical maturation throughout childhood and adolescence in humans. *From Kostović I., & Judaš M. (2015). Embryonic and fetal development of the human cerebral cortex. In: Toga (Ed.), Brain mapping: An encyclopedic reference, Volume 2: Anatomy and physiology, systems (pp. 167–175). London, England: Academic Press with permission.*

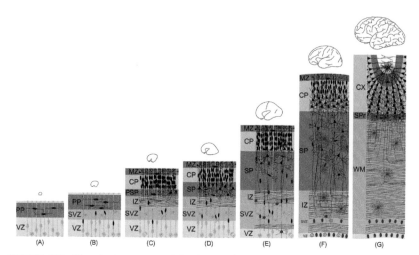

FIGURE 3.2   Transient patterns of lamination in the neocortical cerebral wall from embryonic to late fetal period. Depicted stages are approximately: a) 3PCW, b) 6 PCW, c) 10 PCW, d) 15 PCW, e) 20 PCW, f) 25 PCW and g) Newborn. *VZ*, Ventricular zone and *SVZ*, subventricular zone (green), *PP*, preplate; *SP*, subplate; and *MZ*, marginal zone (blue), *CP*, cortical plate (gray), *IZ*, intermediate zone (fetal "white" matter) (red); progenitor cells (green), early differentiating neurons (blue), CP neurons and migratory neurons (black) and glia (brown). *From Kostović I., & Judaš M. (2015). Embryonic and fetal development of the human cerebral cortex. In: Toga (Ed.), Brain mapping: An encyclopedic reference, Volume 2: Anatomy and physiology, systems (pp. 167–175). London, England: Academic Press with permission.*

an early fetal period characterized by trilaminar cortical organization. These two zones, above and below the CP, are sites of the first cortical synaptogenesis, while there is no synaptogenesis in the CP.

At early fetal period, the dendrites of CP cells (Mrzljak, Uylings, Kostović, & Van Eden, 1988) and presubplate neurons (Kostović & Rakic, 1990) receive early monoaminergic afferents (Kostović & Judaš 2007; Zecevic & Verney, 1995). Furthermore, the immature neural circuitry in the early PFC, arising from modulatory extrathalamic subcortical system, i.e., monoaminergic brainstem tegmentum and cholinergic basal forebrain, produce endogenous spontaneous activity (Feller, 1999; Penn & Shatz, 1999).

At 12–13 PCW the transient fetal compartment, the subplate zone (Kostović & Molliver, 1974; Kostović & Rakic, 1990), starts to form bellow the CP and becomes a landmark of the typical midfetal lamination, as a place of early synaptogenesis and the major connectivity compartment in the neocortical anlage, particularly prominent in the association areas including PFC. Subplate zone, as a "waiting" compartment for ingrowing afferents, including thalamocorticals, has an essential role in the establishment of intracortical and extracortical circuitries (Fig. 3.3).

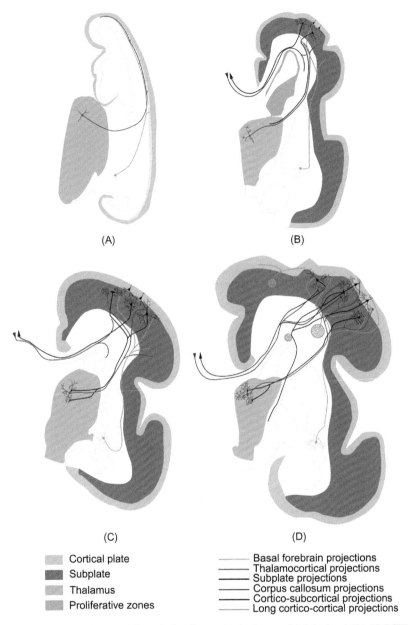

(A)

(B)

(C)

(D)

Cortical plate
Subplate
Thalamus
Proliferative zones

Basal forebrain projections
Thalamocortical projections
Subplate projections
Corpus callosum projections
Cortico-subcortical projections
Long cortico-cortical projections

FIGURE 3.3 **Development of cortical pathways in the human fetal brain at (A) 10 PCW, (B) 20 PCW, (C) 23 PCW, and (D) 28 PCW.** *PCW*, postconceptional weeks. *From Kostović I., & Judaš M. (2015). Embryonic and fetal development of the human cerebral cortex. In: Toga (Ed.), Brain mapping: An encyclopedic reference, Volume 2: Anatomy and physiology, systems (pp. 167–175). London, England: Academic Press with permission.*

Massive ingrowth of thalamocortical afferents from the subplate in the CP occurs between 23 and 26 PCW (Kostović & Judaš 2010, Kostović & Rakic, 1990) and continues until 34 PCW. Using cholinesterase (ChE) reactivity, Kostović and Goldman-Rakic (1983) have described maturation and connections of thalamic mediodorsal (MD) nuclei in primate brain that is the major source of afferents to the prefrontal granular cortex (Goldman-Rakic & Porrino, 1985). They suggested that early ChE activity plays an instrumental role in the frontal lobe development by differentiation of connections between thalamic MD nuclei and PFC. Although the basic areal specifications (protomap hypothesis, Rakic, 1988) by cortical patterning genes occurs as early as the second month of embryonic life in humans, there is an evidence that the thalamic input also plays an important role in cortical areal differentiation (O'Leary, Chou, & Sahara, 2007; O'Leary, Schlaggar & Tuttle, 1994).

Already at the midfetal period, transient fetal zones, particularly MZ (Kostović et al., 2004/05) and prominent subplate zone (Duque, Krsnik, et al., 2016), display regional differences in thickness between dorsolateral, orbitomedial, and orbitolateral prefrontal cortical regions (Kostović 1990, Kostović, Judaš, Radoš, & Hrabač, 2002). At midfetal period, radially migrating neurons end up as prospective layer III pyramidal neurons, a source of associative and commissural pathways (Schwartz & Goldman-Rakic, 1991). These supragranular neurons in layer III establish long cortico-cortical network, essential for the normal cognitive functions.

However, only in late preterm, after 33 PCW there is a growth of inter-hemispheric callosal connections while maturation of long associative corti-cocortical connection shows somewhat later growth schedule (between 36 PCW and term infants) and by birth most of the long corticocortical bundles are visible with modern imaging technics (Huang, Xue, et al., 2009, Huang, Zhang, et al., 2006, Kasprian, Brugger, et al., 2008, Vasung, Huang, et al., 2010). Histological correlates of long corticocortical pathways were traced in experimental primate (Schwartz & Goldman-Rakic, 1984). In human, it is difficult to reconstruct the trajectory and termination because there are resistant for routine histological stains and they are not myelinated, which presents additional obstacle for the visualization.

In preterm infants, PFC still shows transient laminar organization and receives a massive thalamic input from MD nucleus (Kostović & Goldman-Rakic, 1983). The major neurogenetic event is growth of callosal and projection pathways (Kostović & Judaš 2002, Kostović & Rakic, 1984, Kostović & Rakic, 1990). PFC receives nonsensory information via thalamocortical projection (from MD nuclei). It is not likely that sensory information received from somatosensory cortex is conveyed further to PFC because in preterm infants, long corticocortical connections are still in the phase of growth.

During the neonatal period the major feature of the PFC is immature lamination with well-developed granular layer IV as a main target for thalamocortical afferents. Therefore, in newborn brain, well-established tha-lamocortical circuitry enables interaction with other brain areas and sensory environment. However, at birth, neuronal circuitry is still immature demon-strating growth of short corticocortical connections and growth and reorgani-zation of callosal axons.

During early infancy (2−6 months) a massive reorganization of cortico-cortical pathways occurs (growth of short corticocortical connections and retraction of callosal projections) and rapid increase in the number of synap-ses (Petanjek, Judaš, et al., 2011). In parallel with establishment of perma-nent circuitry, there is still transient subplate circuitry present, probably important for the general movements in early infant (Hadders-Algra, 2007).

Late infancy (7−12 months of postnatal age), when transient circuitry is resolved and corticocortical connections are established, coincides with cru-cial timing when PFC starts to exhibit first executive functions. It is a crucial question whether transient cortical circuitry observed in the late fetal and preterm brain is functionally active. This problem is difficult to access because of the limitation in testing cortical function in the late fetal and pre-term brain. However, in primary cortical areas, such as somatosensory, audi-tory, motor, and visual sensory−sensitive cortex, it was possible to evoke cortical response upon peripheral stimulation in early fetal preterm (after 23 PCW) (Fitzgerald, 2005; Khazipov & Luhmann, 2006; Kostović & Judaš, 2007; Novak, Kurtzberg, Kreuzer, & Vaughan, 1989). More substantial evi-dence for development of PFC activity in preterm infants was presented by recent functional magnetic resonance imaging (fMRI) studies in which it was shown that medial prefrontal cortical hubs are active in preterm brain (Fair, Cohen, et al. 2008; Fransson, Skiold, et al., 2007). Because medial pre-frontal cortical areas are involved in different social, decision-making, and cognitive functions, it would be interesting to know how long in which developmental period there is an overlap between transient (preterm) and permanent (child) functions (Kostović & Judaš, 2006). However, immature organization of functional connectivity in preterm infant is different than an adult pattern (Smyser, Snyder, & Neil, 2011). The exact timing of gradual emergence of the adult pattern is better studied in later postnatal phases than during the first year. In this period there is an increasing response to environ-mental stimuli. However, apparent cognitive phase occurs between 7 and 8 postnatal months.

In conclusion, the development of transient spontaneous neuronal cir-cuitry of the human PFC starts before beginning of cognition, already at early fetal period. It is modulated by monoamines and continues during mid-fetal and late fetal period modulated by thalamic input. However, initial cog-nitive circuitry develops during late infancy when all parts of connectivity (long corticocortical pathways, short corticocortical pathways, and interneur-ons), and their synaptic connections reach required level of structural and functional maturity (Kostović & Judaš, 2009). However, maturation of the frontal lobe circuitry continues throughout childhood and adolescence when new cognitive functions develop. Prolonged maturation of cortical circuitry seems to be one of the major features of the human brain development. This phenomenon is particularly pronounced in the association areas of cerebral neocortex, such as prefrontal granular cortex, where characteristic developmental pattern was demonstrated throughout childhood and adolescence (Petanjek, Judaš, Kostović, & Uylings, 2008). This prolonged synaptic production allows environmental influence, including interaction with social environment and modification of neural circuitry underlying cognitive functions. On the other side, this complex and prolonged neurodevelopment in humans also explains vulnerability and susceptibility to certain neurodevelopmental disorders with complex etiology, such as ASD. ASD is a highly heritable neurodevelopment disorder characterized by difficulties in social communication and interaction, language development and repetitive stereotyped behavior, and/or restricted interests. ASD is considered multifactorial disorder, extremely genetically heterogeneous, with strong contribution of copy number variations, single-nucleotide polymorphism, and rare and de novo damaging mutations (Yeh & Weiss, 2016). Current estimations suggest that it could be as many as 300 up to 1000 genes which are targets of rare mutations and which greatly increase risk for ASD (He, Sanders, et al., 2013; Ronemus, Iossifov, Levy, & Wigler, 2014). Giving this genetic and clinical heterogeneity, in the last two decades researchers had some success in identifying clusters of ASD risk genes (Chang, Gilman, Chiang, Sanders, & Vitkup, 2015; Gilman, Iossifov, et al., 2011; Packer, 2016). First transcriptomic analysis of postmortem ASD brain samples has shown that despite heterogeneity there is a common transcriptional profile present in the majority of affected individuals (Voineagu, Wang, et al., 2011). In the ASD brain, regional patterns of gene expression that typically distinguish frontal and temporal cortex are significantly attenuated, suggesting abnormal cortical patterning in ASD brain (Voineagu, Wang, et al., 2011). The arrival of new genetic technologies and analysis tools begins a new era of genomic research that will be beneficiary not just for ASD studies but also for research of other complex disorders with unknown etiology.

METHODOLOGICAL LIMITATIONS OF HUMAN TRANSCRIPTOMIC STUDIES

The precise gene expression profile of the human brain is one of the most intriguing questions in the neuroscience. To solve this question many different methods were used. These methods were often time-consuming and provided the opportunity to study just a few genes in any given sample. Data obtained from those studies did not provide possibility to analyze large-scale changes in the gene expression between different brain areas and different brain disorders. With the advent of methods for the large-scale gene expression, profiling the study of the human brain transcriptome experienced significant boost. Today, two of the most used methods for studying human brain transcriptome are oligonucleotide microarrays and RNA-seq. Both methods have its advantages and disadvantages, with microarrays being easier and faster to analyze and RNA-seq providing more detailed analysis of the transcriptome (for details, see Hitzemann, Darakjian, et al., 2014; Marioni, Mason, Mane, Stephens, & Gilad, 2008).

The analysis of the human brain transcriptome has become an important tool for elucidating the basis of normal brain development and investigating neurobiological basis of major disorders of the nervous system (Mirnics, 2006; Mirnics, Levitt, & Lewis, 2004; Mirnics & Pevsner, 2004). More and more studies of such type are reporting sets of differentially expressed genes (DEXs) either between different brain regions or between controls and affected samples. However, there are many limitations in designing, conducting, and analyzing such experiments. These limitations can be divided in three groups: (1) factors influencing the quality of the RNA analyzed (postmortem interval, premortem events, postmortem handling of the body, pH, climate and seasonal influence, etc.); (2) factors influencing interindividual differences; and (3) factors influencing brain diversity and complexity.

Unlike the DNA, RNA is extremely unstable and susceptible to many postmortem artefacts (Bahn, Augood, Standaert, Starkey, & Emson, 2001; Li, Li, et al., 2004). RNA quality is routinely examined using Agilent's BioAnalyzer (or similar instruments) checking for RNA integrity number (RIN). When dealing with human brain samples RIN > 5 (on the scale of $0-10$) is usually considered satisfactory for further analysis although RIN > 7 is preferred. One of the key questions for all transcriptomic studies is which factors influence the RNA quality the most. Factors such as postmortem sampling interval, premortem events (e.g., agonal state), postmortem handling of the body, climate and seasonal influences, and brain pH are usually considered as major factors influencing the quality of RNA although their importance is still debated and disputed (Popova, Mennerich, Weith, & Quast, 2008).

Another level of complexity added to the studies of the human brain transcriptome is exceptional diversity among analyzed samples. Humans are very diverse species with significantly different life styles. High rate of interindividual variability in analyzed samples (e.g., age, race, medical history, medication history, lifestyle, substance abuse, etc.), when compared with experimental models, can introduce differences in the transcriptome not related to underlying biological basis. Important, but often overlooked, factor that can significantly influence the quality of data and comparison between different studies is anatomical localization of analyzed tissue sample. The transcriptome of different brain areas significantly differ (Hawrylycz, Lein, et al., 2012; Johnson, Kawasawa, et al., 2009; Kang, Kawasawa, et al., 2011; Miller, Ding, et al., 2014; Pletikos, Sousa, et al., 2014), thus comparison between two samples that are not from the same area could provide artificial differences or remove the real differences. The main reason for such vastly different transcriptome profiles between different areas is enormous cellular diversity of the human brain, with each cellular class having its own unique transcriptional profile (Mirnics, 2008). To minimize differences due to the anatomical localization, every sample used for gene expression analysis should be collected by experienced neuroanatomist, based on established neuroanatomical landmarks, and confirmed using standard cytoarchitectonic methods.

Last but not least, the analysis procedure can vastly differ between different studies. Often the data are normalized using different procedures that can artificially produce differences (or remove one). Studies also usually use different values to consider one gene "expressed," or different cutoff values to consider gene differentially expressed (e.g., fold change or false discovery rate correction value). The different analytical procedures can influence the end result and complicate the comparison between different studies. When analyzing and comparing results of transcriptomic studies, one has to bear in mind all the above-mentioned limitations of methodology to fully understand the presented data.

GENE EXPRESSION IN THE CEREBRAL CORTEX OF THE HUMAN BRAIN

The human cerebral cortex is diverse and complex organ, composed of many different cell classes, which develops over protracted period of time (Bystron, Blakemore, et al., 2008; Kostović & Judaš, 2006; Rakic, 2006). The entire cerebral cortex can be subdivided into distinct areas with specific structure and function. Over the years, many attempts to subdivide cerebral cortex, based on the difference in cytoarchitecture or myeloarhitecture, were made (Bailey & von Bonin, 1951; Brodmann, 1909; Vogt & Vogt, 1919; Von Economo & Koskinas, 1925). However, the question regarding the differences in genetic makeup of different cytoarchitectonic areas remains unanswered. With the advent of the large-scale and high-throughput methods to study gene expression profiles, it became possible to answer some of those questions. Furthermore, these methods helped us to better understand the molecular processes leading to the areal specification, sex differences in transcriptomes between cortical areas, establishment of the laterality of brain hemispheres, and the role that different areas are playing in many neurological disorders.

Global Gene Expression Patterns in the Cerebral Cortex

One of the more interesting features of the human cerebral cortex is that it expresses more than 80% of all protein-coding genes present in our genome

(Kang, Kawasawa, et al., 2011; Pletikos, Sousa, et al., 2014). Furthermore, the expression of these genes has precise spatiotemporal regulation producing large number of DEX. Almost 25% of genes are spatially DEX (i.e., being differentially expressed between two neocortical areas in at least one time period) and 85% were temporally DEX (i.e., being differentially expressed between two time periods in any area; Kang, Kawasawa et al., 2011). Although the number of DEX gene is very high, there are not many genes that are specifically expressed in only one neocortical area (Colantuoni, Lipska, et al., 2011; Johnson, Kawasawa, et al. 2009; Kang, Kawasawa, et al., 2011; Pletikos, Sousa, et al., 2014). Interareal differences in the gene expression exhibit the "temporal hourglass pattern," dividing the development of the human cerebral cortex into three distinct periods: (1) the prenatal period characterized by highly dynamic and diverse gene expression pattern, (2) the postnatal period characterized by the uniform gene expression pattern and slow transformation into adult-like pattern, and (3) adulthood characterized by distinct and stable gene expression patterns between different areas (Pletikos, Sousa, et al., 2014). Interestingly, two different areas from the same individual have more similar transcriptome than same areas in two different individuals (Kang, Kawasawa, et al., 2011; Khaitovich, Muetzel, et al., 2004; Pletikos, Sousa, et al., 2014). When comparing similarity of transcriptional profiles between different neocortical areas, the anatomically and functionally related areas have more similar transcriptional profile than more distant areas (Johnson, Kawasawa, et al., 2009; Kang, Kawasawa, et al., 2011; Miller, Ding, et al., 2014; Pletikos, Sousa, et al., 2014).

The structural and functional maturation of different neocortical areas has been described as asynchronous, i.e., primary areas (such as primary motor or somatosensory cortex), are maturing first followed by higher associative areas (Flechsig, 1901; Rapoport & Gogtay, 2008; Sowell, Thompson et al., 2003). When analyzing the global maturation rate of the cortical transcriptome during the prenatal period, different areas have distinct maturational patterns. However, when the maturation of cortical areas during postnatal period is compared, increased synchrony in the transcriptome maturation can be observed with no significant differences between primary and associative areas (Pletikos, Sousa, et al., 2014).

The human brain transcriptome is functionally organized into groups of genes called "modules" that exhibit highly correlated expression levels across different samples (Ihmels, Bergmann, & Barkai, 2004; Oldham, Horvath & Geschwind, 2006; Oldham, Konopka, et al., 2008; Zhang & Horvath, 2005). Genes with the highest degree of connectivity within the module are called "hub-genes," and are generally expected to be more important for the proper function of the entire gene network described by the module. Similar to individual genes, modules also exhibit distinct spatiotemporal pattern (Kang, Kawasawa, et al., 2011; Miller, Ding, et al., 2014; Oldham, Konopka, et al., 2008). It is interesting to note that one gene can be attributed to more than one module, suggesting high degree of functional interconnectivity between different modules. In fact, more than 50% of genes from one module can overlap with other modules (Oldham, Konopka, et al., 2008). However, the high reproducibility of modules between different individuals and platforms suggests that biological processes are at the basis of this functional organization of the transcriptome (Kang, Kawasawa, et al., 2011; Miller, Ding, et al., 2014; Oldham, Konopka, et al., 2008). The functional characterization of genes in modules showed that majority of genes in one module can be attributed to either one cell class (e.g., neurons, astrocytes, and oligodendrocytes) or neuronal process (e.g., neurogenesis, synaptic transmission, and mitochondrial function). Modules that have similar functional characterization usually have higher degree of overlap, and their expression pattern follows similar trajectory (Miller, Ding, et al., 2014; Oldham, Konopka, et al., 2008). Based on the expression of different modules, a prediction is made about the underlying cellular composition of the analyzed area and about the relationships between different cellular types or biological processes in the analyzed samples (Miller, Ding, et al., 2014; Oldham, Konopka, et al., 2008).

Specificities of the Human Neocortical Transcriptome During Prenatal Period

The structural and functional properties of the neocortical areas are primarily determined by the transcriptional profile of developing telencephalic wall. Unlike the adult brain, where transcriptional profile of the neocortical area is mainly determined by the profile of the cerebral cortex, in the developing brain each transient fetal zone has its own transcriptional profile and influences transcriptional profile of the prospective cortical area. These transcriptomes depend on the level of maturity of the analyzed region and its developmental role. Thus, for proper understanding of the human brain development, it is necessary to study the transcriptome of each individual transient zone. A drawback of the transcriptome analysis during development is a lack of defined anatomical landmarks, which makes comparison of sampled areas between different studies difficult, thus hindering the ability to reliably compare results. Due to the limited availability of the human fetal brain tissue, only a few studies have analyzed transcriptome during prenatal period (Colantuoni, Lipska, et al., 2011; Fietz, Lachmann, et al., 2012; Johnson, Kawasawa, et al., 2009; Kang, Kawasawa, et al., 2011; Lambert, Lambot, et al., 2011; Pletikos, Sousa, et al., 2014). The percentage of expressed gene during prenatal period has been reported to be around 75% of total protein coding genes and 35% of them are DEX genes (Johnson, Kawasawa, et al., 2009; Kang, Kawasawa, et al., 2011; Pletikos, Sousa, et al., 2014). Although there is no established cytoarchitectonic division of the human neocortex during development, based on the transcriptional profile, prospective cytoarchitectonic areas can be distinguished (Colantuoni, Lipska, et al., 2011; Johnson, Kawasawa, et al., 2009; Kang, Kawasawa, et al., 2011; Lambert, Lambot, et al., 2011; Miller, Ding, et al., 2014; Pletikos, Sousa, et al., 2014). However, differences in the transcriptomic profile are quite small. When comparing different areas in the PFC during development, only 2% of genes are differentially expressed between areas (Johnson, Kawasawa, et al., 2009), with the biggest differences observed between functionally distinct areas (e.g., orbitofrontal cortex vs dorsolateral PFC).

The alternative gene splicing also contributes to the reported differences between areas. During prenatal development around 5% of genes exhibits differential exon usage (DEU) between areas (Johnson, Kawasawa, et al., 2009; Kang, Kawasawa, et al., 2011). Many of the DEU genes have important neurodevelopmental function. For example, one of the reported DEU genes during prenatal development is *ROBO1*, which is a key axon guidance molecule important for the formation of major cortical projections (Johnson, Kawasawa, et al., 2009). Two isoforms of the protein are produced *ROBO1a* and *ROBO1b*. *ROBO1a* is enriched in the temporal cortex, whereas *ROBO1b* is enriched in the PFC (Johnson, Kawasawa, et al., 2009).

The gene modules reported during fetal brain development are unique to this period. Majority of modules are functionally linked with neuron development and differentiation; cell cycle and mitosis; and cell morphogenesis and adhesion (Johnson, Kawasawa, et al., 2009; Miller, Ding, et al., 2014; Pletikos, Sousa, et al., 2014). Majority of these modules are exclusively expressed during fetal brain development. Furthermore, many modules are enriched in specific areas. In prospective prefrontal areas several modules were enriched with important hub genes such as *CALB1*, *RGS8*, and *PART1* (Johnson, Kawasawa, et al., 2009).

For proper understanding of the human brain development, it is necessary to analyze transcriptome in different transient fetal zones. The analysis of the transient zones transcriptome showed that there are more than 2000 genes enriched in different zones (Miller, Ding, et al., 2014). In every zone a layer enriched genes could be observed, with tendency of functionally similar zones grouping together and exhibit significant overlap of the transcriptome (Fietz, Lachmann, et al., 2012; Miller, Ding, et al., 2014).

The laminar expression profile correlated well with known cellular composition, developmental processes, and maturity level of analyzed zone (Miller, Ding, et al., 2014). Germinal layers are enriched with markers of cortical progenitors (e.g., *PAX6* and *TBR2*) and radial glial cells (e.g., *GFAP*); MZ with markers of Cajal−Retzius cells (e.g., *CALB2*) and pial cells (e.g., *ZIC1*); subplate zone with markers of mature neurons and synaptic transmission (e.g., *NPY, KCNAB1*); and CP with markers of axonal growth and forming connections (in older more mature parts) and metabolic processes (in younger more immature parts; Miller, Ding, et al., 2014). Similar to the layer-enriched gene expression profile, modules also exhibited spatiotemporal layer enrichment and correlate with functional characteristics of the zone in which they are enriched (Miller, Ding, et al., 2014; Qiu, Luo, et al., 2012; Sorensen, Bernard, et al., 2015). The observed laminar changes of the transcriptome can also be translated to the MRI structural studies of human brain development. It has been shown that structural changes in the telencephalic wall during fetal period, as observed by changes in fractional anisotropy (FA) maps, can be linked with the gene expression patterns in the CP (Huang, Jeon, et al., 2013). These genes often exhibit a real enrichment and have important developmental functions. One of the examples is *CNTNAP2*, a gene enriched in the PFC and implicated in the pathogenesis of various neurodevelopmental disorders such as ASD (Huang, Jeon, et al., 2013; Johnson, Kawasawa, et al., 2009; Poot, 2015).

The initial patterning of the telencephalon is one of the developmental processes, which is very difficult to study in the human brain. Majority of data about cortical patterning were obtained from rodent studies and then translated to the human brain proposing several patterning centers and two main gradients of morphogens (rostro−caudal and medial−lateral; O'Leary & Nakagawa, 2002; O'Leary & Sahara, 2008). The analysis of telencephalic transcriptome enabled us to indirectly study cortical patterning in the human brain. The interesting finding of these studies is that in human brain two dominant putative patterning centers are located at frontal and temporal pole (Miller, Ding, et al., 2014). The general rostro−caudal gradient of gene expression observed in many species, including humans, is supplemented with very robust frontal to temporal pole gene expression gradient arching around perisylvian regions (Johnson, Kawasawa, et al., 2009; Miller, Ding, et al., 2014). This has not been described in rodents and could represent evolutionary adaptation for the development of enlarged human neocortex with pronounced temporal cortex. The transcriptomic signature of putative patterning centers and gradients are present throughout all zones of the fetal human telencephalon (Miller, Ding, et al., 2014). In the human brain, in contrast to the rodent brain, there are more rostrally than caudally enriched genes. The biggest difference is observed in the CP suggesting that these genes may be responsible for evolutionary expansion of the PFC in the human brain (Miller, Ding, et al., 2014).

One of the factors shaping transcriptional profile of different areas is regulatory mechanisms of gene expression. Conserved noncoding sequences (CNS; e.g., promotors and enhancers) are genomic parts responsible for the regulation of expression of protein coding genes. The CNS are usually located near genes responsible for important developmental processes (Woolfe, Goodson, et al., 2005). It is interesting to note that human accelerated CNS have predominantly rostral enriched expression pattern (Johnson, Kawasawa, et al., 2009; Lambert, Lambot, et al., 2011; Miller, Ding, et al., 2014), with significant enrichment in the subplate zone, thus suggesting that subplate zone is important for evolutionary development of the human cerebrum, especially PFC (Judaš, Sedmak, & Kostović, 2013; Miller, Ding, et al., 2014).

Specificities of the Human Brain Transcriptome During Postnatal Period

The transcriptome of the human brain in the early postnatal period (infancy and childhood) is rarely studied due to the limited number of available samples. Therefore, the data from these early postnatal developmental periods are often scarce. On the contrary, adult human brain transcriptome has been studied extensively although usually as a part of analysis of various human brain disorders. In the postnatal human brain more than 80% of all protein coding genes are expressed (Hawrylycz, Lein, et al., 2012; Kang, Kawasawa, et al., 2011). The pattern of gene expression in the first few years of life (throughout infancy and childhood) is characterized by the lack of DEX genes between neocortical areas, and this is not observed when comparing other brain regions (Pletikos, Sousa, et al., 2014). After the period of uniform gene expression pattern during infancy and childhood, the intraareal differences in transcriptome can again be seen during adolescence and adulthood although to a lesser extent than in the prenatal period (Pletikos, Sousa, et al., 2014). Notably those transcriptomic changes between different areas can first be observed in adolescence, known as the period that is associated with the onset of many disorders of the nervous system such as schizophrenia (Harris, Lockstone, et al., 2009; Pletikos, Sousa, et al., 2014). Although the early postnatal period is characterized by the uniform gene expression across entire cerebral cortex, the changes of the gene expression in the PFC (and subsequently entire cerebral cortex) happen more rapidly early during this period, with a much slower rate of change during adolescence and adulthood (Colantuoni, Lipska, et al., 2011; Somel, Guo, et al., 2010). The biggest health challenges of the 21st century will be linked to the increased population aging. To successfully combat those challenges, it is important to understand molecular underpinning of the aging process in the brain. Interestingly, there are no genes that are specifically activated during aging processes, and majority of genes involved in these processes are the same genes active during development (Somel, Guo, et al., 2010). However, many genes that exhibit different expression patterns linked with aging in the human brain are reported, especially in the PFC. Furthermore, these patterns were unique to the human brain when compared with our closest living relative chimpanzee (Fraser, Khaitovich, Plotkin, Paabo, & Eisen, 2005). This notion suggests that development and aging are not two distinct processes but one continuum. When comparing different neocortical areas in the postnatal period, the most prominent differences in the transcriptome are seen in the areas located on the medial side of the hemisphere (e.g., medial PFC and primary visual area; Hawrylycz, Lein, et al., 2012; Hawrylycz, Miller, et al., 2015; Khaitovich, Muetzel, et al., 2004; Pletikos, Sousa, et al., 2014).

The enrichment of different gene modules in the postnatal brain correlates well with the anatomical localization of the analyzed samples.

In comparison with other brain areas, the neocortex is enriched with the modules composed of genes involved in the neuronal functioning, neuron specificity, and cellular metabolism (Hawrylycz, Lein, et al., 2012; Kang, Kawasawa, et al., 2011; Pletikos, Sousa, et al., 2014). The functional annotation of gene modules during postnatal period can be summarized as predominantly linked with neuronal and synaptic function, neurotransmitter binding, and ion trafficking (Colantuoni, Lipska, et al., 2011; Kang, Kawasawa, et al., 2011; Pletikos, Sousa, et al., 2014).

One of the major drawbacks of the transcriptomic studies is the use of homogenized tissue samples, thus preventing the analysis of layer- and cell-specific gene expression patterns. The studies in rodents provided evidence about many layer- and cell-specific genes (Molyneaux, Arlotta, Menezes, & Macklis, 2007). Unfortunately, these kind of human brain studies are lacking or dealing only with the few genes obtained from rodent studies. In human brain, the pioneering study of Zeng, Shen, et al. (2012) used in situ hybridization to elucidate cellular gene expression pattern of 1000 genes. Many genes exhibited layer-specific expression, thus enabling precise anatomical and cytoarchitectonical identification of different cortical areas. Furthermore, they confirmed previously known (e.g., *CALB1, CALB2,* and *CCK*) and identified many novel layer and cell type−specific genes (e.g., *KCNC1, KCNC2,* and *GRIK1*) Around 20% of analyzed genes are differentially expressed between human and mouse. However, a substantial number of genes exhibited a wide range of pattern differences, as the expression in different layers, cell groups, or in the level of expression (Zeng, Shen, et al., 2012). These findings indicate that although differences between species can be subtle when analyzing homogenized tissue samples, the distribution of expressed genes within the layers and cell types in the sample can significantly differ between species.

Similar to the prenatal period a significant number of genes (up to 40%) exhibited alternative splicing in the human brain, observable also on the protein level (Mazin, Xiong, et al., 2013). The differences in the alternative splicing follow general trend of gene expression in the PFC with 70% of total splicing variation occurring before 14 years of life (Mazin, Xiong, et al., 2013).

The postnatal period is characterized by the formation, rearrangement, and refinement of synaptic connections and fiber pathways. The precise control of these processes is crucial for normal functioning of the adult cerebral cortex. Among genes involved in synaptic transmission, more than 30% of them exhibits regional differences in the expression pattern (e.g., primary motor cortex is enriched for the neurofilament genes *NEFL, NEFM,* and *NEFH*; Hawrylycz, Lein, et al., 2012). Recent studies showed that gene expression patterns can be linked to functional brain networks observed by fMRI. The study conducted by IMAGEN consortium reported that strength of the functional networks in the cerebrum is correlated with the gene networks linked with synaptic transmission, and that this pattern can be observed across entire life span (Richiardi, Altmann, et al., 2015). Furthermore, many genes that exhibit a link with functional brain networks are also implicated in many neurological diseases whose pathogenesis is, at least in part, attributed to the aberrant brain connectivity (Richiardi, Altmann, et al., 2015). These kind of studies, as well as ones performed during prenatal period (e.g., Huang, Jeon, et al., 2013), are very important as they demonstrate possibility to translate in vitro findings of gene expression to the observable changes on in vivo MRI and provide future directions for transcriptome—MRI correlation studies.

Sex-Biased Gene Expression Patterns and Laterality of the Human Brain Transcriptome

Analysis of the transcriptome revealed a number of genes with sexually dimorphic expression pattern (Kang, Kawasawa, et al., 2011; Reinius & Jazin, 2009, Vawter, Evans, et al., 2004; Weickert, Elashoff, et al., 2009; Yuan, Chen, Boyd-Kirkup, Khaitovich, & Somel, 2012). The largest number of sexually dimorphic genes was located on autosomal chromosomes, followed by Y and X chromosome (Kang, Kawasawa, et al., 2011; Weickert, Elashoff, et al., 2009). More than 75% of the sexually dimorphic genes have been upregulated in the male brains with spatial differences in expression. It is interesting to note that majority of sexually dimorphic genes had sex-biased expression during prenatal development, whereas postnatal period and adulthood, are characterized with only few sex-biased genes (Kang, Kawasawa, et al., 2011; Reinius & Jazin, 2009; Weickert, Elashoff, et al., 2009). As expected the biggest difference in the gene expression levels were observed in Y chromosome sex-biased genes. However, no compensatory upregulation of functional homologues located on X chromosome in female brains have been observed (Kang, Kawasawa, et al., 2011; Vawter, Evans, et al., 2004). The largest number of sexually dimorphic genes is reported in the PFC (Kang, Kawasawa, et al., 2011; Weickert, Elashoff, et al., 2009; Yuan, Chen, et al., 2012). It has also been proposed that the female transcriptome is aging faster than the male transcriptome (i.e., aging changes are observed earlier in the female than in the male brain; Yuan, Chen, et al., 2012). The functional categories that exhibited faster aging in females were associated with neuronal function and metabolic processes (Yuan, Chen, et al., 2012).

Furthermore, a number of genes exhibited sex-biased DEU, although they have comparable levels of gene expression in male and females (Kang, Kawasawa, et al., 2011). The reported data suggest that there are gender-specific alternative splicing of various genes that are usually located on autosomal chromosomes. Intriguingly, some of those genes have been implicated in the pathophysiology of diseases with significant differences in male—female distribution (e.g., *NLGN4X* associated with ASD; Kang, Kawasawa, et al., 2011).

The functional and structural lateralization of the human cerebral cortex has been well documented (Amunts, Schleicher, Ditterich, & Zilles, 2003; Geschwind & Levitsky, 1968; Hayes & Lewis, 1993; Kasprian, Langs, et al., 2011). Since the initial description of functional lateralization of speech- and language-related cortical areas (Broca, 1861; Dax, 1865; Wernicke, 1874) the quest to elucidate the molecular and genetic underpinning of structural and functional laterality has begun. The transcriptome studies of the gene expression laterality in the neocortex are rare, limited by small sample sizes and often with contradictory results (Hawrylycz, Lein, et al., 2012; Johnson, Kawasawa, et al., 2009; Khaitovich, Muetzel, et al., 2004; Lambert, Lambot, et al., 2011; Pletikos, Sousa, et al., 2014; Sun & Walsh, 2006; Sun, Collura, Ruvolo, & Walsh, 2006; Sun, Patoine, et al., 2005). Although initial studies found lateralization of gene expression in early fetal period (Sun & Walsh, 2006; Sun, Collura, et al., 2006; Sun, Patoine, et al., 2005), more recent studies that were conducted on larger sample size could not confirm this finding, thus implying that on the population level neocortical transcriptome is symmetrical throughout entire life span (Hawrylycz, Lein, et al., 2012; Johnson, Kawasawa, et al., 2009; Khaitovich, Muetzel, et al., 2004; Lambert, Lambot, et al., 2011; Pletikos, Sousa, et al., 2014). One of the proposed explanations for the observed laterality is the difference in maturational trajectories between hemispheres. However, no evidence of different maturational trajectories between hemispheres has been observed (Pletikos, Sousa, et al., 2014).

Noncoding RNAs as a Posttranscriptional Regulators of Gene Expression

In the recent years it has been discovered that many of the noncoding RNAs have important role in the posttranscriptional gene expression control. Among them the largest group is microRNAs (miRNA), single-stranded RNA molecules, approximately 22 nucleotides long (Bartel, 2004, 2009). Many of the newly discovered miRNA have significant role in human brain development and disorders (Kosik, 2006, 2009). More than 600 different miRNAs are expressed in the prenatal and in the postnatal human PFC (Berezikov, Thuemmler, et al., 2006; Shao, Hu, et al., 2010). However, more than 80% of observed expression level can be attributed to the 20 highly expressed miRNAs (Shao, Hu, et al., 2010). Similar with protein coding mRNA, the miRNA expression is influenced by age (Somel, Guo, et al., 2010; Wei, Hu, et al., 2015). The expression pattern of miRNAs closely follows the pattern or mRNAs expression, thus indicating that expression profile of mRNAs can be directly influenced by the expression of miRNA (Somel, Guo, et al., 2010). Interestingly, it has been noted that in the aging processes a significant decoupling of mRNA and protein levels happen.

MiRNA play an important role in this process by regulating the amount of available mRNA for translation, thus influencing the protein levels in the brain (Wei, Hu, et al., 2015).

Transcriptomic Studies as a Tool to Study Evolution of the Human Cerebral Cortex

One of the unique features of the humans are cognitive and behavioral traits responsible for development of culture, technology, and society. The fundamental question of the modern neuroscience is what evolutionary changes allowed us to develop these abilities. Unfortunately, the molecular events that led to these changes are still largely unknown. However, it has been suggested that major reason for phenotypic differences are due to the different gene expression between various species (King & Wilson, 1975; Ohno, 1972). The transcriptomic studies allow us to test this hypothesis and to uncover how evolution shaped the human cerebral cortex. Majority of studies are focused on the transcriptome of three species important for neuroscience: mouse as a main experimental model in neuroscience, rhesus monkey as a main primate model, and chimpanzee as our closest evolutionary relative. The transcriptome studies allowed us to analyze differences between species on a large scale and elucidate potential candidate genes responsible for evolutionary changes observed in the human brain. Although, the expression pattern of genes involved in basic neurodevelopmental processes are usually conserved between different species (e.g., *WNT7B* involved in early brain development and dendritic arborization), many subtle differences in the expression patterns between human and model animals can be observed (Enard, Khaitovich, et al., 2002; Khaitovich, Enard, Lachmann, & Paabo, 2006; Khaitovich, Muetzel, et al., 2004; Khaitovich, Tang, et al., 2006; Pletikos, Sousa, et al., 2014). The number of DEXs between humans and other primates are constantly reported around 10% with majority of the DEX genes being upregulated in the human brain (Babbitt, Fedrigo, et al., 2010; Enard, Khaitovich, et al., 2002; Khaitovich, Enard, et al., 2006; Khaitovich, Hellmann, et al., 2005; Khaitovich, Tang, et al., 2006; Preuss, Caceres, Oldham, & Geschwind, 2004; Somel, Franz, et al., 2009). The largest transcriptomic brain differences between human and other species are reported in the cerebral cortex (Caceres, Lachuer, et al., 2003; Enard, Khaitovich, et al., 2002; Khaitovich, Muetzel, et al., 2004; Khaitovich, Tang, et al., 2006; Konopka, Friedrich, et al., 2012). Surprisingly, when comparing differential gene expression between humans and our closest living relative chimpanzee in different organs, the neocortex (i.e., PFC) shows the least differences and liver shows the most (Khaitovich, Hellmann, et al., 2005). However, when comparing differences in the gene expression with the outgroup species (such as rhesus monkey), the human brain transcriptome has more differences (usually upregulation of gene expression) than chimpanzee brain transcriptome, indicating positive selection in the human (Caceres, Lachuer, et al., 2003; Enard, Khaitovich, et al., 2002; Khaitovich, Hellmann, et al., 2005; Khaitovich, Tang, et al., 2006; Somel, Liu, & Khaitovich, 2013; Somel, Liu, et al., 2011). Interestingly, when comparing the difference between areas of the neocortex (e.g., PFC, anterior cingulate cortex, and primary visual cortex) in different species, no significant divergence in the gene expression levels between species were reported with the exception of primary visual cortex (Khaitovich, Muetzel, et al., 2004; Oldham, Horvath, et al., 2006).

However, more recent studies that are using next-generation sequencing to analyze transcriptome data reported significantly larger difference in gene expression levels. The study conducted by Konopka, Friedrich, et al. (2012) reported up to five times more DEX genes between species than previous studies. Furthermore, they reported that the biggest difference in DEX genes was observed in the PFC, i.e., frontal pole (Konopka, Friedrich, et al., 2012). In their report, genes enriched in the fixation point in human lineage were attributed to many important pathways such as neuronal maturation (e.g., *FARP2, RND1*, and *PICK1*), regulation of neuronal projections (e.g., *MAP1B, PLXNB1*, and *PLXNB2*), and axonal components (e.g., *NCAM2, MAP1B*, and *STMN2*). Furthermore, human frontal pole exhibited more complex gene network organization compared with other species. Fifteen modules were identified in the human frontal pole compared with 7 in chimpanzee brain and 6 in macaque brain. Additionally, modules in frontal pole are less evolutionary conserved than in other brain parts (Konopka, Friedrich, et al., 2012).

Although, the level of gene expression patterns and trajectories of expression are conserved between species, more than 75% of expressed genes exhibited substantial differences in timing of expression (Pletikos, Sousa, et al., 2014; Somel, Franz, et al., 2009; Somel, Liu, et al., 2013). The area with the most pronounced differences in the gene expression timing is PFC. Interestingly, the gene network that showed the most significant changes in timing of the gene expression was linked to the synaptic function. The observed changes resulted in the peak expression of synaptic genes around 5 years of life in humans compared with several months in chimpanzee (Liu, Somel, et al., 2012). Lack of significant differences in the gene expression levels between different species indicate that novel functions, which evolved in the human brain, evolved without large-scale changes of functional organization or genetic makeup of these areas (Somel, Liu, et al., 2013).

MiRNAs also exhibit differential expression between species. Approximately 11% of miRNA is differentially expressed between human and chimpanzee PFC, and 30% between human and rhesus monkey PFC (Hu, Guo, et al., 2011). The differential miRNA expression can be linked to the observed differences in both gene and protein expression levels between species. The human brain enriched miRNAs are localized in the neurons and control the expression of genes important for many neuronal functions such as synaptic transmission and proliferation (Hu, Guo, et al., 2011; Liu, Teng, et al., 2010). For example, miR-184 is an miRNA involved in the control of neuronal stem cell proliferation and is highly expressed in the PFC and cerebellum of humans but not of chimpanzees or rhesus monkeys and could potentially be important for expanded neuronal diversity observed in the human brain (Liu, Teng, et al., 2010). However, it is important to note that the observed gene expression differences between species could be explained by increased cellular diversity, more elaborate connections, and expanded set of cortical areas present in the human brain.

CONCLUSION

The Transcriptome Is Important But Just One Piece in the Puzzle of the Development and Function of Human Frontal Cortex

Over the last decade the transcriptomic studies experienced significant boost with the perfection of large-scale and high-throughput techniques such as oligonucleotide microarrays and next-generation sequencing. The wealth of data provided by these studies enabled us to better understand driving forces behind the development of the human cerebral cortex. It also provided us with unique opportunity to study transcriptomic changes between different cortical areas, species, or disorders in fast and efficient way. However, the transcriptome analysis still has many drawbacks, and often the data from two studies are hard to compare due to the use of different platforms or analytical procedures. Furthermore, criteria for considering one gene expressed or DEXs between studies varies greatly, leading to the significantly different results. To fully understand and utilize the data from transcriptomic studies, one must always bear in mind limitations of the methodology. This becomes increasingly important for the experiments trying to elucidate transcriptomic changes in the disorder of the nervous system. Unfortunately, many transcriptomic studies are missing "wider picture." The normal development of the human brain, especially the PFC, is key for proper functioning of the brain in the adult life. The development of the frontal lobe cytoarchitecture (regions, areas, laminas, and moduli) and its connections starts early during fetal period. Various transient fetal zones play important function in the proper development of the cerebral cortex, and damage to one of them will critically damage the development of entire telencephalon. However, due to the lack of human fetal and perinatal tissue sample, these crucial periods of human life are often overlooked and neglected in transcriptomic studies. Importantly, the fetal period is characterized by very dynamic changes in gene expression. Every transient zone has its own unique profile that changes significantly through time. The initial driving forces for the cortical development are endogenous. However, not only gene expression influences brain development at this stage. The early brain circuits are endogenously driven and integrated in transient compartments. They provide signals for many developmental processes. Till date, there is no direct evidence that this early circuitry is predominantly genetically regulated during normal brain development. However, the fact that sensory influences do not evoke responses during early fetal life suggests predominantly genetic control of neurogenetic events. Already at this early life period a unique transcriptomic and connectivity patterns in different cortical areas can be seen. One of the hallmarks of fetal development is the change. The late fetal and early perinatal period is characterized with substantial reorganization of neuronal architecture and connectivity. All neuronal circuitry elements show fast-growing curve during first postnatal year, which corresponds to an early onset of motor, sensory, and environmentally driven developmental processes, followed by socially driven processes in childhood and adolescence. These processes are driven by changes in gene expression. However, the gene expression can also be influenced by environmental factors, where abnormal or detrimental social context can lead to changes in gene expression and disturbances of normal brain development. Therefore, it is important to remember that changes in gene expression are endogenously driven but also significantly influenced by environment, and for the proper understanding of the meaning behind observed changes, one must put it in proper developmental context.

REFERENCES

Amunts, K., Schleicher, A., Ditterich, A., & Zilles, K. (2003). Broca's region: Cytoarchitectonic asymmetry and developmental changes. *The Journal of Comparative Neurology, 465*(1), 72–89.

Babbitt, C. C., Fedrigo, O., Pfefferle, A. D., Boyle, A. P., Horvath, J. E., Furey, T. S., & Wray, G. A. (2010). Both noncoding and protein-coding RNAs contribute to gene expression evolution in the primate brain. *Genome Biology and Evolution, 2*, 67–79.

Bahn, S., Augood, S., Standaert, D. G., Starkey, M., & Emson, P. C. (2001). Gene expression profiling in the post-mortem human brain—No cause for dismay. *Journal of Chemical Neuroanatomy, 22*(1–2), 79–94.

Bailey, P., & von Bonin, G. (1951). *The isocortex of man.* Urbana: University of Illinois Press.

Bartel, D. P. (2004). MicroRNAs: Genomics, biogenesis, mechanism, and function. *Cell, 116*(2), 281–297.

Bartel, D. P. (2009). MicroRNAs: Target recognition and regulatory functions. *Cell, 136*(2), 215–233.

Berezikov, E., Thuemmler, F., van Laake, L. W., Kondova, I., Bontrop, R., Cuppen, E., & Plasterk, R. H. (2006). Diversity of microRNAs in human and chimpanzee brain. *Nature Genetics, 38*(12), 1375–1377.

Boulder Committee (1970). Embryonic vertebrate central nervous system: Revised terminology. *The Anatomical Record, 166*, 257–261.

Broca, P. (1861). Perte de la parole, ramollissement chronique et destruction partielle du lobe anterieur gauche. *Bulletin de la Societe Antropologique, 2*, 235–238.

Brodmann, K. (1909). *Vergleichende Lokalisationslehre der Grosshirnrinde in ihren Prinzipien dargestellt aut Grund des Zellenbaues.* Leipzig: J.A. Barth.

Bystron, I., Blakemore, C., & Rakic, P. (2008). Development of the human cerebral cortex: Boulder Committee revisited. *Nature Reviews Neuroscience, 9*(2), 110–122. Available from http://dx.doi.org/10.1038/nrn2252.

Caceres, M., Lachuer, J., Zapala, M. A., Redmond, J. C., Kudo, L., Geschwind, D. H., & Barlow, C. (2003). Elevated gene expression levels distinguish human from non-human primate brains. *Proceedings National Academy Science of the United States of America, 100*(22), 13030–13035.

Chang, J., Gilman, S. R., Chiang, A. H., Sanders, S. J., & Vitkup, D. (2015). Genotype to phenotype relationships in autism spectrum disorders. *Nature Neuroscience, 18,* 191–198.

Colantuoni, C., Lipska, B. K., Ye, T. Z., Hyde, T. M., Tao, R., Leek, J. T., & Kleinman, J. E. (2011). Temporal dynamics and genetic control of transcription in the human prefrontal cortex. *Nature, 478*(7370), 519-U117

Dax, M. (1865). Lesions de la moitie guache de l'encephale coincidant avec l'oubli des signes de la pensee: Lu au Congres meridional tenu a Montpellier en 1836. *Bulletin hebdomadaire de medecine et de chirurgie 2me serie, 2,* 259–262.

Diamond, A., & Goldman-Rakic, P. S. (1989). Comparison of human infants and rhesus monkeys on Piaget's AB task: Evidence for dependence on dorsolateral prefrontal cortex. *Experimental Brain Research, 74*(1), 24–40.

Duque, A., Krsnik, Z., Kostović, I., & Rakic, P. (2016). Secondary expansion of the transient subplate zone in the developing cerebrum of human and nonhuman primates. *Proceedings of the National Academy of Sciences of the United States of America, 113*(35), 9892–9897.

Enard, W., Khaitovich, P., Klose, J., Zollner, S., Heissig, F., Giavalisco, P., & Paabo, S. (2002). Intra- and interspecific variation in primate gene expression patterns. *Science, 296*(5566), 340–343.

Fair, D. A., Cohen, A. L., Dosenbach, N. U. F., Church, J. A., Miezin, F. M., Barch, D. M., & Schlaggar, B. L. (2008). The maturing architecture of the brain's default network. *Proceedings of the National Academy of Sciences of the United States of America, 105*(10), 4028–4032.

Feller, M. B. (1999). Spontaneous correlated activity in developing neural circuits. *Neuron, 22*(4), 653–656.

Fietz, S. A., Lachmann, R., Brandl, H., Kircher, M., Samusik, N., Schroder, R., & Huttner, W. B. (2012). Transcriptomes of germinal zones of human and mouse fetal neocortex suggest a role of extracellular matrix in progenitor self-renewal. *Proceedings of the National Academy of Sciences of the United States of America, 109*(29), 11836–11841.

Fitzgerald, M. (2005). The development of nociceptive circuits. *Nature Reviews Neuroscience, 6*(7), 507–520.

Flechsig, P. (1901). Developmental (myelogenetic) localisation of the cerebral cortex in the human subject. *Lancet, 158,* 1027–1030.

Fransson, P., Skiold, B., Horsch, S., Nordell, A., Blennow, M., Lagercrantz, H., & Aden, U. (2007). Resting-state networks in the infant brain. *Proceedings of the National Academy of Sciences of the United States of America, 104*(39), 15531–15536.

Fraser, H. B., Khaitovich, P., Plotkin, J. B., Paabo, S., & Eisen, M. B. (2005). Aging and gene expression in the primate brain. *PLoS Biology, 3*(9), e274.

Geschwind, N., & Levitsky, W. (1968). Human brain: Left-right asymmetries in temporal speech region. *Science, 161*(3837), 186–187.

Gilman, S. R., Iossifov, I., Levy, D., Ronemus, M., Wigler, M., & Vitkup, D. (2011). Rare de novo variants associated with autism implicate a large functional network of genes involved in formation and function of synapses. *Neuron, 70*(5), 898–907.

Goldman-Rakic, P. S., & Porrino, L. J. (1985). The primate mediodorsal (MD) nucleus and its projection to the frontal-lobe. *Journal of Comparative Neurology, 242*(4), 535–560.

Hadders-Algra, M. (2007). Putative neural substrate of normal and abnormal general movements. *Neuroscience and Biobehavioral Reviews, 31*(8), 1181–1190.

Harris, L. W., Lockstone, H. E., Khaitovich, P., Weickert, C. S., Webster, M. J., & Bahn, S. (2009). Gene expression in the prefrontal cortex during adolescence: Implications for the onset of schizophrenia. *BMC Medical Genomics, 2*, 28.

Hawrylycz, M., Miller, J. A., Menon, V., Feng, D., Dolbeare, T., Guillozet-Bongaarts, A. L., & Lein, E. (2015). Canonical genetic signatures of the adult human brain. *Nature Neuroscience, 18*(12), 1832–1844.

Hawrylycz, M. J., Lein, E. S., Guillozet-Bongaarts, A. L., Shen, E. H., Ng, L., Miller, J. A., & Jones, A. R. (2012). An anatomically comprehensive atlas of the adult human brain transcriptome. *Nature, 489*(7416), 391–399.

Hayes, T. L., & Lewis, D. A. (1993). Hemispheric differences in layer III pyramidal neurons of the anterior language area. *Archives of Neurology, 50*(5), 501–505.

He, X., Sanders, S. J., Liu, L., De Rubeis, S., Lim, E. T., Sutcliffe, J. S., & Roeder, K. (2013). Integrated model of de novo and inherited genetic variants yields greater power to identify risk genes. *PLoS Genetics, 9*(8), e1003671.

Hitzemann, R., Darakjian, P., Walter, N., Iancu, O. D., Searles, R., & McWeeney, S. (2014). Introduction to sequencing the brain transcriptome. *Brain Transcriptome, 116*, 1–19.

Hu, H. Y., Guo, S., Xi, J., Yan, Z., Fu, N., Zhang, X., & Khaitovich, P. (2011). MicroRNA expression and regulation in human, chimpanzee, and macaque brains. *PLoS Genetics, 7*(10), e1002327.

Huang, H., Zhang, J. Y., Wakana, S., Zhang, W. H., Ren, T. B., Richards, L. J., & Mori, S. (2006). White and gray matter development in human fetal, newborn and pediatric brains. *Neuroimage, 33*(1), 27–38.

Huang, H., Xue, R., Zhang, J. Y., Ren, T. B., Richards, L. J., Yarowsky, P., & Mori, S. (2009). Anatomical characterization of human fetal brain development with diffusion tensor magnetic resonance imaging. *Journal of Neuroscience, 29*(13), 4263–4273.

Huang, H., Jeon, T., Sedmak, G., Pletikos, M., Vasung, L., Xu, X. M., & Mori, S. (2013). Coupling diffusion imaging with histological and gene expression analysis to examine the dynamics of cortical areas across the fetal period of human brain development. *Cerebral Cortex, 23*(11), 2620–2631.

Ihmels, J., Bergmann, S., & Barkai, N. (2004). Defining transcription modules using large-scale gene expression data. *Bioinformatics, 20*(13), 1993–2003.

Johnson, M. B., Kawasawa, Y. I., Mason, C. E., Krsnik, Z., Coppola, G., Bogdanovic, D., & Sestan, N. (2009). Functional and evolutionary insights into human brain development through global transcriptome analysis. *Neuron, 62*(4), 494–509.

Judaš, M., Sedmak, G., & Kostović, I. (2013). The significance of the subplate for evolution and developmental plasticity of the human brain. *Frontiers in Human Neuroscience, 7*, 423.

Kang, H. J., Kawasawa, Y. I., Cheng, F., Zhu, Y., Xu, X. M., Li, M. F., & Sestan, N. (2011). Spatio-temporal transcriptome of the human brain. *Nature, 478*(7370), 483–489.

Kasprian, G., Brugger, P. C., Weber, M., Krssak, M., Krampl, E., Herold, C., & Prayer, D. (2008). In utero tractography of fetal white matter development. *Neuroimage, 43*(2), 213–224.

Kasprian, G., Langs, G., Brugger, P. C., Bittner, M., Weber, M., Arantes, M., & Prayer, D. (2011). The prenatal origin of hemispheric asymmetry: An in utero neuroimaging study. *Cerebral Cortex*, *21*(5), 1076–1083.

Khaitovich, P., Enard, W., Lachmann, M., & Paabo, S. (2006). Evolution of primate gene expression. *Nature Review Genetics*, *7*(9), 693–702.

Khaitovich, P., Hellmann, I., Enard, W., Nowick, K., Leinweber, M., Franz, H., & Paabo, S. (2005). Parallel patterns of evolution in the genomes and transcriptomes of humans and chimpanzees. *Science*, *309*(5742), 1850–1854.

Khaitovich, P., Muetzel, B., She, X. W., Lachmann, M., Hellmann, I., Dietzsch, J., & Paabo, S. (2004). Regional patterns of gene expression in human and chimpanzee brains. *Genome Research*, *14*(8), 1462–1473.

Khaitovich, P., Tang, K., Franz, H., Kelso, J., Hellmann, I., Enard, W., & Paabo, S. (2006). Positive selection on gene expression in the human brain. *Current Biology*, *16*(10), R356–R358.

Khazipov, R., & Luhmann, H. J. (2006). Early patterns of electrical activity in the developing cerebral cortex of humans and rodents. *Trends in Neurosciences*, *29*(7), 414–418.

King, M. C., & Wilson, A. C. (1975). Evolution at 2 levels in humans and chimpanzees. *Science*, *188*(4184), 107–116.

Konopka, G., Friedrich, T., Davis-Turak, J., Winden, K., Oldham, M. C., Gao, F., & Geschwind, D. H. (2012). Human-specific transcriptional networks in the brain. *Neuron*, *75*(4), 601–617.

Kosik, K. S. (2006). The neuronal microRNA system. *Nature Review Neuroscience*, *7*(12), 911–920.

Kosik, K. S. (2009). MicroRNAs tell an evo-devo story. *Nature Review Neuroscience*, *10*(10), 754–759.

Kostović, I. (1990). Structural and histochemical reorganization of the human prefrontal cortex during perinatal and postnatal life. *Progress in Brain Research*, *85*, 223–240.

Kostović, I., & Goldman-Rakic, P. S. (1983). Transient cholinesterase staining in the mediodorsal nucleus of the thalamus and its connections in the developing human and monkey brain. *Journal of Comparative Neurology*, *219*(4), 431–447.

Kostović, I., Jovanov-Milošević, N., Krsnik, Ž., Petanjek, Z., & Judaš, M. (2004). Laminar organization of the marginal zone in the human fetal cortex. *Neuroembryology*, *3*, 19–26.

Kostović, I., & Judaš, M. (2002). Correlation between the sequential ingrowth of afferents and transient patterns of cortical lamination in preterm infants. *Anatomical Record*, *267*(1), 1–6.

Kostović, I., & Judaš, M. (2006). Prolonged coexistence of transient and permanent circuitry elements in the developing cerebral cortex of fetuses and preterm infants. *Developmental Medicine and Child Neurology*, *48*(5), 388–393.

Kostović, I., & Judaš, M. (2007). Transient patterns of cortical lamination during prenatal life: Do they have implications for treatment? *Neuroscience and Biobehavioral Reviews*, *31*(8), 1157–1168.

Kostović, I., & Judaš, M. (2009). Early development of neuronal circuitry of the human prefrontal cortex. In M. S. Gazzaniga (Ed.), *The cognitive neuroscience* (pp. 29–47). Cambridge, Massachusetts, London, England: A Bradford Book, The MIT press.

Kostović, I., & Judaš, M. (2010). The development of the subplate and thalamocortical connections in the human foetal brain. *Acta Paediatrica*, *99*(8), 1119–1127.

Kostović, I., & Judaš, M. (2015). Embryonic and fetal development of the human cerebral cortex. In Toga (Ed.), *Brain mapping: An encyclopedic reference* (Volume 2, pp. 167–175). London, England: Academic Press, Anatomy and Physiology, Systems.

Kostović, I., & Molliver, M. E. (1974). New interpretation of laminar development of cerebral-cortex—Synaptogenesis in different layers of neopallium in human fetus. *Anatomical Record, 178*(2), 395.

Kostović, I., & Rakic, P. (1984). Development of prestriate visual projections in the monkey and human-fetal cerebrum revealed by transient cholinesterase staining. *Journal of Neuroscience, 4*(1), 25–42.

Kostović, I., & Rakic, P. (1990). Developmental history of the transient subplate zone in the visual and somatosensory cortex of the macaque monkey and human brain. *Journal of Comparative Neurology, 297*(3), 441–470.

Kostović, I., Judaš, M., Petanjek, Z., & Šimić, G. (1995). Ontogenesis of goal-directed behavior: anatomo-functional considerations. *The International Journal of Psychophysiology, 19*(2), 85–102.

Kostović, I., Judaš, M., Radoš, M., & Hrabač, P. (2002). Laminar organization of the human fetal cerebrum revealed by histochemical markers and magnetic resonance imaging. *Cerebral Cortex, 12*(5), 536–544.

Lambert, N., Lambot, M. A., Bilheu, A., Albert, V., Englert, Y., Libert, F., & Vanderhaeghen, P. (2011). Genes expressed in specific areas of the human fetal cerebral cortex display distinct patterns of evolution. *PLoS One, 6*(3), e17753.

Li, Y., Li, T., Liu, S. Z., Qiu, M. Y., Han, Z. Y., Jiang, Z. L., & Mao, Y. M. (2004). Systematic comparison of the fidelity of aRNA, mRNA and T-RNA on gene expression profiling using cDNA microarray. *Journal of Biotechnology, 107*(1), 19–28.

Liu, C., Teng, Z. Q., Santistevan, N. J., Szulwach, K. E., Guo, W., Jin, P., & Zhao, X. (2010). Epigenetic regulation of miR-184 by MBD1 governs neural stem cell proliferation and differentiation. *Cell Stem Cell, 6*(5), 433–444.

Liu, X., Somel, M., Tang, L., Yan, Z., Jiang, X., Guo, S., & Khaitovich, P. (2012). Extension of cortical synaptic development distinguishes humans from chimpanzees and macaques. *Genome Research, 22*(4), 611–622.

Marioni, J. C., Mason, C. E., Mane, S. M., Stephens, M., & Gilad, Y. (2008). RNA-seq: An assessment of technical reproducibility and comparison with gene expression arrays. *Genome Research, 18*(9), 1509–1517.

Mazin, P., Xiong, J. Y., Liu, X. L., Yan, Z., Zhang, X. Y., Li, M. S., & Khaitovich, P. (2013). Widespread splicing changes in human brain development and aging. *Molecular Systems Biology*, 9.

Miller, J. A., Ding, S. L., Sunkin, S. M., Smith, K. A., Ng, L., Szafer, A., & Lein, E. S. (2014). Transcriptional landscape of the prenatal human brain. *Nature, 508*(7495), 199–206.

Mirnics, K. (2006). Microarrays in brain research: Data quality and limitations revisited. *Current Genomics, 7*(1), 11–17.

Mirnics, K. (2008). What is in the brain soup? *Nature Neuroscience, 11*(11), 1237–1238.

Mirnics, K., Levitt, P., & Lewis, D. A. (2004). DNA microarray analysis of postmortem brain tissue. *DNA Arrays in Neurobiology, 60*(60), 153.

Mirnics, K., & Pevsner, J. (2004). Progress in the use of microarray technology to study the neurobiology of disease. *Nature Neuroscience, 7*(5), 434–439.

Molyneaux, B. J., Arlotta, P., Menezes, J. R., & Macklis, J. D. (2007). Neuronal subtype specification in the cerebral cortex. *Nature Review Neuroscience, 8*(6), 427–437.

Mrzljak, L., Uylings, H. B., Kostović, I., & Van Eden, C. G. (1988). Prenatal development of neurons in the human prefrontal cortex: I. A qualitative Golgi study. *Journal of Comparative Neurology, 271*(3), 355–386.

Novak, G. P., Kurtzberg, D., Kreuzer, J. A., & Vaughan, H. G., Jr. (1989). Cortical responses to speech sounds and their formants in normal infants: Maturational sequence and spatiotemporal analysis. *Electroencephalography and Clinical Neurophysiology, 73*(4), 295−305.

Ohno, S. (1972). Argument for genetic simplicity of man and other mammals. *Journal of Human Evolution, 1*(6), 651−662.

Oldham, M. C., Horvath, S., & Geschwind, D. H. (2006). Conservation and evolution of gene colexpression networks in human and chimpanzee brains. *Proceedings of the National Academy of Sciences of the United States of America, 103*(47), 17973−17978.

Oldham, M. C., Konopka, G., Iwamoto, K., Langfelder, P., Kato, T., Horvath, S., & Geschwind, D. H. (2008). Functional organization of the transcriptome in human brain. *Nature Neuroscience, 11*(11), 1271−1282.

O'Leary, D. D., Chou, S. J., & Sahara, S. (2007). Area patterning of the mammalian cortex. *Neuron, 56*(2), 252−269.

O'Leary, D. D., & Nakagawa, Y. (2002). Patterning centers, regulatory genes and extrinsic mechanisms controlling arealization of the neocortex. *Current Opinion in Neurobiology, 12*(1), 14−25.

O'Leary, D. D., & Sahara, S. (2008). Genetic regulation of arealization of the neocortex. *Current Opinion in Neurobiology, 18*(1), 90−100.

O'Leary, D. D., Schlaggar, B. L., & Tuttle, R. (1994). Specification of neocortical areas and thalamocortical connections. *Annual Review of Neuroscience, 17*, 419−439.

Packer, A. (2016). Neocortical neurogenesis and the etiology of autism spectrum disorder. *Neuroscience and Biobehavioral Reviews, 64*, 185−195.

Penn, A. A., & Shatz, C. J. (1999). Brain waves and brain wiring: the role of endogenous and sensory-driven neural activity in development. *Pediatric Research, 45*(4 Pt 1), 447−458.

Petanjek, Z., Judas, M., Kostovic, I., & Uylings, H. B. M. (2008). Lifespan alterations of basal dendritic trees of pyramidal neurons in the human prefrontal cortex: A layer-specific pattern. *Cerebral Cortex, 18*(4), 915−929.

Petanjek, Z., Judaš, M., Šimić, G., Rasin, M. R., Uylings, H. B., Rakic, P., & Kostović, I. (2011). Extraordinary neoteny of synaptic spines in the human prefrontal cortex. *Proceedings of the National Academy of Science of the United States of America, 108*(32), 13281−13286.

Pletikos, M., Sousa, A. M. M., Sedmak, G., Meyer, K. A., Zhu, Y., Cheng, F., & Sestan, N. (2014). Temporal specification and bilaterality of human neocortical topographic gene expression. *Neuron, 81*(2), 321−332.

Poot, M. (2015). Connecting the CNTNAP2 networks with neurodevelopmental disorders. *Molecular Syndromology, 6*(1), 7−22.

Popova, T., Mennerich, D., Weith, A., & Quast, K. (2008). Effect of RNA quality on transcript intensity levels in microarray analysis of human post-mortem brain tissues. *BMC Genomics, 9*, 91.

Preuss, T. M., Caceres, M., Oldham, M. C., & Geschwind, D. H. (2004). Human brain evolution: Insights from microarrays. *Nature Review Genetics, 5*(11), 850−860.

Qiu, S., Luo, S., Evgrafov, O., Li, R., Schroth, G. P., Levitt, P., & Wang, K. (2012). Single-neuron RNA-Seq: Technical feasibility and reproducibility. *Frontiers in Genetics, 3*, 124.

Rakic, P. (1988). Specification of cerebral cortical areas. *Science, 241*(4862), 170−176.

Rakic, P. (1995). A small step for the cell, a giant leap for mankind: A hypothesis of neocortical expansion during evolution. *Trends in Neuroscience, 18*(9), 383−388.

Rakic, P. (2006). A century of progress in corticoneurogenesis: From silver impregnation to genetic engineering. *Cerebral Cortex, 16*, I3−I17.

Rapoport, J. L., & Gogtay, N. (2008). Brain neuroplasticity in healthy, hyperactive and psychotic children: Insights from neuroimaging. *Neuropsychopharmacology, 33*(1), 181−197.

Reinius, B., & Jazin, E. (2009). Prenatal sex differences in the human brain. *Molecular Psychiatry, 14*(11), 988−989.

Richiardi, J., Altmann, A., Milazzo, A. C., Chang, C., Chakravarty, M. M., Banaschewski, T., & I. consortium (2015). BRAIN NETWORKS. Correlated gene expression supports synchronous activity in brain networks. *Science, 348*(6240), 1241−1244.

Ronemus, M., Iossifov, I., Levy, D., & Wigler, M. (2014). The role of de novo mutations in the genetics of autism spectrum disorders. *Nature Review Genetics, 15*(2), 133−141.

Schwartz, M. L., & Goldmanrakic, P. S. (1984). Callosal and intrahemispheric connectivity of the prefrontal association cortex in rhesus-monkey—Relation between intraparietal and principal sulcal cortex. *Journal of Comparative Neurology, 226*(3), 403−420.

Schwartz, M. L., & Goldmanrakic, P. S. (1991). Prenatal specification of callosal connections in rhesus-monkey. *Journal of Comparative Neurology, 307*(1), 144−162.

Shao, N. Y., Hu, H. Y., Yan, Z., Xu, Y., Hu, H., Menzel, C., & Khaitovich, P. (2010). Comprehensive survey of human brain microRNA by deep sequencing. *BMC Genomics, 11*, 409.

Silbereis, J. C., Pochareddy, S., Zhu, Y., Li, M., & Sestan, N. (2016). The cellular and molecular landscapes of the developing human central nervous system. *Neuron, 89*(2), 248−268.

Smyser, C. D., Snyder, A. Z., & Neil, J. J. (2011). Functional connectivity MRI in infants: Exploration of the functional organization of the developing brain. *Neuroimage, 56*(3), 1437−1452.

Somel, M., Franz, H., Yan, Z., Lorenc, A., Guo, S., Giger, T., & Khaitovich, P. (2009). Transcriptional neoteny in the human brain. *Proceedings of the National Academy of Science of the United States of America, 106*(14), 5743−5748.

Somel, M., Guo, S., Fu, N., Yan, Z., Hu, H. Y., Xu, Y., & Khaitovich, P. (2010). MicroRNA, mRNA, and protein expression link development and aging in human and macaque brain. *Genome Research, 20*(9), 1207−1218.

Somel, M., Liu, X. L., & Khaitovich, P. (2013). Human brain evolution: Transcripts, metabolites and their regulators. *Nature Reviews Neuroscience, 14*(2), 112−127.

Somel, M., Liu, X. L., Tang, L., Yan, Z., Hu, H. Y., Guo, S., & Khaitovich, P. (2011). MicroRNA-driven developmental remodeling in the brain distinguishes humans from other primates. *PLoS Biology, 9*(12), e1001214.

Sorensen, S. A., Bernard, A., Menon, V., Royall, J. J., Glattfelder, K. J., Desta, T., Hirokawa, K., Mortrud, M., MIller, J. A., Zeng, H., Hohmann, J. G., Jones, A. R., & Lein, E. S. (2015). Correlated gene expression and target specificity demonstrate excitatory projection neuron diversity. *Cereb Cortex, 25*, 433−439.

Sowell, E. R., Thompson, P. M., Welcome, S. E., Henkenius, A. L., Toga, A. W., & Peterson, B. S. (2003). Cortical abnormalities in children and adolescents with attention-deficit hyperactivity disorder. *Lancet, 362*(9397), 1699−1707.

Sun, T., Collura, R. V., Ruvolo, M., & Walsh, C. A. (2006). Genomic and evolutionary analyses of asymmetrically expressed genes in human fetal left and right cerebral cortex. *Cerebral Cortex, 16*(Suppl 1), i18−i25.

Sun, T., Patoine, C., Abu-Khalil, A., Visvader, J., Sum, E., Cherry, T. J., & Walsh, C. A. (2005). Early asymmetry of gene transcription in embryonic human left and right cerebral cortex. *Science, 308*(5729), 1794−1798.

Sun, T., & Walsh, C. A. (2006). Molecular approaches to brain asymmetry and handedness. *Nature Review Neuroscience, 7*(8), 655−662.

Vasung, L., Huang, H., Jovanov-Milosevic, N., Pletikos, M., Mori, S., & Kostović, I. (2010). Development of axonal pathways in the human fetal fronto-limbic brain: Histochemical characterization and diffusion tensor imaging. *Journal of Anatomy, 217*(4), 400–417.

Vawter, M. P., Evans, S., Choudary, P., Tomita, H., Meador-Woodruff, J., Molnar, M., & Bunney, W. E. (2004). Gender-specific gene expression in post-mortem human brain: Localization to sex chromosomes. *Neuropsychopharmacology, 29*(2), 373–384.

Vogt, C., & Vogt, O. (1919). Allgemeine Ergebnisse unserer Hirnforschung. *Journal fur Psychologie und Neurologie, 25*(Suppl. 1), 273–462.

Voineagu, I., Wang, X., Johnston, P., Lowe, J. K., Tian, Y., Horvath, S., & Geschwind, D. H. (2011). Transcriptomic analysis of autistic brain reveals convergent molecular pathology. *Nature, 474*(7351), 380–384.

Von Economo, C., & Koskinas, G. N. (1925). *Die Cytoarchitektonik der Hirnrinde des Erwaschsenen Menschen: Textband und Atlas mit 112 Mikrophotographischen Tafeln.* Vienna: Springer.

Wei, Y. N., Hu, H. Y., Xie, G. C., Fu, N., Ning, Z. B., Zeng, R., & Khaitovich, P. (2015). Transcript and protein expression decoupling reveals RNA binding proteins and miRNAs as potential modulators of human aging. *Genome Biology, 16*, 41.

Weickert, C. S., Elashoff, M., Richards, A. B., Sinclair, D., Bahn, S., Paabo, S., & Webster, M. J. (2009). Transcriptome analysis of male-female differences in prefrontal cortical development. *Molecular Psychiatry, 14*(6), 558–561.

Wernicke, C. (1874). *Der Aphasische Symptomenkomplex: Eine Psychologische Studie auf Anatomischer Basis.* Breslau: Max Cohn & Weigert.

Woolfe, A., Goodson, M., Goode, D. K., Snell, P., McEwen, G. K., Vavouri, T., & Elgar, G. (2005). Highly conserved non-coding sequences are associated with vertebrate development. *PLoS Biology, 3*(1), 116–130.

Yeh, E., & Weiss, L. A. (2016). If genetic variation could talk: What genomic data may teach us about the importance of gene expression regulation in the genetics of autism. *Molecular and Cellular Probes*.

Yuan, Y., Chen, Y. P. P., Boyd-Kirkup, J., Khaitovich, P., & Somel, M. (2012). Accelerated aging-related transcriptome changes in the female prefrontal cortex. *Aging Cell, 11*(5), 894–901.

Zecevic, N., & Verney, C. (1995). Development of the catecholamine neurons in human embryos and fetuses, with special emphasis on the innervation of the cerebral cortex. *Journal of Comparative Neurology, 351*(4), 509–535.

Zeng, H. K., Shen, E. H., Hohmann, J. G., Oh, S. W., Bernard, A., Royall, J. J., & Jones, A. R. (2012). Large-scale cellular-resolution gene profiling in human neocortex reveals species-specific molecular signatures. *Cell, 149*(2), 483–496.

Zhang, B., & Horvath, S. (2005). A general framework for weighted gene co-expression network analysis. *Statistical Applications in Genetics and Molecular Biology, 4*, Article 17.

Chapter 4

A Functional Network Perspective on the Role of the Frontal Lobes in Executive Cognition

Adam Hampshire
The Computational Cognitive and Clinical Neuroimaging Laboratory (C³NL), The Division of Brain Sciences, Imperial College London, London, United Kingdom

THE CLASSIC APPROACH TO FUNCTIONAL BRAIN MAPPING

Early functional magnetic resonance imaging (fMRI) studies of frontal lobe function were largely based on classic modular perspectives, which ascribed specific functions to individual brain regions and their specific connection pathways. Typically, fMRI tasks used carefully designed parametric or subtractive analyses to differentially manipulate established constructs from the cognitive psychology literature, for example, attentional orienting, working memory maintenance, or response inhibition. Rendering changes in blood oxygenation levels in response to these manipulations mapped the putative cognitive constructs onto discrete functional–anatomical modules within the brain. The resultant modular models formed a natural complement to the pre-existing functional lesion maps developed in the course of neuropsychology research, enabling functional–anatomical modules to be defined at finer spatial resolution and their responses to cognitive conditions to be examined in vivo at the second scale temporal resolution. In this manner, distinct aspects of cognitive processing that occurred at different stages of complex executive tasks could be ascribed to different areas of the frontal lobes.

The resultant combination of behavioral construct, cognitive paradigm, and functional–anatomical mapping provided a simple and tractable framework for examining the neural bases of cognitive impairments in clinical populations. Observations from such clinical research in turn informed the refinement of the cognitive models, leading to the generation of testable predictions for further empirical study. This synergistic progression of theoretical and clinical

Executive Functions in Health and Disease. DOI: http://dx.doi.org/10.1016/B978-0-12-803676-1.00004-0

research highlighted the functional complexity of the human lateral frontal cortices. Ultimately, although, it has also changed our notion of what the distinct aspects of human cognition are and of the fundamental functional organizational principles of the brain. The study of the frontal lobes involvement in attentional set shifting provides a good illustration of these developments.

PROBING THE FUNCTIONAL HETEROGENEITY OF THE HUMAN PFC USING AN FMRI OPTIMIZED INTRADIMENSIONAL–EXTRADIMENSIONAL SWITCHING PARADIGM

The intradimensional–extradimensional (IDED) fMRI paradigm (Fig. 4.1) was developed as a neuroimaging-optimized variant on the classic Wisconsin Card Sorting Test (WCST), which is a popular paradigm for assessing executive function (Berg, 1948). The IDED and the WCST were both designed to probe the cognitive processes that enable optimal behavior when dealing with changing conditions. The individual must first derive a rule by exploring possible behaviors and monitoring feedback. They must then exploit that rule to generate rewarding feedback but adapt when the rule is changed and the routine behavior no longer generates optimal feedback. As with many executive paradigms, the WCST is complex by design and this complexity may be considered a two-edged sword; on the one hand, the WCST is sensitive to executive impairments, but on the other hand the performance measures that it takes are heterogeneous; that is, the diverse populations that struggle to perform it can have different underlying neural pathologies. Consequently, the WCST provides a sensitive but nonspecific assessment of executive function.

To address this issue a behavioral paradigm had previously been developed that differentiate between two of the qualitatively distinct aspects of executive function that are tapped by the classic WCST (Dias, Robbins, & Roberts, 1996, 1997): attentional set shifting, the process by which the focus of attention is switched from one stimulus category to another, and reversal learning, the process by which previously rewarded behaviors are overridden when stimulus–response–reward contingencies are changed. Research with nonhuman primates had indicated that lesions within the lateral and orbital frontal cortices differentially affected these executive subprocesses (Collins, Roberts, Dias, Everitt, & Robbins, 1998). In accordance with the classic modular approach, the aim of the fMRI study was to extend the lesion mapping research by further fractionating the task into subprocesses and mapping them to their distinct functional–anatomical substrates within the human brain (Hampshire & Owen, 2006).

Sixteen healthy young adults undertook the initial fMRI study (Fig. 4.1). When analyzing the behavioral data from the fMRI study, individuals were slower to respond when trying to derive the rule by exploration relative to

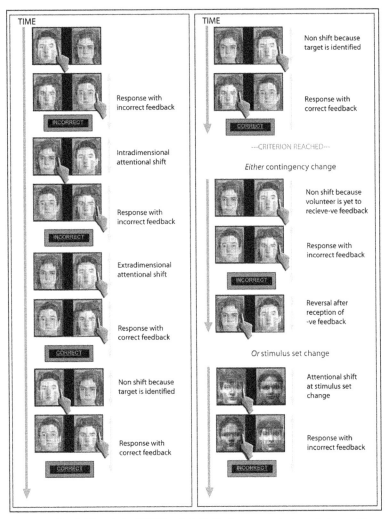

FIGURE 4.1 The fMRI optimized IDED task. Individuals were required to select one of two multidimensional stimuli, consisting of superimposed house-face stimuli, according to a rule that related to just one of these dimensions. For example, the rule could be that selecting Face A would generate positive feedback, whereas selecting Face B would generate negative feedback. The participant was required to derive the rule by a process of trial and error and then to apply it by selecting the stimuli that generate positive feedback. Periodically, the rule changed and the participant was required to derive the new rule. At a coarse grain, the task followed a cycle of exploratory and exploitative behavior. At a finer grain, if the rule is related to the same dimension (e.g., switching from one face to another) this was termed an intradimensional switch, whereas if it is related to a different dimension (e.g., switching from faces to buildings) then this was termed an extradimensional switch. Notably, under the latter conditions, attention must be switched between information coded within quite distinct processing areas of the posterior brain, i.e., the fusiform face area and the parahippocampal place area. When the rule change was accompanied by a new set of stimuli, this was termed stimulus-set change, whereas when it was within the context of the same stimuli, it was termed a reversal. These conditions differ because in the latter case, the previous stimulus-response behavior is still available; therefore, the participant must detect that the previously rewarded behavior is no longer optimal and they must override it. *IDED*, intradimensional–extradimensional; *fMRI*, functional magnetic resonance imaging. *From Hampshire, A., & Owen, A.M. (2006). Fractionating attentional control using event-related fMRI. Cerebral Cortex, 16, 1679–1689.*

when exploiting a rule that had been established based on reception of positive feedback. Contrasting the entire period of time during which the rule was being actively derived by trial and error relative to the period of time when responses were being made routinely based on an established rule activated a widespread network of brain regions, including large swathes of the lateral frontal, medial frontal, and parietal cortices (Fig. 4.2A). At a finer grain, individuals took longer to switch attention between stimuli that were from different as opposed to the same object dimension. On average, they also make more mistakes before deriving the correct rule if an extradimensional switch was required; this was because they used the object dimensions to organize their search, eliminating the stimuli from one dimension (e.g., faces) before exploring the other (e.g., houses). Together these provided measures of "set-like" behavior. When contrasting regional brain activation for events where attention was switched extra- versus intradimensionally, there was a significant increase in the activity within a set of areas that included the anterior insula/inferior frontal operculum and the anterior cingulate cortex (ACC) (Fig. 4.2B). Individuals also were significantly slower to respond when reengaging in exploration behavior do to a change in rule (reversal learning). Contrasting brain activation during reversal events minus stimulus-set change events rendered activation within the lateral frontopolar cortices and posterior parietal cortices bilaterally (Fig. 4.2C). Brain activity also differed during the reception of positive and negative feedback. Specifically, there was heightened activity within the medial orbitofrontal cortex during positive feedback and within the lateral frontal cortices focused on the right dorsolateral prefrontal cortex during negative feedback (Fig. 4.2D).

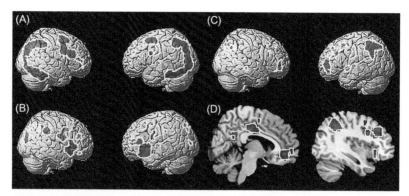

FIGURE 4.2 Functional correlates of IDED task subprocesses. Event-related fMRI contrasts. (A) Exploration minus exploitation of rules. (B) Extradimensional minus intradimensional switching. (C) Contingency reversal minus change of stimulus-set. (D) Positive minus negative (*left*) and negative minus positive (*right*) feedback. *IDED*, intradimensional−extradimensional; *fMRI*, functional magnetic resonance imaging.

These results demonstrate the functional complexity of the human frontal lobes. Different brain regions are active at different stages of the IDED task; they likely support distinct aspects of cognitive information processing. Performance of complex executive tasks likely requires the coordinated processing of many of these brain regions; therefore, clinical populations that struggle with classic tasks such as the WCST or IDED behavioral paradigm may have very different underlying neuropathology.

The IDED paradigm provided a validated tool for probing this heterogeneity. For example, an analysis of older versus younger adults when performing the task showed a pattern of anterior insula/inferior frontal operculum (AIFO) and ACC hypoactivation that was most pronounced during extradimensional switches of attention. Older adults still showed set-like behavior, eliminating stimuli from one dimension before trying those from another. However, their search was generally inefficient, being characterized by more errors when identifying the rewarded stimulus. In contrast, when patients with obsessive compulsive disorder undertook the same task, they showed a pattern of reduced activation within the lateral orbitofrontal and posterior parietal cortices, which was particularly pronounced during reversal learning. Notably, the same pattern of abnormal activation was evident in the first-degree relatives of the patients, providing a functional–anatomical endophenotype. In Parkinson's patients and age-matched controls, there was a relationship between the expression of set-like behavior and the catechol-o-methyl transferase val-158met genotype, which affects frontal lobe dopamine processing. In line with models of frontal cortex dopamine function, the genotype effects were inverted across the two populations. These effects were concomitant with reduced inferior frontal sulcus (IFS) activation. The key point is that although all three populations struggle to perform executive tasks such as the WCST and IDED, the neural systems that underlie these deficits are different, as are the finer grained behavioral characteristics of the behavioral impairments. The modular perspective is useful insofar as it makes such differences transparent and measurable, thereby providing tractable markers for research into the commonalities and heterogeneity of impairments across clinical populations.

LIMITATIONS OF MODULAR PERSPECTIVES

Models that ascribe functional labels to subregions of the human frontal cortices have highlighted important limitations of modular perspectives, namely, such models run the risk of being overspecified both functionally and anatomically. Indeed, these limitations are thrown into sharp relief when results from the field of frontal lobe function are considered holistically (Hampshire & Sharp, 2015). For example, task manipulations designed to tap putatively distinct cognitive subprocesses, such as attentional orienting (Levy & Wagner, 2011; Shulman et al., 2009), target detection (Hampshire,

Duncan, & Owen, 2007; Linden et al., 1999), motor response inhibition (Aron, Robbins, & Poldrack, 2004), and working memory maintenance (D'Esposito, Postle, Ballard, & Lease, 1999; Owen, 1997; Postle & D'Esposito, 2000), have often reported task-evoked activation within the same subregions of the frontal cortices. Consequently, models based on lines of research that focus on any one of these subprocesses have ascribed frontal lobe brain regions with overly specific functions that do not account for their broader involvement in cognition. Conversely, tasks that are designed to tap the same underlying cognitive construct (e.g., motor inhibition) can activate different subregions of the lateral frontal cortices (Simmonds, Pekar, & Mostofsky, 2008). Furthermore, although putatively distinct cognitive functions are often ascribed to specific subregions of the lateral frontal cortices based on the conjunction of prior hypotheses (e.g., from neuropsychological models) and fMRI task-evoked activation, entire distributed networks of brain regions are also typically coactivated under the conditions designed to isolate the module of interest; indeed, this was the case for the IDED fMRI paradigm discussed in the previous section (Fig. 4.2).

Taken together, this triad of observations suggests that our notion of what constitutes the distinct aspects of human cognition corresponds poorly with the underlying functional organization of the frontal lobes. This calls into question the validity of classic modular approaches to mapping frontal lobe function. Simply put, the modular approach has demonstrated the functional complexity of the frontal cortices. In the process, it has identified functionally distinct subregions the activities of which have proven useful as markers for clinical research. However, our understanding of what the distinct role of each area is, and of the network mechanisms that they apply, has been obfuscated by the confusing mass of overspecific functional–anatomical mappings of the fMRI field. This problem is likely to be particularly pronounced when studying frontal lobe brain areas that are involved in high-level executive processes, which generalize across diverse task contexts.

RESPONSE INHIBITION AND THE INFERIOR FRONTAL GYRUS

The debate surrounding the role of the right inferior frontal cortex in response inhibition exemplifies the advantages and limitations of modular perspectives. Motor response inhibition can broadly be defined as the process by which habitual, initiated, or otherwise-dominant behaviors are willfully overridden. The Stop Signal Task (SST) is elegantly designed to assess response inhibition performance (Logan & Cowan, 1984; Verbruggen & Logan, 2008) (Fig. 4.3).

Response inhibition is of great clinical relevance because a number of prominent patient populations are characterized by poor self-control, and they often exhibit abnormally long stop signal reaction time (SSRT), the task's main measure of inhibitory control; a nonexhaustive list includes

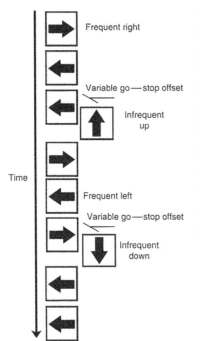

Time

FIGURE 4.3 The SST. During the SST, participants are instructed to respond as quickly as they can by making left or right button presses when presented with frequent left and right "go" stimuli, typically in the form of arrows. Infrequently, a stop cue is presented at a variable offset to the go stimulus. On these stop signal trials, the participant must try to cancel their already initiated response. The go–stop offset may be varied dynamically to produce a 50% failure rate. A simple subtraction of the go–stop offset that produces 50% failure from the mean response time provides an estimate of the stop signal response time: this being interpreted as the time required for the motor response to be countermanded. Behaviorally, SST performance can be described by a horserace model, where two processes (go and stop) compete for completion. *SST,* stop signal task.

attention-deficit hyperactivity disorder (ADHD) patients (Rubia et al., 1999), substance abusers (Smith, Mattick, Jamadar, & Iredale, 2014), binge drinkers (Lopez-Caneda et al., 2012), and pathological gamblers (Lawrence, Luty, Bogdan, Sahakian, & Clark, 2009).

A wealth of evidence has been provided to support the view that the right inferior frontal gyrus (RIFG) plays a key role in response inhibition. For example, a subregion of the RIFG was the most active area of the brain when contrasting stop minus go trials of the SST (Rubia, Smith, Brammer, & Taylor, 2003). This effect was weaker in a variety of impulsivity disorder patient populations, most notably, those who suffer from ADHD (Rubia et al., 1999). Furthermore, pharmacotherapies that are used to treat such populations have been observed to normalize activation within this same brain region (Chamberlain et al., 2009; Rubia, Halari, Mohammad, Taylor, & Brammer, 2011). Finally, it has been reported that lesions within the RIFG volume, but not outside of this volume, are associated with impaired SSRT (Aron, Fletcher, Bullmore, Sahakian, & Robbins, 2003). Together, this "active during and necessary for" profile constituted convincing evidence that the RIFG is necessary for normal motor response inhibition.

The inhibitory control hypothesis provided a systems level interpretation of these results (Aron et al., 2004). It proposed that a module within the RIFG is dedicated to response inhibition and that it is uniquely specialized to this purpose within the human brain. In an extension of this hypothesis, it was reported that during stop-signal trials, there was an increase in the correlation of activity within the RIFG and the subthalamic nucleus, a basal ganglia region that is known to play a role in motor processing. Based on this connectivity result, it was proposed that the RIFG inhibitory module exerts inhibitory control by activating a subthalamic nucleus brake, which brings a halt to ongoing motor processes. This circuit was proposed to include a hyperdirect pathway from the RIFG to the sub thalamic nucleus (STN) (Aron & Poldrack, 2006).

The clinical relevance of motor response inhibition as a construct, the strength of the behavioral RIFG association, and the simplicity of the response inhibition hypothesis formed a popular focus for research with clinical populations. There was a discrete aspect of executive ability that is related to specific functional—anatomical module and its dedicated cortical—subcortical connection, and there was a simple validated paradigm to probe the integrity of that circuit. Others and I have argued that the response inhibition hypothesis shares the common limitations of being functionally overspecified (Chatham et al., 2012; Hampshire & Sharp, 2015; Hampshire, 2015; Sharp et al., 2010).

A BROADER ROLE FOR THE RIFG IN COGNITION?

A primary limitation for the response inhibition hypothesis is that a variety of tasks that are designed to tap other putatively distinct aspects of cognition have been mapped to the RIFG. These include generic attentional (Seeley et al., 2007) and working memory (D'Esposito et al., 1999; Owen, 1997; Petrides, 1994; Postle & D'Esposito, 2000) processes. The study of target detection (Hampshire et al., 2007; Linden et al., 1999) provides a pertinent example of such mappings (Fig. 4.4).

Like the SST, target detection tasks involve monitoring a series of stimuli for an infrequent item that precipitates some planned behavior. However, unlike the SST, that behavior is the execution as opposed to the countermanding of a motor action; therefore, in the former case there is no routine motor action to inhibit. Despite this key difference, a highly similar pattern of activation, centered on the RIFG, has been reported when contrasting fMRI activation during target minus distractor trials. A key question therefore, regards whether (1) the SST measures a discrete impulsivity construct that is supported by a dedicated inhibition module or (2) response inhibition is one example of the type of process that is supported by a more generalizable cognitive control system?

To test directly between these two competing hypotheses, we developed four novel versions of the classic SST (Erika-Florence, Leech, & Hampshire, 2014). In all four versions of the task, the stimulus frequency and timing parameters were matched to those of the classic SST. However, the task was

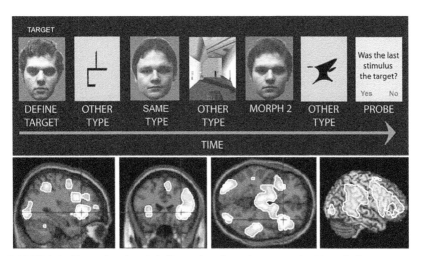

FIGURE 4.4 Target detection. *Left*: Target detection tasks are organized in a similar manner to the SST. The participant is instructed to monitor a sequence of distractor stimuli for an infrequently presented target. However, when the target is detected, the participant is typically required to make some further response, e.g., a button press. *Right*: Contrasting the presentation of targets minus distractors renders activation within a set of brain regions including the RIFG (Hampshire, Thompson, Duncan, & Owen, 2008). *SST,* Stop Signal Task; *RIFG,* right inferior frontal gyrus.

broken down into four sections by blocks of rest, allowing both transient and sustained activation to be examined relative to a resting baseline in a mixed block/event-related design. The four variants of the task differed with respect to the motor control requirements of the task. In one variant "MONITOR" participants were required to silently count the infrequent "stop" stimuli, and no motor responses were required at all. Another variant "INHIBITION" had the same requirements as the original SST, in which responses were made to the frequent left and right "go" cues, and these routine responses were countermanded on reception of an infrequent stop signal. There was a "RESPOND" variant, in which participants only responded to the infrequent stimuli. In this condition, they were required to indicate the direction of the most recent "go" cue; therefore, responses were planned but withheld on all frequent trials and executed only on infrequent trials. A final condition "COMPELX" was similar to respond but required selection from a greater number of possible responses dependent on whether the stop cue (a vertical arrow) was oriented up or down.

Critically, only one of these four variants required the countermanding of a routine/initiated motor response. According to the response inhibition hypothesis, this condition should have elicited the greatest activation selectively within the RIFG, the putative coordinates of the response inhibition module. By contrast, if the RIFG plays a more generic role in cognition, then these coordinates should have been active when the infrequent condition in all four variants of the task.

A side issue that will be revisited is that it remains unclear exactly where within the volume of the RIFG the inhibition module would be located. For example, research with the SST (Hampshire, Chamberlain, Monti, Duncan, & Owen, 2010; Rubia et al., 2001a, 2001b) typically produces peak activation at similar AIFO coordinates as extradimensional switching; this being part of what some refer to as the "salience network" (Seeley et al., 2007). Others have argued that the inhibition module is located at the most dorsal and posterior extent of the RIFG (Aron, Robbins, & Poldrack, 2014). Research with clinical populations such as ADHD patients typically highlights abnormal functional activity at the former location (Rubia et al., 1999), whereas meta-analysis comparing attentional orienting and inhibition paradigms has highlighted the latter location (Levy & Wagner, 2011).

To eschew this issue, we applied spatial-independent component analysis to the voxelwise timecourse data from the lateral frontal cortex volume. Independent component analysis (ICA) is a common method for functionally parcellating a brain volume in a data-driven as opposed to hypothesis-driven (and therefore biased) manner. None of the areas identified by the ICA within the RIFG, or the lateral frontal cortex more generally, showed heightened activation during the INHIBITION relative to the other three variants of the SST. However, there was robust activation within the AIFO for the infrequent versus frequent contrast of all four tasks. Indeed, unconstrained voxelwise analyses showed similar effects throughout much of the frontal cortex volume, with widespread activation for infrequent minus frequent stimuli but no voxels having heightened activation for the INHIBITION task specifically (Fig. 4.5A).

These results highlight the more general role of lateral frontal cortex regions across varied task conditions. However, it remained possible that a specific conjunction of RIFG and STN activity supported response inhibition, representing an inhibition dedicated circuit. To test this we examined the strength of the change in RIFG-STN connectivity on inhibition trials. Again, there was generally an increase in this connectivity strength for infrequent minus frequent trials, regardless of the requirement to inhibit a motor response. Moreover, similar increases in connectivity were more robustly evident between the ICA-defined subregions of the lateral frontal cortex. Notably, the strength of this diffuse network connectivity state correlated with interindividual differences in SSRT, the primary measure of inhibition ability.

In a final test of the inhibitory control hypothesis, we examined how frontal cortex activation changed across the four blocks of each task variant. More specifically, a logical prediction of the inhibition hypothesis was that inhibitory processing should be the greatest when established responses were being overridden. The frequent responses should become more established across the four blocks with practice; it logically follows that RIFG activation

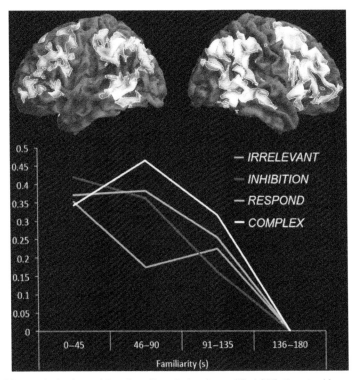

FIGURE 4.5 Activation and learning effects during the modified SST. *Top*: A widespread pattern of activation is evident when contrasting stop minus go trials but also under other task conditions with the same stimulus sequence but no requirement to inhibit a response. *Bottom*: RIFG activation steadily reduces as the SST is practiced practice. *SST*, stop signal task; *RIFG*, right inferior frontal gyrus.

should be the greatest in the final block, reflecting the additional work of the inhibition module. Contrary to this prediction, activation throughout the lateral frontal cortex (LFC) was the strongest in the early blocks, when the task was initially being learned (Fig. 4.5B). This activation profile accords with the PFC having relatively generic role in supporting nonautomated behaviors, e.g., when a novel task is being learnt (Hampshire et al., 2016; Toni & Passingham, 1999; Toni, Ramnani, Josephs, Ashburner, & Passingham, 2001) or a particular task component is more difficult (Duncan & Owen, 2000).

Taken together, these results support the view that motor response inhibition is just one specific, albeit important and clinically relevant, example of the broader class of cognitive processes that are supported by a domain-general neural system. Furthermore, they demonstrate how some cognitive control processes cannot be localized to any one module or connection pathway; instead, they are emergent from rich interactions that occur throughout distributed networks of brain regions.

VOODOO NEUROIMAGING VALIDATIONS OF COGNITIVE CONSTRUCTS

A pertinent side issue in the previous section pertains to the perception that the observation of an fMRI activation cluster represents a form of cognitive construct validation; specifically, if a task or meta-analysis contrast that is designed to tap a putatively distinct aspect of cognition generates activation within a brain region, then this demonstrates that the putative construct must exist as a distinct aspect of cognition because its discrete neuroanatomical module has been located. The confusion regarding where exactly the inhibition module is located exemplifies the limitations of this type of validation. As discussed above, it has been suggested by some that the inhibition module is located within the most dorsal and posterior extent of the RIFG (Aron et al., 2014)—this is based on the meta-analysis conducted by another group (Levy & Wagner, 2011). However, when we applied ICA to decompose the frontal cortex into functionally distinct subregions in a data-driven manner, none of the resultant components had a peak cluster at the expected location of the posterior RIFG module.

Interestingly, the proposed location of the inhibition module centered on the exact overlap area between peak clusters of three distinct ICA components. This was the case when running the ICA model at varying levels of model dimensionality. Furthermore, a highly similar LFC parcellation was evident when applying ICA to data from three different studies, conducted with different individuals undertaking different tasks (Hampshire, 2015). Therefore although the ICA-derived functional parcellation of the RIFG was robust and reproducible, it accorded poorly with functional subdivisions as defined meta-analysis. A pertinent question regarded why this might be the case.

To address this question, I ran a series of simple simulations of four functional—anatomical "modules" with approximately Gaussian spatial distributions. In one simulation, the modules had little spatial overlap with each other. In the other, the modules had more extensive spatial overlap. Conditions were generated in which the levels of task-related activation were varied for these sources and noise added; this provides a crude simulation of how the modules would activate during tasks that involve them to varying levels. One might imagine modules as defined in the classic literature for maintenance and manipulation of information in working memory. Most tasks will tap these processes to some degree, but the mixtures of them will vary differentially dependent on the number of items that are being maintained and the complexity of the manipulation applied to them.

Meta-analysis contrasts were generated across the resultant task-rest activation maps, but the accuracy with which these contrasts captured the underlying balance of demands was varied such that it loaded accurately on one, other, or some mixture of the underlying sources; this may be considered analogous to running empirical meta-analyses in which there is either an accurate notion of what the underlying functional roles of each module are or having a false model in which the putative constructs are misaligned, with the extreme being orthogonal alignment of putative and actual functional dissociations.

Under conditions in which the modules were spatially segregated, the activation clusters that were generated by the meta-analysis contrasts all correspond spatially with the underlying sources although inaccurate contrasts generated multiple distinct clusters. Conversely, when the underlying modules overlap spatially, inaccurate meta-analysis contrasts generated a cluster with a peak located at the intersection between the underlying modules. The location of this varied dependent on how closely the contrast correlated with one or other vector of module-task loadings; that is, the weighting of the mixture defined by the meta-analysis contrast works such as a spotlight, shifting through space from underlying module to another. For comparison, application of spatial ICA correctly localized the underlying spatial modules under both low and high overlap conditions (Fig. 4.6).

This simple simulation provides a simple heuristic for determining whether functional regions of the prefrontal cortex overlap spatially with each other. If simple *t*-test contrasts or meta-analysis contrasts tend to generate peak activation coordinates that are at the intersection of the spatial clusters defined using data-driven methods such as ICA, then there is likely a heavy overlap. This is exactly what is observed for the inhibition module. Such overlap may relate to the spatial smoothing applied during

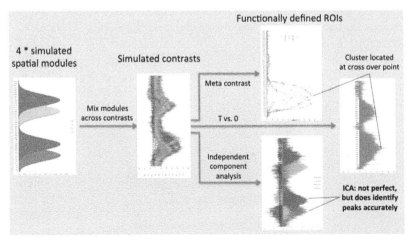

FIGURE 4.6 Simulating metacontrast and data-driven functional parcellations. When there is some degree of spatial overlap between functional areas within the brain, poorly defined meta-analysis and fMRI task contrasts can generate activation clusters that are at the intersection of these functional areas. Data-driven methods such as ICA can prove more robust at identifying the location of functional areas under such conditions. *fMRI*, functional magnetic resonance imaging.

preprocessing, intersubject differences in the geometry of functional brain regions, genuine spatial overlap between functional regions of the brain, or most likely some combination of all the three. Given that this is the case, we must be wary of how we interpret the output of meta-analyses and other function MRI contrasts: we can identify a potentially massive number of spurious functional—anatomical modules under these conditions if our notion of what constitutes a distinct aspect of brain function is flawed. Put simply, when estimating fMRI contrasts, junk in = junk out. Activation blobs from contrasts, models, or meta-analyses do not prove the existence of theoretical cognitive constructs.

A GENERAL INTELLIGENCE SYSTEM WITHIN THE FRONTAL AND PARIETAL CORTICES?

At the opposite extreme to modular perspectives are globalist theories, which posit that a global neural resource supports a wide variety of cognitive demands. In support of this view, it has long been known that a similar pattern of activity is observed across a range of cognitively demanding task contexts (Duncan & Owen, 2000). This pattern of activation has been labeled multiple demand (MD) cortex (Duncan, 2001). MD cortex has a marked correspondence with the pattern of activation observed during the performance of attentional set shifting, response inhibition, and target detection tasks. It includes the AIFO, IFS, ACC, presupplementary motor area (preSMA), and inferior parietal cortex (IPC) (Fig. 4.7). In accordance with a role in supporting highly generalizable processes, MD cortex is more active during the performance of tasks that load heavily on the general intelligence factor "g" (Duncan et al., 2000). Furthermore, it has been reported that lesion volume within MD cortex correlates with the estimated drop in a patients IQ (Woolgar et al., 2010), whereas lesion volume outside of MD cortex does not. Based on this, and electrophysiology research (Freedman, Riesenhuber, Poggio, & Miller, 2001; Miller & Cohen, 2001; Stokes et al., 2013), it has

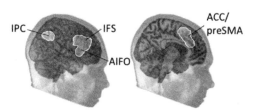

FIGURE 4.7 Multiple demand cortex. Multiple demand cortex is a set of brain regions that are commonly recruited across many task contexts. This includes bilaterally the IPC, AIFO, IFS, ACC, and preSMA. *IPC*, inferior parietal cortex; *AIFO*, anterior insula/inferior frontal operculum; *IFS*, inferior frontal sulcus; *ACC*, anterior cingulate cortex; *preSMA*, presupplementary motor area (preSMA)

been proposed that MD cortex houses a highly flexible processing resource that can rapidly adapt to code for diverse cognitive tasks (Duncan, 2001, 2006). The processing capacity of this resource may underlie the cross correlations in performance measures of diverse tasks, which form the statistical basis of the intelligence construct "g."

Notably, although evidence for this broad involvement in cognition is strong, this does not equate to the MD volume being functionally homogenous. Like executive tasks, IQ test are cognitively complex by design; therefore, they are likely to recruit multiple brain systems that support distinct cognitive processes. Furthermore, in the previous section, I discussed how simulations show that running t-contrasts on activation contrast maps from diverse task contrasts can under some conditions highlight brain areas where functionally distinct modules spatially overlap. In support of this being the case for MD cortex, the task contrasts in the IDED task and target detection task dissociated MD subregions such as the AIFO and IFS. The same is the case during nonverbal reasoning (Hampshire, Thompson, Duncan, & Owen, 2011). Furthermore, data-driven analyses with ICA also dissociate the AIFO and IFS but associate each region with a different functional network (Dosenbach, Fair, Cohen, Schlaggar, & Petersen, 2008; Erika-Florence et al., 2014; Seeley et al., 2007). Thus the brain regions from which the MD cortex is composed are likely organized into two or more functional networks that each support highly generalizable but distinct cognitive subprocesses (Hampshire & Sharp TICS, 2015).

A NETWORK-BASED FRACTIONATION OF HUMAN INTELLIGENCE

The limitations of modular perspectives highlight the broader uncertainties regarding what the core components of human cognition actually are. This uncertainty might be resolved by applying an alternative network centric approach; one that first maps the functional network architecture of the brain in a data-driven manner and then defines cognitive constructs based on the distinct functional role of each network. In effect, this is an inversion of the traditional approach of first defining cognitive constructs and then identifying their functional−anatomical correlates that is unbiased by assumptions regarding what those constructs should be. The strengths of such an approach include that, unlike psychometric constructs which depend on the exact choice of cognitive tests, the network subdivision within the brain appear to be highly consistent across task contexts and indeed even at rest (Smith et al., 2009). Furthermore, such a framework need not discard insights from the neuroimaging literature, as instead, it may be used to reorganize them; specifically, the mass of highly specific functional−anatomical mappings may be associated into broader cognitive constructs using a classification system that is based on functional networks.

The subnetworks of MD cortex form a logical starting point for developing such a classification system due to their particularly broad roles in cognition. Therefore, we conducted a study to determine (1) whether the AIFO and IFS networks formed consistent features of MD cortex across diverse task contexts and (2) whether a cognitive task classification system that was based on the activation profile of the AIFO and IFS networks had behavioral construct validity.

To address the former question, 16 young healthy controls undertook 12 fMRI paradigms of the type that are typically considered akin to general intelligence (Hampshire, Highfield, Parkin, & Owen, 2012). These included fMRI optimized variants of tasks that would classically be categorized as tapping aspects of working memory, reasoning, planning, and attention. Each task had a simple block design in which active task performance was interspersed with periods of rest. This enabled similar task-active versus rest contrasts to be conducted for all 12 tasks. We first examined how functional activity during the performance of the 12 tasks covaried within predefined AIFO, IFS, and IPC regions of interest (ROIs). Specifically, task-rest contrasts for each ROI were averaged across participants, and cross correlations were conducted between them. There were no significant correlation between the AIFO ROIs and IFS or IPC ROIs. However, strong correlations were evident between the AIFO bilaterally and between IFS and IPC bilaterally. This result reemphasized the functionally heterogeneous nature of MD cortex (Crittenden, Mitchell, & Duncan, 2016).

A limitation for this analysis was that functional subdivisions of the brain do not necessarily align with macroscopic structural landmarks. Therefore, a second analysis was run using ICA. Specifically, task-rest contrasts were calculated separately for each task and for each voxel within MD cortex. These were averaged across individuals, and spatial ICA was run across the resultant 12 contrast maps. Similar (but not identical) networks were generated, one including the AIFO bilaterally and the other including the IFS and IPC bilaterally (Fig. 4.8A). The AIFO network also included a region of the ACC and superior frontal sulcus. The IFS network also included a more dorsal/posterior region of the preSMA. These two networks accounted for 90% of the mean task-related activations within MD cortex. They were evident in 13 of 16 subject data sets when analyzed individually. By definition, they represent consistent features across individuals and task contexts. Therefore, they form a sensible basis for beginning to construct a network-oriented system for classifying cognitive tasks.

In support of this view, the manner in which the tasks activated each network was simple and interpretable (Fig. 4.8B). Specifically, the AIFO network was most activated during working memory tasks that involve the encoding and maintenance of task-relevant information, e.g., Spatial Span and Digit Span. Conversely, the IFS network was most activated during more complex tasks that required the transformation of information

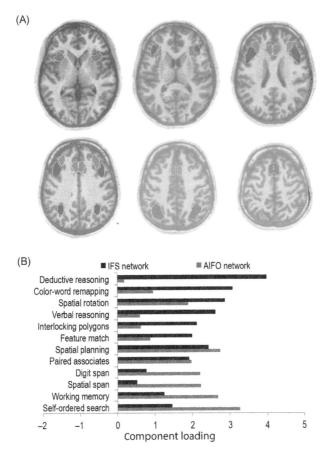

FIGURE 4.8 Distinct functional networks within MD cortex. (A) Spatial ICA subdivides MD cortex into two component networks. (B) Task-related activation levels for the two networks. One network was particularly active during tasks that involved working memory maintenance. The other was particularly active during reasoning, planning, or tasks that otherwise required the transformation of information according to rules. *MD*, multiple demand.

according to rules, e.g., matrix reasoning, grammatical reasoning, mental rotation, and spatial planning. It is tempting based on this observation to infer a two-tier system within MD cortex, consisting of subsystems for maintaining and manipulating information in working memory. Recall from the previous sections although the AIFO network was active during extradimensional switching, response inhibition, and target detection, it also has been closely associated with attentional orienting (Levy & Wagner, 2011) and salience detection (Seeley et al., 2007). A class that bridges working memory maintenance and attentional processes is therefore required if the broader role of the AIFO network in cognition is to be accounted for. Another key limitation of the analysis approach is that it was conducted at the level of task contrasts not fluctuations in activity over time. This may limit the power of the analysis approach to differentiate between functional networks, i.e., some corecruitment may be an artefact of the selection of tasks within the fMRI battery. Most notably the AIFO and superior frontal sulcus often dissociate when applying ICA to fMRI timecourse data and likely support different classes of cognitive processes.

NETWORK-ORIENTED COGNITIVE CONSTRUCTS

Our second question regarded whether a cognitive task classification system that was based on the activation profile of the AIFO and IFS networks had behavioral construct validity. This question pertained to the long running debate regarding the multifactorial nature of human intelligence. Specifically, there have been many neural accounts of human intelligence, and a prominent role for frontal and parietal brain regions has long been a consistent theme (Duncan et al., 2000; Duncan, 2005), although the exact set of frontal and parietal brain regions that have been implicated varies (Jung & Haier, 2007). Given that intelligence had been associated with MD cortex, it was sensible to predict that individual differences in cognitive ability would be organized into factors that corresponded with the cognitive roles of MD subnetworks.

The correspondence between behavioral and neuroimaging data may be compared in different ways. One approach is to examine correlations in individual differences analyses, that is, analyses in which common variance is analyzed between behavioral and imaging measures taken from the same set of individuals. Another approach is to determine whether the structure of interrelationships within each data set, when derived independently, conforms significantly. The former approach is the most commonly applied; however, it assumes that there is a simple linear relationship between imaging measures of a neural system and the processing capacity (or ability) of that system, i.e., if a system is more active or more strongly functionally connected, then it also has greater capacity. We know from the clinical neuroimaging literature that this is an oversimplification. For example, in one study, nocturnal frontal lobe (NFL) alumni who had suffered multiple concussions showed hyperactivation during spatial planning within a functional network that included frontal and parietal brain regions (Hampshire, MacDonald, & Owen, 2013). Conversely, in another two studies, pathological gamblers and Parkinson's patients showed hypoactivation of the same network when performing the same task (Grant et al., 2013; Williams-Gray, Hampshire, Robbins, Owen, & Barker, 2007). All three populations are characterized by executive impairments. These cognitive−neural relationships are almost certainly mediated by different biological factors as they relate to different clinical populations. Across these populations the relationships are not simply nonlinear, they are opposing; thus, if the biological factors underlying normal population variability in cognitive ability also have such complex relationships, they will likely cancel each other out to some degree, reducing any linear relationship between the functional capacity (reflected in ability) and activity or connectivity of a brain network. Furthermore, signal correlated noise in imaging parameters (e.g., global drifts and spike artefacts in fMRI time courses) will tend to inflate estimates of network activity/connectivity, and these in turn can relate to cognition indirectly (i.e., lower IQ individuals tend to move more in the scanner). Given these limitations, it is unsurprising that some recent attempts to relate imaging measures to cognitive abilities at large-scale using linear models have produced correlations that although informative and statistically significant are also of small scale, explaining only small proportions of variance (Smith et al., 2015). Ultimately, large data sets that include direct measures of mediating biological factors (e.g., genotypes) may help us to understand such complexities; however, these are only just beginning to become available to the field.

We eschewed these issues by applying the second approach of comparing the structure of constructs derived behaviorally and via neuroimaging analysis. Our hypothesis was that MD subnetworks have different processing capacities and that due to their broad but dissociable contributions to cognition, they would manifest behaviorally as distinct cognitive abilities. Based on this hypothesis, our prediction was that tasks that tend to heavily recruit one or other MD subnetwork would also tend to cluster onto one or other latent variable when behavioral performances were factor analyzed. To test this prediction, the 12 tasks were adapted so that they could be delivered to gather data from large-scale cohorts via a custom website. One cohort undertook all 12 tasks in fixed sequence, followed by a questionnaire. After data cleaning, this cohort included data from 44,600 individuals. A second cohort consisted of individuals who logged in to a free play site on which they could take the tests in any combination or order. After data cleaning, 60,642 individuals were included who had undertaken two or more tasks.

Principal component analyses were conducted on the cross-correlation matrices of performance measures from each data set. In both cohorts, three significant components were evident that exceed the Kaiser convention threshold, i.e., explaining more variance than was contributed by any one task and therefore by definition being generalizable. When varimax rotation was applied to the three components, there was a close conformity in the pattern of loadings across the two cohorts and the component scores were reciprocally dissociable with respect to questionnaire variables. The factor structure was simple and interpretable. The first two components were qualitatively similar to those from the neuroimaging study, with working memory tasks tending to load onto one, and more complex reasoning and planning tasks tending to load onto the other (Fig. 4.9). This latter result was critical as it demonstrated that the two analyses, of networks and behavioral performances, produced the same cognitive constructs (Hampshire et al., 2012); this was despite the fact that the three data sets (imaging and behavioral) were analyzed completely independently from each other.

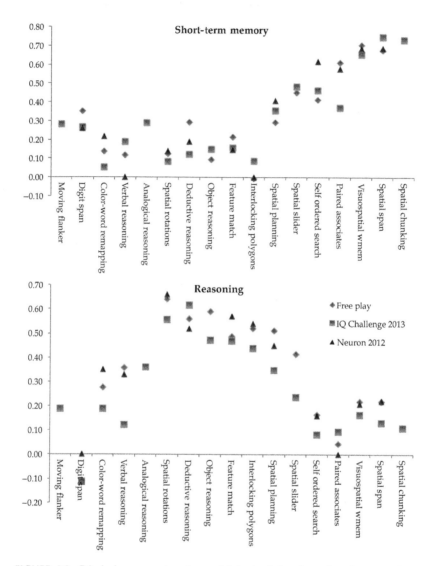

FIGURE 4.9 Principal component analyses of behavioral data from three Internet cohorts. Highly similar behavioral components were evident when applying principal component analysis to data from each of three large-scale Internet cohorts. One component included all of the paradigms in which information had to be manipulated using rules (e.g., reasoning, planning, and rotations tasks). Another included all of the paradigms in which information had to be actively maintained in mind over a delay (e.g., working memory span tasks).

A third behavioral component included all of the tasks that had either number (e.g., digit span) or word (e.g., grammatical reasoning) stimuli. To identify brain regions that had a corresponding profiles, the pattern of task-component loadings was regressed onto each voxel in the brain in a mass univariate analysis. This rendered a network that included regions within temporal cortices bilaterally and the left inferior frontal gyrus. This latter set of brain regions was located primarily outside the MD cortex volume, which explains why they were not evident in the ICA analysis of neuroimaging data.

Taken together, these results support the view that a network-based classification system for cognitive tasks (Laird et al., 2011) is tractable and has behavioral construct validity insofar as it predicts the latent variable structure underlying population variability in intelligence. More broadly, such a system could have considerable value in clinical research, as common functional network abnormalities are evident across different patient populations (Menon, 2011) but also subdivide heterogeneous populations (Nombela et al., 2014). Therefore, they also can form a framework for transferring insights between patient groups or subclassifying them when developing new treatments.

NETWORK DYNAMICS DURING RELATIONAL INTEGRATION

The application of network-based constructs can help organize the space of possible functional—anatomical mappings into a reduced set of cognitive classes (Laird et al., 2011), effectively eschewing the problem of overly specified models of brain functional organization. However, these still represent static functional—anatomical mappings that do no capture the rich dynamic nature of the human brain. Indeed, there is evidence to suggest that some aspects of cognitive information processing cannot be mapped to any specific module or network but, instead, relate to rich interactions that occur across multiple networks. The study of motor response inhibition, as discussed earlier, provided one example where such dynamics appeared key to behavior (Erika-Florence et al., 2014). Specifically, the ability to inhibit a response did not relate to the magnitude of event-related activity within any subregion of the lateral frontal cortices. Instead, it robustly related to the strength of functional connectivity, not across one, but across many frontal cortex subregions. The study of relational integration during reasoning provides further insight into the nature of these dynamics.

Relational integration can be defined as the process by which interdependent subrules of a problem are combined into higher order constructs. A prominent perspective on the neural mechanism that may underlie relational integration was developed from basic principles within the computational psychology literature (Hummel & Holyoak, 1997; Knowlton, Morrison, Hummel, & Holyoak, 2012). It was demonstrated in silico that higher order constructs could be coded in transient couplings between distributed representations of lower order subcomponents. Binding by synchrony provides a likely mechanism for such transient coupling. Specifically, representations of rules pertaining to stimulus dimensions including color, shape, number, and orientation, may be coded across different neural populations. These may transiently be bound by synchronous activity, enabling a potentially massive range of higher order representations to be formed from combination of more basic elements.

It has been proposed that a module located within the anterior lateral prefrontal cortex, often referred to as rostrolateral or frontopolar cortex, supported the formation of higher order representations during relational integration (Ramnani & Owen, 2004). In empirical support of this view, it has been reported that the lateral frontopolar cortices are more active during relational reasoning tasks (Bunge, Helskog, & Wendelken, 2009; Christoff et al., 2001). However, relational reasoning tasks are complex and challenging by design; therefore, from a globalist perspective it could simply be the case that relational integration provides a proxy measure of a more generalizable processes supported by domain general systems; increased difficulty might lead to recruitment of more domain general resources, with a spread toward the more anterior areas of the lateral frontal cortex. In support of this latter view, lateral frontopolar cortex activation has been reported during tasks that have no overt relational reasoning demands (Crittenden & Duncan, 2014). To test between these two competing hypotheses, we developed a novel nonverbal matrix-reasoning task (Parkin, Hellyer, Leech, & Hampshire, 2015) that orthogonally manipulated two aspects of difficulty— the number of subrules that must be solved and the level to which those subrules must be relationally integrated (Fig. 4.10).

Behaviorally, both factors of the design affected performance significantly; therefore, they can be considered to manipulate general difficulty. From the globalist perspective, contrasting along either dimensions of the factorial model should have tapped global resources and rendered more activation within the lateral frontopolar cortices. Conversely, if there was a relational integration module, then only the integration contrast should have rendered frontopolar cortex activation.

Spatial ICA was first applied to functionally parcellate the gray matter volume of the frontal lobes in a data-driven manner. One component included clusters within the lateral frontopolar cortices bilaterally and the posterior dorsolateral prefrontal cortices. The AIFO and IFS subregions described in previous sections of this chapter were again evident in this analysis. Seed analyses were then conducted to map the broader functional networks that each of these frontal lobe areas was most closely associated with. The lateral frontopolar cortex (LFPC) network included bilateral areas within the posterior middle frontal gyrus and posterior parietal cortex. The AIFO network included the ACC and temporal–parietal junction bilaterally. The IFS network included bilateral areas within the mid-ventral caudate and inferior parietal cortices. For further analysis, ROIs were placed at peak coordinates from the ICA and seed analyses and these ROIs were formed into a two-tier network graph, including connections between frontal cortex subregions and connections between frontal and posterior brain regions.

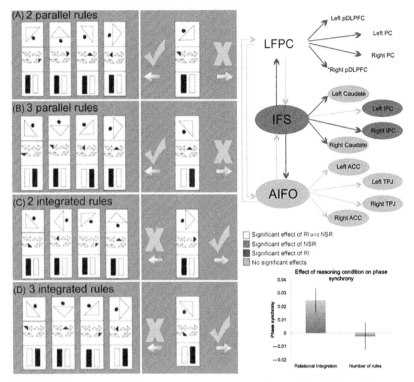

FIGURE 4.10 A novel fMRI relational integration paradigm. *Left*: Relational integration demands and the number of component subrules orthogonally within a 2 × 2 factorial design. Specifically, individuals had to first work out and then apply either two (a&c) or three (b&d) rules that described progressive changes across several matrices, and these rules could either be solvable in parallel (a&b) or one could relate to the output of the other (c&d), thereby requiring their integration. *Right*: The lateral frontopolar cortex and associated network were more active during relational integration and number of subrules contrasts. However, increased functional connectivity was only evident for the relational integration contrast. *fMRI*, functional magnetic resonance imaging; *AIFO*, anterior insula/inferior frontal operculum; *IFS*, inferior frontal sulcus; *IPC*, inferior parietal cortex; *ACC*, anterior cingulate cortex.

In accordance with a role in relational integration, the LFPC and its associated network were significantly more active when contrasting reasoning problems that had high minus low integration demands. However, in accordance with the globalist perspective, this effect was also evident for the orthogonal contrast of reasoning problems that had high minus low numbers of subrules. Furthermore, in accordance with the network perspective, the same pattern of results was evident throughout the broader functional network that was associated with the LFPC in the seed analysis. Thus, increased difficulty lead to the progressive recruitment of functional networks, which each had frontal lobe nodes within the MD volume.

Next, we examined transient changes in the connectivity of the network graph for the relational integration and rule complexity contrasts; this was achieved using psychophysiological interaction models between the three frontal cortex nodes reciprocally and between those nodes and the ROIs that were associated with them in the seed analysis. Critically, intranetwork connections and internetwork functional connectivity of the LFPC and IFS increased for the relational integration contrast only (Fig. 4.10). Furthermore, the strengths of the connectivity effect increased across the duration of the reasoning problem becoming strongest toward the end when subrules were successfully integrated. Thus, although one cognitive demand may recruit the same set of domain general functional networks as another, tapping highly generalizable brain resources, those demands may still evoke alternative processing mechanisms of those networks, as evidenced by qualitatively different connectivity states.

COMBINING MODULAR AND NETWORK PERSPECTIVES

Cognitive processes may best be conceived of as emergent properties of rich interactions that occur throughout functional networks as opposed to within specialized modules. However, this does not preclude the possibility that some nodes with those networks play key roles. Indeed, subclassifying the information processing roles of nodes within complex network architectures forms the focus of graph theory as applied to steady-state resting state connectomes. Over the past few years, such perspectives have also become more common in the study of transient dynamic network connectivity states.

For example, a branch of the computational literature focuses on understanding whole-brain network dynamics at a coarse grain (Deco, Jirsa, McIntosh, Sporns, & Kotter, 2009), that is, as opposed to the fine-grained neural interactions that underlie cognitive information processing in neural network models. Hellyer et al. (2014) provided a pertinent exemplar of how this coarse-grained level of modeling can provide insight normal and pathological brain function. They created a model of the brain in which macroscopic anatomical areas consisted of individual oscillators. These were wired using an empirically derived model of structural connectivity. Analysis of the changing activities of these oscillators produced a model that had significant correspondence to the resting state functional networks that are observed empirically in the human brain. This analysis provided several novel insights. First, it demonstrated how a model with excitatory long distance connections and oscillatory properties can produce multiple functional networks with metastable characteristics. That is, one or other combination of networks may be transiently expressed with the appearance of anticorrelated networks despite there being a lack of inhibitory connections between such anticorrelated networks.

More relevantly, widespread changes in network activity and connectivity were produced when the activities of some but not other oscillators were upregulated. That is, certain brain regions, simply by dint of their placement within the global structural network topology, can orchestrate the widespread activation and functional connectivity states that are associated with cognitive processes such as response inhibition and relational integration. Notably, within the simulation, brain regions corresponding to the AIFO and LFPC formed two such orchestrating nodes.

A logical prediction of this computationally derived observation was that although in our fMRI relational integration study, integration demands were concomitant with widespread changes in network connectivity, the LFPC should have had a causal influence on the broader network state under these conditions. We tested this hypothesis using dynamic causal modeling (Friston, Harrison, & Penny, 2003) with Bayesian model selection (Fig. 4.11).

The Bayesian model selection process strongly favored a model in which integration demands modulated connections along an anterior to posterior axis within the lateral frontal cortices, with the LFPC situated at the apex. Further analysis also favored a model in which the LFPC had a causal influence on the ROIs from the broader functional network identified by seed analysis. This finding demonstrates how the network perspective is able to reconcile models that ascribe specialized functions to specific modules with

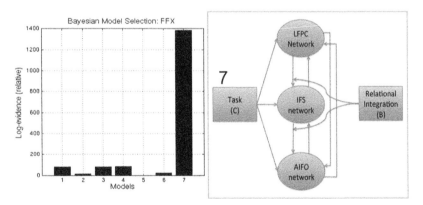

FIGURE 4.11 Dynamic causal modeling of frontal cortex activity during relational integration. Alternative dynamic causal modeling models were constructed in which the AIFO, IFS, and LFPC formed reciprocally interconnected nodes within a directed connectivity network. In all variants of the model, the requirement to undertake a reasoning problem had a driving influence on all three nodes (task). The level of relational integration demands had a modulatory influence on connections between the nodes, and this differed between the models according to the specific connections that were targeted. Bayesian model selection with fixed effects analysis (*left*) favored the "top-down" model (7) (*right*) in which RI modulated connectivity from anterior to posterior regions of the frontal cortex, with the LFPC acting upon IFS and IFS acting upon the AIFO. *AIFO*, anterior insula/inferior frontal operculum; *IFS*, inferior frontal sulcus.

models that consider cognitive processing to emergent from the rich interactions of distributed functional networks.

Based on these results, it is tempting to now define the LFPC as module or node that is specialized for relational reasoning. Notably, however, we have also reported the exact same pattern of causal interactions under simpler task conditions, for example, when simple stimulus—response rules are being learnt through the process of repetition (Hampshire et al., 2016). Thus, just like the static functional—anatomical mappings discussed in earlier sections, it is important to take a broader view when assigning functional labels to dynamic network states. Increased anterior to posterior causal flow within the lateral frontal cortices likely underlies generalizable process, perhaps relating to the temporary maintenance of novel conjunctions between multiple rules, but also of rules with stimuli and responses, within a highly generalizable neural system.

FUNCTIONAL NETWORK MARKERS OF NEUROPATHOLOGY IN RETIRED NFL PLAYERS

The network framework may have considerable value when deriving a deeper understanding of the neural mechanisms that underlie abnormal cognition. For example, it has been reported that after traumatic brain injury, it is a damage to highly connected hub regions of the brain that is most predictive of subsequent cognitive impairments (Fagerholm, Hellyer, Scott, Leech, & Sharp, 2015). Analyses based on network perspectives may also provide tractable measures for practically assessing such abnormalities. More specifically, networks analyses tend to provide rich multivariate measures, and these can be input to machine learning and classification machines. Such multivariate analyses may better cope with the complicating factors that have limited clinical applications of fMRI; e.g., many-to-one mappings between cognitive demands and neural systems and the heterogeneity of disease expression (Paul Matthews & Hampshire, 2016). We provided an example of how this type of approach can prove sensitive to neural abnormalities in a recent study of retired American football players, who had sustained multiple concussions during the course of their NFL careers.

NFL alumni often report suffering from cognitive problems in everyday life, and it is well established that they have a high incidence of chronic traumatic encephalopathy postmortem (Cantu, 2007; McKee et al., 2009); however, structural neuroimaging and neuropsychological assessment studies have failed to provide conclusive evidence of this pathology in vivo. Notably, this combination of observations fits the well-established profile of some forms of executive dysfunction, which can be particularly hard to assess with neuropsychological scales that are applied within the laboratory or clinic (Burgess et al., 2006).

Thirteen retired NFL players and 50 age- and education-matched controls undertook a spatial planning task in the scanner (Hampshire et al., 2013). In accordance with previous studies, the NFL alumni showed little in the way of behavioral impairment on the fMRI paradigm except at the highest level of difficulty. The differences at that behavioral level were too subtle to be of clinical diagnostic value when assessing a given individual. In contrast to these weak behavioral results, the NFL alumni showed hyperactivation and hypoconnectivity within a set of brain regions that correspond with the LFPC network. Notably, the LFPC is vulnerable to neurotrauma due to its placement within the brain; reduced causal connectivity was also evident for this and a dorsolateral prefrontal cortex area (Fig. 4.12).

A linear support vector machine was trained on the combination of network activation and connectivity measures using a robust leave-one-out cross-validation pipeline. Specifically, the machine was trained to classify NFL alumni relative to controls with one individual excluded during the training phase. The trained machine was then used to classify the remaining individual. This process was repeated until each individual had been left out and classified once, providing a classification accuracy rate. To test the statistical significance of classification accuracy, it was compared against a null distribution that was formed by running the same process but with the group labels randomly permuted 1000 times. This approach classified players versus controls with ~90% accuracy, an accuracy rate that was statistically significant relative to the permutation null distribution. Such an accuracy rate would be of far greater clinical diagnostic value than that observed for the behavioral assessment. Furthermore, distance from classification hyperplane correlated with number of times players were taken out of play due to them having suffered a head injury, providing further evidence of the relationship between injury and functional network abnormality.

This study provides one example of how network activity and connectivity can be combined as a sensitive polymarkers of hard to detect damage to executive brain systems. Subsequent studies that have also provided robust network polymarkers in other clinical populations, for example, attentional impairments in ADHD patients (Rosenberg et al., 2016).

CONCLUSION

In this chapter, I have provided a personal perspective on the role of the human frontal cortices in executive function. In the process, I highlighted several points that are relevant to the study of executive dysfunction in clinical populations.

First, the frontal lobe plays a key role in executive function; however, executive function is complex, consisting of distinct classes of cognitive process. The frontal lobes match this complexity as they include multiple distinct subregions. Second, although various patient populations may struggle

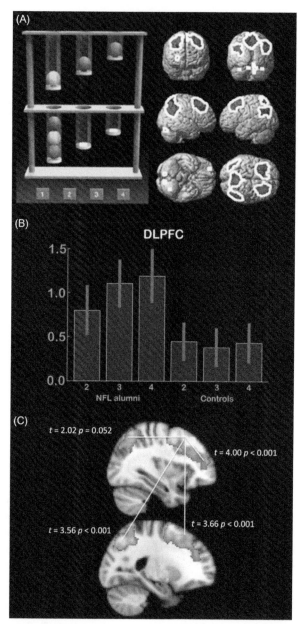

FIGURE 4.12 Frontal lobe hypoconnectivity and hyperactivation in retired NFL players. (A) The fMRI optimized Tower of London Task. Participants are instructed to work out the number of moves required to form the balls in the top panel into the same configuration as the balls in the bottom planning. A control variant of the task (counting) involves calculating the difference in the number of balls in the top and bottom panels. Contrasting planning minus counting trials generates activation within a dorsal frontoparietal network. (B) NFL alumni show significantly heightened activation relative to controls during planning (Hampshire et al., 2013). (C) NFL alumni have reduced functional connectivity relative to controls (assessed using psychophysiological interaction models (Friston et al., 1997) during the planning task. *NFL*, nocturnal frontal lobe; *fMRI*, functional magnetic resonance imaging.

to perform the same classic executive paradigms, their underlying neuropathology can be quite distinct and this heterogeneity is reflected by subtle differences in behavioral abnormalities. Third, our classic conceptualization of what the distinct aspects of executive function are appears to map poorly onto the underlying functional subdivisions of the frontal lobes. Cognitive assessment paradigms that can differentially assess these neural systems and their associated cognitive processes are lacking but could have substantial clinical research and clinical diagnostic value.

Seeking validation of behavioral constructs through identification of neuroanatomical modules is a demonstrably flawed exercise, which has led to a confusing plethora of functional—anatomical mappings; en masse, these mappings effectively obfuscate the underlying functional organization of the frontal lobes. Given that certain functional networks may be considered canonical insofar as they are reliably evident across task contexts, analysis methods, and even the resting state, it may be more tractable to start by reorganizing this space of functional—anatomical mappings based on a network-oriented framework.

Despite having the advantage in terms of consistency, a classification system based purely on static network-cognitive construct mappings can provide only a starting point when understanding the neural mechanisms that underlie executive cognition. Functional networks are dynamic by nature, and some aspects of cognitive processing cannot be mapped to any individual network or brain region; instead some cognitive demands involve widespread network processes, and these are evident as alternative network dynamic states, e.g., synchronous versus asynchronous activity or anterior versus posterior causal flow.

Nonetheless, the network perspective provides a consistent, simplifying, and tractable framework for studying such higher order functional to connectivity state mappings. When studied on this dynamic level, modular and network perspectives cease to appear so conflicted; instead they provide partial and complementary insights into the functioning of complex brain mechanisms. Processes such as motor inhibition and relational reasoning may have their basis in widespread network connectivity states, but particular neuroanatomical nodes such as the AIFO and LFPC play key roles in orchestrating such states and integrating the products of their distributed processing.

The rich descriptions of the network perspectives lend themselves particularly well to robust multivariate analysis approaches. These may overcome limitations that have hampered the transition of fMRI methods from research to clinical applications. For example, they can handle data from clinical populations with pathologies that are heterogeneously expressed across network nodes or cognitive processes that have one-to-many as opposed to one-to-one mappings. In sum, the network perspective holds much promise for clinical research into the frontal lobe mechanisms that underlie executive function and executive dysfunction.

REFERENCES

Aron, A., Robbins, T., & Poldrack, R. (2014). Inhibition and the right inferior frontal cortex: One decade on. *Trends in Cognitive Sciences, 18*(4), 177–185.

Aron, A. R., Fletcher, P. C., Bullmore, E. T., Sahakian, B. J., & Robbins, T. W. (2003). Stop-signal inhibition disrupted by damage to right inferior frontal gyrus in humans. *Nature Neuroscience, 6*, 115–116.

Aron, A. R., & Poldrack, R. A. (2006). Cortical and subcortical contributions to Stop signal response inhibition: Role of the subthalamic nucleus. *Journal of Neuroscience, 26*, 2424–2433.

Aron, A. R., Robbins, T. W., & Poldrack, R. A. (2004). Inhibition and the right inferior frontal cortex. *Trends in Cognitive Sciences, 8*, 170–177.

Berg, E. A. (1948). A simple objective technique for measuring flexibility in thinking. *Journal of General Psychology, 39*, 15–22.

Bunge, S. A., Helskog, E. H., & Wendelken, C. (2009). Left, but not right, rostrolateral prefrontal cortex meets a stringent test of the relational integration hypothesis. *NeuroImage, 46*, 338–342.

Burgess, P. W., Alderman, N., Forbes, C., Costello, A., Coates, L. M., Dawson, D. R., & Channon, S. (2006). The case for the development and use of "ecologically valid" measures of executive function in experimental and clinical neuropsychology. *Journal of the International Neuropsychological Society: JINS, 12*, 194–209.

Cantu, R. C. (2007). Chronic traumatic encephalopathy in the National Football League. *Neurosurgery, 61*, 223–225.

Chamberlain, S. R., Hampshire, A., Muller, U., Rubia, K., Campo, N. D., Craig, K., & Sahakian, B. J. (2009). Atomoxetine modulates right inferior frontal activation during inhibitory control: A pharmacological functional magnetic resonance imaging study. *Biological Psychiatry, 65*(7), 550–555.

Chatham, C. H., Claus, E. D., Kim, A., Curran, T., Banich, M. T., & Munakata, Y. (2012). Cognitive control reflects context monitoring, not motoric stopping, in response inhibition. *PLoS One, 7*, e31546.

Christoff, K., Prabhakaran, V., Dorfman, J., Zhao, Z., Kroger, J. K., Holyoak, K. J., & Gabrieli, J. D. (2001). Rostrolateral prefrontal cortex involvement in relational integration during reasoning. *NeuroImage, 14*, 1136–1149.

Collins, P., Roberts, A. C., Dias, R., Everitt, B. J., & Robbins, T. W. (1998). Perseveration and strategy in a novel spatial self-ordered sequencing task for nonhuman primates: Effects of excitotoxic lesions and dopamine depletions of the prefrontal cortex. *Journal of Cognitive Neuroscience, 10*, 332–354.

Crittenden, B. M., & Duncan, J. (2014). Task difficulty manipulation reveals multiple demand activity but no frontal lobe hierarchy. *Cerebral Cortex, 24*, 532–540.

Crittenden, B. M., Mitchell, D. J., & Duncan, J. (2016). Task encoding across the multiple demand cortex is consistent with a frontoparietal and cingulo-opercular dual networks distinction. *Journal of Neuroscience, 36*, 6147–6155.

Deco, G., Jirsa, V., McIntosh, A. R., Sporns, O., & Kotter, R. (2009). Key role of coupling, delay, and noise in resting brain fluctuations. *Proceedings of the National Academy of Sciences of the United States of America, 106*, 10302–10307.

D'Esposito, M., Postle, B. R., Ballard, D., & Lease, J. (1999). Maintenance versus manipulation of information held in working memory: An event-related fMRI study. *Brain and Cognition, 41*, 66–86.

Dias, R., Robbins, T. W., & Roberts, A. C. (1996). Dissociation in prefrontal cortex of affective and attentional shifts. *Nature, 380*, 69–72.

Dias, R., Robbins, T. W., & Roberts, A. C. (1997). Dissociable forms of inhibitory control within prefrontal cortex with an analog of the Wisconsin Card Sort Test: Restriction to novel situations and independence from "on-line'" processing. *Journal of Neuroscience, 17*, 9285−9297.

Dosenbach, N. U., Fair, D. A., Cohen, A. L., Schlaggar, B. L., & Petersen, S. E. (2008). A dual-networks architecture of top-down control. *Trends in Cognitive Sciences, 12*, 99−105.

Duncan, J. (2001). An adaptive coding model of neural function in prefrontal cortex. *Nature Reviews. Neuroscience, 2*, 820−829.

Duncan, J. (2005). Prefrontal cortex and Spearman's g. In J. Duncan, L. H. Phillips, & P. McLeod (Eds.), *Measuring the mind: Speed, control, and age* (pp. 249−272). Oxford: Oxford University Press.

Duncan, J. (2006). EPS Mid-Career Award 2004: Brain mechanisms of attention. *Quarterly Journal of Experimental Psychology Section B: Comparative and Physiological Psychology, 59*, 2−27.

Duncan, J., & Owen, A. M. (2000). Common regions of the human frontal lobe recruited by diverse cognitive demands. *Trends in Neurosciences, 23*, 475−483.

Duncan, J., Seitz, R. J., Kolodny, J., Bor, D., Herzog, H., Ahmed, A., & Emslie, H. (2000). A neural basis for general intelligence. *Science, 289*, 457−460.

Erika-Florence, M., Leech, R., & Hampshire, A. (2014). A functional network perspective on inhibition and attentional control. *Nature Communications, 5*, 4073.

Fagerholm, E. D., Hellyer, P. J., Scott, G., Leech, R., & Sharp, D. J. (2015). Disconnection of network hubs and cognitive impairment after traumatic brain injury. *Brain: A Journal of Neurology, 138*, 1696−1709.

Freedman, D. J., Riesenhuber, M., Poggio, T., & Miller, E. K. (2001). Categorical representation of visual stimuli in the primate prefrontal cortex. *Science, 291*, 312−316.

Friston, K. J., Buechel, C., Fink, G. R., Morris, J., Rolls, E., & Dolan, R. J. (1997). Psychophysiological and modulatory interactions in neuroimaging. *NeuroImage, 6*, 218−229.

Friston, K. J., Harrison, L., & Penny, W. (2003). Dynamic causal modelling. *NeuroImage, 19*, 1273−1302.

Grant, J. E., Odlaug, B. L., Chamberlain, S. R., Hampshire, A., Schreiber, L., & Won Kim, S. (2013). A proof of concept study of tolcapone for pathological gambling: Relationships with COMT genotype and brain activation. *European Neuropsychopharmacology, 23*(11), 1587−1596.

Hampshire, A. (2015). Putting the brakes on inhibitory models of frontal lobe function. *NeuroImage, 113*, 340−355.

Hampshire, A., Chamberlain, S. R., Monti, M. M., Duncan, J., & Owen, A. M. (2010). The role of the right inferior frontal gyrus: Inhibition and attentional control. *NeuroImage, 50*, 1313−1319.

Hampshire, A., Duncan, J., & Owen, A. M. (2007). Selective tuning of the blood oxygenation level-dependent response during simple target detection dissociates human frontoparietal subregions. *Journal of Neuroscience, 27*, 6219−6223.

Hampshire, A., Hellyer, P. J., Parkin, B., Hiebert, N., MacDonald, P., Owen, A. M., & Rowe, J. (2016). Network mechanisms of intentional learning. *NeuroImage, 127*, 123−134.

Hampshire, A., Highfield, R. R., Parkin, B. L., & Owen, A. M. (2012). Fractionating human intelligence. *Neuron, 76*, 1225−1237.

Hampshire, A., MacDonald, A., & Owen, A. M. (2013). Hypoconnectivity and hyperfrontality in retired professional American football players. *Scientific Reports, 3*, 2972.

Hampshire, A., & Owen, A. M. (2006). Fractionating attentional control using event-related fMRI. *Cerebral Cortex, 16*, 1679–1689.

Hampshire, A., & Sharp, D. J. (2015). Contrasting network and modular perspectives on inhibitory control. *Trends in Cognitive Sciences, 19*(8), 445–452.

Hampshire, A., Thompson, R., Duncan, J., & Owen, A. M. (2008). The target selective neural response—Similarity, ambiguity, and learning effects. *PLoS One, 3*(6), e2520.

Hampshire, A., Thompson, R., Duncan, J., & Owen, A. M. (2011). Lateral prefrontal cortex subregions make dissociable contributions during fluid reasoning. *Cerebral Cortex, 21*, 1–10.

Hellyer, P. J., Shanahan, M., Scott, G., Wise, R. J., Sharp, D. J., & Leech, R. (2014). The control of global brain dynamics: Opposing actions of frontoparietal control and default mode networks on attention. *Journal of Neuroscience, 34*, 451–461.

Hummel, J. E., & Holyoak, K. J. (1997). Distributed representations of structure: A theory of analogical access and mapping. *Psychological Review, 104*, 427–466.

Jung, R. E., & Haier, R. J. (2007). The Parieto-Frontal Integration Theory (P-FIT) of intelligence: converging neuroimaging evidence. *Behavioural and Brain Sciences, 30*, 135–154, discussion 154–187

Knowlton, B. J., Morrison, R. G., Hummel, J. E., & Holyoak, K. J. (2012). A neurocomputational system for relational reasoning. *Trends in Cognitive Sciences, 16*, 373–381.

Laird, A. R., Fox, P. M., Eickhoff, S. B., Turner, J. A., Ray, K. L., McKay, D. R., & Fox, P. T. (2011). Behavioral interpretations of intrinsic connectivity networks. *Journal of Cognitive Neuroscience, 23*, 4022–4037.

Lawrence, A. J., Luty, J., Bogdan, N. A., Sahakian, B. J., & Clark, L. (2009). Impulsivity and response inhibition in alcohol dependence and problem gambling. *Psychopharmacology, 207*, 163–172.

Levy, B. J., & Wagner, A. D. (2011). Cognitive control and right ventrolateral prefrontal cortex: reflexive reorienting, motor inhibition, and action updating. *Annals of the New York Academy of Sciences, 1224*, 40–62.

Linden, D. E. J., Prvulovic, D., Formisano, E., Vollinger, M., Zanella, F. E., Goebel, R., & Dierks, T. (1999). The functional neuroanatomy of target detection: An fMRI study of visual and auditory oddball tasks. *Cerebral Cortex, 9*, 815–823.

Logan, G. D., & Cowan, W. B. (1984). On the ability to inhibit thought and action—A theory of an act of control. *Psychological Review, 91*, 295–327.

Lopez-Caneda, E., Cadaveira, F., Crego, A., Gomez-Suarez, A., Corral, M., Parada, M., & Rodriguez Holguin, S. (2012). Hyperactivation of right inferior frontal cortex in young binge drinkers during response inhibition: a follow-up study. *Addiction, 107*, 1796–1808.

McKee, A. C., Cantu, R. C., Nowinski, C. J., Hedley-Whyte, E. T., Gavett, B. E., Budson, A. E., & Stern, R. A. (2009). Chronic traumatic encephalopathy in athletes: Progressive tauopathy after repetitive head injury. *Journal of Neuropathology and Experimental Neurology, 68*, 709–735.

Menon, V. (2011). Large-scale brain networks and psychopathology: a unifying triple network model. *Trends in Cognitive Sciences, 15*, 483–506.

Miller, E. K., & Cohen, J. D. (2001). An integrative theory of prefrontal cortex function. *Annual Review of Neuroscience, 24*, 167–202.

Nombela, C., Rowe, J. B., Winder-Rhodes, S. E., Hampshire, A., Owen, A. M., Breen, D. P., & Barker, R. A. (2014). Genetic impact on cognition and brain function in newly diagnosed Parkinson's disease: ICICLE-PD study. *Brain: A Journal of Neurology, 137*, 2743–2758.

Owen, A. M. (1997). The functional organization of working memory processes within human lateral frontal cortex: The contribution of functional neuroimaging. *European Journal of Neuroscience, 9,* 1329−1339.

Parkin, B., Hellyer, P. J., Leech, R., & Hampshire, A. (2015). Dynamic network mechanisms of relational integration. *Journal of Neuroscience, 35*(20), 7660−7673.

Matthews, P. M., & Hampshire, A. (2016). Clinical concepts emerging from fMRI functional connectomics. *Neuron, 91*(3), 511−528.

Petrides, M. (1994). Frontal lobes and working memory: Evidence from investigations of the effects of cortical excisions in nonhuman primates. In F. Boller, & J. Grafman (Eds.), *Handbook of neuropsychology* (pp. 59−82). Amsterdam: Elsevier.

Postle, B. R., & D'Esposito, M. (2000). Evaluating models of the topographical organization of working memory function in frontal cortex with event-related fMRI. *Psychobiology, 28,* 132−145.

Ramnani, N., & Owen, A. M. (2004). Anterior prefrontal cortex: insights into function from anatomy and neuroimaging. *Nature Reviews. Neuroscience, 5,* 184−194.

Rosenberg, M. D., Finn, E. S., Scheinost, D., Papademetris, X., Shen, X., Constable, R. T., & Chun, M. M. (2016). A neuromarker of sustained attention from whole-brain functional connectivity. *Nature Neuroscience, 19,* 165−171.

Rubia, K., Halari, R., Mohammad, A. M., Taylor, E., & Brammer, M. (2011). Methylphenidate normalizes frontocingulate underactivation during error processing in attention-deficit/hyperactivity disorder. *Biological Psychiatry, 70,* 255−262.

Rubia, K., Overmeyer, S., Taylor, E., Brammer, M., Williams, S. C., Simmons, A., & Bullmore, E. T. (1999). Hypofrontality in attention deficit hyperactivity disorder during higher-order motor control: A study with functional MRI. *The American Journal of Psychiatry, 156,* 891−896.

Rubia, K., Russell, T., Overmeyer, S., Brammer, M. J., Bullmore, E. T., Sharma, T., & Taylor, E. (2001a). Mapping motor inhibition: Conjunctive brain activations across different versions of go/no-go and stop tasks. *NeuroImage, 13,* 250−261.

Rubia, K., Smith, A., Lidzba, K., Toone, B., Simmons, A., Williams, S. C. R., & Taylor, E. (2001b). Neural substrates of successful versus unsuccessful stopping in a cognitively challenging event related stop task. *NeuroImage, 13,* S351.

Rubia, K., Smith, A. B., Brammer, M. J., & Taylor, E. (2003). Right inferior prefrontal cortex mediates response inhibition while mesial prefrontal cortex is responsible for error detection. *NeuroImage, 20,* 351−358.

Seeley, W. W., Menon, V., Schatzberg, A. F., Keller, J., Glover, G. H., Kenna, H., & Greicius, M. D. (2007). Dissociable intrinsic connectivity networks for salience processing and executive control. *Journal of Neuroscience, 27,* 2349−2356.

Sharp, D. J., Bonnelle, V., De Boissezon, X., Beckmann, C. F., James, S. G., Patel, M. C., & Mehta, M. A. (2010). Distinct frontal systems for response inhibition, attentional capture, and error processing. *Proceedings of the National Academy of Sciences of the United States of America, 107,* 6106−6111.

Shulman, G. L., Astafiev, S. V., Franke, D., Pope, D. L. W., Snyder, A. Z., McAvoy, M. P., & Corbetta, M. (2009). Interaction of stimulus-driven reorienting and expectation in ventral and dorsal frontoparietal and basal ganglia-cortical networks. *Journal of Neuroscience, 29,* 4392−4407.

Simmonds, D. J., Pekar, J. J., & Mostofsky, S. H. (2008). Meta-analysis of Go/No-go tasks demonstrating that fMRI activation associated with response inhibition is task-dependent. *Neuropsychologia, 46,* 224−232.

Smith, J. L., Mattick, R. P., Jamadar, S. D., & Iredale, J. M. (2014). Deficits in behavioural inhibition in substance abuse and addiction: A meta-analysis. *Drug and Alcohol Dependence*, *145*, 1–33.

Smith, S. M., Fox, P. T., Miller, K. L., Glahn, D. C., Fox, P. M., Mackay, C. E., & Beckmann, C. F. (2009). Correspondence of the brain's functional architecture during activation and rest. *Proceedings of the National Academy of Sciences of the United States of America*, *106*, 13040–13045.

Smith, S. M., Nichols, T. E., Vidaurre, D., Winkler, A. M., Behrens, T. E., Glasser, M. F., & Miller, K. L. (2015). A positive-negative mode of population covariation links brain connectivity, demographics and behavior. *Nature Neuroscience*, *18*, 1565–1567.

Stokes, M. G., Kusunoki, M., Sigala, N., Nili, H., Gaffan, D., & Duncan, J. (2013). Dynamic coding for cognitive control in prefrontal cortex. *Neuron*, *78*, 364–375.

Toni, I., & Passingham, R. E. (1999). Prefrontal-basal ganglia pathways are involved in the learning of arbitrary visuomotor associations: A PET study. *Experimental Brain Research*, *127*, 19–32.

Toni, I., Ramnani, N., Josephs, O., Ashburner, J., & Passingham, R. E. (2001). Learning arbitrary visuomotor associations: Temporal dynamic of brain activity. *NeuroImage*, *14*, 1048–1057.

Verbruggen, F., & Logan, G. D. (2008). Response inhibition in the stop-signal paradigm. *Trends in Cognitive Sciences*, *12*, 418–424.

Williams-Gray, C. H., Hampshire, A., Robbins, T. W., Owen, A. M., & Barker, R. A. (2007). Catechol O-methyltransferase Val158Met genotype influences frontoparietal activity during planning in patients with Parkinson's disease. *Journal of Neuroscience*, *27*, 4832–4838.

Woolgar, A., Parr, A., Cusack, R., Thompson, R., Nimmo-Smith, I., Torralva, T., & Duncan, J. (2010). Fluid intelligence loss linked to restricted regions of damage within frontal and parietal cortex PNAS. *Proceedings of the National Academy of Sciences of the United States of America*, *107*(33), 14899–14902.

Chapter 5

Neural Network Models of Human Executive Function and Decision Making

Daniel S. Levine

Department of Psychology, University of Texas at Arlington, Arlington, TX, United States

INTRODUCTION: WHAT ARE NEURAL NETWORKS?

As brain imaging and other techniques have allowed the cognitive neuroscience of executive functions to be better understood, it is natural that more detailed quantitative theories of these functions should be sought. Yet the complexity of billions of neurons and trillions of synapses makes mapping out the relevant pathways and their interactions a daunting task. Hence a wide range of models of different aspects of executive function and decision making have emerged, but the major growth in modeling of those processes is yet to come.

Neural network models ideally should fit both behavioral and neural data and make nontrivial predictions. Yet those are not the only criteria for a computational model. As Meeter, Jehee, and Murre (2007) advocate, a model should also be based on assumptions that make sense from a biological and/or behavioral viewpoint. For these authors argue that it is desirable to have several interconnected and mutually consistent models for the same process at different levels of representation, and such hierarchies of models are particularly useful when some of the relevant data are unavailable, incomplete, or contradictory. A similar point was made by the neural network pioneer Stephen Grossberg (Grossberg, 2006): "One works with large amounts of data because otherwise too many seemingly plausible hypotheses cannot be ruled out."

How do we develop theories of brain–behavior relationships? Elsewhere (Levine, 1999) I have described the theory building process as analogous to the building of the tunnel across the channel between England and France. The theorist starts at both the behavioral and the neural ends, and then builds "tunnels" of connection from each end toward the other.

Executive Functions in Health and Disease. DOI: http://dx.doi.org/10.1016/B978-0-12-803676-1.00005-2

One widely read source on computational modeling of cognitive processes is the two volumes by the PDP Research Group (Rumelhart & McClelland, 1986). Many psychologists, neuroscientists, and philosophers incorrectly equate neural networks with the parallel distributed processing (PDP) networks developed in those books. Hence, many scholars assume that neural networks (1) consist of three layers, called input, hidden, and output layers; (2) have little structure at the start of an operation; and (3) require extensive training, up to hundreds of thousands of learning trials. Yet in fact none of properties (1), (2), and (3) is universally or even generally true of neural networks. There have been computational models, for example, of both innate and learned behaviors, and of both quick decisions from description and slow decisions from feedback. In each case the function constrains the structure of the model, so different neuro-computational structures may model different cognitive tasks. Much of the field's early history is summarized in Levine (1983, 2000).

From the 1980s to the present, neural network models have gradually evolved in the direction of greater fidelity to brain structure and function. Some of the models in this chapter include explicit analogs of specific brain regions, while others have parts representing cognitive entities that are not directly located in the brain. Modeling of executive functions has lagged behind models of lower-level functions like visual perception, motor control, and conditioning, both in biological realism and ability to make testable predictions. Yet often the older models of lower-level functions provide building blocks for early models of higher-level functions.

Techniques such as magnetic resonance scanning of whole brain regions and recording with electrodes from up to 50 neurons at once have made neurophysiology more amenable to quantification. At the same time, advances in computing (personal computers, supercomputers, and interfaces with recording devices) have made simulation of biological data easier and more practical. These technical developments are enabling theorists building on earlier, more abstract cognitive models to create theories with greater explanatory and predictive power.

The term *neural networks* encompasses both theoretical and applied models that provide mechanistic bases for cognitive functions. Functional units in neural networks are often called "nodes" or "units," terms which do not commit the user to assume that units correspond to either single or multiple neurons. Both earlier and more recent models include nodes, connections between nodes, and equations describing interactions of node activities and connection strengths.

In order to classify models of executive functions, we must first specify which cognitive processes do or do not require those functions. Norman and Shallice (1986) described two interacting systems, one for automatic and routine actions and another for actions requiring executive control. They described situations that require the executive system as follows:

1. Those that involve planning or decision making.
2. Those that involve error correction or troubleshooting.
3. Situations where responses are not well-learned or contain novel sequences of actions.
4. Dangerous or technically difficult situations.
5. Situations which require the overcoming of a strong habitual response or resisting temptation (Norman & Shallice, 1986; paraphrased by Wikipedia).

Of these types of situations, the ones that have been most modeled are types 1, 3, and 5. Executive models are now reviewed in that order.

MODELS OF DECISION MAKING

The dominant paradigms in the study of human preference decisions have involved choices between gambles, that is, between options that involve different probabilities of gains or losses. The gains or losses most often have involved money because that is the easiest thing to quantify, but sometimes instead have involved human or animal lives. Researchers in the 1960s and 1970s largely treated probabilistic choices among different resources as equivalent. Yet in this century some points of nonequivalence between resources (e.g., lives versus money) have been studied and modeled, based on differences in the strength of emotion induced by thinking about the possibility of obtaining different resources.

Before the 1960s the dominant quantitative theory of preference decisions was based on calculating the "utility" or value of each possible amount of money or lives and multiplying those utilities by the probability of a gain or loss of that amount, then summing over all possible outcomes (with losses counted as the negative of equal gains). It was assumed that decision makers are rational and choose the gamble with the highest "expected utility" so obtained. Expected utility theory entails several key assumptions. These assumptions include irrelevance of possible outcomes common to the alternatives being considered, and consistency of preferences over different descriptions of the alternatives. Both those assumptions were refuted by many behavioral results, notably by Tversky and Kahneman (1981), and a theoretical paradox noted by Allais (1953).

Allais (1953) noted several situations that violate irrelevance of common outcomes. An example is that if A is certainty of winning $100 million; B is a 10% chance of winning $500 million, 89% chance of $100 million, and 1% of nothing; C is an 11% chance of winning $100 million and 89% of nothing; D is a 10% chance of winning $500 million and 90% of nothing, then most people prefer A to B and prefer D to C. This finding is paradoxical from the rational utility viewpoint because subtracting an 89% chance of winning $100 million from A yields C, and subtracting the same 89% chance of winning $100 million from B yields D.

Tversky and Kahneman (1981) found several results that violate consistency of preferences, one of which involves the *Asian Disease Problem*. In this problem, the experimenter asks participants to decide between two public health measures to combat a disease expected to come to the United States and kill 600 people: one measure will save 200 for sure, whereas the other has a 1/3 probability of saving 600 and 2/3 of saving none. If choices are framed in terms of people saved, participants prefer the safer option of saving fewer for sure, but if they are framed in terms of people dying, participants prefer the risky option that might lead to no deaths.

In addition to framing effects, the Asian Disease Problem highlights the tendency to be risk seeking with losses but risk averse with gains. Those processes demanded a new model, and Kahneman and Tversky (1979) developed a quantitative nonneural theory known as *prospect theory* to account for those effects. The main difference between prospect theory and expected utility theory is that probabilities in prospect theory are nonlinearly weighted. The nonlinear weighting magnifies psychological differences between low nonzero probabilities and impossibility or between high nonunity probabilities and certainty.

Prospect theory has an impressive record of reproducing data, but does not have a natural mechanistic basis that allows it to be mapped easily into a neural network. Moreover, recent results (e.g., Barron & Erev, 2003) suggest that overweighting low and underweighting high probabilities applies only to *decisions from description*, that is, quick real-time choices between two gambles with explicitly presented probabilities. In fact, the weighting sometimes reverses when the same choices are made between gambles with probabilities learned by feedback over repeated trials (*decisions from experience*). Many researchers since the 1980s have developed more neurally plausible theories that explain the same results as prospect theory.

The earliest computational decision theories were largely cognitive and did not include explicit brain regions. Grossberg and Gutowski (1987) modeled framing effects such as are found in the Asian Disease Problem. They noted that choices between gambles depend on the reference point with which the gambles are being compared; for example, in the loss frame of the Asian Disease Problem the two plans are compared with the reference point of no lives lost, whereas in the gain frame the same two plans are compared with the reference point of no lives saved. Such counterfactual comparison is closely related to opponent processing, whereby the removal or reduction of a stimulus of positive or negative hedonic sign generates a transient feeling of the opposite hedonic sign. Grossberg and Gutowski applied to the decision data a version of the *gated dipole*, an opponent processing model developed by Grossberg (1972a, 1972b). The gated dipole involves habituation of chemical transmitters and was originally designed to account for affective contrast in classical conditioning, such as positive reward due to escape from shock or frustration due to absence of expected food.

The *decision field theory* of Busemeyer and Townsend (1993) was designed to model variability of individual preferences and effects of deliberation time on preferences. Busemeyer and Townsend accounted for these effects by making their model dynamic and probabilistic, and including approach and avoidance gradients previously developed in theories of classical conditioning. Roe, Busemeyer, and Townsend (2001) mapped decision field theory into a network model of decisions between options with multiple attributes. This network provides explanations for three effects that violate EU predictions. All three effects involve starting with two dissimilar options A and B (e.g., A is a car that is high in power and low in economy and B is a car that is high in economy and low in power) and adding a third alternative C. The *similarity effect* means that if C is similar in attribute values to A, it competes with A more than with B and so increases the probability of choosing B. The *attraction effect* means that if C is worse than A on all attributes it increases the probability of choosing A. The compromise effect means that if C is intermediate between A and B (e.g., has medium values of both economy and power), it tends to be chosen more than either A or B. Their model was later compared to processes in basal ganglia-thalamocortical loops (Busemeyer, Jessup, Johnson, & Townsend, 2006).

Usher and McClelland (2004) developed a different multiattribute decision model of the compromise, similarity, and attraction effects. Their model includes a value function that is steeper for losses than for gains. This was done to account Tversky and Kahneman's finding of *loss aversion*, the tendency for losses to influence decisions more than gains of the same amount.

Starting about 2004, there have been models of specific decision data that incorporated knowledge about the roles of brain regions. Some of these models simulate the *Iowa Gambling Task* (IGT), the most popular clinical test of decision-making competence. The IGT involves deciding whether decks of cards are good or bad based on feedback from sampling the deck. Other neural network models simulate data on decisions from description, such as the early findings of Tversky, Kahneman, and their colleagues.

Models of the IGT

The IGT incorporates the insight of Damasio (1994) that connections between orbitofrontal cortex (OFC) and amygdala are required for effective decision making, due to the role of these connections in processing emotional and social stimuli. In the IGT (Bechara, Damasio, Damasio, & Anderson, 1994), the participant on each trial must draw a card from one of four decks of cards shown on a computer screen, and each deck provides a different probabilistic distribution of gains and losses of play money. Two of these decks have higher short-term payoffs than the other two, but over time the decks with high immediate payoffs are disadvantageous (i.e., the expected value of earnings from those decks is negative), whereas the decks with low immediate payoffs are advantageous. Hence the IGT is a test of ability to learn from feedback and to inhibit the impulse to pursue short-term gain.

Participants with damage to either OFC or amygdala cannot learn the advantageous strategy effectively. Also, several investigators have studied IGT difficulties in participants who suffer from many conditions including Parkinson's disease, Huntington's disease, alcoholism, and drug abuse. A series of cognitive models based on decision field theory (e.g., Yechiam, Stout, Busemeyer, Rock, & Finn, 2005) have had some success at reproducing these clinical patterns through IGT model parameter variations.

There are at least three IGT models in the literature that include brain regions. These models vary in emphasis but all incorporate a role for OFC or, more broadly, ventromedial prefrontal cortex (VMPFC) in long-term evaluation of the goodness or badness of options. Wagar and Thagard (2004) were particularly interested in reproducing the physiological effects of prefrontal cortex (PFC) and amygdalar lesions. They modeled the influence on IGT choices of covert emotional reactions, as indicated by what Bechara et al. (1994) termed *somatic markers*. Somatic markers are the bodily representations that are gradually built up to stimuli that take on positive or negative emotional significance. Wagar and Thagard's GAGE model includes amygdalar (bodily state), VMPFC (emotional evaluation), and hippocampal (context) influence on throughput of stimulus representations that is governed by the nucleus accumbens of the ventral striatum, which in turn feeds back to VMPFC. Their model includes training episodes of several thousand time steps before the actual running of the deck choices.

While the IGT includes two good and two bad decks, GAGE simplifies it to one good and one bad deck. The model of Levine, Mills, and Estrada (2005) includes all four decks, with one bad deck leading to infrequent large losses and the other to more frequent small losses. This network avoids the deck with frequent losses more than the other bad deck, a result confirmed in human participants by Yechiam and Busemeyer (2005). The network includes anterior cingulate cortex (ACC) for plan generation along with amygdala (two layers of), OFC, and striatum. Striatum is divided into *direct* and *indirect pathways* (Alexander & Crutcher, 1990). The internal globus pallidus (GPi) sends inhibitory projections to mediodorsal thalamus, which in turn excites both PFC and motor cortex. The direct pathway involves inhibition from striatum to inhibitory GPi, so its net effect on cortex is excitatory. The indirect pathway involves inhibition from striatum to external GPi, which inhibits the subthalamic nucleus, which excites mediodorsal thalamus, so its net effect on cortex is inhibitory. The Levine et al. model, which includes plasticity at two loci, does not emphasize somatic markers and does not require training.

The IGT model of Frank and Claus (2006) is part of a general model of connections between OFC and striatum. To a previous model of striatum that was sensitive to frequency but not magnitude of reward and punishment,

Frank and Claus added influences from an OFC that was also sensitive to magnitude. Their combined model also reproduces various conditioning data dealing with reversal and devaluation.

Models of Other Decision Data and Phenomena

Perhaps the most comprehensive brain-based model of decision data to date is the ANDREA model of Litt, Eliasmith, and Thagard (2008). The model of Litt et al. reproduces general phenomena accounted for by prospect theory, including loss aversion and the effects of frames and reference points. The network includes spiking neurons in the amygdala and OFC, representing valuation, and other brain regions such as dorsolateral prefrontal cortex (DLPFC), ACC, striatum, and dopamine and serotonin nuclei.

ANDREA simulates data of Mellers, Schwartz, Ho, and Ritov (1997) on the desirability of dollar outcomes being strongly influenced by comparison with what is expected and with how surprising they are (a low-probability gain being more valued that a high-probability one). Litt et al. explain the Mellers et al. data using a neural model of reward prediction errors (Sutton & Barto, 1998), with dopamine mediating positive prediction errors (Schultz, Apicella, & Ljungberg, 1993) and serotonin mediating negative prediction errors (Daw, Kakade, & Dayan, 2002). The model does not distinguish between decisions from experience and from description.

Another neural-based approach to decision phenomena is found in Levine (2012) and AlQaudi, Levine, and Lewis (2015). This model combines adaptive resonance theory, a neural network theory of hierarchical links between attributes and categories (Carpenter & Grossberg, 1987); the gated dipole theory of counterfactual comparison (Grossberg & Gutowski, 1987); and a psychological account of decision making and memory known as *fuzzy trace theory* (FTT) (e.g., Reyna & Brainerd, 2008). FTT says that we store events simultaneously in two separate memory traces: *verbatim* and *gist* traces. The verbatim trace stores a stimulus exactly as it is presented, including numerical values (e.g., of dollars won or lost or lives saved or lost) and probabilities of those values occurring, whereas the gist trace stores what the person regards as the essential meaning of these stimuli. Levine and colleagues treated gist as a category of possible options with some attributes selectively enhanced. This led to a model network with an adaptive resonance module whose attributes are located in amygdala or a superficial layer of OFC, categories in another layer of OFC, category mismatch signals in ACC, and behavioral decisions filtered through striatal direct and indirect pathways.

The networks of Levine and his colleagues incorporate the FTT explanation for framing effects, which is based on gists that ignore detailed numerical probabilities in favor of the simpler comparison of "some versus none" (possibility of gaining or losing money, saving or losing lives, etc.). That explanation was supported by the results of Reyna and Brainerd (1991) showing that framing effects in the Asian Disease Problem are enhanced by making the possibility of no lives lost or saved more salient and reduced or eliminated by not explicitly presenting that possibility. AlQaudi et al. (2015) simulated that result, and Levine (2012) simulated results of Rottenstreich and Hsee (2001) suggesting that probability weight distortion is larger for more emotional resources (a kiss versus a small amount of money). This model has been applied so far to decisions from description but might extend to decisions from experience with the addition of dopamine-dependent plasticity in corticostriatal synapses (cf. Levine, 2016).

FTT is a dual process theory. Reyna and Brainerd (2008) review data suggesting a gradual shift in predominant processing from verbatim to gist as we develop from childhood to adolescence to adulthood. Gist processing allows us to ignore irrelevant details and see the commonalities that unite many of our experiences, so Reyna and Brainerd regard it as a more advanced form of processing than verbatim. Yet gist processing also makes us vulnerable to some types of errors such as false memories and misleading decision heuristics.

A different dual process theory of decision making is *cognitive-experiential theory* (e.g., Epstein, 1994; see Kahneman, 2011, for a recent variation). The two processes are described by Mukherjee (2010) as follows:

> ... *an associative affect-based mode of decision making (System A) and a deliberative rule-based mode of decision making (System D). Processing in System A is intimately influenced by mood and emotional states of mind and involves how one feels about a particular prospect. On the other hand, processing in System D is analytical in nature and can involve computational operations. (p. 243)*

Epstein (1994) and other proponents of this theory regard System D as more advanced than System A, in contrast to the claims of FTT. Mukherjee (2010) developed a nonneural cognitive model of decisions that combines processing done by the two systems into decisions that synthesize the two modes. The relative strength of the two systems varies in different individuals and different contexts. Mukherjee's model accounts for such data as the effects of emotion in Rottenstreich and Hsee (2001) and the role of irrelevant outcomes in Allais (1953).

The diversity of decision models is partly due to lack of consensus about how the brain processes choice options. How do we select the most relevant attributes of an option? The words "select" and "decision" are not meant to imply that the process is a matter of conscious choice. There is a salience system in the brain, including ACC and anterior insula, which selects some stimuli and attributes as most salient based on emotion, learning, task relevance, and other influences (Menon & Uddin, 2010; Seeley et al., 2007). The salience system in turn influences the brain's executive system. Decision theory would benefit from more results on how the salience system influences selective attention between attributes of a single stimulus, such as an option presented verbally with numbers and probabilities.

MODELS OF SEQUENCE LEARNING AND WORKING MEMORY

Various researchers have built on earlier neural network models of perception and motor control to develop models of learning novel perceptual or motor sequences. Many of those models built on the insight that sequence learning is more a parallel than a serial process. Many early psychologists regarded sequence learning as a serial process based on chains of associations; that is, to learn, say, the sequence ABCD one needs to strengthen the links A-to-B, B-to-C, and C-to-D. Yet Lashley (1951) argued that sequence learning is based not on associative chaining but on parallel representations of the sequence items, all present at the start of the task and excited to different degrees at a given time. His argument was based on characteristic sequence learning errors, which involve reproducing the correct items in the wrong order. Typical errors involve "filling in" previously skipped items; that is, if the sequence is ABCD and the participant has produced A and then C, he or she is most likely to go next to B which has been skipped, rather than D which follows C as associative chaining would predict.

Neurophysiological support for Lashley's parallel representation hypothesis came with studies of Averbeck, Chafee, Crowe, and Georgopoulos (2003) and Averbeck, Crowe, Chafee, and Georgopoulos (2003) on neurons in an area of the PFC (a part of Brodmann area 46) of monkeys. These researchers trained monkeys to draw a set of geometric shapes including a triangle, square, trapezoid, and upside down triangle. Shapes were drawn in blocks of consecutive trials of the same shape, enabling the monkey to anticipate the appropriate shape in the subsequent trial. Analysis of the monkey's hand movements showed that the continuous trajectory was composed of a sequence of individual segments. While the monkeys carried out this task, ensembles of individually isolated single area 46 neurons were recorded. During the period before drawing the segments, it was found that the neural correlates of all the segments were active. The relative strength of the representation of each segment corresponded to the serial position of the segment; that is, prior to the execution of the sequence, the first segment had the strongest representation, the second had the second strongest representation, etc.

Rhodes (2000) and Rhodes, Bullock, Verwey, Averbeck, and Page (2004) developed models of parallel learning of sequence elements, incorporating data about learning to produce sequences of six or fewer key presses or sounds (e.g., Klapp, 1995; Verwey, 1996). These data deal with relationships among various response latencies and how those latencies are affected by the length of the sequence to be learned.

These combined neural and behavioral data motivated a model based on *competitive queuing*. Competitive queuing is defined as follows (Bohland, Bullock, & Guenther, 2010):

> ... *items and their serial order are stored via a primacy gradient utilizing the simultaneous parallel activation of a set of nodes, where relative activation levels of the content-addressable nodes code their relative order in the sequence. This parallel working memory plan ... can be converted to serial performance through an iterative competitive choice process in which i) the item with the highest activation is chosen for performance, ii) the chosen item's activation is then suppressed, and iii) the process is repeated until the sequence reaches completion. (p. 1505)*

Rhodes's competitive queuing model included tentative assignments of functions to brain regions: working memory to DLPFC; chunking of items to parietal cortex; item-by-item learning and chunk learning to cerebellum; and execution to supplementary and presupplementary motor areas, motor cortex, and basal ganglia.

Competitive queuing principles have also informed many models of immediate recall of items presented in short-term memory (Botvinick & Plaut, 2006; Grossberg & Pearson, 2008; Page & Norris, 1998). The Page−Norris model is a cognitive model without brain regions, but set the tone for later models by positing a coding of presented items in a list by relative activation. The Botvinick−Plaut model is a three-layer PDP model (Rumelhart & McClelland, 1986) with concept representations at recurrently connected hidden units. The Grossberg−Pearson model integrates short-term memory with the laminar structure of the cerebral cortex.

Botvinick and Plaut (2006) noted a paradox about interitem associations. The paradox is that while the data previously described refute chaining models, other data involving letter pairs (*bigrams*) point to the importance of learned sequential associations. Specifically, words containing bigrams commonly presented in sequence (such as CK) are easier to remember than words containing less common bigrams (such as KC). Botvinick and Plaut reproduced both data sets using their PDP model. The emergent internal representations code both list items and orders within lists. They noted that their model is compatible with neurophysiological data whereby responses of prefrontal neurons change over several steps of sequence encoding. Yet the requirement of massive amounts of training argues against their model's plausibility as a neural representation of the immediacy of the process of serial recall. So do their learning laws which are based, as are the laws in many PDP models, on back propagation of synaptic weights.

The LIST PARSE network of Grossberg and Pearson (2008) models immediate serial recall by extending to the PFC a type of laminar architecture previously used in models of visual cortex (Grossberg, 1999; Raizada & Grossberg, 2003). In so doing LIST PARSE also can simulate human data on *free recall*, that is, recalling as many items as possible from a list without regard to the order of their presentation, and monkey data on prefrontal neuron response during learning of a motor sequence (Averbeck, Chafee et al., 2003; Averbeck, Crowe et al., 2003).

The LIST PARSE network consists of a cognitive working memory, a motor working memory, and a trajectory generator. The cognitive working memory is assumed to be located in ventrolateral PFC and the principal sulcus, and the motor working memory in DLPFC. Layers 4 through 6 of that part of the network are assumed to be involved in filtering and temporary storage of inputs. Layers 2 and 3 are assumed to group these inputs, as they do in the laminar visual models. The groupings are based on sequential order, and groups form chunks of items that are remembered as units. Grossberg and Pearson (2008) also noted that their model provides a computational implementation of the influential psychological model of working memory due to Baddeley (1986), based on a set of interactions between a central executive controller and two subsidiary systems called the *phonological loop* and *visuospatial sketchpad*.

LIST PARSE does not rely on explicit representations of numerical order. Yet Grossberg and Pearson (2008) noted behavioral data indicating that we do develop representations of positions of items within sequences. For example, when participants recall one list, intrusions from other recently presented lists tend to go into a serial position close to the one they occupied on their correct lists. Also, repeated presentation of an item in the same serial position tends to make that item easier to learn. Based on these data, Grossberg and Pearson suggested future extensions of their network to include joint coding of item, order, and position.

PFC layering also plays a role in the models of PFC−basal ganglia interactions in working memory by Frank, Loughry, and O'Reilly (2001) and O'Reilly and Frank (2006). Frank et al. (2001) considered two paradoxical requirements of working memory: robust maintenance of items and rapid task-relevant updating of memory representations. Based on the capacity of the PFC to sustain representations of sensory events over delays (e.g., Fuster, 1973), these authors assigned robust maintenance to the frontal lobes. Updating they assigned to the basal ganglia based on this region's importance for disinhibiting motor plans whose details are organized elsewhere (Chevalier & Deniau, 1990). Stimuli input to this network are represented twice in PFC, once in a "maintenance" layer (assumed to be in cortical layers 2−3 or 5−6) and once in a "gating" layer (assumed to be in cortical layer 4) influenced by striatum through its disinhibition of thalamus. Inputs recognized as relevant to task performance also have corresponding representations in the striatum. Frank et al. applied this network to sequence working memory tasks such as the *1-2-AX task*, whereby the participant is asked to respond to a sequence A−X if they saw a 1 more recently than a 2 and to a different sequence B−Y if they saw a 2 more recently than a 1.

O'Reilly and Frank (2006) built on Frank et al. (2001) but noted that the earlier article had not answered the question of how the striatum learns which stimuli are relevant. They answered that question using a reward structure developed in a previous model of classical conditioning. The expanded model combining sequence working memory with reward was extended to simulate two other tasks. One of these tasks is called *store-ignore-recall*: storing a particular stimulus called S, maintain and ignoring S over a sequence of other stimuli, and then recalling S when another stimulus called R appears. The other is an analog of Baddeley's (1986) phonological loop, a task that requires encoding and reproducing a sequence of phoneme inputs.

Another sequence model, due to Taylor and Taylor (2000), includes basal ganglia-thalamocortical loops (Alexander, DeLong, & Strick, 1986), emphasizing roles for premotor, supplementary motor, and presupplementary motor cortex. In particular, Taylor and Taylor reproduced many of the monkey data of Tanji and Shima (1994) and Halsband, Matsuzaka, and Tanji (1994) on sequences whose elements were a push, pull, and turn.

The Taylor–Taylor sequence model is a variant of a more general model of the functions of basal ganglia-thalamocortical loops. The sequence data simulations are in two parts, one dealing with motor sequences guided by visual cues and the other dealing with sequences guided by internal cues. The activity patterns of various network nodes reproduced some of the experimentally found cell types. These cell types included initiators that responded to the auditory tone used to signal that the movement would be visually guided; memory cells that indicate which movement is to be made in response to an internal GO signal; premovement cells that are active in response to a GO signal if a specific movement is called for; movement cells that are active while the movement is being made; cells responsive to a specific order of movements; and cells active in the delay between two movements.

MODELS OF OVERCOMING HABITUAL RESPONSES

Prefrontal executive function is particularly needed when the context requires replacing a dominant or habitual response by a novel response. This capacity is tested in both normal and prefrontally damaged individuals in a variety of widely used clinical tasks. Two of these tests, the Wisconsin Card Sorting Test (WCST) and the Stroop Test, have been the subject of extensive computational modeling.

Models of the WCST

The WCST is used by clinical neuropsychologists to test the executive capacity of cognitive flexibility. The WCST task is to classify cards, which differ by three criteria: color, shape, or number of the designs on the face of the cards, with the experimenter changing the criterion used after the participant makes 10 consecutive correct classifications. Damage to the DLPFC impairs WCST performance, leading typically to perseveration on the first classification (e.g., Milner, 1964).

Since the late 1980s, several computational models have simulated typical performance of normal and DLPFC-damaged participants on the WCST. All these models include a node or set of nodes such that "lesions" of those nodes lead to perseverative responses. The earliest WCST models (Dehaene & Changeux, 1991; Kimberg & Farah, 1993; Leven & Levine, 1987; Levine & Prueitt, 1989) were built mainly on abstract neuro-cognitive capacities with loose assignment of modules to brain regions. More recent WCST models (e.g., Amos, 2000; Monchi & Taylor, 1998) include explicit analogs of loops connecting PFC, basal ganglia, and thalamus.

Leven and Levine (1987) and Levine and Prueitt (1989) simulated the card sorting data using a network based on adaptive resonance theory, whereby attribute and category nodes are linked in a hierarchical module (Carpenter & Grossberg, 1987). In their WCST network, attribute nodes code numbers, colors, and shapes, whereas category nodes code template cards with which input cards are classified. For each criterion (color, shape, number), there is a "habit node" and a "bias node." Habit nodes code how often classifications have been made, rightly or wrongly, on the basis of each attribute. Bias nodes additively combine habit node activities with reinforcement signals, then gate the excitatory signals from attributes to categories. A parameter measuring gain of reinforcement signals to bias nodes was varied. The network with high reinforcement gain acts like Milner's normal subjects. The network with low reinforcement gain acts like Milner's frontal patients, learning the first classification as quickly as the normal network but remaining stuck in that classification for the remaining trials.

Perseveration due to frontal damage can be overridden by attraction to novelty. Pribram (1961) kept adding new objects to a scene and each time placed a peanut under the new object, unobserved by a monkey. Then he waited for the monkey to choose which object to lift for food. On the first trial with a novel object present, normal monkeys tended to choose a previously rewarded object, whereas monkeys with OFC lesions chose the novel object immediately. Levine and Prueitt (1989) simulated the novelty data using a *dipole field* (Grossberg, 1980). In a dipole field, each sensory stimulus has an "on" and an "off" channel as in the gated dipole model of counterfactual comparison (Grossberg, 1972b), and each channel becomes transiently active when an input to the other channel is turned off. The gated dipole operates via transmitter habituation; hence, if the outputs of dipoles corresponding to different stimuli compete, novel stimuli that have not been habituated have an advantage over nonnovel stimuli.

Another WCST simulation was developed by Dehaene and Changeux (1991). Dehaene and Changeux's model was intended to represent more general cognitive and inferential capabilities than are manifested by this test. Their model includes representations of the input features, color, shape, and number; rule-coding clusters that represent the three different possible card classification rules; nodes entitled "current intention" that represent dynamic tendencies to follow each of those rules; a reward node; and an error cluster that became active when the network receives feedback that its classification is incorrect.

Dehaene and Changeux's model is based on primary neurophysiological considerations and not on previously established neural network models of simpler cognitive functions. Their memory nodes were found to have activity patterns somewhat like those of DLPFC neurons that remain active during delay tasks (Fuster, 1973), and their model had previously been used to model delayed response deficits with PFC lesions. For explaining responses to unexpected lack of a reward, they include a mechanism analogs to the transmitter depletion in a gated dipole but arguably more biologically realistic, stating that "fast synaptic depression may result from the desensitization of receptor molecules, mediated by their allosteric transitions in the postsynaptic membrane" (p. 75). Yet most parts of Dehaene and Changeux's network can be mapped fairly closely either into Levine and Prueitt's WCST model or their novelty preference model.

Kimberg and Farah (1993) simulated the WCST using a computational model that is not properly a neural network model but based on the artificial intelligence concept of *production system*. A production system combines instructions of the form "If condition X holds, THEN perform action Y" (Kimberg & Farah, 1993, p. 415) with working memory representations. These researchers showed that if prefrontal damage is interpreted as weakening of working memory associations, their production system model can account for results on the WCST, Stroop test, a motor sequencing task, and a context memory task.

Monchi and Taylor (1998) and Monchi, Taylor, and Dagher (2000) emphasized that WCST and other executive tasks activate basal ganglia and thalamus in addition to PFC. They modeled these tasks using analogs of basal ganglia-thalamocortical loops (Alexander et al., 1986), which the same research group used in models of sequence learning (Taylor & Taylor, 2000). The Monchi–Taylor models rely on inhibition and task-selective disinhibition of sensory and attribute representations, via striatal direct and indirect pathways. Monchi and his colleagues also modeled how task selection is disrupted in Parkinson's disease (Owen et al., 1992) and schizophrenia. Both of those conditions tend to involve poor performance on these working memory tasks; Parkinson's disease involves basal ganglia abnormalities (in particular, weakening of the direct pathway) and schizophrenia involves reduced PFC activity.

Another WCST model that was applied to Parkinson's disease and schizophrenia (and also to Huntington's disease) is that of Amos (2000).

Amos's model is clinically focused and anatomically simplified in comparison with Monchi et al.'s: it includes PFC, basal ganglia, and thalamus but not connections from thalamus back to PFC. However, Amos's model makes more accurate predictions about types of error that different patient groups will show on the WCST. Specifically, it predicts that schizophrenics, such as people with DLPFC lesions, will show perseverative errors, classifying cards using rules that were previously correct. Parkinson's and Huntington's patients, on the other hand, will show more random errors because basal ganglia damage will prevent them from selecting responses on the basis of reward.

Clinical concerns were also paramount in the WCST model of Bishara et al. (2010), a cognitive-process model whose nodes do not correspond to brain regions. Their goal was predictability at the level of individuals as well as groups. Their model used four parameters representing decision consistency, attentional focus, sensitivity to reward, and sensitivity to punishment. They found that performance of participants who are substance dependent, on either alcohol or stimulants, could be modeled either by lowered decision consistency or lowered sensitivity to punishment. Another cognitive-process WCST model, by Kaplan, Şengör, Gürvit, Genç, and Güzelis (2006), captured two possible effects of PFC damage: perseveration, associated with loss of executive function due to DLPFC damage; and distractibility, associated with loss of response inhibition due to OFC damage.

All these WCST models have different emphases: some are designed mainly to capture functional properties, others focus on realistic anatomy, and still others are intended to reproduce clinical lesion data. Hence none of these models is yet definitive or generally accepted. While some of the models also reproduce data other than the WCST on cognitive effects of prefrontal damage, none is yet embedded in a comprehensive model of prefrontal executive function.

Models of the Stroop Test

Cohen and Servan-Schreiber (1992), using a back propagation network (Rumelhart & McClelland, 1986), simulated three cognitive tasks that require attention to the current context. One of these was the Stroop Test— previously modeled in Cohen, Dunbar, and McClelland (1990) without reference to frontal involvement—whereby the subject sees the word for a color printed in ink of either the same or a different color, and must state the *color of the ink*. The automatic response, which needs to be inhibited, is to read the word. Hence, reaction time is slower if ink color and word do not match; for example, if the word "red" is written in green ink. People with DLPFC damage, and many schizophrenics, have an even slower reaction time than normals under these incongruent conditions. Cohen and Servan-Schreiber also simulated a *continuous performance* task, whereby subjects were instructed to respond to a target pattern while receiving a steady stream of other stimuli, and a lexical disambiguation task. All these tasks required the subject to perform a nondominant but contextually appropriate response.

Cohen and Servan-Schreiber (1992) simulated deficits of schizophrenics on all three tasks, attributing these deficits to reduced dopamine input to DLPFC. Their network includes a node that influences gains in two competing neural pathways (e.g., in the Stroop test, pathways coding words and colors) and that is assumed to decrease in activity with either DLPFC damage or schizophrenia. Their learning algorithm is anatomically unrealistic, yet they captured important functional relationships for a wide class of tasks involving PFC executive function.

The Stroop model of Kaplan, Şengör, Gürvit, and Güzelis (2007) added recent knowledge about executive brain regions to the models of Cohen and his colleagues. Kaplan et al. did not include explicit brain anatomy but built their model around functional modules corresponding to these roles: sensory and motor networks along with modules for word reading; color naming; habitual responses; directing of attention; inhibition; and error detection. A more biologically realistic extension of Cohen et al. (1990) is due to Herd, Banich, and O'Reilly (2006). Their model includes abstract representations of colors and words in addition to the task and rule representations of the previous model. The refined model explains some previously puzzling functional magnetic resonance imaging (fMRI) data, such as increased activity in regions processing information that the task requires ignoring.

MODELS OF GENERAL COGNITIVE CONTROL

A few researchers have built models that link working memory, attention, and other cognitive control functions. These models show how brain networks are involved in monitoring the environment and task requirements.

Rougier, Noelle, Braver, Cohen, and O'Reilly (2005) noted that some previous models (including those of Cohen et al., 1990 and Dehaene & Changeux, 1991) had posited PFC rule representations that influence processing in the posterior cortex, but had not explained how these rule representations might develop over time. Rougier et al. explained rule formation using a network that includes PFC modulation of posterior cortex. The PFC area incorporates the two complementary functions of maintaining neural activity patterns over time and rapidly updating new representations (cf. Frank et al., 2001). Updating is implemented by an adaptive gating mechanism that mimics functions of the basal ganglia and midbrain dopaminergic nuclei involved in reinforcement learning (Montague, Dayan, & Sejnowski, 1996). The network including PFC, but not the posterior part alone, can extract from task-based training any rule based on selection of one of the features of a stimulus as the most important.

Related models (Brown, Reynolds, & Braver, 2007; Herd et al., 2014) have simulated the process of switching between tasks. The Brown et al. model focuses on cognitive data involving multiple tasks with several stimulus dimensions. The data dealt with costs in reaction time due to several sources: switching tasks, changing desired responses on the same task, and presenting incongruent stimuli. One example of incongruency occurs when "a feature of the target stimulus is associated with an incompatible response according to the currently irrelevant task" (Brown et al., 2007, p. 40). The network designed to simulate these data includes a task-switching subnetwork and a supervisory control system. The network regions are not explicitly assigned to brain regions but are inspired by known regional functions such as the ACC's role in conflict monitoring.

The task-switching model of Herd et al. (2014) is based on models of PFC—basal ganglia interactions in working memory (Frank et al., 2001; O'Reilly & Frank, 2006) and includes individual differences in task-switching ability. Herd et al. reviewed evidence that task-switching ability is separate from, and sometimes even negatively correlated with, other executive functions such as updating and response inhibition. Their model includes a PFC module influencing parietal cortex, and executive function strength relates to strengths of both PFC influence on parietal areas and recurrent connections within PFC. Yet these same recurrent connections can lead to "stickiness" that interferes with task switching. Stickiness can also come from persistence of basal ganglia "go" signals from previous tasks.

More sophisticated extensions of these task control models are found in Collins and Frank (2013) and Ranti, Chatham, and Badre (2015), which extend prefrontal—basal ganglia interactions to multiple hierarchical levels. These authors base their theory on results showing that the PFC is arranged hierarchically, with cognitive processing tending to become more abstract as one moves further forward in the frontal lobe. The PFC region at each level of abstraction is part of a loop that includes a corresponding region of striatum.

The Collins—Frank model is designed to select abstract task sets in response to arbitrary cues and then select actions in response to stimuli once the rule is in effect. Task sets are encoded in PFC. Candidate actions are encoded in "stripes" within premotor cortex, which compete via lateral inhibition. Sensory stimuli are encoded in parietal cortex. As in previous working memory models (e.g., O'Reilly & Frank, 2006), the basal ganglia perform the gating function of selectively inhibiting or disinhibiting action stripes and task sets. Sensory projections to basal ganglia are plastic, with dopamine involved in reinforcement learning. Characteristic errors on complex discrimination tasks are obtained by weakening PFC-to-basal-ganglia connections more than parietal-to-basal-ganglia connections.

Ranti et al. (2015) made minor changes in the Collins—Frank model and applied it to learning a hierarchy of rules. They also did experiments involving visual stimuli that varied along seven dimensions at different levels of abstraction. Their data were reproduced by their network, which exerts parallel cognitive control at all levels by means of multiple interconnected prefrontal−basal-ganglia loops. In the model the highest (most abstract) level is more likely than the others to be engaged first, but only slightly more: the parallel control is paramount.

GENERAL DISCUSSION

The enterprise of modeling high-level cognitive functions such as executive function and decision making is still in its early stages. Yet computational models of lower-level neural processes such as visual pattern perception, motor control, and Pavlovian conditioning have already achieved more success and predictive value, which augurs well for the future of models of the higher-level processes.

Sophisticated theoretical models reproduce data and sometimes lead to novel predictions at both the behavioral and brain imaging levels. Yet as the modeling field evolves, it can increasingly be seen not as a satellite to experimental cognitive neuroscience but as a research program with a life of its own. Theoretical cognitive neuroscience can become an equal partner with the experimental work, just as theoretical physics is now established as an equal partner with experimental physics.

Computational modeling of brain−behavior relationships draws on data from a wide range of sources. These sources include human brain imaging studies (e.g., fMRI, positron emission tomography, electroencephalography, and near-infra red spectroscopy); human patient data; human and animal behavioral studies; animal single-cell recording; and animal lesion studies. The theory helps to tie together data from the different sources.

Modeling can also tie together data from different branches of psychology. For example, a thought experiment in Levine (2000, Chapter 1) asks what processes are needed to decide whether a printed letter of the alphabet should be classified as E or F. It concludes that this depends on combining associative learning at synapses with competition via lateral inhibition. Yet combining association and competition is also required for attentional aspects of Pavlovian conditioning, such as a bell that has been paired with food being attended more than competing stimuli. Cognitive psychologists and behaviorists have often been rivals, but the thought experiment suggests common building blocks between a "cognitive" process (categorization) and a "behavioral" process (conditioning). Within cognitive psychology, models can find common bases for processes sometimes regarded as disparate; note connections between working memory and visual perception in Grossberg and Pearson (2008) and between cognitive control and attention in Herd et al. (2014).

Models of complex cognitive processes rely on repeated use of a "toolkit" of organizing principles. As discussed in the thought experiment of Levine (2000), two of those principles are associative learning (via synaptic plasticity) and competition (via lateral inhibition). Other network organizing principles mentioned in this chapter include opponent processing, reward prediction error, and interlevel resonance. But repeated use of the same principles does not mean that "one size fits all": different cognitive and behavioral requirements often entail different neural architectures.

Sometimes the results of a computational model suggest a novel insight about cognitive processes. An example is discussed in Levine (2011). In the Levine and Prueitt (1989) model of the WCST, when the rule changes from color to shape, color bias gradually decreases while shape bias increases. But in the Milner (1964) version of the test, some cards match a template card on both color and shape. When the simulated participant saw one of those cards and was rewarded for correctly placing it with the shape-matched template, shape bias increased but so did color bias. Hence, ambiguous inputs slowed the change from an obsolete rule to the appropriate rule.

As other chapters of this book indicate, advances in brain imaging since about 2000 have led to an increasing consensus about executive-related functions of specific brain regions such as orbital, dorsolateral, and ventrolateral PFC, ACC, dorsal and ventral striatum, GPi, and posterior parietal cortex. This consensus is reflected in the most recent computational models of these regions and executive processes. Yet the commonest method for studying these functions, fMRI, is a blunt instrument: what it means exactly for a brain region to show greater activity in one task condition than another is controversial. Many studies in the last 5 years have dealt with task-varying connectivity *between* regions, a methodological advance whose full benefits are yet to come.

Moreover, there is no consensus yet on what the "nodes" or "units" in a typical computational model correspond to in the brain. Nodes are generally thought of not as single neurons but as collections of thousands of neurons with some kind of functional boundaries, yet many modelers verify their theories by showing patterns of node activity across time that match some neuronal firing patterns. Some models use actual neuronal spikes whereas others use average spiking frequency over a collection of neurons: modelers disagree on how useful spiking is in understanding cognitive behavior.

Neuro-computational modeling of human executive and decision-making functions is high-risk. But its rewards are likely to be a substantial increase in understanding how these functions work in the brain. Ultimately, this should increase our knowledge about what kinds of interventions, interpersonal as well as pharmaceutical, and in groups and organizations as well as individual lives, can enhance executive performance.

REFERENCES

Alexander, G. E., & Crutcher, M. D. (1990). Functional architecture of basal ganglia circuits: Neural substrates of parallel processing. *Trends in Neurosciences, 13*, 266–271.

Alexander, G. E., DeLong, M. R., & Strick, P. F. (1986). Parallel organization of functionally segregated circuits linking basal ganglia and cortex. *Annual Review of Neuroscience, 9*, 357–381.

Allais, M. (1953). Le comportement de l'homme rationnel devant le risque: Critique des postulats et axioms de l'École Américaine. *Econometrica, 21*, 503–546.

AlQaudi, B., Levine, D. S., & Lewis, F. L. (2015). Neural network model of decisions on the Asian disease problem. *Proceedings of International Joint Conference on Neural Networks, 2015*, 1333–1340.

Averbeck, B. B., Chafee, M. V., Crowe, D. A., & Georgopoulos, A. P. (2003). Neural activity in prefrontal cortex during copying geometrical shapes. I. Single cell studies. *Experimental Brain Research, 150*, 127–141.

Averbeck, B. B., Crowe, D. A., Chafee, M. V., & Georgopoulos, A. P. (2003). Neural activity in macaque prefrontal cortex during copying geometrical shapes. II. Decoding shape segments from neural ensembles. *Experimental Brain Research, 150*, 142–153.

Baddeley, A. D. (1986). *Working memory.* London: Oxford University Press.

Barron, G., & Erev, I. (2003). Small feedback-based decisions and their limited correspondence to description-based decisions. *Journal of Behavioral Decision Making, 16*, 215–233.

Bechara, A., Damasio, A. R., Damasio, H., & Anderson, S. W. (1994). Insensitivity to future consequences following damage to human prefrontal cortex. *Cognition, 50*, 7–15.

Bishara, A. J., Kruschke, J. K., Stout, J. C., Bechara, A., McCabe, D. P., & Busemeyer, J. R. (2010). Sequential learning models for the Wisconsin card sort task: Assessing processes in substance dependent individuals. *Journal of Mathematical Psychology, 54*, 5–13.

Bohland, J. W., Bullock, D., & Guenther, F. H. (2010). Neural representations and mechanisms for the performance of simple speech sequences. *Journal of Cognitive Neuroscience, 22*, 1504–1529.

Botvinick, M. M., & Plaut, D. C. (2006). Short-term memory for serial order: A recurrent neural network model. *Psychological Review, 113*, 201–233.

Brown, J. W., Reynolds, J. R., & Braver, T. S. (2007). A computational neural model of fractionated conflict-control mechanisms in task-switching. *Cognitive Psychology, 55*, 37–85.

Busemeyer, J. R., Jessup, R. K., Johnson, J. G., & Townsend, J. T. (2006). Building bridges between neural models and complex decision making behavior. *Neural Networks, 19*, 1047–1058.

Busemeyer, J. R., & Townsend, J. T. (1993). Decision field theory: A dynamic cognitive approach to decision making in an uncertain environment. *Psychological Review, 100*, 432–459.

Carpenter, G. A., & Grossberg, S. (1987). A massively parallel architecture for a self-organizing neural pattern recognition machine. *Computer Vision, Graphics, and Image Processing, 37*, 54–115.

Chevalier, G., & Deniau, J. M. (1990). Disinhibition as a basic process in the expression of striatal functions. *Trends in Neurosciences, 13*, 277–280.

Cohen, J. D., Dunbar, K., & McClelland, J. L. (1990). On the control of automatic processes: A parallel distributed processing account of the Stroop effect. *Psychological Review, 97*, 332–361.

Cohen, J. D., & Servan-Schreiber, D. (1992). Context, cortex and dopamine: A connectionist approach to behavior and biology in schizophrenia. *Psychological Review, 99*, 45–77.

Collins, A. G. E., & Frank, M. J. (2013). Cognitive control over learning: Creating, clustering, and generalizing task-set structure. *Psychological Review*, *120*, 190−229. Available from http://dx.doi.org/10.1037/a0030852.

Damasio, A. R. (1994). *Descartes' error: Emotion, reason, and the human brain*. New York: Grosset/Putnam.

Daw, N. D., Kakade, S., & Dayan, P. (2002). Opponent interactions between serotonin and dopamine. *Neural Networks*, *15*, 603−616.

Dehaene, S., & Changeux, J.-P. (1991). The Wisconsin card sorting test: Theoretical analysis and modeling in a neural network. *Cerebral Cortex*, *1*, 62−79.

Epstein, S. (1994). Integration of the cognitive and psychodynamic unconscious. *American Psychologist*, *49*, 709−724.

Frank, M. J., & Claus, E. D. (2006). Anatomy of a decision: Striato-orbitofrontal interactions in reinforcement learning, decision making, and reversal. *Psychological Review*, *113*, 300−326.

Fuster, J. M. (1973). Unit activity in prefrontal cortex during delayed-response performance: Neuronal correlates of transient memory. *Journal of Neurophysiology*, *36*, 61−78.

Grossberg, S. (1972a). A neural theory of punishment and avoidance. I. Qualitative theory. *Mathematical Biosciences*, *15*, 39−67.

Grossberg, S. (1972b). A neural theory of punishment and avoidance. II. Quantitative theory. *Mathematical Biosciences*, *15*, 253−285.

Grossberg, S. (1980). How does a brain build a cognitive code? *Psychological Review*, *87*, 1−51.

Grossberg, S. (2006). *My interests and theoretical method*. http://www.cns.bu.edu/Profiles/Grossberg/GrossbergInterests.pdf.

Grossberg, S., & Gutowski, W. (1987). Neural dynamics of decision making under risk: Affective balance and cognitive-emotional interactions. *Psychological Review*, *94*, 300−318.

Grossberg, S., & Pearson, L. R. (2008). Laminar cortical dynamics of cognitive and motor working memory, sequence learning and performance: Toward a unified theory of how the cerebral cortex works. *Psychological Review*, *115*, 677−732. Available from http://dx.doi.org/10.1037/a0012618.

Halsband, U., Matsuzaka, Y., & Tanji, J. (1994). Neuronal activity in the primate supplementary, pre-supplementary and premotor cortex during externally and internally instructed sequential movements. *Neuroscience Research*, *20*, 149−155.

Herd, S. A., Banich, M. T., & O'Reilly, R. C. (2006). Neural mechanisms of cognitive control: An integrative model of Stroop task performance and fMRI data. *Journal of Cognitive Neuroscience*, *18*, 22−32.

Herd, S. A., O'Reilly, R. C., Hazy, T. E., Chatham, C. H., Brant, A. M., & Friedman, N. P. (2014). A neural network model of individual differences in task switching abilities. *Neuropsychologia*, *62*, 375−389.

Kahneman, D. (2011). *Thinking fast and slow*. New York: Farrar, Straus, and Giroux.

Kahneman, D., & Tversky, A. (1979). Prospect theory: An analysis of decision under risk. *Econometrica*, *47*, 263−291.

Kaplan, G. G., Şengör, N. S., Gürvit, H., Genç, İ., & Güzelis, C. (2006). A composite neural network model for perseveration and distractibility in the Wisconsin card sorting test. *Neural Networks*, *19*, 375−387.

Kaplan, G. G., Şengör, N. S., Gürvit, H., & Güzelis, C. (2007). Modelling the Stroop effect: A connectionist approach. *Neurocomputing*, *70*, 1414−1423.

Kimberg, D. Y., & Farah, M. J. (1993). A unified account of cognitive impairments following frontal lobe damage: The role of working memory in complex, organized behavior. *Journal of Experimental Psychology: General, 122,* 411–428.

Klapp, S. T. (1995). Motor response programming during simple and choice-reaction time—The role of practice. *Journal of Experimental Psychology—Human Perception and Performance, 21,* 1015–1027.

Lashley, K. S. (1951). The problem of serial order in behavior. In L. A. Jeffress (Ed.), *Cerebral mechanisms in behavior* (pp. 112–136). New York: Wiley.

Leven, S. J., & Levine, D. S. (1987). *Effects of reinforcement on knowledge retrieval and evaluation. IEEE first international conference on neural networks* (Vol. II, pp. 269–279). San Diego, CA: IEEE/ICNN.

Levine, D. S. (1983). Neural population modeling and psychology: A review. *Mathematical Biosciences, 66,* 1–86.

Levine, D. S. (1999). What are neural networks, and what can they contribute to psychology? *Psychline, 3*(2), 23–30.

Levine, D. S. (2000). *Introduction to neural and cognitive modeling* (2nd ed., Third edition with Taylor & Francis anticipated in 2017). Mahwah, NJ: Lawrence Erlbaum Associates.

Levine, D. S. (July 2011). The pitfalls of doing the right thing for the wrong reason. *Proceedings of International Joint Conference on Neural Networks, 2011,* 886–891.

Levine, D. S. (2012). Neural dynamics of affect, gist, probability, and choice. *Cognitive Systems Research, 15–16,* 57–72. Available from http://dx.doi.org/10.1016/j.cogsys.2011.07.002.

Levine, D.S. (2016). Toward a neuro-developmental theory of decision attribute weighting. To appear in *International joint conference on neural networks 2016.*

Levine, D. S., & Prueitt, P. S. (1989). Modeling some effects of frontal lobe damage: Novelty and perseveration. *Neural Networks, 2,* 103–116.

Litt, A., Eliasmith, C., & Thagard, P. (2008). Neural affective decision theory: Choices, brains, and emotions. *Cognitive Systems Research, 9,* 252–273.

Meeter, M., Jehee, J., & Murre, J. (2007). Neural models that convince: Model hierarchies and other strategies to bridge the gap between behavior and the brain. *Philosophical Psychology, 20,* 749–772.

Mellers, B. A., Schwartz, A., Ho, K., & Ritov, I. (1997). Decision affect theory: Emotional reactions to the outcomes of risky options. *Psychological Science, 8,* 423–429.

Menon, V., & Uddin, L. Q. (2010). Saliency, switching, attention, and control: A network model of insula function. *Brain Structure and Function, 214,* 655–667.

Monchi, O., & Taylor, J. G. (1998). A hard wired model of coupled frontal working memories for various tasks. *Information Sciences Journal, 113,* 221–243.

Monchi, O., Taylor, J. G., & Dagher, A. (2000). A neural model of working memory processes in normal subjects, Parkinson's disease and schizophrenia for fMRI design and predictions. *Neural Networks, 13,* 953–973.

Montague, P. R., Dayan, P., & Sejnowski, T. J. (1996). A framework for mesencephalic dopamine systems based on predictive Hebbian learning. *Journal of Neuroscience, 16,* 1936–1947.

Mukherjee, K. (2010). A dual system model of preferences under risk. *Psychological Review, 177,* 243–255.

Norman, D. A., & Shallice, T. (1986). Attention to action: Willed and automatic control of behaviorIn R. J. Davidson, G. E. Schwartz, & D. Shapiro (Eds.), *Consciousness and self-regulation* (Vol. 4, pp. 1–18). New York: Plenum Press.

Owen, A. M., James, M., Leigh, P. N., Summers, B. A., Marsden, C. D., Quinn, N. P., & Robbins, T. W. (1992). Fronto-striatal cognitive deficits at different stages of Parkinson's disease. *Brain, 115,* 1727–1751.

Page, M., & Norris, D. (1998). The primacy model: A new model of immediate serial recall. *Psychological Review, 105,* 761−781.

Pribram, K. H. (1961). A further experimental analysis of the behavioral deficit that follows injury to the primate frontal cortex. *Journal of Experimental Neurology, 3,* 432−466.

Ranti, C., Chatham, C. H., & Badre, D. (2015). Parallel temporal dynamics in hierarchical cognitive control. *Cognition, 142,* 205−229.

Reyna, V. F., & Brainerd, C. J. (1991). Fuzzy-trace theory and framing effects in choice: Gist extraction, truncation, and conversion. *Journal of Behavioral Decision Making, 4,* 249−262. Available from http://dx.doi.org/10.1002/bdm.3960040403.

Reyna, V. F., & Brainerd, C. J. (2008). Numeracy, ratio bias, and denominator neglect in judgments of risk and probability. *Learning and Individual Differences, 18,* 89−107.

Rhodes, B.J. (2000). Learning-driven changes in the temporal characteristics of serial movement performance: A model based on cortico-cerebellar cooperation. Unpublished Ph.D. dissertation, Boston University.

Rhodes, B. J., Bullock, D., Verwey, W. B., Averbeck, B. B., & Page, M. P. A. (2004). Learning and production of movement sequences: Behavioral, neurophysiological, and modeling perspectives. *Human Movement Science, 23,* 699−746.

Roe, R. M., Busemeyer, J. R., & Townsend, J. T. (2001). Multi-alternative decision field theory: A dynamic connectionist model of decision-making. *Psychological Review, 108,* 370−392.

Rougier, N. P., Noelle, D. C., Braver, T. S., Cohen, J. D., & O'Reilly, R. C. (2005). Prefrontal cortex and flexible cognitive control: Rules without symbols. *Proceedings of the National Academy of Sciences USA, 102,* 7338−7343.

Rumelhart, D. E., & McClelland, J. L. (Eds.), (1986). *Parallel distributed processing* (Vols. 1 and 2). Cambridge, MA: MIT Press.

Schultz, W., Apicella, P., & Ljungberg, T. (1993). Responses of monkey dopamine neurons to reward and conditioned stimuli during successive steps of learning a delayed response task. *Journal of Neuroscience, 13,* 900−913.

Seeley, W. W., Menon, V., Schatzberg, A. F., Keller, J., Glover, G. H., Kenna, H., & Greicius, M. D. (2007). Dissociable intrinsic connectivity networks for salience processing and executive control. *Journal of Neuroscience, 27,* 2349−2365.

Sutton, R. S., & Barto, A. G. (1998). *Reinforcement learning: An introduction.* Cambridge, MA: MIT Press.

Tanji, J., & Shima, K. (1994). Role for supplementary motor area cells in planning several movements ahead. *Nature, 371,* 413−416.

Taylor, N. R., & Taylor, J. G. (2000). Hard-wired models of working memory and temporal sequence storage and generation. *Neural Networks, 13,* 201−224.

Tversky, A., & Kahneman, D. (1981). The framing of decisions and the rationality of choice. *Science, 211,* 453−458.

Usher, M., & McClelland, J. L. (2004). Loss aversion and inhibition in dynamical models of multialternative choice. *Psychological Review, 111,* 757−769.

Verwey, W. B. (1996). Buffer loading and chunking in sequential keypressing. *Journal of Experimental Psychology: Human Perception and Performance, 22,* 544−562.

Yechiam, E., & Busemeyer, J. R. (2005). Comparison of basic assumptions embedded in learning models for experience-based decision making. *Psychonomic Bulletin and Review, 12,* 387−402.

Yechiam, E., Stout, J. C., Busemeyer, J. R., Rock, S. L., & Finn, P. P. (2005). Individual differences in the response to forgone payoffs: An examination of high functioning drug abusers. *Journal of Behavioral Decision Making, 18,* 97−100. Available from http://dx.doi.org/10.1002/bdm.487.

Chapter 6

Crucial Role of the Prefrontal Cortex in Conscious Perception

Seth Lew[1] and Hakwan Lau[1,2]

[1]Psychology Department, University of California Los Angeles, Los Angeles, CA, United States,
[2]Brain Research Institute, University of California Los Angeles, Los Angeles, CA, United States

EARLY NEUROIMAGING EVIDENCE OF PREFRONTAL CORTEX'S INVOLVEMENT IN CONSCIOUS PERCEPTION

Functional magnetic resonance imaging (fMRI) studies since the late 1990s presented findings that areas in the prefrontal cortex (PFC) are associated with conscious perception (Dehaene & Naccache, 2001; Dehaene, Changeux, Naccache, Sackur, & Sergent, 2006; Lumer & Rees, 1999; Rees, Kreiman, & Koch, 2002). For example, one of the earlier studies by Lumer and Rees (1999) identified activity in the extrastriate cortex that correlated with perceptual switching in binocular rivalry and PFC activity that covaried with the activation of the extrastriate cortex. A review (Rees et al., 2002) pooled results from five different neuroimaging studies that identified neural correlates of consciousness and found an overlap of activity in the dorsolateral prefrontal cortex (DLPFC). Dehaene et al. (2006) further reasoned that the involvement of PFC is selective to conscious versus un- or preconscious perception. Specifically, they posited that conscious awareness requires both bottom-up stimulus processing and top-down attention in areas of higher cognition, such as the PFC (Dehaene & Naccache, 2001), a view that we will discuss at the end of this chapter.

In this chapter, we evaluate the status of the claim that PFC is critically involved in conscious perception.

THE "NO-REPORT" ARGUMENT AGAINST PFC'S ROLE IN CONSCIOUSNESS

One argument against PFC's association with consciousness is that the activation of PFC may reflect processes used for self-report instead of conscious perception. Researchers usually make use of participants' self-report

Executive Functions in Health and Disease. DOI: http://dx.doi.org/10.1016/B978-0-12-803676-1.00006-4

to assess their conscious experience of the presented stimuli. These reports are crucial to studies searching for differences in neural activity that track changes in perceptual states while the stimulus is being held constant (Ress, Backus, & Heeger, 2000; Super, Spekreijse, & Lamme, 2001; Tong, Meng, & Blake, 2006). The idea is that if a stimulus remains constant but a person's perceptual experience of it has changed, then any difference in the person's neural activities must be correlated with the difference in their conscious experience. In that way, the parts of the brain that show different levels of activity when a person has different conscious experiences of the same stimulus can be understood as neural correlates of consciousness.

However, some authors have recently argued that the self-report itself can be a confounding factor (Tsuchiya, Wilke, Frässle, & Lamme, 2015). The need to self-report requires employment of neural areas correlated with paying attention to the upcoming stimulus, self-monitoring after sensing the stimulus, accessing the sensory data, and generating and delivering a report, which are processes conceptually distinct from the phenomenon of conscious perception itself. Therefore, the brain areas reported to be neural correlates of consciousness could have wrongly included activity due to demands of self-report rather than conscious perception per se.

To remove confounds associated with self-report, "no-report" paradigms have been developed and used as alternatives to those that require self-report (Tse, Martinez-Conde, Schlegel, & Macknik, 2005). As the name suggests, no-report paradigms remove the reliance on self-report from the participants to determine their perceptual state. Instead, researchers use neural recordings or physiological changes of the participant to infer their perceptual experience. For example, optokinetic nystagmus (i.e., eye movement to follow a moving object while the head remains stationary) and pupil size were used to accurately verify perceptual switching in binocular rivalry in the absence of self-report (Frässle, Sommer, Jansen, Naber, & Einhäuser, 2014). Neural correlates found in no-report paradigms are expected to be more refined than those from report-dependent paradigms because the regions of the brain that activates solely for aspects of self-report would be truncated from the results.

Interestingly, findings from no-report paradigms have revealed consistent activity in the striate and extrastriate cortex but none in the PFC or the parietal cortex that correlated with consciousness (Brascamp, Blake, & Knapen, 2015; Frässle et al., 2014; Kouider, Dehaene, Jobert, & Le Bihan, 2007; Tse et al., 2005). For instance, Tse et al. (2005) took advantage of the same perceptual content of monoptic and dichoptic visual masking to narrow down the areas that might be correlated to consciousness. In monoptic visual masking, the visual stimulus and mask were presented to both eyes, whereas in dichoptic masking, the visual stimulus was presented to one eye and the mask to the other eye. The masked pattern occupied most of the screen but was unattended to by the participant due to their focus on a fixation task. Although there was no need for the participants to report on the masked pattern, it is unlikely that they did not consciously see the pattern, considering it spanned almost the entire screen. The authors found that with monoptic visual masking, visibility of the pattern was correlated with activation throughout the visual pathway. In dichoptic masking, there was only activation beyond V2. Because the perceptual experience between monoptic and dichoptic masking did not change, they reasoned that these results narrowed down the potential brain regions responsible for conscious perception to only the regions activated in both masking conditions: occipital retinotopic areas beyond V2.

A similar masking study using words (Kouider et al., 2007) broadened the scope of the results from Tse et al. (2005). The participants of the study were instructed to perform a semantic decision task on words shown on a screen. Just before the target word was shown, a different priming word was flashed very briefly. Similar to Tse's study, the prime was irrelevant to the task and was unattended to by the participants. Whether they could consciously see the priming word was determined by if it was masked by a string of letters immediately after it was shown. In the subliminal masking condition, the string of letters made the priming word invisible, whereas in the supraliminal masking condition, the absence of the string of letters made the prime visible, although still unattended to by the participants. FMRI results showed that visibility of the prime word was correlated with activity only in occipital and temporal cortices. Extensive repetition enhancement and suppression (i.e., increase or decrease in neural activity) in frontal and parietal cortices suggested that these areas are responsible for conscious access and information processing rather than conscious perception.

Frässle et al. (2014) used the aforementioned correlation of optokinetic nystagmus and pupil size with perceptual switch in binocular rivalry to conduct a study comparing active brain regions in a report-dependent paradigm versus a no-report paradigm. The authors first instructed the participants to report switches in percept by holding down and switching between two buttons. They also kept track of the participants' eye movements and pupil size to get an objective time point of the switch and continuous data of the dominance of the percept at any given time determined by the values of the physical measures. The fMRI data revealed a significant increase of activity in occipital, parietal, and frontal regions that correlated with subjective and objective perceptual switches in active report trials. When participants were no longer asked to respond on buttons, there was a similar activation pattern across the occipital and parietal regions, but there was no longer any significant activity in the frontal region that correlated with rivalry switching. Bilateral activity in the middle frontal gyrus was entirely eliminated. The authors interpreted this negative finding to mean that frontal cortex is not involved in switches in perceptual experience itself but rather in self-monitoring for reporting any such switches.

Another no-report binocular rivalry paradigm yielded negative results (Brascamp et al., 2015). The paradigm incorporated a method of binocular rivalry in which the viewer sees moving dots with each eye that move around randomly in such a way that the viewer cannot know if and when a perceptual switch occurs. To make the changes noticeable, the experimenters simply colored the dots differently in each eye. When viewers could determine when the percepts were changing due to the difference in color of the dots, activity in the PFC, along with other areas of the frontal cortex such as the frontal eye fields, and occipital and parietal cortices was correlated with perceptual switches. However, when the viewers could not know about and therefore could not report perceptual changes, there was no such correlated activity in the frontal cortex. Therefore, the authors reasoned that activity in the frontal cortex was not involved with changes in conscious perception.

RESPONSES TO THE NO-REPORT ARGUMENT

Not being able to find any positive results in PFC after getting rid of subjective report could mean that those areas were correlated with self-report, not consciousness per se. However, while such interpretation of negative findings is reasonable and popular, negative findings are limited in nature, especially when there are clear positive findings from other studies using no-report paradigms. For example, in Lumer and Rees (1999), the pioneering study that revealed a correlation between PFC activity and subjective visual perception, the subjects did not make any reports about perceptual switches during the viewing condition. Yet, they found prefrontal involvement in the absence of self-report that consistently covaried with activity in the extrastriate cortex.

Another evidence for PFC's association with consciousness comes from a study that successfully decoded unattended stimuli from neurons in the PFC (Mante, Sussillo, Shenoy, & Newsome, 2013). The study consisted of taking single- and multiunit recordings from monkeys trained to saccade to a visual target based on either the color or the direction of motion of the majority of moving dots on a display. The color of the fixation cue determined which of the two features—direction of movement or color—the monkeys needed to discriminate. Interestingly, even with no task demand to respond to one of the features, neuronal activity in the frontal eye field could be decoded to extract information about the task-irrelevant feature. Information that was not required to be discriminated on a particular block of trials was also found to be encoded in the PFC, undermining the interpretation of PFC's activity in human conscious perception studies to be reflective of only the self-reports.

Positive activity was revealed when electrocorticogram (ECoG) measurements on surgical epileptics during a no-report visual memory task displayed a late "glow" of late activity in the PFC (Noy et al., 2015). The task required the subjects to click whenever they see an image flash twice in a row on a laptop screen. Even when there was no need to respond because the consecutive images were different, there was activity in the PFC that overlapped in time with activation of higher order visual areas, similar to Lumer's results. Rather than seeing this as evidence of PFC's involvement in conscious perception, the authors interpreted the observed activity in the PFC to be associated with choosing not to make any motor responses. Similar to how making a motor response might need to recruit areas of the PFC, the need to refrain from doing so might have weakly activated the same areas for planning and decision-making. While this is a possible interpretation, it does not rule out the possibility that the PFC activity they found may simply reflect conscious perception even when no explicit response was required. The study by Mante et al. (2013) supports this latter interpretation.

These positive results from no-report paradigms hint that there is an alternative explanation to the other negative findings that are currently seen as evidence against PFC's involvement in consciousness. One such explanation is that the activity in the PFC correlated with conscious perception went unnoticed, perhaps because they are only weakly expressed in some imaging modalities when reporting demand or attention is removed. One way to maximize the sensitivity for the frontal regions in imaging studies would be to target a priori functionally defined regions of interest for each individual. The alternative method of spatially morphing each individual's brain to a normalized template based on anatomical landmarks could introduce errors from potential distortions and mismatches of brain regions. Such errors could lead to a misinterpretation of activity in a certain region of an individual's brain as an activity in a different region in the transformed brain.

Incorporating multivoxel pattern analysis (MVPA), which has been shown to be able to detect and decode information from "silent" sustained activity in the PFC (Stokes, 2015), could also boost the visibility of PFC activity. Stokes found that there is dynamic activity in the PFC that may be hidden from detection methods that measure increases in activity at the population level, such as the fMRI BOLD signals. Recent advancements in MVPA techniques that measure response patterns between voxels instead of their average activity have enabled detection of maintained activity otherwise unrecognizable by fMRI alone. The view that conventional fMRI may just lack sensitivity is also compatible with the fact that Noy et al. (2015) was able to detect activity in the PFC by utilizing ECoG, a more sensitive, intracranial method of measuring brain activity.

THE ARGUMENT BASED ON LESION STUDIES

It has long been argued that PFC lesions reveal no resulting impairment of conscious perception (Pollen, 1995). Even in 1940s and 1950s, bilateral frontal lobectomy, prefrontal topectomy, and lobotomy on humans have left consciousness intact, despite other consequential intellectual and behavioral impairments (Brickner, 1952; Fullton, 1949; Hebb & Penfield, 1940; Mettler, 1949). Although such statements are not the results of modern psychological scrutiny, it seems safe to say from their accounts that the patients were, at the very least, conscious.

More recent cases of patients with PFC damage tell a similar story. In a case study (Markowitsch & Kessler, 2000) of a 27-year-old woman with widespread degeneration in her PFC, the woman performed poorly on tests that measure prefrontal abilities but normally or even superiorly on other memory tests. Her consciousness was left unimpaired despite her selective deficiencies in prefrontal abilities. A different case study (Mataró et al., 2001) of a 81-year-old man 60 years after a severe bilateral lesion in the orbital and dorsolateral frontal regions also recorded behavioral and intellectual disturbances believed to be involved with those regions, such as executive functioning, memory, and motor speed, as well as mood, emotion, and personality. However, his consciousness was still intact.

Also, a "virtual lesion" of the DLPFC induced by transcranial magnetic stimulation (TMS) did not interrupt conscious perception (de Graaf, de Jong, Goebel, van Ee, & Sack, 2011). In this study, participants viewed a bistable display of dots moving in an ambiguous direction (either left or right). TMS to DLPFC had no effect on passive viewing of the bistable display and only affected voluntary perceptual switching. That is, participants could still experience two different percepts but had trouble trying to voluntarily switch from one to the other. These results indicate that disruption of DLPFC activity does not obstruct conscious perception.

RESPONSES TO THE "LESION" ARGUMENT

In stark contrast, there are many reports that magnetic stimulations and lesions of relevant regions within PFC do in fact impair specific aspects of conscious perception (Chiang, Lu, Hsieh, Chang, & Yang, 2014; Del Cul, Dehaene, Reyes, Bravo, & Slachevsky, 2009; Fleming, Ryu, Golfinos, & Blackmon, 2014; Rounis, Maniscalco, Rothwell, Passingham, & Lau, 2010; Turatto, Sandrini, & Miniussi, 2004). Many of these studies report an impairment related to perceptual metacognition. Metacognition here refers to the subjective evaluation of one's own perceptual process, which is usually measured by the correspondence between subjective report and perceptual task performance (Lau & Rosenthal, 2011). Mismatch between subjective confidence and objective performance indicates impaired metacognitive abilities.

Relevance of metacognition in consciousness research is exemplified in blindsight (Weiskrantz, Barbur, & Sahraie, 1995). In blindsight, cortically blind patients perform above chance level at visual discrimination tasks despite their denial of consciously seeing the relevant visual stimuli (Ko & Lau, 2012). Studies with blindsight avoid performance confounds that may be prevalent in other conscious perception paradigms such as backward masking (Lau, 2008) because the performance between blindsight (unconscious perception) and normal vision (conscious perception) can be matched

(Weiskrantz et al., 1995). Poor metacognition has been identified as the potential underlying mechanism responsible for the unconscious perception in blindsight (Ko & Lau, 2012; Persaud et al., 2011), which could be extended to say that impairment in metacognition is an impairment in conscious perception.

TMS to DLPFC decreased metacognitive sensitivity—the correspondence between visibility ratings and task performance—demonstrating PFC's role in metacognition of conscious perception (Rounis et al., 2010). Participants viewed a diamond and a square placed next to each other in either of the two possible orientations in each trial. They were asked to report the visibility of the figures (clear vs unclear) and their orientation (square left and diamond right vs vice versa). TMS induction decreased subjective visibility ratings when the orientation was correctly identified, similar to the discrepancy between poor visibility and high visual discrimination performance observed in blindsight (Ko & Lau, 2012). The mismatch between visibility and task performance caused by disruption of activity in DLPFC confirms previous attribution of poor metacognition in blindsight to PFC activity (Ko & Lau, 2012), ratifying the crucial role of the PFC in metacognitive accuracy of conscious perception.

A different study found a decrease in subjective confidence ratings following repetitive transmagnetic stimulation (rTMS) of the DLPFC (Chiang et al., 2014). The participants were shown a display of dots in two different colors, which moved in different directions. Following the stimulus presentation, they were asked to correctly identify either the direction moved by one of the two groups of colored dots or the color of the dots that moved a certain direction. Also, they were asked to give a confidence rating (confident vs guessing) of their answer to the identification question. Compared to the number of confident and guessed responses of the control groups that did not receive rTMS or received a sham rTMS, the DLPFC rTMS group reported significantly more guesses, reflecting a drop in their confidence in response. Hence, the DLPFC seems to be engaged in determining the quality of metacognitive percepts.

Turatto et al. (2004) also utilized rTMS to temporarily disable the right DLPFC during a visual change detection task, which impaired the ability to perceive changes in conscious visual perception. The study consisted of participants indicating with a key press whether any one of the four faces presented on a screen has changed between the first and second displays separated by a brief interval. Disrupting the right DLPFC significantly lowered the percentage of correct change detection, a clear indication of DLPFC's role in conscious perception of change.

A lesion study (Fleming et al., 2014) has revealed a drop in perceptual metacognitive accuracy upon damage to the PFC. The patients and controls had to decide which of the two circles on the screen contained more dots that briefly flashed inside them and rate their confidence in rating on a scale of 1−6. The patients with anterior PFC lesions had much lower correspondence between their confidence rating and perceptual task performance.

Such lowered metacognitive accuracy was specific to perception tasks (rather than memory tasks) and was not observed in patients with temporal lobe lesions or healthy controls, suggesting a causal role of anterior PFC in perceptual metacognition.

Furthermore, focal PFC lesions had a negative effect on subjective visibility of masked visual stimuli (Del Cul et al., 2009). A single digit was flashed on the screen and shortly after masked with four letters surrounding the target location. A subjective response (see vs did not see target digit) and an objective response (identifying the presented digit) were given verbally after each display. Patients had less accurate objective performance and subjective visibility than controls, conveying that the damaged area in those patients—specifically the left anterior PFC—plays a causal role in conscious perception of masked visual stimuli.

Taken together, it is empirically unsound to deny the role the PFC plays in conscious perception. Such role may be specific, i.e., especially regarding subjective, metacognitive aspects of perception. But if we are concerned with subjective conscious awareness, rather than just perception, these results are clearly relevant.

WHY DO PFC LESIONS PRODUCE SUCH SUBTLE EFFECTS?

Above data shows that disruption of activity within or damage to the PFC only partially impairs conscious perception rather than eliminating it as a whole (i.e., cortical blindness). Severe lesions to many areas of the brain result in near-complete degradation of its functions (Aldrich, Alessi, Beck, Gilman, 1987). If PFC causally contributes to conscious perception, why does not lesion completely remove conscious perception?

Curiously, conscious perception is not the only PFC-dependent operation that does not get completely abolished from PFC damage. A recent finding (Mackey, Devinsky, Doyle, Meager, & Curtis, 2016) shows that even working memory, a classic PFC function, withstands severe damage to the PFC. Mackey et al. (2016) prepared a study with patients with lesions to either the DLPFC or the precentral sulcus (PCS). The patients performed a memory-guided saccade task, in which they were shown a dot on a screen and needed to remember and saccade to its location after a delay period. The average degree of saccade error for PCS lesion patients was significantly higher than that of healthy controls, whereas the patients with DLPFC lesions performed at the same level as the controls. These results highlight that even a reliable function of the DLPFC that has been studied and elucidated in many studies can remain intact after a lesion to the DLPFC. Therefore, the lack of data for a complete elimination of conscious perception following PFC damage should not be a reason to believe that PFC is not responsible for conscious perception; rather, the more appropriate question may be why damage to the PFC does not entirely extinguish at least some of its functions.

To theorize how PFC functions are buffered from physical damage, perhaps it may be useful to consider how brain structures encode the underlying functions. Hebb (1949) famously hypothesized that mental phenomena are results of the networks between nodes (i.e., single neuron or group of neurons) in our brain. This well-accepted basic principle is reflected in many theories of cognitive processing, as in parallel distributed processing (PDP; Thomas & McClelland, 2008). PDP posits that neural networks process multiple pieces of information simultaneously and in parallel, as opposed to models of intelligence that process information serially in a rule-based fashion, such as in a Turing machine.

An important consideration about PDP is how many nodes or neurons are activated to encode a piece of information or a cognitive process. In "sparse" coding, an item or process is coded as an activation of a small number of neurons, even down to a single neuron at an extreme (Olshausen & Field, 1997). Each neuron has a highly selective activation rule, and there is hardly any activational overlap among two different items. An example of sparse coding is seen in simple cells, which are located in the primary visual cortex and only respond to bars of particular orientations. Another example is the famous hypothetical case of a "grandmother" neuron, which responds to nothing but the face of one's grandmother (Gross, 2002). However, in "dense" coding (as contra "sparse" coding; Rigotti et al., 2013), an object or concept is represented by ensemble activity of a large group of neurons, which also carry the shared duty of coding other representations. In some cases, dense coding provides a computational advantage over lower dimensional neural representations to allow for higher cognition of more potential informational states (Fusi, Miller, & Rigotti, 2016).

Identifying the coding mechanism underlying neural networks is valuable because it could explain how "graceful degradation" might work in the PFC. Graceful degradation refers to the overall intact ability of a neural system to carry out its function although its component has been damaged (Rolls, 1994). Such protection of the functionality of the whole system can account for various mental phenomena, such as partial memory and only a partial impairment in relevant functions in patients with brain lesions (Baddeley, 1997). Even under sparse coding, graceful degradation has been believed to be possible (Rolls & Treves, 1990). Given that the PFC likely uses a "dense" coding scheme (Rigotti et al., 2013), meaning that a single representation spreads over many neurons distributed throughout the system, perhaps it is not surprising that damages to PFC often do not produce devastating effects (de Graaf et al., 2011; Mackey et al., 2016). In fact, Rigotti et al. (2013) reported that neurons in the PFC have heterogeneous, mixed selectivity for multiple task-related features and encode information about each feature they respond to. Importantly, they found that even after turning off single-cell selectivity to a feature, information could still be decoded at the population level in the PFC.

Congruent with the foregoing speculations, indeed, bilateral lesion of the relatively sparsely coded primary visual cortex results in detrimental cortical blindness (Aldrich et al., 1987). In contrast, damage to the PFC has been much more lenient in hurting its functions (Mackey et al., 2016) as discussed before. PFC functions have also been shown to be able to recover from unilateral damage because the undamaged side compensates for any losses in functions normally carried out by the damaged side, revealing the flexibility of the PFC's system as a whole (Voytek et al., 2010).

IMPLICATIONS FOR THEORIES OF CONSCIOUSNESS

So far, we have defended PFC's involvement in consciousness from opposing arguments. But such defense also helps us to characterize the extent to which PFC may contribute to conscious perception. From early on, evidence of PFC's activity in conscious perception (Lumer & Rees, 1999) has been interpreted as part of a global workspace for conscious processing across regions of the cortex that provide top-down cognitive processing and attentional amplification necessary for conscious experience (Baars, 1988; Dehaene & Naccache, 2001; Dehaene et al., 2006). Theoretically, one would expect that information reaching the global workspace would lead to superior performance in perceptual and higher cognitive tasks, because the workspace would serve to "ignite" and "broadcast" to amplify such signals. However, it has recently been shown that induction of rTMS on DLPFC resulted in less metacognitive awareness of visual stimuli without lowered task performance (Chiang, Lu, Hsieh, Chang, & Yang, 2014). Because the disruption of PFC activity selectively reduced subjective awareness without lowering performance capacity, and that under no-report situations, PFC activity may be relatively local and weak rather than widespread (Noy et al., 2015), these results seem difficult to interpret in the light of global workspace theory.

On the other end of the spectrum of theories on PFC's importance in conscious perception, first-order theories hold that consciousness solely depends on early sensory activity without any higher levels of cognition. An example of such a view is the popular local recurrency theory (Lamme, 2006). An empirical prediction made by such views is that PFC activity does not play a part in conscious experience. But earlier we reviewed that PFC does play important and specific roles in conscious perception.

The foregoing review suggests that the most plausible view reflecting PFC's involvement may exist somewhere in between global workspace theory and first-order theories. Such model would explain correlated activation of the PFC with conscious perception without attributing too many other cognitive functions to the same mechanisms. Higher order theories of consciousness posit that consciousness is contingent on some higher level activity that makes oneself aware of being in a particular mental state, which makes that mental state conscious (Lau & Rosenthal, 2011). Relating the studies that identified the association between PFC activity and conscious awareness (Rees et al., 2002) to higher order theories, it is likely that such activity occurs in the PFC.

A study (Maniscalco & Lau, 2016) that lends support to higher order theories analyzed the relationship between subjective visibility ratings and objective perceptual processing performance. The authors observed a clear dissociation between visibility rating and task performance, which is difficult to be captured by the most parsimonious computational models that hold task performance and visibility ratings to be based on the same underlying process. The model that fit their data the best was a hierarchical model in which early processing generates the objective perceptual judgment, whereas a later processing stream evaluates those early perceptual processes to generate the subjective judgments. This model predicts that altering the late processing stage would affect only the subjective reports and not the objective task capacity, as congruent with the TMS and lesion results reviewed earlier (Chiang et al., 2014; Del Cul et al., 2009; Fleming et al., 2014; Rounis et al., 2010).

Findings that could uphold or challenge some major theories of consciousness are still emerging. Perhaps it is fair to say that at this point, there is no conclusive victor among the reviewed theories of consciousness. However, there are optimistic signs that one could eventually resolve these differences between the theories through careful consideration of empirical evidence collected using different methods. This review hopefully represents a modest exercise in this spirit.

REFERENCES

Aldrich, M. S., Alessi, A. G., Beck, R. W., & Gilman, S. (1987). Cortical blindness: Etiology, diagnosis, and prognosis. *Annals of Neurology, 21*(2), 149–158.

Baars, B. J. (1988). *A cognitive theory of consciousness*. New York: Cambridge University Press.

Baddeley, A. (1997). *Human memory: Theory and practice*. Boston: Psychology Press.

Brascamp, J., Blake, R., & Knapen, T. (2015). Negligible fronto-parietal BOLD activity accompanying unreportable switches in bistable perception. *Nature Neuroscience, 18*, 1672–1678.

Brickner, R. M. (1952). Brain of patient A. After bilateral frontal lobectomy; status of frontal-lobe problem. *A.M.A. Archives of Neurology and Psychiatry, 68*, 293–313.

Chiang, T. C., Lu, R. B., Hsieh, S., Chang, Y. H., & Yang, Y. K. (2014). Stimulation in the dorso-lateral prefrontal cortex changes subjective evaluation of percepts. *PLoS One, 9*(9), e106943.

de Graaf, T. A., de Jong, M. C., Goebel, R., van Ee, R., & Sack, A. T. (2011). On the functional relevance of frontal cortex for passive and voluntarily controlled bistable vision. *Cerebral Cortex, 21*, 2322–2331.

Dehaene, S., Changeux, J., Naccache, L., Sackur, J., & Sergent, C. (2006). Conscious, preconscious, and subliminal processing: A testable taxonomy. *Trends in Cognitive Sciences, 10*(5), 204–211.

Dehaene, S., & Naccache, L. (2001). Towards a cognitive neuroscience of consciousness: Basic evidence and a workspace framework. *Cognition, 79*(1), 1–37.

Del Cul, A., Dehaene, S., Reyes, P., Bravo, E., & Slachevsky, A. (2009). Causal role of prefrontal cortex in the threshold for access to consciousness. *Brain, 132*(9), 2531–2540.

Fleming, S. M., Ryu, J., Golfinos, J. G., & Blackmon, K. E. (2014). Domain-specific impairment in metacognitive accuracy following anterior prefrontal lesions. *Brain, 137*(10), 2811–2822.

Fulton, J. F. (1949). *Functional localization in relation to frontal lobotomy*. New York: Oxford University Press.

Fusi, S., Miller, E. K., & Rigotti, M. (2016). Why neurons mix: High dimensionality for higher cognition. *Current Opinion in Neurobiology, 37*, 66–74.

Frässle, S., Sommer, J., Jansen, A., Naber, M., & Einhäuser, W. (2014). Binocular rivalry: Frontal activity relates to introspection and action but not to perception. *The Journal of Neuroscience, 34*(5), 1738–1747.

Gross, C. G. (2002). Genealogy of the "grandmother cell." *Neuroscientist, 8*(5), 512–518.

Hebb, D. O. (1949). *The organization of behavior: A neuropsychological approach*. New York: John Wiley & Sons.

Hebb, D. O., & Penfield, W. (1940). Human behavior after extensive bilateral removal from the frontal lobes. *Archives of Neurology and Psychiatry, 42*, 421–438.

Ko, Y., & Lau, H. (2012). A detection theoretic explanation of blindsight suggests a link between conscious perception and metacognition. *Philosophical Transactions of the Royal Society B, 367*, 1401–1411.

Kouider, S., Dehaene, S., Jobert, A., & Le Bihan, D. (2007). Cerebral bases of subliminal and supraliminal priming during reading. *Cerebral Cortex, 17*(9), 2019–2029.

Lamme, V. A. (2006). Towards a true neural stance on consciousness. *Trends in Cognitive Sciences, 10*, 494–501.

Lau, H., & Rosenthal, D. (2011). Empirical support for higher-order theories of conscious awareness. *Trends in Cognitive Sciences, 15*(8), 365–373.

Lau, H. C. (2008). Are we studying consciousness yet? In L. Weiskrantz, & M. David (Eds.), *Frontiers of consciousness: Chichele lectures* (pp. 245–258). New York, NY: Oxford University Press.

Lumer, E. D., & Rees, G. (1999). Covariation of activity in visual and prefrontal cortex associated with subjective visual perception. *Proceedings of the National Academy of Sciences of the United States of America, 96*(4), 1669–1673.

Mackey, W. E., Devinsky, O., Doyle, W., Meager, M. R., & Curtis, C. E. (2016). Human dorsolateral prefrontal cortex is not necessary for spatial working memory. *The Journal of Neuroscience, 36*(10), 2847–2856.

Maniscalco, B., & Lau, H. (2016). The signal processing architecture underlying subjective reports of sensory awareness. *Neuroscience of Consciousness, 2016*, 1–17.

Mante, V., Sussillo, D., Shenoy, K. V., & Newsome, W. T. (2013). Context-dependent computation by recurrent dynamics in prefrontal cortex. *Nature, 503*(7474), 78–84.

Markowitsch, H. J., & Kessler, J. (2000). Massive impairment in executive functions with partial preservation of other cognitive functions: The case of a young patient with severe degeneration of the prefrontal cortex. *Experimental Brain Research, 133*, 94–102.

Mataró, M., et al. (2001). Long-term effects of bilateral frontal brain lesion: 60 years after injury with an iron bar. *Archives of Neurology, 58*, 1139–1142.

Mettler, F.A. (1949). Selective partial ablation of the frontal cortex, a correlative study of its effects on human psychotic subjects, New York: Hoebar.

Noy, N., Bickel, S., Zion-Golumbic, E., Harel, M., Golan, T., Davidesco, I., & Mehta, A. D. (2015). Ignition's glow: Ultra-fast spread of global cortical activity accompanying local "ignitions" in visual cortex during conscious visual perception. *Consciousness and Cognition, 35*, 206–224.

Olshausen, B. A., & Field, D. J. (1997). Sparse coding with an overcomplete basis set: A strategy employed by V1? *Vision Research, 37*(23), 3311–3325.

Persaud, N., Davidson, M., Maniscalco, B., Mobbs, D., Passingham, R. E., Cowey, A., & Lau, H. (2011). Awareness-related activity in prefrontal and parietal cortices in blindsight reflects more than superior visual performance. *Neuroimage, 58*(2), 605–611.

Pollen, D. A. (1995). Cortical areas in visual awareness. *Nature, 377*(6547), 293–295.

Ress, D., Backus, B. T., & Heeger, D. J. (2000). Activity in primary visual cortex predicts performance in a visual detection task. *Nature Neuroscience, 3*(9), 940–945.

Rees, G., Kreiman, G., & Koch, C. (2002). Neural correlates of consciousness in humans. *Nature Reviews Neuroscience, 3*(4), 261–270.

Rigotti, M., Barak, O., Warden, M. R., Wang, X. J., Daw, N. D., Miller, E. K., & Fusi, S. (2013). The importance of mixed selectivity in complex cognitive tasks. *Nature, 497*(7451), 585–590.

Rolls, E. T. (1994). Brain mechanisms for invariant visual recognition and learning. *Behavioural Processes, 33*(1-2), 113–138.

Rolls, E. T., & Treves, A. (1990). The relative advantages of sparse versus distributed encoding for associative neuronal networks in the brain. *Network: Computation in Neural Systems, 1*(4), 407–421.

Rounis, E., Maniscalco, B., Rothwell, J. C., Passingham, R. E., & Lau, H. (2010). Theta-burst transcranial magnetic stimulation to the prefrontal cortex impairs metacognitive visual awareness. *Cognitive Neuroscience, 1*(3), 165–175.

Stokes, M. G. (2015). 'Activity-silent' working memory in prefrontal cortex: A dynamic coding framework. *Trends in Cognitive Sciences, 19*(7), 394–405.

Super, H., Spekreijse, H., & Lamme, V. A. (2001). Two distinct modes of sensory processing observed in monkey primary visual cortex (V1). *Nature Neuroscience, 4*, 304–310.

Thomas, M. S., & McClelland, J. L. (2008). *Connectionist models of cognition. The Cambridge handbook of computational psychology.* New York: Cambridge University Press.

Tong, F., Meng, M., & Blake, R. (2006). Neural bases of binocular rivalry. *Trends in Cognitive Sciences, 10*(11), 502–511.

Tse, P. U., Martinez-Conde, S., Schlegel, A. A., & Macknik, S. L. (2005). Visibility, visual awareness, and visual masking of simple unattended targets are confined to areas in the occipital cortex beyond human V1/V2. *Proceedings of the National Academy of Sciences of the United States of America, 102*(47), 17178–17183.

Tsuchiya, N., Wilke, M., Frässle, S., & Lamme, V. A. (2015). No-report paradigms: Extracting the true neural correlates of consciousness. *Trends in Cognitive Sciences, 19*(12), 757–770.

Turatto, M., Sandrini, M., & Miniussi, C. (2004). The role of the right dorsolateral prefrontal cortex in visual change awareness. *Neuroreport, 15*(16), 2549–2552.

Voytek, B., Davis, M., Yago, E., Barceló, F., Vogel, E. K., & Knight, R. T. (2010). Dynamic neuroplasticity after human prefrontal cortex damage. *Neuron, 68*(3), 401–408.

Weiskrantz, L., Barbur, J. L., & Sahraie, A. (1995). Parameters affecting conscious versus unconscious visual discrimination with damage to the visual cortex (V1). *Proceedings of the National Academy of Sciences of the United States of America, 92*, 6122–6126.

Chapter 7

Neurodevelopment of the Executive Functions

Layne Kalbfleisch
Department of Pediatrics, The George Washington School of Medicine and Health Sciences, Washington, DC, United States

INTRODUCTION

Like many of the definitions associated with the constructs and principles of learning, executive functions do not have a universally agreed upon definition, although they have been shown to emerge hierarchically (Tillman, Brocki, Sorensen, & Lundervold, 2015) and derive from separate relationships within regional areas of the brain's resting state networks (Zhao et al., 2016). Irrespective of which definition one ascribes to, executive functions are how the brain uses its natural capacities to set and to reach goals in a dynamic environment. For example, Miyake et al. (2000) provide evidence that some of the skills that constitute executive function are dissociable into *inhibition* (a capacity to rebuff distraction and resist prepotent response), *shift* (a capacity to move smoothly between tasks, routines, or contexts), and *working memory* (a capacity to hold and manipulate multiple ideas). This conception has drawn consensus, as many cognitive tasks used to assess executive function in the developmental, neuropsychological, and neuroimaging literatures tap into and assess these functions to inform the foundations of executive function (Best & Miller, 2010; Gallant, 2016; Hoffman, Schmeichel, & Baddeley, 2012; Smolker, Depue, Reineberg, Orr, & Banich, 2015). Modern neuroscience presents evidence that plasticity can be modified by manipulating the internal and external environment. We also have much evidence that executive functions manage the interplay of internal and external environmental factors affecting developmental plasticity and learning. In general, the important task at hand is to determine how executive functions emerge and comingle with general (i.e., inhibitory control) and specific (i.e., language) cognitive processes in early life to promote competence across life and to determine the extent to which plasticity can be beneficially modified through training.

Executive Functions in Health and Disease. DOI: http://dx.doi.org/10.1016/B978-0-12-803676-1.00007-6

143

DEFINING AND LOCATING EXECUTIVE FUNCTIONS

Executive functions derive, in part, from a diverse number of regions in the brain's frontal lobes. To look at a physical brain, the frontal lobes may appear undifferentiated, folds of neocortical tissue coiled neatly in the skull. Functionally, however, that tissue is diverse, containing a suite of functions that sum to what are commonly referred to as the executive functions (Duncan & Owen, 2000; Hampshire, Thompson, Duncan, & Owen, 2011). Indeed, those functions enable us to manage ourselves and to engage with the environment (Kalbfleisch & Loughan, 2011). Knowledge of the neural systems of these functions and how they unfold in the brain and emerge in behavior is under active investigation, and we are cautioned from inferring that only the frontal lobes support the executive functions (Alvarez & Emory, 2006; Smolker et al., 2015). The frontal lobes, however, can be likened to a "conductor" or an orchestrator of these skills (Goldberg, 2001). An inherent paradox of the executive functions is that some aspects of these skills have a heritable trace, such as the predictive validity of the delay of gratification (Mischel, Ayduk, Bemran, Casey, Gotlib, et al., 2011), yet there is also evidence that some skills can be improved and trained in certain contexts (Diamond, 2013; Karbach & Unger, 2014; Karbach, Strobach, & Schubert, 2014; Klingberg, 2010).

Executive function skills initially emerge through simpler challenges from the environment. For example, a 3- or 4-year old child can shift between two choices but would have difficulty in managing more. At the age of 8 years, children still do not appear to have mature metacognition on a task that asks them to shift among tasks. They do not detect their errors well (Crone, Wendelken, Donohue, van Leijenhorst, & Bunge, 2006). It is useful to note that children are highly engaged in reinforcement learning at early ages, acquiring the "behavioral policies" that executive functions require. This demonstrates a form of early self-manipulation of plasticity in response to the environment and relates with what we know about managing children's environments to impact learning and development. By the age of 15 years, this skill is not measurably different from young adults (Huizinga, Dolan, & van der Molan, 2006), which is interesting in light of the fact that children and adults share common neural systems for flexible rule use that are established in the brain by the age of 8 years (Wendelken, Munakata, Baym, Souza, & Bunge, 2012). Flexible rule use requires a person to switch rules as dictated by the task and apply them appropriately, even in the face of distraction. The neural systems that support this function in children and adults lie in the left hemisphere's dorsolateral prefrontal cortex, posterior parietal cortex, and presensory motor area, a region that overlaps its membership in networks of developing self-control (Berkman, Graham, & Fisher, 2012). The developmental difference is determined by time and how quickly a person can switch between or among rules. In this study, children (ages

8−13 years) were slower than adults (ages 20−27 years) at representing rule(s) and switching effectively. This is one instance where one of the foundations of higher level skills is in place quite early in life and experience increases their efficiency. Studies of reasoning in young children, ages 5−7 years, and in conditions such as attention-deficit hyperactivity disorder, show that the executive functions themselves develop hierarchically and exert contingencies on learning (Tillman et al., 2015; Zaitchik, Iqbal, & Carey, 2014). The fact that certain reasoning skills are present at early ages despite these executive immaturities is an important cognitive dynamic yet to be fully explained by modern neuroscience. Although, a recent study in 20-year-old young adults describes a relationship between behavioral performance on certain executive function skills (measures of total executive function, planning, working memory, short-term memory, inhibition, and switch were taken from the Cambridge Neuropsychological Test Automated Battery, or CANTAB) and the brain's resting state networks, making the important distinction that different skills correspond to various locations in prefrontal cortex and also correspond to regional network patterns in the resting state map, not the global network itself (Zhao et al., 2016). This perhaps provides insight into previous findings that report idiosyncratic relationships among strong and weak executive functions in children with high-functioning autism (Kalbfleisch & Loughan, 2011; Kalbfleisch, 2013). In this study, children with high-functioning autism that had stronger verbal skills (higher verbal intelligence scores) exhibited fewer executive function deficits than their autistic peers with average verbal ability. Negative correlations between verbal intelligence and planning and monitoring scores from the Brief Rating Scale of Executive Function (BRIEF), a measure designed to provide an ecologically valid assessment of behavioral regulation and metacognitive capacity, suggest that verbal ability may protect or preserve some executive skills in disability. This holds promise for leveraging intellectual strengths in high-functioning autism by promoting their transfer to improve social competence, particularly in light of the fact that real-world executive function deficits have been shown to increase as these children grow into adolescence (Rosenthal et al., 2013). Executive functions in disabilities such as attention-deficit hyperactivity disorder and autism often elude neat characterization (Dajani, Llabre, Nebel, Mostofsky, & Uddin, 2016), but some have shown that inhibitory control in early childhood can predict working memory function in adolescents with attention deficits (Tillman et al., 2015). The junctures of perceptual skills with cognitive skills such as short term and working memory illustrate the initial dependence of these skills on one another as basic blocks in the larger skill suite. Once these skills become linked and interdependent, explaining relationships among them becomes more complex.

For instance, recent work in the study of short-term memory illustrates that the quality of item-context binding, the strength of the affiliation of an item or object with its context, strongly influences the fidelity of short-term memory (Libby, Hannula, & Ranganath, 2014) across the life span (Fandakova, Sander, Werkle-Bergner, & Shing, 2014). Fandakova et al. (2014) used structural equation modeling to demonstrate that item-context binding processes are weaker in both children and older adults. Item-context binding appears to be optimized by the middle teen years (ages 13−15 years) persisting through young adulthood (ages 20−25 years). Short-term memory permits a person to form and remember rich and recent memories. Bell, Roer, and Buchner (2013) demonstrated that the associations being formed between an item and various features of its context, for instance, spatial location, serial position, or background color, can be disrupted with irrelevant speech. Just as noise can disrupt this early and critical stage of memory formation, it is a feature of distraction that can challenge other metacognitive processes closely related to short-term memory, such as working memory. Working memory supports the amount of information one can accurately hold immediately available during problem solving. This is an important feature of executive function often truncated in early life with various developmental and learning disorders, such as attention-deficit disorder, autism (Dajani et al., 2016), and deafness (Boutla, Supalla, Newport, & Bavalier, 2004), and has been widely studied as a foundational skill for higher level thinking (Kane & Engel, 2002; Klingberg, 2014).

Efforts to map the human brain across development portray the neural systems of working memory to show that these systems experience tuning and initial optimization roughly between the ages of 7 and 22 years (Darki & Klingberg, 2015), that working memory related to visual and spatial context develops between the ages of 8 and 18 years (Dumontheil & Klingberg, 2012), and that task demand and complexity determine the extent of neural recruitment, where more (neural recruitment) does not equal best (most fast and accurate responses) (Klingberg, Forssberg, & Westerberg, 2002). There are contextual challenges to probing various skills and features of executive function, what is a logical or "cool" task to one person may carry "hot" emotional tone or promote a motivational aspect to another (Welsh & Peterson, 2014). One experiment may involve a task that precisely isolates an important perceptual process that many other skills build on such as response conflict probed with a dot motion task (Wendelken, Ditterich, Bunge, & Carter, 2009), but the task itself has little value in assessing executive function in a learning setting. Whereas other experiments more closely relate basic function to a consequential behavior or skill such as to test working memory for faces or scenes (Wendelken, Baym, Gazzaley, & Bunge, 2011). There are seemingly straightforward versions of tasks that test inhibitory control, such as Mischel's marshmallow test (Mischel & Mischel, 1983) that has stood the test of time as a fundamental experimental paradigm that also elicits a feature of "hot" control, managing inhibitory control in the face of acutely attractive appetitive reward. Or, Zelazo's card sort task (1995) that introduces deceptively simple instructions to resist or disregard a feature of the task at hand, representing a behavioral challenge that draws on motivated reasoning and focus in response to cognitive demand. More complex response inhibition tasks, such as Luria's tapping test (Weiner, Hynan, Rossetti, & Falkowski, 2011), the Day/Night task (Gerstadt, Hong, & Diamond, 1994), and Dimensional Change Card Sort (Garon, Bryson, & Smith, 2008), each require increasingly effortful forms of inhibition and working memory and demonstrate that different ages achieve different levels of mastery. Finally, there are executive function tasks that map slightly better to the real-world that promote ecological validity by task requirements such as route finding (Boyd & Sautter, 1993) and completing multiple errands (Shallice & Burgess, 1991). Although, recent work challenges some existing measures of executive function by failing to find a predictive relationship between some psychometric instruments (Sorting and Tower tests on the Delis–Kaplan Executive Function System (D-KEFS), and the self-report measure of the BRIEF (Behavior Rating Inventory of Executive Function) and college preparatory school performance (Boschloo, Krabbendam, Aben, de Groot, & Jolles, 2014). Many argue that it is difficult to dissociate the cognitive requirements of each of these and other tasks as a "pure" task that taps merely one function (e.g., inhibitory control) or elicits a common emotional or motivational tone. The challenge in understanding the neurodevelopment of executive functions is to determine a collective matrix of information that holds where development, skill, and environmental opportunity and complexity converge for either success or failure, in the conditions of health and disease and across life. Read the National Center for Education Research monograph by Zelazo, Blair, and Willoughby (2016) for a comprehensive treatment of executive functions and implications for education and society. From simple challenges and interactions with the environment early in life, the primary skills of executive function (i.e., inhibitory control) emerge in response to cognitive, behavioral, and emotional demands, and develop and differentiate into multiple capacities (i.e., shift, emotional control, and working memory) to contend with complexity.

GRAY MATTER, WHITE MATTER, AND EXECUTIVE FUNCTION

A discussion about the neurodevelopment of the executive functions is first best understood in the context of what is known about the general principles and stages of human brain development. For instance, Deoni, Dean, Remer, Dirks, and O'Muircheartaigh (2015) found no differences between the left and right hemispheres in the rate of development when 34 regions of the brain were compared for evidence of cortical myelination and increases in gray matter volume. However, they detected differences in laterality in some structures related to executive function in early development. For example, maturation between the ages of 0 and 2 years in both males and females were characterized by left lateralized activity in the inferior and superior frontal gyri, areas known to later support working memory during the reasoning process in both hemispheres (Kalbfleisch et al., 2013; Kalbfleisch, Van Meter, & Zeffiro, 2006, 2007; Wendelken, O'Hare, Whitaker, Ferrer, & Bunge, 2011) and known to be correlated with intellectual aptitude and fluid reasoning skills later in life (Geake & Hansen, 2005, 2010). Shaw (2007) and Shaw, Greenstein, Lerch, Clasen, Lenroot, et al. (2006) outlined dynamic processes associated with gray matter changes in the lateral prefrontal cortex that appear to impact the connectivity of this region and converge anatomically around the age of 12 years. Although the study could not draw inferences about behavior from the observed changes, it sets the stage for examination of the influence of genes and individual differences on changes and timing differences occurring in cortical thickness throughout various regions of the brain and not just the absolute measure at a given point in time.

A few points about this physiological result are meaningful to the discussion of the development of executive functions in contexts such as social cognition and bilingualism, two cortical challenges from the environment. First, Mills, Lalonde, Clasaen, Giedd, and Blakemore (2014) highlighted specific changes in gray matter volume and cortical thickness in a network of areas associated with social cognition in the brain that undergo a protracted period of development defined by decreases in volume and cortical thickness from childhood into the early 20s (medial Brodmann Area 10, temporoparietal junction, and the posterior temporal sulcus) and increased gray matter volume into adolescence and in cortical thickness through early adulthood (anterior temporal cortex). Blakemore and Mills (2014) suggest that adolescence brings a period of increasing executive function proficiencies and sensitivity to social dynamics and that these changes influence the convergence of these processes to optimize cognitive function into adulthood. Second, there is a body of evidence that a bilingual brain contends with general distraction more efficiently. Jasinska and Pettito (2013) distinguish that bilinguals who are exposed to their second language later (age 4 years or beyond) tend to recruit executive function regions as opposed to early second language learners (exposed from birth) whose brains showed adaptations in the classic language areas. Abutalebi et al. (2012) posit that the robustness of local gray matter volume in the anterior cingulate cortex is related to this bilingual proficiency. An extensive review article by Barac, Bialystok, Castro, and Sanchez (2014) reports that bilingual children outperform monolingual children from the first year of life on measures of nonverbal executive control and that experience with more than one language changes brain function. Lastly, a diffusion tensor study by Mohades et al. (2015) portrays differences in white matter development of the left inferior—occipito—frontal fasciculus that favors enhanced function in bilingual adolescents (ages 10—13 years).

Myelination of the prefrontal and posterior association cortices is among the developmental processes that are the last to mature as adolescence begins. Cortical thinning occurs with synaptic pruning and is the primary process by which the adolescent brain refines itself (Sowell, Thompson, & Toga, 2004). The means by which the brain in early childhood develops is due to changes in cortical myelin that influence and promote gray matter volume. Across the life span, cortical myelination increases up until age 40 years and then begins to decrease with age (Grydeland, Walhovd, Tamnes, Westlye, & Fjell, 2013). In sum, sweeping changes in the brain occur early in the human life span that impact individual tissue types. Presenting them in discussion addresses the distinctness of each process (gray matter pruning vs white matter tract development), but the cognitive and behavioral consequences on executive function are not as clearly distinguished.

A structural neuroimaging study examining responses to reward and novelty seeking found that reward behavior is primarily associated with white matter integrity across the brain and could not be explained by age, sex, alcohol use, or trait anxiety (Bjornebekk, Westlye, Fjell, Grydeland, & Walhovd, 2012). This is evidence that some of how humans relate to social reward is not solely a learned behavior but one guided by quantitative differences in white matter microcircuitry in the brain. White matter connects various regions of the brain and facilitates domain general and specific skill pathways that are distinct from one another such as working memory and reading skill (Niogi & McCandliss, 2006). The delay of gratification, known to be a source of individual differences in humans (Mischel, Ayduk, Bemran, Casey, Gotlib, et al., 2011), is based on an ability to turn one's attention away from temptation. This attentional resistance is associated with the strength of a neural system that affiliates the nucleus accumbens, a structure in the brain that supports reward-based behaviors such as interest and curiosity, with regions in the parietal and frontal cortices that promote self-control (Luerssen, Gyurak, Ayduk, Wendelken, & Bunge, 2015). Finally, white matter maturation has also been identified as the means by which processing speed supports reasoning ability (Ferrer et al., 2013). To advance the discussion and address separate executive functions, one of the simplest ways to conceptualize this suite of skills is to differentiate between regulating oneself and contending with features of the environment although, pragmatically, these skills are inextricably linked (Austin, Groppe, & Elsner, 2014).

INFLUENCE AND INTERPLAY OF INTERNAL AND EXTERNAL ENVIRONMENTAL FACTORS

Certain attention skills in early life set the stage for more complex skills to emerge as a child explores and interacts with his or her environment (Posner, Rothbart, Sheese, & Voelker, 2014). Westlye, Grydeland, Walhovd, and Fjell (2011) were able to demonstrate that the skills probed by the Attention Network Test, shown to successfully train these skills (alerting, orienting, and conflict response) in children as young as 6 years of age (Lewis, Reeve, & Johnson, 2016; Rueda, Fan, McCandliss, Halparin, Gruber, Lercari & Posner, 2004), remain reliably stable across adulthood (in subjects 20–84 years of age), relating this consistency to cortical maturation and the foundation for visual spatial attention in adults. This team also demonstrated that error processing and cognitive control measured by performance on a flanker task are associated with the degree of intracortical myelinization in the posterior cingulate cortex, increased amplitude, and higher levels of cortical myelin independent of general ability and adjacent white matter myelin (Grydeland, Westlye, Walhovd, & Fjell, 2016).

Research from social affective neuroscience shows us the neural systems that support how a person affiliates or relates to their social environment (Norris, Chen, Zhu, Small, & Cacioppo, 2004). The quality or dynamic of a social relationship is one of the very first properties coded in the brain (Norris et al., 2004). Consequently, this influences the amount of attention available for other things happening in that interaction or within the environment. Perhaps the effect observed for socially disadvantaged children is pointing to an improved attention state that frees up their minds for learning instead of monitoring the climate for social value (Quirin, Gruber, Kuhl, & Dusing, 2013). For example, physical pain and the social pain of rejection are processed in the same neural system (Cacioppo et al., 2013). Thus, it is plausible that what these interventions address for disadvantaged children is the stress and distraction associated with a feeling of "other" in the classroom. Later in life, a person's perceived control, physical health, and level of fitness have been shown to moderate age-related changes in memory (Infurna & Gerstorf, 2013).

One of the skills of adolescence is learning to successfully manage inhibition in the face of emotion, social complexity, and cognitive demand. In an experiment that varied cues signaling safety or threat, adolescents in this study (males, in particular) were highly reactive to threats, even when asked not to respond to them (Dreyfuss et al., 2014). When compared to adults and children, their brains showed greater sensitivity to these cues. Salience is a way to describe the impact on attention of something that attracts a majority of one's cognitive resources. In this case, threat signals are salient enough to earn a response from an adolescent despite other competing information (i.e., the instruction not to respond to a threat signal if one has been presented). The capacity to manage impulsivity and to resolve an action despite competing information is part of the maturation process of executive function. A functional magnetic resonance imaging (fMRI) experiment involving people between the ages of 6 and 23 years old exposed participants to neutral and aversive images. Changes in neural systems illustrated that adolescents increasingly represent and engage distributed areas that move from ventral to dorsal to process emotional stimuli, perhaps lessening the sensory affective impact of negative emotional information on the brain (Silvers, Insel, Powers, Franz, Helion, et al., 2016).

Research on how priming can influence emotion perception is another example that neuroscience has officially departed from understanding that there is 1:1 ratio between one brain function and one brain area or system (Sass, Kircher, Gauggel, & Habel, 2014). What are some of the known conditions that promote or prohibit transfer? The Yerkes Dodson curve that outlines the curvilinear relationship between good (engaged, motivated, and anticipatory) and bad (anxious, afraid, uncertain, and paralyzed) stress shows us that one can possess a skill and not be able to use it or possess the means to learn but be put in a circumstance that makes it impossible (Mattaralla, Micke, Mateo, Kozak, Foster, & Beilock, 2011; Wang et al., 2015). For instance, research on stereotype threat (Forbes & Leitner, 2014; Rydell, Van Loo, & Boucher, 2014) and sensitive periods in affective development of fear learning in adolescence (Hartley & Lee, 2015) illustrates that shapes how one responds to stress (Pearlin, 1989; Wheaton, 1996). The 2-year longitudinal study that tested an intervention for social emotional learning reports that children from lower socioeconomic backgrounds showed greater achievement in math although the improvement did not generalize to all children in the intervention group (Rimm-Kaufmann et al., 2014). Stories abound about children who are quite savvy with numbers, games, and street mathematics in their cultural contexts who come to school and do poorly during formal training (Nunes, Schliemann, & Carraher, 1993). In school, differences in the perception of task difficulty can be enough to stratify the competency of a classroom of students as problems that are harder to solve require greater support from working memory systems in the brain (Kalbfleisch, Van Meter, & Zeffiro, 2007). In a study that examined a case of prolonged stress in medical students preparing for examinations, the prefrontal cortex experienced plastic changes that negatively impacted general attentional control but were also shown to be reversible by a period of low stress and recovery (Liston, McEwen, & Casey, 2009). In the world outside school, we learn to adapt and cope and, over time, adopt a set of routines (skills, mind-sets, and responses) that are consistent with our temperament, ability, preferences, and experience.

UNDERSTANDING HOW EXECUTIVE FUNCTION TRAINING MAY AFFECT LEARNING

How might we better understand what executive function may contribute to learning? Although it has been suggested that executive function may be a proxy for influences such as socioeconomic status or parent level of education (Jacob & Parkinson, 2015), perhaps one aspect of executive function provides a clearer picture of the relationship between cognitive capacity and academic achievement. For example, *self-regulation* is defined as the capacity to respond to reactivity, impose effortful control, and regulate attention (Posner, Rothbart, & Tang, 2013; Rothbart, Sheese, Rueda, & Posner, 2011) and incorporates the dissociable skills referenced by Miyake et al. (2000). Studies of the development of attention and self-regulation in early childhood show that early success with these competencies is related to adult success (Moffitt et al., 2011). In early childhood, *orienting* attention is the main job of the brain at that state of maturation, and even this skill is different among children who come from various socioeconomic backgrounds (Stevens, Lauinger, & Neville, 2009). The classroom "trains" this aspect of attention by helping children to know what features of the environment and learning to focus on. Formal learning engages *alerting* attention, a part of a larger network of functions that support processes of effortful control and an ability to reflect rather than react. These processes begin to develop in the first 3–4 years of life (Rothbart et al., 2011) and are applied and developed throughout childhood (Posner & Rothbart, 2014). Although randomized controlled intervention experiments attempting to examine the relationship of executive function capacity to school performance have not yielded wholesale improvements in executive function in kindergarten-aged school children and show low correlation with academic achievement at approximately 0.03 for reading and math (Jacob & Parkinson, 2015), collectively these studies have shown that positive gains happen for the children who are most disadvantaged (Blair & Raver, 2014; Jacob & Parkinson, 2015; Paunesku et al., 2015; Rimm-Kaufmann et al., 2014). A measure that includes a self-referent could account for additional variance (Belland, Kim, & Hannafin, 2013; Botvinick & Braver, 2015).

The executive functions determine, in part, how (well) an individual engages in the environment. Poorer executive function is associated with conditions and outcomes such as obesity (Crescioni, Ehrlinger, Alquist, Conlon, & Baumeister, 2011), substance abuse (Riggs, Spruijt-Metz, Sakuma, Chou, & Pentz, 2010), job success (Bailey, 2007), and public safety (Denson et al., 2011). In childhood, executive functions help to determine school readiness (Blair & Razza, 2007) and later competence in skills such as math and reading (Borella, Carretti, & Pelgrina, 2010). In adults, there are a few training phenomenon that demonstrate the malleability of self-regulation skills. Computer video games and meditation have shown promise in promoting self-management skills in practical contexts such as weight loss (Kuo, Lee, & Chiou, 2016) and developing self-talk and imagery strategies to refine competitive advantage (Lane et al., 2016). An important developmental question and one that could impact how and when we teach certain skills is how do executive functions interface with more specific processing skills? In one case, cortical thickness in areas that support executive control (lateral frontal, right inferior frontal, and anterior cingulate) and alerting (parietal) provide the foundation for visual spatial attention in adults

(Westlye et al., 2011). In an fMRI study of adults 18—46 years of age, environmental cues were determined to differentially support performance on a visual matrix reasoning task (Kalbfleisch et al., 2013). Certain basic features of our physical environment, color, and visual contrast can either promote or inhibit efficient reasoning and problem solving (Kalbfleisch et al., 2013). Kalbfleisch and colleagues (2013) dissociated contributions from mutually supportive areas of visual and frontal cortices during problem solving on the task. When color was used as the main organizing feature of the matrix problem, it elicited a "reasoning heuristic" such that color collapsed complexity so that the superior frontal gyrus and color visual areas supported the most efficient performance as evidenced by speed and accuracy. Alternatively, the visual contrast condition drew upon a neural system composed of the early visual and lateral frontal cortices, illustrating a "sensory heuristic," whereby the frontal lobes were detecting the visual load of the problem and were less efficient at problem solving in these trials of the task. Another opportunity to observe how executive functions "play" with more domain-specific skills is in the case of bilingualism.

There is evidence that the brain's sensitive period ("preferred" time to learn) for learning multiple languages peaks around late puberty, although a hard and fast range of time is not specified by science to date (Jasinska & Petitto, 2013). Yet, multilingual learning from the start of formal school is not mandated in all systems of education. Indeed, one of the brain areas that facilitates language learning, Broca's area, has been shown to reserve and organize functional space in its tissue when languages are learned (Kim, Relkin, Lee, & Hirsch, 1997). In this landmark study, Kim was able to show that when a person had learned two languages approximately in time, that knowledge/skill could be functionally observed in the brain stored in adjacent tissue. For those in the study who learned a second language much later, these tissue areas were separate from one another. While interesting to an eye trained to understand images from brain scanning, is this meaningful? A robust literature on the relationship between multilingualism and executive function capacity shows that people who speak more than one language demonstrate enhanced executive function capacities for cognitive control (Garbin et al., 2010) and task switching (Barac & Bialystok, 2012), even at early stages of bilingualism (Rodríguez-Pujadas et al., 2013). Bilingualism has also been shown to influence neural systems for reading (Jasinska & Petitto, 2014). One longitudinal study that followed 61 French-speaking 5-year-olds enrolled in English immersion across 3 years demonstrated that the competencies associated with their early L2 vocabulary learning were associated with phonological short-term memory and speech perception for language skills and auditory attention and flexibility for general executive functions (Nicolay & Poncelet, 2013). In addition, neuroimaging studies show that dual language learning alters the cortical thickness of gray matter in certain cortical regions (Klein, Mok, Chen, & Watkinds, 2014) and in white matter pathways in the developing brain (Muhades et al., 2015). Thus, dual language capacity is proving to be a competency that optimizes and supports the development of other domain-specific (i.e., reading) and general skills (cognitive flexibility and attention).

The associated neurology of language function (Brun et al., 2009; Choi et al., 2010) and how the brain processes language is different for men than it is for women (Harrington & Farias, 2008). This difference has been observed in children who are school-aged (ages 9–15 years old) in studies that examined phonological and prosodic processing of language (Bitan, Lifshitz, Breznitz, & Booth, 2010) and auditory and visual processing of words (Burman, Bitan, & Booth, 2008). Bitan and colleagues (2010) showed that while the brains of females illustrate greater levels of connectivity between language processing areas, that greater connectivity can slow performance time if verbal intelligence is low. In another example, children were shown to access orthographic processing during a language task that did not require it. They were prompted to indicate a rhyming match between word pairs that were conflicting or not conflicting either visually or aurally such as "pint/mint" (conflicting) or "gate/hate" (not conflicting). As children become proficient at reading, processes for written, read (orthographic), and spoken (phonological) language interact more strongly (Cone, Burman, Bitan, Bolger, & Booth, 2008; Zecker, 1991). This additional processing slowed performance and particularly influenced examples in the task that presented ambiguity or conflict between the word pairs.

Emerging evidence shows that bilingualism tunes the anterior cingulate cortex, the part of the brain associated with conflict monitoring (Abutalebi, 2012), inhibitory control during auditory comprehension (Blumenfeld & Marian, 2011), cognitive control and task switching (Luk, Green, Abutalebi, & Grady, 2011). How does bilingualism's advantage play out across the life span? It alters children's frontal lobe function for attentional control (Arredondo, Hu, Satterfield, & Kovelman, 2016) and protects anterior temporal lobe integrity in aging (Abutalebi et al., 2014). It also promotes white matter integrity into aging (Luk, Bialystok, Craik, & Grady, 2011). Green and Abutalebi (2013) posit the adaptive control hypothesis as the means by which dual language learners gain in domain-specific (languages) and general skills such as goal maintenance, conflict monitoring, interference suppression, salient cue detection, selective response inhibition, task disengagement, task engagement, and opportunistic planning. Their model asserts that language control processes adapt to contextual demands and that the means by which the executive functions improve may not be from corollary or independent skills but embedded control processes already in use that reflexively adapt across many of these types of executive demands.

Similar to emerging data on the benefits of musical training (Slater et al., 2015; Tierney, Krizman, Skoe, Johnston, & Kraus, 2013), bilingualism may optimize the brain's capacity to resist distraction (Kapa & Columbo, 2013).

In one study, musically trained adults outperformed adults with no music training on behavioral measures of cognitive flexibility, working memory, and verbal fluency (Zuk, Benjamin, Kenyon, & Gaab, 2014). Children tested in the same study showed superior behavioral performance on measures of verbal fluency and processing speed and enhanced neural activity in brain areas supporting task switching and rule representation. Slater et al. (2015) found that at-risk children, after 1 year of musical training, were better at keeping a beat. A longitudinal study across 2 years that included children and young adults ages 6−25 years found significant improvement effects from music practice that increased executive function capacities for working memory (visual and verbal), processing speed, and reasoning (Bergman Nutley, Darki, & Klingberg, T., 2014). In his 2009 commentary, Levitin (2012) poses the question what it means to be musical? Inherent in this set of traits and skills is a brain more resilient to outside distraction and irrelevant noise. Another important feature of the executive functions is that they are likely to be the gatekeepers of higher level skills and promote transfer between domains as a learner matures and acquires new skill and broader experience. We understand that *transfer*, the level of competence that allows a person to take what is learned in one setting and apply it to another, is most likely to occur when a learner understands the general principles underlying their learning (Bransford, Brown, & Cocking, 1999). Learning at this level seeds rote fact into memory and builds on prior knowledge that aligns learning with the development of a skill or a talent (for instance, see Kalbfleisch, 2009; Kalbfleisch, 2004; Khalil, Minces, McLoughlin, & Chiba, 2013). There is emerging evidence that early childhood is a time when reasoning, symbolic representation, and communication skills can be taught and learned preceding expected, protracted stages of neural development (Gogtay et al., 2006; Kundakovic & Champagne, 2015; Lee, Wallace, Raznahan, Clasen, & Giedd, 2014; Lu et al., 2009) for certain types of skills that emerge across childhood and early life (DeWind & Brannon, 2012; Gadzichowski, Pasnak, & Kidd, 2013; Kidd et al., 2012; Kidd et al., 2013, 2014; Pasnak et al., 2014). Furthermore, neuroscience is showing us that just because there is not a significant effect in a randomized controlled intervention examining how executive function relates to academic achievement (Jacob & Parkinson, 2015), it does not mean there are not meaningful changes occurring in neuroplasticity (Posner et al., 2014). The measures took place at different scales, in different contexts, and with different assessment criteria.

Consequently, the executive functions are the closest fundamental proxy for understanding the neural basis of complex learning that we have. Promoting skill transfer is an exercise of process and practice more than the making of a product. For example, if a child learns to dribble a basketball on a court in their school gym, with practice, he/she retains the ability to dribble the ball at home in the driveway, on another court at the school in grandma's hometown or in the local park. In each of these cases, a good game and some fun may ensue (the product), but it is the practice and the process of dribbling that led to that competency and the person's ability to execute dribbling behavior in each of those different contexts. And yet, a metaanalysis reveals that attempts to study the relationship between executive functions and academic achievement fall short at the causal level (Jacob & Parkinson, 2015), although an intervention with exercise for children with attention-deficit hyperactivity disorder has shown an ability to improve inhibitory control and cognitive flexibility in 7–9 year-old-children (Scudder et al., 2014). More evidence for the stability of early life factors includes documented cortical changes observed in groups of low and high general cognitive ability when variables such as birthweight and parental education are taken into account and illustrate a consistent and stable influence across life (Walhovd, Krogsrud, Amlien, Bartsch, Bjornerud, et al., 2016). Finally, there is evidence that individual differences in executive functions are stable in late adolescence but can still be influenced by the environment (Friedman et al., 2016). In sum, it is an achievement that we can outline the developmental trajectories and persistence of executive functions and that we have some ideas as to how the environment can promote or inhibit their capacities. Still, a caveat emerges from the realm of formal education. For instance, inhibition develops through systems devoted to acquiring early expertise. This has been shown to interfere with the learning of certain scientific concepts that are taught later in childhood (Masson & Pesenti, 2014; Brault Foisy, Potvin, Riopel, & Masson, 2015; Potvin, Termel, & Masson, 2014). This is a time when the practice of the basic skill (inhibition) overrides memory processes devoted to learning and comprehension. This purportedly happens as a result of the salience of surface features of a problem that become distractors during problem solving (Stavy, Goel, Critchley, & Dolan, 2006). Recent research is beginning to demonstrate that intuitive interference can be halted with a disruptive warning at the correct time (Babai, Shalev, & Stavy, 2015; Stavy & Babai, 2010). Thus, having robust executive function skills is necessary to learn and to achieve but not sufficient. The comprehensive understanding of how executive function skills may influence plasticity can help researchers and educators map and account for the dynamic environmental factors, variability of neural structures, and nonintrospectable processes as part of the experimental context and, eventually, pedagogy and curriculum development. Taken together, they are at the center of our "endogenous heuristic" (Kalbfleisch, 2008), the map inherent in our neural development that, as we improve our methodological specificity to uncover it, will support our efforts to discern the predictive validity of education and training tailored to promote skill development and anticipate obstacles to learning and life quality across the life span.

REFERENCES

Abutalebi, J., Canini, M., Della Rosa, P. A., Sheung, L. P., Green, D. W., & Weekes, B. S. (2014). Bilingualism protects anterior temporal lobe integrity in aging. *Neurobiology of Aging, 35*(9), 2126−2133. Available from http://dx.doi.org/10.1016/j.neurobiolaging.2014.03.010.

Abutalebi, J., Della Rosa, P. A., Green, D. W., Hernandez, M., Scifo, P., Keim, R., & Costa, A. (2012). Bilingualism tunes the anterior cingulate cortex for conflict monitoring. *Cerebral Cortex, 22*(9), 2076−2086. Available from http://dx.doi.org/10.1093/cercor/bhr287.

Abutalebi, J., Guidi, L., Borsa, V., Canini, M., Della Rosa, P. A., Parris, B. A., & Weekes, B. S. (2015). Bilingualism provides a neural reserve for aging populations. *Neuropsychologia, 69*, 201−210. Available from http://dx.doi.org/10.1016/j.neuropsychologia.2015.01.040.

Alvarez, J. A., & Emory, E. (2006). Executive function and the frontal lobes: A meta-analytic. *Neuropsychology Review, 16*(1), 17−42.

Arredondo, M. M., Hu, X. S., Satterfield, T., & Kovelman, I. (2016). Bilingualism alters children's frontal lobe functioning for attentional control. *Developmental Science*. Available from http://dx.doi.org/10.1111/desc.12377.

Austin, G., Groppe, K., & Elsner, B. (2014). The reciprocal relationship between executive function and theory of mind in middle childhood: A 1-year longitudinal perspective. *Frontiers in Psychology, 5*, 655. Available from http://dx.doi.org/10.3389/fpsyg.2014.00655.

Babai, R., Shalev, E., & Stavy, R. (2015). A warning intervention improves students' ability to overcome intuitive interference. *ZDM Mathematics Education, 47*, 735. Available from http://dx.doi.org/10.1007/s11858-015-0670-y.

Bailey, C. E. (2007). Cognitive accuracy and intelligent executive function in the brain and in business. *Annals of the New York Academy of Sciences, 1118*, 122−141.

Barac, R., & Bialystok, E. (2012). Bilingual effects on cognitive and linguistic development: Role of language, cultural background, and education. *Child Development, 83*(2), 413−422. Available from http://dx.doi.org/10.1111/j.1467-8624.2011.01707.x.

Barac, R., Bialystok, E., Castro, D. C., & Sanchez, M. (2014). The cognitive development of young dual language learners: A critical review. *Early Childhood Research Quarterly, 29*(4), 699−714.

Bell, R., Roer, J. P., & Buchner, A. (2013). Irrelevant speech disrupts item-context binding. *Experimental Psychology, 60*(5), 376−384. Available from http://dx.doi.org/10.1027/1618-3169/a000212.

Belland, B. R., Kim, C., & Hannafin, M. J. (2013). A framework for designing scaffolds that improve motivation and cognition. *Educational Psychologist, 48*(4), 243−270.

Bergman Nutley, S., Darki, F., & Klingberg, T. (2014). Music practice is associated with development of working memory during childhood and adolescence. *Frontiers in Human Neuroscience, 7*, 926. Available from http://dx.doi.org/10.3389/fnhum.2013.00926.

Berkman, E. T., Graham, A. M., & Fisher, P. A. (2012). Training self-control: A domain-general translational neuroscience approach. *Child Developmental Perspectives, 6*(4), 374−384.

Best, J. R., & Miller, P. H. (2010). A developmental perspective on executive function. *Child Development, 81*(6), 1641−1660. Available from http://dx.doi.org/10.1111/j.1467-8624.2010.01499.x.

Bitan, T., Lifshitz, A., Breznitz, Z., & Booth, J. R. (2010). Bidirectional connectivity between hemispheres occurs at multiple levels in language processing but depends on sex. *Journal of Neuroscience, 30*(35), 11576−11585. Available from http://dx.doi.org/10.1523/JNEUROSCI.1245-10.2010.

Bjornebekk, A., Westlye, L. T., Fjell, A. M., Grydeland, H., & Walhovd, K. B. (2012). Social reward dependence and brain white matter microstructure. *Cerebral Cortex*, *22*(11), 2672–2679. Available from http://dx.doi.org/10.1093/cercor/bhr345.

Blair, C., & Raver, C. C. (2014). Closing the achievement gap through modification of neuro-cognitive and neuroendocrine function: Results from a cluster randomized controlled trial of an innovative approach to the education of children in kindergarten. *PLoS One*, *9*(11), e112393. Available from http://dx.doi.org/10.1371/journal.pone.0112393.

Blair, C., & Razza, R. P. (2007). Relating effortful control, executive function, and false-belief understanding to emerging math and literacy ability in kindergarten. *Child Development*, *8*, 647–663.

Blakemore, S. J., & Mills, K. L. (2014). Is adolescence a sensitive period for sociocultural processing? *Annual Review of Psychology*, *65*, 187–207. Available from http://dx.doi.org/10.1146/annurev-psych-010213-115202.

Blumenfeld, H. K., & Marian, V. (2011). Bilingualism influences inhibitory control in auditory comprehension. *Cognition*, *118*(2), 245–257. Available from http://dx.doi.org/10.1016/j.cognition.2010.10.012.

Borella, E., Carretti, B., & Pelgrina, S. (2010). The specific role of inhibition in reading comprehension in good and poor comprehenders. *Journal of Learning Disabilities*, *43*, 541–552.

Boschloo, A., Krabbendam, L., Aben, A., de Groot, R., & Jolles, J. (2014). Sorting Test, Tower Test, and BRIEF-SR do not predict school performance of healthy adolescents in preuniversity education. *Frontiers in Psychology*, *5*, 287. Available from http://dx.doi.org/10.3389/fpsyg.2014.00287.

Botvinick, M., & Braver, T. (2015). Motivation and cognitive control: From behavior to neural mechanism. *Annual Review of Psychology*, *66*, 83–113. Available from http://dx.doi.org/10.1146/annurev-psych-010814-015044.

Boutla, M., Supalla, T., Newport, E. L., & Bavalier, D. (2004). Short-term memory span: Insights from sign language. *Nature Neuroscience*, *7*(9), 997–1002. Available from http://dx.doi.org/10.1038/nn1298.

Boyd, T. M., & Sautter, S. W. (1993). Route-finding: A measure of everyday executive functioning in the head-injured adult. *Applied Cognitive Psychology*, *7*(2), 171–181. Available from http://dx.doi.org/10.1002/acp.23500700208.

Bransford, J. D., Brown, A. L., & Cocking, R. R. (1999). *How people learn: Brain, mind, experience, and school*. Washington, DC: National Academy Press.

Brault Foisy, L. M., Potvin, P., Riopel, M., & Masson, S. (2015). Is inhibition involved in overcoming a common physics misconception in mechanics? *Trends in Neuroscience and Education*, *4*(1–2), 26–36.

Brun, C. C., Leporé, N., Luders, E., Chou, Y. Y., Madsen, S. K., Toga, A. W., & Thompson, P. M. (2009). Sex differences in brain structure in auditory and cingulate regions. *Neuroreport*, *20*(10), 930–935.

Burman, D. D., Bitan, T., & Booth, J. R. (2008). Sex differences in neural processing of language among children. *Neuropsychologia*, *46*(5), 1349–1362. Available from http://dx.doi.org/10.1016/j.neuropsychologia.2007.12.021.

Cacioppo, S., Frum, C., Asp, E., Weiss, R. M., Lewis, J. W., & Cacioppo, J. T. (2013). A quantitative meta-analysis of functional imaging studies of social rejection. *Scientific Reports*, *3*, 2027. Available from http://dx.doi.org/10.1038/srep02027.

Choi, C. H., Lee, J. M., Koo, B. B., Park, J. S., Kim, D. S., Kwon, J. S., & Kim, I. Y. (2010). Sex differences in the temporal lobe white matter and the corpus callosum: A diffusion tensor tractography study. *Neuroreport*, *21*(1), 73–77. Available from http://dx.doi.org/10.1097/WNR.0b013e3283345eb0.

Cone, N. E., Burman, D. D., Bitan, T., Bolger, D. J., & Booth, J. R. (2008). Developmental changes in brain regions involved in phonological and orthographic processing during spoken language processing. *NeuroImage, 41*(2), 623−635. Available from http://dx.doi.org/10.1016/j.neuroimage.2008.02.055.

Crescioni, A. W., Ehrlinger, J., Alquist, J. L., Conlon, K. E., Baumeister, R. F., et al. (2011). High trait self-control predicts positive health behaviors and success in weight loss. *Journal of Health Psychology, 16*, 750−759.

Crone, E., Wendelken, C., Donohue, S., van Leijenhorst, L., & Bunge, S. A. (2006). Neurocognitive development of the ability to manipulate information in working memory. *Proceedings of the National Academy of Sciences of the United States of America, 103*(24), 9315−9320.

Dajani, D. R., Llalbre, M. M., Nebel, M. B., Mostofsky, S. H., & Uddin, L. Q. (2016). Heterogeneity of executive functions among comorbid neurodevelopmental disorders. *Scientific Reports, 9*(6), 36566−36580.

Darki, F., & Klingberg, T. (2015). The role of fronto-parietal and fronto-striatal networks in the development of working memory: A longitudinal study. *Cerebral Cortex, 25*(6), 1587−1595. Available from http://dx.doi.org/10.1093/cercor/bht352.

Deoni, S. C. L., Dean, D. C., III, Remer, J., Dirks, H., & O'Muircheartaigh, J. (2015). Cortical maturation and myelination in healthy toddlers and young children. *NeuroImage, 115*, 147−161. Available from http://dx.doi.org/10.1016/j.neuroimage.2015.04.058.

Dewind, N. K., & Brannon, E. M. (2012). Malleability of the approximate number system: Effects of feedback and training. *Frontiers in Human Neuroscience, 6*, 68. Available from http://dx.doi.org/10.3389/fnhum.2012.00068.

Diamond, A. (2011). Interventions shown to aid executive function development in children 4 to 12 years old. *Science, 333*(6045), 959−964. Available from http://dx.doi.org/10.1126/science.1204529.

Diamond, A. (2013). Executive functions. *Annual Review of Psychology, 64*, 135−168. Available from http://dx.doi.org/10.1146/annurev-psych-113011-143750.

Dreyfuss, M., Caudle, J., Drysdale, A. T., Johnston, N. E., Cohen, A. O., Somerville, L. H., & Casey, B. J. (2014). Teens impulsively react rather than retreat from threat. *Developmental Neuroscience, 36*(3-4), 220−227.

Dumontheil, I., & Klingberg, T. (2012). Brain activity during a visuospatial working memory task predicts arithmetical performance 2 years later. *Cerebral Cortex, 22*(5), 1078−1085. Available from http://dx.doi.org/10.1093/cercor/bhr175.

Duncan, J., & Owen, A. M. (2000). Common regions of the human frontal lobe recruited by diverse cognitive demands. *Trends in Neuroscience, 23*(10), 475−483.

Fandakova, Y., Sander, M. C., Werkle-Bergner, M., & Shing, Y. L. (2014). Age differences in short-term memory binding are related to working memory performance across the lifespan. *Psychology and Aging, 29*(1), 140−149. Available from http://dx.doi.org/10.1037/a0035347.

Ferrer, E., Whitaker, K. J., Steele, J. S., Green, C. T., Wendelken, C., & Bunge, S. A. (2013). White matter maturation supports the development of reasoning ability through its influence on processing speed. *Developmental Science, 16*(6), 941−951. Available from http://dx.doi.org/10.1111/desc.12088.

Fjell, A. M., Walhovd, K. B., Brown, T. T., Kuperman, J. M., Chung, Y., Hagler, D. J., & Dale, A. M. (2012). Multimodal imaging of the self-regulating developing brain. *Proceedings of the National Academy of Sciences of the United States of America, 109*(48), 19620−19625. Available from http://dx.doi.org/10.1073/pnas.1208243109.

Forbes, C. E., & Leitner, J. B. (2014). Stereotype threat engenders neural attentional bias toward negative feedback to undermine performance. *Biological Psychology, 102*, 98−107. Available from http://dx.doi.org/10.1016/j.biopsycho.2014.07.007.

Friedman, N. P., Miyake, A., Altamirano, L. J., Corley, R. P., Young, S. E., Rhea, S. A., & Hewitt, J. K. (2016). Stability and change in executive function abilities from late adolescence to early adulthood: A longitudinal twin study. *Developmental Psychology, 52*(2), 326−340. Available from http://dx.doi.org/10.1037/dev0000075.

Gadzichowski, K. M., Pasnak, R., & Kidd, J. K. (2013). What's odd about that? Exploring preschoolers' ability to apply the oddity principle to stimuli differing in colour, size, or form. *European Journal of Developmental Psychology, 10*, 739−751.

Gallant, S. N. (2016). Mindfulness meditation practice and executive functioning: Breaking down the benefit. *Consciousness and Cognition, 4*, 116−130.

Garbin, G., Sanjuan, A., Forn, C., Bustamante, J. C., Rodríguez-Pujadas, A., Belloch, V., & Avila, C. (2010). Bridging language and attention: Brain basis of the impact of bilingualism on cognitive control. *NeuroImage, 53*(4), 1272−1278. Available from http://dx.doi.org/10.1016/j.neuroimage.2010.05.078.

Garon, N., Bryson, S. E., & Smith, I. M. (2008). Executive function in pre-schoolers: A review using an integrative framework. *Psychological Bulletin, 134*, 31−60.

Geake, J., & Hansen, P. (2005). Neural correlates of intelligence as revealed by fMRI of fluid analogies. *NeuroImage, 26*(2), 555−564.

Geake, J., & Hansen, P. (2010). Functional neural correlates of fluid and crystallized analogizing. *NeuroImage, 49*(4), 3489−3497.

Gerstadt, C. L., Hong, Y. J., & Diamond, A. (1994). The relationship between cognition and action: Performance of children 3.5-7 years old on a Stroop-like day-night test. *Cognition, 53*, 129−153.

Gogtay, N., Nugent, T. F., 3rd, Herman, D. H., Ordonez, A., Greenstein, D., Hayashi, K. M., & Thompson, P. M. (2006). Dynamic mapping of normal human hippocampal development. *Hippocampus, 16*(8), 664−672.

Goldberg, E. (2001). *The executive brain: Frontal lobes and the civilized mind*. New York, NY: Oxford University Press.

Green, D. W., & Abutalebi, J. (2013). Language control in bilinguals: The adaptive control hypothesis. *Journal of Cognitive Psychology, 25*(5), 515−530. Available from http://dx.doi.org/10.1080/20445911.2013.796377.

Grydeland, H., Walhovd, K. B., Tamnes, C. K., Westlye, L. T., & Fjell, A. M. (2013). Intracortical myelin links with performance variability across the human lifespan: Results from T1 and T2-weighted MRI myelin mapping and diffusion tensor imaging. *Journal of Neuroscience, 33*(47), 18618−18630. Available from http://dx.doi.org/10.1523/JNEUROSCI.2811-13.2013.

Grydeland, H., Westlye, L. T., Walhovd, K. B., & Fjell, A. M. (2016). Intracortical posterior cingulate myelin content relates to error processing: Results from T1 and T2-weighted MRI myelin mapping and electrophysiology in healthy adults. *Cerebral Cortex, 26*(6), 2402−2410. Available from http://dx.doi.org/10.1093/cercor/bhv065.

Hampshire, A., Thompson, R., Duncan, J., & Owen, A. M. (2011). Lateral prefrontal cortex subregions make dissociable contributions during fluid reasoning. *Cerebral Cortex, 21*(1), 1−10. Available from http://dx.doi.org/10.1093/cercor/bhq085.

Harrington, G. S., & Farias, S. T. (2008). Sex differences in language processing: Functional MRI methodological considerations. *Journal of Magnetic Resonance Imaging, 27*(6), 1221−1228. Available from http://dx.doi.org/10.1002/jmri.21374.

Hartley, C. S., & Lee, F. S. (2015). Sensitive periods in affective development: Nonlinear maturation of fear learning. *Neuropsychopharmacology: Official Publication of the American College of Neuropsychopharmacology, 40*(1), 50−60. Available from http://dx.doi.org/10.1038/npp.2014.179.

Hoffman, W., Schmeichel, B. J., & Baddeley, A. D. (2012). Executive functions and self-regulation. *Trends in Cognitive Sciences, 16*(3), 174−180. Available from http://dx.doi.org/10.1016/j.tics.2012.01.006.

Huizinga, M., Dolan, C. V., & van der Molen, M. W. (2006). Age-related change in executive function: Developmental trends and a latent variable analysis. *Neuropsychologia, 44*(11), 2017−2036.

Infurna, F. J., & Gerstorf, D. (2013). Linking perceived control, physical activity, and biological health to memory change. *Psychology and Aging, 28*(4), 1147−1163. Available from http://dx.doi.org/10.1037/a0033327.

Jacob, R., & Parkinson, J. (2015). The potential for school-based interventions that target executive function to improve academic achievement: A review. *Review of Educational Research, 85*(4), 512−552. Available from http://dx.doi.org/10.3102/0034654314561338.

Jasinska, K., & Petitto, L. A. (2013). How age of bilingual exposure can change the neural systems for language in the developing brain: A functional near infrared spectroscopy investigation of syntactic processing in monolingual and bilingual children. *Developmental Cognitive Neuroscience, 6*, 87−101. Available from http://dx.doi.org/10.1016/j.dcn.2013.06.005.

Kalbfleisch, M. L. (2004). The functional neural anatomy of talent. *The Anatomical Record, 277B*(1), 21−36. Available from http://dx.doi.org/10.1002/ar.b.20010.

Kalbfleisch, M.L. (2008). Getting to the heart of the brain: Using cognitive neuroscience to explore the nature of human ability and performance. In: Kalbfleisch, L. (Ed.) Special issue on the cognitive neuroscience of giftedness. *Roeper Review*, 30 (3), 162−170. Available from http://dx.doi.org/10.1080/02783190802199321.

Kalbfleisch, M. L. (2009). The neural plasticity of giftedness. In L. Shavanina (Ed.), *International handbook on giftedness* (pp. 275−293). New York, NY: Springer Science.

Kalbfleisch, M. L. (2013). Twice exceptional learners. In J. A. Plucker, & C. M. Callahan (Eds.), *Critical issues and practices in gifted education* (*Second Edition*, pp. 269−287). Waco, TX: Prufrock Press.

Kalbfleisch, M. L., Debettencourt, M. T., Kopperman, R., Banasiak, M., Roberts, J. M., & Halavi, M. (2013). Environmental influences on neural systems of relational complexity. *Frontiers in Psychology, 4*, 631. Available from http://dx.doi.org/10.3389/fpsyg.2013.00631.

Kalbfleisch, M. L., & Loughan, A. R. (2011). Impact of IQ discrepancy on executive function in high-functioning autism: Insight into twice exceptionality, online *Journal of Autism and Developmental Disorders, 42*, 390−400. http://dx.doi.org/10.1007/s10803-011-1257-2 (in print, 2012, 42, pp. 390-400)

Kalbfleisch, M. L., Van Meter, J. W., & Zeffiro, T. A. (2006). The influences of task difficulty and response correctness on neural systems supporting fluid reasoning, online, 2007 print *Cognitive Neurodynamics, 1*(1), 71−84. Available from http://dx.doi.org/10.1007/s11571-006-9007-4

Kane, M. J., & Engel, R. W. (2002). The role of the prefrontal cortex in working-memory capacity, executive attention and general fluid intelligence: An individual differences perspective. *Psychonomic Bulletin and Review, 9*(4), 637−671.

Kapa, L. L., & Columbo, J. (2013). Attentional control in early and later bilingual children. *Cognitive Development, 28*(3), 233−246. Available from http://dx.doi.org/10.1016/j.cogdev.2013.01.011.

Karbach, J., Strobach, T., & Schubert, T. (2014). Adaptive working memory training benefits reading, but not mathematics in middle childhood. *Child Neuropsychology, 21*(3), 285−301.

Karbach, J., & Unger, K. (2014). Executive control training from middle childhood to adolescence. *Frontiers in Psychology, 5*, 390. Available from http://dx.doi.org/10.3389/fpsyg.2014.00390.

Khalil, A. K., Minces, V., McLoughlin, G., & Chiba, A. (2013). Group rhythmic synchrony and attention in children. *Frontiers in Psychology*, *4*, 564. Available from http://dx.doi.org/10.3389/fpsyg.2013.00564.

Kidd, J. K., Carlson, A. G., Gadzichowski, K. M., Boyer, C. E., Gallington, D. A., & Pasnak, R. (2013). Effects of patterning instruction on the academic achievement of first grade children. *Journal of Research in Childhood Education*, *27*, 224–238.

Kidd, J. K., Curby, T. W., Boyer, C. E., Gadzichowski, K. M., Gallington, D. A., Machado, J. A., & Pasnak, R. P. (2012). Benefits of interventions focused on oddity and seriation, literacy, or numeracy. *Early Education and Development*, *23*, 900–918.

Kidd, J. K., Pasnak, R., Gadzichowski, K. M., Gallington, D. A., McKnight, P. E., Boyer, C. E., & Carlson, A. (2014). Instructing first-grade children on patterning improves reading and mathematics. *Early Education and Development*, *25*, 134–151.

Kim, K. H., Relkin, N. R., Lee, K. M., & Hirsch, J. (1997). Distinct cortical areas associate with native and second languages. *Nature*, *388*(6638), 171–174.

Klein, D., Mok, K., Chen, J. K., & Watkinds, K. E. (2014). Age of language learning shapes brain structure: A cortical thickness study of bilingual and monolingual individuals. *Brain and Language*, *31*, 20–24. Available from http://dx.doi.org/10.1016/j.bandl.2013.05.014.

Klingberg, T. (2010). Training and plasticity of working memory. *Trends in Cognitive Science*, *14*(7), 317–324, doi 10.1016/j.tics.2010.05.002.

Klingberg, T., Forssberg, H., & Westerberg, H. (2002). Increased brain activity in frontal and parietal cortex underlies the development of visuospatial working memory capacity during childhood. *Journal of Cognitive Neuroscience*, *14*(1), 1–10.

Kundakovic, M., & Champagne, F. A. (2015). Early-life experience, epigenetics, and the developing brain. *Neuropsychopharmacology: Official Publication of the American College of Neuropsychopharmacology*, *40*(1), 141–153. Available from http://dx.doi.org/10.1038/npp.2014.140.

Kuo, H. C., Lee, C. C., & Chiou, W. B. (2016). The power of the virtual ideal self in weight control: Weight-reduced avatars can enhance the tendency to delay gratification and regulate dietary practices. *Cyberpsychology, Behaviour and Social Networking*, *19*(2), 80–85. Available from http://dx.doi.org/10.1089/cyber.2015.0203.

Lane, A. M., Totterdell, P., MacDonald, I., Devonport, T. J., Friesen, A. P., Beedie, C. J., & Nevill, A. (2016). Brief online training enhances competitive performance: Findings of the BBC Lab UK Psychological Skills Intervention Study. *Frontiers in Psychology*, *7*, 413. Available from http://dx.doi.org/10.3389/fpsyg.2016.00413.

Lee, N. R., Wallace, G. L., Raznahan, A., Clasen, L. S., & Giedd, J. N. (2014). Trail making test performance in youth varies as a function of anatomical coupling between the prefrontal cortex and distributed cortical regions. *Frontiers in Psychology*, *5*(496). Available from http://dx.doi.org/10.3389/fpsyg.2014.00496.

Levitin, D. J. (2012). What does it mean to be musical? *Neuron*, *73*(4), 633–637. Available from http://dx.doi.org/10.1016/j.neuron.2012.01.017.

Lewis, F. C., Reeve, R. A., & Johnson, K. A. (2016). A longitudinal analysis of attention networks in 6 to 11 year old children. *Child Neuropsychology*, *24*, 21.

Li, L., Abutalebi, J., Zou, L., Yan, X., Liu, L., Feng, X., & Ding, G. (2015). Bilingualism alters brain functional connectivity between "control" regions and "language" regions: Evidence from bimodal bilinguals. *Neuropsychologia*, *71*, 236–247. Available from http://dx.doi.org/10.1016/j.neuropsychologia.2015.04.007.

Libby, L. A., Hannula, D. E., & Ranganath, C. (2014). Medial temporal lobe coding of item and spatial information during relational binding in working memory. *Journal of Neuroscience,* *34*(43), 14233–14342. Available from http://dx.doi.org/10.1523/JNEUROSCI.5341-13.2014.

Liston, C., McEwen, B. S., & Casey, B. J. (2009). Psychosocial stress reversibly disrupts prefrontal processing and attentional control. *Proceedings of the National Academy of Sciences* *of the United States of America, 106*(3), 912–917. Available from http://dx.doi.org/10.1073/pnas.0807041106.

Luerssen, A., Gyurak, A., Ayduk, O., Wendelken, C., & Binge, S. A. (2015). Delay of gratification in childhood linked to cortical interactions with the nucleus accumbens. *Social* *Cognitive and Affective Neuroscience, 10*(12), 1769–1776. Available from http://dx.doi.org/10.1093/scan/nsv068.

Luk, G., Bialystok, E., Craik, F. I., & Grady, C. L. (2011). Lifelong bilingualism maintains white matter integrity in older adults. *Journal of Neuroscience, 31*(46), 16808–16813. Available from http://dx.doi.org/10.1523/JNEUROSCI.4563-11.2011.

Luk, G., Green, D. W., Abutalebi, J., & Grady, C. (2011). Cognitive control for language switching in bilinguals: A quantitative meta-analysis of functional neuroimaging studies. *Language* *and Cognitive Processes, 27*(10), 1479–1488. Available from http://dx.doi.org/10.1080/01690965.2011.613209.

Masson, N., & Pesenti, M. (2014). Attentional bias induced by solving simple and complex addition and subtraction problems. *The Quarterly Journal of Experimental Psychology, 67*(8), 1514–1526. Available from http://dx.doi.org/10.1080/17470218.2014.903985.

Mattarella-Micke, M., Mateo, J., Kozak, M. N., Foster, K., & Beilock, S. L. (2011). Choke or thrive? The relation between salivary cortisol and math performance depends on individual differences in working memory and math-anxiety. *Emotion, 11*(4), 1000–1005. Available from http://dx.doi.org/10.1037/a0023224.

Mills, K. L., Dumontheil, I., Speekenbrink, M., & Blakemore, S. J. (2015). Multitasking during social interactions in adolescence and early adulthood. *Royal Society of Open Science, 2,* 150117. Available from http://dx.doi.org/10.1098/rsos.150117.

Mills, K. L., Lalonde, F., Clasaen, L. S., Giedd, J. N., & Blakemore, S. J. (2014). Developmental changes in the structure of the social brain in late childhood and adolescence. *Social Cognitive and Affective Neuroscience, 9*(1), 123–131. Available from http://dx.doi.org/10.1093/scan/nss113.

Mischel, W., Ayduk, O., Berman, M. G., Casey, B. J., Gotlib, I. H., Jonides, J., & Shoda, Y. (2011). 'Willpower' over the life span: Decomposing self-regulation. *Social Cognitive and* *Affective Neuroscience, 6*, 252–256. Available from http://dx.doi.org/10.1093/scan/nsq081.

Mischel, W., & Mischel, H. N. (1983). Development of children's knowledge of self-control strategies. *Child Development, 54*, 603–619.

Miyake, A., Friedman, N. P., Emerson, M. J., Witzki, A. H., Howerter, A., & Wager, T. D. (2000). The unity and diversity of executive functions and their contributions to complex "frontal lobe" tasks: A latent variable analysis. *Cognitive Psychology, 41*, 49–100.

Moffitt, T. E., Arseneault, L., Belsky, D., Dickson, N., Hancox, R. J., Harrington, H., & Caspi, A. (2011). A gradient of childhood self-control predicts health, wealth, and public safety. *Proceedings of the National Academy of Sciences of the United States of America,* *108*(7), 2693–2698.

Mohades, S. G., Van Schuerbeek, P., Rosseel, Y., Van De Craen, P., Luypaert, R., & Baeken, C. (2015). White-matter development is different in bilingual and monolingual children: A longitudinal DTI study. *PLoS One, 10*(2), e0117968. Available from http://dx.doi.org/10.1371/journal.pone.0117968.

Nicolay, A. C., & Poncelet, M. (2013). Cognitive abilities underlying second-language vocabulary acquisition in an early second-language immersion education context: A longitudinal study. *Journal of Experimental Child Psychology, 115*(4), 655−671. Available from http://dx.doi.org/10.1016/j.jecp.2013.04.002.

Niogi, S. N., & McCandliss, B. D. (2006). Left lateralized white matter microstructure accounts for individual differences in reading ability and disability. *Neuropsychologia, 44*(11), 2178−2188.

Norris, C. J., Chen, E. E., Zhu, D. C., Small, S. L., & Cacioppo, J. T. (2004). The interaction of social and emotional processes in the brain. *Journal of Cognitive Neuroscience, 16*(10), 1818−1829.

Nunes, T., Schliemann, A. D., & Carraher, D. W. (1993). *Street mathematics and school mathematics*. New York, NY: Cambridge University Press.

Paunesku, D., Walton, G. M., Romero, C., Smith, E. N., Yeager, D. S., & Dweck, C. S. (2015). Mind-set interventions are a scalable treatment for academic underachievement. *Psychological Science, 26*(6), 784−793. Available from http://dx.doi.org/10.1177/0956797615571017.

Pearlin, L. I. (1989). The sociological study of stress. *Journal of Health and Social Behavior, 30*(3), 241−256.

Posner, M. I., & Rothbart, M. K. (2014). Attention to learning of school subjects. *Trends in Neuroscience and Education, 3*(1), 14−17.

Posner, M. I., Rothbart, M. K., Sheese, B. E., & Voelker, P. (2014). Developing attention: Behavioral and brain mechanisms. *Advances in Neuroscience (Hindawi), 2014*, 405094.

Posner, M. I., Rothbart, M. K., & Tang, Y. (2013). Developing self-regulation in early childhood. *Trends in Neuroscience and Education, 2*(3−4), 107−110.

Potvin, P., Termel, E., & Masson, S. (2014). Linking neuroscientific research on decision making to the educational context of novice students assigned to a multiple-choice scientific task involving common misconceptions about electrical circuits. *Frontiers in Human Neuroscience, 8*, 14. Available from http://dx.doi.org/10.3389/fnhum.2014.00014.

Quirin, M., Gruber, T., Kuhl, J., & Dusing, R. (2013). Neural correlates of social motivation: An fMRI study on power versus affiliation. *International Journal of Psychophysiology: Official Journal of the International Organization of Psychophysiology, 88*(3), 289−295. Available from http://dx.doi.org/10.1016/j.ijpsycho.2012.07.003.

Riggs, N. R., Spruijt-Metz, D., Sakuma, K. K., Chou, C. P., & Pentz, M. A. (2010). Executive cognitive function and food intake in children. *Journal of Nutrition Education and Behavior, 42*, 398−403.

Rimm-Kaufmann, S. E., Larsen, R. A. A., Baroody, A. E., Curby, T. W., Thomas, J. B., Meritt, E. G., & DeCoster, J. (2014). Efficacy of the responsive classroom approach: Results from a 3-year longitudinal randomized controlled trial. *American Educational Research Journal, 51*(3), 567−603. Available from http://dx.doi.org/10.3102/0002831214523821.

Rodríguez-Pujadas, A., Sanjuán, A., Ventura-Campos, N., Román, P., Martin, C., Barceló, F., & Avila, C. (2013). Bilinguals use language-control brain areas more than monolinguals to perform non-linguistic switching tasks. *PLoS One, 8*(9), e73028. Available from http://dx.doi.org/10.1371/journal.pone.0073028.

Roer, J. P., Bell, R., & Buchner, A. (2014). Please silence your cell phone: Your ringtone captures other people's attention. *Noise & Health, 16*, 34−39.

Rosenthal, M., Wallace, G. L., Lawson, R., Wills, M. C., Dixon, E., Yerys, B. E., & Kenworthy, L. (2013). Impairments of real-world executive function increase from childhood to adolescence in autism spectrum disorders. *Neuropsychology, 27*(1), 13−18. Available from http://dx.doi.org/10.1037/a0031299.

Rothbart, M. K., Sheese, B. E., Rueda, M. R., & Posner, M. I. (2011). Developing mechanisms of self-regulation in early life. *Emotion Review: Journal of the International Society for Research on Emotion, 3*(2), 207−213.

Rueda, M. R., Rothbart, M. K., McCandliss, B. D., Saccomanno, L., & Posner, M. I. (2005). Training, maturation, and genetic influences on the development of executive attention. *Proceedings of the National Academy of Sciences of the United States of America, 102,* 14931−14936.

Rydell, R. J., Van Loo, K. J., & Boucher, K. L. (2014). Stereotype threat and executive functions: Which functions mediate different threat-related outcomes? *Personality and Social Psychology Bulletin, 40*(3), 377−390. Available from http://dx.doi.org/10.1177/0146167213513475.

Sass, K., Kircher, T., Gauggel, S., & Habel, U. (2014). An fMRI-study on semantic priming of panic-related information in depression without comorbid anxiety. *Psychiatry Research, 222* (1−2), 37−42. http://dx.doi.org/10.1016/j.pscychresns.2014.02.008

Scudder, M. R., Lambourne, K., Drollette, E. S., Herrmann, S. D., Washburn, R. A., Donnelly, J. E., & Hillman, C. H. (2014). Aerobic capacity and cognitive control in elementary school-age children. *Medicine and Science in Sports and Exercise, 46*(5), 1025−1035. Available from http://dx.doi.org/10.1249/MSS.0000000000000199.

Shallice, T., & Burgess, P. W. (1991). Deficits in strategy application following frontal lobe damage in man. *Brain, 114,* 727−741.

Shaw, P. (2007). Intelligence and the developing human brain. *BioEssays: News and Reviews in Molecular, Cellular and Developmental Biology, 29*(10), 962−973. Available from http://dx.doi.org/10.1002/bies.20641.

Shaw, P., Greenstein, D., Lerch, J., Clasen, L., Lenroot, R., Gogtay, N., & Giedd, J. (2006). Intellectual ability and cortical development in children and adolescents. *Nature, 440*(7084), 676−679. Available from http://dx.doi.org/10.1038/nature04513.

Silvers, J. A., Insel, C., Powers, A., Franz, P., Helion, C., Martin, R., & Ochsner, K. N. (2016). The transition from childhood to adolescence is marked by a general decrease in amygdala reactivity and an affect-specific ventral-to-dorsal shift in medial prefrontal recruitment. *Developmental Cognitive Neuroscience.* Available from http://dx.doi.org/10.1016/j.dcn.2016.06.005.

Slater, J., Skoe, E., Strait, D. L., O'Connell, S., Thompson, E., & Kraus, N. (2015). Music training improves speech-in-noise perception: Longitudinal evidence from a community-based music program. *Behavioural Brain Research, 291,* 244−252. Available from http://dx.doi.org/10.1016/j.bbr.2015.05.026.

Slater, J., Tierney, A., & Kraus, N. (2013). At-risk elementary school children with one year of classroom music instruction are better at keeping a beat. *PLoS One, 8*(10), e77250. Available from http://dx.doi.org/10.1371/journal.pone.0077250.

Smolker, H. R., Depue, B. E., Reineberg, A. E., Orr, J. M., & Banich, M. T. (2015). Individual differences in regional prefrontal gray matter morphometry and fractional anisotropy are associate with different constructs of executive function. *Brain Structure & Function, 220*(3), 1291−1306. Available from http://dx.doi.org/10.1007/s00429-014-0723-y.

Sowell, E. R., Thompson, P. M., & Toga, A. W. (2004). Mapping changes in the human cortex throughout the span of life. *The Neuroscientist: A Review Journal Bringing Neurobiology, Neurology and Psychiatry, 10*(4), 372−392.

Stavy, R., & Babai, R. (2010). Overcoming intuitive interference in mathematics: Insights from behavioral, brain imaging and intervention studies. *ZDM Mathematics Education, 42,* 621−633. Available from http://dx.doi.org/10.1007/s11858-010-0251-zdoi .

Stavy, R., Goel, V., Critchley, H., & Dolan, R. (2006). Intuitive interference in quantitative reasoning. *Brain Research, 1073–1074*, 383–388.

Stevens, C., Lauinger, B., & Neville, H. (2009). Differences in the neural mechanisms of selective attention in children from different socioeconomic backgrounds: An event-related brain potential study. *Developmental Science, 12*(4), 634–646. Available from http://dx.doi.org/ 10.1111/j.1467-7687.2009.00807.x.

Tang, Y. Y., Posner, M. I., & Rothbart, M. K. (2014). Meditation improves self-regulation over the life span. *Annals of the New York Academy of Sciences, 1307*, 104–111. Available from http://dx.doi.org/10.1111/nyas.12227.

Tang, Y. Y., Rothbart, M. K., & Posner, M. I. (2012). Neural correlates of establishing, maintaining, and switching brain states. *Trends in Cognitive Sciences, 16*(6), 330–337. Available from http://dx.doi.org/10.1016/j.tics.2012.05.001.

Tierney, A., Krizman, J., Skoe, E., Johnston, K., & Kraus, N. (2013). High school music classes enhance the neural processing of speech. *Frontiers in Psychology, 4*, 855. Available from http://dx.doi.org/10.3389/fpsyg.2013.00855.

Tillman, C., Brocki, K. C., Sorensen, L., & Lundervold, A. J. (2015). A longitudinal examination of the developmental executive function hierarchy in children with externalizing problems. *Journal of Attention Disorders, 19*(6), 496–506. Available from http:// dx.doi.org/10.1177/1087054713488439.

Tran, C. D., Arredondo, M. M., & Yoshida, H. (2015). Differential effects of bilingualism and culture on early attention: A longitudinal study in the U.S., Argentina, and Vietnam. *Frontiers in Psychology, 6*(795). Available from http://dx.doi.org/10.3389/fpsyg. 2015.00795.

Walhovd, K. B., Krogsrud, S. K., Amlien, I. K., Bartsch, H., Bjørnerud, A., Due-Tønnessen, P., & Fjell, A. M. (2016). Neurodevelopmental origins of lifespan changes in brain and cognition. *Proceedings of the National Academy of Sciences of the United States of America, 113*(33), 9357–9362. Available from http://dx.doi.org/10.1073/pnas.1524259113.

Wang, X. L., Du, M. Y., Chen, T. L., Chen, Z. Q., Huang, X. Q., Luo, Y., & Gong, Q. Y. (2015). Neural correlates during working memory processing in major depressive disorder. *Progress in Neuro-Psychopharmacology & Biological Psychiatry, 56*, 101–108. Available from http://dx.doi.org/10.1016/j.pnpbp.2014.08.011.

Weiner, M. F., Hynan, L. S., Rossetti, H., & Falkowski, J. (2011). Luria's three-step test: What is it and what does it tell us?. *International Psychogeriatrics, 23*(10), 1602–1606. Available from http://dx.doi.org/10.1017/S1041610211000767.

Welsh, M., & Peterson, E. (2014). Issues in the conceptualization and assessment of hot executive functions in childhood. *Journal of the International Neuropsychological Society: JINS, 20*(2), 152–156. Available from http://dx.doi.org/10.1017/S1355617713001379.

Wendelken, C., Baym, C. L., Gazzaley, A., & Bunge, S. A. (2011). Neural indices of improved attentional modulation over middle childhood. *Developmental Cognitive Neuroscience, 1*(2), 175–186. Available from http://dx.doi.org/10.1016/j.dcn.2010.11.001.

Wendelken, C., Ditterich, J., Bunge, S. A., & Carter, C. S. (2009). Stimulus and response conflict processing during perceptual decision making. *Cognitive Affective Behavioral Neuroscience, 9*(4), 434–447.

Wendelken, C., O'Hare, E. D., Whitaker, K. J., Ferrer, E., & Bunge, S. A. (2011). Increased functional selectivity over development in rostrolateral prefrontal cortex. *Journal of Neuroscience, 31*(47), 17260–17268.

Wendelken, C., Munakata, Y., Baym, C., Souza, M., & Bunge, S. A. (2012). Flexible rule use: Common neural substrates in children and adults. *Developmental Cognitive Neuroscience*, 2(3), 329−339. Available from http://dx.doi.org/10.1016/j.dcn.2012.02.001.

Westlye, L. T., Grydeland, H., Walhovd, K. B., & Fjell, A. M. (2011). Associations between regional cortical thickness and attentional networks as measured by the attention network test. *Cerebral Cortex*, 21(2), 345−356. Available from http://dx.doi.org/10.1093/cercor/bhq101.

Wright, A., & Diamond, A. (2014). An effect of inhibitory load in children while keeping working memory load constant. *Frontiers in Psychology*, 5, 213. Available from http://dx.doi.org/10.3389/fpsyg.2014.00213.

Zaitchik, D., Iqbal, Y., & Carey, S. (2014). The effect of executive function on biological reasoning in young children: An individual differences study. *Child Development*, 85(1), 160−175. Available from http://dx.doi.org/10.1111/cdev.12145.

Zelazo, P. D., Blair, C. B., & Willoughby, M. T. (2016). *Executive function: Implications for education (NCER 2017-2000)*. Washington, DC: National Center for Education Research, Institute of Education Sciences, US Department of Education.

Zhao, J., Liu, J., Jiang, X., Zhou, G., Chen, G., Ding, X. P., & Lee, K. (2016). Linking resting-state networks in the prefrontal cortex to executive function: A functional near infrared spectroscopy study. *Frontiers in Human Neuroscience*, 10, 452. Available from http://dx.doi.org/10.3389/fnins.2016.00452.

Zuk, J., Benjamin, C., Kenyon, A., & Gaab, N. (2014). Behavioral and neural correlates of executive functioning in musicians and non-musicians. *PLoS One*, 9(6), e99868. http://dx.doi.org/10.1371/journal.pone.0099868. Erratum in: PLoS One. 2015;10(9):e0137930.

FURTHER READING

Abutalebi, J., Guidi, L., Borsa, V., Canini, M., Della Rosa, P. A., Parris, B. A., & Weekes, B. S. (2015). Bilingualism provides a neural reserve for aging populations. *Neuropsychologia*, 69, 201−210. Available from http://dx.doi.org/10.1016/j.neuropsychologia.2015.01.040.

Diamond, A. (2011). Interventions shown to aid executive function development in children 4 to 12 years old. *Science*, 333(6045), 959−964. Available from http://dx.doi.org/10.1126/science.1204529.

Fiell, A. M., Walhovd, K. B., Brown, T. T., Kuperman, J. M., Chung, Y., Hagler, D. J., & Dale, A. M. (2012). Multimodal imaging of the self-regulating developing brain. *Proceedings of the National Academy of Sciences of the United States of America*, 109(48), 19620−19625. Available from http://dx.doi.org/10.1073/pnas.1208243109.

Li, L., Abutalebi, J., Zou, L., Yan, X., Liu, L., Feng, X., & Ding, G. (2015). Bilingualism alters brain functional connectivity between "control" regions and "language" regions: Evidence from bimodal bilinguals. *Neuropsychologia*, 71, 236−247. Available from http://dx.doi.org/10.1016/j.neuropsychologia.2015.04.007.

Mills, K. L., Dumontheil, I., Speekenbrink, M., & Blakemore, S. J. (2015). Multitasking during social interactions in adolescence and early adulthood. *Royal Society of Open Science*, 2, 150117. Available from http://dx.doi.org/10.1098/rsos.150117.

Roer, J. P., Bell, R., & Buchner, A. (2014). Please silence your cell phone: Your ringtone captures other people's attention. *Noise & Health*, 16, 34−39.

Rueda, M. R., Rothbart, M. K., McCandliss, B. D., Saccomanno, L., & Posner, M. I. (2005). Training, maturation, and genetic influences on the development of executive attention. *Proceedings of the National Academy of Sciences of the United States of America*, 102, 14931−14936.

Slater, J., Tierney, A., & Kraus, N. (2013). At-risk elementary school children with one year of classroom music instruction are better at keeping a beat. *PLoS One, 8*(10), e77250. Available from http://dx.doi.org/10.1371/journal.pone.0077250.

Tang, Y. Y., Posner, M. I., & Rothbart, M. K. (2014). Meditation improves self-regulation over the life span. *Annals of the New York Academy of Sciences, 1307,* 104–111. Available from http://dx.doi.org/10.1111/nyas.12227.

Tang, Y. Y., Rothbart, M. K., & Posner, M. I. (2012). Neural correlates of establishing, maintaining, and switching brain states. *Trends in Cognitive Sciences, 16*(6), 330–337. Available from http://dx.doi.org/10.1016/j.tics.2012.05.001.

Tran, C. D., Arredondo, M. M., & Yoshida, H. (2015). Differential effects of bilingualism and culture on early attention: A longitudinal study in the U.S., Argentina, and Vietnam. *Frontiers in Psychology, 6*(795). Available from http://dx.doi.org/10.3389/fpsyg.2015.00795.

Washington, S. D., Gordon, E. M., Brar, J., Warburton, S., Sawyer, A. T., Wolfe, A., Mease-Ference, E. R., Girton, L., Hailu, A., Mbwana, J., Gaillard, W. D., Kalbfleisch, M. L., & Van Meter, J. W. (2014). Dysmaturation of the default mode network in autism. *Human Brain Mapping, 35*(4), 1284–1296. Available from http://dx.doi.org/10.1002/hbm.22252.

Wright, A., & Diamond, A. (2014). An effect of inhibitory load in children while keeping working memory load constant. *Frontiers in Psychology, 5,* 213. Available from http://dx.doi.org/10.3389/fpsyg.2014.00213.

Chapter 8

Executive Functions and Neurocognitive Aging

R. Nathan Spreng[1,2], Leena Shoemaker[3] and Gary R. Turner[3]

[1]*Department of Human Development, Cornell University, Ithaca, NY, United States,*
[2]*Human neuroscience Institute, Cornell University, Ithaca, NY, United States,*
[3]*Department of Psychology, York University, Toronto, ON, Canada*

INTRODUCTION

Executive functions (EFs) are integrative processes that guide goal-directed and purposeful behavior (Cicerone et al., 2011). These cognitive abilities are essential for maintaining functional independence in older adulthood (Cahn-Weiner, Boyle, & Malloy, 2002), yet show a consistent, near-linear, decline from middle adulthood onward. Indeed, EF loss is considered to be a hallmark of cognitive aging (Park, Polk, Mikels, Taylor, & Marshuetz, 2001). While the behavioral trajectory of executive functioning in older adulthood has been well characterized (Baltes & Lindenberger, 1997; Buckner, 2004; Hasher & Zacks, 1988; Miyake et al., 2000; Park et al., 2001; Salthouse, 1996), research is just beginning to link these cognitive changes to changes in brain structure and function. Establishing this link is becoming increasingly important as older adults, their families, and health care providers are looking to "brain science" for answers on how to slow the pace of cognitive decline. In this chapter we review how neurocognitive aging research is bridging this gap, leading to new approaches and strategies for preserving executive functioning—and prolonging functional independence—in later life.

More than a century and a half of neuropsychological research has implicated the frontal lobes of the brain in executive, goal-directed, control of behavior (Stuss & Levine, 2002). The advent of neuroimaging tools, enabling researchers to obtain in vivo measures of structure and function across the whole brain, has broadened this association, demonstrating that executive functioning is not simply the result of frontal lobe activity per se but rather an emergent property of interactions between the frontal lobes and posterior brain regions. Structural brain imaging research has shown that over the course of the adult life span, there is loss of cortical and white matter volume within

Executive Functions in Health and Disease. DOI: http://dx.doi.org/10.1016/B978-0-12-803676-1.00008-8

169

the frontal lobes of the brain, and these changes also follow a near-linear trajectory (Rodrigue, Kennedy, & Raz, 2005). This suggests that age-related declines in executive control may simply proceed in lock step with loss of frontal brain volume. However, brain structure is a poor predictor of cognition, with many older adults showing remarkable preservation of cognitive abilities despite significant brain volume loss (Snowdon, 1997). This dissociation between changes in brain structure and cognition has led researchers to investigate brain function as a potential mediator of age-related cognitive decline (Stern et al., 2005).

Many functional neuroimaging studies have now reported changes in brain function during cognitive task performance in older versus younger adults (Cabeza, 2002; Davis, Dennis, Daselaar, Fleck, & Cabeza, 2008; Park & Reuter-Lorenz, 2009; Reuter-Lorenz & Cappell, 2008; Reuter-Lorenz & Park, 2014; Spreng, Wojtowicz, & Grady, 2010). Within the domain of executive functioning, research has primarily focused on age-related changes in brain activity associated with specific executive control processes, such as working memory and inhibition (see Turner & Spreng, 2012 for a review). More recently, researchers have recognized that goal-directed control of behavior involves constant, reciprocal, and dynamic communication between frontal cortices and posterior brain regions. As such, changes in functional connectivity, within or between functionally connected assemblies or networks, of brain regions may provide a more powerful marker of age-related declines in executive control (Gallen, Turner, Adnan, & D'Esposito, 2016; Grady, 2012; Spreng & Schacter, 2012; Turner & Spreng, 2015).

Here we review executive functioning and aging through the lens of functional brain changes that occur across the adult life span. We begin the chapter with an update of our metaanalytic review of all functional neuroimaging studies investigating age-related changes in *brain activity* across three executive control domains: working memory, inhibition, and task switching (Turner & Spreng, 2012). We next explore how research investigating changes in *functional connectivity* between brain regions is leading to increasing mechanistic accounts of age-related cognitive decline. In the concluding section of the chapter we review how these advances are informing the design of interventions to slow the pace of decline and enhance executive control functioning in older adulthood.

FUNCTIONAL BRAIN CHANGES AND EXECUTIVE FUNCTIONING: A METAANALYTIC REVIEW

As noted in the Introduction, studies of age-related functional brain changes have focused mainly on specific executive control processes. While there is no universally accepted schema for identifying component processes of executive control, one of the most influential has been the fractionated account proposed by Miyake et al. (2000). The authors used factor analytic methods to contrast a unitary versus a fractionated model of executive functioning in younger adults. Their findings suggested that executive functioning was not a unitary cognitive construct but rather comprised three dissociable processes: updating in working memory, inhibition, and task switching. Other process-specific accounts of executive control have been proposed. One model suggests that task switching may not be a dissociable process but rather an emergent capacity drawing upon inhibition and working memory processes (Diamond, 2013). Others have argued that working memory capacity is superordinate, akin to fluid intelligence or G (Conway, Kane, & Engle, 2003; Duncan et al., 2000). Miyake et al. (2000) updated their original fractionation model identifying a common EF component that almost perfectly correlated with their original inhibition factor. The updated model now includes this unitary EF component and two dissociable subcomponents: task switching and working memory (see Friedman & Miyake, 2016; Miyake & Friedman, 2012 for reviews).

Despite these various schema, the majority of published studies of functional brain activity associated with executive control functions have investigated the three processes associated with the original fractionated account (Miyake et al., 2000). Indeed, in a metaanalysis of brain activity and executive control functions in young adults, more than three-quarters (349 of 457) of the studies reviewed investigated task switching (mental flexibility), inhibition, and working memory (Niendam et al., 2012). Therefore, we selected this original fractionated model as the basis for our prior metaanalytic review of functional brain changes associated with executive functioning in older adults (Turner & Spreng, 2012). At the time of our original review, there were too few published studies investigating age-related functional brain changes during task switching, so we limited our analysis to published studies involving either working memory or inhibition tasks.

Our original metaanalysis included 30 studies (19 working memory and 11 inhibition) that met criterion for inclusion (see Executive functions, brain activity and aging: An updated metaanalytic review, and Turner & Spreng, 2012). For younger adults, we observed increased activation in frontal and parietal brain regions associated with working memory, right lateralized activation in inferior frontal gyrus, and supplemental motor areas for inhibition tasks. These findings were consistent with the results of a large metaanalysis of executive functioning in younger adults (Niendam et al., 2012). When contrasted with young, aging was associated with greater recruitment of dorsolateral prefrontal cortex (PFC) bilaterally (right greater than left) during working memory tasks, consistent with previous reports (Reuter-Lorenz & Cappell, 2008; Reuter-Lorenz et al., 2000; Rypma & D'Esposito, 2000; Smith, Jonides, Marshuetz, & Koeppe, 1998; Wager & Smith, 2003). Inhibition was associated with greater activity in the right inferior frontal gyrus, inferior frontal junction, and in the left medial superior frontal gyrus in older adults. We interpreted this pattern of increased recruitment as "young-plus," i.e., overrecruitment of regions associated with inhibitory control in younger adults (Simmonds, Pekar, & Mostofsky, 2008).

When we directly contrasted patterns of activity between working memory and inhibition in each age group, the spatial separation in the pattern of functional brain response across the two executive control processes appeared to be largely maintained from younger to older adulthood, consistent with a process-specific account of age-related functional brain changes. To our knowledge, this was the first quantitative review to report that functional brain changes associated with specific executive control processes may not follow a common trajectory across the adult life span.

From the time of our initial review, several more reports have been published investigating functional brain changes during working memory and inhibition in older and younger adults. Critically, in updating our review we were also able to identify a sufficient number of age-related task switching studies to include this executive process in our revised metaanalysis. We report the findings of this updated analysis in the next section.

EXECUTIVE FUNCTIONS, BRAIN ACTIVITY, AND AGING: AN UPDATED METAANALYTIC REVIEW

Here we report the findings of an updated metaanalytic review of all functional neuroimaging studies investigating age-related changes in brain activity associated with the three executive control processes: working memory, inhibition, and task switching (Miyake et al., 2000). We replicate the methods reported in Turner and Spreng (2012) and describe core aspects of the review procedure here for comprehensiveness. Additional details may be found in the original published report.

Metaanalysis Methods

Selection of Studies

Neuroimaging studies examining aging and executive functioning were selected using a systematic search process. To update our previous analysis (Turner & Spreng, 2012), search criteria for working memory and inhibition were reentered covering the time period from April 2010 to May 2016. To capture studies investigating task switching, we covered the full time period of our previous review (January 1982 to May 2016). Peer-reviewed articles, published in English, were selected from the search results of three separate databases: Medline, PsycINFO, and Science Citation Index. Searches were conducted using the following terms: (1) Keyword: "age" <OR> "aging" <OR> "ageing" <OR> "age-related" <OR> "older adults" <OR> "adult life-span"; AND (2) Keyword: "neuroimaging" <OR> "cerebral blood flow" <OR> "fMRI" <OR> "functional magnetic resonance imaging" <OR> "PET" <OR> "positron emission tomography"; AND (3) Population: "human." A second search specifically targeted EF with the added search term, Topic: "executive" <OR> "working memory" <OR>

"inhibition." To identify task switching studies, we conducted a third search with the following search terms: "task switching" OR reconfiguration OR "mental flexibility" OR "cognitive flexibility" OR "rule set" OR "reversal learning" OR "attention switching" OR "Wisconsin Card Sorting Task" OR "Trail making task." For this updated review, 9308 independent reports were identified across both searches.

Only studies that reported both healthy young and healthy old adult group results were included. Theoretical papers and reviews were excluded. Studies that reported combined group results and a region-of-interest analysis, reported only brain-behavior correlations, or did not report activation foci as 3D coordinates in stereotaxic space were excluded because these studies could not be meaningfully analyzed with our metaanalytic software (see below). For studies that contained multiple nonindependent contrasts, to limit the contribution of any one set of participants to the pool of foci, we selected the contrast with the lowest level baseline. We selected these lower level contrasts because functional brain activity is reduced in older relative to younger adults at higher levels of task challenge as performance limits are exceeded (Cappell, Gmeindl, & Reuter-Lorenz, 2010). Inclusion of only high-level contrasts would confound age-related brain changes with potential ceiling effects on behavioral tasks. For studies containing multiple independent samples, peak activation foci from each sample were included. Three papers for working memory and one inhibition study met criteria for inclusion and were added to those reported in our original publication. A total of 11 papers were identified as meeting our criteria for task switching (Table 8.1). Next, all experiments were allocated to working memory ($n = 22$), inhibition ($n = 14$), or task switching analyses ($n = 11$). In cases where allocation to either category was unclear, we assigned the study based on the author's characterization.

Creation of Activation Likelihood Estimation (ALE) Maps

The activation likelihood estimation (ALE) method provides a voxel-based metaanalytic technique for functional neuroimaging data (Laird et al., 2005; Turkeltaub, Eden, Jones, & Zeffiro, 2002). The software (GingerALE v1.1; BrainMap) computes statistically significant concordance in the pattern of brain activity across any number of independent experiments. Additionally, GingerALE can compute statistically significant differences in the pattern of brain activity between two sets of data from several independent experiments. ALE maps are derived based on foci of interest, which comprise statistically significant peak activation locations from published studies. Independent group analysis peak foci (Working memory/Inhibition/Task switching > Control task in Younger; WM/Inhibition/Task switching task > Control task in Older) were extracted from each study. Where studies reported within- and between-group peak foci (i.e., combined Younger/Older,

TABLE 8.1 Details of Metaanalysis Studies Included in the Review

Study Number	First Author	Year	Executive Control Process	Paradigm
Working Memory				
1	Anguera	2011	Spatial working memory	Delayed spatial rotation task
2	Bennet	2013	Verbal working memory	Sternberg task
3	Cabeza	2004	Verbal working memory	Delayed word recognition
4	Emery	2008	Verbal working memory	Letter-number sequencing
5	Freo	2005	Face working memory	Delayed match to sample
6	Grady	1998	Face working memory	Delayed match to sample
7	Grossman	2002	Verbal working memory	Sentence comprehension
8	Haut	2005	Verbal working memory	Letter-number sequencing (WAIS)
9	Holtzer	2009	Nonverbal working memory	Sternberg task (nonverbal)
10	Johnson	2004	Verbal working memory	Refresh task
11	Nagel	2009	Spatial working memory	Delayed spatial recognition
12	Otsuka	2006	Complex verbal working memory	Reading span
13	Park	2010	Nonverbal working memory	Delayed recognition
14	Paxton	2008	Verbal working memory	Continuous performance task (AX-CPT)
15	Podell	2012	Verbal working memory	Updating task
16	Raye	2008	Verbal working memory	Refresh task
17	Reuter-Lorenz	2000	Verbal working memory	Delayed latter recognition

(Continued)

TABLE 8.1 (Continued)

Study Number	First Author	Year	Executive Control Process	Paradigm
17	Reuter-Lorenz	2000	Spatial working memory	Delayed spatial recognition
18	Ricciardi	2009	Face working memory	Delayed match to sample
19	Rypma	2001	Verbal working memory	Sternberg task
20	Schneider-Garces	2010	Verbal working memory	Sternberg Task
21	Smith	2001	Complex working memory	Operation span (mathematical problem solving)
Inhibition				
1	Colcombe	2005	Response inhibition (sensory)	Flanker task
2	Jonides	2000	Response inhibition (sensory)	Delayed word recognition (with recency manipulation)
3	Korsch	2014	Response inhibition (sensory/motor)	Flanker task with response conflict
4	Lee	2006	Response inhibition (motor)	Simon task (with response conflict)
5	Madden	2002	Inhibition (distractor items)	Visual search
6	Mathis	2009	Response inhibition (semantic)	Stroop task (Incongruent vs neural)
7	Meinzer	2009	Response inhibition (semantic)	Category fluency
8	Mell	2009	Response inhibition (sensory)	Probabilistic object reversal
9	Milham	2002	Response inhibition (semantic)	Stroop task
10	Nielson	2004	Response inhibition (motor)	Go–no-go task

(*Continued*)

TABLE 8.1 (Continued)

Study Number	First Author	Year	Executive Control Process	Paradigm
11	Paxton	2008	Response inhibition (sensory)	Continuous performance task (AX-CPT)
12	Prakash	2009	Response inhibition (semantic)	Stroop task
13	Zhu	2010	Response inhibition (sensory)	Flanker task
14	Zysset	2007	Response inhibition (semantic)	Stroop task
Task Switching				
1	DiGirolamo	2001	Task switch (semantic)	Numerical (odd/even)
2	Esposito	1999	Set-shifting	Wisconsin Card Sorting Task
3	Gazes	2012	Task switch (feature)	Letter–color switch
4	Gold	2013	Task switch (feature)	Color–shape switch
5	Steffener	2014	Task switch (feature)	Letter–color switch
6	Jimura	2010	Task switch (semantic)	Semantic classification
7	Martins	2012	Set-shifting	Wisconsin Word Sorting Task
8	Nagahama	1997	Set-shifting	Wisconsin Card Sorting Task
9	Nashiro	2013	Set-shifting	Emotional reversal learning
10	Townsend	2006	Task switch (modality)	Auditory/visual attention task
11	Zhu	2014	Task switch (feature)	Color–shape switch

Younger > Older, and Older > Younger), foci from the combined task effects were allocated to both groups and task by age interaction foci (i.e., between-group effects) were allocated to each respective age group, consistent with previous methods (Spreng, Wojtowicz, et al., 2010). Nine separate ALE analyses were conducted in total, each yielding an ALE map and corresponding cluster report: (1–3) Working Memory in Younger, Older, and comparing Younger to Older; (4–6) Inhibition in Younger, Older, and comparing Younger to Older; (7–9) Task switching in Younger, Older, and comparing Younger to Older.

Before the analysis, coordinates reported in Montreal Neurological Institute space were converted to Talairach coordinates using the Lancaster transformation (Laird et al., 2010; Lancaster et al., 2007). In the approach taken by ALE, localization probability distributions for the foci are modeled at the center of 3D Gaussian functions, where the Gaussian distributions are summed across the experiments to generate a map of interstudy consistencies that estimate the likelihood of activation for each focus (the ALE statistic). The foci were modeled using a full-width half-maximum value of 8 mm^3. We then compared the summary of observations against a null distribution, determined through 5000 permutations of randomly generated foci identical in number to those being tested. To determine reliable differences in brain activity between younger and older adults, we tested the null hypothesis that the two sets of foci were randomly distributed and the observed difference between them was zero. For all analyses, the false discovery rate method was used to correct for multiple comparisons at $P < .05$ and subjected to a cluster size threshold of 100 mm^3 (Laird et al., 2005). Anatomical labels were applied to the clusters by using the Talairach Daemon and visual inspection of the ALE maps that were imported into FSLview v3.1 (Smith et al., 2004). Coordinates are reported in Talairach space (Talairach & Tournoux, 1988). All ALE maps were transformed from a volume image to an average multifiducial surface map using the Caret software (Van Essen, 2005) for presentation.

Metaanalysis Results

Younger Adults

Consistent with our original review, younger adults showed increased activation in frontal and parietal brain regions associated with working memory, and right lateralized activation in the inferior frontal gyrus and supplemental motor areas for inhibition tasks. Task switching was associated with left dorsolateral prefrontal, bilateral parietal, and dorsal anterior cingulate activation (see Fig. 8.1, Table 8.2). These findings are again consistent with a metaanalytic review of EFs in young adults (Niendam et al., 2012).

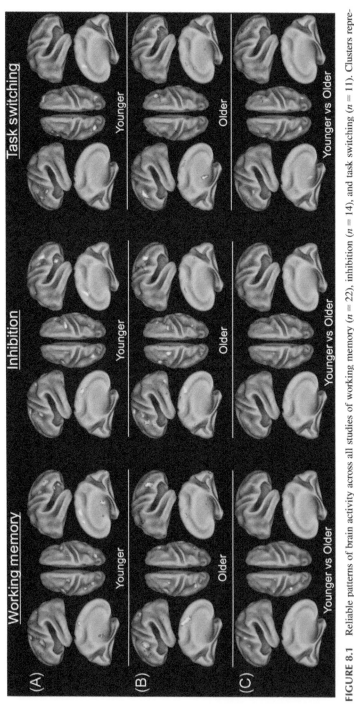

FIGURE 8.1 Reliable patterns of brain activity across all studies of working memory ($n = 22$), inhibition ($n = 14$), and task switching ($n = 11$). Clusters represent areas where activity was greater during executive function than baseline tasks. (A) Activation likelihood clusters for young adults. (B) Older adults. (C) ALE clusters displaying reliable differences between younger and older subjects (warm colors: Younger adults > Older adults; cool colors: Older adults > Younger adults). Activation likelihood clusters (false discovery rate, $P < .05$) are shown on an average multifiducial partially inflated surface map in Caret (Van Essen, 2005).

TABLE 8.2 Regions of Activation Demonstrating Significant Differences Between Young and Older Adults During Working Memory (A), Inhibition (B), and Task Switching (C)

Lat	Region	BA	x	y	z
A. Working Memory					
Young > Old					
L	Precentral gyrus	6	−42	0	28
L	Precentral gyrus	6	−50	−4	42
R	Frontal white matter		36	26	20
L	Anterior insula	13	−38	18	8
R	Inferior parietal lobule	40	32	−50	38
L	Inferior parietal lobule	40	−40	−38	38
L	Superior temporal gyrus	38	−44	20	−24
R	Caudate		14	−6	16
L	Caudate		−16	−2	18
Old > Young					
R	Middle frontal gyrus	46	46	26	22
R	Middle frontal gyrus	46	36	38	2
L	Inferior frontal gyrus	9	−36	8	30
L	Inferior frontal gyrus	47	−46	20	−4
R	Medial frontal gyrus	32	2	8	44
L	Medial frontal gyrus	32	−6	10	44
L	Precuneus	7	−24	−64	34
B. Inhibition					
Young > Old					
R	Inferior occipital gyrus	19	38	−76	0
Old > Young					
R	Middle frontal gyrus	6	28	−2	56
R	Middle frontal gyrus	6	48	2	32
R	Inferior frontal gyrus	9	54	8	36
L	Inferior frontal gyrus	44	−56	12	16
L	Superior frontal gyrus	6	−4	28	54
C. Task Switching					
Young > Old					
L	Superior frontal gyrus	10	−34	50	22
L	Middle frontal gyrus	9	−38	28	32

(Continued)

TABLE 8.2 (Continued)

Lat	Region	BA	x	y	z
L	Inferior frontal gyrus	9	−46	14	20
L	Precentral gyrus	6	−40	−2	36
R	Angular gyrus	39	30	−54	34
R	Superior parietal lobule	7	32	−64	44
L	Superior parietal lobule	7	−28	−62	44
Old > Young					
R	Middle frontal gyrus	8/9	38	28	38
R	Inferior frontal gyrus	46	46	32	12
R	Inferior frontal gyrus	13	38	24	10
L	Superior frontal gyrus	6	−4	8	54
R	Superior occipital gyrus	19	32	−78	24
R	Cerebellum		28	−50	−12

Lat, laterality; *L,* left; *R,* right; *BA,* Brodmann area; *X,* right/left coordinate; *Y,* anterior/posterior coordinate; *Z,* inferior/superior coordinate; *Vol,* volume.

Older Adults

(1) Working memory. Consistent with our previous report, older adults showed significantly greater activation than young in dorsal and anterior PFC brain regions bilaterally during working memory tasks (Fig. 8.1, column 1 and Table 8.2A). (2) Inhibition. Older adults showed more activity in the right inferior frontal gyrus, near the inferior frontal junction and in the left medial superior frontal gyrus, presupplementary motor area region during inhibition tasks. These results were consistent with the "young-plus" pattern we identified in our previous report (Fig. 8.1, column 2 and Table 8.2B). (3) Task switching. Activation differences during task switching in older versus younger adults were observed in right dorsolateral PFC and left superior medial brain regions (Fig. 8.1, column 3 and Table 8.2C).

Here we report the results of an updated metaanalytic review of age-related brain activation changes associated with the three executive control processes: working memory, inhibition, and task switching. In our previous report, working memory and inhibition showed dissociable patterns of brain activity in young, consistent with a fractionated account of executive functioning (Miyake et al., 2000). Not surprisingly, the addition of four studies to our initial review of working memory and inhibition did not significantly alter these findings. In a novel extension of this metaanalysis, activity associated with task switching closely overlapped those regions of the PFC observed during working memory in young.

While these updated results support our earlier conclusion that executive functioning is dissociable into component processes with respect to brain function in younger adults, here we also observed a pattern of increasing overlap or dedifferentiated brain activity during working memory and task switching in older adults. These findings advance our understanding of executive functioning in the aging brain in two ways. First, they suggest that working memory may emerge as a superordinate control process in older adulthood. In both our previous study and in the current findings, we observed increased bilateral PFC activation during working memory for older adults. Here we also observed a similar pattern of bilateral PFC recruitment in older adults during task switching. Increased PFC activation during executive control processing has been reported previously for older adults (Reuter-Lorenz & Cappell, 2008; Spreng, Wojtowicz, et al., 2010). Although we did not observe a similar pattern of increased bilateral PFC activity for inhibition, there is evidence from studies of younger adults that more complex inhibition tasks are associated with increased recruitment of dorsolateral PFC regions, potentially reflecting increased working memory demand (Simmonds et al., 2008). The inhibition studies included in our review may have involved simpler or more "pure inhibition" demands and thereby did not tax working memory resources or engage dorsolateral PFC regions in young or older adults. However, the pattern of dedifferentiated brain activity between working memory and task switching suggests that the age-related recruitment of dorsolateral PFC observed for both control processes may reflect greater reliance on working memory resources to implement executive or goal-directed control of behavior in older adulthood.

A second important finding from this updated review was the observation of age-related increases in superior medial PFC (msPFC)/dorsal anterior cingulate cortex (dACC) for all three control processes. This region has been implicated in initiation tasks such as word generation in younger adults (Niendam et al., 2012). Lesions to this region have been associated with slowed processing particularly during more complex tasks reflecting inefficient access to stored representations or action schema necessary to guide responses in a goal-directed manner (Stuss et al., 2005). Overrecruitment of this region may reflect increased reliance on representational schema to support executive functioning in older adulthood, a hypothesis we have proposed in our recent work (Turner & Spreng, 2015; and see below).

Together, the results of the original and updated metaanalyses reviewed in this section provide a process-specific account of age-related changes in functional brain activity during executive functioning. Although we have interpreted these results as evidence for increasing reliance on working memory and internal representational schema, the findings do not provide a mechanistic account of how these changes are reflected in brain function. Put another way, although brain activation maps tell us where executive functioning is "located" in older adults, they remain silent with respect to how executive control emerges from these activation patterns. Understanding how executive control is implemented in the brain is essential if we are to identify predictive neural markers of cognitive decline, or design brain-based, targeted intervention strategies. To better address this question, we next turn to investigations of how spatially distributed brain regions communicate through functionally connected networks. We postulate that age-related changes in the brain's functional network architecture may be an important neural mechanism associated with age-related decline in executive functioning.

BRAIN NETWORKS AND EXECUTIVE FUNCTIONS IN OLDER ADULTHOOD

Interactions among spatially distributed brain regions, or collections of regions, enable goal-directed modulation of neural activity based on goal states (Chao & Knight, 1995; Lorenc, Lee, Chen, & D'Esposito, 2015). Altered functional connectivity has been associated with poor goal-directed modulation of brain activity or interactivity, providing a putative neural mechanism of EF decline in older adulthood (Gazzaley, Cooney, McEvoy, Knight, & D'Esposito, 2005; Park et al., 2004; Payer et al., 2006). In this section we review how age-related changes in functional connectivity between frontal and posterior brain regions, and among distributed brain networks, lead to reduced goal-directed modulation of brain activity, providing a putative neural mechanism underlying EF decline in aging.

Goal-Directed Perceptual Processing

Age-related reductions in the modulation of neural activity in perceptual processing regions based on task goals have been associated with age-related declines in executive control (Gazzaley & D'Esposito, 2007). Payer et al. (2006) reported reduced selectivity in neural responses in category-selective regions of visual association cortex (VAC) in older relative to younger subjects during a working memory task. This reduced selectivity of neural response was accompanied by enhanced activity in PFC, which the authors interpreted as compensatory modulation of posterior brain regions in response to degraded perceptual representations. Gazzaley et al. (2005) reported a similar pattern of age-related deficits in the modulation of neural responses within the VAC. The authors observed age-related reductions in goal-directed modulation of perceptual cortices that resulted in poor filtering of goal-irrelevant (i.e., distracting) stimuli. In a follow-up study, Gazzaley, Sheridan, Cooney, and D'Esposito (2007) observed increased functional connectivity between lateral PFC and VAC regions during goal-directed responding on a selective working memory task, suggesting that top-down modulation is implemented through functional connections between frontal and posterior cortices. This causal modulatory influence of PFC on posterior cortices has been confirmed in animal models (Fuster, Bauer, & Jervey, 1985), human lesion studies, and using transcranial magnetic stimulation methods (Lorenc et al., 2015).

In a recent review, Li and Reickmann (2014) reported that impaired modulatory influence from frontal cortices attenuates neural responsiveness to afferent signaling in posterior brain regions, producing poorly regulated (i.e., noisy) information processing. They emphasize the role of dopamine in modulating the integrity of neural representations through top-down (i.e., PFC-derived) biasing of goal-relevant versus irrelevant representations. This biasing mechanism serves to allocate limited cognitive resources to goal-relevant information processing, facilitating executive control of behavior.

In this neuromodulation account of executive functioning, increased engagement of lateral PFC brain regions, as we reported in our metaanalytic review above, may reflect increased demands for modulation of perceptual brain regions based on the current goals held in working memory. This provides a mechanistic account of goal-directed control in older adulthood. Degraded functional interactions between frontal and posterior brain regions lead to poor filtering of goal-relevant from irrelevant representations, producing a noisier cognitive landscape (Schmitz, Dixon, Anderson, & De Rosa, 2014). In this account, poor goal-directed modulation of perceptual processing regions results in poor suppression of irrelevant stimuli, leading to distractibility, poor concentration, and off-task behavior, which are the common symptoms of executive dysfunction.

Goal-Directed Modulation of Network Dynamics

In the previous section we discussed aging and executive functioning from the perspective of top-down, or goal-directed, control of perceptual processing. More recently, goal-directed control of behavior has been associated with interactions among spatially distributed brain regions that are intrinsically organized into large-scale, interacting networks (Corbetta & Shulman, 2002; Fox et al., 2005; Spreng, Sepulcre, Turner, Stevens, & Schacter, 2013; Vincent, Kahn, Snyder, Raichle, & Buckner, 2008). Age-related changes in functional connectivity, or network interactivity, has been associated with age-related declines in executive functioning (Gallen et al., 2016; Geerligs, Renken, Saliasi, Maurits, & Lorist, 2015; Geerligs, Saliasi, Maurits, & Lorist, 2012; Grady, Sarraf, Saverino, & Campbell, 2016; Lustig et al., 2003; Madden et al., 2010; Persson, Lustig, Nelson, & Reuter-Lorenz, 2007; Sambataro et al., 2010; Spreng & Schacter, 2012; Turner & Spreng, 2015). Our work has begun to explore how changes in network organization or interactivity may impact goal-directed cognition in older adulthood. Specifically, how does goal-directed modulation of neural network dynamics change from younger to older adulthood and how do these changes manifest as age-related decline in executive functioning?

Numerous models of the brain's functional network architecture have been developed using both task (Spreng, Stevens, Chamberlain, Gilmore, & Schacter, 2010) and resting-state (Power et al., 2011; Yeo et al., 2011) fMRI data. Our work has focused on a functional network model of goal-directed cognition that includes three interacting brain networks: dorsal attention, default, and frontal–parietal control (Spreng, Stevens, et al., 2010; Vincent et al., 2008). The dorsal attention network (DAN) is engaged during externally directed attentional tasks and comprised functionally connected brain regions including visual motion area, frontal eye fields, superior parietal lobule, intraparietal sulcus, and ventral premotor cortex. The default mode network (DMN) is hypothesized to be involved in accessing stored representations and is suppressed by externally oriented cognitive processes (Corbetta & Shulman, 2002). Anticorrelations between DAN and DMN networks are considered to be a core neural mechanism supporting executive functioning (see Grady, 2012, for review). The DMN network includes ventral medial PFC, posterior cingulate cortex, retrosplenial cortex, posterior inferior parietal lobule, and lateral temporal pole. A third, frontoparietal control network (FPCN), couples with these two networks to implement the cognitive control processes necessary to maintain goals, inhibit distractions, and shift behavior in the service of goal attainment (Spreng, Stevens, et al., 2010; Vincent et al., 2008). Critically, the FPCN network includes regions of the dorsolateral and dorsal medial PFC, as well as dACC; all regions identified as being overactive in older adults during EF tasks in our metaanalytic review.

DAN and DMN are associated with attention to perceptual features of the environmental or stored representational knowledge respectively. The FPCN is active for both attention states, suggesting that this network may play a modulatory role in shifting the focus of attention (Spreng, Stevens, et al., 2010). FPCN coupling could facilitate the updating of goal states, integrating information from the immediate environment with internal representations of past experience and future desires. Furthermore, coupling of FPCN with default and DAN could help to expand or stabilize the mental workspace by associating the contents of working memory with stored representations, mediated through FPCN–DMN coupling, or by facilitating external cueing strategies to refresh working memory, mediated through FPCN–DAN coupling. This dynamic network coupling may facilitate goal-directed control by increasing working memory capacity to maintain increasingly complex goal hierarchies.

In this model, neuromodulation occurs at the network level, with frontal and parietal brain regions of the FPCN implicated in the goal-directed modulation of neural processing in other brain regions, which are also organized into functional networks (e.g., DAN and DMN). Consistent with this network modulation account, the FPCN is the only network containing dual-aligned nodes, brain regions functionally connected to both DAN and DMN regions facilitating attention to external stimuli or internal mnemonic representations, respectively (Spreng et al., 2013).

Drawing upon this interacting network model of goal-directed cognition, we investigated interactions among these brain networks in younger and older adults while they performed two planning tasks. The Tower of London task (Shallice, 1982) required participants to attend to perceptual features of an array to plan a series of actions that would transform the configuration of the array from the starting to a target goal state. In contrast, an autobiographical planning task (e.g., "How will I exercise more") required participants to attend to stored representational knowledge, such as recall of past behaviors, identification of potential hurdles, and desired goal states, to plan for a future goal (Spreng & Schacter, 2012; Spreng, Stevens, et al., 2010). Unlike younger subjects, older adults failed to modulate network dynamics based on changing task goals. Specifically, older adults failed to decouple default and frontal–parietal brain regions as the task goal shifted from the internal/personal to external/visuospatial task (Spreng & Schacter, 2012). This "stickiness" of DMN coupling may reflect reduced suppression of these brain regions during executive control tasks in older adulthood (Hansen et al., 2014; Lustig et al., 2003; Persson et al., 2007) or reduced differentiation among functional networks (Chan, Park, Savalia, Petersen, & Wig, 2014; Geerligs et al., 2015; Grady et al., 2016; Sambataro et al., 2010; Spreng & Schacter, 2012; Spreng, Stevens, Viviano, & Schacter, 2016).

While suppression and dedifferentiation explanations are consistent with our findings of poor goal-directed DN modulation, these accounts are more descriptive and do not speak to *how* network modulation is implemented in the brain or how this neural mechanism is altered in older adulthood. Our work provides a more mechanistic account, suggesting that goal direction is implemented through the dynamic modulation of FPCN, DAN, and DMN interactions. More specifically, we maintain that this interactivity is mediated through dual-aligned nodes of the FPCN, which modulate the activation (or suppression) of DAN and DMN regions and facilitate the transfer of information from the internal or external milieu to cognitive control regions (Spreng et al., 2013).

Thus far in this chapter we have demonstrated that older adults show increased recruitment of frontal brain regions and poor modulation of network interactivity during executive control tasks. Our recent work suggests that these two patterns may be linked. We end this section of the chapter by describing a novel network-based hypothesis of executive control functioning in older adulthood: the Default-Executive Coupling Hypothesis of Aging (DECHA)

Default-Executive Coupling Hypothesis of Aging

As we reported in our metaanalysis (see Executive Functions, Brain Activity, and Aging: An Updated Metaanalytic Review section), aging is associated with increased activity in frontal brain regions during executive control processing. We also provided evidence of reduced DN flexibility during goal-directed cognitive tasks in a recent study investigating executive control functions during the Tower of London task (Shallice, 1982; and see above) across multiple levels of planning challenge (e.g., 3−6 move puzzles). Younger subjects demonstrated increased bilateral activation of frontal brain regions and increased DMN suppression as planning complexity increased. In contrast, older adults failed to modulate brain activity in these areas based on planning challenge, demonstrating increased PFC activity and reduced default suppression at lower levels of task challenge relative to younger subjects. Furthermore, while younger adults demonstrated increased functional connectivity between frontal brain regions during more complex planning tasks, older adults showed increasing connectivity between frontal and DMN brain regions (Turner & Spreng, 2015).

Based on these findings, we proposed the DECHA. This account suggests that increased prefrontal activation and increased frontal−default interactions cooccur and are functionally coupled during goal-directed tasks in older adults. This account reconciles two of the most persistent findings in studies of functional brain changes in older adulthood: enhanced bilateral prefrontal recruitment (reviewed in Executive Functions, Brain Activity, and Aging: An Updated Metaanalytic Review section) and altered network dynamics (reviewed in Brain Networks and Executive Functions in Older Adulthood section). Cognitively, we interpret these intersecting functional brain patterns as support for our earlier contention that sustaining stable representations in working memory is increasingly challenging in older adulthood, resulting in increased PFC activity. At the same time, as control processes decline with age (Park et al., 2001), working memory may become increasingly dependent on the vast accumulation of stored representational knowledge, which is implemented through increased frontal−default coupling.

In younger adults, we have shown that DN engagement can facilitate working memory when access to stored representations is goal relevant (Spreng et al., 2014). In older adulthood, age-related declines in working memory, or control processes generally, may increase reliance on stored representational knowledge, mediated by the DMN (Andrews-Hanna, Smallwood, & Spreng, 2014). As we discussed above, the increased frontal engagement observed in our metaanalysis suggests greater engagement of working memory resources. Increased default coupling may support the formation, maintenance, and stability of goal hierarchies in working memory by linking goal states with stored representational knowledge. Consistent with this hypothesis, dual-aligned nodes within the FPCN include both the msPFC and dACC that are functionally connected to the DMN (Spreng et al., 2013). Interestingly, these regions showed consistent age-related increases in activation for all three control processes included in our metaanalysis (see Executive Functions, Brain Activity, and Aging: An Updated Metaanalytic

Review section and Fig. 8.1). This may suggest that these regions within dorsal–medial PFC serve as a hub for access to, and/or transfer of, representational knowledge to lateral prefrontal brain regions in support of goal formation, updating, and maintenance in working memory.

Our exploration and validation of the DECHA model is ongoing, and mapping these functional brain changes to cognitive processes remains speculative. However, we believe that investigating process-specific changes in brain network activation, as well as alterations in functional network interactions, will lead to a more comprehensive understanding of the neural mechanisms supporting goal-directed cognition and how these change with age. In the concluding section of the chapter, we review some of our translational work, in which we are drawing upon these mechanistic accounts of age-related changes in executive functioning to develop and measure the efficacy of training interventions. We end with a brief review of future directions, promoting further research to elucidate the functional brain mechanisms associated with executive control in older adulthood and leading to more targeted intervention strategies to prevent or slow the pace of age-related decline.

AGING, BRAIN FUNCTION, AND EXECUTIVE CONTROL: CONCLUSIONS AND FUTURE DIRECTIONS

In this chapter we reviewed how age-related changes in executive functioning, a hallmark of cognitive aging, are associated with changes in brain function from young to older adulthood. We investigated this question from two perspectives. First we examined how aging is associated with process-specific changes in brain activity during executive or goal-directed cognitive control. In a metaanalytic review, contrasting brain activity associated with working memory, inhibition, and task switching in younger and older adults, we reported a common pattern of increased activation in lateral (working memory and task switching) and medial (all three processes) frontal brain regions. Second, we explored how age-related changes in functional connectivity among distributed brain regions may be an important neural mechanism underlying executive control decline in older adulthood. Specifically we reviewed evidence that reduced functional connectivity between frontal and posterior brain regions is associated with poor goal-directed filtering of perceptual inputs, leading to distractions and off-task behaviors, both of which are hallmarks of executive dysfunction. We also described how goal-directed modulation of brain network dynamics is reduced in older adulthood. Poor modulation of default and frontal–parietal control network coupling based on task context suggests that older adults may engage stored representational knowledge to support executive control in the face of declining control resources. Consistent with these findings, we have proposed a DECHA, suggesting that increased frontal brain activity and reduced modulation of DN connectivity are functionally coupled and provide a core neural mechanism of executive control decline in older adulthood.

Characterizing the relationship between executive control and brain function in older adulthood is a complex endeavor. This work requires investigations of both brain activation and functional connectivity to elucidate the neural mechanisms associated with age-related cognitive decline. However, these efforts also hold considerable translational potential. Understanding how executive control is implemented in the brain, and how these mechanisms are altered in aging and brain disease, is opening new avenues for intervention design.

By identifying specific neural mechanisms and functional neural markers that characterize the implementation of executive control in the brain, we have designed a brain-based cognitive intervention to enhance goal-directed selective attention in brain-injured and healthy aging populations. The intervention, goal-based attention regulation (GOALS, Novakovic-Agopian et al., 2011), targets top-down neuromodulation through an active process of redirection of attention to goal-relevant stimuli, in effect, training participants to selectively filter "noise" (nonrelevant information). The intervention protocol have proven highly efficacious, improving executive control functioning (Novakovic-Agopian et al., 2011) and goal-directed modulation of brain activity in posterior visual cortices (Chen et al., 2011) in acquired brain injury patients. We are now investigating the efficacy of this intervention for enhancing goal-directed attention in healthy older adults with similarly encouraging results (Adnan, Chen, Novakovic-Agopian, D'Esposito, & Turner, in press; Turner et al., in press).

These rehabilitation studies highlight the significant translational potential of studying functional brain mechanisms to guide the design of more targeted and efficacious intervention protocols. Indeed, an emerging frontier in cognitive rehabilitation neuroscience involves the application of neurostimulation methods to alter brain function in place of, or as an adjunct to, standard behavioral or pharmacological therapies (Fox et al., 2014). These methods are critically dependent on a mechanistic understanding of how cognitive functions are implemented in the functional architecture of the brain. Planned studies in our laboratory will draw upon the DECHA model to guide neurostimulation protocols. For example, stimulating dual-aligned nodes of the FPCN (see Brain Networks and Executive Functions in Older Adulthood section) may serve to enhance information flow among brain networks, allowing more rapid integration of internally generated and externally perceived information, necessary to guide adaptive, goal-directed behavior. We believe that these neurostimulation methods represent an important new frontier in cognitive intervention research and that their success is critically dependent on a mechanistic understanding of how cognitive processes are implemented in brain's functional architecture.

To conclude, executive functioning is perhaps the highest cognitive achievement in human evolution. The capacity to guide our behavior by our goals, and overcome reflexive, automatic, or hard-wired reactions, frees us from rigid stimulus-response behaviors and enables us to flexibly navigate the challenges and obstacles on our way to a desired future. There is a certain irony, then, in the fact that our most advanced cognitive capacity is also the most vulnerable as we age.

With dramatic increases in life expectancy in most areas of the western world, the cost of age-related declines in executive functioning and associated loss of functional independence will rapidly mount, impacting the health care system, burdening families and care givers, and ultimately harming the health and dignity of older individuals. In this context, developing interventions to remediate, or slow the pace of, EF decline in older adulthood is of the utmost urgency. Here we have provided a comprehensive review of executive functioning, viewed through the lens of functional brain changes in older adulthood. We maintain that improving our understanding of how executive functioning is implemented in the aging brain offers the most direct, efficient, and efficacious approach to sustaining and enhancing this capacity well into advanced age.

REFERENCES

Adnan, A., Chen, A.J., Novakovic-Agopian, T., D'Esposito, M., & Turner, G.R. (in press). Brain changes following attention regulation training in older adults.

Andrews-Hanna, J. R., Smallwood, J., & Spreng, R. N. (2014). The default network and self-generated thought: Component processes, dynamic control, and clinical relevance. *Annals of the New York Academy of Sciences, 1316*(1), 29−52.

Anguera, J. A., Reuter-Lorenz, P. A., Willingham, D. T., & Seidler, R. D. (2011). Failure to engage spatial working memory contributes to age-related declines in visuomotor learning. *Journal of Cognitive Neuroscience, 23*(1), 11−25.

Baltes, P. B., & Lindenberger, U. (1997). Emergence of a powerful connection between sensory and cognitive functions across the adult life span: A new window to the study of cognitive aging? *Psychology and Aging, 12*(1), 12−21.

Bennett, I. J., Rivera, H. G., & Rypma, B. (2013). Isolating age-group differences in working memory load-related neural activity: Assessing the contribution of working memory capacity using a partial-trial fMRI method. *Neuroimage, 72*, 20−32.

Buckner, R. L. (2004). Memory and executive function in aging and AD: Multiple factors that cause decline and reserve factors that compensate. *Neuron, 44*(1), 195−208.

Cabeza, R. (2002). Hemispheric asymmetry reduction in older adults: The HAROLD model. *Psychology and Aging, 17*(1), 85−100.

Cabeza, R., Daselaar, S. M., Dolcos, F., Prince, S. E., Budde, M., & Nyberg, L. (2004). Task-independent and task-specific age effects on brain activity during working memory, visual attention and episodic retrieval. *Cerebral Cortex, 14*(4), 364−375.

Cahn-Weiner, D. A., Boyle, P. A., & Malloy, P. F. (2002). Tests of executive function predict instrumental activities of daily living in community-dwelling older individuals. *Applied Neuropsychology, 9*(3), 187−191.

Cappell, K. A., Gmeindl, L., & Reuter-Lorenz, P. A. (2010). Age differences in prefrontal recruitment during verbal working memory maintenance depend on memory load. *Cortex: A Journal Devoted to the Study of the Nervous System and Behavior, 46*(4), 462−473.

Chan, M. Y., Park, D. C., Savalia, N. K., Petersen, S. E., & Wig, G. S. (2014). Decreased segregation of brain systems across the healthy adult lifespan. *Proceedings of the National Academy of Sciences of the United States of America, 111*(46), E4997−5006.

Chao, L. L., & Knight, R. T. (1995). Human prefrontal lesions increase distractibility to irrelevant sensory inputs. *Neuroreport, 6*(12), 1605−1610.

Chen, A. J., Novakovic-Agopian, T., Nycum, T. J., Song, S., Turner, G. R., Hills, N. K., et al. (2011). Training of goal-directed attention regulation enhances control over neural processing for individuals with brain injury. *Brain, 134*(Pt 5), 1541−1554.

Cicerone, K. D., Langenbahn, D. M., Braden, C., Malec, J. F., Kalmar, K., Fraas, M., et al. (2011). Evidence-based cognitive rehabilitation: Updated review of the literature from 2003 through 2008. *Archives of Physical Medicine and Rehabilitation, 92*(4), 519−530.

Colcombe, S. J., Kramer, A. F., Erickson, K. I., & Scalf, P. (2005). The implications of cortical recruitment and brain morphology for individual differences in inhibitory function in aging humans. *Psychology and Aging, 20*(3), 363−375.

Conway, A. R., Kane, M. J., & Engle, R. W. (2003). Working memory capacity and its relation to general intelligence. *Trends in Cognitive Sciences, 7*(12), 547−552.

Corbetta, M., & Shulman, G. L. (2002). Control of goal-directed and stimulus-driven attention in the brain. *Nature Reviews. Neuroscience, 3*(3), 201−215.

Davis, S. W., Dennis, N. A., Daselaar, S. M., Fleck, M. S., & Cabeza, R. (2008). Que PASA? The posterior-anterior shift in aging. *Cerebral Cortex, 18*(5), 1201−1209.

Diamond, A. (2013). Executive functions. *Annual Review of Psychology, 64*, 135−168.

DiGirolamo, G. J., Kramer, A. F., Barad, V., Cepeda, N. J., Weissman, D. H., Milham, M. P., et al. (2001). General and task-specific frontal lobe recruitment in older adults during executive processes: A fMRI investigation of task-switching. *Neuroreport, 12*(9), 2065−2071.

Duncan, J., Seitz, R. J., Kolodny, J., Bor, D., Herzog, H., Ahmed, A., et al. (2000). A neural basis for general intelligence. *Science (New York, N.Y.), 289*(5478), 457−460.

Emery, L., Heaven, T. J., Paxton, J. L., & Braver, T. S. (2008). Age-related changes in neural activity during performance matched working memory manipulation. *Neuroimage, 42*(4), 1577−1586.

Esposito, G., Kirkby, B. S., Van Horn, J. D., Ellmore, T. M., & Berman, K. F. (1999). Context-dependent, neural system-specific neurophysiological concomitants of ageing: Mapping PET correlates during cognitive activation. *Brain, 122*(Pt 5), 963−979.

Fox, M. D., Buckner, R. L., Liu, H., Chakravarty, M. M., Lozano, A. M., & Pascual-Leone, A. (2014). Resting-state networks link invasive and noninvasive brain stimulation across diverse psychiatric and neurological diseases. *Proceedings of the National Academy of Sciences of the United States of America, 111*(41), E4367−4375.

Fox, M. D., Snyder, A. Z., Vincent, J. L., Corbetta, M., Van Essen, D. C., & Raichle, M. E. (2005). The human brain is intrinsically organized into dynamic, anticorrelated functional networks. *Proceedings of the National Academy of Sciences of the United States of America, 102*(27), 9673−9678.

Freo, U., Ricciardi, E., Pietrini, P., Schapiro, M. B., Rapoport, S. I., & Furey, M. L. (2005). Pharmacological modulation of prefrontal cortical activity during a working memory task in young and older humans: A PET study with physostigmine. *The American Journal of Psychiatry, 162*(11), 2061−2070.

Friedman, N. P., & Miyake, A. (2016). Unity and diversity of executive functions: Individual differences as a window on cognitive structure. *Cortex; a Journal Devoted to the Study of the Nervous System and Behavior.*

Fuster, J. M., Bauer, R. H., & Jervey, J. P. (1985). Functional interactions between inferotemporal and prefrontal cortex in a cognitive task. *Brain Research, 330*(2), 299–307.

Gallen, C. L., Turner, G. R., Adnan, A., & D'Esposito, M. (2016). Reconfiguration of brain network architecture to support executive control in aging. *Neurobiology of Aging, 44,* 42–52.

Gazes, Y., Rakitin, B. C., Habeck, C., Steffener, J., & Stern, Y. (2012). Age differences of multivariate network expressions during task-switching and their associations with behavior. *Neuropsychologia, 50*(14), 3509–3518.

Gazzaley, A., Cooney, J. W., McEvoy, K., Knight, R. T., & D'Esposito, M. (2005). Top-down enhancement and suppression of the magnitude and speed of neural activity. *Journal of Cognitive Neuroscience, 17*(3), 507–517.

Gazzaley, A., & D'Esposito, M. (2007). Top-down modulation and normal aging. *Annals of the New York Academy of Sciences, 1097,* 67–83.

Gazzaley, A., Sheridan, M. A., Cooney, J. W., & D'Esposito, M. (2007). Age-related deficits in component processes of working memory. *Neuropsychology, 21*(5), 532–539.

Geerligs, L., Renken, R. J., Saliasi, E., Maurits, N. M., & Lorist, M. M. (2015). A Brain-Wide Study of Age-Related Changes in Functional Connectivity. *Cerebral Cortex, 25*(7), 1987–1999.

Geerligs, L., Saliasi, E., Maurits, N. M., & Lorist, M. M. (2012). Compensation through increased functional connectivity: Neural correlates of inhibition in old and young. *Journal of Cognitive Neuroscience, 24*(10), 2057–2069.

Gold, B. T., Kim, C., Johnson, N. F., Kryscio, R. J., & Smith, C. D. (2013). Lifelong bilingualism maintains neural efficiency for cognitive control in aging. *The Journal of Neuroscience, 33*(2), 387–396.

Grady, C. (2012). The cognitive neuroscience of ageing. *Nature Reviews. Neuroscience, 13*(7), 491–505.

Grady, C., Sarraf, S., Saverino, C., & Campbell, K. (2016). Age differences in the functional interactions among the default, frontoparietal control, and dorsal attention networks. *Neurobiology of Aging, 41,* 159–172.

Grady, C. L., McIntosh, A. R., Bookstein, F., Horwitz, B., Rapoport, S. I., & Haxby, J. V. (1998). Age-related changes in regional cerebral blood flow during working memory for faces. *Neuroimage, 8*(4), 409–425.

Grossman, M., Smith, E. E., Koenig, P., Glosser, G., DeVita, C., Moore, P., et al. (2002). The neural basis for categorization in semantic memory. *Neuroimage, 17*(3), 1549–1561.

Hansen, N. L., Lauritzen, M., Mortensen, E. L., Osler, M., Avlund, K., Fagerlund, B., et al. (2014). Subclinical cognitive decline in middle-age is associated with reduced task-induced deactivation of the brain's default mode network. *Human Brain Mapping, 35*(9), 4488–4498.

Hasher, L., & Zacks, R. T. (1988). Working memory, comprehension, and aging: A review and a new view. In G. H. Brower (Ed.), *The Psychology of Learning and Motivation* (pp. 193–225). San Diego, CA: Academic Press.

Haut, M. W., Kuwabara, H., Moran, M. T., Leach, S., Arias, R., & Knight, D. (2005). The effect of education on age-related functional activation during working memory. *Aging, Neuropsychology and Cognition, 12,* 216–229.

Holtzer, R., Rakitin, B. C., Steffener, J., Flynn, J., Kumar, A., & Stern, Y. (2009). Age effects on load-dependent brain activations in working memory for novel material. *Brain Research, 1249,* 148–161.

Jimura, K., & Braver, T. S. (2010). Age-related shifts in brain activity dynamics during task switching. *Cerebral Cortex, 20*(6), 1420–1431.

Johnson, M. K., Mitchell, K. J., Raye, C. L., & Greene, E. J. (2004). An age-related deficit in prefrontal cortical function associated with refreshing information. *Psychological Science, 13*(2), 127–132.

Jonides, J., Marshuetz, C., Smith, E. E., Reuter-Lorenz, P. A., Koeppe, R. A., & Hartley, A. (2000). Age differences in behavior and PET activation reveal differences in interference resolution in verbal working memory. *Journal of Cognitive Neuroscience, 12*(1), 188–196.

Korsch, M., Fruhholz, S., & Herrmann, M. (2014). Ageing differentially affects neural processing of different conflict types-an fMRI study. *Frontiers in Aging Neuroscience, 6*, 57.

Laird, A. R., Fox, P. M., Price, C. J., Glahn, D. C., Uecker, A. M., Lancaster, J. L., et al. (2005). ALE meta-analysis: Controlling the false discovery rate and performing statistical contrasts. *Human Brain Mapping, 25*(1), 155–164.

Laird, A. R., Robinson, J. L., McMillan, K. M., Tordesillas-Gutierrez, D., Moran, S. T., Gonzales, S. M., et al. (2010). Comparison of the disparity between Talairach and MNI coordinates in functional neuroimaging data: Validation of the Lancaster transform. *Neuroimage, 51*(2), 677–683.

Lancaster, J. L., Tordesillas-Gutierrez, D., Martinez, M., Salinas, F., Evans, A., Zilles, K., et al. (2007). Bias between MNI and Talairach coordinates analyzed using the ICBM-152 brain template. *Human Brain Mapping, 28*(11), 1194–1205.

Lee, T. M., Zhang, J. X., Chan, C. C., Yuen, K. S., Chu, L. W., Cheung, R. T., et al. (2006). Age-related differences in response regulation as revealed by functional MRI. *Brain Research, 1076*(1), 171–176.

Li, S. C., & Rieckmann, A. (2014). Neuromodulation and aging: Implications of aging neuronal gain control on cognition. *Current Opinion in Neurobiology, 29*, 148–158.

Lorenc, E. S., Lee, T. G., Chen, A. J., & D'Esposito, M. (2015). The Effect of Disruption of Prefrontal Cortical Function with Transcranial Magnetic Stimulation on Visual Working Memory. *Frontiers in Systems Neuroscience, 9*, 169.

Lustig, C., Snyder, A. Z., Bhakta, M., O'Brien, K. C., McAvoy, M., Raichle, M. E., et al. (2003). Functional deactivations: Change with age and dementia of the Alzheimer type. *Proceedings of the National Academy of Sciences of the United States of America, 100*(24), 14504–14509.

Madden, D. J., Costello, M. C., Dennis, N. A., Davis, S. W., Shepler, A. M., Spaniol, J., et al. (2010). Adult age differences in functional connectivity during executive control. *Neuroimage, 52*(2), 643–657.

Madden, D. J., Turkington, T. G., Provenzale, J. M., Denny, L. L., Langley, L. K., Hawk, T. C., et al. (2002). Aging and attentional guidance during visual search: Functional neuroanatomy by positron emission tomography. *Psychology and Aging, 17*(1), 24–43.

Martins, R., Simard, F., Provost, J. S., & Monchi, O. (2012). Changes in regional and temporal patterns of activity associated with aging during the performance of a lexical set-shifting task. *Cerebral Cortex, 22*(6), 1395–1406.

Mathis, K. W., & Molina, P. E. (2009). Central acetylcholinesterase inhibition improves hemodynamic counterregulation to severe blood loss in alcohol-intoxicated rats. *American Journal of Physiology. Regulatory, Integrative and Comparative Physiology, 297*(2), R437–445.

Meinzer, M., Flaisch, T., Wilser, L., Eulitz, C., Rockstroh, B., Conway, T., et al. (2009). Neural signatures of semantic and phonemic fluency in young and old adults. *Journal of Cognitive Neuroscience, 21*(10), 2007–2018.

Mell, T., Wartenburger, I., Marschner, A., Villringer, A., Reischies, F. M., & Heekeren, H. R. (2009). Altered function of ventral striatum during reward-based decision making in old age. *Frontiers in Human Neuroscience, 3*, 34.

Milham, M. P., Erickson, K. I., Banich, M. T., Kramer, A. F., Webb, A., Wszalek, T., et al. (2002). Attentional control in the aging brain: Insights from an fMRI study of the Stroop task. *Brain and Cognition, 49*(3), 277−296.

Miyake, A., & Friedman, N. P. (2012). The nature and organization of individual differences in executive functions: Four general conclusions. *Current Directions in Psychological Science: A Journal of the American Psychological Society, 21*(1), 8−14.

Miyake, A., Friedman, N. P., Emerson, M. J., Witzki, A. H., Howerter, A., & Wager, T. D. (2000). The unity and diversity of executive functions and their contributions to complex "Frontal Lobe" tasks: A latent variable analysis. *Cognitive Psychology, 41*(1), 49−100.

Nagahama, Y., Fukuyama, H., Yamauchi, H., Katsumi, Y., Magata, Y., Shibasaki, H., et al. (1997). Age-related changes in cerebral blood flow activation during a Card Sorting Test. *Experimental Brain Research, 114*(3), 571−577.

Nagel, I. E., Preuschhof, C., Li, S. C., Nyberg, L., Backman, L., Lindenberger, U., et al. (2009). Performance level modulates adult age differences in brain activation during spatial working memory. *Proceedings of the National Academy of Sciences of the United States of America, 106*(52), 22552−22557.

Nashiro, K., Sakaki, M., Nga, L., & Mather, M. (2013). Age-related similarities and differences in brain activity underlying reversal learning. *Frontiers in Integrative Neuroscience, 7*, 37.

Nielson, K. A., Langenecker, S. A., Ross, T. J., Garavan, H., Rao, S. M., & Stein, E. A. (2004). Comparability of functional MRI response in young and old during inhibition. *Neuroreport, 15*(1), 129−133.

Niendam, T. A., Laird, A. R., Ray, K. L., Dean, Y. M., Glahn, D. C., & Carter, C. S. (2012). Meta-analytic evidence for a superordinate cognitive control network subserving diverse executive functions. *Cognitive, Affective & Behavioral Neuroscience, 12*(2), 241−268.

Novakovic-Agopian, T., Chen, A. J., Rome, S., Abrams, G., Castelli, H., Rossi, A., et al. (2011). Rehabilitation of executive functioning with training in attention regulation applied to individually defined goals: A pilot study bridging theory, assessment, and treatment. *The Journal of Head Trauma Rehabilitation, 26*(5), 325−338.

Otsuka, Y., Osaka, N., Morishita, M., Kondo, H., & Osaka, M. (2006). Decreased activation of anterior cingulate cortex in the working memory of the elderly. *Neuroreport, 17*(14), 1479−1482.

Park, D. C., Polk, T. A., Hebrank, A. C., & Jenkins, L. J. (2010). Age differences in default mode activity on easy and difficult spatial judgment tasks. *Frontiers in Human Neuroscience, 3*, 75.

Park, D. C., Polk, T. A., Mikels, J. A., Taylor, S. F., & Marshuetz, C. (2001). Cerebral aging: Integration of brain and behavioral models of cognitive function. *Dialogues in Clinical Neuroscience, 3*(3), 151−165.

Park, D. C., Polk, T. A., Park, R., Minear, M., Savage, A., & Smith, M. R. (2004). Aging reduces neural specialization in ventral visual cortex. *Proceedings of the National Academy of Sciences of the United States of America, 101*(35), 13091−13095.

Park, D. C., & Reuter-Lorenz, P. (2009). The adaptive brain: Aging and neurocognitive scaffolding. *Annual Review of Psychology, 60*, 173−196.

Paxton, J. L., Barch, D. M., Racine, C. A., & Braver, T. S. (2008). Cognitive control, goal maintenance, and prefrontal function in healthy aging. *Cerebral Cortex, 18*(5), 1010–1028.

Payer, D., Marshuetz, C., Sutton, B., Hebrank, A., Welsh, R. C., & Park, D. C. (2006). Decreased neural specialization in old adults on a working memory task. *Neuroreport, 17* (5), 487–491.

Persson, J., Lustig, C., Nelson, J. K., & Reuter-Lorenz, P. A. (2007). Age differences in deactivation: A link to cognitive control? *Journal of Cognitive Neuroscience, 19*(6), 1021–1032.

Podell, J. E., Sambataro, F., Murty, V. P., Emery, M. R., Tong, Y., Das, S., et al. (2012). Neurophysiological correlates of age-related changes in working memory updating. *Neuroimage, 62*(3), 2151–2160.

Power, J. D., Cohen, A. L., Nelson, S. M., Wig, G. S., Barnes, K. A., Church, J. A., et al. (2011). Functional network organization of the human brain. *Neuron, 72*(4), 665–678.

Prakash, R. S., Erickson, K. I., Colcombe, S. J., Kim, J. S., Voss, M. W., & Kramer, A. F. (2009). Age-related differences in the involvement of the prefrontal cortex in attentional control. *Brain and Cognition, 71*(3), 328–335.

Raye, C. L., Mitchell, K. J., Reeder, J. A., Greene, E. J., & Johnson, M. K. (2008). Refreshing one of several active representations: Behavioral and functional magnetic resonance imaging differences between young and older adults. *Journal of Cognitive Neuroscience, 20*(5), 852–862.

Reuter-Lorenz, P. A., & Cappell, K. A. (2008). Neurocognitive aging and the compensation hypothesis. *Current Directions in Psychological Science, 17*(3), 177–182.

Reuter-Lorenz, P. A., Jonides, J., Smith, E. E., Hartley, A., Miller, A., Marshuetz, C., et al. (2000). Age differences in the frontal lateralization of verbal and spatial working memory revealed by PET. *Journal of Cognitive Neuroscience, 12*(1), 174–187.

Reuter-Lorenz, P. A., & Park, D. C. (2014). How does it STAC up? Revisiting the scaffolding theory of aging and cognition. *Neuropsychology Review, 24*(3), 355–370.

Ricciardi, E., Pietrini, P., Schapiro, M. B., Rapoport, S. I., & Furey, M. L. (2009). Cholinergic modulation of visual working memory during aging: A parametric PET study. *Brain Research Bulletin, 79*(5), 322–332.

Rodrigue, K. M., Kennedy, K. M., & Raz, N. (2005). Aging and longitudinal change in perceptual-motor skill acquisition in healthy adults. *Journals of Gerontology. Series B, Psychological Sciences and Social Sciences, 60*(4), P174–181.

Rypma, B., & D'Esposito, M. (2000). Isolating the neural mechanisms of age-related changes in human working memory. *Nature Neuroscience, 3*(5), 509–515.

Rypma, B., Prabhakaran, V., Desmond, J. E., & Gabrieli, J. D. (2001). Age differences in prefrontal cortical activity in working memory. *Psychology and Aging, 16*(3), 371–384.

Salthouse, T. A. (1996). The processing-speed theory of adult age differences in cognition. *Psychological Review, 103*(3), 403–428.

Sambataro, F., Murty, V. P., Callicott, J. H., Tan, H. Y., Das, S., Weinberger, D. R., et al. (2010). Age-related alterations in default mode network: Impact on working memory performance. *Neurobiology of Aging, 31*(5), 839–852.

Schmitz, T. W., Dixon, M. L., Anderson, A. K., & De Rosa, E. (2014). Distinguishing attentional gain and tuning in young and older adults. *Neurobiology of Aging, 35*(11), 2514–2525.

Schneider-Garces, N. J., Gordon, B. A., Brumback-Peltz, C. R., Shin, E., Lee, Y., Sutton, B. P., et al. (2010). Span, CRUNCH, and beyond: Working memory capacity and the aging brain. *Journal of Cognitive Neuroscience, 22*(4), 655–669.

Shallice, T. (1982). Specific impairments of planning. *Philosophical Transactions of the Royal Society of London. Series B, Biological Sciences, 298*(1089), 199–209.

Simmonds, D. J., Pekar, J. J., & Mostofsky, S. H. (2008). Meta-analysis of Go/No-go tasks demonstrating that fMRI activation associated with response inhibition is task-dependent. *Neuropsychologia, 46*(1), 224–232.

Smith, Jonides, J., Marshuetz, C., & Koeppe, R. A. (1998). Components of verbal working memory: Evidence from neuroimaging. *Proceedings of the National Academy of Sciences of the United States of America, 95*(3), 876–882.

Smith, E. E., Geva, A., Jonides, J., Miller, A., Reuter-Lorenz, P., & Koeppe, R. A. (2001). The neural basis of task-switching in working memory: Effects of performance and aging. *Proceedings of the National Academy of Sciences of the United States of America, 98*(4), 2095–2100.

Smith, S. M., Jenkinson, M., Woolrich, M. W., Beckmann, C. F., Behrens, T. E., Johansen-Berg, H., et al. (2004). Advances in functional and structural MR image analysis and implementation as FSL. *Neuroimage, 23*(Suppl 1), S208–219.

Snowdon, D. A. (1997). Aging and Alzheimer's disease: Lessons from the Nun Study. *The Gerontologist, 37*(2), 150–156.

Spreng, R. N., DuPre, E., Selarka, D., Garcia, J., Gojkovic, S., Mildner, J., et al. (2014). Goal-congruent default network activity facilitates cognitive control. *The Journal of Neuroscience, 34*(42), 14108–14114.

Spreng, R. N., & Schacter, D. L. (2012). Default Network Modulation and Large-Scale Network Interactivity in Healthy Young and Old Adults. *Cerebral Cortex, 22*, 2610–2621.

Spreng, R. N., Sepulcre, J., Turner, G. R., Stevens, W. D., & Schacter, D. L. (2013). Intrinsic architecture underlying the relations among the default, dorsal attention, and frontoparietal control networks of the human brain. *Journal of Cognitive Neuroscience, 25*(1), 74–86.

Spreng, R. N., Stevens, W. D., Chamberlain, J. P., Gilmore, A. W., & Schacter, D. L. (2010). Default network activity, coupled with the frontoparietal control network, supports goal-directed cognition. *Neuroimage, 53*(1), 303–317.

Spreng, R. N., Stevens, W. D., Viviano, J. D., & Schacter, D. L. (2016). Attenuated anticorrelation between the default and dorsal attention networks with aging: Evidence from task and rest. *Neurobiology of Aging, 45*, 149–160.

Spreng, R. N., Wojtowicz, M., & Grady, C. L. (2010). Reliable differences in brain activity between young and old adults: A quantitative meta-analysis across multiple cognitive domains. *Neuroscience and Biobehavioral Reviews, 34*(8), 1178–1194.

Steffener, J., Barulli, D., Habeck, C., & Stern, Y. (2014). Neuroimaging explanations of age-related differences in task performance. *Frontiers in Aging Neuroscience, 6*, 46.

Stern, Y., Habeck, C., Moeller, J., Scarmeas, N., Anderson, K. E., Hilton, H. J., et al. (2005). Brain networks associated with cognitive reserve in healthy young and old adults. *Cerebral Cortex, 15*(4), 394–402.

Stuss, D. T., Alexander, M. P., Shallice, T., Picton, T. W., Binns, M. A., Macdonald, R., et al. (2005). Multiple frontal systems controlling response speed. *Neuropsychologia, 43*(3), 396–417.

Stuss, D. T., & Levine, B. (2002). Adult clinical neuropsychology: Lessons from studies of the frontal lobes. *Annual Review of Psychology, 53*, 401–433.

Talairach, J., & Tournoux, P. (1988). *Co-planar stereotaxic atlas of the human brain (M. Rayport, Trans.)*. Stuttgart: Georg Thieme Verlag.

Townsend, J., Adamo, M., & Haist, F. (2006). Changing channels: An fMRI study of aging and cross-modal attention shifts. *Neuroimage, 31*(4), 1682–1692.

Turkeltaub, P. E., Eden, G. F., Jones, K. M., & Zeffiro, T. A. (2002). Meta-analysis of the functional neuroanatomy of single-word reading: Method and validation. *Neuroimage, 16*(3 Pt 1) 765–780.

Turner, G.R., Novakovic-Agopian, T., Kornblith, E., Madore, M., Adnan, A., D'Esposito, M., et al. (in press). Goal-oriented attention regulation (GOALS) training in older adults.

Turner, G. R., & Spreng, R. N. (2012). Executive functions and neurocognitive aging: Dissociable patterns of brain activity. *Neurobiology of Aging, 33*(4), 826 e821-813.

Turner, G. R., & Spreng, R. N. (2015). Prefrontal engagement and reduced default network suppression co-occur and are dynamically coupled in older adults: The Default-Executive Coupling Hypothesis of Aging. *Journal of Cognitive Neuroscience, 27*(12), 2462–2476.

Van Essen, D. C. (2005). A population-average, landmark- and surface-based (PALS) atlas of human cerebral cortex. *Neuroimage, 28*(3), 635–662.

Vincent, J. L., Kahn, I., Snyder, A. Z., Raichle, M. E., & Buckner, R. L. (2008). Evidence for a frontoparietal control system revealed by intrinsic functional connectivity. *Journal of Neurophysiology, 100*(6), 3328–3342.

Wager, T. D., & Smith, E. E. (2003). Neuroimaging studies of working memory: A meta-analysis. *Cognitive, Affective & Behavioral Neuroscience, 3*(4), 255–274.

Yeo, B. T., Krienen, F. M., Sepulcre, J., Sabuncu, M. R., Lashkari, D., Hollinshead, M., et al. (2011). The organization of the human cerebral cortex estimated by intrinsic functional connectivity. *Journal of Neurophysiology, 106*(3), 1125–1165.

Zhu, D. C., Zacks, R. T., & Slade, J. M. (2010). Brain activation during interference resolution in young and older adults: An fMRI study. *Neuroimage, 50*(2), 810–817.

Zhu, Z., Hakun, J. G., Johnson, N. F., & Gold, B. T. (2014). Age-related increases in right frontal activation during task switching are mediated by reaction time and white matter microstructure. *Neuroscience, 278*, 51–61.

Zysset, S., Schroeter, M. L., Neumann, J., & Yves von Cramon, D. (2007). Stroop interference, hemodynamic response and aging: An event-related fMRI study. *Neurobiol Aging, 28*(6), 937–946.

Chapter 9

Assessment of Executive Functions in Research

Yana Suchy, Madison A. Niermeyer and Rosemary E. Ziemnik
Department of Psychology, University of Utah, Salt Lake City, UT, United States

CONCEPTUALIZING EXECUTIVE FUNCTIONS IN THE RESEARCH CONTEXT

Executive functioning (or functions; EF) is a complex neurocognitive construct that made its debut in the scientific literature in the 1970s (Luria, 1973; Pribram, 1973), in the initial attempts to provide a conceptual framework for the deficits observed in patients with frontal lobe damage. From the very beginning, it came to be recognized that EF was not like other neurocognitive domains, in that it was less related to test scores and more related to "how a person goes about doing something" (Lezak, 1982). Another difference between EF and other neurocognitive domains lies in its persistent defiance of models and definitions (Suchy, 2009). In fact, in the four decades since EF was first introduced, researchers have not yet been able to agree on such basic premises as whether the construct is unitary versus multifaceted, or whether the construct should be delineated by the boundaries of the frontal lobes (i.e., the "frontal lobe functions" Stuss & Alexander, 2000) versus by its presumed evolutionary purpose (i.e., those abilities that allow one to plan, organize, and successfully execute purposeful, goal-directed, and future-oriented actions) (Cummings & Miller, 2007; Gazzaley, D'Esposito, Miller, & Cummings, 2007). Despite this lack of agreement on a definition, the early EF research investigated a fairly consistent set of questions, having to do primarily with gaining better understanding of the nature of deficits associated with frontal lobe lesions and with the development of tests that would be sensitive to such deficits. This research was virtually completely confined within the disciplines of clinical neuropsychology and behavioral neuroscience, and the nature of the research questions themselves de facto defined the construct.

However, in the past 15−20 years, other disciplines have evidenced an exponentially growing interest in EF. Outside clinical neuropsychology,

Executive Functions in Health and Disease. DOI: http://dx.doi.org/10.1016/B978-0-12-803676-1.00009-X

EF came to be investigated as the potential "silver bullet" in the search for causes for antisocial acts in criminals (Blair & Cipolotti, 2000; Brower & Price, 2001), behavioral problems in conduct-disordered children (Hobson, Scott, & Rubia, 2011; Stevens, Kaplan, & Hesselbrock, 2003), or failures to adhere to medical regimens among a variety of nonneurologic patient populations (Miller et al., 2012), to name a few. Additionally, individual differences in EF have come to be viewed as major contributors to personality and subtle inherent weaknesses in EF as risk factors for the development of psychopathology (Snyder, Miyake, & Hankin, 2015). This proliferation of research questions has resulted in a proliferation of definitions and models of EF, some of which bear little resemblance to the original conceptualizations that stemmed from impairments seen in patients with brain damage. Thus, researchers interested in incorporating EF into their study designs are faced with having to choose not only from an array of assessment methods but also from an array of EF models and definitions.

While full overview of the many models and definitions of EF is beyond the scope of this chapter, suffice it to say that they range from highly parsimonious unifaceted models that propose a single unifying neurocognitive ability (Baddeley, 1998; Baddeley, Chincotta, & Adlam, 2001) to models that are quite complex and include multiple subdomains of EF, each further divided into multiple elemental processes (Suchy, 2015). When selecting a theoretical framework for their research, researchers should carefully consider whether a model they are selecting is clinical, cognitive, or developmental in its origin, so as to select the best fit for their research question.

Clinical models typically originate in clinical neuropsychology and tend to be comprehensive, including multiple facets or subdomains of EF that correspond, at least to some extent, to deficits seen in patient populations. Such models often include both cognitive control and behavioral control processes although this distinction is often only implied. Examples of such models include those by Lezak, Howieson, Bigler, and Tranel (2012), Stuss (2011), and Suchy (2015). In contrast, *cognitive models* are typically derived from research conducted with healthy populations (typically college students) and originate in cognitive psychology or cognitive neuroscience. Such models tend to be more parsimonious (sometimes unifaceted) and reductionistic and at times propose components of EF that are purely cognitive in nature (i.e., excluding behavioral control, although, once again, this may only be implied). Such models are frequently developed and validated using factor analytic procedures, with the focus on individual differences in healthy populations. A prominent example of such models is that used by Miyake and Friedman in their work (Friedman et al., 2006; Miyake et al., 2000). Lastly, there is increasing emergence of models that are *developmental* in nature and rely on examination of EF maturation in healthy children or teens. These models often refer to constructs such as "self-regulation" or "self-control," as well as integration of cognitive and emotional processes (Diamond, 2013; Duckworth & Seligman, 2005; see Suchy, Ziemnik, and Niermeyer, 2017, in this volume for an additional discussion of challenges in defining EF). Before choosing tools for use in a given study, researchers need to carefully consider the nature of their research question, so as to select the most appropriate model or definition of EF.

TOOLS AVAILABLE FOR EXECUTIVE FUNCTIONS ASSESSMENT

In this section, we examine three broad categories of EF measures: clinical, experimental, and self-report. Each category is associated with a unique set of pros and cons, and, once again, careful consideration of these in the context of one's research question is needed.

Clinical Measures of Executive Functioning

Clinical measures of EF are those that have been developed for use in clinical settings and are used for purposes of diagnosis, assessment of current functional potential, prediction of future functional potential, measuring treatment response, localizing brain lesions, and clinical correlation with imaging findings (Harvey, 2012). A prominent example of clinical measures of EF is the Delis−Kaplan Executive Function System battery (D-KEFS; Delis, Kaplan, & Kramer, 2001). Although many EF tests were historically designed to differentiate patients with frontal lobe lesions from those characterized by diffuse or posterior brain damage, it is well recognized that performance on these measures can be adversely affected by damage in a variety of brain areas (Channon & Crawford, 1999; Robinson, Shallice, Bozzali, & Cipolotti, 2012). Because these tests have been developed for clinical decision-making, there is greater emphasis on sensitivity to dysfunction than specificity to discrete elemental processes. In other words, if the original goal was to identify patients with lesions in the frontal lobes, then the best tests would have to be those that tap *multiple* frontal lobe processes. Consequently, it is ill-advised to assume that one can isolate discrete components of EF with any one clinical measure, although there is some variability among tests in terms of their specificity.

In addition to limitations and variability in specificity, tests also vary in their sensitivity to EF impairment across different populations. For example, some tests may be quite sensitive for use with older adults but quite insensitive when used with younger adults (Niermeyer, Suchy, & Ziemnik, 2016). Relatedly, to maximize the tests' ability to differentiate between healthy and brain-damaged populations, these tests tend to be somewhat less sensitive to normal individual differences among healthy individuals. For all these reasons, different measures are differentially effective in identifying clinical syndromes, and multiple tests are usually needed to deduce a cognitive deficit or to discern normal individual differences (Burgess, Alderman, Evans, Emslie, & Wilson, 1998; Homack, Lee, & Riccio, 2005).

Importantly, performance on clinical measures of EF necessarily relies on a number of lower order cognitive processes. This is because, to complete any EF task, the examinee must be able to understand test instructions, perceive test stimuli, attend appropriately, and use the requisite response modality (e.g., language, graphomotor skills, etc.). In addition, because many tests of EF are timed, speed of processing necessarily confounds results. For these reasons, it is key that such nonexecutive process be also assessed and accounted for. For more discussion of this topic, see Challenges and Considerations in Test Selection section.

There are four major advantages of clinical measures, as compared to experimental measures: (1) they have been standardized, which increases the replicability and comparability of findings across studies, (2) they have been well characterized regarding various psychometric properties, such as reliabilities, factor structure, and the magnitudes of practice effects, (3) they have been validated for specific clinical uses, which facilitates interpretation of findings, and (4) they have been normed, which allows for comparison with an age-matched (and sometimes education, gender, and/or ethnicity-matched) comparison groups. Because the degree to which demographic matching is available differs across tests, the importance of demographic matching for any given study question should be a consideration in test selection. Importantly, the ability to compare participant performance to norms is superior to simple comparison to a control group, as it allows the determination of whether the target group's performance is within a normal versus an impaired range. In other words, it is possible for a target population to differ from a control group but still fall within a normal range. For more discussion of this topic, see Interpretive Considerations section.

Clinical measures have several disadvantages. First, they cannot be readily acquired by nonclinical researchers, as they are protected not only by copyright laws but also by test security guidelines (American Psychological Association, 2010). Second, they are proprietary and thus not available free of charge. The cost of clinical tests varies but typically involves not only the cost of the test itself but also the cost of response booklets, which, too, are protected by copyright. And lastly, the majority of clinical measures are administered in a paper and pencil format and as such require quite a bit of investment in examiner training and careful monitoring to ensure that standardized administration procedures are followed throughout the study duration.

Experimental Measures of Executive Functioning

Experimental measures of EF typically involve relatively simple responses during relatively simple tasks. They are often designed with the intention of isolating some presumed components of EF, most typically switching, inhibitory control, and working memory, and are almost always administered via computer. Some classic examples include the Stroop task (Stroop, 1935) or the various flanker tasks (Posner & Dehaene, 1994) presumed to measure inhibition, the Operation Span (Engle, 2002) or the Letter Memory Task (Morris & Jones, 1990) presumed to measure working memory, or the various switching tasks (Meiran, Chorev, & Sapir, 2000; Sohn & Anderson, 2001) presumed to measure cognitive flexibility. Some tasks that were originally developed for research purposes have since become available for clinical usage and thus have gained all the advantages and disadvantages of typical clinical measure. An example of such a test is the Iowa Gambling task (Bechara, Damasio, Tranel, & Damasio, 2005), presumed to measure emotional decision-making, which, according to some conceptualizations, falls under the EF umbrella (Suchy, 2015).

Experimental tasks yield a number of advantages. First, they facilitate understanding of the contribution of discrete neurocognitive processes to the construct of EF. Second, because isolation of discrete processes sometimes relies on a subtraction methodology, nonexecutive contributions to performance are in some cases already controlled for. For example, the various versions of the switching task isolate the so called "switching cost," which is the difference between performance of the same task without versus with switching (Meiran et al., 2000; Sohn & Anderson, 2001). Third, because they are typically administered via computer, they obviate the need for extensive test administration training. However, there are some disadvantages: Measuring discrete EF subcomponents means that many other important aspects of EF may be missed, and this can sometimes lead to inappropriately simplistic conclusions or interpretations about the structure of EF. Also, a more global EF deficit that results from a cumulative effect of a number of slight weaknesses is likely to be missed. Lastly, many experimental computer-administered tasks require a high number of trials, resulting in long testing sessions.

Self- and Informant-Reports

Self-report scales of EF require respondents to rate themselves on behaviors that are presumed to be subserved by EF. These scales typically inquire about the frequency with which certain types of EF lapses occur. Similarly, informant-reports ask family members, close acquaintances, or teachers to rate the patient's frequency of various behaviors that involve EF. Many measures are available in both self- and informant-report versions. Common examples of EF rating scales are the Behavior Rating Inventory of Executive Function (BRIEF; Guy, Gioia, & Isquith, 2004), the Frontal Systems Behavior Scale (FrSBe; Grace & Malloy, 2001), the Executive Function Index (Spinella, 2005), the Dysexecutive Questionnaire

(DEX; Burgess, Alderman, Wilson, Evans, & Emslie, 1996), and Brock Adaptive Functioning Questionnaire (BAFQ; Dywan & Segalowitz, 1996).

A primary advantage to informant- and self-reports is that they are extremely easy to administer. Additionally, they have been purported to have better ecological validity than performance-based measures, as they inquire about actual daily functioning (Gioia, Isquith, Guy, & Kenworthy, 2000; Puente, Cohen, Aita, & Brandt, 2016). Finally, the reported reliabilities of self-report scales tend to be higher than those of performance-based tests (Malloy & Grace, 2005).

Nevertheless, there are some limitations to self- and informant-reports. Most notably, they rely on subjective judgments and are vulnerable to memory failures, personal biases, and poor self-awareness, or outright purposeful misdirection on part of the examinee (Edmonds, Delano-Wood, Galasko, Salmon, & Bondi, 2014; Farias, Mungas, & Jagust, 2005). In addition, self-reports have shown to have very low correlations with objective test performance (Bogod, Mateer, & MacDonald, 2003; Burgess et al., 1998; Nęcka, Lech, Sobczyk, & Śmieja, 2012), and it is not clear whether they tap personality traits and temperament, or actual cognitive abilities.

CHALLENGES AND CONSIDERATIONS IN TEST SELECTION

There are a number of common pitfalls that researchers should be wary of when selecting tests of EF for their research project. Some common mistakes include (1) selection of EF tests that are *not* appropriate for the populations being studied and/or for the research question, (2) failing to consider the appropriateness of the test's norms, (3) failing to consider test reliability, and (4) failing to assess other cognitive processes that confound performance on tests of EF. Each of these pitfalls and related issues are discussed below.

Matching the Method to the Population(s) and Research Question(s)

A common challenge researchers face is appropriate matching of the method of EF assessment to the population(s) being studied. One way this issue can manifest is floor and ceiling effects. A test is said to have a *high floor* when many participants achieve a score near the bottom of all possible scores, and a *low ceiling* when many participants achieve a score near the top of all possible scores (Brooks, Strauss, Elisabeth, Iverson, & Slick, 2009). This limited variability not only greatly constricts the range of available scores but also violates the assumption of normality upon which many statistical methods depend, thereby leading to an underestimation of effects. Researchers should recognize that this applies not only to tools used to compare means, such as *t*-tests and the analysis of variance but also to correlation and regression analyses (Rorden, Bonilha, & Nichols, 2007; Tabachnick & Fidell, 2013).

One example of this mismatch is the use of the Wisconsin Card Sorting Test (WCST; Heaton, Chelune, Talley, Kay, & Curtiss, 1993) to assess EF in a neurologically healthy young adult sample. As a clinical measure, the WCST was designed to be relatively easy for healthy individuals, while being sensitive to damage in the frontal lobes. Consequently, the scores it produces are often not normally distributed in healthy populations. This can be easily gleaned by looking at the WCST manual (Heaton et al., 1993). For example, a perfect score of 6/6 categories completed corresponds to a percentile rank of >16 for adults between the ages of 20 and 59 years (regardless of education). This suggests that 84% of neurologically normal adults are likely to achieve this perfect score. Thus, it should not be surprising that studies that find individual differences on other tests of EF fail to find results for the WCST (Cowles, 2012; Hildebrand, 1997; Parada et al., 2012; Webb, 2004).

The problem with inappropriate matching of tests and populations becomes magnified when multiple cognitive measures are used with the goal of characterizing a cognitive *profile*. In such situations, spurious profiles may emerge simply because one measure is appropriately matched to the population at hand (and thus is appropriately sensitive to individual or group differences), whereas another measure is not appropriate (and thus unable to discriminate among individuals or groups). Interpreting results from such mismatched batteries as reflecting a particular cognitive profile (e.g., saying that groups differ on one cognitive ability but not on another) is inappropriate, and researchers should be wary of drawing such conclusions. Instead, a more appropriate interpretation would be that the first *test* was sensitive enough to detect EF differences between the groups, whereas the second test was not (Brooks et al., 2009).

In addition to ensuring that the EF measures match the studied population, researchers should also consider whether their assessment tools match the research question. For example, is the researcher using EF tests with the goal of (1) identifying EF differences between two neurologic populations, (2) examining the structure of the EF construct among healthy individuals, or (3) validating a newly developed EF test? For the first question, the measures should be selected based on the known level of impairment of the two populations, such that they would be maximally discriminable and would not result in a ceiling or a floor effect in either group. Additionally, the researcher needs to have a good theoretical sense of which aspects of EF are likely to be different for the two groups because many populations differ in some, but not all, aspects of EF (Happé, Booth, Charlton, & Hughes, 2006; Levy & Chelune, 2007). For the second question, experimental tasks may be the best choice, as many clinical measures are designed to identify impairment, and as such may be minimally discriminable with respect to subtle individual differences. The second question would also require careful conceptualization of EF, and the researcher should consider which one of the many available

EF models will be theoretically most meaningful. Once a model is selected, then the selection of measures should logically follow. The third question would require that the researcher carefully consider which aspects of EF the new measure taps into. The researcher should then select previously validated EF tests that are presumed to tap into not only the same aspects of EF as the new test but, if possible, also different aspects of EF to establish discriminant validity.

A common example of a mismatch between the tool and the purpose of assessment is the use of a screening measure when attempting to assess *subtle group differences.* Screening tools are popular in research settings because they take little time to administer and often promise to tap into several cognitive domains. Thus, for example, a researcher interested in examining individual differences in EF among older adults may be tempted to use the Montreal Cognitive Assessment (MoCA; Nasreddine et al., 2005), which is a neuropsychological screening tool that has been praised (Lam et al., 2013) for having more EF items than its counterpart, the Mini-Mental Status Examination (Folstein, Folstein, & McHugh, 1975). However, because the MoCA was developed to *screen for impairment,* it, virtually by definition, will not tap into subtle individual variability.

Considering the Appropriateness of Test Norms

When selecting clinical measures of EF, researchers should also always consider whether the norms of the tests they are using are appropriately representative of the research participants in terms of demographic variables such as age, education, socioeconomic status, and ethnicity (Campbell Jr. et al., 2002). A thorough treatment of the way in which these demographic variables intersect with neuropsychological research is beyond the scope of this chapter. However, researchers are encouraged to seek out literature about how these topics interface with their specific research area and take time to learn about the demographic characteristics of the samples upon which specific EF measures were developed and normed.

There are some additional important considerations when using standardized EF scores based on norms. In particular, when multiple measures are used (whether for the purpose of examining profiles or for the purpose of creating a composite across several measures), researchers need to examine how similar the normative samples for the measures are. For example, let us say a researcher uses two EF tests, one normed on a sample of older adults who are free of any medical or neurologic conditions and the other normed on a sample that is representative of the general population of older adults (and thus contains individuals with medical and neurologic conditions). Because of this difference, the same level of ability on the first test will translate into a lower age-corrected standard score than that on the second test (Brooks et al., 2009). Additional normative issues that need to be carefully considered when selecting tests include whether norms for two different tests use different age bands, or whether two tests rely on different subsets of demographic characteristics (e.g., age and education vs age and gender). To avoid problems with relying on norms that are *not* mutually comparable, researchers may wish to opt for batteries of EF that are conormed, such as the D-KEFS (Delis et al., 2001).

Considering Test Reliability

Another common problem with the measurement of EF in research is using only one measure to capture the entire EF construct. First of all, as already alluded to earlier, it is unlikely that any single measure will assess all components of EF (Ogilvie, Stewart, Chan, & Shum, 2011). Second, using a single test is likely to compromise the reliability of EF measurement, as suggested by a recent meta-analysis that has shown that clinical measures of EF have lower test−retest reliability than do tests of other neuropsychological domains (Calamia, Markon, & Tranel, 2013). Although low test−retest reliability may simply reflect limited construct stability, internal consistency of EF measures reported in test manuals is often also quite modest (Suchy, 2015). In a research context, this is particularly problematic as low reliabilities increase the probability of failing to detect effects that exist.

Fortunately, research suggests that both test−retest and internal consistency reliabilities can be improved by creating a composite score from multiple EF measures (Ettenhofer, Hambrick, & Abeles, 2006; Suchy, 2015). Importantly, creating a composite allows researchers to report the actual reliabilities in their sample, rather than relying on the information presented in the test manual, as considerable deviations from manual-reported reliabilities have been found in clinical populations (Piovesana, Ross, Whittingham, Ware, & Boyd, 2015). Of note, many experimental measures of EF do not have the same psychometric information available as do clinical tests, and their reliabilities are frequently unknown and unreported. Researchers are urged to compute reliabilities of different trial types on experimental tasks they use and report those in their methods section.

Including Measures of Component Processes and Intelligence

Another pitfall that can greatly limit interpretation is failing to include measures of component processes that contribute to performance on EF tests, and measures of certain foundational abilities, such as IQ. As mentioned earlier, it is well accepted in neuropsychology that cognition is hierarchically structured (Stuss, Picton, & Alexander, 2001), and that it is extremely difficult to measure EF in isolation. Deficits in lower order abilities such as processing speed, basic attention, visual perception, and language can masquerade as deficits in EF if not properly controlled (for a more thorough discussion, see Suchy et al., 2017, in this volume). Researchers are in a much stronger position to draw conclusions about EF if they have separate measures of these component processes and can therefore control for them statistically. The logic of hierarchical regression lends itself nicely to this approach. Researchers who include measures of component processes can enter them into the regression equation followed by EF to determine whether EF explains unique variance in the outcome (Euler, Niermeyer, & Suchy, 2015; Franchow & Suchy, 2015). Of note, although many experimental measures already control for component processes as they rely on subtraction of one task condition from another, it is nevertheless important to be vigilant to confounds on tests that do not rely on subtraction, such as the popular Operation Span test.

Researchers are also encouraged to consider and measure IQ when studying EF. Intelligence has been shown to account for both unique (beyond EF) and overlapping variance in functional outcomes (e.g., medication adherence), both for older adults (Hart & Bean, 2011; Puente, Lindbergh, & Miller, 2015) and for a number of clinical populations (Maeda et al., 2006; Martinez-Aran et al., 2009; Perna, Loughan, & Talka, 2012; Suchy, Turner, Queen, Durracio, Wiebe, Butner et al., 2016). There is also some functional magnetic resonance imaging evidence showing that individuals with higher IQ use fewer EF resources when performing challenging tasks, perhaps due to more efficient use of strategies (Graham et al., 2010). Collectively these findings suggest that IQ can be an important mediator and moderator between EF and many outcomes of interest (Graham et al., 2010; Hart & Bean, 2011). Of note, assessment of IQ does not necessarily always require administration of a full intelligence battery; rather, a screening tool of crystallized intelligence, such as vocabulary, world knowledge, or even simple sight reading, may suffice (Lezak *et al.* 2012; Olsen et al., 2015).

INTERPRETIVE CONSIDERATIONS

When reporting and interpreting the results of EF assessment, researchers need to carefully attend to several issues. Although we have touched upon some of these earlier in this chapter, we believe that they each warrant a more in-depth treatment.

Impairments Versus Group Differences

It is not uncommon for researchers to describe group differences in their writing as reflecting a "deficit" or "impairment" in one group relative to the other group. The term "impairment" implies that a person cannot function normally or that he or she performs in a range that is sufficiently below age-matched peers, so as to be of clinical significance. A statistically significant difference between two groups is not sufficient to draw such a conclusion, especially if the comparison is based on experimental tasks or on raw scores from clinical measures. There are several reasons for this. First, many perfectly healthy and normal groups differ when compared on their cognitive performance. For example, middle-aged adults commonly differ from young adults on many cognitive measures, including those of EF. However, it would be inappropriate to simply assume that, by virtue of being middle-aged, one is impaired. An even more extreme example pertains to sex differences: Research shows that women outperform men on certain verbal tests and men outperform women on certain tests of visual−spatial abilities (Torres et al., 2006). Once again, however, these subtle, albeit statistically significant, differences do not render either group "impaired."

Second, even a group difference that is of clinically significant magnitude does not always warrant the label of impairment. Consider, for example, a comparison between two highly educated samples: Physicians who are healthy versus physicians who had suffered a mild myocardial infarction. If we assume that physicians are cognitively about $1-2$ standard deviations (SD) above the population mean, then even a loss of function corresponding to 1.5 SD, which is certainly clinically significant, would not render the more poorly performing group "impaired."

The best ways to address these issues is to examine standardized scores based on normative comparisons. To demonstrate this, we provide a concrete example from our own research (Suchy, Kraybill, & Franchow, 2011a). In a sample of community-dwelling older adults, we examined the association of IQ with insight about one's limitations in performing instrumental activities of daily living. We found that lower IQ was in fact associated with poorer insight. Had we examined raw scores only, we might have been tempted to assume that below average IQ relates to poor insight. However, examination of standard scores revealed a very different interpretation: The group that scored in the average range exhibited poor insight, and those with good insight were in the above average to superior range. In other words, the results were not driven by a deficit but rather by a strength, and examination of standard scores allowed more nuanced, and more accurate, interpretation of the results.

Interpretation of Repeat Assessments

Many research designs require that tests be administered more than once. In clinical neuropsychology, it is well recognized that a second administration of the same test is typically associated with an improvement in performance, known as a practice effect. There are several issues about practice effects that are relevant here. First, measures of fluid abilities, such as EF, tend to exhibit larger practice effects than do tests that are less complex or that rely on crystalized abilities (Wechsler, 2008). Thus, one needs to guard against inappropriately interpreting differential practice effects of EF, relative to other domains. Second, the size of practice effects depends not only on the particular cognitive domain or measure but also on certain characteristics of the test taker, such as their age, educational background, level of intellectual functioning, or diagnosis (Duff et al., 2007; Duff et al., 2008; Thaler, Hill, Duff, Mold, & Scott, 2015). Third, a practice effect is not a unitary construct. For example, we have previously hypothesized that both learning and reaction to task novelty contribute to practice effects (Suchy, Kraybill, & Franchow, 2011b); recently, we have confirmed that not only do these two processes contribute *differentially* to practice effects on *different* tests but also that they are differentially affected by general cognitive status (Thorgusen, Suchy, Chelune, & Baucom, 2016). In other words, when it comes to practice effects, one size does not fit all. Thus, it is important that the effects of practice be carefully considered by using well-established methods for interpreting results of serial assessment, so as to account for factors that could confound interpretation (Chelune, 2003; Sawrie, Chelune, Naugle, & Lueders, 1996).

In addition to the general issues with practice effects, some tests of EF have the added complication that they cannot be easily readministered without fundamentally affecting the construct that is being assessed. Specifically, some tests inherently require that examinees engage in novel reasoning and problem solving; once a problem is solved, the second administration only measures lower order processes and possibly memory. Common tests that are particularly vulnerable to this threat to construct validity are the WCST (Heaton et al., 1993); the Halstead Category Test (Reitan & Wolfson, 1993); and the Sorting, Twenty Questions, Word Context, Tower, and Proverb tests from the D-KEFS battery (Delis et al., 2001).

Limitations in Interpreting Factor Structures

Another issue, which is likely less appreciated by researchers outside of clinical neuropsychology, is the fact that neuropsychological tests can have different underlying factor structures in different populations. This has been clearly demonstrated with memory. In most individuals (including many clinical populations), immediate and delayed recall scores are very closely related to one another and therefore load onto a single factor. However, for individuals with disorders characterized by rapid forgetting due to mesial temporal lobe dysfunction (e.g., Alzheimer's disease), these constructs load onto separate factors (Delis, Jacobson, Bondi, Hamilton, & Salmon, 2003). This notion also applies to measures of EF. For example, Goldman et al. (1996) found that, for healthy controls, all WCST variables loaded onto a single factor, whereas for two samples of neurological patients (patients with diffuse lesions and focal frontal lesions), the variables fell on two separate factors.

These findings highlight the limitations of using normal or mixed clinical populations to investigate the underlying structure of cognition. Given that the structure of EF is far from being agreed upon by the broader neuropsychological community (Suchy, 2015), researchers interested in advancing our knowledge on this topic need to avoid generalizing their findings to other populations; in fact, it is likely that the interpretations of most factor analytic findings are truly accurate only when they limit their comments to the *factor structure of a given battery of tests in a given population* (Shura, Rowland, & Yoash-Gantz, 2015), rather than presuming to explain the structure of the construct.

Recognizing the Difference between Self-report and Performance-based Measures

Lastly, researchers should be very clear in their writing about whether they are investigating participants' subjective self-reported EF or objective EF performance. This is important not only because each assessment approach is likely to yield different results (Suchy et al., 2016) but also because the reporting of results can be confusing or even misleading. Specifically, it is the case that findings based on self-report tools are sometimes referred to in the literature (or in article abstracts) simply as "executive functioning," giving the impression that performance-based measures of EF were used. This is problematic because, as stated above, numerous studies have shown that the relationship between self-reported and objective measures of EF is weak to nonexistent (Bogod et al., 2003; Burgess et al., 1998; Nęcka et al., 2012; Wingo, Kalkut, Tuminello, Asconape, & Han, 2013). This has been shown for healthy adults using both clinical measures of EF (Wingo et al., 2013)and experimental measures designed to isolate more discrete executive cognitive functions (Nęcka et al., 2012). Clinical populations show a similar pattern (Bogod et al., 2003; Burgess et al., 1998). In fact, a recent meta-analysis estimated that the average correlations between the BRIEF, a commonly used self-report measure of EF, and performance-based measures are as little as 0.19 (Toplak, West, & Stanovich, 2013). Factors that may contribute to this lack of association include differences in the abilities captured by these methods, reporting biases influenced by personality (e.g., healthy individuals who are higher on neuroticism are likely to endorse more dysfunction), and, for patient populations, a lack of insight, which itself results from neuropathology.

Informant-based subjective reports of an individual's EF (e.g., filled out by a parent, teacher, or spouse) may map onto performance measures slightly better. However, research on the strength of this association is mixed, and differences exist among different types of informants (e.g., parents vs teachers; Wochos, Semerjian, & Walsh, 2014). When taken together, research suggests only weak to modest correlations between these types of rating scales and performance-based EF measures (Bogod et al., 2003; Burgess et al., 1998; Chaytor, Schmitter-Edgecombe, & Burr, 2006).

CONCLUSIONS

Assessment of EF for research purposes can take on several different forms, relying on clinical measures of EF, experimental tasks, or self- and informant-reports. Each approach is characterized by a different set of advantages and disadvantages. Researchers need to carefully consider which of these approaches best fits their research question and study design. Additionally, researchers need to make sure that they select tests that are appropriate for the population they use in their research, taking care to avoid floor or ceiling effects. When relying on clinical measures, researches are encouraged to rely on norms to help them interpret results but are also cautioned to become familiar with the normative samples and normative structures of different tests, so as to ensure comparability across standard scores. A number of psychometric issues also need to be considered, including reliabilities, practice effects, and the contributions of lower order component processes to EF test performance. Lastly, generalization of factor analytic findings to other populations or to the EF construct more globally is discouraged.

REFERENCES

American Psychological Association. (2010). Maintaining test security. In: *Ethical principles of psychologists and code of conduct*, Washington, D.C.

Baddeley, A. D. (1998). The central executive: A concept and some misconceptions. *Journal of the International Neuropsychological Society*, 4(5), 523–526. Retrieved from http://dx.doi.org/10.1017/S135561779800513X.

Baddeley, A. D., Chincotta, D., & Adlam, A. (2001). Working memory and the control of action: Evidence from task switching. *Journal of Experimental Psychology: General*. US: American Psychological Assn, US, http://www.apa.org. Retrieved from http://www.apa.org.

Bechara, A., Damasio, H., Tranel, D., & Damasio, A. R. (2005). The Iowa Gambling task and the somatic marker hypothesis: Some questions and answers. *Trends in Cognitive Sciences*, 9, 159–162. Available from http://dx.doi.org/10.1016/j.tics.2005.02.002.

Blair, R. J. R., & Cipolotti, L. (2000). Impaired social response reversal. A case of "acquired sociopathy." *Brain: A Journal of Neurology*, 123(6)1122–1141. Retrieved from http://doi.org/10.1093/brain/123.6.1122.

Bogod, N. M., Mateer, C. A., & MacDonald, S. W. (2003). Self-awareness after traumatic brain injury: A comparison of measures and their relationship to executive functions. *Journal of the International Neuropsychological Society*, 9, 450–458. Available from http://dx.doi.org/10.1017/S1355617703930104.

Brooks, B. L., Strauss, E. S., Elisabeth, M. S., Iverson, G. L., & Slick, D. J. (2009). Developments in neuropsychological assessment: Refining psychometric and clinical interpretive methods. *Canadian Psychology*, 50, 196–209. Available from http://dx.doi.org/10.1037/a0016066.

Brower, M. C., & Price, B. H. (2001). Neuropsychiatry of frontal lobe dysfunction in violent and criminal behaviour: A critical review. *Journal of Neurology, Neurosurgery & Psychiatry, 71*(6), 720−726. Retrieved from http://www.bmjpg.com.

Burgess, P. W., Alderman, N., Evans, J., Emslie, H., & Wilson, B. A. (1998). The ecological validity of tests of executive function. *Journal of the International Neuropsychological Society: JINS, 4,* 547−558. Available from http://dx.doi.org/10.1017/S1355617798466037.

Burgess, P. W., Alderman, N., Wilson, B. A., Evans, J. J., & Emslie, H. (1996). *The dysexecutive questionnaire. Behavioural assessment of the dysexecutive syndrome.* Bury St. Edmunds, UK: Thames Valley Test Company.

Calamia, M., Markon, K., & Tranel, D. (2013). The robust reliability of neuropsychological measures: Meta-analyses of test-retest correlations. *The Clinical Neuropsychologist, 27,* 1077−1105. Available from http://dx.doi.org/10.1080/13854046.2013.809795.

Campbell, A. L., Jr., Ocampo, C., DeShawn Rorie, K., Lewis, S., Combs, S., Ford-Booker, P., & Hastings, A. (2002). Caveats in the neuropsychological assessment of African Americans. *Journal of the National Medical Association, 94,* 591−601.

Channon, S., & Crawford, S. (1999). Problem-solving in real-life-type situations: The effects of anterior and posterior lesions on performance. Neuropsychologia. United Kingdom: Elsevier Science. Retrieved from http://www.elsevier.com.

Chaytor, N., Schmitter-Edgecombe, M., & Burr, R. (2006). Improving the ecological validity of executive functioning assessment. *Archives of Clinical Neuropsychology, 21,* 217−227. Available from http://dx.doi.org/10.1016/j.acn.2005.12.002.

Chelune, G. J. (2003). Assessing reliable neuropsychological change. In R. D. Franklin (Ed.), *Prediction in forensic and neuropsychology: Sound statistical practices* (pp. 123−147). Mahwah, NJ: Lawrence Erlbaum Associates Publishers.

Cowles, M. L. (2012). The relationship between physical fitness and executive control functioning in young adults. *Dissertation Abstracts International, The Sciences and Engineering, 73*(6-B), 3972.

Cummings, J. L., & Miller, B. L. (2007). Conceptual and clinical aspects of the frontal lobes. *The human frontal lobes: Functions and disorders* (2nd ed., Retrieved from http://search.ebscohost.com/login.aspx?direct=true&db=psyh&AN=2006-23347-002&site=ehost-live). New York, NY: Guilford Press.

Delis, D. C., Jacobson, M., Bondi, M. W., Hamilton, J. M., & Salmon, D. P. (2003). The myth of testing construct validity using factor analysis or correlations with normal or mixed clinical populations: Lessons from memory assessment. *Journal of the International Neuropsychological Society, 9,* 936−946. Available from http://dx.doi.org/10.1017/S1355617703960139.

Delis, D., Kaplan, E., & Kramer, J. (2001). *Delis-Kaplan Executive Function System: Examiner's manual.* San Antonio, TX: The Psychological Corporation.

Diamond, A. (2013). Executive functions. *Annual Review of Psychology, 64,* 135−168.

Duckworth, A. L., & Seligman, M. E. P. (2005). Self-discipline outdoes IQ in predicting academic performance of adolescents. *Psychological Science, 16*(12), 939.

Duff, K., Beglinger, L. J., Schultz, S. K., Moser, D. J., McCaffrey, R. J., Haase, R. F., & Paulsen, J. S. (2007). Practice effects in the prediction of long-term cognitive outcome in three patient samples: A novel prognostic index. *Arch Clin Neuropsychol, 22*(1), 15−24. Retrieved from http://www.ncbi.nlm.nih.gov/entrez/query.fcgi?cmd=Retrieve&db=PubMed&dopt=Citation&list_uids=17142007

Duff, K., Beglinger, L. J., Van Der Heiden, S., Moser, D. J., Arndt, S., Schultz, S. K., & Paulsen, J. S. (2008). Short-term practice effects in amnestic mild cognitive impairment: Implications for diagnosis and treatment. *International Psychogeriatrics, 20*(5), 986−999. Retrieved from http://dx.doi.org/10.1017/S1041610208007254.

Dywan, J., & Segalowitz, S. J. (1996). Self- and family ratings of adaptive behavior after traumatic brain injury: Psychometric scores and frontally generated ERPs. *The Journal of Head Trauma Rehabilitation*, *11*, 79–95. Available from http://dx.doi.org.ez.statsbiblioteket. dk:2048/10.1097/00001199-199604000-00008.

Edmonds, E. C., Delano-Wood, L., Galasko, D. R., Salmon, D. P., & Bondi, M. W. (2014). Subjective cognitive complaints contribute to misdiagnosis of mild cognitive impairment. *Journal of the International Neuropsychological Society: JINS*, *20*, 836–847. Available from http://dx.doi.org/10.1017/S135561771400068X.

Engle, R. W. (2002). Working memory capacity as executive attention. *Current Directions in Psychological Science*, *11*, 19–23. Available from http://dx.doi.org/10.1111/1467-8721.00160.

Ettenhofer, M. L., Hambrick, D. Z., & Abeles, N. (2006). Reliability and stability of executive functioning in older adults. *Neuropsychology*, *20*, 607–613. Available from http://dx.doi.org/10.1037/0894-4105.20.5.607.

Euler, M., Niermeyer, M., & Suchy, Y. (2015). Neurocognitive and neurophysiological correlates of motor planning during familiar and novel contexts. *Neuropsychology*, *30*(1), 109–119.

Farias, S. T., Mungas, D., & Jagust, W. (2005). Degree of discrepancy between self and other-reported everyday functioning by cognitive status: Dementia, mild cognitive impairment, and healthy elders. *International Journal of Geriatric Psychiatry*, *20*, 827–834. Available from http://dx.doi.org/10.1002/gps.1367.

Folstein, M. F., Folstein, S. E., & McHugh, P. R. (1975). "Mini-mental state". A practical method for grading the cognitive state of patients for the clinician. *Journal of Psychiatric Research*, *12*, 189–198. Available from http://dx.doi.org/10.1016/0022-3956(75)90026-6

Franchow, E. I., & Suchy, Y. (2015). Naturally-occurring expressive suppression in daily life depletes executive functioning. *Emotion*, *15*(1), 78–89.

Friedman, N. P., Miyake, A., Corley, R. P., Young, S. E., DeFries, J. C., & Hewitt, J. K. (2006). Not all executive functions are related to intelligence. *Psychological Science*, *17*(2), 172–179.

Gazzaley, A., D'Esposito, M., Miller, B. L., & Cummings, J. L. (2007). Unifying prefrontal cortex function: Executive control, neural networks, and top-down modulation. *The human frontal lobes: Functions and disorders* (2nd ed., Retrieved from <http://search.ebscohost.com/login.aspx?direct=true&db=psyh&AN=2006-23347-013&site=ehost-live>). New York, NY: Guilford Press.

Gioia, G. A., Isquith, P., Guy, S. C., & Kenworthy, L. (2000). *The behavior rating inventory of executive function. Professional manual*. Lutz, FL: Psychological Assessment Resources.

Goldman, R. S., Axelrod, B. N., Heaton, R. K., Chelune, G. J., Curtiss, G., Kay, G. G., & Thompson, L. L. (1996). Latent structure of the WCST with the standardization samples. *Assessment*, *3*, 73–78. Available from http://dx.doi.org/10.1177/107319119600300108.

Grace, J., & Malloy, P. F. (2001). *Frontal systems behavior scale (FrSBe): Professional manual*. Lutz, FL: Psychological Assessment Resources.

Graham, S., Jiang, J., Manning, V., Nejad, A. B., Zhisheng, K., Salleh, S. R., & McKenna, P. J. (2010). IQ-related fMRI differences during cognitive set shifting. *Cerebral Cortex*, *20*(3), 641–649. Available from http://dx.doi.org/10.1093/cercor/bhp130.

Guy, S. C., Gioia, G. A., & Isquith, P. K. (2004). *Behavior rating inventory of executive function: Self-report version*. Lutz, FL: Psychological Assessment Resources.

Happé, F., Booth, R., Charlton, R., & Hughes, C. (2006). Executive function deficits in autism spectrum disorders and attention-deficit/hyperactivity disorder: Examining profiles across domains and ages. *Brain and Cognition, 61*(1), 25−39. Available from http://dx.doi.org/ 10.1016/j.bandc.2006.03.004.

Hart, R. P., & Bean, M. K. (2011). Executive function, intellectual decline and daily living skills. *Aging, Neuropsychology, and Cognition, 18*(1), 64−85. Available from http://dx.doi. org/10.1080/13825585.2010.510637.

Harvey, P. D. (2012). Clinical applications of neuropsychological assessment. *Dialogues in Clinical Neuroscience, 14*, 91−99.

Heaton, R. K., Chelune, G. J., Talley, J. L., Kay, G. G., & Curtiss, G. (1993). *Wisconsin Card Sorting Test manual: Revised and expanded.* Odessa, FL: Psychological Assessment Resources Inc.

Hildebrand, B. (1997). Neuropsychological predictors of academic success: Use of Controlled Oral Word Association Test, Trailmaking Test, and Wisconsin Card Sorting Test as measures of academic success among community college students. *Dissertation Abstracts International, The Sciences and Engineering, 57*(8-B), 5380.

Hobson, C. W., Scott, S., & Rubia, K. (2011). Investigation of cool and hot executive function in ODD/CD independently of ADHD. *Journal of Child Psychology and Psychiatry, 52*(10) 1035−1043. Retrieved from http://search.ebscohost.com/login.aspx?direct=true&db= psyh&AN=2011-20427-004&site=ehost-live.

Homack, S., Lee, D., & Riccio, C. A. (2005). Test review: Delis-Kaplan executive function system. *Journal of Clinical and Experimental Neuropsychology, 27*, 599−609. Available from http://dx.doi.org/10.1080/13803390490918444.

Lam, B., Middleton, E., Masellis, M., Stuss, T., Harry, D., Kiss, A., & Black, E. (2013). Criterion and convergent validity of the Montreal cognitive assessment with screening and standardized neuropsychological testing. *Journal of the American Geriatrics Society, 61*, 2181.

Levy, J. A., & Chelune, G. J. (2007). Cognitive-behavioral profiles of neurodegenerative dementias: Beyond Alzheimer's disease. *Journal of Geriatric Psychiatry and Neurology, 20*(4), 227−238. Retrieved from http://search.ebscohost.com/login.aspx?direct=true&db= psyh&AN=2007-18275-005&site=ehost-live

Lezak, M. D. (1982). The problem of assessing executive functions. *International Journal of Psychology, 17*(2), 281−297 . Retrieved from http://dx.doi.org/10.1080/00207598208247445.

Lezak, M. D., Howieson, D. B., Bigler, E. D., & Tranel, D. (2012). Neuropsychological Assessment *(Fifth).* New York, New York: Oxford University Press.

Luria, A. R. (1973). *The frontal lobes and the regulation of behavior. Psychophysiology of the frontal lobes.* Oxford, England: Academic Press. Retrieved from http://search.ebscohost. com/login.aspx?direct=true&db=psyh&AN=1974-05772-010&site=ehost-live.

Maeda, K., Kasai, K., Watanabe, A., Henomatsu, K., Rogers, M. A., & Kato, N. (2006). Effect of subjective reasoning and neurocognition on medication adherence for persons with schizophrenia. *Psychiatric Services (Washington, D.C.), 57*, 1203−1205. Available from http://dx.doi.org/10.1176/appi.ps.57.8.1203.

Malloy, P., & Grace, J. (2005). A review of rating scales for measuring behavior change due to frontal systems damage. *Cognitive and Behavioral Neurology, 18*, 18−27. Available from http://dx.doi.org/10.1097/01.wnn.0000152232.47901.88.

Martinez-Aran, A., Scott, J., Colom, F., Torrent, C., Tabares-Seisdedos, R., Daban, C., & Vieta, E. (2009). Treatment nonadherence and neurocognitive impairment in bipolar disorder. *Journal of Clinical Psychiatry*, *70*, 1017–1023. Available from http://dx.doi.org/ 10.4088/JCP.08m04408.

Meiran, N., Chorev, Z., & Sapir, A. (2000). *Component processes in task switching*. Cognitive Psychology. United Kingdom: Elsevier Science. Retrieved from http://www.elsevier.com.

Miller, M. M., Rohan, J. M., Delamater, A., Shroff-Pendley, J., Dolan, L. M., Reeves, G., & Drotar, D. (2012). Changes in executive functioning and self-management in adolescents with type 1 diabetes: A growth curve analysis. *Journal of Pediatric Psychology*, *38*(1), 18–29. Available from http://dx.doi.org/10.1093/jpepsy/jss100.

Miyake, A., Friedman, N. P., Emerson, M. J., Witzki, A. H., Howerter, A., & Wager, T. D. (2000). The unity and diversity of executive functions and their contributions to complex "Frontal Lobe" tasks: A latent variable analysis. *Cognitive Psychology*, *41*(1), 49–100.

Morris, N., & Jones, D. M. (1990). Memory updating in working memory: The role of the central executive. *British Journal of Psychology*, *81*, 111–121. Available from http://dx.doi. org/10.1111/j.2044-8295.1990.tb02349.x.

Nasreddine, Z. S., Phillips, N. A., Bedirian, V., Charbonneau, S., Whitehead, V., Collin, I., & Chertkow, H. (2005). The Montreal Cognitive Assessment, MoCA: A brief screening tool for mild cognitive impairment. *Journal of the American Geriatrics Society*, *53*, 695–699. Available from http://dx.doi.org/10.1111/j.1532-5415.2005.53221.x.

Nęcka, E., Lech, B., Sobczyk, N., & Śmieja, M. (2012). How much do we know about our own cognitive control? *European Journal of Psychological Assessment*, *28*, 240–247. Available from http://dx.doi.org/10.1027/1015-5759/a000147.

Niermeyer, M. A., Suchy, Y., & Ziemnik, R. E. (2016). Motor sequencing in older adulthood: Relationships with executive functioning and effects of complexity. *The Clinical Neuropsychologist*, *17*, 1–21.

Ogilvie, J. M., Stewart, A. L., Chan, R. C. K., & Shum, D. H. K. (2011). Neuropsychological measures of executive function and antisocial behavior: A meta-analysis. *Criminology: An Interdisciplinary Journal*, *49*(4), 1063–1107 . Retrieved from http://search.ebscohost.com/ login.aspx?direct=true&db=psyh&AN=2011-29135-007&site=ehost-live.

Olsen, J. P., Fellows, R. P., Rivera-Mindt, M., Morgello, S., Byrd, D. A., & Manhattan HIV Brain Bank (2015). Reading ability as an estimator of premorbid intelligence: Does it remain stable among ethnically diverse HIV + adults? *The Clinical Neuropsychologist*, *29* (7), 1034–1052. Available from http://dx.doi.org/10.1080/13854046.2015.1122085.

Parada, M., Corral, M., Mota, N., Crego, A., Rodríguez Holguín, S., & Cadaveira, F. (2012). Executive functioning and alcohol binge drinking in university students. *Addictive Behaviors*, *37*, 167–172. Available from http://dx.doi.org/10.1016/j.addbeh.2011.09.015.

Perna, R., Loughan, A. R., & Talka, K. (2012). Executive functioning and adaptive living skills after acquired brain injury. *Applied Neuropsychology: Adult*, *19*(4), 263–271. Available from http://dx.doi.org/10.1080/09084282.2012.670147.

Piovesana, A. M., Ross, S., Whittingham, K., Ware, R. S., & Boyd, R. N. (2015). Stability of executive functioning measures in 8–17-year-old children with unilateral cerebral palsy. *The Clinical Neuropsychologist*, *29*(1), 133–149. Available from http://dx.doi.org/10.1080/ 13854046.2014.999125.

Posner, M. I., & Dehaene, S. (1994). Attentional networks. *Trends in Neurosciences*, *17*(2), 75–79. Retrieved from http://dx.doi.org/10.1016/0166-2236(94)90078-7.

Pribram, K. H. (1973). *The primate frontal cortex: Executive of the brain. Psychophysiology of the frontal lobes.* Oxford, England: Academic Press. Retrieved from http://search.ebscohost. com/login.aspx?direct=true&db=psyh&AN=1974-05772-014&site=ehost-live.

Puente, A. N., Cohen, M. L., Aita, S., & Brandt, J. (2016). Behavioral ratings of executive functioning explain instrumental activities of daily living beyond test scores in Parkinson's disease. *The Clinical Neuropsychologist, 30*(1), 95−106. Available from http://dx.doi.org/ 10.1080/13854046.2015.1133847.

Puente, A. N., Lindbergh, C. A., & Miller, L. S. (2015). The relationship between cognitive reserve and functional ability is mediated by executive functioning in older adults. *The Clinical Neuropsychologist, 29*(1), 67−81. Available from http://dx.doi.org/10.1080/ 13854046.2015.1005676.

Reitan, R. M., & Wolfson, D. (1993). *The Halstead-Reitan Neuropsychological Test Battery: Theory and clinical interpretation* (2nd ed.). Tucson, Arizona: Neuropsychology Press.

Robinson, G., Shallice, T., Bozzali, M., & Cipolotti, L. (2012). The differing roles of the frontal cortex in fluency tests. *Brain: A Journal of Neurology, 135*(7), 2202−2214 . Retrieved from http://search. ebscohost.com/login.aspx?direct=true&db=psyh&AN=2012-17218-020&site=ehost-live.

Rorden, C., Bonilha, L., & Nichols, T. E. (2007). Rank-order versus mean based statistics for neuroimaging. *NeuroImage, 35,* 1531−1537. Available from http://dx.doi.org/10.1016/ j.neuroimage.2006.12.043.

Sawrie, S. M., Chelune, G. J., Naugle, R. I., & Lueders, H. O. (1996). Empirical methods for assessing meaningful neuropsychological change following epilepsy surgery. *Journal of the International Neuropsychological Society, 2*(6), 556−564. Retrieved from http://dx.doi.org/ 10.1017/S1355617700001739.

Shura, R. D., Rowland, J. A., & Yoash-Gantz, R. E. (2015). Factor structure and construct validity of the Behavioral Dyscontrol Scale-II. *The Clinical Neuropsychologist, 29*(1), 82−100. Available from http://dx.doi.org/10.1080/13854046.2015.1007169.

Snyder, H. R., Miyake, A., & Hankin, B. L. (2015). Advancing understanding of executive function impairments and psychopathology: Bridging the gap between clinical and cognitive approaches. *Frontiers in Psychology, 6.* Available from http://dx.doi.org/10.3389/ fpsyg.2015.00328.

Sohn, M.-H., & Anderson, J. R. (2001). *Task preparation and task repetition: Two-component model of task switching. Journal of Experimental Psychology: General.* US: American Psychological Assn, US, http://www.apa.org. Retrieved from http://www.apa.org.

Spinella, M. (2005). Self-rated executive function: Development of the executive function index. *The International Journal of Neuroscience, 115,* 649−667. Available from http://dx.doi.org/ 10.1080/00207450590524304.

Stevens, M. C., Kaplan, R. F., & Hesselbrock, V. M. (2003). Executive-cognitive functioning in the development of antisocial personality disorder. *Addictive Behaviors, 28*(2), 285−300. Retrieved from http://search.ebscohost.com/login.aspx?direct=true&db=psyh&AN=2003- 04996-007&site=ehost-live.

Stroop, J. R. (1935). Stroop color word test. *J. Exp. Physiol., 18,* 643−662. Available from http://dx.doi.org/10.1007/978-0-387-79948-3.

Stuss, D. T. (2011). Functions of the frontal lobes: Relation to executive functions. *Journal of the International Neuropsychological Society, 17*(5), 759−765. Retrieved from http://search. ebscohost.com/login.aspx?direct=true&db=psyh&AN=2011-21369-001&site=ehost-live.

Stuss, D. T., & Alexander, M. P. (2000). Executive functions and the frontal lobes: A conceptual view. *Psychological Research/Psychologische Forschung, 63*(3), 289−298. Retrieved from http://dx.doi.org/10.1007/s004260050007.

Stuss, D. T., Picton, T. W., & Alexander, M. P. (2001). Consciousness, self-awareness, and the frontal lobes. In S. P. Salloway, P. F. Malloy, & J. D. Duffy (Eds.), *The frontal lobes and neuropsychiatric illness* (pp. 101−109). Arlington, VA: American Psychiatric Publishing, Inc.

Suchy, Y. (2009). Executive functioning: Overview, assessment, and research issues for non-neuropsychologists. *Annals of Behavioral Medicine*, *37*(2), 106−116.

Suchy, Y. (2015). *Executive functions: A comprehensive guide for clinical practice.* New York, NY: Oxford University Press.

Suchy, Y., Kraybill, M. L., & Franchow, E. (2011a). Instrumental activities of daily living among community-dwelling older adults: Discrepancies between self-report and performance are mediated by cognitive reserve. *Journal of Clinical and Experimental Neuropsychology*, *33*(1), 92−100.

Suchy, Y., Kraybill, M. L., & Franchow, E. I. (2011b). Practice effect and beyond: Reaction to novelty as an independent predictor of cognitive decline among older adults. *Journal of the International Neuropsychological Society*, *17*, 1−11.

Suchy, Y., Turner, S., Queen, T., Durracio, K., Wiebe, D., Perrin, W., & Micheal, S. (2016). The relation of questionnaire and performance-based measures of executive functioning with type 1 diabetes outcomes among late adolescents. *Health Psychology*, *35*(7), 661−669.

Suchy, Y., Ziemnik, R. E., & Niermeyer, M. A. (2017). Assessment of executive functions in clinical settings. In E. Goldberg (Ed.), *Executive functions in health and disease.* New York, NY: Luria Neuroscience Institute.

Tabachnick, B. G., & Fidell, L. S. (2013). *Using multivariate statistics* (6th ed.). Boston, MA: Pearson Education.

Thaler, N. S., Hill, B. D., Duff, K., Mold, J., & Scott, J. G. (2015). Repeatable Battery for the Assessment of Neuropsychological Status (RBANS) intraindividual variability in older adults: Associations with disease and mortality. *Journal of Clinical and Experimental Neuropsychology*, *37*(6), 622−629. Available from http://dx.doi.org/10.1080/13803395.2015.1039962.

Thorgusen, S. R., Suchy, Y., Chelune, G. J., & Baucom, B. R. (2016). Neuropsychological practice effects in the context of cognitive decline: Contributions from learning and task novelty. *Journal of the International Neuropsychological Society*, *22*(4), 453−466. Available from http://dx.doi.org/10.1017/S1355617715001332.

Toplak, M. E., West, R. F., & Stanovich, K. E. (2013). Do performance-based measures and ratings of executive function assess the same construct. *Journal of Child Psychology and Psychiatry*, *54*(2), 131−143. Available from http://dx.doi.org/10.1111/jcpp.12001.

Torres, A., Gómez-Gil, E., Vidal, A., Puig, O., Boget, T., & Salamero, M. (2006). [Gender differences in cognitive functions and influence of sex hormones]. *Actas Espanolas de Psiquiatria*, *34*(6)408−415. Retrieved from http://www.ncbi.nlm.nih.gov/pubmed/17117339.

Webb, R. M. (2004). Emotional processing and college grade point average. *Dissertation Abstracts International, The Sciences and Engineering*, *65*(6-A), 2091.

Wechsler, D. (2008). *Wechsler Adult Intelligence Scale-4th edition: Technical and interpretative manual.* San Antonio, TX: Psychological Corporation.

Wingo, J., Kalkut, E., Tuminello, E., Asconape, J., & Han, S. D. (2013). Executive functions, depressive symptoms, and college adjustment in women. *Applied Neuropsychology. Adult*, *20*, 136−144. Available from http://dx.doi.org/10.1080/09084282.2012.670154.

Wochos, G. C., Semerjian, C. H., & Walsh, K. S. (2014). Differences in parent and teacher rating of everyday executive function in pediatric brain tumor survivors. *The Clinical Neuropsychologist*, *28*(8), 1243−1257. Available from http://dx.doi.org/10.1080/13854046.2014.971875.

Part II

Executive Functions in Disease

Chapter 10

Cognitive, Emotional, and Behavioral Inflexibility and Perseveration in Neuropsychiatric Illness

Daniel S. Weisholtz[1], John F. Sullivan[1,2], Aaron P. Nelson[2], Kirk R. Daffner[1] and David A. Silbersweig[1,2]

[1]*Department of Neurology, Brigham & Women's Hospital, Harvard Medical School, Boston, MA, United States,* [2]*Department of Psychiatry, Brigham & Women's Hospital, Harvard Medical School, Boston, MA, United States*

Cognitive and behavioral flexibility is a core adaptive function of the executive control system in the human brain. Executive functions include a set of processes that allow for context-appropriate volitional control in "nonroutine situations" (Daffner & Searl, 2008; Daffner & Willment, 2014). Goal-directed behavior requires not only an ability to represent a goal and then generate a plausible sequence of actions that must be accomplished to achieve it but also an ability to prioritize goals (represent the relative value of various goals at a given time), initiate a goal-directed process, and maintain goal pursuit in the face of unexpected environmental factors that might otherwise command attention. Too much environmental dependency will result in distractibility, a tendency for tasks to be interrupted, and, ultimately, an inability to complete a complex task sequence aimed toward a particular goal. This can manifest clinically as impulsivity, where the individual quickly shifts tasks in response to a novel stimulus, leaving the prior task sequence incomplete. However, one must also be able to discontinue an activity, switching to a different task when appropriate. An excessively rigid adherence to a predetermined task sequence or a previously valued goal prevents an individual from appropriately responding to changing environmental contingencies. For example, a behavior sequence aimed toward finding food may need to be temporarily suspended in the face of a predatory attack, where escape from danger becomes a suddenly more urgent goal. Similarly, changing environmental contingencies may necessitate a redetermination of

Executive Functions in Health and Disease. DOI: http://dx.doi.org/10.1016/B978-0-12-803676-1.00010-6

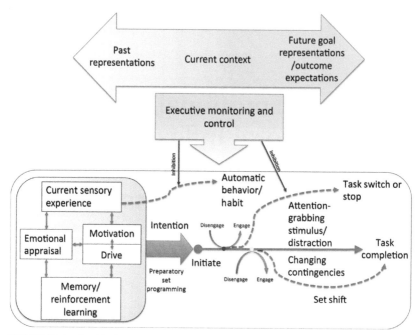

FIGURE 10.1 Graphical representation of a model of cognitive operations necessary to initiate and sustain flexible goal-directed behavior. Bidirectional arrows indicate interacting modules, while unidirectional left-to-right blue arrows indicate the sequence of events as they play out over time, in the context of feedback. Solid unidirectional arrows indicate the intended path toward task completion, while dashed arrows indicate possible ways in which the individual may deviate from the intended path. Red arrows indicate inhibitory processes. A plan is formulated on the basis of a representation of the temporal sequence of events from representation of past experiences to future goal representations and outcome expectations. Before initiation of any behavior, the intention to act is formed, driven by the motivation to achieve the goal, this being influenced by basic drives, and integrated emotional and cognitive appraisals of the desired goal, the currently experienced situation, and past experience. Once the task is initiated, the individual is sensitive to changing contingencies and may adapt his or her strategy to the new environment in order to achieve the goal a different way (set shift). The task may not be completed (and the goal not achieved) if the individual reverts to automatic responses or habit, if he/she can't adequately sequence or shift, or if the initially goal-directed behavior is derailed by an attention-grabbing stimulus that is not over-ridden by the superordinate goal set.

the sequence of steps needed to achieve a goal (a change in strategy) (Fig. 10.1). For example, if one's typical route to work requires him or her to cross a particular bridge, the sudden discovery that the bridge is closed for construction necessitates a search for an alternate route. Finding a different bridge to cross is a better solution to this problem than either abandoning the goal (giving up and going home) or persisting in the old plan despite the new information, a potentially dangerous prospect.

Successful cognitive and behavioral flexibility depends on a delicate interplay among a variety of neural networks (Fig. 10.2). Basic drives are mediated at the level of the hypothalamus while motivated behavior is

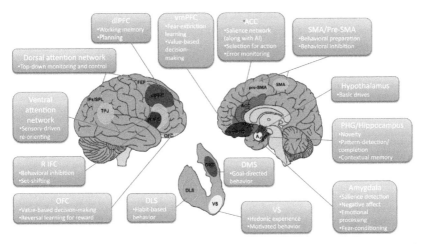

FIGURE 10.2 Brain regions relevant to cognitive, emotional, and behavioral flexibility and some of their functions. (dlPFC−dorsolateral prefrontal cortex; vmPFC−ventromedial prefrontal cortex; ACC−anterior cingulate cortex; sgACC−subgenual anterior cingulate cortex; SMA−supplementary motor area; PHG−parahippocampal gyrus; A−amygdala; H−hypothalamus; DMS−dorsomedial striatum; VS−ventral striatum; DLS−dorsolateral striatum; OFC−orbitofrontal cortex; R IFC−right inferior frontal cortex; FEF−frontal eye fields; IPs/SPL−intraparietal sulcus/superior parietal lobule; TPJ−temporoparietal junction).

determined via interactions between the ventral striatum and its limbic, cortical, and subcortical connections, as well as the closely related mesolimbic and mesocortical dopamine projections. Effective environmental responsiveness during a goal-directed activity depends on the ability of a salience network to effectively capture attention in the face of a worthy distractor. This requires a network of brain regions, including the anterior insula and dorsal anterior cingulate cortex (ACC) (Uddin, 2015), which is involved in detecting salient environmental stimuli and influencing the balance between two attention networks—one involved in top-down attention control (the dorsal frontoparietal attention network) and the other involved in sensory-driven reorientation of attention (the right ventral frontoparietal network) (Corbetta & Shulman, 2002). If task switching is to occur, there must be a disengagement from the previous task to pursue a new task, a process that may require inhibitory mechanisms implemented in the right inferior frontal cortex (IFC) (Dajani & Uddin, 2015). Sometimes, flexibility entails an ability to change strategies on the fly while completing a task. Set-shifting, unlike task-shifting, involves a change in approach toward accomplishing the same goal, as opposed to a shift from pursuing one goal to another. This is typically exemplified by the Wisconsin Card Sorting Test (WCST), which requires subjects to perceive a change in the rules governing successful performance of the task (in this case, a change in which stimulus attributes determine the correct way to sort the cards) and to adapt to this change by shifting attention from one category of stimulus attributes to another to continue to perform the task successfully. Set-shifting also seems to involve the IFC (Konishi, Nakajima, & Uchida, 1998). The IFC, particularly on the right, appears to be an important node in the intersecting networks mediating salience detection, environmentally dependent attention shifting, task switching, and set-shifting. In addition, this region has been consistently implicated as an important cortical area mediating motor inhibition, along with several other brain areas such as the supplementary motor area (SMA), pre-SMA, and interconnected basal ganglia regions (Aron, Robbins, & Poldrack, 2014; Bari & Robbins, 2013; Chambers, Garavan, & Bellgrove, 2009). Thus, the right IFC likely plays a role in cognitive and behavioral inhibition beyond the purely motor domain. Inhibition is an important aspect of cognitive and behavioral flexibility, and a failure to inhibit a prepotent response may manifest clinically as perseveration. A failure of inhibition is only one putative mechanism by which perseveration may occur although. In other circumstances, repetitive behavior may be the result of an inappropriately increased drive maintaining the activity, a failure to disengage, a failure to engage in something new, or possibly a failure to switch.

Impairment in cognitive and behavioral flexibility may result from an impaired ability to modify one's behavior in response to negative outcomes brought about by it. This inability to learn from one's own mistakes may be viewed as a failure of instrumental learning. A healthy individual should have the capacity to determine the value of various behavioral options on the basis of experience, to make choices on the basis of those judgments, and to adapt future choices to changing circumstances, understanding that what was once a good choice may not always be a good choice. An individual who continues to make the same bad choices again and again, despite clearly undesirable outcomes each time, demonstrates a pathological form of perseverative behavior. This may result from an inability to represent future consequences of one's behavior and/or to be guided by those representations. Sigmund Freud recognized this phenomenon in 1920, referring to it as a "compulsion to repeat," and this observation has been reaffirmed, reanalyzed, and reconceptualized throughout the history of modern psychodynamic psychiatry (Levy, 2000). Behaviorists have conceptualized the phenomenon as a failure to adaptively respond to changing stimulus-outcome (S-O) or response-outcome (R-O) contingencies (Izquierdo, Brigman, Radke, Rudebeck, & Holmes, 2017). Reversal learning paradigms have been used to test humans and laboratory animals in their ability to learn which stimulus response results in a reward and then to adapt their behavior when a new response becomes rewarded instead. The orbitofrontal cortex (OFC) has been consistently implicated as a region of importance for mediating reversal learning (Izquierdo et al., 2017). The OFC plays an important role in value-based decision-making (Wallis, 2011). Neurons in the OFC can respond to reward-predicting stimuli that drive reward-seeking behavior and can track reward value across reversal learning (Moorman & Aston-Jones, 2014). Neurons in the ventromedial prefrontal cortex (vmPFC) are sensitive to internally driven motivational factors influencing value judgments such as satiety (a food reward is less valuable if the animal is satiated), whereas lateral OFC neurons are more sensitive to environmentally driven factors (Bouret & Richmond, 2010). Damage to the vmPFC in humans affects value-based decision-making, such that patients become insensitive to future positive or negative consequences with their decisions guided primarily by short-term factors (Bechara, Damasio, Damasio & Anderson, Apr-1994; Bechara, Tranel, & Damasio, 2000). This is exemplified by poor performance on the Iowa Gambling Task, where patients repeatedly make choices associated with high reward but high risk, a strategy that fails in the long run. While healthy individuals soon learn to avoid these choices, patients with vmPFC lesions fail to learn from their prior bad decisions (Bechara et al., Apr-1994) (this has forensic implications, as an individual's culpability may be viewed differently if a brain lesion has compromised his or her decision-making ability). Similarly, in reversal learning tasks, OFC-lesioned animals fail to exhibit an appropriate behavior change in response to negative reinforcement. This may lead to perseveration on a "devalued" choice. It should be noted, however, that when multiple options are available, rather than perseveration, these animals may demonstrate less stable choices than nonlesioned animals, referred to as increased switching behavior (Noonan, Kolling, Walton, & Rushworth, 2012).

In this chapter, we examine a variety of forms of cognitive, emotional, and behavioral perseveration in neuropsychiatric disease and explore the various mechanisms believed to account for these phenomena. In many neuropsychiatric illnesses, impairments of flexibility in one form or another account for a significant restriction in the range of reactions, feelings, and self-generated behaviors an individual may exhibit, leading to a breakdown in social and occupational functioning, and in many cases, significant suffering. Perseveration, in its broadest conceptualization, can occur at a variety of levels of organization from simple motor behaviors (i.e., tics), verbal utterances, complex cognitions (i.e., obsessions in obsessive compulsive disorder (OCD), perseverative rumination in mood and anxiety disorders, and fixed delusions in psychosis), complex behaviors (i.e., compulsions in OCD and addiction), and perseveration of affect in mood and anxiety disorders. In the subsequent sections, we review the ways in which these various forms of perseveration may manifest in different disease states and explore the similarities and differences between their putative mechanisms. While there is much that remains unknown, a common theme across these conditions is abnormal functioning of the frontal lobes.

PERSEVERATION AS A MANIFESTATION OF FRONTAL LOBE IMPAIRMENT

Frontal Lobe Lesions

Destructive lesions of the frontal lobes have been associated with a variety of cognitive, emotional, and behavioral impairments that to some extent depend on which regions of the frontal lobes are damaged. While lesions to the posterior portions of the lobe can directly impair motor function, more anterior (prefrontal) lesions can impair goal-directed behavior and cognitive flexibility even while basic motor functions remain intact. Increased environmental or stimulus dependency is common in patients with prefrontal lesions, and there may be an increase in automatic behavior relative to volitional goal-directed behavior. Luria (1976) attributed simple motor perseverations to lesions in posterior areas of the frontal lobe affecting the proximal motor circuitry. More subtle perseverations such as intrusion errors, where a previously correct action occurs inappropriately in response to a different stimulus, were attributed to more anterior lesions affecting hierarchically higher order behavior systems. These sorts of perseveration may be seen as the converse of the stimulus-bound behaviors described by Lhermitte such as utilization behavior (Lhermitte, 1983) and imitation behavior (Lhermitte, Pillon, & Serdaru, 1986). Utilization behavior describes the phenomenon in which patients with frontal lobe damage automatically grasp objects presented to them and/or exhibit purposeless but complex gestures or movements appropriate to the object but inappropriate to the context. Imitation behavior refers to the purposeless mimicking of the gestures of an examiner that can be seen in some patients with frontal lobe lesions. These phenomena were classically attributed to a release of parietal lobe inhibition by the frontal lobe. They may also be seen as a consequence of the hierarchical organization of the brain whereby the prefrontal cortex (PFC) facilitates flexible goal-directed behaviors by modulating or inhibiting the relatively "hard-wired," innate, or overlearned motor programs that are encoded in premotor basal ganglia circuits and initiated via interactions between the premotor cortices and the parietotemporal sensory cortices. An example of some of these automatic programs may be exemplified by the stereotyped automatic motor behaviors known as ictal automatisms that can manifest during temporal lobe or frontal lobe seizures and can be experimentally elicited with electrical stimulation of the ACC (Talairach, Bancaud, & Geier, 1973). Pathological imitation behavior may also be mediated, in part, by the inappropriate release or activation of a system of frontal and parietal mirror neurons that can code for both one's own actions and the actions of another and that, in healthy individuals, may play a role in imitative learning (Iacoboni, 2005). Destruction of PFC may inappropriately release these more automatic behaviors (and primitive reflexes) that normally occur only when modulatory influence from the PFC is minimal. While perseverative behavior does not appear to exhibit the same sort of environmental dependency as utilization behavior and imitation behavior, these three phenomena share the commonality that the associated behavior is not goal directed, is restricted in scope, and is not context appropriate. They illustrate the importance of the frontal lobes in mediating flexible goal-directed behaviors.

Schizophrenia

Schizophrenia is a chronic mental illness characterized by a constellation of cognitive, affective, perceptual, linguistic, and motor symptoms. Despite its reputation as the "graveyard of neuropathologists" due to the absence of clear morphological changes on histopathology (Harrison, 1999), with the help of modern neuroimaging technology, it has come to be seen as a disorder characterized by prominent frontal lobe impairment (Weinberger & Berman, 1988; Weinberger, Berman, & Zec, 1986). More specific neural abnormalities have been identified by studying specific symptoms and schizophrenia subsyndromes. The symptoms of schizophrenia have commonly been grouped into three categories: positive symptoms, negative symptoms, and cognitive and behavioral disorganization. Positive symptoms include hallucinations, which are characterized by internally generated perceptual experiences that occur in the absence of external stimuli and delusions, which are defined as fixed false beliefs that are not amenable to change even in the setting of conflicting evidence. Negative symptoms include a variety of symptoms attributed to a loss of function such as a decrease in self-initiated purposeful activities (avolition), as well as diminished speech, emotional expression, and social engagement. Disorganization in schizophrenia is characterized by "loosening of associations," where the connections between thoughts become fragmented, at times so severely that speech can become incomprehensible and behavior may become abnormal and unpredictable. Rarely, behavior may become so limited such that there is a near absence of volitional interaction with the environment (catatonia). Schizoaffective disorder may be diagnosed if a major depressive or manic episode coincides.

Studies using factor analysis or principal components analysis to investigate the underlying structure of psychotic illness have generally supported the symptom domains described earlier as at least partially independent of each other (Liddle, 1987; Potuzak, Ravichandran, Lewandowski, Ongur, & Cohen, 2012). Affective symptoms may represent a fourth domain, particularly when patients with schizoaffective disorder are included (Potuzak et al., 2012). Symptoms within these domains tend to cooccur but may appear or remit independently from symptoms in other domains. Converging evidence from a variety of functional neuroimaging studies has identified specific patterns of dysfunction in the different schizophrenia subsyndromes although inconsistent results are still common (Goghari, Sponheim, & MacDonald, 2010). The disorganization subsyndrome has been linked with abnormal functioning of the dorsolateral prefrontal cortex (DLPFC) during executive functioning tasks, whereas dysfunction of the ventrolateral prefrontal cortex (VLPFC) during executive function tasks may be more associated with the negative subsyndrome. An association between the positive subsyndrome and abnormalities of medial prefrontal cortex (mPFC), amygdala, hippocampus, and parahippocampal gyrus function has been found during emotional tasks, with the medial temporal lobe abnormalities most prominent when paranoid symptoms were considered.

Patients with schizophrenia exhibit a variety of types of perseveration similar to those seen in patients with frontal lobe lesions. These include verbal perseveration at multiple levels of language processing (morphemes, phonemes, phrases, or syntax), simple motor perseveration and stereotypy, perseveration for complex behaviors, and impaired set shifting, as can be seen with perseverative errors on the WCST (Crider, 1997). Perseveration may be one manifestation of a broader impairment of executive functioning in schizophrenia (Dawes, Jeste, & Palmer, 2011; Zec, 1995) where impaired abstraction and cognitive flexibility are prominent relative weakness (Dawes et al., 2011). Executive function deficits are more common in older patients and patients with more severe disease, and they tend to correlate with negative symptoms and disorganization more than with positive symptoms (Chan, Chen, Cheung, Chen, & Cheung, 2006; O'Leary et al., 2000).

Schizophrenia patients have been found to have reduced DLPFC regional cerebral blood flow (rCBF) while performing the WCST, and rCBF abnormalities in the DLPFC correlated with perseverative error (Weinberger & Berman, 1988; Weinberger et al., 1986), suggesting dysfunction in this region may be related to the perseverative error. More modern studies utilizing higher resolution techniques have provided supporting evidence (Riehemann et al., 2001). For example, decreased gray matter volume in portions of the DLPFC has been shown to correlate with poorer performance on the WCST in patients with schizophrenia (Bonilha, Molnar, & Horner, 2008; Wilmsmeier, Ohrmann, & Suslow, 2010). Perseverative error may be related to difficulty in generating a plan, as patients with a tendency to perseverate on the WCST also tend to have difficulty using internally generating semantic ordering on the California Verbal Learning Test (Lanser, Berger, Ellenbroek, Cools, & Zitman, 2002). Perseveration on the WCST can also be seen in patients with bipolar disorder and major depression (Waford & Lewine, 2010), possibly related to specific types of impairment of frontal lobe functioning in these patient populations as well.

More recently, neuroimaging research on executive functioning in schizophrenia has moved away from the WCST due to the complexity of this task. The multiple cognitive functions required for successful performance of the task can be difficult to disentangle, limiting the ability of neuroimagers to tease out specific functional networks. However, the specific task chosen for functional neuroimaging studies can impact which brain regions are found to show abnormal patterns of activation in schizophrenia, as each task probes the specific brain regions and networks involved in the performance of that particular task. In go/no-go tasks, which are designed to test a subject's ability to inhibit a prepotent response, a variety of functional imaging studies have implicated dysfunctional ACC for the impaired error monitoring seen in schizophrenia (Carter, MacDonald, Ross, & Stenger, 2001; Laurens, Ngan, Bates, Kiehl, & Liddle, 2003; Polli, Barton, & Thakkar, 2008; Rubia, Russell, & Bullmore, 2001). A metaanalysis of functional neuroimaging studies of executive function in schizophrenia using a variety of tasks probing different aspects of executive functioning identified a broader set of abnormalities in largely prefrontal—subcortical areas including DLPFC, VLPFC, ACC, and thalamus (Minzenberg, Laird, Thelen, Carter, & Glahn, 2009). It should be noted, though, that executive dysfunction in schizophrenia, while prominent, may be a manifestation of a more global intellectual deficit rather than a selective impairment (Laws, 1999).

Positive symptoms in schizophrenia have not generally been shown to correlate with executive function impairments as measured on neuropsychological tests including tests of cognitive flexibility (Clark, Warman, & Lysaker, 2010), and frontal lobe dysfunction has not been as prominent finding in association with the positive subsyndrome of schizophrenia. However, delusions may reflect a selective impairment in cognitive flexibility that is not accessed by standard examinations. A rigidity of thought leaves these patients impervious to reason regarding their specific delusions. Thus, although they may exhibit less motor and cognitive perseveration of the sort tested for in standard neuropsychological tests, they seem to lack the capacity to revise their delusional beliefs even in the face of clearly conflicting evidence. Delusional patients demonstrate abnormal reasoning, and their decision-making is characterized by reduced information gathering before reaching conclusions. This has been called the "jumping to conclusions" bias. In addition, schizophrenia patients demonstrate increased confidence in those conclusions despite objectively reduced accuracy (Garety, Hemsley, & Wessely, 1991) and impaired ability to integrate disconfirmatory evidence (Woodward, Moritz, Menon, & Klinge, 2008). Thus, the delusions persist, unshakably.

Coltheart has proposed a two-factor hypothesis to explain the neuropsychological basis of delusion formation, suggesting that there may be both a cognitive bias driving misinterpretation of information and another abnormality accounting for the failure to correct this misinterpretation (Coltheart, 2007; Coltheart, 2010; Coltheart, Menzies, & Sutton, 2010). In schizophrenia, abnormal phasic dopamine release from ventral tegmental neurons projecting to the ventral striatum may serve as the neural basis for a misattribution of salience to irrelevant stimuli (Kapur, 2003). Such misattribution of salience can lead to erroneous impressions about the world that may serve as the basis for paranoid delusions and delusions of reference (in which a feature of the person's environment is erroneously believed to carry special personal significance). Temporolimbic hyperactivity, a finding that has been consistently recognized in schizophrenic patients with positive symptoms (Epstein, Stern, & Silbersweig, 1999; Goghari et al., 2010; Liddle et al., 1992; Silbersweig, Stern, & Frith, 1995), may contribute to the intense negative affect that often accompanies these delusions. This is particularly the case with paranoid delusions, where fear of persecution is a prominent theme. Other neurological abnormalities may underlie different types of delusions such as delusional misidentification (Coltheart, 2010) or delusions of control (Frith, 2005). Inappropriate misattribution of salience may lead to erroneous ideas, such as the notion that an innocent bystander bears ill will toward the individual. This sort of false idea only becomes a delusion if it becomes intransigent. It is Coltheart's second factor—the failure to appropriately evaluate and reject the idea—that leads to its persistence. The right frontal lobe, and in particular, the right DLPFC has been proposed as a putative locus mediating this failure (Coltheart, 2010). The right DLPFC has been shown to activate when feedback contradicts a current hypothesis (Fletcher, Anderson, & Shanks, 2001) and delusion severity correlates with abnormal responses to prediction error in the lateral PFC (Corlett, Murray, & Honey, 2007). The authors interpreted this finding as a failure of frontostriatal involvement in prediction error–dependent causal associative learning. It should be noted that this lateral PFC region overlaps with both the right DLPFC region associated with contradiction of a hypothesis and the right IFC region discussed earlier regarding salience detection, attention-shifting, set-shifting, and behavioral inhibition (Aron et al., 2014). Thus, delusion formation may be related to dysfunction in key brain regions associated with cognitive flexibility. Indeed, patients with right frontal lobe damage may be particularly prone to delusion formation (Signer, 1994). However, the perseverance of delusional belief is not likely related to simple hypofunctioning of frontal circuits, as the lateral PFC was not found to be hypofunctioning in the prediction error task but, instead, activated to both surprising and unsurprising events to an equal degree in patients. The implication here is that increased and indiscriminate salience tagging leads to a reduced signal-to-noise ratio and thus a failure to discriminate prediction errors warranting hypothesis revision from expected, unsurprising, hypothesis-confirming events.

A related theory by Fletcher and Frith (2009) combines Coltheart's two factors, attempting to explain delusion formation as a single deficit in Bayesian inference, i.e., abnormal predictive coding. According to this theory, a noisy prediction error signal from dopamine neurons in the midbrain influences reasoning such that evidence in favor of a theory is given undue weight, whereas evidence against the theory is discounted. A tendency to form associations when none are warranted can, over time, significantly influence one's explanatory model of the world that is then used to interpret and integrate day-to-day prediction errors. "The repeated occurrence of the faulty signal in essence may render the world baffling and unreliable, providing ever greater challenges to the sufferer's explanatory models."

In summary, patients with schizophrenia demonstrate a variety of repetitive, perseverative utterances, behaviors, and cognitions, ranging from simple motor stereotypies to complex but rigidly fixed delusions. Many of these perseverative behaviors are similar to what is seen in patients with frontal lobe lesions and likely reflect the hypofunction of various regions of PFC that are seen in the negative and disorganized schizophrenia subsyndromes. Psychosis also represents a type of cognitive and perceptual inflexibility (with delusions and hallucinations) where prefrontal executive deficits are accompanied by aberrant activity in limbic and sensory cortices (Silbersweig & Stern, 1996).

PERSEVERATION AS A FORM OF HABITUAL BEHAVIOR AND FRONTAL–SUBCORTICAL DYSFUNCTION

Normal human behavior is not strictly goal-directed, and the model described in the beginning of this chapter governing goal-directed behavior is most relevant to complex and novel tasks. Much of human behavior is rote, well-practiced/over-learned, and can be categorized as habit, requiring little attention, planning, or forethought. Many tasks required of us are not novel but repetitive and do not require a complex process of weighing the values of various options each time they are performed. Consider, for example, the need to go to work each morning. Initially, the best method of transportation, as well as the best time to leave the house, the best route to take, etc., must be determined However, once the strategy is worked out, there is rarely a need to continue to consider all of these factors on a daily basis, and usually the morning routine becomes a matter of habit that requires scarcely a thought (unless an unanticipated obstacle presents itself, as discussed earlier). Habits serve an important role for the individual, as they can be performed quite expertly with a great deal of computational efficiency, while requiring minimal cognitive resources that can then be redirected elsewhere. Perseverative behaviors and cognitions in a variety of neuropsychiatric disorders may be attributed to abnormalities in the neural systems mediating the balance between habitual and goal-directed behavior.

A key difference between habitual behavior and goal-directed behavior is that habits operate more or less purely based on experience and can be modeled as a type of reinforcement learning where choices are made because they were previously reinforced. Habit is inflexible and tends to operate according to stimulus-response associations. It has been referred to as "model-free learning." In contrast, flexible goal-directed behavior tends to operate according to response-outcome associations. A response is chosen because the expected outcome associated with that choice is desired. This requires a cognitive representation of a goal, and as such, it is future oriented. Goal-directed behavior not only takes into account experiences but also determines a set of current options from which to choose and then calculates the value of each choice on the basis of the values of outcomes expected from each choice. This has the potential to become computationally sophisticated if a long chain of causal relationships must be anticipated for each option to determine the likely resultant outcomes, but it allows for adaptive flexibility despite the high computational cost. For example, "if I set my alarm clock 15 minutes later, I will get more sleep, but then I will likely miss the first train. The next train after that will likely get me to work too late for my first meeting. On the other hand, if I take the bus, I can get more sleep and still arrive at work in time for my first meeting." In computational terms, goal-directed decision-making has been conceptualized as "model-based learning" because a model of causal relations is formulated to make the best choice (Dolan & Dayan, 2013; Gillan, Robbins, Sahakian, van den Heuvel, & van Wingen, 2016).

Operationally, goal-directed behavior can be assessed by devaluing a reinforcer after training. For example, a behavior that is directed toward the goal of obtaining food will become less likely if the animal is satiated and no longer desires the food. Conversely, habitual behavior will continue even when the outcome is no longer desired. Normal human behavior depends on an intricate balance between goal-directed and habitual behavior and an ability to transition from one to the other. There is evidence from animal and human neuroscience literature that goal-directed behavior is supported by a dorsomedial striatal circuit, whereas habit-based behavior is supported by a dorsolateral striatal circuit. With extensive training, there is transfer of processing from dorsomedial to dorsolateral striatum as behavior transitions from goal directed to habit based (Dolan & Dayan, 2013). In humans, this translates into caudate-based circuits supporting goal-directed behavior (Tricomi, Delgado, & Fiez, 2004), while putamen-based circuits support the more automatic stimulus-response habit system (Tricomi, Balleine, & O'Doherty, 2009).

These dissociations can be seen in selected frontal regions, connected to these basal ganglia-thalamic circuits, as well. Killcross and Coutureau (2003) found that lesions to mouse prelimbic mPFC induce lack of sensitivity to goal value, whereas lesions to infralimbic cortex result in retained sensitivity to goal value but impaired expression of habitual behavior. In humans, the vmPFC has been shown to respond selectively to valued versus devalued choices in a functional magnetic resonance imaging (fMRI) study of goal-directed learning (Valentin, Dickinson, & O'Doherty, 2007). This contrasts with the findings in the mouse lesion study by Killcross and Coutureau (2003), as vmPFC is generally considered homologous with infralimbic cortex in the mouse. This suggests a possible breakdown in functional homology in the frontal lobes, as there is a wealth of literature documenting the role of the vmPFC in value-based decision-making (see discussion in introductory section). The strength of white matter connections between posterior putamen and premotor cortex may predict vulnerability to "slips of action" toward habitual but no-longer-rewarding outcomes, whereas strength of white matter connections between caudate and vmPFC can be protective (de Wit et al., 2012). Thus, the strength of these complementary, and in some cases, competing frontostriatal pathways may help to determine an individual's susceptibility to slipping into habitual behavior in a context when goal-directed behavior may be more desirable. This may underlie some of the problems experienced by patients with disorders such as addiction, OCD, trichotillomania, eating disorders, and others, where habitual behaviors supersede goal-directed behaviors to the detriment of the individual.

Addiction

Addiction is characterized by the perseverative repetition of a behavior, despite negative consequences. According to the American Society of Addiction Medicine, addiction is defined as a pathological pursuit of reward and/or relief by substance abuse and other behaviors. Addiction is further characterized by the inability to consistently abstain, impaired behavioral control, craving, diminished recognition of significant problems with one's behaviors and interpersonal relationships, and a dysfunctional emotional response (http://www.asam.org/quality-practice/definition-of-addiction). Although addiction is not a Diagnostic and Statistical Manual of Mental Disorder (DSM) diagnosis, the DSM-5 (American Psychiatric Association, 2013) recognizes a variety of substance use disorders, some of which overlap with concepts of addiction. Although, in most cases, addiction refers to compulsive use of chemical substances such as heroin, alcohol, or cocaine that activate the brain's reward circuitry (i.e., dopaminergic projections from the ventral tegmental area to the nucleus accumbens), addictions can be seen with a variety of behaviors that may similarly activate the brain's reward circuitry, such as eating, shopping, sexual behaviors, gambling, and internet gaming, among others (the last two are recognized as separate disorders in the DSM-5). Each of these behaviors, whether or not it involves an exogenous psychoactive substance, has reinforcing properties that can motivate its repetition. This may be seen as (dysfunctional) goal-directed behavior.

However, as an addiction develops, compulsive and repetitive behavior continues even as the behavior ceases to be rewarding or useful (the goal has been devalued and yet the behavior persists). Habit-related behavior supersedes other goal-directed behaviors to such a degree, that there may be a loss of voluntary control. Prefrontal influence over behavior is reduced while striatal control becomes dominant. Although the nucleus accumbens (within the ventral striatum) and the interconnected OFC are likely critical to the reinforcement of addictive behaviors (instrumental learning), the dorsomedial striatum and interconnected mPFC and ultimately dorsolateral striatum are likely involved in mediating the perseverative drug-seeking behavior of the addict (Everitt & Robbins, 2005).

Coupled with the compulsive behaviors described above, there is often an impairment in inhibitory control that leaves chronic drug users susceptible to impulsive decisions (Chambers et al., 2009). This is likely driven by impairments in brain networks mediating response inhibition. Supporting this are studies showing hypoactivation in the right ACC (Kaufman, Ross, Stein, & Garavan, 2003) and the left ACC, right pre-SMA, and DLPFC (Hester & Garavan, 2004) in cocaine users performing a go/no-go task. Bechara (2005) has proposed a role for vmPFC dysfunction in the impaired decision-making and breakdown in goal-directed behavior seen with addicts, observing that their performance on the Iowa Gambling Task is similarly impaired to that of patients with vmPFC lesions who make decisions based on immediate rewards without reflecting on the long-term consequences of their decisions. Thus, patients with addiction find it difficult to resist their compulsive tendencies, particularly in the face of cues that are associated with drug-related behaviors, and they may continue to relapse into old patterns even after a conscious decision to abstain has been made.

Obsessive Compulsive Disorder and Tourette Syndrome

OCD and Tourette Syndrome (TS) represent a spectrum of neuropsychiatric illness characterized by repetitive unwanted behaviors and cognitions that can cause significant distress and/or be time-consuming or overwhelming enough to impair social or occupational functioning. TS is characterized by recurrent tics—sudden, rapid recurrent motor movements or vocalizations that are experienced as essentially involuntary but can be suppressed, at least temporarily, demonstrating some degree of volitional control. OCD is characterized by recurrent obsessions—intrusive thoughts, urges, or images that are difficult to suppress, and compulsions, or repetitive behaviors that the individual feels driven to complete even if he does not want to. OCD compulsions are similar to the compulsions experienced in addiction in that the individual feels a loss of control. However, the ego-dystonic compulsions in OCD tend to be behaviors that are not necessarily thrilling or pleasurable and include perseverative checking, counting, ordering, or cleaning behaviors or repetitive mental acts. Many of these behaviors have some value, if performed occasionally, but in OCD, they are repeated unnecessarily and to the detriment of the individual. Patients may view these behaviors as aimed at reducing anxiety or avoiding some sort of dreaded consequence of not completing the behavior (Association, 2013). In this sense, there is some similarity with the chronic stage of addiction, in which the behavior may no longer be particularly rewarding but serves to reduce the craving and other associated unpleasant symptoms. There is compelling evidence that obsessions, compulsions, and tics represent a spectrum from higher order cognitions to simple movements, where the underlying pathology is a compulsive need to repeatedly perform an unnecessary activity. More than half of patients with TS have obsessions and compulsions, and about 30% meet the diagnostic criteria for OCD. Tics and tic-like compulsions can be seen in OCD (Diniz, Rosario-Campos, & Hounie, 2006), and the pediatric autoimmune neuropsychiatric disorder associated with *Streptococcus* (PANDAS) is associated with both OCD and tics (Lombroso & Scahill, 2008). Thus, there is considerable overlap between these disorders.

Both TS and OCD may be viewed as disorders of the corticostriatal circuitry. A metaanalysis of neuroimaging studies reported reduced volumes of the left ACC and bilateral OFC in patients with OCD, and symptom reduction has been achieved with surgical procedures disrupting connections between frontal cortex and subcortical structures (Brown et al., 2016) implicating frontal subcortical circuits as important mediators of symptom generation in OCD. Optogenetic stimulation of the lateral OFC−striatal pathway has been shown to suppress compulsive behaviors in a mouse model (Burguiere, Monteiro, Feng, & Graybiel, 2013). On functional imaging studies, OCD patients tend to show abnormalities in the caudate and OFC, and, in particular, the medial OFC. Symptom provocation studies have generally shown hyperactivity in the mOFC and caudate in patients with OCD that can be reduced with successful therapy (Gillan et al., 2016). TS has also been associated with dysfunctional cortico-striato-pallito-thalamo-cortical networks (Worbe, Marrakchi-Kacem, & Lecomte, 2015; Yael, Vinner, & Bar-Gad, 2015).

Various neurobiological models have been proposed to explain the perseverative obsessions and compulsions in OCD, several of which are reviewed by Barahona-Correa, Camacho, Castro-Rodrigues, Costa, and Oliveira-Maia (2015) and include an imbalance between a hyperactive OFC and ACC and a hypoactive DLPFC, failure of inhibition at the level of the ventral pallidum, or an imbalance between the excitatory direct and inhibitory indirect pathways through the basal ganglia.

Increasing evidence has suggested that OCD is characterized by an imbalance between habit learning and flexible goal-directed behavior systems (Gillan & Robbins, 2014; Gillan et al., 2016; Graybiel & Rauch, 2000). Although OCD patients show hyperactivity in mOFC, a region generally associated with goal-directed behavior, OCD patients exhibit deficits in a variety of paradigms intended to test their ability to modulate their stimulus-response behaviors according to changes in the value of an expected outcome. OCD patients appear to be more susceptible to stimulus-response patterns of behavior and less susceptible to stimulus-outcome−driven behavior, and thus may persist in patterns that cease to have any purpose (Gillan et al., 2016; Gillan, Papmeyer, & Morein-Zamir, 2011). This occurs, in particular, in the setting of positive reinforcement learning, and the enhancement of habitual behavior in OCD correlates with greater compulsivity severity scores (Voon, Baek, & Enander, 2015). Interestingly, there is a valence effect, and the opposite pattern appears to be true in tasks measuring reactivity to loss as opposed to reward—thus, greater goal-directed learning from loss-outcomes may be seen in OCD.

Neuropsychological testing in patients with OCD reveals difficulties on tasks of executive functioning requiring cognitive flexibility (Gruner & Pittenger, 2017; Kashyap, Kumar, Kandavel, & Reddy, 2013). Patients are prone to perseveration errors on a delayed alternation task (Moritz, Hottenrott, & Randjbar, 2009) and exhibit impairment in response inhibition tasks (McLaughlin et al., 2016). Abnormal functional connectivity has been seen between the right IFC and the caudate during avoidance learning in patients with OCD, and this was found to predict later habit formation (Gillan, Apergis-Schoute, & Morein-Zamir, 2015), suggesting that impaired inhibitory influence from the right IFC on corticostriatal circuits may play a role in driving habit formation.

It may be that the obsessions and compulsions in OCD (and possibly the tics in TS) are driven by an overactive habit circuit involving the mOFC and various portions of the striatum, and the loss of voluntary control is associated with a transition from more dorsomedial portions of the striatum (caudate) to dorsolateral striatum (putamen). Impaired inhibitory control from the right IFC, pre-SMA, and subthalamic nucleus fails to block these inappropriate behaviors from being impulsively pursued despite the fact that they may conflict with the individual's goals.

EMOTIONAL AND COGNITIVE PERSEVERATION IN DISORDERS OF MOOD AND ANXIETY WITH FRONTOLIMBIC DYSFUNCTION

Emotional fluctuations are part of normal human experience, and extreme emotional responses may be appropriate in certain circumstances (e.g., loss of a loved one or a life-threatening attack). Although emotional reactions can be useful in the short term and emotional appraisals of environmental stimuli can help to guide appropriate behavior, significant suffering can result when negative emotions occur (or recur) outside the appropriate circumstances and cannot be easily ameliorated. Several psychiatric disorders are characterized by abnormally persistent negative emotional states, in which recurrent negative thoughts or feelings occur either without provocation or with only minor triggers. This represents a form of emotional and cognitive inflexibility (and thus repetition) somewhat different from the forms described above, but that nevertheless significantly impacts the range of responses an individual may be able to generate to his environment.

Impaired Fear Extinction in Posttraumatic Stress Disorder

Posttraumatic stress disorder (PTSD) is an anxiety disorder associated with an abnormal response to a traumatic experience after which there is persistent, intrusive, recurrent, distressing memories, dreams, or flashbacks of the trauma, along with persistent emotional reactivity to stimuli that serve as reminders of the trauma. This may lead to depressed mood, avoidant behaviors, and distorted cognitions. In all of these disorders, patients become stuck in recurrent patterns of negative emotional responses and cognitions.

Functional neuroimaging studies in PTSD have shown hyperreactivity of the amygdala, particularly in response to emotional stimuli (Etkin & Wager, 2007; Protopopescu, Pan, & Tuescher, 2005), and this can be ameliorated with CBT (Felmingham, Kemp, & Williams, 2007). The amygdala is a gray matter structure in the mesial temporal lobe whose functions have been most closely associated with negative emotions, and in particular, fear (Sah, Faber, Lopez De Armentia, & Power, 2003). In contrast, there is hypoactivity in the vmPFC, a frontal lobe region that projects densely to the amygdala (Ghashghaei, Hilgetag, & Barbas, 2007) and serves a modulatory role on amygdala reactivity. PTSD symptom severity has been shown to correlate positively with amygdalar responses to emotional, and particularly trauma-specific stimuli (Hughes & Shin, 2011; Protopopescu et al., 2005), and to correlate negatively with vmPFC activity (Dickie, Brunet, Akerib, & Armony, 2008), highlighting an inverse relationship between these two brain regions, where the vmPFC activation may serve a protective role, reducing symptom severity by mitigating the amygdalar hyperresponsivity. Thus, the persistence of emotional/limbic hyperreactivity in PTSD may relate to impaired functioning of the vmPFC.

A large body of human and animal literature has shown that the amygdala serves a critical role in the learning of fear memories, and the expression of fear-related behaviors and autonomic responses (LeDoux, 2003, 2007). The neural circuitry underlying the potentiated amygdala response after fear-learning has been elucidated using Pavlovian fear conditioning tasks, where an aversive unconditioned stimulus (US) is paired with a neutral conditioned stimulus (CS) that, after repeated trials, comes to elicit a fear response similar to that of the US. After fear conditioning has been completed, the CS may be paired with a nonaversive stimulus and the subsequent learning of the new association serves to extinguish the emotional association with the US (extinction learning). This is a form of emotional reversal learning that likely depends on the vmPFC and its connections with the amygdala (Milad et al., 2007; Milad, Rosenbaum, & Simon, 2014), and serves as a model for how we learn about safety and come to no longer fear what we once feared. Top-down modulation and plasticity are involved. Patients with PTSD are resistant to fear extinction, as indexed by persistently abnormal autonomic responses to the CS after extinction learning (Blechert, Michael, Vriends, Margraf, & Wilhelm, 2007), and impaired fear extinction due to an abnormal vmPFC-amygdala circuit has been proposed as an explanation for the persistence of abnormal emotional reactivity in PTSD. Patients appear to be unable to effectively learn that they are safe from danger. It has even been argued that impaired structural integrity of a pathway from the vmPFC to the amygdala (as measured with diffusion tensor imaging) may underlie trait anxiety in healthy individuals (Kim & Whalen,

2009). While much remains uncertain regarding the detailed neurocircuitry underlying PTSD, the literature reviewed above demonstrates the importance of frontal lobe modulation of the limbic system in dampening emotional responses and enabling behavioral flexibility. Impaired frontal modulation may lead to the perpetuation of maladaptive emotions.

Rumination in Generalized Anxiety Disorder

Patients with generalized anxiety disorder (GAD) experience persistent excessive worry "more days than not for at least 6 months" about a variety of unrelated tasks, activities, or circumstances. The individual with GAD finds it difficult to control these worries, which are characterized by excessive, recurrent, negative thoughts, often associated with physical and cognitive symptoms such as muscle tension, sleep disturbance, difficulty concentrating, and fatigue.

GAD is a somewhat more heterogeneous and less well-understood disorder than PTSD, but some of the same concepts discussed with regard to PTSD have been applied to GAD. Increased amygdala responses have been seen in some studies of patients with GAD (McClure, Monk, & Nelson, 2007; Monk, Telzer, & Mogg, 2008) although this has not been an entirely consistent finding (Blair, Shaywitz, & Smith, 2008; Whalen, Johnstone, & Somerville, 2008). Support for a general deficit in emotion regulation has come from studies demonstrating reduced activation of dorsolateral and dorsomedial PFC during emotion tasks (Ball, Ramsawh, Campbell-Sills, Paulus, & Stein, 2013; Etkin, Prater, Hoeft, Menon, & Schatzberg, 2010; Palm, Elliott, McKie, Deakin, & Anderson, 2011). Etkin and colleagues showed reduced DLPFC-amygdala connectivity in a resting state fMRI study of GAD patients (Etkin, Prater, Schatzberg, Menon, & Greicius, 2009) and abnormal ACC-amygdala connectivity during an emotional conflict task (Etkin et al., 2010) suggesting a role for impaired frontal modulation of the amygdala in the pathophysiology of GAD. Amygdala hyperactivity has also been seen in major depressive disorder (MDD), particularly when subjects are presented with stimuli that have negative emotional valence, and this has been viewed as neural evidence of processing bias for negative information (Price & Drevets, 2012; Suslow, Konrad, & Kugel, 2010; Victor, Furey, Fromm, Ohman, & Drevets, 2010).

While emotional dysregulation may be a prominent aspect of GAD symptomatology, amygdalar hyperactivity may not be as crucial component of the pathophysiology as it appears to be in PTSD and may be less relevant to the cardinal symptom of GAD, which is excessive worry or rumination. Rumination typically takes the form of perseverative thoughts related to the anticipation of negative future outcomes. Individuals with GAD often perceive the worries as serving a beneficial purpose, despite evidence to the contrary and despite the distress they cause. This differentiates the ruminations of GAD from the obsessions in OCD. While perseverative thoughts occur in both conditions, the ruminations of GAD patients are generally considered by the individual to be in line with his or her goals (i.e., they are ego-syntonic), whereas the obsessions of OCD patients are typically unwanted and are perceived as an intrusion that is in conflict with the individual's goals (ego-dystonic). In both conditions, the perseverative cognitions may be intrusive and difficult for the individual to control.

It has been argued that excessive worry in GAD reflects an ineffective cognitive attempt to avoid a perceived threat. Another potential explanation for rumination highlights the role of "intolerance of uncertainty," in which the ruminative worry is intended to help the individual cope with, or prevent, a feared event (Behar, DiMarco, Hekler, Mohlman, & Staples, 2009). A similar type of ego-syntonic perseverative rumination can be seen in MDD, although the nature of the ruminative thoughts may differ somewhat. In MDD, ruminative thoughts tend to focus on pessimistic appraisals of future possibilities, regrets, guilt-ridden self-assessments, and suicidal thoughts. A tendency to ruminate can predict onset of depression in adolescents (Stange, Connolly, & Burke, 2016; Stone, Hankin, Gibb, & Abela, 2011) and may be a core aspect of this illness.

Several neuroimaging studies have attempted to investigate the neural underpinnings of rumination. Paulesu, Sambugaro, and Torti (2010) used fMRI to image GAD patients and healthy control subjects during a task intended to induce worry-like mental activity. ACC and dorsomedial PFC activated in association with worry in both healthy controls and GAD patients, but the activity persisted during the resting state scans that followed the worrying phase in the GAD patients only. This persistent activation was found to correlate with scores on the Penn State Worry Questionnaire and was believed to reflect the tendency for GAD patients worry perseveratively. Andreescu, Gross, and Lenze (2011) used pulsed arterial spin labeling MRI to measure rCBF during a worry induction and worry suppression task in elderly subjects with and without GAD. During the worry suppression task, GAD patients failed to show activation in the left lateral PFC and dorsal ACC, as did the nonanxious controls, potentially implicating dysfunctional prefrontal modulatory systems as a cause for the difficulty GAD patients experience in suppressing worries.

Perseveration of Mood and Rumination in Depression

The prototypical mood disorder, MDD, is characterized by at least one episode lasting at least 2 weeks, where an individual has a persistently negative emotional state "most of the day, nearly every day," with often unrealistic feelings of hopelessness, worthlessness, or guilt. In addition, individuals with depression may experience a variety of other symptoms including diminished energy or appetite, diminished interest in pleasurable activities (anhedonia), and impaired sleep (Association, 2013).

MDD is associated with a persistent attentional bias toward negative information (De Raedt & Koster, 2010) and difficulty escaping from negative moods. This disorder represents a key example of what we refer to as perseveration of negative mood, which may result from a failure of frontal modulatory influences on limbic/emotional neural circuitry. The negative appraisal and attentional bias and the perseveration of negative mood may be related. In a mood-induction study, Clasen, Wells, Ellis, and Beevers (2013) induced a sad mood in patients with MDD and healthy controls and found that attentional biases for sad and fear stimuli were associated, in the patients more than in the controls, with slower recovery from the induced negative mood. They also found that in MDD patients, the degree of mood recovery 12 min after induction was negatively correlated with the severity of the MDD. MDD patients have difficulty disengaging attention from negative stimuli (Leyman, De Raedt, Schacht, & Koster, 2007). They have been shows to look longer at images with dysphoric themes during a naturalistic visual scanning task (Eizenman, Yu, & Grupp, 2003) and to exhibit impaired inhibition of negative affect in negative affect priming (NAP) tasks (Goeleven, De Raedt, Baert, & Koster, 2006; Joormann, 2004) and impaired ability to ignore previously learned negative words when trying to recall a new word list (Joormann & Gotlib, 2008). In an event-related fMRI study in which subjects performed an emotion identification task, depressed patients showed amygdala responses to emotional trials that persisted into the next nonemotional trial, considerably longer than what was seen in nondepressed control subjects (Siegle, Steinhauer, Thase, Stenger, & Carter, 2002). Amygdala–prefrontal connectivity has also been shown to be aberrant in MDD (Carballedo, Scheuerecker, & Meisenzahl, 2011; Connolly, Wu, & Ho, 2013; Kong, Chen, & Tang, 2013). Taken together, these data suggest that the persistence of negative affect seen in patients with MDD may relate to both abnormal persistence of bottom-up emotional processing and a problem with inhibition of attentional processes engaged in the processing of negative information (De Raedt & Koster, 2010).

Patients with MDD do not exhibit global cognitive impairment, as patients with schizophrenia seem to (Laws, 1999), and despite the concentration difficulties that are characteristic of depressive episodes, working memory tasks have not consistently shown deficits in depression (De Raedt & Koster, 2010). However, executive function deficits have been found in patients with MDD (Karabekiroglu, Topcuoglu, Gimzal Gonentur, & Karabekiroglu, 2010), including difficulties with attentional set shifting (Murphy, Sahakian, & Rubinsztein, 1999). Perseverative errors on the WCST have been shown to correlate with the number of depressive episodes an individual has experienced (Karabekiroglu et al., 2010), and poor attentional shifting is a risk factor for the development of a first major depressive episode in adolescence (Stange et al., 2016). MDD patients were slower than healthy controls on a task-switching paradigm designed to assess cognitive flexibility, and they failed to activate a region of anterior PFC that was activated by controls in this task (Remijnse, van den Heuvel, & Nielen, 2013). Thus, a case can be made that the difficulty depressed patients have in shifting away from negative emotional states may due to an impairment of frontally mediated processes governing cognitive flexibility.

The difficulty depressed patients experience in disengaging from perseverative thoughts (rumination) may also be related to impairment in similar processes. Dysphoric people who ruminate were shown to commit significantly more perseverative errors and failed to maintain set more often on the WCST than nonruminators (Davis & Nolen-Hoeksema, 2000), and depressive rumination was associated with difficulty inhibiting prior mental sets, as opposed to difficulty switching to a new set, on a task switching paradigm designed to distinguish these two types of impairments (Whitmer & Banich, 2007). A deficit in inhibiting an irrelevant task was seen in high ruminators who were dysphoric but not necessarily depressed (Owens & Derakshan, 2013), and impaired inhibition for emotional words on the NAP task is seen in ruminators relative to nonruminators even after controlling for differences in depression severity (Joormann, 2006).

As with rumination in GAD, depressive rumination has been associated with abnormalities in medial prefrontal regions. Patients in the midst of a major depressive episode were given self-focused cues known to provoke rumination and showed less activation than nondepressed control subjects in an area of the dorsomedial PFC that has been associated with positive self-referential thought. Activity in this area negatively correlated with rumination scores (Johnson, Nolen-Hoeksema, Mitchell, & Levin, 2009). Dorsomedial PFC has been shown to be hypoactive in a variety of tasks in patients with MDD, while more ventral parts of the medial PFC such as the subgenual ACC tend to be hyperactive in depression (Fitzgerald, Laird, Maller, & Daskalakis, 2008; Price & Drevets, 2012) and in normal sadness (Mayberg, Liotti, & Brannan, 1999). In addition, increased and sustained amygdala reactivity has been associated with trait rumination (Mandell, Siegle, Shutt, Feldmiller, & Thase, 2014; Ray et al., 2005). Taken together, this evidence broadly suggests that impairments in medial regions of PFC can lead to reduced cognitive and emotional flexibility in a variety of disorders of mood and anxiety. This manifests as perseverative negative emotional experience and perseverative negative cognitions in the form of rumination. This form of inflexibility manifests primarily in the emotional domain but is not exclusive to this domain, as evidenced by the impairments in cognitive tests such as the WCST mentioned earlier. Whether the cognitive problems some patients exhibit on these tests is secondary to the emotional dysfunction or the cause of it can be studied, but the relationship between cognitive and emotional symptoms may have to do with the fact that frontal systems mediating cognitive and emotional flexibility are closely interconnected and possibly interdependent.

CONCLUSION

The massive expansion of the frontal lobes has been crucial for the evolution of the human capacity to interact flexibly with our environment and with each other. The human capacity for nuanced adaptive behavior is a critical trait, and yet the frontal lobe areas and networks that make this possible have evolved to interact with and modulate more primitive existing limbic—subcortical brain structures that were likely already specialized for mediating adaptive behavior via innate and learned pre-scripted programs and stimulus-response associations in our distant ancestors. In light of this organizational structure (Lautin, 2007), it should not be surprising that when sectors of frontal lobe fail to function properly, more primitive neural systems predominate and flexibility gives way to more automatic behavior and cognition. While birds, reptiles, and other nonmammalian vertebrates may be able to function quite well without a frontal lobe (and in fact without much semblance of a cerebral cortex), humans have evolved to depend on it, and a variety of neuropsychiatric syndromes and disorders can manifest as a result of the disruption of frontal lobe function, either as a consequence of structural damage or genetic, neurodevelopmental, or environmental factors. These disorders may manifest as a tendency to get stuck in maladaptive patterns, such as repetitive and useless behaviors or cognitive processes, abnormally intransigent false beliefs, and abnormally hyperactive, persistent, and dysregulated emotional responses, all of which can cause enormous suffering and difficulty functioning in society. A neuroscience-based understanding of many of these diseases and symptom complexes remains in its infancy, and treatments are only just beginning to be developed to target-specific brain regions and neural networks on the basis of the evidence of their dysfunction in these diseases. And yet, the treatments that have been effective so far are likely acting on these networks, either by targeting transmitter systems that impact frontolimbic functioning (a bottom-up treatment approach) or by targeting the abnormal executive functions themselves (a top-down treatment approach). Cognitive behavior therapy, although not developed on the basis of principles rooted in neuroscience, likely exerts its beneficial effects by helping patients to enhance the functioning of the various frontal lobe systems discussed in this chapter (Franklin, Carson, & Welch, 2016) and by helping patients to find compensatory strategies—in essence teaching patients to make use of their better functioning systems to compensate for those that are impaired. Continued advancement in the neuroscience of executive function and dysfunction will lead to the development of new evidence-based strategies for both biological and psychotherapy-oriented treatment approaches for perseverative neuropsychiatric symptoms and syndromes.

REFERENCES

Andreescu, C., Gross, J. J., Lenze, E., et al. (2011). Altered cerebral blood flow patterns associated with pathologic worry in the elderly. *Depression and Anxiety, 28*(3), 202−209.

Aron, A. R., Robbins, T. W., & Poldrack, R. A. (2014). Inhibition and the right inferior frontal cortex: One decade on. *Trends in Cognitive Sciences, 18*(4), 177−185.

American Psychiatric Association. 2013. *Diagnostic and Statistical Manual of Mental Disorders.* 5th ed. Washington, DC.

Ball, T. M., Ramsawh, H. J., Campbell-Sills, L., Paulus, M. P., & Stein, M. B. (2013). Prefrontal dysfunction during emotion regulation in generalized anxiety and panic disorders. *Psychological Medicine, 43*(7), 1475−1486.

Barahona-Correa, J. B., Camacho, M., Castro-Rodrigues, P., Costa, R., & Oliveira-Maia, A. J. (2015). From thought to action: How the interplay between neuroscience and phenomenology changed our understanding of obsessive-compulsive disorder. *Frontiers in Psychology, 6*, 1798.

Bari, A., & Robbins, T. W. (2013). Inhibition and impulsivity: Behavioral and neural basis of response control. *Progress in Neurobiology, 108*, 44−79.

Bechara, A. (2005). Decision making, impulse control and loss of willpower to resist drugs: A neurocognitive perspective. *Nature Neuroscience, 8*(11), 1458−1463.

Bechara, A., Damasio, A. R., Damasio, H., & Anderson, S. W. (1994). Insensitivity to future consequences following damage to human prefrontal cortex. *Cognition, 50*(1−3), 7−15.

Bechara, A., Tranel, D., & Damasio, H. (2000). Characterization of the decision-making deficit of patients with ventromedial prefrontal cortex lesions. *Brain, 123*(Pt 11), 2189−2202.

Behar, E., DiMarco, I. D., Hekler, E. B., Mohlman, J., & Staples, A. M. (2009). Current theoretical models of generalized anxiety disorder (GAD): Conceptual review and treatment implications. *Journal of Anxiety Disorders, 23*(8), 1011−1023.

Blair, K., Shaywitz, J., Smith, B. W., et al. (2008). Response to emotional expressions in generalized social phobia and generalized anxiety disorder: Evidence for separate disorders. *The American Journal of Psychiatry, 165*(9), 1193−1202.

Blechert, J., Michael, T., Vriends, N., Margraf, J., & Wilhelm, F. H. (2007). Fear conditioning in posttraumatic stress disorder: Evidence for delayed extinction of autonomic, experiential, and behavioural responses. *Behaviour Research and Therapy, 45*(9), 2019−2033.

Bonilha, L., Molnar, C., Horner, M. D., et al. (2008). Neurocognitive deficits and prefrontal cortical atrophy in patients with schizophrenia. *Schizophrenia Research, 101*(1−3), 142−151.

Bouret, S., & Richmond, B. J. (2010). Ventromedial and orbital prefrontal neurons differentially encode internally and externally driven motivational values in monkeys. *Journal of Neuroscience, 30*(25), 8591−8601.

Brown, L. T., Mikell, C. B., Youngerman, B. E., Zhang, Y., McKhann, G. M., 2nd, & Sheth, S. A. (2016). Dorsal anterior cingulotomy and anterior capsulotomy for severe, refractory obsessive-compulsive disorder: A systematic review of observational studies. *Journal of Neurosurgery, 124*(1), 77−89.

Burguiere, E., Monteiro, P., Feng, G., & Graybiel, A. M. (2013). Optogenetic stimulation of lateral orbitofronto-striatal pathway suppresses compulsive behaviors. *Science, 340*(6137), 1243−1246.

Carballedo, A., Scheuerecker, J., Meisenzahl, E., et al. (2011). Functional connectivity of emotional processing in depression. *Journal of Affective Disorders, 134*(1−3), 272−279.

Carter, C. S., MacDonald, A. W., 3rd, Ross, L. L., & Stenger, V. A. (2001). Anterior cingulate cortex activity and impaired self-monitoring of performance in patients with schizophrenia: An event-related fMRI study. *The American Journal of Psychiatry, 158*(9), 1423−1428.

Chambers, C. D., Garavan, H., & Bellgrove, M. A. (2009). Insights into the neural basis of response inhibition from cognitive and clinical neuroscience. *Neuroscience & Biobehavioral Reviews, 33*(5), 631−646.

Chan, R. C., Chen, E. Y., Cheung, E. F., Chen, R. Y., & Cheung, H. K. (2006). The components of executive functioning in a cohort of patients with chronic schizophrenia: A multiple single-case study design. *Schizophrenia Research, 81*(2−3), 173−189.

Clark, L. K., Warman, D., & Lysaker, P. H. (2010). The relationships between schizophrenia symptom dimensions and executive functioning components. *Schizophrenia Research, 124* (1-3), 169−175.

Clasen, P. C., Wells, T. T., Ellis, A. J., & Beevers, C. G. (2013). Attentional biases and the persistence of sad mood in major depressive disorder. *Journal of Abnormal Psychology, 122*(1), 74−85.

Coltheart, M. (2007). Cognitive neuropsychiatry and delusional belief. *The Quarterly Journal of Experimental Psychology (Hove), 60*(8), 1041−1062.

Coltheart, M. (2010). The neuropsychology of delusions. *Annals of the New York Academy of Sciences, 1191*, 16−26.

Coltheart, M., Menzies, P., & Sutton, J. (2010). Abductive inference and delusional belief. *Cognitive Neuropsychiatry, 15*(1), 261−287.

Connolly, C. G., Wu, J., Ho, T. C., et al. (2013). Resting-state functional connectivity of subgenual anterior cingulate cortex in depressed adolescents. *Biological Psychiatry, 74*(12), 898−907.

Corbetta, M., & Shulman, G. L. (2002). Control of goal-directed and stimulus-driven attention in the brain. *Nature Reviews Neuroscience, 3*(3), 201−215.

Corlett, P. R., Murray, G. K., Honey, G. D., et al. (2007). Disrupted prediction-error signal in psychosis: Evidence for an associative account of delusions. *Brain, 130*(Pt 9), 2387−2400.

Crider, A. (1997). Perseveration in schizophrenia. *Schizophrenia Bulletin, 23*(1), 63−74.

Daffner, K. R., & Searl, M. M. (2008). The dysexecutive syndromesIn G. Goldenberg, & B. L. Miller (Eds.), *Neuropsychology and Behavioral Neurology* (Vol. 88, pp. 249−267). Elsevier.

Daffner, K. R., & Willment, K. C. (2014). Executive control, the regulation of goal-directed behaviors, and the impact of dementing illness. In B. Dickerson, & A. Atri (Eds.), *Dementia: Comprehensive principles and practices.* Oxford University Press.

Dajani, D. R., & Uddin, L. Q. (2015). Demystifying cognitive flexibility: Implications for clinical and developmental neuroscience. *Trends in Neuroscience, 38*(9), 571−578.

Davis, R. N., & Nolen-Hoeksema, S. (2000). Cognitive inflexibility among ruminators and non-ruminators. *Cognitive Therapy and Research, 24*(6), 699−711.

Dawes, S. E., Jeste, D. V., & Palmer, B. W. (2011). Cognitive profiles in persons with chronic schizophrenia. *Journal of Clinical and Experimental Neuropsychology, 33*(8), 929−936.

De Raedt, R., & Koster, E. H. (2010). Understanding vulnerability for depression from a cognitive neuroscience perspective: A reappraisal of attentional factors and a new conceptual framework. *Cognitive, Affective, & Behavioral Neuroscience, 10*(1), 50−70.

de Wit, S., Watson, P., Harsay, H. A., Cohen, M. X., van de Vijver, I., & Ridderinkhof, K. R. (2012). Corticostriatal connectivity underlies individual differences in the balance between habitual and goal-directed action control. *Journal of Neuroscience, 32*(35), 12066−12075.

Dickie, E. W., Brunet, A., Akerib, V., & Armony, J. L. (2008). An fMRI investigation of memory encoding in PTSD: Influence of symptom severity. *Neuropsychologia, 46*(5), 1522−1531.

Diniz, J. B., Rosario-Campos, M. C., Hounie, A. G., et al. (2006). Chronic tics and Tourette syndrome in patients with obsessive-compulsive disorder. *Journal of Psychiatric Research, 40*(6), 487−493.

Dolan, R. J., & Dayan, P. (2013). Goals and habits in the brain. *Neuron, 80*(2), 312–325.

Eizenman, M., Yu, L. H., Grupp, L., et al. (2003). A naturalistic visual scanning approach to assess selective attention in major depressive disorder. *Psychiatry Research, 118*(2), 117–128.

Epstein, J., Stern, E., & Silbersweig, D. (1999). Mesolimbic activity associated with psychosis in schizophrenia. Symptom-specific PET studies. *Annals of the New York Academy of Sciences, 877*, 562–574.

Etkin, A., Prater, K. E., Hoeft, F., Menon, V., & Schatzberg, A. F. (2010). Failure of anterior cingulate activation and connectivity with the amygdala during implicit regulation of emotional processing in generalized anxiety disorder. *American Journal of Psychiatry, 167*(5), 545–554.

Etkin, A., Prater, K. E., Schatzberg, A. F., Menon, V., & Greicius, M. D. (2009). Disrupted amygdalar subregion functional connectivity and evidence of a compensatory network in generalized anxiety disorder. *Archives of General Psychiatry, 66*(12), 1361–1372.

Etkin, A., & Wager, T. D. (2007). Functional neuroimaging of anxiety: A meta-analysis of emotional processing in PTSD, social anxiety disorder, and specific phobia. *American Journal of Psychiatry, 164*(10), 1476–1488.

Everitt, B. J., & Robbins, T. W. (2005). Neural systems of reinforcement for drug addiction: From actions to habits to compulsion. *Nature Neuroscience, 8*(11), 1481–1489.

Felmingham, K., Kemp, A., Williams, L., et al. (2007). Changes in anterior cingulate and amygdala after cognitive behavior therapy of posttraumatic stress disorder. *Psychological Science, 18*(2), 127–129.

Fitzgerald, P. B., Laird, A. R., Maller, J., & Daskalakis, Z. J. (2008). A meta-analytic study of changes in brain activation in depression. *Human Brain Mapping, 29*(6), 683–695.

Fletcher, P. C., Anderson, J. M., Shanks, D. R., et al. (2001). Responses of human frontal cortex to surprising events are predicted by formal associative learning theory. *Nature Neuroscience, 4*(10), 1043–1048.

Fletcher, P. C., & Frith, C. D. (2009). Perceiving is believing: A Bayesian approach to explaining the positive symptoms of schizophrenia. *Nature Reviews Neuroscience, 10*(1), 48–58.

Franklin, G., Carson, A. J., & Welch, K. A. (2016). Cognitive behavioural therapy for depression: Systematic review of imaging studies. *Acta Neuropsychiatrica, 28*(2), 61–74.

Frith, C. (2005). The self in action: Lessons from delusions of control. *Conscious Cognition, 14* (4), 752–770.

Garety, P. A., Hemsley, D. R., & Wessely, S. (1991). Reasoning in deluded schizophrenic and paranoid patients. Biases in performance on a probabilistic inference task. *Journal of Nervous and Mental Disease, 179*(4), 194–201.

Ghashghaei, H. T., Hilgetag, C. C., & Barbas, H. (2007). Sequence of information processing for emotions based on the anatomic dialogue between prefrontal cortex and amygdala. *NeuroImage, 34*(3), 905–923.

Gillan, C. M., Apergis-Schoute, A. M., Morein-Zamir, S., et al. (2015). Functional neuroimaging of avoidance habits in obsessive-compulsive disorder. *American Journal of Psychiatry, 172* (3), 284–293.

Gillan, Claire M., Papmeyer, Martina, Morein-Zamir, Sharon, et al. (2011). Disruption in the balance between goal-directed behavior and habit learning in obsessive-compulsive disorder. *American Journal of Psychiatry, 168*(7), 718–726.

Gillan, C. M., & Robbins, T. W. (2014). Goal-directed learning and obsessive-compulsive disorder. *Philosophical Transactions of the Royal Society B: Biological Sciences, 369*(1655).

Gillan, C. M., Robbins, T. W., Sahakian, B. J., van den Heuvel, O. A., & van Wingen, G. (2016). The role of habit in compulsivity. *European Neuropsychopharmacology*, *26*(5), 828−840.

Goeleven, E., De Raedt, R., Baert, S., & Koster, E. H. (2006). Deficient inhibition of emotional information in depression. *Journal of Affective Disorders*, *93*(1−3), 149−157.

Goghari, V. M., Sponheim, S. R., & MacDonald, A. W., 3rd (2010). The functional neuroanatomy of symptom dimensions in schizophrenia: A qualitative and quantitative review of a persistent question. *Neuroscience & Biobehavioral Reviews*, *34*(3), 468−486.

Graybiel, A. M., & Rauch, S. L. (2000). Toward a neurobiology of obsessive-compulsive disorder. *Neuron*, *28*(2), 343−347.

Gruner, P., & Pittenger, C. (2017). Cognitive inflexibility in obsessive-compulsive disorder. *Neuroscience*, *345*, 243−255.

Harrison, P. J. (1999). The neuropathology of schizophrenia. A critical review of the data and their interpretation. *Brain*, *122*(Pt 4), 593−624.

Hester, R., & Garavan, H. (2004). Executive dysfunction in cocaine addiction: Evidence for discordant frontal, cingulate, and cerebellar activity. *Journal of Neuroscience*, *24*(49), 11017−11022.

Hughes, K. C., & Shin, L. M. (2011). Functional neuroimaging studies of post-traumatic stress disorder. *Expert Review of Neurotherapeutics*, *11*(2), 275−285.

Iacoboni, M. (2005). Neural mechanisms of imitation. *Current Opinion in Neurobiology*, *15*(6), 632−637.

Izquierdo, A., Brigman, J. L., Radke, A. K., Rudebeck, P. H., & Holmes, A. (2017). The neural basis of reversal learning: An updated perspective. *Neuroscience*, *345*, 12−26.

Johnson, M. K., Nolen-Hoeksema, S., Mitchell, K. J., & Levin, Y. (2009). Medial cortex activity, self-reflection and depression. *Social Cognitive and Affective Neuroscience*, *4*(4), 313−327.

Joormann, J. (2004). Attentional bias in dysphoria: The role of inhibitory processes. *Cognition & Emotion*, *18*(1), 125−147.

Joormann, J. (2006). Differential effects of rumination and dysphoria on the inhibition of irrelevant emotional material: Evidence from a negative priming task. *Cognitive Therapy and Research*, *30*(2), 149−160.

Joormann, J., & Gotlib, I. H. (2008). Updating the contents of working memory in depression: Interference from irrelevant negative material. *Journal of Abnormal Psychology*, *117*(1), 182−192.

Kapur, S. (2003). Psychosis as a state of aberrant salience: A framework linking biology, phenomenology, and pharmacology in schizophrenia. *American Journal of Psychiatry*, *160*(1), 13−23.

Karabekiroglu, A., Topcuoglu, V., Gimzal Gonentur, A., & Karabekiroglu, K. (2010). [Executive function differences between first episode and recurrent major depression patients]. *Turkish Journal of Psychiatry*, *21*(4), 280−288, Winter.

Kashyap, H., Kumar, J. K., Kandavel, T., & Reddy, Y. C. (2013). Neuropsychological functioning in obsessive-compulsive disorder: Are executive functions the key deficit? *Comprehensive Psychiatry*, *54*(5), 533−540.

Kaufman, J. N., Ross, T. J., Stein, E. A., & Garavan, H. (2003). Cingulate hypoactivity in cocaine users during a GO-NOGO task as revealed by event-related functional magnetic resonance imaging. *Journal of Neuroscience*, *23*(21), 7839−7843.

Killcross, S., & Coutureau, E. (2003). Coordination of actions and habits in the medial prefrontal cortex of rats. *Cerebral Cortex*, *13*(4), 400−408.

Kim, M. J., & Whalen, P. J. (2009). The structural integrity of an amygdala-prefrontal pathway predicts trait anxiety. *Journal of Neuroscience, 29*(37), 11614–11618.

Kong, L., Chen, K., Tang, Y., et al. (2013). Functional connectivity between the amygdala and prefrontal cortex in medication-naive individuals with major depressive disorder. *Journal of Psychiatry & Neuroscience, 38*(6), 417–422.

Konishi, S., Nakajima, K., Uchida, I., et al. (1998). Transient activation of inferior prefrontal cortex during cognitive set shifting. *Nature Neuroscience, 1*(1), 80–84.

Lanser, M. G., Berger, H. J., Ellenbroek, B. A., Cools, A. R., & Zitman, F. G. (2002). Perseveration in schizophrenia: Failure to generate a plan and relationship with the psychomotor poverty subsyndrome. *Psychiatry Research, 112*(1), 13–26.

Laurens, K. R., Ngan, E. T., Bates, A. T., Kiehl, K. A., & Liddle, P. F. (2003). Rostral anterior cingulate cortex dysfunction during error processing in schizophrenia. *Brain, 126*(Pt 3), 610–622.

Lautin, A. L. (2001). *Chapter 3: MacLean's limbic system. The Limbic Brain.* New York, N.Y: Kluwer Academic/Plenum Publishers.

Laws, K. R. (1999). A meta-analytic review of Wisconsin Card Sort studies in schizophrenia: General intellectual deficit in disguise? *Cognitive Neuropsychiatry, 4*(1), 1–30, discussion 31–35.

LeDoux, J. (2003). The emotional brain, fear, and the amygdala. *Cellular and Molecular Neurobiology, 23*(4–5), 727–738.

LeDoux, J. (2007). The amygdala. *Current Biology, 17*(20), R868–874.

Levy, M. S. (2000). A conceptualization of the repetition compulsion. *Psychiatry, 63*(1), 45–53, Spring.

Leyman, L., De Raedt, R., Schacht, R., & Koster, E. H. (2007). Attentional biases for angry faces in unipolar depression. *Psychological Medicine, 37*(3), 393–402.

Lhermitte, F. (1983). 'Utilization behaviour' and its relation to lesions of the frontal lobes. *Brain, 106*(Pt 2), 237–255.

Lhermitte, F., Pillon, B., & Serdaru, M. (1986). Human autonomy and the frontal lobes. Part I: Imitation and utilization behavior: A neuropsychological study of 75 patients. *Annals of Neurology, 19*(4), 326–334.

Liddle, P. F. (1987). The symptoms of chronic schizophrenia. A re-examination of the positive-negative dichotomy. *British Journal of Psychiatry, 151*, 145–151.

Liddle, P. F., Friston, K. J., Frith, C. D., Hirsch, S. R., Jones, T., & Frackowiak, R. S. (1992). Patterns of cerebral blood flow in schizophrenia. *British Journal of Psychiatry, 160*, 179–186.

Lombroso, P. J., & Scahill, L. (2008). Tourette syndrome and obsessive-compulsive disorder. *Brain and Development, 30*(4), 231–237.

Luria, A. R. (1976). *The working brain: An introduction to neuropsychology.* New York, NY: Basic Books.

Mandell, D., Siegle, G. J., Shutt, L., Feldmiller, J., & Thase, M. E. (2014). Neural substrates of trait ruminations in depression. *Journal of Abnormal Psychology, 123*(1), 35–48.

Mayberg, H. S., Liotti, M., Brannan, S. K., et al. (1999). Reciprocal limbic-cortical function and negative mood: Converging PET findings in depression and normal sadness. *American Journal of Psychiatry, 156*(5), 675–682.

McClure, E. B., Monk, C. S., Nelson, E. E., et al. (2007). Abnormal attention modulation of fear circuit function in pediatric generalized anxiety disorder. *Archives of General Psychiatry, 64*(1), 97–106.

McLaughlin, N. C., Kirschner, J., Foster, H., O'Connell, C., Rasmussen, S. A., & Greenberg, B. D. (2016). Stop signal reaction time deficits in a lifetime obsessive-compulsive disorder sample. *Journal of the International Neuropsychological Society, 22*(7), 785–789.

Milad, M. R., Rosenbaum, B. L., & Simon, N. M. (2014). Neuroscience of fear extinction: Implications for assessment and treatment of fear-based and anxiety related disorders. *Behaviour Research and Therapy, 62*, 17–23.

Milad, M. R., Wright, C. I., Orr, S. P., Pitman, R. K., Quirk, G. J., & Rauch, S. L. (2007). Recall of fear extinction in humans activates the ventromedial prefrontal cortex and hippocampus in concert. *Biological Psychiatry, 62*(5), 446–454.

Minzenberg, M. J., Laird, A. R., Thelen, S., Carter, C. S., & Glahn, D. C. (2009). Meta-analysis of 41 functional neuroimaging studies of executive function in schizophrenia. *Archives of General Psychiatry, 66*(8), 811–822.

Monk, C. S., Telzer, E. H., Mogg, K., et al. (2008). Amygdala and ventrolateral prefrontal cortex activation to masked angry faces in children and adolescents with generalized anxiety disorder. *Archives of General Psychiatry, 65*(5), 568–576.

Moorman, D. E., & Aston-Jones, G. (2014). Orbitofrontal cortical neurons encode expectation-driven initiation of reward-seeking. *Journal of Neuroscience, 34*(31), 10234–10246.

Moritz, S., Hottenrott, B., Randjbar, S., et al. (2009). Perseveration and not strategic deficits underlie delayed alternation impairment in obsessive-compulsive disorder (OCD). *Psychiatry Research, 170*(1), 66–69.

Murphy, F. C., Sahakian, B. J., Rubinsztein, J. S., et al. (1999). Emotional bias and inhibitory control processes in mania and depression. *Psychological Medicine, 29*(6), 1307–1321.

Noonan, M. P., Kolling, N., Walton, M. E., & Rushworth, M. F. (2012). Re-evaluating the role of the orbitofrontal cortex in reward and reinforcement. *European Journal of Neuroscience, 35*(7), 997–1010.

O'Leary, D. S., Flaum, M., Kesler, M. L., Flashman, L. A., Arndt, S., & Andreasen, N. C. (2000). Cognitive correlates of the negative, disorganized, and psychotic symptom dimensions of schizophrenia. *Journal of Neuropsychiatry & Clinical Neurosciences, 12*(1), 4–15, Winter.

Owens, M., & Derakshan, N. (2013). The effects of dysphoria and rumination on cognitive flexibility and task selection. *Acta Psychologica (Amsterdam), 142*(3), 323–331.

Palm, M. E., Elliott, R., McKie, S., Deakin, J. F., & Anderson, I. M. (2011). Attenuated responses to emotional expressions in women with generalized anxiety disorder. *Psychological Medicine, 41*(5), 1009–1018.

Paulesu, E., Sambugaro, E., Torti, T., et al. (2010). Neural correlates of worry in generalized anxiety disorder and in normal controls: A functional MRI study. *Psychological Medicine, 40*(1), 117–124.

Polli, F. E., Barton, J. J., Thakkar, K. N., et al. (2008). Reduced error-related activation in two anterior cingulate circuits is related to impaired performance in schizophrenia. *Brain, 131*(Pt 4), 971–986.

Potuzak, M., Ravichandran, C., Lewandowski, K. E., Ongur, D., & Cohen, B. M. (2012). Categorical vs dimensional classifications of psychotic disorders. *Comprehensive Psychiatry, 53*(8), 1118–1129.

Price, J. L., & Drevets, W. C. (2012). Neural circuits underlying the pathophysiology of mood disorders. *Trends in Cognitive Sciences, 16*(1), 61–71.

Protopopescu, X., Pan, H., Tuescher, O., et al. (2005). Differential time courses and specificity of amygdala activity in posttraumatic stress disorder subjects and normal control subjects. *Biological Psychiatry, 57*(5), 464–473.

Ray, R. D., Ochsner, K. N., Cooper, J. C., Robertson, E. R., Gabrieli, J. D., & Gross, J. J. (2005). Individual differences in trait rumination and the neural systems supporting cognitive reappraisal. *Cognitive, Affective, & Behavioral Neuroscience, 5*(2), 156–168.

Remijnse, P. L., van den Heuvel, O. A., Nielen, M. M., et al. (2013). Cognitive inflexibility in obsessive-compulsive disorder and major depression is associated with distinct neural correlates. *PLoS One, 8*(4), e59600.

Riehemann, S., Volz, H. P., Stutzer, P., Smesny, S., Gaser, C., & Sauer, H. (2001). Hypofrontality in neuroleptic-naive schizophrenic patients during the Wisconsin Card Sorting Test—A fMRI study. *European Archives of Psychiatry and Clinical Neuroscience, 251*(2), 66−71.

Rubia, K., Russell, T., Bullmore, E. T., et al. (2001). An fMRI study of reduced left prefrontal activation in schizophrenia during normal inhibitory function. *Schizophrenia Research, 52* (1−2), 47−55.

Sah, P., Faber, E. S., Lopez De Armentia, M., & Power, J. (2003). The amygdaloid complex: Anatomy and physiology. *Physiological Reviews, 83*(3), 803−834.

Siegle, G. J., Steinhauer, S. R., Thase, M. E., Stenger, V. A., & Carter, C. S. (2002). Can't shake that feeling: Event-related fMRI assessment of sustained amygdala activity in response to emotional information in depressed individuals. *Biological Psychiatry, 51*(9), 693−707.

Signer, S. F. (1994). Localization and lateralization in the delusion of substitution. Capgras symptom and its variants. *Psychopathology, 27*(3−5), 168−176.

Silbersweig, D., & Stern, E. (1996). Functional neuroimaging of hallucinations in schizophrenia: Toward an integration of bottom-up and top-down approaches. *Molecular Psychiatry, 1*(5), 367−375.

Silbersweig, D. A., Stern, E., Frith, C., et al. (1995). A functional neuroanatomy of hallucinations in schizophrenia. *Nature, 378*(6553), 176−179.

Stange, J. P., Connolly, S. L., Burke, T. A., et al. (2016). Inflexible cognition predicts first onset of major depressive episodes in adolescence. *Depression and Anxiety, 33*(11), 1005−1012.

Stone, L. B., Hankin, B. L., Gibb, B. E., & Abela, J. R. (2011). Co-rumination predicts the onset of depressive disorders during adolescence. *Journal of Abnormal Psychology, 120*(3), 752−757.

Suslow, T., Konrad, C., Kugel, H., et al. (2010). Automatic mood-congruent amygdala responses to masked facial expressions in major depression. *Biological Psychiatry, 67*(2), 155−160.

Talairach, J., Bancaud, J., Geier, S., et al. (1973). The cingulate gyrus and human behaviour. *Electroencephalography and Clinical Neurophysiology, 34*(1), 45−52.

Tricomi, E., Balleine, B. W., & O'Doherty, J. P. (2009). A specific role for posterior dorsolateral striatum in human habit learning. *European Journal of Neuroscience, 29*(11), 2225−2232.

Tricomi, E. M., Delgado, M. R., & Fiez, J. A. (2004). Modulation of caudate activity by action contingency. *Neuron, 41*(2), 281−292.

Uddin, L. Q. (2015). Salience processing and insular cortical function and dysfunction. *Nature Reviews Neuroscience, 16*(1), 55−61.

Valentin, V. V., Dickinson, A., & O'Doherty, J. P. (2007). Determining the neural substrates of goal-directed learning in the human brain. *Journal of Neuroscience, 27*(15), 4019−4026.

Victor, T. A., Furey, M. L., Fromm, S. J., Ohman, A., & Drevets, W. C. (2010). Relationship between amygdala responses to masked faces and mood state and treatment in major depressive disorder. *Archives of General Psychiatry, 67*(11), 1128−1138.

Voon, V., Baek, K., Enander, J., et al. (2015). Motivation and value influences in the relative balance of goal-directed and habitual behaviours in obsessive-compulsive disorder. *Translational Psychiatry, 5*, e670.

Waford, R. N., & Lewine, R. (2010). Is perseveration uniquely characteristic of schizophrenia? *Schizophrenia Research, 118*(1−3), 128−133.

Wallis, J. D. (2011). Cross-species studies of orbitofrontal cortex and value-based decision-making. *Nature Neuroscience*, *15*(1), 13–19.

Weinberger, D. R., & Berman, K. F. (1988). Speculation on the meaning of cerebral metabolic hypofrontality in schizophrenia. *Schizophrenia Bulletin*, *14*(2), 157–168.

Weinberger, D. R., Berman, K. F., & Zec, R. F. (1986). Physiologic dysfunction of dorsolateral prefrontal cortex in schizophrenia. I. Regional cerebral blood flow evidence. *Archives of General Psychiatry*, *43*(2), 114–124.

Whalen, P. J., Johnstone, T., Somerville, L. H., et al. (2008). A functional magnetic resonance imaging predictor of treatment response to venlafaxine in generalized anxiety disorder. *Biological Psychiatry*, *63*(9), 858–863.

Whitmer, A. J., & Banich, M. T. (2007). Inhibition versus switching deficits in different forms of rumination. *Psychological Science*, *18*(6), 546–553.

Wilmsmeier, A., Ohrmann, P., Suslow, T., et al. (2010). Neural correlates of set-shifting: Decomposing executive functions in schizophrenia. *Journal of Psychiatry & Neuroscience*, *35*(5), 321–329.

Woodward, T. S., Moritz, S., Menon, M., & Klinge, R. (2008). Belief inflexibility in schizophrenia. *Cognitive Neuropsychiatry*, *13*(3), 267–277.

Worbe, Y., Marrakchi-Kacem, L., Lecomte, S., et al. (2015). Altered structural connectivity of cortico-striato-pallido-thalamic networks in Gilles de la Tourette syndrome. *Brain*, *138*(Pt 2), 472–482.

Yael, D., Vinner, E., & Bar-Gad, I. (2015). Pathophysiology of tic disorders. *Movement Disorders*, *30*(9), 1171–1178.

Zec, R. F. (1995). Neuropsychology of schizophrenia according to Kraepelin: Disorders of volition and executive functioning. *European Archives of Psychiatry and Clinical Neuroscience*, *245*(4–5), 216–223.

Chapter 11

Functional Neuroimaging of Deficits in Cognitive Control

Melissa-Ann Mackie[1,2] and Jin Fan[1,2,3,4]

[1]*The Graduate Center, The City University of New York, New York, NY, United States,*
[2]*Department of Psychology, Queens College, The City University of New York,*
Queens, NY, United States, [3]*Department of Psychiatry, Icahn School of Medicine at*
Mount Sinai, New York, NY, United States, [4]*Department of Neuroscience, Icahn School*
of Medicine at Mount Sinai, New York, NY, United States

DEFINITION OF COGNITIVE CONTROL

On a daily basis, the brain receives a vast amount of input information that far exceeds the limited processing capacity of the conscious mind. Therefore, cognitive control is required to flexibly allocate mental resources to guide thought and action in the service of goal-directed behavior, to select information that will reach conscious mind (Badre, 2008; Fan, 2014; Koechlin, Ody, & Kouneiher, 2003; Mackie, Van Dam, & Fan, 2013; Miller & Cohen, 2001; Posner & Snyder, 1975). Efficient information processing and behavioral response depend to a great extent on the integrity of cognitive control (Mackie & Fan, 2016). This ability for control over information processing underlies our ability engage in the high-level cognitive processes known as "executive functions," which have been typically attributed to the frontal lobes (Miller & Cohen, 2001). Cognitive control, which is the underlying core of executive functions, has been described in terms of a widespread network of brain regions, including frontoparietal and subcortical brain structures (Cole & Schneider, 2007; Esterman, Chiu, Tamber-Rosenau, & Yantis, 2009; Fan, 2014; Fassbender et al., 2006; Niendam et al., 2012).

Other approaches to defining cognitive control have been proposed. Many of them have been grounded in task-based ways that are focused on response inhibition or on neuroanatomical underpinnings constrained to prefrontal cortex (PFC), particularly anterior cingulate and dorsolateral prefrontal cortices (ACCs and dlPFCs) (Botvinick, Braver, Barch, Carter, & Cohen, 2001; Brown & Braver, 2005; Kerns et al., 2004; Kim, Chung, & Kim, 2013; MacDonald, Cohen, Stenger, & Carter, 2000). Such approaches have been

Executive Functions in Health and Disease. DOI: http://dx.doi.org/10.1016/B978-0-12-803676-1.00011-8

restricted to specific functions of cognitive control and tasks known to elicit activation in confined neuroanatomical areas (Mackie et al., 2013). In a broader sense, cognitive control is required for a wide range of goal-directed cognitive processes, beyond the inhibition of irrelevant stimuli. In search of a parsimonious factor structure of the construct, a three-factor model has been described that includes cognitive flexibility (shifting), updating of information in the conscious mind, and inhibition of unwanted responses (Friedman & Miyake, 2016; Miyake et al., 2000). However, these factors are not entirely dissociable, suggesting an underlying commonality.

Functionally, cognitive control can be considered as a set of processes that are implemented under conditions of increased uncertainty about competing choices or actions within a given context (Fan, 2014; Mushtaq, Bland, & Schaefer, 2011). Uncertainty can be conceptualized at various levels, from a low level of sensory prediction to higher level outcome prediction (Bach & Dolan, 2012). Under conditions of uncertainty, there is typically competition for mental resources in the brain, which may or may not involve the conscious mind. Cognitive control serves to reduce uncertainty in decision-making by prioritizing information to reach conscious awareness. As previously mentioned, tasks investigating cognitive control often involve some type of conflict between stimulus dimensions or between stimulus and response (Li, Nan, Wang, & Liu, 2014). However, conflict is just one type of case with an increase in uncertainty for which cognitive control may be used (Fan, 2014).

Cognitive control is implemented by attentional functions (Mackie et al., 2013; Posner & Snyder, 1975) of alerting, orienting, and executive control (Fan, McCandliss, Sommer, Raz, & Posner, 2002; Posner & Petersen, 1990). These attentional functions serve to reduce uncertainty in temporal, spatial, and response domains. For example, alerting reduces the temporal uncertainty of stimuli, orienting serves as spotlight to focus on information that is selected, and executive control acts to bias cognitive processing toward task-relevant stimuli when there is competition between processes. These attentional functions are well positioned to serve as the common thread underlying cognitive control (Feldman & Friston, 2010; Mackie et al., 2013). Consequently, the brain mechanisms of cognitive control often include brain regions that are reliably associated with these attentional functions (Cole & Schneider, 2007; Dosenbach & Petersen, 2009; Dosenbach et al., 2006; Dosenbach, Fair, Cohen, Schlaggar, & Petersen, 2008; Ochsner, Hughes, Robertson, Cooper, & Gabrieli, 2009; Xuan et al., 2016).

INFORMATION THEORY APPROACH TO COGNITIVE CONTROL

It is clear that the brain is an information processing entity. Less intuitive is what this means in terms of how "information" is represented and processed in the brain. Theoretical approaches that use concrete and quantifiable definitions of information are needed to begin understanding the vast, nebulous, set of processes undertaken by the mind, the majority of which occur below the threshold of our conscious awareness. Such a computational approach is provided by information theory. It was first used to describe signals being transmitted from a source to a receiver across a noisy channel with limited capacity (Shannon, 1948). Its application to cognitive control is clear when we consider that goal-relevant information (signal) must be prioritized and transferred within the context of goal-irrelevant information (noise) in a limited capacity channel to the conscious mind. Therefore, cognitive control can be considered to be a limited capacity integrative interface between information input and the mind that dynamically facilitates information processing by prioritizing the transfer of relevant information and suppressing the transfer of irrelevant information to further processing stages (Fan, 2014).

We recently proposed an information theory-based account of cognitive control. Uncertainty can be quantified in terms of *information entropy*, which is tied to the probability of the occurrence of events (Shannon, 1948). This allows us to computationally consider the minimum amount of information that must be processed to make a judgment about the nature of an event. In computing and digital communication, a "bit" is the basic unit of information. Information contained within various types or sequences of events can be estimated in unit bits that provides a more concrete understanding of computational requirements of various task. How quickly we are able to make these judgments relies on the rate of information transfer or the average amount of information transmitted per unit time, in bits per second (bps), is related to the capacity of the channel.

There are two main concepts in information theory: surprise and entropy. *Surprise* refers to information contained in the occurrence of a certain type of event, and is defined as: $I(x_i) = -\log_2 p(x_i)$, where $p(x_i)$ is the probability of the occurrence of event x_i. The base 2 logarithm transformation produces information quantified in bits. Low probability events are associated with high surprise values. For example, in a sequence of events that require a high frequency of "right" responses (e.g., 87.5% right, 12.5% left), a stimulus requiring a "left" response would have a higher surprise value (3 bits) than the "right" response stimulus (0.19 bits). *Entropy* is the information contained in a sequence of events (as opposed to a specific event type), and is defined as: $H(X) = E(I(X)) = -\sum_{i=1}^{n} p(x_i) \log_2 p(x_i)$. It therefore reflects the weighted average of surprise across all types of events in a sequence. Low entropy values are associated with predictable sequences. For example, in the example mentioned above, the overall entropy for this sequence is 0.54 bits, with a high probability of a "right" response event. Maximum entropy occurs when all event types are equally probable. In the example above, entropy would be the highest (1 bit) when "left" and "right" response events occur with equal frequency and are therefore less predictable.

As previously mentioned, the information described above is transmitted through a noisy channel with limited capacity. Cognitive control, too, is known to be a limited-capacity psychological construct (Posner & Snyder, 1975). In instances where the required information transfer rate exceeds the capacity of the channel, there should be diminished channel efficiency and an increase in error, associated with performance costs (Fan, 2014). A recent study challenged perceptual decision-making under time constraints and estimated the average capacity of the cognitive control system as $\sim 3-4$ bps (Wu, Dufford, Mackie, Egan, & Fan, 2016). This capacity is far lower than what has been previously described for sensory systems, reading (Pierce & Karlin, 1957), and motor control (Fitts, 1954). This relatively restricted capacity may be due to neural constraints related to a relatively high biological cost of continued representation of information within the conscious mind (Cowan, 2001; Wu, Dufford, Egan, et al., in press).

Revisiting the tasks typically used to investigate cognitive control within this framework, behavioral manipulations can be reconceptualized in terms of uncertainty in information theory. For example, the "switch cost" typically associated with set-shift tasks reflects the cost of a channel switch or increased information associated with an infrequent event (switch trials may be less frequent than "stay" trials), with associated increased entropy typically ranging from 1 to 3 bits (Cooper, Garrett, Rennie, & Karayanidis, 2015; Fan, 2014). Similarly, undetermined response and choice selection reflect increased uncertainty as the number of possible responses increases. In a go/no-go task, the no-go trials (20%) are far less frequent than go trials (80%) and carry a relatively high surprise value (~ 2.3 bits for no-go compared to ~ 0.3 bits for go). In an oddball task, the low-frequency oddball event, by definition, has a high surprise value. Another example is the Wisconsin Card Sorting Test (Berg, 1948), which is commonly applied to the study of cognitive control and flexibility, and involves sorting cards according to rules the participant must infer based on the feedback from the examiner. The initial entropy of this task is high because participants must deal with uncertainty related to both the number of piles and the number of dimensions on which the cards may be sorted. Once the dimension is inferred, entropy is reduced but increases again when a rule change occurs. Dealing with these types of dynamic changes in uncertainty requires cognitive control to monitor and flexibly adjust performance in the service of uncertainty reduction (Berg, 1948; Miyake et al., 2000; Van Eylen et al., 2011). Previous studies have successfully applied this quantification to the study of cognitive control in healthy individuals and patient populations (Barcelo & Knight, 2007; Cooper et al., 2015; Cooper, Darriba, Karayanidis, & Barceló, 2016; Fan et al., 2014; Fan, Guise, Liu, & Wang, 2008; Just, Keller, Malave, Kana, & Varma, 2012; Mackie et al., 2013).

THE COGNITIVE CONTROL NETWORK

Decades of research have demonstrated the necessity of the frontal lobes in performing these typical executive function tasks. For example, the Tower of London (Shallice, 1982), Trail Making Test (Reitan, 1958), WCST (Berg, 1948),

Stroop Test (Stroop, 1935), and others have been shown to be sensitive to frontal lobe deficits. However, the involvement of the frontal lobes has not always been so clear. While many studies have been able to demonstrate that frontal lesions can impair performance on executive control tasks, these tests have also been sensitive to lesions in other brain regions (Anderson, Damasio, Jones, & Tranel, 1991; Dunbar & Sussman, 1995; Rossi, Pessoa, Desimone, & Ungerleider, 2009). Within a more contemporary view of the neural under-pinnings of the cognitive control, which is the core of the executive functions, we now understand that cognitive control does not arise solely from frontal lobe function but rather from an extended network of regions that involve frontoparietal and subcortical regions (Fan, 2014; Niendam et al., 2012).

There is an existing body of evidence for a large-scale cognitive control network (CCN) that is involved in cognitively demanding tasks that require uncertainty reduction and response generation (Corbetta & Shulman, 2002; Hopfinger, Buonocore, & Mangun, 2000; Minzenberg, Laird, Thelen, Carter, & Glahn, 2009; Niendam et al., 2012). In neuroimaging studies of cognitive control, a positive linear relationship has been observed between uncertainty quantified as entropy and activation in frontal regions such as the ACC, anterior insula (AI), frontal eye fields (FEF), and dlPFC, parietal regions including areas near/along the intraparietal sulcus (IPS), and subcortical regions such as thalamus, basal ganglia, and cerebellum (Fan, 2014; Heyder, Suchan, & Daum, 2004; Strange, Duggins, Penny, Dolan, & Friston, 2005; Thakkar, van den Heiligenberg, Kahn, & Neggers, 2014; Xuan et al., 2016). These regions comprise parts of the frontoparietal (Corbetta & Shulman, 1998; Fan, 2014) and cingulo-opercular (Dosenbach et al., 2007; Dosenbach et al. 2008) networks that have been implicated in the implemen-tation of cognitive control.

In previous studies of cognitive control, there has been much attention focused on the ACC, the anterior portion of the cingulate gyrus, which is highly interconnected with other neocortical, limbic, and subcortical regions. Activation of the ACC has been previously associated with the presence of conflict, but we previously demonstrated that the ACC may also be reliably activated under uncertainty without the presence of conflict, suggesting a broader role for this region in cognitive control (Fan et al., 2014). Consistent with our information theory account of cognitive control, ACC activation is often associated with tasks requiring low-frequency (i.e., high surprise) responses (Braver, 2001). It is also activated to a greater degree during ran-dom sequences (i.e., high entropy) than fixed sequences (Koechlin, Corrado, Pietrini, & Grafman, 2000) and by stimulus novelty (Berns, Cohen, & Mintun, 1997). Increased activation of the CCN, particularly of ACC and AI, is associated with cognitive control under conditions of increased uncertainty, including channel switching and selection, and a high rate of information transmission (Fan, 2014). Furthermore, in a recent multilevel mediation analysis study, the CCN mediated the relationship between the manipulation of uncertainty and increased behavioral response times (Hick's law) (Wu, Dufford, Egan, et al., in press).

Within each body of literature investigating neural underpinnings of neurotypical cognitive control and deficits in psychiatric disorders, there is great variability in the experimental questions being addressed and the psychometric tools used to examine them, making it difficult to draw conclusions across individual studies. Metaanalysis of neuroimaging studies allows us to overcome this problem of inconsistency by examining consistent patterns of activation across studies. Here, we describe the results of metaanalyses using the activation likelihood estimate (ALE) method (Turkeltaub, Eden, Jones, & Zeffiro, 2002) of neuroimaging studies of cognitive control in both healthy and neuropsychiatric populations (described in the Appendix). The ALE technique models each reported significant focus of activation within a study as the center of a Gaussian probability distribution, and whole-brain statistical maps can be generated for the likelihood of activation for each voxel across the entire set of studies in a metaanalysis with an estimated probability (ALE statistic) of the significance of these results.

First, to confirm the involvement of distant CCN regions in tasks requiring cognitive control, we conducted ALE metaanalysis of 59 patient studies that reported contrasts for healthy controls (HC) only with an uncertainty manipulation relative to a control condition (see Appendix A for the complete list and analysis parameters). The analysis included 1183 foci from 101 experiments and a total of 1617 participants. Results (Fig. 11.1 and Table 11.1) confirm the involvement of widespread regions of cortex including frontal regions, such as ACC, AI, dlPFC, and FEF; posterior parietal and temporoparietal regions; and, subcortically, thalamus and basal ganglia as the CCN in cognitive control. In the subsequent sections, we explore deficits in terms of activation in specific regions of the CCN in three neuropsychiatric populations relative to HC.

COGNITIVE CONTROL NETWORK DEFICITS IN PATIENT POPULATIONS

The brain needs to efficiently process information for optimal behavioral responses. Contexts that require the implementation of cognitive control are typically high-demand, high-uncertainty situations, in which it is necessary to process goal-oriented information, stay on task, and/or reorient attention to other environmentally salient stimuli if necessary (Fan, 2014; Mackie et al., 2013; Mushtaq et al., 2011). Whereas cognitive control is typically efficiently deployed in healthy, typically developing (TD) individuals, it can often be disrupted in neurodevelopmental and psychiatric populations, resulting in both cognitive and behavioral impairment (Burden et al., 2009; Mackie & Fan, 2016; Minshew & Goldstein, 1998; Poljac & Bekkering, 2012; Rowe, Lavender, & Turk, 2006; Shapiro, Wong, & Simon, 2013;

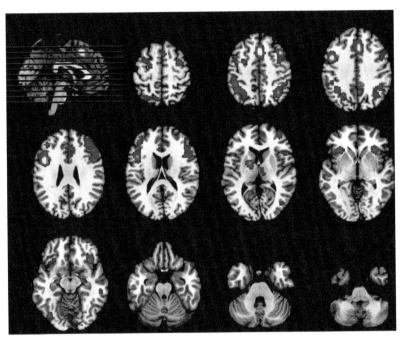

FIGURE 11.1   Brain regions that constitute the CCN; results of ALE metaanalysis from healthy controls only. *ALE*, activation likelihood estimate; *CCN*, cognitive control network.

Vaidya et al., 2005). It is clear that in some specific psychiatric populations, behavioral responses are less than optimal, and given that the CCN mediates the relationship between uncertainty and response generation (Wu, Dufford, Egan, et al., in press), we can consider abnormality of the CCN as a likely candidate for cognitive and behavioral abnormalities in these populations.

A previous metaanalysis of structural neuroimaging studies across a variety of psychiatric disorders revealed reduced gray matter volume in dorsal ACC and AI bilaterally, and that these volumetric differences were associated with executive function deficits (Goodkind et al., 2015), shedding light on the common finding of executive dysfunction in individuals with psychiatric disorders. Indeed, many studies investigating cognitive control deficits in patient populations have reported either hypo- or hyperactivation of these core structures relative to HC. We examine patterns of abnormal response within the CCN across several major neuropsychiatric disorders, as reported in the subsequent sections.

AUTISM SPECTRUM DISORDER

Autism spectrum disorder (ASD) is a neurodevelopmental disorder characterized by impairments in social and communicative skills, accompanied by

TABLE 11.1 Results of ALE Metaanalysis of Neuroimaging Studies of Cognitive Control in Healthy Controls

	L/R	BA	MNI x	MNI y	MNI z	ALE ($\times 10^{-2}$)	Volume (mm³)
Middle frontal gyrus	R	9	40	16	48	5.3	21,848
Inferior frontal gyrus pars triangularis	R	45	48	28	24	5.0	
Inferior frontal gyrus pars opercularis	R	44	52	14	28	4.0	
Inferior frontal gyrus	R	9	50	10	30	3.9	
Middle frontal gyrus	R	46	40	52	8	3.5	
Middle frontal gyrus	R	6	34	−2	56	3.4	
Precentral gyrus	R	6	48	4	44	2.4	
Middle frontal gyrus	R	8	30	18	50	1.9	
Precentral gyrus	L	6	−44	6	34	7.4	18,848
Inferior frontal gyrus	L	9	−46	12	22	5.7	
Superior frontal gyrus	L	6	−24	−4	54	3.6	
Middle frontal gyrus	L	9	−38	38	28	3.1	
Middle frontal gyrus	L	46	−40	44	18	2.8	
Inferior parietal lobule	L	40	−38	−52	42	5.1	13,304
Precuneus	L	7	−28	−66	42	3.0	
Superior parietal lobule	L	7	−28	−64	54	2.9	
Supramarginal gyrus	L	40	−56	−44	36	2.4	

(Continued)

TABLE 11.1 (Continued)

	L/R	BA	MNI x	y	z	ALE ($\times 10^{-2}$)	Volume (mm³)
Supplementary motor area	L	8	2	18	48	7.6	12,664
Anterior cingulate gyrus	L	24	−6	28	22	2.3	
Precuneus	R	19	34	−60	44	5.1	7616
Inferior parietal lobule	R	40	44	−46	42	3.8	
Supramarginal gyrus	R	40	52	−36	44	2.4	
Insula	L	13	−32	24	−4	3.7	4864
Superior temporal gyrus	L	38	−52	14	−16	2.8	
Insula	R	13	38	26	−12	4.5	4320
Globus pallidus	L	−	−16	0	6	4.6	3032
Fusiform gyrus	L	19	−40	−76	−12	3.1	1088
Middle occipital gyrus	R	19	44	−74	4	2.8	912
Middle frontal gyrus	R	10	38	58	−8	2.6	840
Middle temporal gyrus	R	21	56	−32	−12	2.8	808
Thalamus (medial dorsal nucleus)	R	−	8	−18	8	2.1	616
Superior temporal pole	R	38	54	22	−20	2.9	584
Parahippocampal gyrus	L	34	−22	−2	−16	2.2	360

Note: A threshold of $P < 0.005$ with minimum cluster size of 250 mm³ was applied. Structures listed below those with a volume listed were within the same cluster with different local maxima. ALE, activation likelihood estimate; BA, Brodmann area; MNI, Montreal Neurological Institute.

highly restricted interests and/or stereotyped, repetitive behaviors (Wang et al., 2008). It has long been observed that individuals with ASD may resemble "frontal lobe" patients in their presentation (Damasio & Maurer, 1978), leading to the development of the executive dysfunction theory of autism (Hughes, Russell, & Robbins, 1994; Ozonoff, Pennington, & Rogers, 1991). Specifically, this has been framed in terms of a deficit in cognitive flexibility, resulting in difficulty with adaptively responding to dynamic environments (Geurts, Corbett, & Solomon, 2009; Kleinhans, Akshoomoff, & Delis, 2005; Memari et al., 2013; Van Eylen et al., 2011). However, individuals with ASD have also been shown to have a reduced efficiency and capacity for cognitive control under time constraints (Mackie & Fan, 2016) and deficits that may be accounted for by abnormal recruitment of CCN hubs and/ or abnormal patterns of functional connectivity among them. Attentional deficits and reduced ACC activation during conflict processing in ASD have been demonstrated (Fan, 2013; Fan, Bernardi, Van Dam, et al., 2012).

However, there is great inconsistency in the ASD literature regarding the presence/nature of cognitive control deficits in this population and the underlying neural mechanisms (Mackie & Fan, 2016). Here we conducted meta analyses of 24 neuroimaging studies (see the list in the Appendix) investigating cognitive control in ASD, including those with social/emotional stimuli. The analysis of activations that were greater in TD controls relative to patients with ASD (TD > ASD) included 24 contrasts with 186 foci and 636 participants. The analysis of activations that were greater in ASD relative to TD controls (ASD > TD) included 12 contrasts with 60 foci and 280 participants. See Fig. 11.2 and Table 11.2 for the results.

The TD > ASD comparison revealed a pattern of ASD hypoactivation of anterior regions, such as ACC, AI, supplementary motor area (SMA), and left dlPFC, and posterior regions of IPS, precuneus, superior temporal gyrus (STG), extrastriate areas, and cerebellum. Hypoactivation in ACC and AI is consistent with previous findings (Fan, Bernardi, Van Dam, et al., 2012) and may underlie previously demonstrated difficulties with uncertainty processing (Mackie & Fan, 2016). Furthermore, reduced activation was observed in a number of regions implicated in cognitive flexibility. For example, dlPFC has often been attributed this function, possibly by overcoming ongoing inhibition to facilitate a set-switch (Dreher & Berman, 2002). IPS and angular gyrus are known to be involved in disengaging and moving attentional focus (Braver, Reynolds, & Donaldson, 2003; Corbetta, Kincade, Ollinger, McAvoy, & Shulman, 2000; Seghier, 2013), cognitive behavioral integration (Gottlieb, 2007), and response under uncertainty (Nee, Wager, & Jonides, 2007; Seghier, 2013; Wager et al., 2005). Together, inferior parietal and temporo-parietal regions (consisting of angular and supramarginal gyri) have been implicated in bottom-up reflexive orienting to task-relevant information (Ciaramelli, Grady, & Moscovitch, 2008; Seghier, 2013; Wu et al., 2015), which is important for cognitive flexibility under dynamic conditions. Furthermore, functional connectivity of precuneus with superior frontal gyrus has also been shown to be involved in cognitive set-shifting (Nagahama et al., 1999). Interestingly, some of these regions (e.g., supramarginal gyrus) are also involved in social cognition (Deschamps, Baum, & Gracco, 2014;

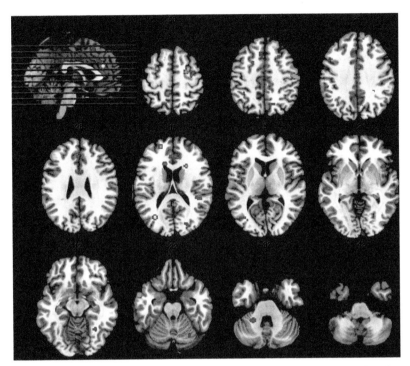

FIGURE 11.2 ALE metaanalysis results showing regions that are likely to be activated to a greater degree in controls relative to participants with ASD (warm colors) and likely to be activated to a greater degree in ASD compared to controls (cool colors). *ALE*, activation likelihood estimate; *ASD*, autism spectrum disorder.

Koster-Hale & Saxe, 2013; Salmon et al., 1996), which is notably impaired in ASD. Observed ASD hypoactivation in fusiform gyrus may reflect the inclusion of studies with facial stimuli to which participants with ASD show an atypical neural response (Pierce, 2001). Overall, these results confirm a pattern of reduced activation in a wide range of CCN regions, most notably ACC, AI, IPS, and dlPFC, relative to neurotypical controls under conditions of uncertainty (Fan, Bernardi, Dam, et al., 2012; Kana, Keller, Minshew, & Just, 2007; Koshino et al., 2005; Shafritz, Dichter, Baranek, & Belger, 2008).

The ASD > TD comparison revealed a pattern of ASD hyperactivation in right primary motor and somatosensory areas, FEF bilaterally, and caudate nucleus. The most striking pattern was hyperactivation (or most likely less deactivation) of areas associated with the resting state default mode network (DMN; including PCC, mPFC, and temporal pole) under conditions requiring cognitive control. The DMN and CCN are known to have an antagonistic relationship, such that increases in CCN activation are typically associated with deactivation of the DMN, and this relationship is associated with efficiency of behavioral performance (Di & Biswal, 2014). This atypical pattern of DMN

TABLE 11.2 Results of ALE Metaanalysis of Neuroimaging Studies of Cognitive Control in ASD Compared to TD Controls

	L/R	BA	MNI x	MNI y	MNI z	ALE $(\times 10^{-2})$	Volume (mm^3)
TD > ASD							
Anterior cingulate gyrus	L	32	−2	36	24	2.1	1824
Anterior cingulate gyrus	R	24	4	34	14	1.0	
Angular gyrus	L	39	−32	−68	16	2.4	888
Middle occipital gyrus	L	37	−46	−70	6	1.0	
Superior frontal gyrus	L	46	−22	52	22	2.3	888
Supplementary motor area	L	8	−6	24	46	1.2	816
Anterior cingulate gyrus	R	24	2	0	36	1.4	720
Cerebellum	L	−	−24	−44	−30	1.6	712
Superior temporal gyrus	R	41	48	−38	14	1.3	656
Fusiform gyrus	L	37	−44	−56	−16	1.3	504
Middle frontal gyrus	L	6	−28	0	60	1.7	488
Precuneus	R	7	12	−64	44	1.1	480
Inferior parietal lobule	L	40	−52	−34	42	1.7	464
Anterior cingulate gyrus	L	32	−14	22	20	1.5	424
Lingual gyrus	L	18	−24	−86	−6	1.5	400
Fusiform gyrus	R	37	32	−58	−14	1.3	384
Middle frontal gyrus	L	9	−48	12	36	1.4	376
Insula	L	13	−44	−10	10	1.3	344
Cerebellum	R	−	28	−66	−20	1.1	336
Precuneus	L	7	−14	−58	56	1.2	320

(Continued)

TABLE 11.2 (Continued)

	L/R	BA	MNI x	y	z	ALE ($\times 10^{-2}$)	Volume (mm³)
Insula	R	13	42	16	−2	1.1	304
Supramarginal gyrus	R	40	28	−42	44	1.4	216
Supplementary motor area	R	8	24	18	48	1.1	280
Middle occipital gyrus	R	17	26	−82	16	1.1	272
ASD > TD							
Precentral gyrus	R	3	52	−14	48	1.1	1064
Postcentral gyrus	R	2	58	−18	50	1.1	
Superior frontal gyrus	R	6	22	−6	58	1.0	1056
Medial frontal gyrus	R	8	10	52	36	1.5	760
Middle temporal gyrus	L	21	−58	2	−24	1.4	728
Superior frontal gyrus	L	6	−18	8	52	1.2	664
Posterior cingulate gyrus	L	29	2	−48	16	1.1	624
Caudate nucleus	R	−	23	19	19	1.0	256

Note: A threshold of $P < 0.005$ with minimum cluster size of 250 mm³ was applied. Structures listed below those with a volume listed were within the same cluster with different local maxima. *ASD*, autism spectrum disorder; *BA*, Brodmann area; *MNI*, Montreal Neurological Institute; *TD*, typically developing controls.

regions under conditions requiring cognitive control supports previous findings that a "failure to deactivate" the DMN in individuals with ASD was associated with inefficient behavioral performance and greater severity of ASD symptoms (Kennedy, Redcay, & Courchesne, 2006; Spencer et al., 2012). The finding of hyperactivation of primary motor and somatosensory regions is consistent with previously reported atypical recruitment of low-level brain regions when cognitive control is required (Lee et al., 2007; Ring et al., 1999). Hyperactivation of the FEF, a region typically associated with attentional spatial and feature selection (Desimone & Duncan, 1995; Rossi et al., 2009) together with under-utilization of areas involved in attentional shifts mentioned earlier, may account for attentional hyperfocus previously noted in this population (Belmonte & Yurgelun-Todd, 2003; Brown & Bebko, 2012; Townsend, Harris, & Courchesne, 1996; Wainwright & Bryson, 1996).

Taken together, these results confirm previously described patterns of underactivation in core CCN regions and less deactivation in DMN regions under conditions of uncertainty in ASD (Spencer et al., 2012). These patterns of activation/deactivation, together with atypical patterns of functional connectivity (Just et al., 2012; Khan et al., 2013), may underlie observed deficits in the efficiency and capacity of information processing in this population (Mackie & Fan, 2016). Within the information theory framework, the integrity and efficiency of both long- and short-range connections is directly related to the capacity or "bandwidth" available for information transfer under time constraints (Fan, 2014; Just et al., 2012; Mackie & Fan, 2016; Wu, Dufford, Mackie, et al., 2016). These functional brain differences have been shown to be related to both behavioral task performance and clinical symptom severity (Fan, Bernardi, Van Dam, et al., 2012). For example, there is a negative relationship between ACC activation and scores on the restricted interests/repetitive behavior subscale of the Autism Diagnostic Interview (Shafritz et al., 2008). Furthermore, abnormal connectivity among core CCN regions is associated with higher behavioral error rates (Solomon et al., 2013), higher social/communication (Schipul & Just, 2016), and restricted interest/repetitive behavior symptom report (Zhou, Shi, Cui, Wang, & Luo, 2016) and therefore likely contributes to the clinical presentation of the disorder.

SCHIZOPHRENIA

Schizophrenia (SZ) is a debilitating psychiatric condition that is characterized by the presence of delusions, hallucinations, and/or disorganized thought/behavior within the context of significant functional impairment (Association, 2013). Impairments in cognitive control and executive functions have been described in terms of the disorganized thought and behavior central to SZ, within the context of significant attentional impairment (Minzenberg et al., 2009; Nuechterlein et al., 2015; Spagna et al., 2015). Furthermore, functional "hypofrontality" and reduced frontal lobe gray matter volume have previously been described (Andreasen et al., 1997; Carter et al., 1998; Ingvar & Franzén, 1974; Weinberger, Berman, & Frith, 1996). However, this pattern of hypofrontality has not been consistently observed (Curtis et al., 1999; Walter et al., 2003), and the CCN correlates of impaired cognitive control remain unclear.

Here, we report the results of an ALE metaanalysis of 46 neuroimaging studies (see Appendix) investigating cognitive control in SZ (Fig. 11.3 and

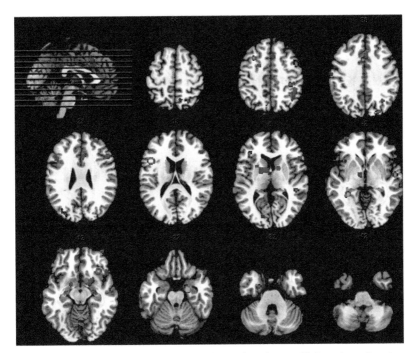

FIGURE 11.3   ALE metaanalysis results showing regions that are likely to be activated to a greater degree in controls relative to participants with schizophrenia (warm colors) and likely to be activated to a greater degree in schizophrenia relative to controls (cool colors). *ALE*, activation likelihood estimate.

Table 11.3). The analysis of activations that were greater for HC relative to individuals with SZ (HC > SZ) included 46 experiments, 292 foci, and 845 participants. The analysis of activations that were greater in SZ relative to HC (SZ>HC) included 30 experiments, 163 foci, and 476 participants.

The HC>SZ comparison revealed hypoactivation in frontal regions, such as right ACC/SMA and AI, and dlPFC and orbitofrontal regions bilaterally. Posterior regions included superior temporal pole, right IPS, and superior parietal lobule (SPL) bilaterally, right angular gyrus and precuneus. Subcortically, basal ganglia and thalamus hypoactivation were also identified. These findings confirm previously described underrecruitment of high-level frontal regions under conditions of uncertainty in SZ (Minzenberg et al., 2009; Perlstein, Dixit, Carter, Noll, & Cohen, 2003). Furthermore, hypoactivation in basal ganglia and thalamus highlights an underuse of core subcortical CCN regions that form parts of a fronto-striatal-thalamic-cortical loop and demonstrates functional abnormalities affecting each level of this circuit that is known to be involved in cognitive control (Sui et al., 2015; van Schouwenburg, Aarts, & Cools, 2010).

TABLE 11.3 Results of ALE Metaanalysis of Neuroimaging Studies of SZ Compared to HC Using Tasks With an Uncertainty Manipulation

	L/R	BA	MNI			ALE $(\times 10^{-2})$	Volume (mm^3)
			x	y	z		
HC > SZ							
Globus pallidus	L	—	−18	0	4	2.1	3712
Caudate nucleus	L	—	−8	2	6	1.8	
Thalamus	L	—	−10	−8	−2	1.4	
Inferior frontal gyrus pars opercularis	L	44	−46	14	18	3.1	2584
Anterior cingulate gyrus	R	24	4	22	32	2.2	2528
Supplementary motor area	R	8	4	18	48	1.5	
Superior temporal pole	R	38	54	22	−20	1.6	2224
Inferior frontal gyrus	R	47	50	24	−10	1.3	
Insula	R	13	48	18	−8	1.2	
Inferior parietal lobule	R	40	44	−44	46	1.7	1872
Inferior parietal lobule	R	39	40	−60	48	1.0	
Middle frontal gyrus	R	9	46	30	22	1.5	1720
Middle frontal gyrus	L	47	−36	62	−10	2.0	1704
Globus pallidus	R	—	18	6	−10	1.6	1624
Inferior frontal gyrus (orbitofrontal)	R	47	34	26	−14	2.2	1224
Superior parietal lobule	L	7	−28	−68	52	1.5	824
Inferior frontal gyrus pars triangularis	R	45	54	24	8	1.5	736

(Continued)

TABLE 11.3 (Continued)

	L/R	BA	MNI x	y	z	ALE ($\times 10^{-2}$)	Volume (mm^3)
Precuneus	L	7	−10	−72	54	1.8	648
Superior temporal pole	L	38	−52	16	−10	1.1	576
Inferior frontal gyrus pars opercularis	L/R	44	−58	14	12	1.0	
Thalamus (medial dorsal nucleus)	L	−	0	−16	6	1.3	480
Caudate nucleus	R	−	14	4	6	1.4	464
Gyrus rectus	L	11	−2	52	−26	1.6	424
Globus pallidus	L	−	−18	2	−14	1.5	424
Angular gyrus	R	39	34	−60	36	1.4	392
Middle frontal gyrus	R	46	26	50	30	1.3	304
Superior parietal lobule	R	7	22	−64	60	1.0	280
SZ > HC							
Parahippocampal gyrus - (amygdala)	R	−	22	−8	−20	2.1	1336
Precentral gyrus	R	6	48	4	52	1.6	1304
Superior temporal gyrus	R	22	56	−8	6	1.5	1256
Precuneus	R	7	8	−60	54	1.4	1040
Postcentral gyrus	R	3	36	−32	52	1.4	1008
Hippocampus	L	−	−32	−42	0	1.7	840
Superior temporal gyrus	R	41	48	−34	4	1.3	832
Superior occipital gyrus	L	19	−36	−74	30	1.0	704
Middle occipital gyrus	L	19	−28	−84	26	1.0	

(Continued)

TABLE 11.3 (Continued)

	L/R	BA	MNI x	MNI y	MNI z	ALE ($\times 10^{-2}$)	Volume (mm³)
Superior occipital gyrus	R	19	24	−82	36	1.2	624
Anterior cingulate gyrus	L	24	−2	14	36	1.4	624
Lingual gyrus	L	18	−16	−82	4	1.2	472
Middle frontal gyrus	L	6	−30	16	50	1.3	464
Precentral gyrus	L	3	−62	−12	42	1.2	416
Inferior frontal gyrus pars triangularis	L	45	−38	34	10	1.0	400
Insula	L	13	−34	18	−8	1.0	296
Parahippocampal gyrus	L	35	−24	−4	−32	1.0	288

Note: A threshold of $P < 0.005$ with minimum cluster size of 250 mm³ was applied. Structures listed below those with a volume listed were within the same cluster with different local maxima. *ALE,* activation likelihood estimate; *BA,* Brodmann area; *HC,* healthy controls; *MNI,* Montreal Neurological Institute; *SZ,* schizophrenia.

The SZ > HC analysis revealed hyperactivation of primary motor and somatosensory regions, precuneus, and temporal and occipital regions. Amygdala and parahippocampal regions were notably hyperactivated in SZ. There was a cluster of ACC activation in this analysis, which was more posterior than that observed in the HC > SZ analysis. A similar observation in a previous metaanalysis was localized to the ventrolateral prefrontal cortex (vlPFC) (Minzenberg et al., 2009). Similar to the pattern described above in ASD, within in the context of underactivation of high-level control regions, there was increased reliance on lower level regions under uncertainty (Fassbender, Scangos, Lesh, & Carter, 2014; Kim et al., 2003; Kühn & Gallinat, 2013; Quintana et al., 2003). The observed hyperactivation or failure to deactivate the STG has been previously proposed as a finding specific to SZ: whereas there is usually an inverse relationship between PFC and STG under increasing cognitive load conditions, this pattern is not seen in SZ (Meyer-Lindenberg et al., 2001; Walter, Vasic, Hose, Spitzer, & Wolf, 2007). However, the finding that ACC was not reliably underactivated across studies in the patient group leaves opens the question of the functional abnormalities of this structure in SZ. Furthermore, reduced recruitment of CCN regions may be associated with reduced regulation of structures, such as the amygdala (Banich et al., 2009; Cole, Repovš, & Anticevic, 2014), which was notably hyperactive in the patient group.

Taken together, these results partially support the hypofrontality previously described, as it relates to dorsal and lateral regions of PFC. However, the role of the ACC is less clear. In contesting the hypofrontality theory of SZ, others have provided evidence of a U-shaped curve pattern of frontal region (typically dlPFC) recruitment such that hypofrontality might be seen at levels of low cognitive load and hyperfrontality when the capacity of cognitive control is exceeded, reflecting greater effort of these regions to produce a level of behavioral performance comparable to HC (Callicott et al., 2003; Van Snellenberg et al., 2016; Walter, Vasic, et al., 2007). This inefficiency in information processing is likely related to the demonstrated abnormal recruitment of key CCN regions.

DEPRESSION

Major depressive disorder (MDD) is a mood disorder characterized by multiple episodes of a combination of vegetative, affective, somatic, and/or cognitive symptoms (Association, 2013). It has been suggested that MDD is associated with a failure to effectively regulate negative thought and affect via top-down control mechanisms (Johnstone, van Reekum, Urry, Kalin, & Davidson, 2007). The role of cognitive control in emotional regulation has been consistently demonstrated (Banich et al., 2009; Green & Malhi, 2006; Marinier Iii, Laird, & Lewis, 2009; Ochsner & Gross, 2005; Ochsner, Silvers, & Buhle, 2012; Ray & Zald, 2012; Taylor & Liberzon, 2007). Executive dysfunction has also been reported and is considered a primary symptom of the disorder as included in the diagnostic criteria, i.e., difficulty with concentration and/or making decisions (Rogers et al., 2004; Walter, Wolf, Spitzer, & Vasic, 2007; Wang et al., 2008). Furthermore, MDD is associated with difficulty disengaging attention from negative thoughts and feelings. It is well established that negative affect interacts with cognitive processes (Gray, 2001; Gray, Braver, & Raichle, 2001), and it has been suggested that MDD is associated with a failure to efficiently regulate negative thoughts and affect. However, the role of the CCN in this disorder remains unclear. Because it is primarily a mood disorder, studies of cognitive control often include emotional stimuli that examine the neural underpinnings with control over negatively valenced emotional information (Dichter, Felder, & Smoski, 2009; Fales et al., 2008; Grimm et al., 2009; Lawrence et al., 2004; Wang et al., 2008; Whalley, Rugg, Smith, Dolan, & Brewin, 2009).

Here, we report the results of ALE metaanalyses of 24 neuroimaging studies of cognitive control in MDD (see the list in Appendix) relative to HC. The analysis of activations that were greater in HC relative to individuals with MDD (HC > MDD) included 29 contrasts, 130 foci, and 510 participants. The analysis of activations that were greater in patients relative to HC (MDD > HC) included 33 contrasts, 130 foci, and 695 participants. Results are presented in Fig. 11.4 and Table 11.4.

The HC > MDD analysis revealed hypoactivation in MDD of frontal dlPFC regions bilaterally, and dorsal and rostral ACC. Posterior regions included fusiform gyrus bilaterally and superior and middle temporal regions. Subcortically, there was hypoactivation of caudate nucleus, pulvinar, and thalamus in MDD. The dorsal and rostral portions of ACC have been associated with cognitive and emotional control, respectively (Matthews, Paulus, Simmons, Nelesen, & Dimsdale, 2004). Frontostriatal involvement was again demonstrated with hypoactivation of the caudate nucleus, a basal ganglia region often associated with response under uncertainty (Grahn, Parkinson, & Owen, 2008). Furthermore, dlPFC hypoactivation in MDD was restricted to the left hemisphere, and left PFC activity has been associated with greater ability to regulate negative affect (Jackson, Cavanagh, & Scott, 2003).

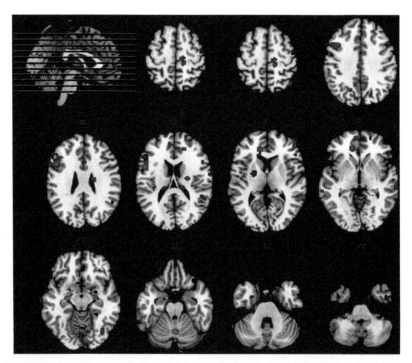

FIGURE 11.4 ALE metaanalysis results showing regions that likely to be activated to a greater degree in controls relative to participants with major depression (warm colors) and likely to be activated to a greater degree in MDD relative to controls (cool colors). *ALE*, activation likelihood estimate; *MDD*, major depressive disorder.

TABLE 11.4 Results of ALE Metaanalysis of Neuroimaging Studies of Major Depression Compared to Healthy Controls Using Tasks With an Uncertainty Manipulation

			MNI				
	L/R	BA	x	y	z	ALE $(\times 10^{-2})$	Volume (mm^3)
HC > DEP							
Inferior frontal gyrus	L	9	−50	14	32	2.2	6712
Inferior frontal gyrus	L	44	−52	8	20	2.0	
Middle frontal gyrus	L	9	−42	14	36	1.5	
Middle frontal gyrus	L	8	−44	14	40	1.5	
Anterior cingulate gyrus	L	32	−12	38	4	3.3	2088
Caudate nucleus	R	−	20	−12	24	1.1	1040
Middle frontal gyrus	R	46	50	54	8	1.3	1000
Inferior frontal gyrus	R	46	46	42	4	1.0	
Paracentral lobule	R	4	16	−28	60	1.0	904
Medial frontal gyrus	L	10	−6	56	0	1.1	728
Precuneus	L	7	−18	−64	40	1.0	696
Anterior cingulate gyrus	L	32	−6	46	22	1.0	616
Fusiform gyrus	R	19	38	−72	−12	1.0	544
Fusiform gyrus	L	19	−50	−60	−8	1.0	504
Middle temporal gyrus	R	22	66	−40	2	1.0	448
Superior temporal gyrus	R	42	50	−42	16	1.0	448
Inferior frontal gyrus pars triangularis	R	45	46	30	2	1.0	440

(Continued)

TABLE 11.4 (Continued)

	L/R	BA	MNI			ALE (×10⁻²)	Volume (mm³)
			x	y	z		
Anterior cingulate gyrus	L	24	2	18	26	1.0	440
Pulvinar	R	–	16	– 32	8	1.0	368
Thalamus	R	–	12	– 28	0	1.0	
Middle temporal gyrus	L	21	– 66	– 34	– 8	1.0	352
Cingulate gyrus	L	31	– 4	– 22	42	1.0	344
Inferior frontal gyrus	R	9	52	18	18	1.0	312
DEP > HC							
Inferior frontal gyrus pars triangularis	L	46	– 52	26	24	3.5	2872
Middle frontal gyrus	L	9	– 58	14	36	1.0	
Putamen	L	–	– 16	8	– 8	1.0	1120
Precentral gyrus	R	6	46	– 10	56	1.0	808
Subgenual cingulate gyrus	L	25	– 6	14	– 18	1.4	744
Globus pallidus	L	–	– 22	– 2	6	1.2	744
Parahippocampal gyrus	R	36	26	– 42	8	1.2	696
Inferior frontal gyrus (orbitofrontal)	R	47	36	26	– 20	1.3	640
Precentral gyrus	R	4	34	– 10	46	1.0	640
Superior parietal lobule	L	7	– 30	– 54	48	1.1	640
Putamen	R	7	26	– 2	– 8	1.2	608
Gyrus rectus	R	11	4	40	– 14	1.0	600
Caudate nucleus	R	–	12	8	2	1.0	536

(Continued)

TABLE 11.4 (Continued)

	L/R	BA	MNI			ALE $(\times 10^{-2})$	Volume (mm^3)
			x	y	z		
Middle temporal gyrus	R	20	44	−4	−40	1.0	528
Precentral gyrus	L	6	−56	4	20	1.0	496
Amygdala	L	–	−18	−6	−24	1.0	488
Angular gyrus	R	39	52	−52	28	1.0	416

Note: A threshold of $P < 0.01$ with minimum cluster size of 300 mm^3 was applied. Structures listed below those with a volume listed were within the same cluster with different local maxima. *ALE,* activation likelihood estimate; *BA,* Brodmann area; *DEP,* depression; *HC,* healthy controls; *MNI,* Montreal Neurological Institute.

The MDD > HC analysis revealed hyperactivation of an area of the left vlPFC, just anterior and inferior to the dlPFC cluster described earlier. This region is associated with response inhibition particularly on go/no-go tasks (Aron, Robbins, & Poldrack, 2004; Dillon & Pizzagalli, 2007). Posterior regions included right angular gyrus and left SPL. Amgydala was also notably hyperactivated in MDD. Hyperactivation of basal ganglia regions such as globus pallidus, caudate nucleus, and putamen was also observed. Increased activation of a region of orbitofrontal cortex located in the subgenual ACC region was also observed and has long been implicated in the neurobiology of MDD (Steele, Currie, Lawrie, & Reid, 2007)

Taken together, these findings suggest that in MDD, dlPFC and dorsal and rostral ACC regions are underactive, whereas vlPFC, limbic cingulate, and basal ganglia regions are overactive, possibly reflecting an increased need to regulate emotion to complete cognitive tasks (Fitzgerald & Laird, 2008; Kühn & Gallinat, 2013; Palmer, Crewther, & Carey, 2014). A prominent model of emotional control implicates dlPFC in emotion regulation (Ochsner & Gross, 2005), and a role for this region in failure to regulate negative affect in depression has been previously suggested (Grimm et al., 2008; Koenigs & Grafman, 2009). Early positron emission tomographic studies demonstrated hypometabolism in dlPFC in depression, and an imbalance in the interactions between rostral ACC, dlPFC, and vmPFC in depression constitutes a popular model of the disorder (Mayberg, 1997). Underrecruitment of ACC activation in depression for tasks of executive function has also been previously demonstrated (Harvey et al., 2005).

These differences in functional anatomy are also associated with behavioral performance and clinical symptom severity. For example, increased left dlPFC activation in depression was associated with behavioral performance that was comparable to controls, and increased activation in the subgenual region of the ACC was positively correlated with depressive symptoms (Walter, Wolf, et al., 2007). Other studies have demonstrated that right dlPFC signal change was correlated with scores on the Beck Depression Inventory (Grimm et al., 2008), and slow behavioral performance was associated with hypoactivity in key CCN regions, in addition to increased deactivation in CCN regions for emotional control (Wang et al., 2008). Difference in dlPFC recruitment for cognitive control over emotional stimuli has also been shown to vary as a function of severity of depressive symptoms (Beevers, Clasen, Stice, & Schnyer, 2010).

COMMON DEFICITS IN THE COGNITIVE CONTROL NETWORK DEFICITS ACROSS THE THREE DISORDERS

To identify common regions of hypo- and hyperactivation across the three disorders described earlier, we completed additional pooled metaanalyses of contrasts of activations that were greater for HC relative to all three patient groups combined (controls > patients) and for patients relative to controls (patients > controls). The controls > patients analysis included 100 contrasts, 610 foci, and 2030 participants. The patients > controls analysis included 76 contrasts, 355 foci, and 1490 participants. Results are shown in Fig. 11.5 and Table 11.5.

The controls > patients analysis revealed left dlPFC, dorsal and rostral ACC, SMA, right orbitofrontal cortex, and right insula. Posterior regions included right IPS, right temporal−parietal junction, left precuneus, and middle occipital regions. Subcortically, left caudate, globus pallidus, and thalamus were also identified. Overall, the results showed a similar pattern as described above in terms of hypofrontality in widespread CCN regions common across the three patient groups.

The patients > controls analysis revealed clusters in the amygdala, vmPFC, vlPFC, in addition to a generally similar pattern to that described above in terms of hyperactivation/failure to deactivate lower level and limbic regions. There was a small cluster in the middle cingulate region, posterior to the clusters identified that were more likely to be activated for controls.

Overall, the results confirm a common pattern across disorders of hypoactivation within key CCN regions (both cortical and subcortical) and hyperactivation of lower order and limbic brain regions for conditions requiring cognitive control. This appears to reflect either a failure to deactivate DMN regions (Backes et al., 2014; Kennedy et al., 2006) or a failure to efficiently regulate limbic and early sensory regions to prioritize information that reaches conscious awareness (Harvey et al., 2005). Although there is a clear pattern of commonality across disorders, there may also be disorder-specific patterns of atypical recruitment.

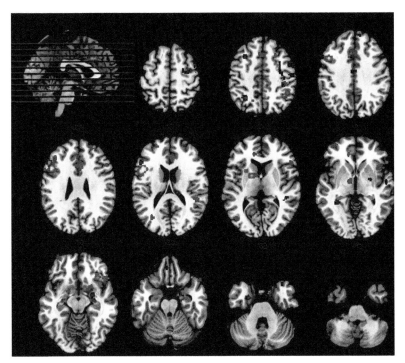

FIGURE 11.5 ALE metaanalysis results showing regions that are likely to be activated to a greater degree in controls relative to all patient groups combined (warm colors) and likely to be activated to a greater degree in patients relative to controls (cool colors). *ALE*, activation likelihood estimate.

DISCUSSION

The review and metaanalysis of neuroimaging studies of cognitive control in three neuropsychiatric disorders were aimed to address the question of the role of the CCN in regulating adaptive behavior under dynamic conditions of uncertainty. Across the three disorders of ASD, SZ, and MDD, atypical patterns of CCN region recruitment were identified, most notably in ACC, AI, dlPFC, basal ganglia, and thalamus. ACC, AI, and thalamus as parts of the cingulo-opercular network are believed to monitor baseline uncertainty (Fan, 2014) and indicate the need for the implementation of cognitive control (Dosenbach et al., 2006; Nelson et al., 2010). DlPFC, as part of a frontoparietal network allows for flexible adjustment of behavior, supposedly by overcoming inhibition of previously task-irrelevant cognitive and motor programs (Dreher & Berman, 2002). The basal ganglia, known for its involvement in the coordination of motor behavior, has also been implicated in the coordination of thought (Miller & Buschman, 2007), and dysfunction in this structure can lead to disorganized thinking as seen in SZ. Across

TABLE 11.5 Results of ALE Metaanalysis of Pooled Data From All Three Patient Groups (ASD, SZ, and DEP) Compared to Controls

	L/R	BA	MNI x	MNI y	MNI z	ALE ($\times 10^{-2}$)	Volume (mm³)
HC > All Patient Groups							
Inferior frontal gyrus	L	9	−46	14	20	3.8	6912
Middle frontal gyrus	L	9	−48	16	32	3.2	
Precentral gyrus	L	9	−44	12	36	2.9	
Anterior cingulate gyrus	R	24	4	20	32	3.0	4160
Supplementary motor area	R	8	0	20	52	1.9	
Anterior cingulate gyrus	L	32	−8	16	40	1.5	
Inferior frontal gyrus	R	47	34	26	−14	2.6	3392
Insula	R	13	44	18	−4	1.7	
Globus pallidus	L	−	−18	2	6	2.8	3016
Thalamus	L	−	−10	−6	−2	2.0	
Caudate nucleus	L	−	−8	2	6	1.9	
Putamen	L	−	−26	10	8	1.7	
Middle frontal gyrus	L	10	−36	62	−10	2.0	1392
Anterior cingulate gyrus	L	24	−2	36	24	2.2	1368
Inferior parietal lobule	R	40	46	−44	46	2.2	1360
Angular gyrus	L	30	−32	−68	16	2.5	1136
Middle occipital gyrus	L	37	−44	−72	8	1.9	
Putamen	R	−	24	12	−8	1.8	1000
Superior temporal gyrus	R	41	48	−38	16	2.1	776

(Continued)

TABLE 11.5 (Continued)

	L/R	BA	MNI x	y	z	ALE $(\times 10^{-2})$	Volume (mm^3)
Middle frontal gyrus	R	9	50	22	26	1.6	744
Thalamus (medial dorsal nucleus)	L	–	0	−18	8	1.8	584
Superior frontal gyrus	L	46	−22	52	22	2.3	440
Inferior frontal gyrus pars triangularis	R	45	54	24	8	1.8	424
Superior frontal gyrus	R	46	24	52	28	1.6	368
Precuneus	L	7	−8	−70	54	1.9	368
Superior frontal gyrus	R	6	24	18	48	1.7	304
All Patient Groups > HC							
Precentral gyrus	R	6	34	−8	54	1.6	2448
Postcentral gyrus	R	3	36	−32	52	1.5	
Superior frontal gyrus	R	6	24	−8	58	1.1	
Middle frontal gyrus	R	6	30	8	50	1.1	
Precentral gyrus	R	4	38	−18	46	1.1	
Amygdala	R	–	22	−8	20	2.4	2344
Putamen	R	–	26	−2	−8	1.8	
Parahippocampal gyrus	R	28	18	2	−22	1.1	
Inferior frontal gyrus pars triangularis	L	45	−52	26	24	3.7	2200
Superior parietal lobule	L	7	−30	−54	48	1.7	752
Superior temporal gyrus	R	22	56	−8	−6	1.5	704

(Continued)

TABLE 11.5 (Continued)

	L/R	BA	MNI x	y	z	ALE ($\times 10^{-2}$)	Volume (mm³)
Parahippocampal gyrus	L	28	−24	−2	32	1.6	608
Superior temporal gyrus	R	41	46	−36	6	1.4	600
Middle temporal gyrus	R	22	54	−36	4	1.1	
Medial frontal gyrus	L	11	−4	42	−20	1.5	576
Middle frontal gyrus	L	8	−30	18	50	1.6	568
Anterior cingulate gyrus	L	24	−2	14	36	1.4	480
Hippocampus	L	−	−32	−42	0	1.7	456
Inferior frontal gyrus	L	44	−38	18	0	1.0	344
Insula	L	13	−38	18	0	1.0	
Superior frontal gyrus	L	6	−26	−6	66	1.3	328
Cingulate gyrus	R	31	2	−10	40	1.3	320
Cingulate gyrus	L	31	−2	−10	38	1.2	
Superior temporal pole	R	38	36	20	−32	1.4	312
Superior frontal gyrus	R	9	10	52	36	1.5	312

Note: A threshold of $p < .005$ with minimum cluster size of 300 mm³ was applied. Structures listed below those with a volume listed were within the same cluster with different local maxima. *ALE,* activation likelihood estimate; *ASD,* autism spectrum disorder; *BA,* Brodmann area; *DEP,* depression; *HC,* healthy controls; *MNI,* Montreal Neurological Institute; *SZ,* schizophrenia.

disorders, it appears that there are deficits in the ability to efficiently implement cognitive control when needed, flexibly adapt to dynamic task responses, and coordinate among various thoughts and possible actions. The results also confirm previously observed patterns of fronto-striatal-thalamic-cortical loop dysfunction in individual disorders (Arnsten & Rubia, 2012; Grinband, Hirsch, & Ferrera, 2006; Köhler, Bär, & Wagner, 2016;

Saalmann, Pinsk, Wang, Li, & Kastner, 2012; Van Der Werf et al., 2003; van Schouwenburg et al., 2013) and demonstrate that in addition to seemingly ubiquitous ACC and AI involvement in neuropsychiatric disorders (Goodkind et al., 2015), there is also involvement at other levels of the CCN. However, the level at which disruptions to cognitive control occurs remain unclear. It may be that dysfunction of one or more of these regions is reflected in other areas further down the loop, or there may be abnormal functionality of some combination of these core regions individually. These hypotheses remain to be tested.

In addition to CCN hypoactivity, a pattern of hyperactivity/failure to deactivate lower level sensory, DMN, and limbic regions was also observed within each of the three disorders. Within ASD, the failure to deactivate PCC was prominent, in SZ, superior temporal and parahippocampal regions were indicated, and in depression, vmPFC, temporoparietal, and parahippocampal regions were atypically recruited. The vmPFC and superior temporal regions have been implicated in self-referential processing (Eilam-Stock et al., 2014; Koenigs & Grafman, 2009; Kühn & Gallinat, 2013). Atypical self-referential processing is well known in MDD in the form of rumination, while atypical self-referential processing in SZ (Liu, Corbera, & Wexler, 2014) is believed to be reflected hallucinatory content (Jardri, Thomas, Delmaire, Delion, & Pins, 2013; Sass & Borda, 2015). In ASD, a paucity of self-referential thought has been previously suggested (Eilam-Stock et al., 2014). It is possible that disorder-specific differences in recruitment of these DMN regions reflect differences in clinical features related to generation and/or response to internal stimuli across the disorders (Walter, Vasic, et al., 2007).

The breakdown in the relationship between CCN and DMN in these disorders is reminiscent of early observations of Hughlings Jackson (1881, 1896) that disruption of function at higher levels of cortical organization results in a release from inhibition of the lower levels, an explanation he used to describe the "negative" and "positive" symptoms of brain dysfunction. It is well known that that the CCN also exerts its influence on lower level sensory regions to modulate the processing of task-relevant sensory information (Crottaz-Herbette & Menon, 2006; Lee et al., 2012; Noudoost & Moore, 2011; Vossel, Weidner, Driver, Friston, & Fink, 2012; Walsh, Buonocore, Carter, & Mangun, 2011), and that it has an antagonistic relationship with DMN under conditions requiring cognitive control (Di & Biswal, 2014; Hellyer et al., 2014). It has recently been demonstrated that the DMN contributes in part to cognitive control at the stage of the representation of uncertainty in the brain but not at the stage of response generation (Wu, Dufford, Egan, et al., in press). In the absence of an adequate level of CCN regulation, internal thoughts and feelings and external task-irrelevant sensory information may compete with task-relevant stimuli for limited attentional resources. This difficulty optimizing the trade-off between attending to internal and external information may lead to inefficient behavioral performance.

By now, it is abundantly clear that cognitive control is not just "cognitive" alone. It interacts with other essential functions, e.g., memory (Raj & Bell, 2010), emotional control (Ochsner & Gross, 2005; Ochsner et al., 2009), and social functioning (Austin, Groppe, & Elsner, 2014; Fizke, Barthel, Peters, & Rakoczy, 2013; Gilotty, Kenworthy, Sirian, Black, & Wagner, 2002; Leung, Vogan, Powell, Anagnostou, & Taylor, 2015). Social situations are high in uncertainty, and successful social behavior requires flexible adaptation to variable social contexts (Calabrese & Berger, 1975; Lamm & Singer, 2010). Lower efficiency of cognitive control, combined with a reduced upper limit of information processing capacity, may negatively impact the cognitive flexibility required for smooth social interaction (Mackie & Fan, 2016). The rostral "limbic" and caudal "cognitive" portions of the ACC (Bush, Luu, & Posner, 2000) have been shown to have antagonistic relationships (Drevets & Raichle, 1998; Price, Carmichael, & Drevets, 1996), but both contribute to emotional processing and control (Etkin, Egner, & Kalisch, 2011; Etkin, Egner, Peraza, Kandel, & Hirsch, 2006). A previous metaanalysis of studies examining brain regions involved in reappraisal of negative stimuli revealed a network with large overlap with the CCN (Messina, Bianco, Sambin, & Viviani, 2015). Similarly, ventral PFC interacts with amygdala (Siegle, Thompson, Carter, Steinhauer, & Thase, 2007) and subcortical regions (thalamus and caudate) for emotion regulation (Wager, Davidson, Hughes, Lindquist, & Ochsner, 2008). Disruption to these regions or their connections may lead to varieties of dysfunction in emotional experience and reappraisal, which can occur in psychiatric disorders (Wager et al., 2008), and the ability to regulate emotion may be a protective factor against psychopathology (Aldao, Nolen-Hoeksema, & Schweizer, 2010). Indeed, when emotional content enters the conscious mind, it requires concerted effort and attention devoted to reappraisal to regulate affect (Ochsner & Gross, 2005).

The analyses here were confined to a limited subset of known disorders involving cognitive control. There are clearly others, notably attention-deficit hyperactivity disorder, in which a similar pattern of brain response to uncertainty has already been documented (Rubia et al., 1999; Schulz, Newcorn, Fan, Tang, & Halperin, 2005; Schulz, Tang, et al., 2005). Anxiety disorders, such as obsessive compulsive disorder (Berlin et al., 2015; de Vries et al., 2014; Koçak, Özpolat, Atbaşoğlu, & Çiçek, 2011), panic disorder (Dresler et al., 2012), and specific phobias (Del Casale et al., 2012), notably include a substantial emotion—cognition interaction, with great difficulty regulating negative emotion in relation to internal and external stimuli in the context of atypical CCN recruitment (Simmons, Matthews, Paulus, & Stein, 2008). CCN dysfunction has also been noted in bipolar disorder (Fernández-Corcuera et al., 2013; Gruber, Rogowska, & Yurgelun-Todd, 2004; Matsuo et al., 2007), bulimia nervosa (Peñas-Lledí, Loeb, Martin, & Fan, 2013), and borderline personality disorder (Koenigsberg et al., 2014; van Zutphen, Siep, Jacob, Goebel, & Arntz, 2015), among others. The precise nature of the common involvement of this brain network in such a diverse array of symptom presentations remains to be clarified.

In summary, the present review and metaanalyses highlight the role of the CCN across various psychiatric and neurodevelopmental disorders and support the assertion that atypical recruitment of one or more of these cognitive control regions can lead to inefficiency in goal-relevant information processing under conditions of uncertainty. Uncertainty reduction requiring cognitive control results from the coordinated action of distant cortical and subcortical brain regions and is not limited to the frontal lobes.

APPENDIX A SUPPLEMENTAL METHOD

All metaanalyses were completed using the ALE technique (Turkeltaub et al., 2002), using the BrainMap GingerALE software (www.brainmap.org/ale) version 2.3.6. Using the coordinates reported in the studies below, two separate metaanalyses were conducted, one using foci reported for the control group greater than the patient group and another for patient group greater than the control group. For the pooled HC analysis that is used to confirm the CCN regions, one metaanalysis using only foci reported for HC was conducted (i.e., within-subjects only). Consequently, there is significant overlap in the studies reported for the control and patient analyses listed below. For the pooled patient analysis, all control > patient and patient > control foci were combined, and two separate analyses were conducted on the pooled data. For studies with coordinates reported in Talairach space, they were converted to the Montreal Neurological Institute (MNI) using the Talairach to MNI conversion tool in GingerALE. For each analysis, ALE probability values were generated for each voxel by modeling each coordinate with an equal weighting using a 3D Gaussian probability density function with maximum full width at half maximum = 10.

Studies included in ALE meta-analyses
Healthy Controls
Autism Spectrum Disorder
Schizophrenia
Major Depressive Disorder

REFERENCES

Aldao, A., Nolen-Hoeksema, S., & Schweizer, S. (2010). Emotion-regulation strategies across psychopathology: A meta-analytic review. *Clinical Psychology Review*, *30*(2), 217–237. Available from http://dx.doi.org/10.1016/j.cpr.2009.11.004.

Anderson, S. W., Damasio, H., Jones, R. D., & Tranel, D. (1991). Wisconsin Card Sorting Test performance as a measure of frontal lobe damage. *Journal of Clinical and Experimental Neuropsychology*, *13*(6), 909–922. Available from http://dx.doi.org/10.1080/01688639108405107.

Andreasen, N. C., O'Leary, D. S., Flaum, M., Nopoulos, P., Watkins, G. L., Ponto, L. L. B., & Hichwa, R. D. (1997). Hypofrontality in schizophrenia: Distributed dysfunctional circuits in neuroleptic-naïve patients. *The Lancet*, *349*(9067), 1730–1734. Available from http://dx.doi. org/10.1016/S0140-6736(96)08258-X.

Arnsten, A. F. T., & Rubia, K. (2012). Neurobiological circuits regulating attention, cognitive control, motivation, and emotion: Disruptions in neurodevelopmental psychiatric disorders. *Journal of the American Academy of Child and Adolescent Psychiatry*, *51*(4), 356–367. Available from http://dx.doi.org/10.1016/j.jaac.2012.01.008.

Aron, A. R., Robbins, T. W., & Poldrack, R. A. (2004). Inhibition and the right inferior frontal cortex. *Trends in Cognitive Sciences*, *8*(4), 170–177. Available from http://dx.doi.org/ 10.1016/j.tics.2004.02.010.

Association, A. P. (2013). *Diagnostic and Statistical Manual of Mental Disorders* (5th ed). Arlington, VA: American Psychiatric Publishing.

Austin, G., Groppe, K., & Elsner, B. (2014). The reciprocal relationship between executive function and theory of mind in middle childhood: A 1-year longitudinal perspective. *Frontiers in Psychology*, *5*(JUN), 1–11. Available from http://dx.doi.org/10.3389/fpsyg. 2014.00655.

Bach, D. R., & Dolan, R. J. (2012). Knowing how much you don't know: A neural organization of uncertainty estimates. *Nature Reviews Neuroscience*, *13*(8), 572–586. Retrieved from http://dx.doi.org/10.1038/nrn3289.

Backes, H., Dietsche, B., Nagels, A., Stratmann, M., Konrad, C., Kircher, T., & Krug, A. (2014). Increased neural activity during overt and continuous semantic verbal fluency in major depression: Mainly a failure to deactivate. *European Archives of Psychiatry and Clinical Neuroscience*, *264*(7), 631–645. Available from http://dx.doi.org/10.1007/s00406-014-0491-y.

Badre, D. (2008). Cognitive control, hierarchy, and the rostro, caudal organization of the frontal lobes. *Trends in Cognitive Sciences*, *12*(5), 193–200. Available from http://dx.doi.org/ 10.1016/j.tics.2008.02.004.

Banich, M. T., Mackiewicz, K. L., Depue, B. E., Whitmer, A. J., Miller, G. A., & Heller, W. (2009). Cognitive control mechanisms, emotion and memory: A neural perspective with implications for psychopathology. *Neuroscience and Biobehavioral Reviews*, *33*(5), 613–630. Available from http://dx.doi.org/10.1016/j.neubiorev.2008.09.010.

Barcelo, F., & Knight, R. T. (2007). An information-theoretical approach to contextual processing in the human brain: Evidence from prefrontal lesions. *Cerebral Cortex*, *17*(SUPPL. 1), 51–60. Available from http://dx.doi.org/10.1093/cercor/bhm111.

Beevers, C. G., Clasen, P., Stice, E., & Schnyer, D. (2010). Depression symptoms and cognitive control of emotion cues: A functional magnetic resonance imaging study. *Neuroscience*, *167* (1), 97–103. Available from http://dx.doi.org/10.1016/j.neuroscience.2010.01.047.

Belmonte, M. K., & Yurgelun-Todd, D. A. (2003). Functional anatomy of impaired selective attention and compensatory processing in autism. *Cognitive Brain Research*, *17*(3), 651–664. Available from http://dx.doi.org/10.1016/s0926-6410(03)00189-7.

Berg, E. A. (1948). A simple objective technique for measuring flexibility in thinking. *The Journal of General Psychology*, *39*(1), 15–22. Available from http://dx.doi.org/10.1080/ 00221309.1948.9918159.

Berlin, H. A., Schulz, K. P., Zhang, S., Turetzky, R., Rosenthal, D., & Goodman, W. (2015). Neural correlates of emotional response inhibition in obsessive-compulsive disorder: A preliminary study. *Psychiatry Research*, *234*(2), 259–264. Available from http://dx.doi.org/ 10.1016/j.pscychresns.2015.09.019.

Berns, G. S., Cohen, J. D., & Mintun, M. A. (1997). Brain regions responsive to novelty in the absence of awareness. *Science (New York, N.Y.), 276*(5316), 1272−1275. Available from http://dx.doi.org/10.1126/science.276.5316.1272.

Botvinick, M. M., Braver, T. S., Barch, D. M., Carter, C. S., & Cohen, J. D. (2001). Conflict monitoring and cognitive control. *Psychological Review, 108*(3), 624−652. Available from http://dx.doi.org/10.1037//0033-295x.108.3.624.

Braver, T. S. (2001). The role of the prefrontal cortex in cognitive control: A cognitive neuroscience perspective. *Brain and Cognition, 47*(1−2), 6−7, Retrieved from <Go to ISI>:// WOS:000172021100008.

Braver, T. S., Reynolds, J. R., & Donaldson, D. I. (2003). Neural mechanisms of transient and sustained cognitive control during task switching. *Neuron, 39*(4), 713−726. Available from http://dx.doi.org/10.1016/s0896-6273(03)00466-5.

Brown, J. W., & Braver, T. S. (2005). Learned predictions of error likelihood in the anterior cingulate cortex. *Science, 307*(5712), 1118−1121. Retrieved from http://search.ebscohost.com/ login.aspx?direct=true&db=a9h&AN=16250247&site=ehost-live.

Brown, S. M. M., & Bebko, J. M. M. (2012). Generalization, overselectivity, and discrimination in the autism phenotype: A review. *Research in Autism Spectrum Disorders, 6*(2), 733−740. Available from http://dx.doi.org/10.1016/j.rasd.2011.10.012.

Burden, M. J., Andrew, C., Saint-Amour, D., Meintjes, E. M., Molteno, C. D., Hoyme, H. E., & Jacobson, S. W. (2009). The effects of fetal alcohol syndrome on response execution and inhibition: An event-related potential study. *Alcoholism, Clinical and Experimental Research, 33*(11), 1994−2004. Available from http://dx.doi.org/10.1111/j.1530-0277. 2009.01038.x.

Bush, G., Luu, P., & Posner, M. I. (2000). Cognitive and emotional influences in anterior cingulate cortex. *Trends in Cognitive Sciences, 4*(6), 215−222. Available from http://dx.doi.org/ 10.1016/s1364-6613(00)01483-2.

Calabrese, R., & Berger, C. (1975). Uncertainty reduction theory.

Callicott, J. H., Mattay, V. S., Verchinski, B. A., Marenco, S., Egan, M. F., & Weinberger, D. R. (2003). Complexity of prefrontal cortical dysfunction in schizophrenia: More than up or down. *American Journal of Psychiatry, 160*(12), 2209−2215. Available from http://dx.doi. org/10.1176/appi.ajp.160.12.2209.

Carter, C. S., Perlstein, W., Ganguli, R., Brar, J., Mintun, M., & Cohen, J. D. (1998). Functional hypofrontality and working memory dysfunction in schizophrenia. *American Journal of Psychiatry, 155*(9), 1285−1287. Available from http://dx.doi.org/10.1176/ajp.155.9.1285.

Ciaramelli, E., Grady, C. L., & Moscovitch, M. (2008). Top-down and bottom-up attention to memory: A hypothesis (AtoM) on the role of the posterior parietal cortex in memory retrieval. *Neuropsychologia, 46*(7), 1828−1851. Available from http://dx.doi.org/10.1016/j. neuropsychologia.2008.03.022.

Cole, M. W., Repovš, G., & Anticevic, A. (2014). The frontoparietal control system: A central role in mental health. *The Neuroscientist: A Review Journal Bringing Neurobiology, Neurology and Psychiatry, 20*(6), 652−664. Available from http://dx.doi.org/10.1177/ 1073858414525995.

Cole, M. W., & Schneider, W. (2007). The cognitive control network: Integrated cortical regions with dissociable functions. *NeuroImage, 37*(1), 343−360. Available from http://dx.doi.org/ 10.1016/j.neuroimage.2007.03.071.

Cooper, P. S., Darriba, Á., Karayanidis, F., & Barceló, F. (2016). Contextually sensitive power changes across multiple frequency bands underpin cognitive control. *NeuroImage, 132,* 499−511. Available from http://dx.doi.org/10.1016/j.neuroimage.2016.03.010.

Cooper, P. S., Garrett, P. M., Rennie, J. L., & Karayanidis, F. (2015). Task uncertainty can account for mixing and switch costs in task-switching. *PLoS One, 10*(6), e0131556. Available from http://dx.doi.org/10.1371/journal.pone.0131556.

Corbetta, M., Kincade, J. M., Ollinger, J. M., McAvoy, M. P., & Shulman, G. L. (2000). Voluntary orienting is dissociated from target detection in human posterior parietal cortex. *Nature Neuroscience, 3*(3), 292−297. Retrieved from http://www.ncbi.nlm.nih.gov/cgi-bin/Entrez/referer?http://www.nature.com/cgi-taf/DynaPage.taf%3ffile=/neuro/journal/v3/n3/abs/nn0300_292.html.

Corbetta, M., & Shulman, G. L. (1998). Human cortical mechanisms of visual attention during orienting and search. *Philosophical Transactions of the Royal Society of London. Series B, Biological Sciences, 353*(1373), 1353−1362. Available from http://dx.doi.org/10.1098/rstb.1998.0289.

Corbetta, M., & Shulman, G. L. (2002). Control of goal-directed and stimulus-driven attention in the brain. *Nature Reviews Neuroscience, 3*(3), 201−215. Available from http://dx.doi.org/10.1038/nrn755.

Cowan, N. (2001). Metatheory of storage capacity limits. *Behavioral and Brain Sciences, 24* (01), 154−176.

Crottaz-Herbette, S., & Menon, V. (2006). Where and when the anterior cingulate cortex modulates attentional response: Combined fMRI and ERP evidence. *Journal of Cognitive Neuroscience, 18*(5), 766−780. Available from http://dx.doi.org/10.1162/jocn.2006.18.5.766.

Curtis, V. A., Bullmore, E. T., Morris, R. G., Brammer, M. J., Williams, S. C. R., Simmons, A., & McGuire, P. K. (1999). Attenuated frontal activation in schizophrenia may be task dependent. *Schizophrenia Research, 37*(1), 35−44. Available from http://dx.doi.org/10.1016/S0920-9964(98)00141-8.

Damasio, A. R., & Maurer, R. G. (1978). A neurological model for childhood autism. *Archives of Neurology, 35*(12), 777−786. Retrieved from http://dx.doi.org/10.1001/archneur.1978.00500360001001.

Del Casale, A., Ferracuti, S., Rapinesi, C., Serata, D., Piccirilli, M., Savoja, V., & Girardi, P. (2012). Functional neuroimaging in specific phobia. *Psychiatry Research, 202*(3), 181−197. Available from http://dx.doi.org/10.1016/j.pscychresns.2011.10.009.

Deschamps, I., Baum, S. R., & Gracco, V. L. (2014). On the role of the supramarginal gyrus in phonological processing and verbal working memory: Evidence from rTMS studies. *Neuropsychologia, 53*, 39−46. Available from http://dx.doi.org/10.1016/j.neuropsychologia.2013.10.015.

Desimone, R., & Duncan, J. (1995). Neural mechanisms of selective visual-attention. *Annual Review of Neuroscience, 18*, 193−222. Available from http://dx.doi.org/10.1146/annurev.neuro.18.1.193.

de Vries, F. E., de Wit, S. J., Cath, D. C., van der Werf, Y. D., van der Borden, V., van Rossum, T. B., & van den Heuvel, O. A. (2014). Compensatory frontoparietal activity during working memory: An endophenotype of obsessive-compulsive disorder. *Biological Psychiatry, 76* (11), 878−887. Available from http://dx.doi.org/10.1016/j.biopsych.2013.11.021.

Di, X., & Biswal, B. B. (2014). Modulatory interactions between the default mode network and task positive networks in resting-state. *PeerJ, 2*, e367. Available from http://dx.doi.org/10.7717/peerj.367.

Dichter, G. S., Felder, J. N., & Smoski, M. J. (2009). Affective context interferes with cognitive control in unipolar depression: An fMRI investigation. *Journal of Affective Disorders, 114* (1−3), 131−142. Available from http://dx.doi.org/10.1016/j.jad.2008.06.027.

Dillon, D. G., & Pizzagalli, D. A. (2007). Inhibition of action, thought, and emotion: A selective neurobiological review. *Applied and Preventive Psychology*, *12*(3), 99−114. Available from http://dx.doi.org/10.1016/j.appsy.2007.09.004.

Dosenbach, N. U. F., Fair, D. A., Cohen, A. L., Schlaggar, B. L., & Petersen, S. E. (2008). A dual-networks architecture of top-down control. *Trends in Cognitive Sciences*, *12*(3), 99−105. Available from http://dx.doi.org/10.1016/j.tics.2008.01.001.

Dosenbach, N. U. F., Fair, D. A., Miezin, F. M., Cohen, A. L., Wenger, K. K., Dosenbach, R. A. T., & Petersen, S. E. (2007). Distinct brain networks for adaptive and stable task control in humans. *Proceedings of the National Academy of Sciences*, *104*(26), 11073−11078. Available from http://dx.doi.org/10.1073/pnas.0704320104.

Dosenbach, N.U.F., & Petersen, S.E. (2009). Attentional networks. In: Editor-in-chief, X. A., R. S. Larry (Eds.), *Encyclopedia of neuroscience* (pp. 655−660). Oxford: Academic Press. Available from http://dx.doi.org/10.1016/b978-008045046-9.00204-7.

Dosenbach, N. U. F., Visscher, K. M., Palmer, E. D., Miezin, F. M., Wenger, K. K., Kang, H. S. C., & Petersen, S. E. (2006). A core system for the implementation of task sets. *Neuron*, *50*(5), 799−812. Available from http://dx.doi.org/10.1016/j.neuron.2006.04.031.

Dreher, J.-C., & Berman, K. F. (2002). Fractionating the neural substrate of cognitive control processes. *Proceedings of the National Academy of Sciences of the United States of America*, *99*(22), 14595−14600. Available from http://dx.doi.org/10.1073/pnas.222193299.

Dresler, T., Hindi Attar, C., Spitzer, C., Löwe, B., Deckert, J., Büchel, C., & Fallgatter, A. J. (2012). Neural correlates of the emotional Stroop task in panic disorder patients: An event-related fMRI study. *Journal of Psychiatric Research*, *46*(12), 1627−1634. Available from http://dx.doi.org/10.1016/j.jpsychires.2012.09.004.

Drevets, W. C., & Raichle, M. E. (1998). Reciprocal suppression of regional cerebral blood flow during emotional versus higher cognitive processes: Implications for interactions between emotion and cognition. *Cognition and Emotion*, *12*(3), 353−385.

Dunbar, K., & Sussman, D. (1995). Toward a cognitive account of frontal lobe function: Simulating frontal lobe deficits in normal subjects. *Annals of the New York Academy of Sciences*, *769*(1), 289−304. Available from http://dx.doi.org/10.1111/j.1749-6632.1995.tb38146.x.

Eilam-Stock, T., Xu, P., Cao, M., Gu, X., Van Dam, N. T., Anagnostou, E., & Fan, J. (2014). Abnormal autonomic and associated brain activities during rest in autism spectrum disorder. *Brain*, *137*(1), 153−171. Available from http://dx.doi.org/10.1093/brain/awt294.

Esterman, M., Chiu, Y.-C., Tamber-Rosenau, B. J., & Yantis, S. (2009). Decoding cognitive control in human parietal cortex. *Proceedings of the National Academy of Sciences of the United States of America*, *106*(42), 17974−17979. Available from http://dx.doi.org/10.1073/pnas.0903593106.

Etkin, A., Egner, T., & Kalisch, R. (2011). Emotional processing in anterior cingulate and medial prefrontal cortex. *Trends in Cognitive Sciences*, *15*(2), 85−93. Available from http://dx.doi.org/10.1016/j.tics.2010.11.004.

Etkin, A., Egner, T., Peraza, D. M., Kandel, E. R., & Hirsch, J. (2006). Resolving emotional conflict: A role for the rostral anterior cingulate cortex in modulating activity in the amygdala. *Neuron*, *51*(6), 871−882. Available from http://dx.doi.org/10.1016/j.neuron.2006.07.029.

Fales, C. L., Barch, D. M., Rundle, M. M., Mintun, M. A., Snyder, A. Z., Cohen, J. D., & Sheline, Y. I. (2008). Altered emotional interference processing in affective and cognitive-control brain circuitry in major depression. *Biological Psychiatry*, *63*(4), 377−384. Available from http://dx.doi.org/10.1016/j.biopsych.2007.06.012.

Fan, J. (2013). Attention network deficits in autism spectrum disorders. *The Neuroscience of Autism Spectrum Disorders*, 110, 155−167. Available from http://dx.doi.org/10.1016/B978-0-12-391924-3.00010-7.

Fan, J. (2014). An information theory account of cognitive control. *Frontiers in Human Neuroscience*, 8(680). Available from http://dx.doi.org/10.3389/fnhum.2014.00680.

Fan, J., Bernardi, S., Dam, N. T., Anagnostou, E., Gu, X., Martin, L., & Hof, P. R. (2012). Functional deficits of the attentional networks in autism. *Brain and Behavior*, 2(5), 647−660. Available from http://dx.doi.org/10.1002/brb3.90.

Fan, J., Guise, K. G., Liu, X., & Wang, H. (2008). Searching for the majority: Algorithms of voluntary control. *PLoS One*, 3(10). Available from http://dx.doi.org/10.1371/journal.pone.0003522.

Fan, J., McCandliss, B. D., Sommer, T., Raz, A., & Posner, M. I. (2002). Testing the efficiency and independence of attentional networks. *Journal of Cognitive Neuroscience*, 14(3), 340−347. Retrieved from http://www.ncbi.nlm.nih.gov/entrez/query.fcgi?cmd=Retrieve&db=PubMed&dopt=Citation&list_uids=11970796.

Fan, J., Van Dam, N. T., Gu, X., Liu, X., Wang, H., Tang, C. Y., & Hof, P. R. (2014). Quantitative characterization of functional anatomical contributions to cognitive control under uncertainty. *Journal of Cognitive Neuroscience*, 26(7), 1490−1506. Available from http://dx.doi.org/10.1162/jocn.

Fassbender, C., Scangos, K., Lesh, T. A., & Carter, C. S. (2014). RT distributional analysis of cognitive-control-related brain activity in first-episode schizophrenia. *Cognitive, Affective, & Behavioral Neuroscience*, 175−188. Available from http://dx.doi.org/10.3758/s13415-014-0252-4.

Fassbender, C., Simoes-Franklin, C., Murphy, K., Hester, R., Meaney, J., Robertson, I. H., & Garavan, H. (2006). The role of a right fronto-parietal network in cognitive control: Common activations for cues-to-attend and response inhibition. *Journal of Psychophysiology*, 20(4), 286−296. Available from http://dx.doi.org/10.1027/0269-8803.20.4.286.

Feldman, H., & Friston, K. J. (2010). Attention, uncertainty, and free-energy. *Frontiers in Human Neuroscience*, 4, 215. Available from http://dx.doi.org/10.3389/fnhum.2010.00215.

Fernández-Corcuera, P., Salvador, R., Monté, G. C., Salvador Sarró, S., Goikolea, J. M., Amann, B., & Pomarol-Clotet, E. (2013). Bipolar depressed patients show both failure to activate and failure to de-activate during performance of a working memory task. *Journal of Affective Disorders*, 148(2−3), 170−178. Available from http://dx.doi.org/10.1016/j.jad.2012.04.009.

Fitts, P. M. (1954). The information capacity of the human motor system in controlling the amplitude of movement*Journal of Experimental Psychology*. US: American Psychological Association. Available from http://dx.doi.org/10.1037/h0055392.

Fitzgerald, P., & Laird, A. (2008). A meta-analytic study of changes in brain activation in depression. *Human Brain*, 29(6), 683−695. Available from http://dx.doi.org/10.1002/hbm.20426.A.

Fizke, E., Barthel, D., Peters, T., & Rakoczy, H. (2013). Executive function plays a role in coordinating different perspectives, particularly when one's own perspective is involved. *Cognition*, 130(3), 315−334. Available from http://dx.doi.org/10.1016/j.cognition.2013.11.017.

Friedman, N. P., & Miyake, A. (2016). Unity and diversity of executive functions: Individual differences as a window on cognitive structure. *Cortex*. Available from http://dx.doi.org/10.1016/j.cortex.2016.04.023.

Geurts, H. M., Corbett, B., & Solomon, M. (2009). The paradox of cognitive flexibility in autism. *Trends in Cognitive Sciences, 13*(2), 74−82. Available from http://dx.doi.org/10.1016/j.tics.2008.11.006.

Gilotty, L., Kenworthy, L., Sirian, L., Black, D. O., & Wagner, A. E. (2002). Adaptive skills and executive function in autism spectrum disorders. *Child Neuropsychology: A Journal on Normal and Abnormal Development in Childhood and Adolescence, 8*(4), 241−248. Available from http://dx.doi.org/10.1076/chin.8.4.241.13504.

Goodkind, M., Eickhoff, S. B., Oathes, D. J., Jiang, Y., Chang, A., Jones-hagata, L. B., & Etkin, A. (2015). *Identification of a Common Neurobiological Substrate for Mental Illness, 5797,* 1−11. Available from http://dx.doi.org/10.1001/jamapsychiatry.2014.2206.

Gottlieb, J. (2007). From thought to action: The parietal cortex as a bridge between perception, action, and cognition. *Neuron, 53*(1), 9−16. Available from http://dx.doi.org/10.1016/j.neuron.2006.12.009.

Grahn, Ja, Parkinson, J. A., & Owen, A. M. (2008). The cognitive functions of the caudate nucleus. *Progress in Neurobiology, 86*(3), 141−155. Available from http://dx.doi.org/10.1016/j.pneurobio.2008.09.004.

Gray, J. R. (2001). Emotional modulation of cognitive control: Approach-withdrawal states double-dissociate spatial from verbal two-back task performance. *Journal of Experimental Psychology-General, 130*(3), 436−452. Available from http://dx.doi.org/10.1037/0096-3445.130.3.436.

Gray, J. R., Braver, T. S., & Raichle, M. E. (2001). Effects of state and trait emotion on cognitive control: FMRI evidence for selective interactions in dorsolateral prefrontal and anterior cingulate cortex. *NeuroImage, 13*(6, Supplement), 412. http://dx.doi.org/10.1016/s1053-8119(01)91755-0.

Green, M. J., & Malhi, G. S. (2006). Neural mechanisms of the cognitive control of emotion. *Acta Neuropsychiatrica, 18*(3-4), 144−153. Available from http://dx.doi.org/10.1111/j.1601-5215.2006.00149.x.

Grimm, S., Beck, J., Schuepbach, D., Hell, D., Boesiger, P., Bermpohl, F., & Northoff, G. (2008). Imbalance between left and right dorsolateral prefrontal cortex in major depression is linked to negative emotional judgment: An fMRI study in severe major depressive disorder. *Biological Psychiatry, 63*(4), 369−376. Available from http://dx.doi.org/10.1016/j.biopsych.2007.05.033.

Grimm, S., Boesiger, P., Beck, J., Schuepbach, D., Bermpohl, F., Walter, M., & Northoff, G. (2009). Altered negative BOLD responses in the default-mode network during emotion processing in depressed subjects. *Neuropsychopharmacology: Official Publication of the American College of Neuropsychopharmacology, 34*(4), 932−943. Available from http://dx.doi.org/10.1038/npp.2008.81.

Grinband, J., Hirsch, J., & Ferrera, V. P. (2006). A neural representation of categorization uncertainty in the human brain. *Neuron, 49*(5), 757−763. Available from http://dx.doi.org/10.1016/j.neuron.2006.01.032.

Gruber, S. A., Rogowska, J., & Yurgelun-Todd, D. A. (2004). Decreased activation of the anterior cingulate in bipolar patients: An fMRI study. *Journal of Affective Disorders, 82*(2), 191−201. Available from http://dx.doi.org/10.1016/j.jad.2003.10.010.

Harvey, P. O., Fossati, P., Pochon, J. B., Levy, R., LeBastard, G., Lehéricy, S., & Dubois, B. (2005). Cognitive control and brain resources in major depression: An fMRI study using the n-back task. *NeuroImage, 26*(3), 860−869. Available from http://dx.doi.org/10.1016/j.neuroimage.2005.02.048.

Hellyer, P. J., Shanahan, M., Scott, G., Wise, R. J. S., Sharp, D. J., & Leech, R. (2014). The control of global brain dynamics: Opposing actions of frontoparietal control and default mode networks on attention. *Journal of Neuroscience, 34*(2), 451–461. Available from http://dx. doi.org/10.1523/JNEUROSCI.1853-13.2014.

Heyder, K., Suchan, B., & Daum, I. (2004). Cortico-subcortical contributions to executive control. *Acta Psychologica, 115*(2–3), 271–289. Available from http://dx.doi.org/10.1016/ j.actpsy.2003.12.010.

Hopfinger, J. B., Buonocore, M. H., & Mangun, G. R. (2000). The neural mechanisms of top-down attentional control. *Nature Neuroscience, 3*(3), 284–291. Available from http://dx.doi. org/10.1038/72999.

Hughes, C., Russell, J., & Robbins, T. W. (1994). Evidence for executive dysfunction in autism. *Neuropsychologia, 32*(4), 477–492. Available from http://dx.doi.org/10.1016/0028-3932(94) 90092-2.

Hughlings Jackson, J. (1881). On temporary paralysis after epileptiform and epileptic seizures; a contribution to the study of dissolution of the nervous system. *Brain, 3*(4), 433–451.

Hughlings Jackson, J. (1896). Neurological fragments. *The Lancet, 148*(3824), 1662–1664.

Ingvar, D., & Franzén, G. (1974). Distribution of cerebral activity in chronic schizophrenia. *The Lancet, 304*(7895), 1484–1486. Available from http://dx.doi.org/10.1016/S0140-6736(74) 90221-9.

Jackson, A., Cavanagh, J., & Scott, J. (2003). A systematic review of manic and depressive prodromes. *Journal of Affective Disorders, 74*(3), 209–217. Available from http://dx.doi.org/ 10.1016/S0165-0327(02)00266-5.

Jardri, R., Thomas, P., Delmaire, C., Delion, P., & Pins, D. (2013). The neurodynamic organization of modality-dependent hallucinations. *Cerebral Cortex (New York, N.Y.: 1991), 23*(5), 1108–1117. Available from http://dx.doi.org/10.1093/cercor/bhs082.

Johnstone, T., van Reekum, C. M., Urry, H. L., Kalin, N. H., & Davidson, R. J. (2007). Failure to regulate: counterproductive recruitment of top-down prefrontal-subcortical circuitry in major depression. *The Journal of Neuroscience: The Official Journal of the Society for Neuroscience, 27*(33), 8877–8884. Available from http://dx.doi.org/10.1523/JNEUROSCI.2063-07.2007.

Just, M. A., Keller, T. A., Malave, V. L., Kana, R. K., & Varma, S. (2012). Autism as a neural systems disorder: A theory of frontal-posterior underconnectivity. *Neuroscience and Biobehavioral Reviews, 36*(4), 1292–1313. Available from http://dx.doi.org/10.1016/j.neubiorev.2012.02.007.

Kana, R. K., Keller, T. A., Minshew, N. J., & Just, M. A. (2007). Inhibitory control in high-functioning autism: Decreased activation and underconnectivity in inhibition networks. *Biological Psychiatry, 62*(3), 198–206. Available from http://dx.doi.org/10.1016/j. biopsych.2006.08.004.

Kennedy, D. P., Redcay, E., & Courchesne, E. (2006). Failing to deactivate: Resting functional abnormalities in autism. *Proceedings of the National Academy of Sciences of the United States of America, 103*(21), 8275–8280. Available from http://dx.doi.org/10.1073/pnas. 0600674103.

Kerns, J. C., Cohen, J. D., MacDonald Iii, A. W., Cho, R. Y., Stenger, V. A., & Carter, C. S. (2004). Anterior cingulate conflict monitoring and adjustments in control. *Science, 303* (5660), 1023–1026. Retrieved from http://search.ebscohost.com/login.aspx?direct= true&db=a9h&AN=12350803&site=ehost-live.

Khan, S., Gramfort, A., Shetty, N. R., Kitzbichler, M. G., Ganesan, S., Moran, J. M., & Kenet, T. (2013). Local and long-range functional connectivity is reduced in concert in autism spectrum disorders. *Proceedings of the National Academy of Sciences of the United States of America, 110*(8), 3107–3112. Available from http://dx.doi.org/10.1073/pnas.1214533110.

Kim, C., Chung, C., & Kim, J. (2013). Task-dependent response conflict monitoring and cognitive control in anterior cingulate and dorsolateral prefrontal cortices. *Brain Research, 1537*, 216−223. Available from http://dx.doi.org/10.1016/j.brainres.2013.08.055.

Kim, J.-J., Kwon, J. S., Park, H. J., Youn, T., Kang, D. H., Kim, M. S., & Lee, M. C. (2003). Functional disconnection between the prefrontal and parietal cortices during working memory processing in schizophrenia: A [15(O)]H2O PET study. *The American Journal of Psychiatry, 160*(5), 919−923. Available from http://dx.doi.org/10.1176/appi.ajp.160.5.919.

Kleinhans, N., Akshoomoff, N., & Delis, D. C. (2005). Executive functions in autism and Asperger's disorder: Flexibility, fluency, and inhibition. *Developmental Neuropsychology, 27*(3), 379−401. Available from http://dx.doi.org/10.1207/s15326942dn2703_5.

Koçak, O. M., Özpolat, A. Y., Atbaşoğlu, C., & Çiçek, M. (2011). Cognitive control of a simple mental image in patients with obsessive−compulsive disorder. *Brain and Cognition, 76*(3), 390−399. Available from http://dx.doi.org/10.1016/j.bandc.2011.03.020.

Koechlin, E., Corrado, G., Pietrini, P., & Grafman, J. (2000). Dissociating the role of the medial and lateral anterior prefrontal cortex in human planning. *Proceedings of the National Academy of Sciences of the United States of America, 97*(13), 7651−7656. Available from http://dx.doi.org/10.1073/pnas.130177397.

Koechlin, E., Ody, C., & Kouneiher, F. (2003). The architecture of cognitive control in the human prefrontal cortex. *Science, 302*(5648), 1181−1185. Available from http://dx.doi.org/10.1126/science.1088545.

Koenigs, M., & Grafman, J. (2009). The functional neuroanatomy of depression: Distinct roles for ventromedial and dorsolateral prefrontal cortex. *Behavioural Brain Research, 201*(2), 239−243. Available from http://dx.doi.org/10.1016/j.bbr.2009.03.004.

Koenigsberg, H. W., Denny, B. T., Fan, J., Liu, X., Guerreri, S., Mayson, S. J., & Siever, L. J. (2014). The neural correlates of anomalous habituation to negative emotional pictures in borderline and avoidant personality disorder patients. *American Journal of Psychiatry, 171* (1), 82−90. Available from http://dx.doi.org/10.1176/appi.ajp.2013.13070852.

Köhler, S., Bär, K.-J., & Wagner, G. (2016). Differential involvement of brainstem noradrenergic and midbrain dopaminergic nuclei in cognitive control. *Human Brain Mapping,* . Available from http://dx.doi.org/10.1002/hbm.23173.

Koshino, H., Carpenter, P. A., Minshew, N. J., Cherkassky, V. L., Keller, T. A., & Just, M. A. (2005). Functional connectivity in an fMRI working memory task in high-functioning autism. *NeuroImage, 24*(3), 810−821. Available from http://dx.doi.org/10.1016/j.neuroimage.2004.09.028.

Koster-Hale, J., & Saxe, R. (2013). Functional neuroimaging of theory of mind. In S. Baron-Cohen, M. Lombardo, & H. Tager-Flusberg (Eds.), *Understanding Other Minds* (3rd edn, pp. 132−163). Oxford, United Kingdom: Oxford University Press.

Kühn, S., & Gallinat, J. (2013). Resting-state brain activity in schizophrenia and major depression: A quantitative meta-analysis. *Schizophrenia Bulletin, 39*(2), 358−365. Available from http://dx.doi.org/10.1093/schbul/sbr151.

Lamm, C., & Singer, T. (2010). The role of anterior insular cortex in social emotions. *Brain Structure & Function, 214*(5−6), 579−591. Retrieved from http://search.ebscohost.com/login.aspx?direct=true&db=mnh&AN=20428887&site=ehost-live.

Lawrence, N. S., Williams, A. M., Surguladze, S., Giampietro, V., Brammer, M. J., Andrew, C., & Phillips, M. L. (2004). Subcortical and ventral prefrontal cortical neural responses to facial expressions distinguish patients with bipolar disorder and major depression. *Biological Psychiatry, 55*(6), 578−587. Available from http://dx.doi.org/10.1016/j.biopsych.2003.11.017.

Lee, A. K. C., Rajaram, S., Xia, J., Bharadwaj, H., Larson, E., Hämäläinen, M. S., & Shinn-Cunningham, B. G. (2012). Auditory selective attention reveals preparatory activity in different cortical regions for selection based on source location and source pitch. *Frontiers in Neuroscience, 6*(January), 190. Available from http://dx.doi.org/10.3389/fnins.2012.00190.

Lee, P. S., Foss-Feig, J., Henderson, J. G., Kenworthy, L. E., Gilotty, L., Gaillard, W. D., & Vaidya, C. J. (2007). Atypical neural substrates of embedded figures task performance in children with autism spectrum disorder. *NeuroImage, 38*(1), 184−193. Available from http://dx.doi.org/10.1016/j.neuroimage.2007.07.013.

Leung, R. C., Vogan, V. M., Powell, T. L., Anagnostou, E., & Taylor, M. J. (2015). The role of executive functions in social impairment in autism spectrum disorder. *Child Neuropsychology, 22*(3), 336−344. Available from http://dx.doi.org/10.1080/09297049. 2015.1005066.

Li, Q., Nan, W., Wang, K., & Liu, X. (2014). Independent processing of stimulus-stimulus and stimulus-response conflicts. *PLoS One, 9*(2), e89249. Available from http://dx.doi.org/ 10.1371/journal.pone.0089249.

Liu, J., Corbera, S., & Wexler, B. E. (2014). Neural activation abnormalities during self-referential processing in schizophrenia: An fMRI study. *Psychiatry Research, 222*(3), 165−171. Available from http://dx.doi.org/10.1016/j.pscychresns.2014.04.003.

MacDonald, A. W., Cohen, J. D., Stenger, V. A., & Carter, C. S. (2000). Dissociating the role of the dorsolateral prefrontal and anterior cingulate cortex in cognitive control. *Science, 288* (5472), 1835−1838. Available from http://dx.doi.org/10.1126/science.288.5472.1835.

Mackie, M.-A., & Fan, J. (2016). Reduced efficiency and capacity of cognitive control in autism spectrum disorder. *Autism Research, 9*(3), 403−414. Available from http://dx.doi.org/ 10.1002/aur.1517.

Mackie, M.-A., Van Dam, N. T., & Fan, J. (2013). Cognitive control and attentional functions. *Brain and Cognition, 82*(3), 301−312. Available from http://dx.doi.org/10.1016/j. bandc.2013.05.004.

Marinier Iii, R. P., Laird, J. E., & Lewis, R. L. (2009). A computational unification of cognitive behavior and emotion. *Cognitive Systems Research, 10*(1), 48−69. Available from http://dx. doi.org/10.1016/j.cogsys.2008.03.004.

Matsuo, K., Glahn, D. C., Peluso, M. A. M., Hatch, J. P., Monkul, E. S., Najt, P., & Soares, J. C. (2007). Prefrontal hyperactivation during working memory task in untreated individuals with major depressive disorder. *Molecular Psychiatry, 12*(2), 158−166. Available from http://dx.doi.org/10.1038/sj.mp.4001894.

Matthews, S. C., Paulus, M. P., Simmons, A. N., Nelesen, R. A., & Dimsdale, J. E. (2004). Functional subdivisions within anterior cingulate cortex and their relationship to autonomic nervous system function. *NeuroImage, 22*(3), 1151−1156. Available from http://dx.doi.org/ 10.1016/j.neuroimage.2004.03.005.

Mayberg, H. S. (1997). Limbic-cortical dysregulation: A proposed model of depression. *The Journal of Neuropsychiatry and Clinical Neurosciences, 9*(3), 471−481.

Memari, A. H., Ziaee, V., Shayestehfar, M., Ghanouni, P., Mansournia, M. A., & Moshayedi, P. (2013). Cognitive flexibility impairments in children with autism spectrum disorders: Links to age, gender and child outcomes. *Research in Developmental Disabilities, 34*(10), 3218−3225. Available from http://dx.doi.org/10.1016/j.ridd.2013.06.033.

Messina, I., Bianco, S., Sambin, M., & Viviani, R. (2015). Executive and semantic processes in reappraisal of negative stimuli: Insights from a meta-analysis of neuroimaging studies. *Frontiers in Psychology, 6*(956), 974−983. Available from http://dx.doi.org/10.3389/ fpsyg.2015.00956.

Meyer-Lindenberg, A., Polin, J. B., Kohn, P. D., Holt, J. L., Egan, M. F., Weinberger, D. R., & Berman, K. F. (2001). Evidence for abnormal cortical functional connectivity during working memory in schizophrenia. *American Journal of Psychiatry, 158*(11), 1809–1817. Available from http://dx.doi.org/10.1176/appi.ajp.158.11.1809.

Miller, E. K., & Buschman, T. J. (2007). Chapter 10—Bootstrapping your brain: How interactions between the frontal cortex and basal ganglia may produce organized actions and lofty thoughts. In P. K. Raymond, L. M. Joe, A. R. P. K., Jr, & Joe L. Martinez, Jr. (Eds.), *Neurobiology of Learning and Memory* (Second Edition, pp. 339–354). Burlington: Academic Press. Available from http://dx.doi.org/10.1016/b978-012372540-0/50011-x.

Miller, E. K., & Cohen, J. D. (2001). An integrative theory of prefrontal cortex function. *Annual Review of Neuroscience, 24*(1), 167–202. Retrieved from http://www.ncbi.nlm.nih.gov/pubmed/11283309.

Minshew, N. J., & Goldstein, G. (1998). Autism as a disorder of complex information processing. *Mental Retardation and Developmental Disabilities Research Reviews, 4,* 129–136.

Minzenberg, M. J., Laird, A. R., Thelen, S., Carter, C. S., & Glahn, D. C. (2009). Meta-analysis of 41 functional neuroimaging studies of executive function in schizophrenia. *Archives of General Psychiatry, 66*(8), 811–822. Available from http://dx.doi.org/10.1001/archgenpsychiatry.2009.91.

Miyake, A., Friedman, N. P., Emerson, M. J., Witzki, A. H., Howerter, A., & Wager, T. D. (2000). The unity and diversity of executive functions and their contributions to complex "Frontal Lobe" tasks: A latent variable analysis. *Cognitive Psychology, 41*(1), 49–100. Available from http://dx.doi.org/10.1006/cogp.1999.0734.

Mushtaq, F., Bland, A. R., & Schaefer, A. (2011). Uncertainty and cognitive control. *Frontiers in Psychology, 2,* 249. Available from http://dx.doi.org/10.3389/fpsyg.2011.00249.

Nagahama, Y., Okada, T., Katsumi, Y., Hayashi, T., Yamauchi, H., Sawamoto, N., & Shibasaki, H. (1999). Transient neural activity in the medial superior frontal gyrus and precuneus time locked with attention shift between object features. *NeuroImage, 10*(2), 193–199. Available from http://dx.doi.org/10.1006/nimg.1999.0451.

Nee, D. E., Wager, T. D., & Jonides, J. (2007). Interference resolution: Insights from a meta-analysis of neuroimaging tasks. *Cognitive, Affective, & Behavioral Neuroscience, 7*(1), 1–17. Available from http://dx.doi.org/10.3758/CABN.7.1.1.

Nelson, S. M., Dosenbach, N. U. F., Cohen, A. L., Wheeler, M. E., Schlaggar, B. L., & Petersen, S. E. (2010). Role of the anterior insula in task-level control and focal attention. *Brain Structure & Function, 214*(5-6), 669–680. Available from http://dx.doi.org/10.1007/s00429-010-0260-2.

Niendam, T. A., Laird, A. R., Ray, K. L., Dean, Y. M., Glahn, D. C., & Carter, C. S. (2012). Meta-analytic evidence for a superordinate cognitive control network subserving diverse executive functions. *Cognitive, Affective, & Behavioral Neuroscience, 12*(2), 241–268. Available from http://dx.doi.org/10.3758/s13415-011-0083-5.

Noudoost, B., & Moore, T. (2011). Control of visual cortical signals by prefrontal dopamine. *Nature, 474*(7351), 372–375. Available from http://dx.doi.org/10.1038/nature09995.

Nuechterlein, K. H., Green, M. F., Calkins, M. E., Greenwood, T. A., Gur, R. E., Gur, R. C., & Braff, D. L. (2015). Attention/vigilance in schizophrenia: Performance results from a large multi-site study of the Consortium on the Genetics of Schizophrenia (COGS). *Schizophrenia Research, 163*(1–3), 38–46. Available from http://dx.doi.org/10.1016/j.schres.2015.01.017.

Ochsner, K. N., & Gross, J. J. (2005). The cognitive control of emotion. *Trends in Cognitive Sciences, 9*(5), 242–249. Available from http://dx.doi.org/10.1016/j.tics.2005.03.010.

Ochsner, K. N., Hughes, B., Robertson, E. R., Cooper, J. C., & Gabrieli, J. D. E. (2009). Neural systems supporting the control of affective and cognitive conflicts. *Journal of Cognitive Neuroscience, 21*(9), 1842–1855. Retrieved from http://search.ebscohost.com/login.aspx?direct=true&db=a9h&AN=43226795&site=ehost-live.

Ochsner, K. N., Silvers, J. A., & Buhle, J. T. (2012). Functional imaging studies of emotion regulation: A synthetic review and evolving model of the cognitive control of emotion. *Annals of the New York Academy of Sciences, 1251*, E1–24. Available from http://dx.doi.org/10.1111/j.1749-6632.2012.06751.x.

Ozonoff, S., Pennington, B. F., & Rogers, S. J. (1991). Executive function deficits in high-functioning autistic individuals: Relationship to theory of mind. *Journal of Child Psychology And Psychiatry, And Allied Disciplines, 32*(7), 1081–1105. Retrieved from http://search.ebscohost.com/login.aspx?direct=true&db=mnh&AN=1787138&site=ehost-live.

Palmer, S. M., Crewther, S. G., & Carey, L. M. (2014). A meta-analysis of changes in brain activity in clinical depression. *Frontiers in Human Neuroscience, 8*, 1045. Available from http://dx.doi.org/10.3389/fnhum.2014.01045.

Peñas-Lledí, E. M., Loeb, K. L., Martin, L., & Fan, J. (2013). Anterior cingulate activity in bulimia nervosa: A fMRI case study. *Eating and Weight Disorders—Studies on Anorexia, Bulimia and Obesity, 12*(4), e78–e82. Available from http://dx.doi.org/10.1007/BF03327599.

Perlstein, W. M., Dixit, N. K., Carter, C. S., Noll, D. C., & Cohen, J. D. (2003). Prefrontal cortex dysfunction mediates deficits in working memory and prepotent responding in schizophrenia. *Biological Psychiatry, 53*(1), 25–38. http://dx.doi.org/10.1016/S0006-3223(02)01675-X.

Pierce, J. R., & Karlin, J. E. (1957). Reading rates and the information rate of a human channel. *Bell System Technical Journal, 36*(2), 497–516. Available from http://dx.doi.org/10.1002/j.1538-7305.1957.tb02409.x.

Pierce, K. (2001). Face processing occurs outside the fusiform 'face area' in autism: Evidence from functional MRI. *Brain, 124*(10), 2059–2073. Available from http://dx.doi.org/10.1093/brain/124.10.2059.

Poljac, E., & Bekkering, H. (2012). A review of intentional and cognitive control in autism. *Frontiers in Psychology, 3*, 436. Available from http://dx.doi.org/10.3389/fpsyg.2012.00436.

Posner, M. I., & Petersen, S. E. (1990). The attention system of the human brain. *Annual Review of Neuroscience, 13*, 25–42. Available from http://dx.doi.org/10.1146/annurev.neuro.13.1.25.

Posner, M. I., & Snyder, C. R. R. (1975). Attention and cognitive control. In R. L. Solso (Ed.), *Information Processing and Cognition: The Loyola Symposium*. Lawrence Erlbaum.

Price, J. L., Carmichael, S. T., & Drevets, W. C. (1996). Networks related to the orbital and medial prefrontal cortex; a substrate for emotional behavior? *Progress in Brain Research, 107*, 523–536. Retrieved from http://www.ncbi.nlm.nih.gov/pubmed/8782540.

Quintana, J., Wong, T., Ortiz-Portillo, E., Kovalik, E., Davidson, T., Marder, S. R., & Mazziotta, J. C. (2003). Prefrontal-posterior parietal networks in schizophrenia: Primary dysfunctions and secondary compensations. *Biological Psychiatry, 53*(1), 12–24. Available from http://dx.doi.org/10.1016/S0006-3223(02)01435-X.

Raj, V., & Bell, M. A. (2010). Cognitive processes supporting episodic memory formation in childhood: The role of source memory, binding, and executive functioning. *Developmental Review, 30*(4), 384–402. Available from http://dx.doi.org/10.1016/j.dr.2011.02.001.

Ray, R. D., & Zald, D. H. (2012). Anatomical insights into the interaction of emotion and cognition in the prefrontal cortex. *Neuroscience & Biobehavioral Reviews, 36*(1), 479–501. Available from http://dx.doi.org/10.1016/j.neubiorev.2011.08.005.

Reitan, R. M. (1958). Validity of the Trail Making Test as an indicator of organic brain damage. *Perceptual and Motor Skills*, *8*, 271–276. Available from http://dx.doi.org/10.2466/PMS.8.7.271-276.

Ring, H. A., Baron-Cohen, S., Wheelwright, S., Williams, S. C. R., Brammer, M., Andrew, C., & Bullmore, E. T. (1999). Cerebral correlates of preserved cognitive skills in autism. *Brain*, *122* (7), 1305–1315. Available from http://dx.doi.org/10.1093/brain/122.7.1305.

Rogers, M. A., Kasai, K., Koji, M., Fukuda, R., Iwanami, A., Nakagome, K., & Kato, N. (2004). Executive and prefrontal dysfunction in unipolar depression: A review of neuropsychological and imaging evidence. *Neuroscience Research*, *50*(1), 1–11. Available from http://dx.doi.org/10.1016/j.neures.2004.05.003.

Rossi, A. F., Pessoa, L., Desimone, R., & Ungerleider, L. G. (2009). The prefrontal cortex and the executive control of attention. *Experimental Brain Research*, *192*(3), 489–497. Available from http://dx.doi.org/10.1007/s00221-008-1642-z.The.

Rowe, J., Lavender, A., & Turk, V. (2006). Cognitive executive function in Down's syndrome. *The British Journal of Clinical Psychology / the British Psychological Society*, *45*(Pt 1), 5–17. Available from http://dx.doi.org/10.1348/014466505X29594.

Rubia, K., Overmeyer, S., Taylor, E., Brammer, M., Williams, S. C., Simmons, A., & Bullmore, E. T. (1999). Hypofrontality in attention deficit hyperactivity disorder during higher-order motor control: A study with functional MRI. *The American Journal of Psychiatry*, *156*(6), 891–896. Available from http://dx.doi.org/10.1176/ajp.156.6.891.

Saalmann, Y. B., Pinsk, Ma, Wang, L., Li, X., & Kastner, S. (2012). The pulvinar regulates information transmission between cortical areas based on attention demands. *Science*, *337* (6095), 753–756. Available from http://dx.doi.org/10.1126/science.1223082.

Salmon, E., Linden, M. Van, Der, Collette, F., Delfiore, G., Maquet, P., Degueldre, C., & Luxen, A. (1996). Regional brain activity during working memory tasks. *Brain*, *119*(pt 5), 1617–1625.

Sass, L. A., & Borda, J. P. (2015). Phenomenology and neurobiology of self-disorder in schizophrenia: Secondary factors. *Schizophrenia Research*, *169*(1), 474–482. Available from http://dx.doi.org/10.1016/j.schres.2015.09.025.

Schipul, S. E., & Just, M. A. (2016). Diminished neural adaptation during implicit learning in autism. *NeuroImage*, *125*, 332–341. Available from http://dx.doi.org/10.1016/j.neuroimage.2015.10.039.

Schulz, K. P., Newcorn, J. H., Fan, J., Tang, C. Y., & Halperin, J. M. (2005). Brain activation gradients in ventrolateral prefrontal cortex related to persistence of ADHD in adolescent boys. *Journal of the American Academy of Child and Adolescent Psychiatry*, *44*(1), 47–54. Available from http://dx.doi.org/10.1097/01.chi.0000145551.26813.f9.

Schulz, K. P., Tang, C. Y., Fan, J., Marks, D. J., Newcorn, J. H., Cheung, A. M., & Halperin, J. M. (2005). Differential prefrontal cortex activation during inhibitory control in adolescents with and without childhood attention-deficit/hyperactivity disorder. *Neuropsychology*, *19*(3), 390–402. Available from http://dx.doi.org/10.1037/0894-4105.19.3.390.

Seghier, M. L. (2013). The angular gyrus: Multiple functions and multiple subdivisions. *The Neuroscientist: A Review Journal Bringing Neurobiology, Neurology and Psychiatry*, *19*(1), 43–61. Available from http://dx.doi.org/10.1177/1073858412440596.

Shafritz, K. M., Dichter, G. S., Baranek, G. T., & Belger, A. (2008). The neural circuitry mediating shifts in behavioral response and cognitive set in autism. *Biological Psychiatry*, *63*(10), 974–980. Available from http://dx.doi.org/10.1016/j.biopsych.2007.06.028.

Shallice, T. (1982). Specific impairments of planning. *Philosophical Transactions of the Royal Society of London B: Biological Sciences*, *298*(1089), 199–209. Retrieved from http://rstb.royalsocietypublishing.org/content/298/1089/199.abstract.

Shannon, C. E. (1948). A mathematical theory of communication. *Bell System Technical Journal, 27*(3), 379−423.

Shapiro, H. M., Wong, L. M., & Simon, T. J. (2013). A cross-sectional analysis of the development of response inhibition in children with chromosome 22q11.2 deletion syndrome. *Frontiers in Psychiatry, 4*(August), 81. Available from http://dx.doi.org/10.3389/fpsyt.2013.00081.

Siegle, G. J., Thompson, W., Carter, C. S., Steinhauer, S. R., & Thase, M. E. (2007). Increased amygdala and decreased dorsolateral prefrontal BOLD responses in unipolar depression: Related and independent features. *Biological Psychiatry, 61*(2), 198−209. Available from http://dx.doi.org/10.1016/j.biopsych.2006.05.048.

Simmons, A., Matthews, S. C., Paulus, M. P., & Stein, M. B. (2008). Intolerance of uncertainty correlates with insula activation during affective ambiguity. *Neuroscience Letters, 430*(2), 92−97. Available from http://dx.doi.org/10.1016/j.neulet.2007.10.030.

Solomon, M., Yoon, J. H., Ragland, J. D., Niendam, T. A., Lesh, T. A., Fairbrother, W., & Carter, C. S. (2013). The development of the neural substrates of cognitive control in adolescents with autism spectrum disorders. *Biological Psychiatry, 76*(5), 1−10. Available from http://dx.doi.org/10.1016/j.biopsych.2013.08.036.

Spagna, A., Dong, Y., Mackie, M.-A., Li, M., Harvey, P. D., Tian, Y., & Fan, J. (2015). Clozapine improves the orienting of attention in schizophrenia. *Schizophrenia Research, 168* (1−2), 285−291. Available from http://dx.doi.org/10.1016/j.schres.2015.08.009.

Spencer, M. D., Chura, L. R., Holt, R. J., Suckling, J., Calder, A. J., Bullmore, E. T., & Baron-Cohen, S. (2012). Failure to deactivate the default mode network indicates a possible endophenotype of autism. *Molecular Autism, 3*(1), 15. Available from http://dx.doi.org/10.1186/2040-2392-3-15.

Steele, J. D., Currie, J., Lawrie, S. M., & Reid, I. (2007). Prefrontal cortical functional abnormality in major depressive disorder: A stereotactic meta-analysis. *Journal of Affective Disorders, 101*(1-3), 1−11. Available from http://dx.doi.org/10.1016/j.jad.2006.11.009.

Strange, B. A., Duggins, A., Penny, W., Dolan, R. J., & Friston, K. J. (2005). Information theory, novelty and hippocampal responses: Unpredicted or unpredictable? *Neural Networks, 18*(3), 225−230. Available from http://dx.doi.org/10.1016/j.neunet.2004.12.004.

Stroop, J. R. (1935). Studies of interference in serial verbal reactions. *Journal of Experimental Psychology, 18*, 643−662.

Sui, J., Pearlson, G. D., Du, Y., Yu, Q., Jones, T. R., Chen, J., & Calhoun, V. D. (2015). In search of multimodal neuroimaging biomarkers of cognitive deficits in schizophrenia. *Biological Psychiatry*. Available from http://dx.doi.org/10.1016/j.biopsych.2015.02.017.

Taylor, S. F., & Liberzon, I. (2007). Neural correlates of emotion regulation in psychopathology. *Trends in Cognitive Sciences, 11*(10), 413−418. Available from http://dx.doi.org/10.1016/j.tics.2007.08.006.

Thakkar, K. N., van den Heiligenberg, F. M. Z., Kahn, R. S., & Neggers, S. F. W. (2014). Frontal-subcortical circuits involved in reactive control and monitoring of gaze. *Journal of Neuroscience, 34*(26), 8918−8929. Available from http://dx.doi.org/10.1523/JNEUROSCI.0732-14.2014.

Townsend, J., Harris, N. S., & Courchesne, E. (1996). Visual attention abnormalities in autism: Delayed orienting to location. *Journal of the International Neuropsychological Society, 2*, 541−550.

Turkeltaub, P. E., Eden, G. F., Jones, K. M., & Zeffiro, T. A. (2002). Meta-analysis of the functional neuroanatomy of single-word reading: Method and validation. *NeuroImage, 16*(3 Pt 1), 765−780. Available from http://dx.doi.org/10.1006/nimg.2002.1131.

Vaidya, C. J., Bunge, S. A., Dudukovic, N. M., Zalecki, C. A., Elliott, G. R., & Gabrieli, J. D. E. (2005). Altered neural substrates of cognitive control in childhood ADHD: Evidence from functional magnetic resonance imaging. *The American Journal of Psychiatry, 162*(9), 1605−1613. Available from http://dx.doi.org/10.1176/appi.ajp.162.9.1605.

Van Der Werf, Y. D., Scheltens, P., Lindeboom, J., Witter, M. P., Uylings, H. B. M., & Jolles, J. (2003). Deficits of memory, executive functioning and attention following infarction in the thalamus; a study of 22 cases with localised lesions. *Neuropsychologia, 41*(10), 1330−1344. http://dx.doi.org/10.1016/S0028-3932(03)00059-9.

Van Eylen, L., Boets, B., Steyaert, J., Evers, K., Wagemans, J., & Noens, I. (2011). Cognitive flexibility in autism spectrum disorder: Explaining the inconsistencies? *Research in Autism Spectrum Disorders, 5*(4), 1390−1401. Available from http://dx.doi.org/10.1016/j.rasd.2011.01.025.

van Schouwenburg, M., Aarts, E., & Cools, R. (2010). Dopaminergic modulation of cognitive control: Distinct roles for the prefrontal cortex and the basal ganglia. *Current Pharmaceutical Design, 16*(18), 2026−2032. Retrieved from http://www.ncbi.nlm.nih.gov/pubmed/20370667.

van Schouwenburg, M. R., Onnink, A. M. H., ter Huurne, N., Kan, C. C., Zwiers, M. P., Hoogman, M., & Cools, R. (2013). Cognitive flexibility depends on white matter microstructure of the basal ganglia. *Neuropsychologia, 53*, 171−177. Available from http://dx.doi.org/10.1016/j.neuropsychologia.2013.11.015.

Van Snellenberg, J. X., Girgis, R. R., Horga, G., van de Giessen, E., Slifstein, M., Ojeil, N., & Abi-Dargham, A. (2016). Mechanisms of working memory impairment in schizophrenia. *Biological Psychiatry, 80*(8), 617−626. Available from http://dx.doi.org/10.1016/j.biopsych.2016.02.017.

van Zutphen, L., Siep, N., Jacob, G. A., Goebel, R., & Arntz, A. (2015). Emotional sensitivity, emotion regulation and impulsivity in borderline personality disorder: A critical review of fMRI studies. *Neuroscience and Biobehavioral Reviews, 51*, 64−76. Available from http://dx.doi.org/10.1016/j.neubiorev.2015.01.001.

Vossel, S., Weidner, R., Driver, J., Friston, K. J., & Fink, G. R. (2012). Deconstructing the architecture of dorsal and ventral attention systems with dynamic causal modelling. *Journal of Neuroscience, 32*(31), 10637−10648. Available from http://dx.doi.org/10.1523/JNEUROSCI.0414-12.2012.

Wager, T. D., Davidson, M. L., Hughes, B. L., Lindquist, M. A., & Ochsner, K. N. (2008). Prefrontal-subcortical pathways mediating successful emotion regulation. *Neuron, 59*(6), 1037−1050. Available from http://dx.doi.org/10.1016/j.neuron.2008.09.006.

Wager, T. D., Sylvester, C.-Y. C., Lacey, S. C., Nee, D. E., Franklin, M., & Jonides, J. (2005). Common and unique components of response inhibition revealed by fMRI. *NeuroImage, 27* (2), 323−340. Available from http://dx.doi.org/10.1016/j.neuroimage.2005.01.054.

Wainwright, J. A., & Bryson, S. E. (1996). Visual-spatial orienting in autism. *Journal of Autism and Developmental Disorders, 26*(4), 423−438. Retrieved from http://www.ncbi.nlm.nih.gov/pubmed/20623169.

Walsh, B. J., Buonocore, M. H., Carter, C. S., & Mangun, G. R. (2011). Integrating conflict detection and attentional control mechanisms. *Journal of Cognitive Neuroscience, 23*(9), 2191−2201. Available from http://dx.doi.org/10.1162/jocn.2010.21595.

Walter, H., Vasic, N., Hose, A., Spitzer, M., & Wolf, R. C. (2007). Working memory dysfunction in schizophrenia compared to healthy controls and patients with depression: Evidence from event-related fMRI. *NeuroImage, 35*(4), 1551−1561. Available from http://dx.doi.org/10.1016/j.neuroimage.2007.01.041.

Walter, H., Wolf, R. C., Spitzer, M., & Vasic, N. (2007). Increased left prefrontal activation in patients with unipolar depression: An event-related, parametric, performance-controlled fMRI study. *Journal of Affective Disorders, 101*(1–3), 175–185. Available from http://dx.doi.org/10.1016/j.jad.2006.11.017.

Walter, H., Wunderlich, A. P., Blankenhorn, M., Schäfer, S., Tomczak, R., Spitzer, M., & Grön, G. (2003). No hypofrontality, but absence of prefrontal lateralization comparing verbal and spatial working memory in schizophrenia. *Schizophrenia Research, 61*(2-3), 175–184. http://dx.doi.org/10.1016/S0920-9964(02)00225-6.

Wang, L., LaBar, K. S., Smoski, M., Rosenthal, M. Z., Dolcos, F., Lynch, T. R., & McCarthy, G. (2008). Prefrontal mechanisms for executive control over emotional distraction are altered in major depression. *Psychiatry Research—Neuroimaging, 163*(2), 143–155. Available from http://dx.doi.org/10.1016/j.pscychresns.2007.10.004.

Weinberger, D. R., Berman, K. F., & Frith, C. (1996). Prefrontal function in schizophrenia: Confounds and controversies [and discussion]. *Philosophical Transactions of the Royal Society of London B: Biological Sciences, 351*(1346), 1495–1503. Retrieved from http://rstb.royalsocietypublishing.org/content/351/1346/1495.abstract.

Whalley, M. G., Rugg, M. D., Smith, A. P. R., Dolan, R. J., & Brewin, C. R. (2009). Incidental retrieval of emotional contexts in post-traumatic stress disorder and depression: An fMRI study. *Brain and Cognition, 69*(1), 98–107. Available from http://dx.doi.org/10.1016/j.bandc.2008.05.008.

Wu, Q., Chang, C.-F., Xi, S., Huang, I.-W., Liu, Z., Juan, C.-H., & Fan, J. (2015). A critical role of temporoparietal junction in the integration of top-down and bottom-up attentional control. *Human Brain Mapping, 36*(11), 4317–4333. Available from http://dx.doi.org/10.1002/hbm.22919.

Wu, T., Dufford, A.J., Egan, L.J., Mackie, M.-A., Chen, C., Yuan, C., & Fan, J. (2017). Hick's law is mediated by the cognitive control network in the brain (in press).

Wu, T., Dufford, A.J., Mackie, M.-A., Egan, L.J., & Fan, J. (2016). The capacity of cognitive control estimated from a perceptual decision making task. *Scientific Reports* 6: 34025

Xuan, B., Mackie, M.-A., Spagna, A., Wu, T., Tian, Y., Hof, P. R., & Fan, J. (2016). The activation of interactive attentional networks. *NeuroImage, 129*, 308–319. Available from http://dx.doi.org/10.1016/j.neuroimage.2016.01.017.

Zhou, Y., Shi, L., Cui, X., Wang, S., & Luo, X. (2016). Functional connectivity of the caudal anterior cingulate cortex is decreased in autism. *PloS One, 11*(3), e0151879. Available from http://dx.doi.org/10.1371/journal.pone.0151879.

FURTHER READING

Abler, B., Erk, S., Herwig, U., & Walter, H. (2007). Anticipation of aversive stimuli activates extended amygdala in unipolar depression. *Journal of Psychiatric Research, 41*, 511–522.

Agam, Y., Joseph, R. M., Barton, J. J. S., & Manoach, D. S. (2010). Reduced cognitive control of response inhibition by the anterior cingulate cortex in autism spectrum disorders. *NeuroImage, 52*, 336–347.

Audenaert, K., et al. (2002). SPECT neuropsychological activation procedure with the Verbal Fluency Test in attempted suicide patients. *Nuclear Medicine Communications, 23*, 907–916.

Backes, H., et al. (2014). Increased neural activity during overt and continuous semantic verbal fluency in major depression: Mainly a failure to deactivate. *European Archives of Psychiatry and Clinical Neuroscience, 264*, 631–645.

Belmonte, M. K., & Yurgelun-Todd, D. A. (2003). Functional anatomy of impaired selective attention and compensatory processing in autism. *Cognitive Brain Research, 17*, 651–664.

Bertocci, M.A. Abnormal anterior cingulate cortical activity during emotional n-back task performance distinguishes bipolar from unipolar depressed females, *Psychological Medicine* **42**(7), 2012, 1417–1428.

Bird, G., Catmur, C., Silani, G., Frith, C., & Frith, U. (2006). Attention does not modulate neural responses to social stimuli in autism spectrum disorders. *NeuroImage, 31*, 1614–1624.

Broome, M. R., et al. (2009). Neural correlates of executive function and working memory in the 'at-risk mental state'. *The British Journal of Psychiatry, 194*, 25–33.

Callicott, J. H., et al. (2003). Complexity of prefrontal cortical dysfunction in schizophrenia: More than up or down. *The American Journal of Psychiatry, 160*, 2209–2215.

Chantiluke, K., et al. (2014). Disorder-specific functional abnormalities during temporal discounting in youth with Attention Deficit Hyperactivity Disorder (ADHD), Autism and comorbid ADHD and Autism. *Psychiatry Research: Neuroimaging, 223*, 113–120.

Curtis, V. A., et al. (1998). Attenuated frontal activation during a verbal fluency task in patients with schizophrenia. *The American Journal of Psychiatry, 155*, 1056–1063.

Dichter, G. S., & Belger, A. (2007). Social stimuli interfere with cognitive control in autism. *NeuroImage, 35*, 1219–1230.

Dichter, G. S., & Belger, A. (2008). Atypical modulation of cognitive control by arousal in autism. *Psychiatry Research: Neuroimaging, 164*, 185–197.

Dichter, G. S., Felder, J. N., & Smoski, M. J. (2009). Affective context interferes with cognitive control in unipolar depression: An fMRI investigation. *Journal of Affective Disorders, 114*, 131–142.

Elliott, R., Rubinsztein, J. S., Sahakian, B. J., & Dolan, R. J. (2002). The neural basis of mood-congruent processing biases in depression. *Archives of General Psychiatry, 59*, 597–604.

Elliott, R., Sahakian, B. J., Michael, A., Paykel, E. S., & Dolan, R. J. (1998). Abnormal neural response to feedback on planning and guessing tasks in patients with unipolar depression. *Psychological Medicine, 28*, 559–571.

Fales, C. L., et al. (2008). Altered emotional interference processing in affective and cognitive-control brain circuitry in major depression. *Biological Psychiatry, 63*, 377–384.

Fan, J., et al. (2012). Functional deficits of the attentional networks in autism. *Brain and Behavior, 2*, 647–660.

Fernández-Corcuera, P., et al. (2013). Bipolar depressed patients show both failure to activate and failure to de-activate during performance of a working memory task. *Journal of Affective Disorders, 148*, 170–178.

Fitzgerald, P. B., et al. (2008). An fMRI study of prefrontal brain activation during multiple tasks in patients with major depressive disorder. *Human Brain Mapping, 29*, 490–501.

Fitzgerald, P. B., Laird, A. R., Maller, J., & Daskalakis, Z. J. (2008). A meta-analytic study of changes in brain activation in depression. *Human Brain Mapping, 29*, 683–695.

Fu, C. H. Y., et al. (2005). Effects of psychotic state and task demand on prefrontal function in schizophrenia: An fMRI study of overt verbal fluency. *The American Journal of Psychiatry, 162*, 485–494.

Gaffrey, M. S., et al. (2008). Atypical participation of visual cortex during word processing in autism: An fMRI study of semantic decision. *Neuropsychologia, 45*, 1672–1684.

Garrett, A., et al. (2011). Aberrant brain activation during a working memory task in psychotic major depression. *The American Journal of Psychiatry, 168*, 173–182.

Gilbert, S. J., Bird, G., Brindley, R., Frith, C. D., & Burgess, P. W. (2008). Atypical recruitment of medial prefrontal cortex in autism spectrum disorders: An fMRI study of two executive function tasks. *Neuropsychologia*, *46*, 2281–2291.

Gomot, M., et al. (2006). Change detection in children with autism: An auditory event-related fMRI study. *NeuroImage*, *29*, 475–484.

Gomot, M., Belmonte, M. K., Bullmore, E. T., Bernard, F. A., & Baron-Cohen, S. (2008). Brain hyper-reactivity to auditory novel targets in children with high-functioning autism. *Brain*, *131*, 2479–2488.

Hamilton, L. S., et al. (2009). Alterations in functional activation in euthymic bipolar disorder and schizophrenia during a working memory task. *Human Brain Mapping*, *30*, 3958–3969.

Harvey, P. O., et al. (2005). Cognitive control and brain resources in major depression: An fMRI study using the n-back task. *NeuroImage*, *26*, 860–869.

Heckers, S., et al. (2004). Anterior cingulate cortex activation during cognitive interference in schizophrenia. *The American Journal of Psychiatry*, *161*, 707–715.

Hill, E. L., & Bird, C. M. (2006). Executive processes in Asperger syndrome: Patterns of performance in a multiple case series. *Neuropsychologia*, *44*, 2822–2835.

Holmes, A. J., et al. (2005). Prefrontal functioning during context processing in schizophrenia and major depression: An event-related fMRI study. *Schizophrenia Research*, *76*, 199–206.

Honey, G. D. (2003). The functional neuroanatomy of schizophrenic subsyndromes. *Psychological Medicine*, *33*(6), 1007–1018.

Honey, G. D., et al. (1999). Differences in frontal cortical activation by a working memory task after substitution of risperidone for typical antipsychotic drugs in patients with schizophrenia. *Proceedings of the National Academy of Sciences of the United States of America*, *96*, 13432–13437.

Honey, G. D., Bullmore, E. T., & Sharma, T. (2002). De-coupling of cognitive performance and cerebral functional response during working memory in schizophrenia. *Schizophrenia Research*, *53*, 45–56.

Johnson, M. R., et al. (2006). A functional magnetic resonance imaging study of working memory abnormalities in schizophrenia. *Biological Psychiatry*, *60*, 11–21.

Just, M. A., Cherkassky, V. L., Keller, T. A., Kana, R. K., & Minshew, N. J. (2007). Functional and anatomical cortical underconnectivity in autism: Evidence from an fMRI study of an executive function task and corpus callosum morphometry. *Cerebral Cortex*, *17*, 951–961.

Kaladjian, A., et al. (2007). Blunted activation in right ventrolateral prefrontal cortex during motor response inhibition in schizophrenia. *Schizophrenia Research*, *97*, 184–193.

Kana, R. K., Keller, T. A., Minshew, N. J., & Just, M. A. (2007). Inhibitory control in high-functioning autism: Decreased activation and underconnectivity in inhibition networks. *Biological Psychiatry*, *62*, 198–206.

Kennedy, D. P., Redcay, E., & Courchesne, E. (2006). Failing to deactivate: Resting functional abnormalities in autism. *Proceedings of the National Academy of Sciences of the United States of America*, *103*, 8275–8280.

Kenworthy, L., et al. (2013). Aberrant neural mediation of verbal fluency in autism spectrum disorders. *Brain and Cognition*, *83*, 218–226.

Kerns, J. C., et al. (2004). Anterior cingulate conflict monitoring and adjustments in control. *Science*, *303*, 1023–1026.

Kiehl, K. A., & Liddle, P. F. (2001). An event-related functional magnetic resonance imaging study of an auditory oddball task in schizophrenia. *Schizophrenia Research*, *48*, 159–171.

Kim, J.-J., et al. (2003). Functional disconnection between the prefrontal and parietal cortices during working memory processing in schizophrenia: A [15(O)]H2O PET study. *The American Journal of Psychiatry, 160,* 919–923.

Koshino, H., et al. (2005). Functional connectivity in an fMRI working memory task in high-functioning autism. *NeuroImage, 24,* 810–821.

Koshino, H., et al. (2008). fMRI investigation of working memory for faces in autism: Visual coding and underconnectivity with frontal areas. *Cerebral Cortex, 18,* 289–300.

Kumari, V., et al. (2006). Neural dysfunction and violence in schizophrenia: An fMRI investigation. *Schizophrenia Research, 84,* 144–164.

Langenecker, S. A., et al. (2007). Frontal and limbic activation during inhibitory control predicts treatment response in major depressive disorder. *Biological Psychiatry, 62,* 1272–1280.

Laurens, K. R., Kiehl, K. A., Ngan, E. T. C., & Liddle, P. F. (2005). Attention orienting dysfunction during salient novel stimulus processing in schizophrenia. *Schizophrenia Research, 75,* 159–171.

Laurens, K. R., Ngan, E. T. C., Bates, A. T., Kiehl, K. A., & Liddle, P. F. (2003). Rostral anterior cingulate cortex dysfunction during error processing in schizophrenia. *Brain, 126*(pt 3), 610–622. Available from http://dx.doi.org/10.1093/brain/awg056.

Lee, T. W., Liu, H. L., Wai, Y. Y., Ko, H. J., & Lee, S. H. (2013). Abnormal neural activity in partially remitted late-onset depression: An fMRI study of one-back working memory task. *Psychiatry Research: Neuroimaging, 213,* 133–141.

Lesh, T. A., et al. (2013). Proactive and reactive cognitive control and dorsolateral prefrontal cortex dysfunction in first episode schizophrenia. *NeuroImage: Clinical, 2,* 590–599.

Macdonald, A., et al. (2005). Specificity of prefrontal dysfunction in never-medicated patients with first-episode psychosis. *The American Journal of Psychiatry, 162,* 475–484.

Manoach, D. S., et al. (2000). Schizophrenic subjects show aberrant fMRI activation of dorsolateral prefrontal cortex and basal ganglia during working memory performance. *Biological Psychiatry, 48,* 99–109.

Manoach, D. S., et al. (2005). Intact hemispheric specialization for spatial and shape working memory in schizophrenia. *Schizophrenia Research, 78,* 1–12.

Marquand, A. F., Mourão-Miranda, J., Brammer, M. J., Cleare, A. J., & Fu, C. H. Y. (2008). Neuroanatomy of verbal working memory as a diagnostic biomarker for depression. *Neuroreport, 19,* 1507–1511.

Matsuo, K., et al. (2007). Prefrontal hyperactivation during working memory task in untreated individuals with major depressive disorder. *Molecular Psychiatry, 12,* 158–166.

Matsuo, K., et al. (2013). Stable signatures of schizophrenia in the cortical-subcortical-cerebellar network using fMRI of verbal working memory. *Schizophrenia Research, 151,* 133–140.

Matthews, S., et al. (2009). Inhibition-related activity in subgenual cingulate is associated with symptom severity in major depression. *Psychiatry Research: Neuroimaging, 172,* 1–6.

Mcdowell, J. E., et al. (2002). Neural correlates of refixation saccades and antisaccades in normal and schizophrenia subjects. *Biological Psychiatry, 51*(3), 216–223.

Meisenzahl, E. M., et al. (2006). Effects of treatment with the atypical neuroleptic quetiapine on working memory function: A functional MRI follow-up investigation. *European Archives of Psychiatry and Clinical Neuroscience, 256,* 522–531.

Mendrek, A., et al. (2004). Changes in distributed neural circuitry function in patients with first-episode schizophrenia. *The British Journal of Psychiatry, 185,* 205–214.

Mendrek, A., et al. (2005). Dysfunction of a distributed neural circuitry in schizophrenia patients during a working-memory performance. *Psychological Medicine, 35,* 187–196.

Meyer-Lindenberg, A., et al. (2001). Evidence for abnormal cortical functional connectivity during working memory in schizophrenia. *The American Journal of Psychiatry, 158,* 1809–1817.

Mitterschiffthaler, M. T., et al. (2008). Neural basis of the emotional Stroop interference effect in major depression. *Psychological Medicine, 38,* 247–256.

Okada, G., Okamoto, Y., Morinobu, S., Yamawaki, S., & Yokota, N. (2003). Attenuated left prefrontal activation during a verbal fluency task in patients with depression. *Neuropsychobiology, 47,* 21–26.

Pedersen, A., et al. (2012). Anterior cingulate cortex activation is related to learning potential on the WCST in schizophrenia patients. *Brain and Cognition, 79,* 245–251.

Perlstein, W. M., Carter, C. S., Noll, D. C., & Cohen, J. D. (2001). Relation of prefrontal cortex dysfunction to working memory and symptoms in schizophrenia. *The American Journal of Psychiatry, 158,* 1105–1113.

Perlstein, W. M., Dixit, N. K., Carter, C. S., Noll, D. C., & Cohen, J. D. (2003). Prefrontal cortex dysfunction mediates deficits in working memory and prepotent responding in schizophrenia. *Biological Psychiatry, 53,* 25–38.

Pompei, F., et al. (2011). Familial and disease specific abnormalities in the neural correlates of the Stroop Task in Bipolar Disorder. *NeuroImage, 56,* 1677–1684.

Quintana, J., et al. (2003). Prefrontal-posterior parietal networks in schizophrenia: Primary dysfunctions and secondary compensations. *Biological Psychiatry, 53,* 12–24.

Raemaekers, M., et al. (2002). Neuronal substrate of the saccadic inhibition deficit in schizophrenia investigated with 3-dimensional event-related functional magnetic resonance imaging. *Archives of General Psychiatry, 59,* 313–320.

Ragland, J. D., et al. (1998). Frontotemporal cerebral blood flow change during executive and declarative memory tasks in schizophrenia: A positron emission tomography study. *Neuropsychology, 12,* 399–413.

Rubia, K., et al. (2001). An fMRI study of reduced left prefrontal activation in schizophrenia during normal inhibitory function. *Schizophrenia Research, 52,* 47–55.

Sabatino, A., et al. (2013). Functional neuroimaging of social and nonsocial cognitive control in autism. *Journal of Autism and Developmental Disorders, 43,* 2903–2913.

Sabri, O., et al. (2003). A truly simultaneous combination of functional transcranial Doppler sonography and H(2)(15)O PET adds fundamental new information on differences in cognitive activation between schizophrenics and healthy control subjects. *Journal of Nuclear Medicine, 44,* 671–681.

Sapara, A., et al. (2014). Preservation and compensation: The functional neuroanatomy of insight and working memory in schizophrenia. *Schizophrenia Research, 152,* 201–209.

Schipul, S. E., & Just, M. A. (2016). Diminished neural adaptation during implicit learning in autism. *NeuroImage, 125,* 332–341.

Schmitz, N., et al. (2006). Neural correlates of executive function in autistic spectrum disorders. *Biological Psychiatry, 59,* 7–16.

Schneider, F., et al. (2007). Neural correlates of working memory dysfunction in first-episode schizophrenia patients: An fMRI multi-center study. *Schizophrenia Research, 89,* 198–210.

Shafritz, K. M., Bregman, J. D., Ikuta, T., & Szeszko, P. R. (2015). Neural systems mediating decision-making and response inhibition for social and nonsocial stimuli in autism. *Progress in Neuro-Psychopharmacology & Biological Psychiatry, 60,* 112–120.

Shafritz, K. M., Dichter, G. S., Baranek, G. T., & Belger, A. (2008). The neural circuitry mediating shifts in behavioral response and cognitive set in autism. *Biological Psychiatry, 63,* 974–980.

Siegle, G. J., Thompson, W., Carter, C. S., Steinhauer, S. R., & Thase, M. E. (2007). Increased amygdala and decreased dorsolateral prefrontal BOLD responses in unipolar depression: Related and independent features. *Biological Psychiatry*, *61*, 198−209.

Solomon, M., et al. (2009). The neural substrates of cognitive control deficits in autism spectrum disorders. *Neuropsychologia*, *47*, 2515−2526.

Solomon, M., et al. (2013). The development of the neural substrates of cognitive control in adolescents with autism spectrum disorders. *Biological Psychiatry*, *76*, 1−10.

Subramaniam, K., et al. (2014). Intensive cognitive training in schizophrenia enhances working memory and associated prefrontal cortical efficiency in a manner that drives long-term functional gains. *NeuroImage*, *99*, 281−292.

Ungar, L., Nestor, P. G., Niznikiewicz, M. A., Wible, C. G., & Kubicki, M. (2010). Color Stroop and negative priming in schizophrenia: An fMRI study. *Psychiatry Research: Neuroimaging*, *181*, 24−29.

Vogan, V. M., et al. (2014). The neural correlates of visuo-spatial working memory in children with autism spectrum disorder: Effects of cognitive load. *Journal of Neurodevelopmental Disorders*, *6*, 19.

Wagner, G., et al. (2006). Cortical inefficiency in patients with unipolar depression: An event-related fMRI study with the Stroop task. *Biological Psychiatry*, *59*, 958−965.

Walsh, N. D., et al. (2007). A longitudinal functional magnetic resonance imaging study of verbal working memory in depression after antidepressant therapy. *Biological Psychiatry*, *62*, 1236−1243.

Walter, H., et al. (2003). No hypofrontality, but absence of prefrontal lateralization comparing verbal and spatial working memory in schizophrenia. *Schizophrenia Research*, *61*, 175−184.

Walter, H., Vasic, N., Hose, A., Spitzer, M., & Wolf, R. C. (2007). Working memory dysfunction in schizophrenia compared to healthy controls and patients with depression: Evidence from event-related fMRI. *NeuroImage*, *35*, 1551−1561.

Walter, H., Wolf, R. C., Spitzer, M., & Vasic, N. (2007). Increased left prefrontal activation in patients with unipolar depression: An event-related, parametric, performance-controlled fMRI study. *Journal of Affective Disorders*, *101*, 175−185.

Wang, L., et al. (2008). Depressive state- and disease-related alterations in neural responses to affective and executive challenges in geriatric depression. *The American Journal of Psychiatry*, *165*, 863−871.

Weiss, E. (2004). Brain activation patterns during a verbal fluency test? A functional MRI study in healthy volunteers and patients with schizophrenia. *Schizophrenia Research*, *70*, 287−291.

Weiss, E. M., et al. (2003). Brain activation patterns during a selective attention test-a functional MRI study in healthy volunteers and patients with schizophrenia. *Psychiatry Research*, *123*, 1−15.

Weiss, E. M., et al. (2007). Brain activation patterns during a selective attention test — a functional MRI study in healthy volunteers and unmedicated patients during an acute episode of schizophrenia. *Psychiatry Research: Neuroimaging*, *154*, 31−40.

Wilmsmeier, A., et al. (2010). Neural correlates of set-shifting: Decomposing executive functions in schizophrenia. *Journal of Psychiatry & Neuroscience*, *35*, 321−329.

Wykes, T., et al. (2002). Effects on the brain of a psychological treatment: Cognitive remediation therapy. Functional magnetic resonance imaging in schizophrenia. *The British Journal of Psychiatry*, *181*, 144−152.

Yerys, B. E., et al. (2015). Neural correlates of set-shifting in children with autism. *Autism Research, 8*(4), 386–397. Available from http://dx.doi.org/10.1002/aur.1454.

Yoo, S.-S., et al. (2005). Working memory processing of facial images in schizophrenia: FMRI investigation. *International Journal of Neuroscience, 115,* 351–366.

Zandbelt, B. B., Van Buuren, M., Kahn, R. S., & Vink, M. (2011). Reduced proactive inhibition in schizophrenia is related to corticostriatal dysfunction and poor working memory. *Biological Psychiatry, 70,* 1151–1158.

Chapter 12

Executive Function in Striatal Disorders

João J. Cerqueira and Nuno Sousa
*Neuroscience Domain, University of Minho and ICVS/3B's - PT Government Associate
Laboratory, Braga/Guimarães, Portugal*

ANATOMICAL AND FUNCTIONAL ORGANIZATION OF THE STRIATUM

The basal ganglia are a collection of nuclei in the depth of the brain that include the caudate nucleus, the putamen, the globus pallidus, the nucleus accumbens (NAcc), striatal cells of the olfactory tubercle, the subthalamic nucleus, and two-related structures of the midbrain, the substantia nigra (SN) and the ventral tegmental area (VTA). A short note to highlight that in the traditional concept of the basal ganglia, the amygdala is also included in the basal ganglia, composing the archistriatum. The pallidum, rich in projecting γ-aminobutyric acid (GABA)-ergic neurons with large dendritic fields, is the main output region of the dorsal basal ganglia, while the striatum, comprising the caudate and the putamen, is composed mainly of smaller, also GABAergic, medium spiny neurons, and its main receptive field (Haber, 2003). The ventral component has the NAcc as the receptor portion and the pars reticulata of the SN as the main output. Functionally, the different basal ganglia structures are organized in topographically organized corticobasal loops that operate in a parallel architecture. Distinct frontal cortical regions (in a ventral/rostral to dorsocaudal gradient) project to specific areas of the striatum (in a corresponding ventromedial to dorsolateral gradient) that in turn project intensely to the pallidum/SN pars reticulata. The latter and the internal portion of the pallidum then send their projections to distinct thalamic regions (in a dorsomedial to ventrolateral gradient) from where information reaches back to the cortex. This pathway is usually called the "direct pathway" and arises mainly from striatal medium spiny neurons rich in D1 type dopamine receptors. On the contrary, striatal medium spiny neurons rich in D2 type dopamine receptors give rise to projections to the external portion of the pallidum. This projects mostly to the subthalamic nucleus that in turn sends projections back to the internal pallidum, from where

Executive Functions in Health and Disease. DOI: http://dx.doi.org/10.1016/B978-0-12-803676-1.00012-X

information reaches the thalamus and the cortex (this constitutes the "indirect pathway") (Graybiel, 1995).

Midbrain basal ganglia (VTA and SN pars compacta) are mainly dopaminergic and project intensely to the striatum, with which they also form topographically organized loops (Haber, 2003). These dopaminergic projections to the striatum exert a key modulatory influence upon the activity of cortico-basal ganglia loops and can be grouped into two main bundles: the mesolimbic projection from the VTA to the ventral striatum (comprising the NAcc, the medioventral regions of the caudate and putamen, and the striatal cells of the olfactory tubercule) and the nigrostriatal pathway from the SN pars compacta to the dorsal regions of the caudate and putamen. Of note, by acting on both D1 (facilitatory) and D2 (inhibitory) receptors in striatal medium spiny neurons, nigrostriatal dopamine favors activity in the direct ("D1 rich") over the indirect ("D2 rich") pathway, for example, facilitating movement (in the dorsolateral striatum). On the contrary, the impact of mesolimbic dopamine in the balance between the direct and indirect pathways is not as clear because in the ventral striatum not only indirect pathway medium spiny neurons express both D1 and D2 receptors in abundance but also the result of D1 and D2 activation seems to be similar, mediating incentive salience and reward (Soares-Cunha, Coimbra, Sousa, Rodrigues, 2016).

Besides their location in the striatum and the dopamine receptor subtype they express, striatal medium spiny neurons can also be classified according to their location in acetylcholinesterase-rich (matrisomes) or acetylcholinesterase-poor (patches or striosomes) areas of the striatum. Indeed, recent evidence indicates that matrisomes cells receive projections from the frontal sensorimotor cortices, involved in motor planning and action execution, and the midbrain dopaminergic nuclei and participate in cortico-basal loops. However, striosome cells receive heavy projections from "limbic" (nonmotor) frontal areas and project mainly to the midbrain dopaminergic nuclei, thereby directly modulating the activity of the matrisome cells (Crittenden & Graybiel, 2011).

As gleaned from their close interconnections with the frontal cortical regions, the basal ganglia are strongly implicated in executive functions. The dorsolateral regions of the striatum have strong ties with the sensorimotor cortices and are deeply involved not only in the control of movement but also in commanding habitual behaviors (Dias-Ferreira et al., 2009). More central regions, including the dorsomedial striatum, receive heavy projections from the dorsolateral prefrontal cortices (dorsomedial prefrontal in rodents) and the anterior cingulate cortex and are involved in cognitive functions such as goal-directed behavior, cognitive flexibility, and working memory tasks (Voorn, Vanderschuren, Groenewegen, Robbins, & Pennartz, 2004). Finally, ventral striatal regions are tightly linked to the ventromedial prefrontal and agranular insular cortices and play a key role in the processing of reward, reinforcement, and feedback (Soares-Cunha et al. 2016). As already mentioned above, this dorsolateral to ventromedial organization of striatal inputs and functions applies particularly to cells in matrisomes, whereas striosomes receive mainly input from the orbitofrontal cortices (agranular insula) and exert a modulatory influence upon corticobasal loops, being critical for appropriate action selection and decision-making (Crittenden & Graybiel, 2011; Morgado, Sousa, & Cerqueira, 2015b). Given this organization, it is not surprising that conditions affecting the striatum, including movement disorders such as Parkinson's disease (PD) or Huntington's disease (HD), psychiatric disorders such as obsessive compulsive disorder or chronic stress exposure, are associated with executive dysfunction, the details of which will be reviewed in the subsequent sections.

EXECUTIVE DYSFUNCTION IN PARKINSON'S DISEASE

It has long been recognized that besides the cardinal motor manifestations, PD patients present a constellation of nonmotor symptoms, many of which are clearly present even in the prodromal phases of the disease (Chaudhuri & Schapira, 2009). Cognitive deficits are one of the cardinal nonmotor manifestations of PD, and its presence is associated with increased morbidity (Williams-Gray, Foltynie, Brayne, Robbins, & Barker, 2007) and, even more, predicts future mortality (Forsaa, Larsen, Wentzel-Larsen, & Alves, 2010). Patients with early PD have an estimated prevalence of cognitive deficits of 20%–30% (Aarsland & Kurz, 2010) although the nature of the deficits exhibits marked variations. While some patients have a more "posterior cortical" pattern, affecting semantic fluency and visuoconstructional abilities, most have a more frontal type, with marked deficits in phonemic fluency, attention, working memory, set shifting, and cognitive/behavioral flexibility which are signatures of executive dysfunction (Bugalho & Vale, 2011). Interestingly, it seems that early presence of the latter might be associated with a polymorphism in the Catechol-O-Methyl-Transferase (COMT) gene (Val(158)Met) and an altered risk of dementia (Williams-Gray et al., 2009).

Numerous studies have tried to elucidate the nature of executive function deficits in patients with PD at different stages of disease. To make sense from this set of data, a meta-analysis by Kudlicka, Clare, and Hindle (2011) reviewed results from the 33 published studies conducted exclusively on early stage (Hoehn & Yahr I–III) nondemented drug-naïve. It showed that compared with age, gender, and education-matched controls, early PD patients show significant deficits in prototypical measures of executive function, as assessed by the Trail Making Test (TMT), the Wisconsin Card Sorting Test (WCST), the Stroop test, the Digit-span backward test, and phonemic fluency, with the Stroop test showing the highest effect size (together with semantic fluency, a measure of more posterior cortical processing). Of note, most frontal (executive) deficits in PD patients seem to be ameliorated with dopamine replacement therapy, suggesting them to be primarily mediated by an hypodopaminergic state on the relevant corticobasal loops, contrary to more posterior cortical functions such as visual memory that seem to worsen after therapy initiation (Miah, Olde Dubbelink, Stoffers, Deijen, & Berendse, 2012).

Patients with PD have difficulties in learning from intrinsic cues, which sometimes are equated as a deficit in the internal control of attention. In an elucidating experiment, the decreased performance of PD patients on a computerized Stroop task in which the relevant stimulus attribute was only stated once at the beginning of each set of trials (as it is usually done) was completely reverted by giving an external cue before each trial indicating the relevant stimulus attribute (Brown & Marsden, 1988). This decreased ability to respond to internal cues seems also critical for the difficulties in performing the WCST, which are commonly reported in PD patients. In this test, subjects have to classify cards according to a given rule (based on color, shape, or number) that changes periodically but is never explicitly stated; instead, it has to be inferred from the feedback received by the patient, as every decision of the patient is immediately classified as correct or wrong. PD patients need more cards (feedback events) to learn the first rule and learn fewer rules than matched controls but do not perform more preservative errors, showing that it is actually a deficit in the self-directed formation of strategies/learning and not behavioral rigidity per se that drives PD patients' performance in the test (Taylor, Saint-Cyr, & Lang, 1986). Interestingly, this difficulty with self-directed learning seems to parallel a similar deficit in self-initiated actions (versus extrinsically initiated ones) that is well described and clinically relevant in PD patients (used often to overcome, e.g., the freezing of gait) and which was attributed to a underactivation of the putamen (together with the dorsolateral prefrontal cortex and supplementary motor area) during the former but not the latter (Jahanshahi et al., 1995).

Patients with PD, especially if untreated, also have impairments in attentional set-shifting, the ability to change the focus of attention from a relevant cue to a previously irrelevant cue. Moreover, this is particularly evident in face of extrinsic cues (and not internal ones) suggesting it to be independent of the above-discussed internal control deficit (Fimm, Bartl, Zimmermann, & Wallesch, 1994). Significantly, as before, patients seem to have special difficulties in paying attention to a formerly irrelevant stimulus and not a tendency to perseverate (Owen, Roberts, Hodges, & Robbins, 1993). More importantly, these deficits are completely reverted by dopaminergic treatment and immediately reinstated upon treatment cessation, suggesting that their emergence is highly dependent on the hypodopaminergic status on the dorsolateral prefrontal cortex to dorsal caudate (dorsomedial striatum) cortical loop, a major target of the nigrostriatal system primarily affected in PD (Cools, Barker, Sahakian, & Robbins, 2001). While most types of cognitive flexibility are affected in PD patients, probabilistic reversal learning, a measure of cognitive flexibility more dependent on stimulus/reward associations and the orbitofrontal to ventral striatum loop (whose major dopaminergic input, the mesolimbic/mesocortical pathways, is relatively more preserved), is considerably spared in the untreated patient population (Cools *et al.* 2001). Treated patients display notable impairments in this type of reversal learning, probably due to an excessive dopaminergic activity in relatively spared regions disrupting the fine balance between D1 and D2 receptor activation and appropriate feedback interpretation (Cools *et al.* 2001).

A hallmark of proper executive functioning is the ability to overcome automatic responses suppressing them whenever circumstances make them inadequate, exerting what has been coined as "inhibitory control." Research data reveal that this ability is strongly impaired in PD patients, which have impaired performance even in a simple go/no-go task (Cooper, Sagar, Tidswell, and Jordan, 1994) and in a more demanding conditional stop signal task (Obeso, Wilkinson, & Jahanshahi, 2011b). Importantly, difficulties in suppressing inappropriate responses seem to be generalized across multiple cognitive and motor domains in PD patients and might constitute a hallmark of the disease (Obeso et al., 2011a). Significantly and counterintuitively, one study suggested that these deficits might not to be amenable to modulation by dopaminergic replacement therapy (Obeso et al. 2011a).

Planning, the ability to foresee a sequence of actions and their respective consequences and select the best sequence to achieve a given goal, is a critical activity for everyday living and an important outcome of executive functioning. Problem solving tasks such as the Tower of London and the similar have been traditionally used to assess planning, but this ability has recently been highlighted as important for prospective memory and assessed in this context in more relevant real-life scenarios in PD (Kliegel, Altgassen, Hering, & Rose, 2011). While untreated patients with mild PD perform similarly to controls in a Tower of London task and thus seem to have intact planning abilities, patients with more severe disease needed a higher number of moves to complete the task, similar to patients with frontal lobe lesions (Owen et al., 1992). In line with this, the presence of these deficits in PD patients correlated with a decreased activation of the prefrontal-cortical-striatal loop (Lewis, Dove, Robbins, Barker, & Owen, 2003). Interestingly, dopaminergic treatment (in both mild and severe patients) selectively increased the time of initial thinking/planning in contrast with frontal lobe lesions in which this period remained unaffected, suggesting that initial problem analysis is independent from overall test performance and disturbed by dopaminergic imbalances (Owen et al., 1992). The additional time needed for treated patients to analyze a problem might be related to a difficulty in foreseeing the future and the consequences of their actions. In a revealing experiment, medicated PD patients showed difficulties in imagining novel and plausible future scenarios given their current life plans, an impairment that was correlated with decreased performance in well-known battery of executive function (de Vito et al., 2012). As stated, planning deficits have been more recently equated with failures in tasks of prospective memory, the ability to project tasks and appointments in the future and remember to accomplish them at the appropriate time. Prospective memory is also impaired in PD patients, particularly when exclusively relying on internal cues (e.g., without external reminders, alarms, and other prompts) (Kliegel et al., 2011). Interestingly, similar to previous executive function deficits, it was also shown to be restored upon dopaminergic treatment (Costa, Peppe, Caltagirone, & Carlesimo, 2008).

Decision-making, the ability to adequately choose the most favorable from a set of possible options, is highly complex executive function, which has been subject to intense research in the last decades. The most common situation, value-based decision-making tasks, involves information processing in a corticobasal loop (pavlovian, goal directed, or habit based) to weigh the expected value (benefit−cost) of each option against its associated uncertainty (risk), predictability (temporal discount), and social implications (Rangel, Camerer, & Montague, 2008), making it highly susceptible to striatal dysfunction. In face of this, the contradictory findings regarding PD patients' performance in the widely accepted Iowa Gambling Task, a classical decision-making test, with five studies suggesting no impairment and three revealing decreased performance (reviewed in Poletti, Cavedini, & Bonuccelli, 2011), appear as a surprise. Indeed, there were no significant differences among patient populations in the different studies that could explain the discrepant results. However, one must bear in mind that, although widely used as a single decision-making test, the Iowa Gambling task can conceptually be considered as having essentially two components. While the first choices consist of decisions based on ambiguity (as the subject has no a priori information of the risks and benefits of each option) and can thus be compared with the rule learning processes in the WCST, later choices are essentially a risk-based decision-making test (Brand, Recknor, Grabenhorst, & Bechara, 2007). Thus, while the first part is likely to be impaired in PD patients, performance on the second part relies heavily on the orbitofrontal cortex (and its connections with the ventral striatum; Seguin, Arseneault, and Tremblay, 2007), an area relatively spared in PD. This may also explain why results regarding PD patients' impairment in another risk-based test, the Cambridge Gambling Task, also gave contradictory results, with one study finding impaired performance (Cools, Barker, Sahakian, & Robbins, 2003) and another failing to do so (Delazer et al., 2009). Of note, it has been suggested that reward uncertainty (risk) is encoded in the orbitofrontal cortex to ventral striatum circuitry, reward expectation is encoded in the anterior cingulate cortex by mesocortical dopamine, and reward predictability is computed by a dorsolateral prefrontal cortex to dorsal striatum loop (Doya, 2008), which would be preferentially affected in PD. In line with this, PD patients off dopaminergic drugs seem to consistently have deficits in the

Game of Dice task (Boller et al., 2014; Brand et al., 2004) where reward is foreseeable (and predictable), thus recruiting the dorsal striatum loop. Of note, feedback processing problems, as mentioned before, might also account for some of the difficulties in these tasks (Brand et al., 2004). Indeed, it has even been proposed that decision-making deficits in PD patients are not generalized but focus particularly in two critical stages of the process: cost-−benefit analysis and outcome evaluation (learning from feedback) (Ryterska, Jahanshahi, & Osman, 2014). However, a recent study showed that improved performance on the Game of Dice task upon dopaminergic therapy or deep brain stimulation was not due to an improvement in the use of feedback (Boller et al., 2014).

Deep brain stimulation is highly effective in controlling motor signs and symptoms of PD patients, allowing significant reductions in dopaminergic dosage. In decision-making tasks such as the Game of Dice, deep brain stimulation seems also to reverse PD-associated deficits (Boller et al., 2014; Brandt et al., 2015) and might be more effective than dopaminergic treatment alone (Brandt et al., 2015), which has produced conflicting results (Euteneuer et al., 2009; Boller et al., 2014; Brandt et al., 2015). Interestingly, one recent study showed that initiation of deep brain stimulation and the concomitant reduction of dopaminergic medication were associated with improved (similar to non-PD controls) performance in the Iowa Gambling task (Castrioto et al., 2015).

The impact of PD treatments in decision-making tasks has recently been subject to intense scrutiny, given the reports of increased pathological gambling, pathological shopping, and hypersexuality upon treatment with dopamine agonists. However, the mechanisms underlying pathological gambling (and the other altered behaviors) are more similar to those underlying addictive behaviors and/or impulse control disorders (critically depending on the ventral striatum, the insular cortex, and mesolimbic dopamine) (Clark & Dagher, 2014), which are beyond the scope of this review. It is important to point that the enhancement of such behaviors seems exclusive of dopamine agonists and not the dopamine precursor levodopa, suggesting that they originate from a disrupted balance in the activation of different receptor subtypes and not from a general hyperdopaminergic state (Moore, Glenmullen, & Mattison, 2014). In line with this, it was shown that the risk of enhancing such disruptive behaviors was proportional to the selectivity for dopamine D3 (vs D2) receptors (Seeman, 2015).

To finalize, we will consider habit formation in patients with PD. As dopaminergic loss affects the putamen more (dorsolateral striatum) than the caudate (dorsomedial striatum), it selectively damages the habit-based action control loop while preserving goal-directed actions (Redgrave et al., 2010). This neuroanatomical findings correlate well with the fact that PD patients require more attentional control (and thus higher cognitive demand) even when executing simple everyday activities that should be entirely automatic (under the sensorimotor dorsolateral loop). Interestingly, this need for higher control for routine actions them taxes executive control in patients and might be in part responsible for their executive dysfunction (Dirnberger & Jahanshahi, 2013).

EXECUTIVE DYSFUNCTION IN HUNTINGTON'S DISEASE

HD is an autosomal dominant neurodegenerative disease caused by an abnormal expansion of a CAG repeat in the gene coding the protein huntingtin (Walker, 2007). Although its pathophysiology is poorly understood, it is well documented that the dorsal striatum is a key target of the disease, with a selective degeneration of the dorsal versus the ventral striatum, although other cortical and subcortical structures are also affected (Waldvogel, Kim, Tippett, Vonsattel, & Faull, 2015). Given its anatomical targets, it is not surprising that executive dysfunction, together with movement disturbances (chorea), are two of the main features of HD (Walker, 2007). Of note, while both Parkinson's and Huntington's disorders target the dorsal striatum, the former affects both the motor and the associative striatum, while the latter seems to be more selective (particularly at disease onset) for the dorsomedial, associative, striatum (Waldvogel et al., 2015). More importantly, while the loss of dopaminergic projections in PD results in decreased activity in the direct pathway but increased activity of the indirect pathway, loss of striatal cells (more intense in the striosomes) in HD induces decreased activity in the direct pathway but mostly in the indirect pathway (Joel, 2001). In light of these, it is not surprising that while both disorders impact executive function, the specificities of their impact are distinct.

The early recognition of executive deficits as a hallmark of HD led to the inclusion of three neuropsychological tests specifically addressing such deficits—phonemic verbal fluency, the Stroop task, and the symbol digit modalities test (SDMT)—in the Unified HD rating scale, a consensus standardized assessment first proposed in 1996 (Huntington Study Group, 1996).

Deficits in phonemic verbal fluency and the Stroop task, which require the activation of the left dorsolateral frontal areas and associated striatal circuits, are common in patients with HD. More importantly, they can even be detected in the presymptomatic stage (Holl, Wilkinson, Tabrizi, Painold, & Jahanshahi, 2013), when verbal fluency seems to be the most severely affected executive function (Unmack Larsen, Vinther-Jensen, Gade, Nielsen, & Vogel, 2015). The SDMT is considered a general measure of executive function and attention and, similarly to verbal fluency, was found to be impaired not only in patients but also in asymptomatic carriers (Unmack Larsen et al., 2015). Of note, longitudinal decline in this easy to perform test was able to successfully predict clinical disease onset in asymptomatic carriers (Hart et al., 2014) and, more importantly, distinguish asymptomatic carriers from noncarriers in one study (Lemiere, Decruyenaere, Evers-Kiebooms, Vandenbussche, & Dom, 2004) but not in a more recent one

(Hart, Middelkoop, Jurgens, Witjes-Ané, & Roos, 2011). Interestingly, despite being a written test, SDMT performance decline was shown to be independent of motor abilities, which increases its robustness in assessing patients' executive functioning (Hart et al., 2014).

As already highlighted, planning abilities are an important component of prospective memory and are key for everyday activities. When assessed on the Tower of London task, a decreased ability to plan ahead (without an increased planning time) is already present in early stage HD patients and does not decline as the disease progresses (Mörkl et al., 2016). Strikingly, these results are exactly the opposite of those obtained by PD patients, who require additional planning time but have intact planning abilities (reviewed earlier). Of interest, performance on this, and on the similar planning test Tower of Hanoi, by early disease stage patients was highly correlated with caudate atrophy, a signature of HD but not with putamen atrophy (Watkins et al., 2000; Peinemann et al., 2005), whereas PD patients' striatal dysfunction mainly affects the putamen (Redgrave et al., 2010). Moreover, the fact that caudate atrophy starts in its most dorsolateral portion and progresses to the ventromedial part later in the disease course (Holl et al., 2013) might also explain why decision-making abilities, as assessed by gambling tasks, are preserved in patients with early disease (Watkins et al., 2000; Holl et al., 2013) but affected in patients with more advanced disease (Campbell, Stout, & Finn, 2004; Busemeyer & Stout, 2002; Stout, Rodawalt, & Siemers, 2001). In line with this, performance on this task was correlated with disease stage (Stout et al., 2001) likely reflecting the underlying progression of caudate damage and the impairment of the risk-assessing ventral corticostriatal loop. Despite this, it is important to note that a recent study found no increased incidence of gambling behavior in HD patients (Kalkhoven, Sennef, Peeters, & van den Bos, 2014) reinforcing the idea that such behaviors are linked to a specific dopaminergic dysregulation at not to a global dysfunction of the ventral corticostriatal loop.

EXECUTIVE DYSFUNCTION IN CHRONIC STRESS

Chronic exposure to stress dramatically alters brain structure and induces several cognitive and behavior impairments (Sousa & Almeida, 2012). Stress-induced changes in the structure of the brain are precise as they selectively target regions participating in some functional networks but not in others; in this regard, stress-induced brain dysfunction is more a disorder of circuits than of specific isolated regions (for an integrative view, see Sousa, 2016). In what concerns the striatum, chronic stress induces an atrophy of the medium spiny neurons dendritic trees and a volume reduction in the striatal component of the associative/goal-directed corticobasal loop (caudate nucleus), in parallel with similar changes in the corresponding cortical regions (dorsolateral prefrontal cortex) (Cerqueira, Mailliet, Almeida, Jay, & Sousa, 2007) and opposite changes in the striatal component of the sensorimotor/habit-based corticobasal loop (putamen) (Soares et al, 2012; Dias-Ferreira et al., 2009). This dual effect is also present in the NAcc (part of the ventral striatum) where chronic stress induces an hypertrophy of the core part, in parallel with similar changes in the corresponding cortical areas of the limbic corticobasal loop (orbitofrontal cortex) (Morgado et al., 2015a; Liston et al., 2006) and opposite changes in the shell region (Taylor et al., 2014). Given the profound morphological changes induced by chronic stress in the striatum and the key role of this region in several executive functions, it is not surprising that stress has a profound effect in such functions in both humans and rodents. Although this review is focused in human data, the subsequent paragraphs will also discuss data from the animal models, inasmuch as they are much more extensive and seem, so far, to be in line with the scarce human data available (see, e.g., Dias-Ferreira et al., 2009 and Soares et al., 2012).

In an interesting Swedish study, chronically stressed patients were found to be significantly impaired in a phonemic fluency task and in tests assessing working memory, attention, and behavioral flexibility such as the SDMT, the TMT part B, and tests of divided attention (Öhman, Nordin, Bergdahl, Birgander, & Neely, 2007). Working memory deficits were also found in a study comparing family caregivers of older adults with high levels of psychological distress with matched controls without distress (MacKenzie, Wiprzycka, Hasher, & Goldstein, 2009), whereas attention-shifting deficits were reported in patients with chronic burnout syndrome (Sandström, Rhodin, Lundberg, Olsson, & Nyberg, 2005) and subjects experimentally exposed to 1 month of chronic psychosocial stress (Liston, McEwen, & Casey, 2009). The latter experiment also revealed these deficits to be completely reversible after a stress-free period of similar duration and correlated with a disturbance in the connection between several cortical areas and the dorsolateral prefrontal cortex, part of the associative/goal-directed circuit (Liston et al., 2009). Unfortunately, these authors did not assess any subcortical structures, although the striatum was also likely to be involved. Of note, attentional disturbances induced by chronic stress might also be related with an increased activity of several resting state networks and a decreased ability to deactivate them upon task initiation (Soares et al., 2013).

The above-mentioned findings were extensively replicated in rodents, as chronically stressed animals were shown to have worse working memory performance (Cerqueira et al., 2007; Mizoguchi et al., 2000), decreased behavioral flexibility (Cerqueira et al., 2007), reduced ability to adapt behavior to environmental cues (Morgado, Silva, Sousa, & Cerqueira, 2012), and impaired attentional set shifting ability (Liston et al., 2006) compared with nonstressed animals. More importantly, these chronic stress-induced behavior deficits were also found to be reversible (Cerqueira et al., 2007; Morgado *et al.* 2012) and to correlate with atrophy of the medial (dorsolateral in humans) prefrontal cortex (Cerqueira et al., 2007; Liston et al., 2006). As before, unfortunately no study has tried to correlate these behaviors with the well-described stress-induced changes in the dorsomedial striatum (Dias-Ferreira et al., 2009), a key projection target of the dorsomedial prefrontal cortex and likely contributor to these executive functions.

In contrast to patients with PD (see Executive Dysfunction in Parkinson's Disease), chronically stressed individuals display an increased tendency to form habits, thus freeing cognitive resources for dealing with the stressful condition. Compared with nonstressed individuals and after only a very short (30 minutes) learning period, chronically stressed young adults kept pressing a button to receive an hypercaloric reward (instead of a neutral one) even when fed to satiety or even when action was required, two characteristics of habitual responses (Soares et al., 2012). Significantly, this accelerated formation of habits in chronically stressed individuals was correlated with a decreased activity in the goal-directed/associative network, including the caudate nucleus, and an increased activity in the habit-based/sensorimotor network, including the putamen, during the actual decision period (Soares et al., 2012). In line with this, chronically stressed subjects also had enlarged putamina, atrophied caudate nucleus, and dorsolateral prefrontal cortex (Soares et al., 2012). Importantly, these changes and the corresponding behavioral alterations where completely reversed after a stress-free period (Soares et al., 2012). As before, the same alterations were reported in a study in which rats had to learn to press a lever to receive a food: after 12 days of learning (but not after 7 days) chronically stressed animals displayed habit-based behaviors while controls were still goal-directed (Dias-Ferreira et al., 2009). As already mentioned, these differences were related with a selective atrophy of the dorsomedial striatum/caudate (and the dendritic trees of its medium spiny neurons) and hypertrophy of the dorsolateral striatum/putamen (and the dendritic trees of its neurons), underlying the shift from the goal-directed to the habit-based circuit (Dias-Ferreira et al., 2009).

Finally, chronic stress also affects decision-making, particularly under risk. In humans, higher perceived chronic stress levels were correlated (albeit moderately and more in women) with increased risk-taking behavior (preference for more risky choices), although no correlation was found between behavior and hair cortisol levels, as a biological measure of chronic stress in the past few months (Ceccato, Kudielka, & Schwieren, 2016). In line with this, researchers also found that in older persons (older than 58 years) the extent of the diurnal cortisol decrease (which is inversely correlated with a chronically stressed status) was inversely correlated with risk-taking behavior, particularly for men (Weller et al., 2014). Interestingly, these results seem in contradiction with those from rodent studies, showing that chronic stress exposure induced a decreased preference for risky choices that was correlated with a hypertrophy of the lateral orbitofrontal cortex and a hypodopaminergic status on this region (Morgado et al., 2015a). More importantly, it was also shown that acute administration of a D2/D3 dopamine agonist immediately before testing was able to completely revert such chronic stress-induced changes (Morgado et al., 2015a). However, as already discussed earlier, differences between studies might stem from different interpretations of risk. Indeed, while reward uncertainty (amount of reward) is encoded in the orbitofrontal cortex to ventral striatum circuitry, reward (un)predictability (reward or no reward) is computed by a dorsolateral prefrontal cortex to dorsal striatum loop (Doya, 2008). Bearing this in mind and the fact that chronic stress exposure induces hypertrophy of the limbic loop (orbitofrontal cortex and NAcc core) and atrophy of the associative loop (prefrontal cortex and dorsomedial striatum), it is not surprising that in the rodent task, assessing preference for reward uncertainty, animals appear less risk-prone, whereas in the human tasks, assessing preferences for reward predictability, animals appears more risk-prone, displaying "impaired" performance.

FINAL WORDS

The striatum is a complex set of structures, highly interconnected with prefrontal cortical areas in spiraling (more than parallel) circuits (Joel, 2001). These relations give this region of the brain a central position to influence executive functions and perhaps justify why cognitive disorders in which these deficits predominate over memory complaints are often called subcortical dementias. Executive function deficits are, indeed, a hallmark of striatal disorders, although clinical manifestations vary according to the preferential subareas and circuits affected. Despite these differences, analysis of three prototypical examples of striatal dysfunction (PD, HD, and chronic stressed) allows us to take some general conclusions. In the first place, almost independent of the nature and location of the damage, all striatal disorders seem to impact more general abilities such as phonemic fluency, working memory, behavioral flexibility, and attention. Second, the degree to which more complex functions such as planning, habit formation, and deciding in ambiguous, uncertain, or unpredictable situations are affected is critically dependent on the circuits affected and is mostly disorder specific, the overall pattern being commonly an early specific marker of the disease. Overall, these findings should prompt us to include more standardized assessments of these executive functions in the clinical evaluation of our patients with striatal disorders, not only because these seem to be more disease specific but also because they are more closely related with the patients' activities of daily living.

REFERENCES

Aarsland, D., & Kurz, M. W. (2010). The epidemiology of dementia associated with Parkinson's disease. *Brain Pathology, 20*(3), 633—639.

Boller, J. K., Barbe, M. T., Pauls, K. A. M., Reck, C., Brand, M., Maier, F., ... Kalbe, E. (2014). Decision-making under risk is improved by both dopaminergic medication and subthalamic stimulation in Parkinson's disease. *Experimental Neurology, 254*, 70—77.

Brand, M., Labudda, K., Kalbe, E., Hilker, R., Emmans, D., Fuchs, G., ... Markowitsch, H. J. (2004). Decision-making impairments in patients with Parkinson's disease. *Behavioural Neurology*, *15*, 77–85.

Brand, M., Recknor, E. C., Grabenhorst, F., & Bechara, A. (2007). Decisions under ambiguity and decisions under risk: Correlations with executive functions and comparisons of two different gambling tasks with implicit and explicit rules. *Journal of Clinical and Experimental Neuropsychology*, *29*(1), 86–99.

Brandt, J., Rogerson, M., Al-Joudi, H., Reckess, G., Shpritz, B., Umeh, C. C., ... Mari, Z. (2015). Betting on DBS: Effects of subthalamic nucleus deep brain stimulation on risk-taking and decision-making in patients with Parkinson's disease. *Neuropsychology*, *29*(4), 622–631.

Brown, R. G., & Marsden, C. D. (1988). Internal versus external cues and the control of attention in Parkinson's disease. *Brain: A Journal of Neurology*, *111*(Pt 2), 323–345.

Bugalho, P., & Vale, J. (2011). Brief cognitive assessment in the early stages of Parkinson disease. *Cognitive and Behavioral Neurology: Official Journal of the Society for Behavioral and Cognitive Neurology*, *24*(4), 169–173.

Busemeyer, J. R., & Stout, J. C. (2002). A contribution of cognitive decision models to clinical assessment: Decomposing performance on the Bechara gambling task. *Psychological Assessment*, *14*(3), 253–262.

Campbell, M., Stout, J. C., & Finn, P. (2004). Reduced autonomic responsiveness to gambling task losses in Huntington's disease. *Journal of the International Neuropsychological Society*, *10*(2), 239–245.

Castrioto, A., Funkiewiez, A., Debû, B., Cools, R., Lhommée, E., Ardouin, C., ... Krack, P. (2015). Iowa gambling task impairment in Parkinson's disease can be normalised by reduction of dopaminergic medication after subthalamic stimulation. *Journal of Neurology, Neurosurgery, and Psychiatry*, *86*, 186–190.

Ceccato, S., Kudielka, B. M., & Schwieren, C. (2016). Increased risk taking in relation to chronic stress in adults. *Frontiers in Psychology*, *6*(JAN), 1–13.

Cerqueira, J. J., Mailliet, F., Almeida, O. O. F. X., Jay, T. M., & Sousa, N. (2007). The prefrontal cortex as a key target of the maladaptive response to stress. *The Journal of Neuroscience: The Official Journal of the Society for Neuroscience*, *27*(11), 2781–2787.

Chaudhuri, K. R., & Schapira, A. H. (2009). Non-motor symptoms of Parkinson's disease: Dopaminergic pathophysiology and treatment. *The Lancet Neurology*, *8*(5), 464–474.

Clark, C. A., & Dagher, A. (2014). The role of dopamine in risk taking: A specific look at Parkinson's disease and gambling. *Frontiers in Behavioral Neuroscience*, *8*(May), 1–12.

Cools, R., Barker, R. A., Sahakian, B. J., & Robbins, T. W. (2001). Enhanced or impaired cognitive function in Parkinson's disease as a function of dopaminergic medication and task demands. *Cerebral Cortex*, *11*(12), 1136–1143.

Cools, R., Barker, R. A., Sahakian, B. J., & Robbins, T. W. (2003). L-Dopa medication remediates cognitive inflexibility, but increases impulsivity in patients with Parkinson's disease. *Neuropsychologia*, *41*(11), 1431–1441.

Cooper, J. A., Sagar, H. J., Tidswell, P., & Jordan, N. (1994). Slowed central processing in simple and go/no-go reaction time tasks in Parkinson's disease. *Brain*, *117*, 517–529.

Costa, A., Peppe, A., Caltagirone, C., & Carlesimo, G. A. (2008). Prospective memory impairment in individuals with Parkinson's disease. *Neuropsychology*, *31*(3), 157–163.

Crittenden, J. R., & Graybiel, A. M. (2011). Basal ganglia disorders associated with imbalances in the striatal striosome and matrix compartments. *Frontiers in Neuroanatomy*, *5*, 59.

de Vito, S., Gamboz, N., Brandimonte, M. A., Barone, P., Amboni, M., & Della Sala, S. (2012). Future thinking in Parkinson's disease: An executive function? *Neuropsychologia, 50*(7), 1494–1501.

Delazer, M., Sinz, H., Zamarian, L., Stockner, H., Seppi, K., Wenning, G. K., ... Poewe, W. (2009). Decision making under risk and under ambiguity in Parkinson's disease. *Neuropsychologia, 47*(8–9), 1901–1908.

Dias-Ferreira, E., Sousa, J. C., Melo, I., Morgado, P., Mesquita, A. R., Cerqueira, J. J., ... Sousa, N. (2009). Chronic stress causes frontostriatal reorganization and affects decision-making. *Science, 325*(5940), 621–625.

Dirnberger, G., & Jahanshahi, M. (2013). Executive dysfunction in Parkinson's disease: A review. *Journal of Neuropsychology, 7*, 193–224.

Doya, K. (2008). Modulators of decision making. *Nature in Neuroscience, 11*(4), 410–416.

Euteneuer, F., Schaefer, F., Stuermer, R., Boucsein, W., Timmermann, L., Barbe, M. T., ... Kalbe, E. (2009). Dissociation of decision-making under ambiguity and decision-making under risk in patients with Parkinson's disease: A neuropsychological and psychophysiological study. *Neuropsychologia, 47*(13), 2882–2890.

Fimm, B., Bartl, G., Zimmermann, P., & Wallesch, C. W. (1994). Different mechanisms underly shifting set on external and internal cues in Parkinson's disease. *Brain and Cognition, 25*, 287–304.

Forsaa, E. B., Larsen, J. P., Wentzel-Larsen, T., & Alves, G. (2010). What predicts mortality in Parkinson disease? A prospective population-based long-term study. *Neurology, 75*(14), 1270–1276.

Graybiel, A. M. (1995). The basal ganglia. *Trends in Neurosciences, 18*(2), 60–62.

Haber, S. N. (2003). The primate basal ganglia: Parallel and integrative networks. *Journal of Chemical Neuroanatomy, 26*(4), 317–330.

Hart, E., Middelkoop, H., Jurgens, C. K., Witjes-Ané, M. N. W., & Roos, R. A. C. (2011). Seven-year clinical follow-up of premanifest carriers of Huntington's disease. *PLoS Currents, 3*, 1–14.

Hart, E. P., Dumas, E. M., Schoonderbeek, A., Wolthuis, S. C., Van Zwet, E. W., & Roos, R. A. C. (2014). Motor dysfunction influence on executive functioning in manifest and premanifest Huntington's disease. *Movement Disorders, 29*(3), 320–326.

Holl, A. K., Wilkinson, L., Tabrizi, S. J., Painold, A., & Jahanshahi, M. (2013). Selective executive dysfunction but intact risky decision-making in early Huntington's disease. *Movement Disorders, 28*(8), 1104–1109.

Huntington Study Group (1996). Unified Huntington's disease rating scale: Reliability and consistency. *Movement Disorders, 11*(2), 136–142.

Jahanshahi, M., Jenkins, I. H., Brown, R. G., Marsden, C. D., Passingham, R. E., & Brooks, D. J. (1995). Self-initiated versus externally triggered movements 1. An investigation using measurement of regional cerebral blood-flow with pet and movement-related potentials in normal and Parkinson's disease subjects. *Brain, 118*, 913–933.

Joel, D. (2001). Open interconnected model of basal ganglia-thalamocortical circuitry and its relevance to the clinical syndrome of Huntington's disease. *Movement Disorders, 16*(3), 407–423.

Kalkhoven, C., Sennef, C., Peeters, A., & van den Bos, R. (2014). Risk-taking and pathological gambling behavior in Huntington's disease. *Frontiers in Behavioral Neuroscience, 8*, 103.

Kliegel, M., Altgassen, M., Hering, A., & Rose, N. S. (2011). A process-model based approach to prospective memory impairment in Parkinson's disease. *Neuropsychologia, 49*(8), 2166–2177.

Kudlicka, A., Clare, L., & Hindle, J. V. (2011). Executive functions in Parkinson's disease: Systematic review and meta-analysis. *Movement Disorders, 26*(13), 2305–2315.

Lemiere, J., Decruyenaere, M., Evers-Kiebooms, G., Vandenbussche, E., & Dom, P. D. R. (2004). Cognitive changes in patients with Huntington's disease (HD) and asymptomatic carriers of the HD mutation. *Journal of Neurology, 251*(8), 935–942.

Lewis, S. J. G., Dove, A., Robbins, T. W., Barker, R. A., & Owen, A. M. (2003). Cognitive impairments in early Parkinson's disease are accompanied by reductions in activity in frontostriatal neural circuitry. *The Journal of Neuroscience: The Official Journal of the Society for Neuroscience, 23*(15), 6351–6356.

Liston, C., McEwen, B. S., & Casey, B. J. (2009). Psychosocial stress reversibly disrupts prefrontal processing and attentional control. *Proceedings of the National Academy of Sciences of the United States of America, 106*(3), 912–917.

Liston, C., Miller, M. M., Goldwater, D. S., Radley, J. J., Rocher, A. B., Hof, P. R., ... Mcewen, B. S. (2006). Stress-induced alterations in prefrontal cortical dendritic morphology predict selective impairments in perceptual attentional set-shifting. *Journal of Neuroscience, 26*(30), 7870–7874.

MacKenzie, C. S., Wiprzycka, U. J., Hasher, L., & Goldstein, D. (2009). Associations between psychological distress, learning, and memory in spouse caregivers of older adults. *Journals of Gerontology - Series B Psychological Sciences and Social Sciences, 64*(6), 742–746.

Miah, I. P., Olde Dubbelink, K. T., Stoffers, D., Deijen, J. B., & Berendse, H. W. (2012). Early-stage cognitive impairment in Parkinson's disease and the influence of dopamine replacement therapy. *European Journal of Neurology, 19*(3), 510–516.

Mizoguchi, K., Yuzurihara, M., Ishige, A., Sasaki, H., Chui, D. H., & Tabira, T. (2000). Chronic stress induces impairment of spatial working memory because of prefrontal dopaminergic dysfunction. *The Journal of Neuroscience: The Official Journal of the Society for Neuroscience, 20*(4), 1568–1574.

Moore, T. J., Glenmullen, J., & Mattison, D. R. (2014). Reports of pathological gambling, hypersexuality, and compulsive shopping associated with dopamine receptor agonist drugs. *JAMA Intern Med., 22314*(12), 1930–1933.

Morgado, P., Marques, F., Ribeiro, B., Leite-Almeida, H., Pêgo, J. M., Rodrigues, A. J., ... Cerqueira, J. J. (2015a). Stress induced risk-aversion is reverted by D2/D3 agonist in the rat. *European Neuropsychopharmacology, 25*(10), 1744–1752.

Morgado, P., Silva, M., Sousa, N., & Cerqueira, J. J. (2012). Stress transiently affects pavlovian-to-instrumental transfer. *Frontiers in Neuroscience, 6*, 93.

Morgado, P., Sousa, N., & Cerqueira, J. J. (2015b). The impact of stress in decision making in the context of uncertainty. *Journal of Neuroscience Research, 93*(6), 839–847.

Mörkl, S., Müller, N. J., Blesl, C., Wilkinson, L., Tmava, A., Wurm, W., ... Painold, A. (2016). Problem solving, impulse control and planning in patients with early- and late-stage Huntington's disease. *European Archives of Psychiatry and Clinical Neuroscience, 266*(7), 663–671.

Obeso, I., Wilkinson, L., Casabona, E., Bringas, M. L., Álvarez, M., Álvarez, L., ... Jahanshahi, M. (2011a). Deficits in inhibitory control and conflict resolution on cognitive and motor tasks in Parkinson's disease. *Experimental Brain Research, 212*(3), 371–384.

Obeso, I., Wilkinson, L., & Jahanshahi, M. (2011b). Levodopa medication does not influence motor inhibition or conflict resolution in a conditional stop-signal task in Parkinson's disease. *Experimental Brain Research, 213*(4), 435–445.

Öhman, L., Nordin, S., Bergdahl, J., Birgander, L. S., & Neely, A. S. (2007). Cognitive function in outpatients with perceived chronic stress. *Scandinavian Journal of Work, Environment and Health*, *33*(3), 223–232.

Owen, A. M., James, M., Leigh, P. N., Summers, B. A., Marsden, C. D., Quinn, N. P., ... Robbins, T. W. (1992). Fronto-striatal cognitive deficits at different stages of Parkinson's disease. *Brain*, *115*, 1727–1751.

Owen, A. M., Roberts, A. C., Hodges, J. R., & Robbins, T. W. (1993). Contrasting mechanisms of impaired attentional set-shifting in patients with frontal lobe damage or Parkinson's disease. *Brain*, *116*(5), 1159–1175.

Peinemann, A., Schuller, S., Pohl, C., Jahn, T., Weindl, A., & Kassubek, J. (2005). Executive dysfunction in early stages of Huntington's disease is associated with striatal and insular atrophy: A neuropsychological and voxel-based morphometric study. *Journal of the Neurological Sciences*, *239*(1), 11–19.

Poletti, M., Cavedini, P., & Bonuccelli, U. (2011). Iowa gambling task in Parkinson's disease. *Journal of Clinical and Experimental Neuropsychology*, *33*(4), 395–409.

Rangel, A., Camerer, C., & Montague, P. R. (2008). Neuroeconomics: The neurobiology of value-based decision-making. *Nature Reviews Neuroscience*, *9*(7), 545–556.

Redgrave, P., Rodriguez, M., Smith, Y., Rodriguez-Oroz, M., Lehericy, S., Bergman, H., ... Obeso, J. (2010). Goal-directed and habitual control in the basal ganglia: Implications for Parkinson's disease. *Nature Reviews Neuroscience*, *11*, 760–772.

Ryterska, A., Jahanshahi, M., & Osman, M. (2014). Decision-making impairments in Parkinson's disease as a by-product of defective cost-benefit analysis and feedback processing. *Neurodegenerative Disease Management*, *4*(4), 317–327.

Sandström, A., Rhodin, I. N., Lundberg, M., Olsson, T., & Nyberg, L. (2005). Impaired cognitive performance in patients with chronic burnout syndrome. *Biological Psychology*, *69*(3), 271–279.

Seeman, P. (2015). Parkinson's disease treatment may cause impulse-control disorder via dopamine D3 receptors. *Synapse*, *69*(4), 183–189.

Seguin, J., Arseneault, L., & Tremblay, R. (2007). The contribution of "cool" and "hot" components of decision-making in adolescence: Implications for psychopathology. *Cognitive Development*, *22*, 530–543.

Soares, J. M., Sampaio, A., Ferreira, L. M., Santos, N. C., Marques, F., Palha, J. A., ... Sousa, N. (2012). Stress-induced changes in human decision-making are reversible. *Translational Psychiatry*, *2*(7), e131.

Soares, J. M., Sampaio, A., Ferreira, L. M., Santos, N. C., Marques, P., Marques, F., ... Sousa, N. (2013). Stress impact on resting state brain networks. *PLoS One*, *8*(6), e66500.

Soares-Cunha, C., Coimbra, B., Sousa, N., & Rodrigues, A. J. (2016). Reappraising striatal D1- and D2-neurons in reward and aversion. *Neuroscience and Biobehavioral Reviews*, *68*, 370–386.

Sousa, N. (2016). The dynamics of the stress neuromatrix. *Molecular Psychiatry*, *21*(February 2015), 1–11.

Sousa, N., & Almeida, O. F. X. (2012). Disconnection and reconnection: The morphological basis of (mal)adaptation to stress. *Trends in Neurosciences*, *35*(12), 742–751.

Stout, J. C., Rodawalt, W. C., & Siemers, E. R. (2001). Risky decision making in Huntington's disease. *Journal of the International Neuropsychological Society: JINS*, *7*(1), 92–101.

Taylor, A., Saint-Cyr, A., & Lang, E. (1986). Frontal lobe dysfunction in Parkinson's disease. *Brain*, *109*, 845–883.

Taylor, S. B., Anglin, J. M., Paode, P. R., Riggert, A. G., Olive, M. F., & Conrad, C. D. (2014). Chronic stress may facilitate the recruitment of habit- and addiction-related neurocircuitries through neuronal restructuring of the striatum. *Neuroscience, 280*, 231–242.

Unmack Larsen, I., Vinther-Jensen, T., Gade, A., Nielsen, J. E., & Vogel, A. (2015). Assessing impairment of executive function and psychomotor speed in premanifest and manifest Huntington's disease gene-expansion carriers. *Journal of the International Neuropsychological Society, 21*(3), 193–202.

Voorn, P., Vanderschuren, L. J. M. J., Groenewegen, H. J., Robbins, T. W., & Pennartz, C. M. A. (2004). Putting a spin on the dorsal-ventral divide of the striatum. *Trends in Neurosciences, 27*(8), 468–474.

Waldvogel, H. J., Kim, E. H., Tippett, L. J., Vonsattel, J.-P. G., & Faull, R. L. M. (2015). The neuropathology of Huntington's disease. *Current Topics in Behavioral Neuroscience, 22*, 33–80.

Walker, F. O. (2007). Huntington's disease. *Lancet, 369*(9557), 218–228.

Watkins, L. H. A., Rogers, R. D., Lawrence, A. D., Sahakian, B. J., Rosser, A. E., & Robbins, T. W. (2000). Impaired planning but intact decision making in early Huntington's disease: Implications for specific fronto-striatal pathology. *Neuropsychologia, 38*(8), 1112–1125.

Weller, J. A., Buchanan, T. W., Shackleford, C., Morganstern, A., Hartman, J. J., Yuska, J., & Denburg, N. L. (2014). Diurnal cortisol rhythm is associated with increased risky decision-making in older adults. *Psychology and Aging, 29*(2), 271–283.

Williams-Gray, C. H., Evans, J. R., Goris, A., Foltynie, T., Ban, M., Robbins, T. W., . . . Barker, R. A. (2009). The distinct cognitive syndromes of Parkinson's disease: 5 year follow-up of the CamPaIGN cohort. *Brain, 132*(11), 2958–2969.

Williams-Gray, C. H., Foltynie, T., Brayne, C. E. G., Robbins, T. W., & Barker, R. A. (2007). Evolution of cognitive dysfunction in an incident Parkinson's disease cohort. *Brain, 130*(7), 1787–1798.

Chapter 13

Neurodevelopmental Disorders and the Frontal Lobes

Masao Aihara
Graduate Faculty of Interdisciplinary Research, University of Yamanashi, Yamanashi, Japan

INTRODUCTION

Knowledge of neuroanatomy has contributed to the understanding of frontal lobe functions (Fuster, 2015). The prefrontal cortex (PFC) is neuroanatomically divided into the following regions: the dorsolateral PFC, the orbitofrontal cortex, the ventrolateral PFC, and the medial PFC (Fig. 13.1). The PFC receives input from the sensory association regions of the cortex (cognitive circuit) and is also connected to the premotor and motor regions and the striatum (frontostriatum circuit). Subcortical bidirectional connections are present with the amygdala via the dorsomedial nucleus of the thalamus (emotional circuit), with the hypothalamus via the insula (somatic marker), and with the hippocampus via the cingulate cortex (memory circuit).

The PFC, which is critical for the temporal organization of cognitive processes, is among the last cortical regions to reach full functional maturity (Fuster, 2015; Stuss & Knight, 2013). Therefore, prefrontal functions show an unusually long period of plasticity and vulnerability in which neurons and glia are easily affected by internal and external insults (Dobbing & Sands, 1971). Furthermore, early frontal lesions can result in deficits that are not immediately apparent, but that predispose an individual to later developmental problems such as learning disorder (LD), attention-deficit hyperactivity disorder (ADHD), and even problems with moral judgment (Anderson, Bechara, Damasio, Tranel, & Damasio, 1999; Barkley & Fischer, 2010; Barkley, 1997). To fully appreciate the implications of developmental problems in children with frontal lobe damage, hypothesis-driven studies are needed to explore functions such as executive function during childhood, rather than relying solely on traditional intelligence tests.

Executive function, the principal function of the PFC, is the ability to temporally organize purposeful behavior, language, and reasoning (Fuster, 2015; Goldberg, 2009; Stuss & Knight, 2013). Executive function is believed

Executive Functions in Health and Disease. DOI: http://dx.doi.org/10.1016/B978-0-12-803676-1.00013-1

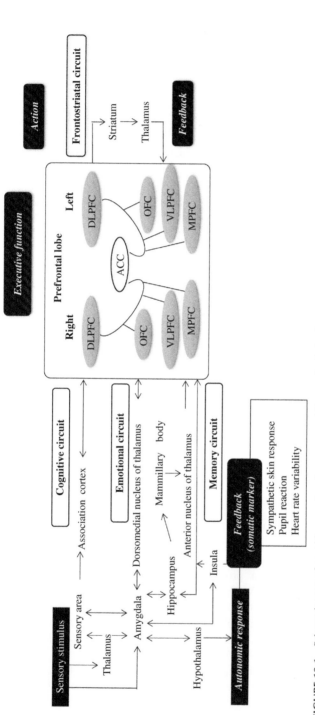

FIGURE 13.1 Schematic map of cognitive, emotional, memory, and frontostriatal circuit connectivity to the prefrontal cortex for executive function. *DLPFC,* dorsolateral prefrontal cortex; *OFC,* orbitofrontal cortex; *VLPFC,* ventrolateral prefrontal cortex; *MPFC,* medial prefrontal cortex; *ACC,* anterior cingulate cortex.

to be composed of three measurable components. (1) Response/behavior inhibition—Inhibition control is necessary when processing involves sustained attention and working memory (Goto et al., 2010; Smith, Johnstone, & Barry, 2004) and depends on the function of the ventrolateral PFC (Brodmann (BA) 47) (Matsubara, Yamaguchi, Xu, & Kobayashi, 2004; Yasumura et al., 2014). (2) Decision-Making: In daily life, we perform repeated decision-making, considering several choices and uncertain circumstances. The orbitofrontal cortex (BA 11, 12) is an important region for the ability to predict future reward/punishment expectations (Damasio, 1994; Manes et al., 2002). (3) Temporal integration: This function is the ability to carry out new and goal-directed behavior or reasoning (Fuster, 2015; Goldberg, 2009; Stuss & Knight, 2013). The dorsolateral PFC (BA 8, 9, and 46) is important for working memory tasks that involve bridging/comparison of temporally separate information.

This chapter deals with response/behavior inhibition by using a memory-guided saccade task (MGST), decision-making by using autonomic responses to aversive visual stimuli, and temporal integration (an ability to organize reasoning) by using a cognitive bias task (CBT).

RESPONSE/BEHAVIOR INHIBITION

In current cognitive theory, the core symptoms in ADHD are considered to be caused by abnormal selection and maintenance of motor responses to stimuli, due to a failure to inhibit or delay behavioral responses (Barkley & Fischer, 2010; Barkley, 1997; Bush et al., 1999; Inoue, Inagaki, Gunji, Furushima, & Kaga, 2008; Jonkman, 2006). Behavior inhibition involves three processes: inhibiting the initial prepotent response; stopping an ongoing response; and interference control from disruption (Barkley, 1997), which is also hypothesized to lead to secondary impairment in executive functions such as working memory, planning, temporal integration, internal speech, and decision-making.

With this background, the aims of this study were to investigate the development of voluntary control of saccades in normal children using an MGST to compare saccade parameters of reflexive deficits in response inhibition between ADHD and control groups and to identify areas involved in the dysfunctional nervous system in children with ADHD (Goto et al., 2010).

Subjects and Methods

Fifteen right-handed subjects (all boys; age range, 6–8 years old) were recruited as controls to investigate saccade development. In addition, 10 children (all boys; age range, 6–8 years old) with ADHD participated in the study.

Each subject was seated upright in a dental chair equipped with a chin rest in the dark, facing a display placed 100 cm away from the eyes. In each trial,

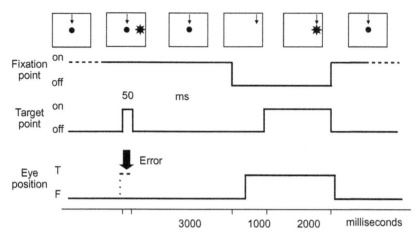

FIGURE 13.2   Representation of memory-guided saccade task. Fixation point illumination (fixation point), target position (target point), and optimal eye position (eye position) tracing are shown. Eye movements are shown for when subjects performed erroneously (↓, anticipatory error).

a central fixation point (FP) first appeared in the straight-ahead position at the center of the screen. Visual targets were presented at a location 20 degrees to the right or left of the central FP. Task presentation was performed in the order detailed below and was maintained across subjects. In the MGST, the subject was instructed to fixate on a central FP, while a lateral target was flashed in a randomly presented direction for a period of 50 ms, saccade to which is prohibited (Fig. 13.2). When the central FP was switched off for 3 seconds after the flashed target disappeared, the subject was required to make a saccade to the remembered position of the flash. The lateral target was then switched on 1 second after disappearance of the central FP, and the subject could make a corrective saccade if so desired. If a saccade was made to the flash while the FP was on, it was judged as an anticipatory error. Eye movements were measured by electrooculography in only the horizontal direction with a bandwidth ranging between direct current and 10 Hz.

Differences Between ADHD and Controls

Mean saccade latency in the MGST was generally longer in ADHD patients (434.7 ± 113.5 ms) compared with controls (338.9 ± 73.5 ms; $P < .05$). Significant differences were found between the two groups in accuracy ($P < .05$). The ADHD group ($59.4\% \pm 18.2\%$) showed a significantly higher percentage of anticipatory errors than controls ($17.8\% \pm 11.9\%$) ($P < .01$).

We found that ADHD children showed significantly more anticipatory errors in the MGST compared with controls. This finding is consistent with the results of previous studies (Manes et al., 2002; Matsubara et al., 2004) and indicates deficits in response inhibition. Current neuropsychological theories emphasize behavior inhibition as the primary deficit in ADHD (Barkley, 1997; Sonuga-Barke, 2003; Sonuga-Barke, Bitsakou, & Thompson, 2010). The three interrelated processes were postulated by Barkley (1997) to constitute response inhibition. Impairment in interference control of this delay from disruption by competing events and responses, representing one of the three response inhibitions, is believed to lead to an anticipatory error in the MGST. Functional imaging in humans and electrophysiological studies in monkeys have shown the presence of a neural network between the frontal eye field (FEF) and parietal area that functions during the MGST (Connolly, Goodale, Menon, & Munoz, 2002; Everling & Munoz, 2000). The FEF is involved in motor planning, whereas the parietal area encodes the spatial location of the relevant sensory stimuli. Therefore, the neural network between the FEF and parietal area is believed to be disrupted by a failure of interference control in ADHD children.

DECISION-MAKING

In daily life, we consciously or unconsciously perform repeated decision-making when considering several choices. To make decisions and perform in uncertain circumstances, deliberation about possible future consequences using probabilistic estimations of both reward and risk is required. The recent somatic marker hypothesis (SMH) proposed by Damasio, Tranel, and Damasio (1990), Bechara, Damasio, Tranel, and Damasio (2005), and Bechara and Damasio (2005) is one idea that may explain the processes of human decision-making. The key idea of the SMH is that the process of decision-making that takes place in the ventromedial PFC, insula, anterior cingulate cortex, and amygdala is influenced by marker signals that arise during autonomic responses such as sympathetic skin responses (SSR) (Aihara, Sata, Osada, Ozoki, & Nakazawa, 1998). Subjects with ventromedial PFC lesions tend to make dangerous decisions and also show a failure of the psychophysiological response (i.e., skin conductance response) (Bechara, Tranel, & Damasio, 2000; Damasio et al., 1990).

Subjects and Methods

Eighteen children aged 6−17 years old (mean age: 10.2 ± 3.7 years) were recruited as controls. We also examined three children aged 13−15 years old with lesions of the frontal−emotional circuit revealed by magnetic resonance imaging (MRI; Fig. 13.3) who all showed conduct disorder. For this study, we originally drew 50 different types of pictures. To standardize the pictures, we evaluated them with a survey consisting of two axes, arousal and valence, modified by the method of the International Affective Picture System, which is used widely to standardize emotional

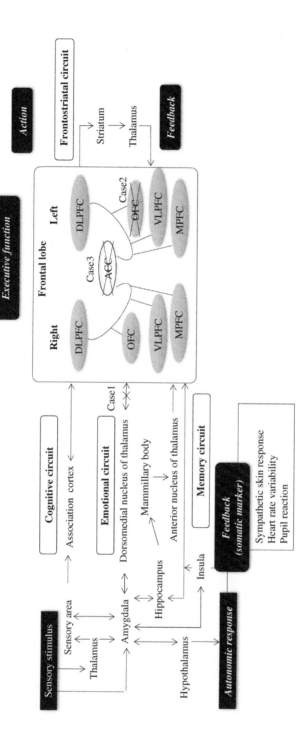

FIGURE 13.3 Schematic map of three patients with frontal lesions. *DLPFC*, dorsolateral prefrontal cortex; *OFC*, orbitofrontal cortex; *VLPFC*, ventrolateral prefrontal cortex; *MPFC*, medial prefrontal cortex; *ACC*, anterior cingulate cortex.

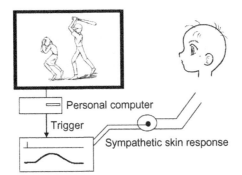

FIGURE 13.4 Schematic representation of the sympathetic skin response measurement system.

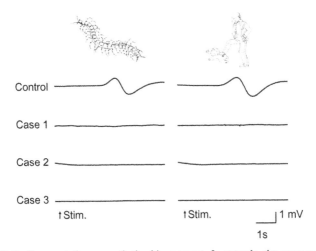

FIGURE 13.5 Representative sympathetic skin response. In controls, the appearance of SSR for aversive/immoral pictures is remarkable. In contrast, all patients with frontal lesions failed to respond to the same picture stimuli. *SSR*, sympathetic skin response.

visual stimuli (Lang, Bradley, & Cuthbert, 1999). The pictures were presented on a monitor for 1.5 seconds each, and the interval between each picture varied randomly from 10 to 14 seconds to avoid anticipatory response (Fig. 13.4).

Differences Between the Frontal Lesion Group and Controls

In normal controls, SSR always appeared 1.5–2 seconds after the presentation of aversive/immoral visual stimuli (Fig. 13.5). However, SSR did not appear in any patients with frontal lesions, although surprisingly, all of them could judge that each picture was aversive or immoral. This is why the lateral PFC may contribute to decision-making regarding veridical information. Failure of a contribution of the frontal–emotional circuit to decision-making may explain the patient's behavior (i.e., conduction disorder). This finding seems to be in agreement with the SMH proposed by Damasio et al. (1990), Bechara et al. (2005), and Bechara and Damasio (2005).

TEMPORAL INTEGRATION (AN ABILITY TO ORGANIZE REASONING)

Some researchers have hypothesized two functionally and neurally distinct cognitive selection mechanisms involving the prefrontal lobes: those involving processing based on internal representations, e.g., planning (context-dependent reasoning), and those involving exploratory processing of novel cognitive situations (context-independent reasoning) (Goldberg & Costa, 1981; Milner & Petrides, 1984; Petrides & Milner, 1982). Goldberg et al. recently refined the CBT for use as an activation procedure representing contextual reasoning and concluded that extreme context-dependent and context-independent response selection biases are linked to the left and right frontal systems, respectively, in right-handed male subjects (Goldberg & Podell, 1995; Goldberg, 2009; Goldberg, Podell, Harner, Riggio, & Lovell, 1994; Podell, Lovell, Zimmerman, & Goldberg, 1995). Based on these findings, we used the CBT to explore development of lateralization in the frontal lobes as a function of age (Aihara, Aoyagi, Goldberg, & Nakazawa, 2003; Aoyagi, Aihara, Goldberg, & Nakazawa, 2005; Shimoyama et al., 2004).

Subjects and Methods

Subjects included 37 right-handed healthy children and adolescents (all male; age range, 5–18 years) and 19 adult males aged 20–30 years who served as controls. We also examined 12 male children with focal frontal lobe lesions/epileptic foci and further divided them according to the laterality of frontal pathology based on the presentation of seizures, 3D MRI, and ictal electroencephalography/single photon emission computed tomography studies. The study included eight children with left frontal lobe lesions/epileptic foci (mean age: 13.1 ± 2.3 years) and four with right frontal lobe lesions/epileptic foci (mean age: 12.8 ± 3.1 years).

A modified version of the original task developed by Goldberg et al. (1994) was designed for children (modified CBT; mCBT). Computer-presented "cards" in the mCBT differed dichotomously in four respects: shape (circle vs square), color (red vs blue), number (one vs two), and shading (outline only vs homogeneously filled). Thus, 16 different stimuli can be presented. A trial involved presentation of the target card alone followed by two choice cards below it (Fig. 13.6). An investigator instructed the subject to look at the target and then select the choice that he preferred. The 30 trial sequences that followed were the same for all subjects.

FIGURE 13.6 Example of a cognitive bias task trial. A trial involves presentation of the target alone, with two choices immediately added below the target in vertical alignment. Here, if a subject selects the upper choice as his preference, the similarity index is three (similar in shape, color, and number, but not in shading). In these examples, the actual color of all figures was red.

An index of similarity to the target that was designed never to be equal between the two choices offered was determined for the subject's choice in each trial. The index ranged from four for identical stimuli to zero for stimuli differing in all four possible respects. All interchoice similarity index values and target-to-choice similarity index values were equally represented and counterbalanced throughout the trial sequence. The mCBT raw score was the sum of similarity indices across trials and was designed to range from 30 to 90. High and low raw scores implied, respectively, consistently similar and consistently dissimilar choices, indicating a target-driven selection bias. A middle-range score (around 60) implied that choices were unrelated to corresponding targets (indifferent selection bias). The converted mCBT score was computed as the absolute value of the deviation of the raw score from the midpoint of the raw score scale, equal to 60. On the converted scale, ranging from 0 to 30, a high score implied a context-dependent response selection bias and a low score, a context-independent bias, irrespective of the direction of deviation from the midpoint.

Developmental Changes in Cognitive Reasoning

The mCBT converted score is shown as a function of age in Fig. 13.7. A significant increase in scores was observed with age ($P < .01$). Scores in

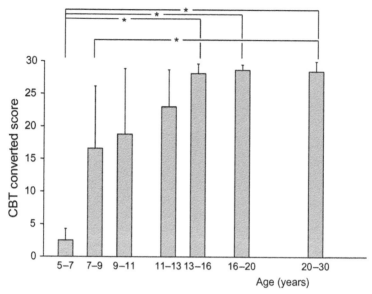

FIGURE 13.7   Converted scores for the modified cognitive bias task as a function of age. The data are presented as median $\pm$ standard error of measurement. $^*P < .05$.

children between 7 and 13 years of age showed much greater interindividual variation than those in other age groups. The youngest children (5–7 years) had a lower converted score than other groups aged 11 years to adulthood ($P < .01$; Mann–Whitney U test with Bonferroni correction, $P < .05$ vs groups aged older than 13 years). Beginning between 7 and 12 years, scores increased as a function of age and reached adult levels by age 13–16 years. We confirmed that all subjects were able to discriminate the four dichotomies in two control tasks and showed, by design, a middle-range raw score (around 60) in the task without presentation of a target.

The youngest children in our study displayed extremely context-independent responses, whereas adolescents and adults responded in an extremely context-dependent manner. This pattern supports the hypothesis that the locus of cortical control in right-handed male subjects shifts from the right to the left frontal lobe as cognitive contextual reasoning develops.

Lesion Study

The right-sided lesions/epileptic foci (RLF) subjects had a higher converted score (mean: 26.8 ± 2.2) than the left-sided lesions/epileptic foci (LLF) subjects (mean: 7.75 ± 6.3). We confirmed that all subjects were able to discriminate the four dichotomies in the control task. Our study revealed that just as lateralized prefrontal lesions produce extreme and opposite response biases in the CBT in right-handed adults, similar patterns are observed in children. The effects of lateralized frontal lobe lesions/epileptic foci were different. CBT converted scores did not change in RLF subjects, but they decreased in LLF subjects relative to a matched control group. Similar studies in children with LD, ADHD, and autistic disorder may shed light on basic questions regarding the effects of abnormal development of lateralized frontal lobe functions on clinical symptoms (Jourdan, Cutini, Weber, & Schroeter, 2009; Tamura, Kitamura, Endo, Abe, & Someya, 2012; Tando et al., 2014).

CONCLUSION

Our studies suggest that frontal lobe functions develop gradually, with spurts between 7 and 12 years of age, reaching completion after adolescence. Thus, frontal lobe function shows increased vulnerability and plasticity in the second decade of life.

ACKNOWLEDGMENTS

The author thanks all the participants in these studies. These works were supported by Grants-in-Aid for Scientific Research (C) (22591124), an Intramural Research Grant (28−7) for Neurological and Psychiatric Disorders of NCNP, and a grant for Interdisciplinary Research of Yamanashi University.

CONFLICT OF INTEREST

The author has no conflict of interest to disclose.

REFERENCES

Aihara, M., Aoyagi, K., Goldberg, E., & Nakazawa, S. (2003). Age shifts frontal cortical control in a cognitive bias task from right to left: Part I. Neuropsychological study. *Brain and Development, 25*, 555−559.

Aihara, M., Sata, Y., Osada, M., Ozoki, Y., & Nakazawa, S. (1998). The effects of higher cortical functions on sympathetic skin responses. In I. Hashimoto, & R. Kakigi (Eds.), *Recent advances in human neurophysiology* (pp. 1089−1094). Amsterdam: Elsevier.

Anderson, S. W., Bechara, A., Damasio, H., Tranel, D., & Damasio, A. R. (1999). Impairment of social and moral behavior related to early damage in human prefrontal cortex. *Nature Neuroscience, 2*, 1032−1037.

Aoyagi, K., Aihara, M., Goldberg, E., & Nakazawa, S. (2005). Lateralization of the frontal lobe functions elicited by a cognitive bias task is a fundamental process. Lesion study. *Brain and Development, 27*, 419−423.

Barkley, R. A. (1997). Behavioral inhibition, sustained attention, and executive functions: Constructing a unifying theory of ADHD. *Psychological Bulletin, 121*, 65−94.

Barkley, R. A., & Fischer, M. (2010). The unique contribution of emotional impulsiveness to impairment in major life activities in hyperactive children as adults. *Journal of the American Academy of Child and Adolescent Psychiatry, 49*, 503−513.

Bechara, A., & Damasio, A. R. (2005). The somatic marker hypothesis: A neural theory of economic decision. *Games and Economic Behavior*, *52*, 336–372.

Bechara, A., Damasio, H., Tranel, D., & Damasio, A. R. (2005). The Iowa Gabling task and the somatic marker hypothesis: Some questions and answers. *Trends in Cognitive Sciences*, *9*, 159–162.

Bechara, A., Tranel, D., & Damasio, H. (2000). Characterization of the decision-making impairment of patients with bilateral lesions of the ventromedial prefrontal cortex. *Brain*, *123*, 2189–2202.

Bush, G., Frazier, J. A., Rauch, S. L., Seidman, L. J., Whalen, P. J., Jenike, M. A., & Biederman, J. (1999). Anterior cingulate cortex dysfunction in attention-deficit/hyperactivity disorder revealed by fMRI and the Counting Stroop. *Biological Psychiatry*, *45*, 1542–1552.

Connolly, J. D., Goodale, M. A., Menon, R. S., & Munoz, D. P. (2002). Human fMRI evidence for the neural correlates of preparatory set. *Nature Neuroscience*, *5*, 1345–1352.

Damasio, A. R. (1994). *Decartes' error: Emotion, reason, and the human brain*. New York: Grosset/Putnam.

Damasio, A. R., Tranel, D., & Damasio, H. (1990). Individual with sociopathic behavior caused by frontal damage fail to responds autonomically to social stimuli. *Behavioural Brain Research*, *41*, 81–94.

Dobbing, J., & Sands, J. (1971). Vulnerability of developing brain: The effect of nutritional growth retardation on the timing of the brain growth spurt. *Biology of the Neonate*, *19*, 363–378.

Everling, S., & Munoz, D. P. (2000). Neuronal correlates for preparatory set associated with pro-saccades and anti-saccades in the primate frontal eye field. *Journal of Neuroscience*, *20*, 387–400.

Fuster, J. M. (2015). *The prefrontal cortex* (5th ed). Amsterdam: Academic Press.

Goldberg, E. (2009). *The new executive brain: Frontal lobes in a complex world*. New York: Oxford University Press.

Goldberg, E., & Costa, L. D. (1981). Hemispheric differences in the acquisition and use of descriptive systems. *Brain and Language*, *14*, 144–173.

Goldberg, E., & Podell, K. (1995). Lateralization in the frontal lobes. In H. H. Jasper, S. Riggio, & P. S. Goldman-Rakic (Eds.), *Epilepsy and the functional anatomy of the frontal lobe* (pp. 85–96). New York: Raven.

Goldberg, E., Podell, K., Harner, R., Riggio, S., & Lovell, M. (1994). Cognitive bias, functional cortical geometry, and the frontal lobes laterality, sex, and handedness. *Journal of Cognitive Neuroscience*, *6*, 276–296.

Goto, Y., Hatakeyama, K., Kitama, T., Sato, Y., Kanemura, H., Aoyagi, K., & Aihara, M. (2010). Saccade eye movements as a quantitative measure of frontostriatal network in children with ADHD. *Brain and Development*, *32*, 347–355.

Inoue, Y., Inagaki, M., Gunji, A., Furushima, W., & Kaga, M. (2008). Response switching process in children with attention-deficit-hyperactivity disorder on the novel continuous performance test. *Developmental Medicine & Child Neurology*, *50*, 462–466.

Jonkman, L. M. (2006). The development of preparation, conflict monitoring and inhibition from early childhood to young adulthood: A Go/Nogo ERP study. *Brain Research*, *1097*, 181–193.

Jourdan, M. S., Cutini, S., Weber, P., & Schroeter, M. L. (2009). Right prefrontal brain activation due to Stroop interference is altered in attention-deficit hyperactivity disorder—A functional near-infrared spectroscopy study. *Psychiatry Research*, *173*, 190–195.

Lang, P. J., Bradley, M. M., & Cuthbert, B. N. (1999). *International affective picture system (IAPS): Instruction manual and affective ratings.* Technical Report A-4. Gainesville, FL: The Center for Research in Psychophysiology, University of Florida.

Manes, F., Sahakia, B., Clark, L., Rogers, R., Antoun, N., & Aitken, M. (2002). Decision-making processes following damage to the prefrontal cortex. *Brain, 15,* 624–639.

Matsubara, M., Yamaguchi, S., Xu, J., & Kobayashi, S. (2004). Neural correlates for the suppression of habitual behavior: A functional MRI study. *Journal of Cognitive Neuroscience, 16,* 944–954.

Milner, B., & Petrides, M. (1984). Behavioural effects of frontal lobe lesions in man. *Trends in Neurosciences, 7,* 403–440.

Petrides, M., & Milner, B. (1982). Deficits on subject-ordered tasks after frontal- and temporal-lobe lesions in man. *Neuropsychologia, 20,* 249–262.

Podell, K., Lovell, M., Zimmerman, M., & Goldberg, G. (1995). The cognitive bias task and lateralized frontal lobe functions in males. *The Journal of Neuropsychiatry & Clinical Neurosciences, 7,* 491–501.

Shimoyama, H., Aihara, M., Fukuyama, H., Hashikawa, K., Aoyagi, K., Goldberg, E., & Nakazawa, S. (2004). Context-dependent reasoning in a cognitive bias task Part . SPECT activation study. *Brain Dev, 26,* 37–42.

Smith, J. L., Johnstone, S. J., & Barry, R. J. (2004). Inhibitory processing during the Go/NoGo task: An ERP analysis of children with attention-deficit/hyperactivity disorder. *Clinical Neurophysiology, 115,* 1320–1331.

Sonuga-Barke, E. (2003). The dual pathway model of AD/HD: An elaboration of neuro-developmental characteristics. *Neuroscience & Biobehavioral Reviews, 27,* 593–604.

Sonuga-Barke, E., Bitsakou, P., & Thompson, M. (2010). Beyond the dual pathway model: Evidence for the dissociation of timing, inhibition, and delay-related impairments in attention-deficit/hyperactivity disorder. *Journal of the American Academy of Child and Adolescent Psychiatry, 49,* 345–355.

Stuss, D. T., & Knight, R. T. (Eds.), (2013). *Principles of frontal lobe function* (2nd ed.). New York: Oxford University Press.

Tamura, R., Kitamura, H., Endo, T., Abe, R., & Someya, T. (2012). Decreased leftward bias of prefrontal activity in autism spectrum disorder revealed by functional near-infrared spectroscopy. *Psychiatry Research, 203,* 237–240.

Tando, T., Kaga, Y., Ishii, S., Aoyagi, K., Sano, F., Kanemura, H., & Aihara, M. (2014). Developmental changes in frontal lobe function during a verbal fluency task: A multichannel near-infrared spectroscopy study. *Brain and Development, 36,* 844–852.

Yasumura, A., Kokubo, N., Yamamoto, H., Yasumura, Y., Nakagawa, E., Kaga, M., & Inagaki, M. (2014). Neurobehavioral and hemodynamic evaluation of Stroop and reverse Stroop interference in children with attention-deficit/hyperactivity disorder. *Brain and Development, 36,* 97–106.

Chapter 14

Executive Control and Emerging Behavior in Youth With Tourette's Syndrome

Kjell Tore Hovik[1,2]

[1]*Division of Mental Health Care, Innlandet Hospital Trust, Sanderud, Norway,* [2]*Department of Neurology, Innlandet Hospital Trust, Elverum, Norway*

INTRODUCTION

Most people know what a "tic" is and probably even know somebody who tics. A typical response to a person afflicted with tics by a person who does not tic himself or herself is simply "Stop it already!" But it is not that simple. The research issues surrounding the repetitive twitches and utterances referred to as "tics" raise profound existential questions about the nature of willful control over our thoughts, feelings, and behavior. The uncontrollable jerks and quirks seem to be signals originating from what Oliver Sacks in his famous article Witty Ticcy Ray refers to as the interface between body and mind "...where the basic affective and instinctual determinants of personality are lodged" (Sacks, 1981). The impulse to twitch in persons with a tic disorder usually starts intermittently at an early age, and the tics often increase in intensity during the teenage years. An interesting question for me was thus what consequence can such a persistent, unwanted, and unavoidable urge have on the development of everyday decision-making during an important transitional period from childhood to adulthood? Could a trail be followed from neurobiological twitch to intellectual itch?

Type and frequency of tics is central to diagnosing the mental illness Tourette's syndrome (TS). Due to the interaction of a wide range of genetic, environmental, and emerging factors believed to influence tic expression in TS, this complex disorder is considered a model for understanding developmental psychopathology. This chapter, which is based on research conducted during my graduate work in collaboration with Innlandet Hospital Trust and the University of Oslo, examines the effect an emerging factor related to disease expression in young persons with TS can have on decision-making over a 2-year period.

Executive Functions in Health and Disease. DOI: http://dx.doi.org/10.1016/B978-0-12-803676-1.00014-3

The chapter begins with a brief introduction to the complex mental condition referred to as TS. I then describe the terms *executive functions* (EF) and *executive control*, which are central concepts in neuropsychology and used in various theoretical approaches to frame the idea of mental control over behavior. A brief description of the age range and developmental period commonly considered as the peak period of tic behavior is given to provide an idea of the many change processes taking place in the brain during this critical period of development. Evidence about factors known to influence tic expression is described, followed by a description of how compensatory brain processes may be thought to develop as a result of persistent, uncontrollable behaviors. I then describe the background and details of my research as a doctoral student studying TS and other neurodevelopmental disorders and look closer at an interesting finding relating to a pattern of decision-making behavior that emerged in the children with TS over a 2-year period. The resulting behavioral tendency is hypothesized to be the outcome of a compensatory response arising to counter the uncontrollable urge to tic.

TOURETTE'S SYNDROME IN BRIEF

TS is a childhood-onset, neurodevelopmental disorder characterized by the presence of chronic motor and phonic tics (Plessen, 2013). Tics are rapid repetitive movements and vocalizations that occur in bouts of waxing and waning intensity (Leckman, 2003). The unwanted movements are often a source of distress for the child and are commonly suppressible for short periods of time (Leckman, Bloch, Scahill, & King, 2006). In addition to tics, the disorder is associated with a range of social, emotional, and behavioral problems that are often more troublesome for the child than the tics themselves (Singer, 2005).

A number of disorders commonly cooccur in children with TS, and the lifetime prevalence of any psychiatric comorbidity in individuals with TS is 85.7% (Hirschtritt et al., 2015). The most commonly reported comorbidities are attention-deficit hyperactivity disorder (ADHD), obsessive compulsive disorder (OCD), depression, anger control problems, and self-injurious behaviors (Freeman et al., 2000). TS plus ADHD is considered a more severe condition than TS alone (Freeman & Tourette Syndrome International Database, 2007; Spencer et al., 1998), and some research suggests that distinguishing the approximately 40% of children with TS without ADHD from the 60% of children with TS plus ADHD is important for predicting short- and long-term prognoses and treatment (Denckla, 2006).

Evidence supports TS being a biological, often inherited disorder of the brain; yet the precise etiology and underlying neurobiological mechanisms remain enigmatic (Ganos, Roessner, & Munchau, 2013; Leckman, 2003). The heredity and genetic basis of TS are under active investigation (Abelson et al., 2005). Multiple studies suggest that the heritability of TS is as high as 60% (Davis et al., 2013). Research into possible causes of tics ranges from investigating the role of the dopaminergic system and autoimmune responses and infections to prenatal and perinatal factors, as well as genetic factors (Ali, Morrison, & Cavanna, 2013).

TS is estimated to affect approximately 1% of schoolchildren across all nationalities and socioeconomic classes (Robertson, Eapen, & Cavanna, 2009; Stern, Burza, & Robertson, 2005). The prevalence of all tic disorders is even higher than 1%. An epidemiological study conducted in Sweden indicated that up to 6.6% of 7- to 15-year-old youth had experienced some kind of tic disorder during the previous 12 months (Khalifa & Von Knorring, 2003). The lifetime prevalence of some form of tic disorder has been estimated to be as high as 20% (Bloch & Leckman, 2009).

EXECUTIVE FUNCTIONS IN TOURETTE'S SYNDROME

Mental processes involved in the monitoring and regulation of cognition, emotion, and behavior develop throughout childhood and adolescence and are referred to as EF, *cognitive control or executive control* (Anderson, 2002; Elliott, 2003; Miller & Cohen, 2001; Vohs & Baumeister, 2004). EF deficits are common in individuals with TS (Rasmussen, Soleimani, Carroll, & Hodlevskyy, 2009) and can cause considerable suffering for those afflicted and their families (Leckman et al., 2006). There is general consensus that core components of EF include inhibition, working memory, and mental flexibility (Best & Miller, 2010; Diamond, 2013), whereas the term is also used in an even broader context to encompass brain processes involved in monitoring and regulating emotion and behavior (Eisenberg & Spinrad, 2004; Moriguchi, Chevalier, & Zelazo, 2016).

The prefrontal cortex (PFC) and basal ganglia (e.g., striatum) are central in the mediation of brain processes involved in EF and regulate both voluntary movement and also higher mental processes that control cognition, decision-making, the planning of complex behavior, and neuropsychiatric symptoms (Bonelli & Cummings, 2007; Elliott, 2003; Koechlin, Ody, & Kouneiher, 2003). Importantly, neuroimaging studies have found that the functioning of the PFC and the basal ganglia is closely related to the tic generation and tic severity experienced by young individuals with TS (Baym, Corbett, Wright, & Bunge, 2008).

EF plays a central role in mediating between competing top-down and bottom-up influences in the PFC (Hanif et al., 2012; Hofmann, Schmeichel, & Baddeley, 2012; Koechlin et al., 2003). Bottom-up influences refer to lower level processes (e.g., automatic processes, sensory and emotional activation), whereas top-down influences refer to higher level goals (e.g., adhering to cultural norms, delaying gratification, etc.) (Aron, 2007; Pashler, Johnston, & Ruthruff, 2001). EF are key components of self-control and self-regulation, with broad and significant implications in our everyday lives (Miyake & Friedman, 2012). Converging evidence from several research fields suggest a model whereby the frontal cortex is involved in representing relevant thoughts and guiding appropriate behaviors, and the basal ganglia are involved in the management of competing action alternatives (Casey, Tottenham, & Fossella, 2002). As most human behavior reflects the joint impact of higher level goals (top-down influences) and recent stimuli (bottom-up influences) (Pashler et al., 2001), understanding EF and executive control in children with TS is relevant for the early treatment, follow-up, and well-being of these youth. The top-down/bottom-up framework provides a flexible approach to understanding impaired executive control of behavior and self-regulatory failure in both psychiatric and normal populations of young people (Banich, 2009; Heatherton & Wagner, 2011).

A CRITICAL PERIOD OF DEVELOPMENT

Children and adolescents with TS experience varying degrees of severity and intensity of tics concurrently with advances in their executive control abilities. Whereas the typical age of onset for tics is 5−7 years, the condition usually reaches its most severe intensity around the ages of 10−12 years (Felling & Singer, 2011). Tics diminish significantly by the age of 18 years in a majority of cases, with as many as 50% reporting being virtually tic free by the second decade of life (Robertson et al., 2009). The waxing and waning of tics is thus taking place at the same time as dramatic, cognitive developments are taking place in the youth with TS. A study comparing disabling features of the disorder in persons with TS older and younger than 18 years reported that subjects younger than 18 years reported more frequent problems with temper control and aggressive behaviors compared with adults with TS (Wand, Matazow, Shady, Furer, & Staley, 1993), suggesting a lessening of behavior problems with age. In contrast, a recent longitudinal study of children with TS reported an increase in emotional problems over a 4-year period during these formative years (Hoekstra, Lundervold, Lie, Gillberg, & Plessen, 2013). Less than 20% of adults diagnosed with TS in childhood report clinically impairing tics in adulthood (Leckman et al., 2006). Thus, these early years for youth with TS seem to be a period when underlying mechanisms influencing tics, cognition, emotion, and behavior are undergoing rapid developmental change processes simultaneously.

A qualitative shift in the nature of thinking takes place in the transition from childhood to adulthood, in which developing children and adolescents progressively enhance their ability to think and act in a more controlled and strategic manner (Blakemore & Choudhury, 2006). Self-reflection and self-monitoring abilities are essential to being able to control thoughts, feelings, and behavior, and the developmental improvements in these metacognitive abilities taking place during these childhood years (via higher levels of conscious awareness and better calibration of monitoring systems) can be spectacular (Lyons & Zelazo, 2011).

Underlying the dramatic cognitive development during these early teen-age years are significant changes taking place in the structure and synaptic density of the PFC, which continues into early adulthood (Petanjek et al., 2011). Cognitive improvements with age in young individuals is believed to be the result of maturation of executive control circuits, in which the frontal cortices become more efficiently connected to the striatum and to the sensorimotor cortices (Eapen & Crncec, 2009; Leckman et al., 2006; Marsh, Zhu, Wang, Skudlarski, & Peterson, 2007). The implication of research on typically developing children is that the functional brain circuits necessary for the control and regulation of behavior increase in efficiency throughout childhood and adolescence (Blakemore & Choudhury, 2006) and are not fully developed until late adolescence or early adulthood (Luna, Garver, Urban, Lazar, & Sweeney, 2004).

Another important developmental factor in children and adolescents with TS is the effect hormones are having on their rapidly developing brains. The significant gender imbalance (ratio of 5:1 of boys to girls) in individuals with TS suggests that sexual hormones are playing a role in the phenomenol-ogy of tics and symptom presentation. Whereas the influence on brain devel-opment from exposure to sex hormones in the prenatal phase is well established, it is now hypothesized that adolescence is a second so-called organizational period in which sex hormones play a decisive role in refining brain functioning (Berenbaum & Beltz, 2011). The effect of this hormonal influence on brain development is taking place precisely during a period of time when children with TS are experiencing a peak in tic intensity and fre-quency (ages 10–12 years) (Felling & Singer, 2011). The precise role of sex hormones in brain development of children with TS, however, is unclear.

Humans, in general, and children, in particular, excel at adapting and adjusting to their environment, and adaption and adjustment is essential to understanding a child's developmental trajectory (Povinelli & Bering, 2002). Despite the large literature on EF and executive control in children, no truly developmental account of EF across childhood and adolescence exists (Best & Miller, 2010). Neural, physiological, and behavioral systems are self-organizing and self-regulating and will likely influence each other in the developmental process (Stern, Blair, & Peterson, 2008). Stressful conditions (e.g., the persistent urge to tic) can generate responses in the form of thoughts, feelings, and behavior, some of which may become habitual and influence the developmental course of the individual child. When accounting for the origins of behavior, it is important to emphasize the increasingly complex self-organization of the developing individual (Greenberg, 2014; Overton, 2013).

Children with TS have normal levels of intelligence (Singer, 2005), yet struggle with controlling unwanted tics on a daily basis. Although the tics are transiently suppressible (Bloch & Leckman, 2009), the repeated suppres-sion of tics has been shown to influence their neurobiology (Jackson,

Mueller, Hambleton, & Hollis, 2007; Jackson et al., 2011; Mueller, Jackson, Dhalla, Datsopoulos, & Hollis, 2006). It is thus reasonable to suspect that youth with TS may develop compensatory cognitive, emotional, and behavioral characteristics in response to the persistent act of suppressing tics (e.g., higher frontal activation to suppress tics, outbursts of emotion, and overly cautious response tendencies) (Baym et al., 2008; Jackson et al., 2011; Mueller et al., 2006; Serrien, Orth, Evans, Lees, & Brown, 2005). The success of a compensatory response could then become a persistent behavioral trait through reinforcement. Interestingly, the same neural mechanism involved in the generation of tics (cortical-striatal-thalamocortical "CSTC" circuits) underlies habit formation (Leckman & Riddle, 2000). The feedback loops responsible for converting novel actions into automatic actions may thus also be playing a role in the repetitive nature of a tic.

Anyone with a temper or anyone who knows someone struggling with sudden, uncontrollable emotional outbursts understands intuitively that control over behavior in many contexts involves a balance between reason and emotion. Responding in highly activating and emotionally salient situations is usually more difficult to fine-tune than selecting between matter-of-fact alternatives in calm surroundings. Thus, a differentiation is also made between executive control that involves decision-making under "cold" circumstances and decision-making under "hot" contexts. Most neurocognitive tests assessing EF engage cognitive processes with little emotional salience and are therefore referred to as cold EF (Chan, Shum, Toulopoulou, & Chen, 2008). Cold EF processes include inhibition, working memory (updating), and mental flexibility (Miyake & Friedman, 2012).

EF tasks involving stronger affective salience (e.g., decision-making paradigms) are referred to as hot EF. Hot EF activates areas of the brain that regulate emotions and the brain's reward systems (e.g., orbitofrontal cortex, ventral striatum, and the limbic system) (Castellanos, Sonuga-Barke, Milham, & Tannock, 2006). Decision-making tasks typically require a choice between competing alternatives involving risk or reward to maximize outcome and thus test sensitivities to reinforcement contingencies (Chan et al., 2008). The relationship between choices and outcomes in these tasks depends on a close interplay between brain regions mediating both cognition and emotion (Bechara, 1997; Bechara, Damasio, Tranel, & Damasio, 2005; Heilman et al., 2010; Maia & McClelland, 2004). The difference between cognitive and more emotional processing in decision-making tasks is often referred to as the difference between hot and cold EF (Prencipe et al., 2011; Zelazo & Carlson, 2012; Zelazo, Qu, & Kesek, 2010).

A clear dissociation between different frontal brain areas involved in cold processing (medial orbitofrontal, rostral anterior cingulated, and posterior cingulated) and hot processing (dorsal anterior cingulated, supplementary motor area, insula, precentral, and fusiform gyri) has been shown by using functional magnetic resonance imaging, where salience plays a key role in allocating attentional, motivational, and computational processes (Litt, Plassmann, Shiv, & Rangel, 2011). Disadvantageous decision-making is a central challenge in adolescence and is closely associated with risky behavior and poor choices that can prove detrimental later in life (Smith, Xiao, & Bechara, 2012). Impulse dysregulation is closely associated with risk-taking behavior and self-injurious behavior in children with TS (Mathews et al., 2004), and there is convincing evidence showing risky behavior to be common in children/adolescents with ADHD as well (Groen, Gaastra, Lewis-Evans, & Tucha, 2013). Decision-making tasks are common in research involving children with ADHD, as hot EF processes have for some time been believed to constitute a promising endophenotype explaining ADHD symptoms (Castellanos et al., 2006; Sonuga-Barke, 2003). Due to the high incidence of ADHD in children with TS, untangling the specific symptom profile in children with TS is imperative to understanding the full range of risk factors associated with the disorder.

Early adolescence coincides with asymmetric neural development in which relatively overactive striatal regions create impulsive reward-driven responses that may go "unchecked" by the slower developing inhibitory mechanisms in the frontal cortex (Smith et al., 2012). The uneven developmental trajectory emerging during childhood and adolescence in brain regions involved in the top-down control of behavior is in strong contrast with the linear development of memory, speed of processing, and other cognitive abilities (Smith et al., 2012). An uneven development in the complex balance of top-down and bottom-up executive abilities during this period of childhood and adolescence may permit a larger range of internal and external factors to exert a stronger influence on the course of emerging behavioral characteristics (Casey, Jones, & Hare, 2008).

In general, the many developmental influences on brain function in children and adolescents with TS are critical to the course of their condition and future well-being (Stern et al., 2008). One aspect complicating the effort to gain an understanding of these many influences is differing maturational trajectories among various brain functions. In a study involving typically developing children aged 8–15 years, improvements in cold EF tasks occurred earlier in the age range and improvements in hot EF tasks occurred later (Prencipe et al., 2011). The authors of the latter study maintain that although similar abilities may underlie both hot and cold EF tasks, their study shows that hot EF abilities develop more slowly, which may have implications for the risky behavior often observed during adolescence. It is likely that experiences and influences during these childhood and adolescent years affect an individual differently depending on the maturation and balance of hot and cold EF abilities. Children with impaired top-down control over bottom-up influences may be more vulnerable to the negative effects of adverse events and less resilient than children with a higher level of top-down control (Maier, 2015). The spectacular increase in physical strength and drive for independence during adolescence, in combination with immature cognitive, emotional, and behavioral control, represent a tremendous potential for serious negative consequences for the health and well-being of developing youth (Boyer, 2006), particularly those with an excessively imbalanced behavior regulating brain system.

MANY FACTORS INFLUENCE TIC EXPRESSION

The complexity of TS requires an approach to understanding the condition that accounts for many factors influencing the development, course, and prognosis of persons suffering from TS (Robertson, 2000). The biopsychosocial approach emphasizes multiple factors influencing tics and cognitive, emotional, and behavioral development in children with TS (Suls & Rothman, 2004). Three central factors in the biopsychosocial view will be described in the following: the biological, the psychological, and the social. This will be followed by a description of how a dual-process view may conceptualize the daily decision-making challenges facing children with TS.

A neurobiological model of the disorder conceptualizes tics as a difficulty in inhibiting sensory urges and behavior (O'Connor, 2002). Paralimbic and sensory association areas are implicated in the generation of a tic, which is believed to be similar to movements triggered internally by unpleasant sensations (e.g., an itch or a blink) (Bohlhalter et al., 2006). Tic symptoms may thus be fragments of innate behavior, and the sensory urges preceding tics may be internal cues involved in the assembly of behavioral sequences. There is no consensus, however, on the primary site of neurobiological dysfunction, which may lie in the failure to regulate impulses rather than the generation of impulses. In other words, tics can be understood as a relative impairment in top-down control over certain bottom-up impulses.

Several lines of evidence suggest that abnormal basal ganglia functioning is the main reason for the involuntary tic movements experienced in subjects with TS (Albin & Mink, 2006; Ganos et al., 2013; Jackson et al., 2007). The basal ganglia function as a central switching mechanism, involved in the selection and regulation of goal-directed movements (Mink, 2003; Redgrave, Prescott, & Gurney, 1999) and habit learning (Marsh, Alexander, Packard, Zhu, & Peterson, 2005). Children and adults with TS are often impaired in striatum-based habit learning (Marsh et al., 2004). A considerable amount of research has been devoted to understanding TS as a problem involving the basal ganglia and may involve structures, neurotransmitters, or both. Dopamine and other neurotransmitters regulate messages transmitted along a critical frontostriatal brain circuit (basal ganglia, thalamus, PFC, and other cortex regions), which influences movement, thoughts, judgment, and behavior sequences (Marsh, Maia, & Peterson, 2009; Swerdlow & Young, 2001). Faulty dopamine regulation at critical points in this circuit could permit unwanted thoughts and behaviors to slip unfiltered through (Mink, 2001; Zinner, 2004).

Dopamine neurons play an important role in mood regulation and decision-making (Ikemoto, Yang, & Tan, 2015; Tye et al., 2013), and are believed to be dysfunctional in both TS (Palminteri et al., 2009) and in ADHD (Solanto, 2002; Volkow et al., 2009).

Animal studies have shown that stereotyped behaviors arise from the basal ganglia following the application of stimulants (Kelley, Lang, & Gauthier, 1988) or dopamine receptor agonists (Canales & Iversen, 2000). Dopaminergic dysfunction is thus a leading candidate for investigation as a source of tics, as dopamine is among the numerous neurotransmitters known to participate in the transmission of messages through CSTC circuits (Leckman, 2003). Lesions to the basal ganglia in humans produce or exacerbate tic-like behaviors (Dale, 2003; Gomis, Puente, Pont-Sunyer, Oliveras, & Roquer, 2008).

A cognitive psychophysiological model of the disorder conceptualizes tic habits as a function of cognitive factors such as perfectionist concerns and heightened sensory awareness and self-attention, as well as physiological factors such as high level of motor activation and accompanying elevated muscle tension (O'Connor, 2002). Whereas the onset and generation of tics has a fundamental biological component, severity can be influenced by a variety of psychological factors, as tics may improve with concentration, distraction, or physical exercise and may worsen with stress, fatigue, or excitement (Bloch & Leckman, 2009; Nixon, Glazebrook, Hollis, & Jackson, 2014). Cooccurring conditions (e.g., ADHD and OCD) can have a significant impact on lowering the quality of life for children with TS (Bernard et al., 2009), as do anxiety and depression symptoms, which are known to exacerbate existing behavioral problems in youth in general (Eysenck, Derakshan, Santos, & Calvo, 2007; Wagner, Müller, Helmreic, Muss, & Tadic, 2015). The precise importance of a range of psychological factors that influence tics symptoms, however, remains unclear.

Social and related factors such as family relationships may influence the impact TS has on a child (Carter et al., 2000). Although the onset of TS does not seem to be related solely to stressful life events (Horesh, Zimmerman, Steinberg, Yagan, & Apter, 2008), evidence suggests that negative life events involving social influences during adolescence influence the course and severity of tics (Steinberg, Shmuel-Baruch, Horesh, & Apter, 2013). A study conducted involving 60 patients aged 7–17 years with TS or a chronic tic disorder reported a close association between negative life events involving friends and the severity of vocal tics, and between major life events and the severity of motor tics (Steinberg et al., 2013). Psychosocial stress and social problems interacting with genetic vulnerability are known to influence the development of comorbidities and impact on the long-term outcomes for children with TS (Lin et al., 2002).

A dual-process approach (Grafman & Krueger, 2006) may serve as a useful framework for conceptualizing and understanding the top-down/bottom-up dichotomy of volitional control in children in general and children with TS in particular. This theory is based on studies reporting that patients with prefrontal lesions perform similarly to typically developing children on response tasks that measure speed of completion, but do significantly worse when the measure depends on an individual's ability to recruit prefrontal resources to respond accurately (Vendrell et al., 1995). Separate and competing response systems (reflective and explicit vs reflexive and automatic) are presumably involved in responding fast or in responding accurately. Although important criticisms of the dual-process approach are made (Bargh & Ferguson, 2000; Osman, 2004), the view provides a simple dichotomy of executive control in which to understand the conflicting behavioral manifestations of automatic versus controlled behaviors.

A prominent dual-process model in the field of cognitive neuroscience, which offers a framework for understanding executive control over cognition and emotion is the Iterative Reprocessing Model (Cunningham, Zelazo, Packer, & Van Bavel, 2007; Zelazo & Cunningham, 2007). According to this model, attitudes and evaluations are constructed through the reprocessing (iteration) of information. Fast automatic evaluations involve few iterations, whereas multiple iterations result in more nuanced evaluations that influence and are influenced by more reflective processes (Cunningham et al., 2007). One can imagine that the continuum from quick and automatic evaluations to nuanced and reflective evaluations in volitional control will vary considerably based on a wide range of cognitive, emotional, and contextual factors. The model provides a framework for understanding the complex and intertwined web of automatic and control processes influencing behavior in children in general and specifically in children with impaired EF and executive control.

BRAIN ADAPTATION AND COMPENSATORY BEHAVIOR

Brain adaptability is an important aspect to account for when considering developmental trajectories and psychopathology. Brain adaptability refers to the consequence of vulnerabilities in gene expression and abnormalities of central structures combining over time through development to find unique phenotypic combinations (Johnson, Jones, & Gliga, 2015). The idea is that the brain may be compensating and adapting to better deal with difficulties it is experiencing. The Johnson et al. (2015) study suggests principles for understanding the developmental consequences of widespread early atypical synaptic function. Atypical synaptic function is common in neurodevelopmental disorders, such as TS, and refers to the way cells communicate with each other. The authors propose that key behavioral features of neurodevelopmental disorders are not the direct result of ongoing neural pathology, not gene-specific, but the end result of the brain's adaptation in the developmental process to irregularities. In other words, an end result of the interplay between emerging structures and processes interacting with their environment.

Adaptability and an individual's control over mental processes is a central area of research in TS. The presence of tics in a child or adolescent suggests an inability to willfully stop or control unwanted movements. Performing an urge to tic most commonly can be delayed. However, the inability to inhibit completely specific movements such as a tic raises the issue of what cognitive processes underlie the ability to inhibit any impulse to act. Whereas some research has indicated response inhibition difficulties in children with TS (Crawford, Channon, & Robertson, 2005; Muller et al., 2003), recent research has documented enhanced inhibitory abilities in children with TS (Jackson et al., 2007; Mueller et al., 2006). The recent findings suggest that the brain is adapting to inhibition difficulties in children with TS. Increased activation in the direct pathway through the basal ganglia and compensatory activation in the PFC and subthalamic nucleus has been shown in children with TS during EF or executive control tasks (Baym et al., 2008). In the latter study, higher tic activity was associated with enhanced activation of dopaminergic nuclei and stronger engagement of the left PFC in the children with TS compared with typically developing children. Inhibitory mechanisms have been a focus of research in TS (Eddy, Rizzo, & Cavanna, 2009), but the precise nature of inhibitory control in TS remains one of the many unresolved issues surrounding the disorder (Robertson, 2000; Singer, 2005).

FINDINGS FROM RESEARCH PROJECT INVESTIGATING EF AND COGNITIVE CONTROL IN TS

From the literature we know that the ability to exert executive control over aspects of cognition, emotion, and behavior in children and adolescents with TS deviates from typically developing children. Knowledge about these processes and their development over time in young persons with TS is scarce and is essential for understanding and treating this group of vulnerable children. As part of the doctoral research project in psychology "Emotional and cognitive development in children and adolescents with neuropsychiatric disorders," I set out to investigate executive control of cognition, emotion, and behavior in youth with TS, and did so based on cross-sectional and longitudinal investigations over a 2-year period. Details regarding demographics, diagnostics, neuropsychological measures, and results of the studies can be reviewed in three papers published in connection with my graduate work (Hovik et al., 2014; Hovik et al., 2015; Hovik, Plessen, Skogli, Andersen, & Oie, 2016).

In brief, the findings in the first paper indicated that children with TS were superior in inhibiting a prepotent verbal response compared to typically developing children, and that comorbid ADHD in the children with TS negatively influenced performance. In the second paper, there was evidence of a considerable overlap of everyday behavior regulation problems and metacognitive difficulties among the children with neurodevelopmental disorders. All of the children with neurodevelopmental disorders were rated by their parents as having significantly more everyday behavior problems compared with typically developing children on all of the subscales. The symptom overlap made differentiation difficult on individual rating scales. By applying paired scale configurations, however, we found evidence that the children with TS had relatively more emotional control difficulties compared with the children suffering from other neurodevelopmental conditions. Difficulty controlling mood, agitation, and excitement in everyday situations involving high affective salience was thus found to be particularly challenging for the children with TS.

Having found that the children with TS excelled at inhibiting impulsive responses on cold tasks (first study), but nonetheless experienced problems controlling their emotions (second study), I was interested in investigating in children with TS the balance of control on a more emotionally salient task that requires decision-making based on an assessment of benefit versus risk.

The computer-based Hungry Donkey Task (HDT) (Crone & van der Molen, 2004) is a children's version of the Iowa Gambling Task (IGT) (Bechara, Damasio, Damasio, & Anderson, 1994). The basic format of IGT (gambling) is retained, but the HDT (a prosocial game) is considered to be a more appropriate decision-making task for children (Crone & van der Molen, 2004). The HDT was used as a measure of decision-making efficiency. Participants are asked to help a hungry donkey to collect as many apples as possible by choosing one of four doors (A, B, C, and D). The amount of wins and losses varied between choices, and overall gains/losses were displayed with a red/green bar at the bottom of the screen. Doors A and B represent disadvantageous choices (resulting in overall loss), and Doors C and D represent advantageous choices (resulting in overall gain). The selection of Doors A and C involve infrequent but higher level losses, whereas the selection of doors B and D involve frequent but lower level losses. The task ends after the completion of 150 trials. As the risk parameters are uncertain at the start of the task, early choices are considered to be decision-making under ambiguity, whereas later choices are considered to be decision-making under risk (Brand, Recknor, Grabenhorst, & Bechara, 2007). The number of advantageous choices (Doors C and D) in the last four blocks was summed to represent a measure of "Advantageous choices." It was further subdivided. We termed results for Door C a "Safer Choice," based on the logic that by selecting this door the subject ensures a steady gain in outcome by having to endure regularly occurring low-level losses. We termed Door D a "Riskier Choice," because, although it offers the same overall gain as Door C, the subject must endure sudden, large losses. The two advantageous doors thus offer differing "gain versus pain" schedules and ratios. For a detailed account of the HDT, see Crone & van der Molen (2004).

Table 14.1 below provides demographic characteristics for the sample with means, standard deviations, and analyses of variance according to group and assessment time.

TABLE 14.1 Demographic Characteristics of Matched Samples: Means, Standard Deviations and ANOVAs for Groups and Assessment Time

Variable	Baseline (T1)					Follow-up (T2)				
	TS [a] (n = 19)	ADHD-C [b] (n = 33)	Typically Developing Children (n = 50)	Group Comparisons Chi-square/F	P	TS (n = 19)	ADHD-C (n = 33)	Typically Developing Children (n = 50)	Group Comparisons Chi-square/F	P
Sex (m/f)	16/3	20/13	32/18	(2, 102) = 3.4	not significant	16/3	20/13	32/18	(2, 102) = 3.4	not significant
Age in months	147 (27)	144 (26)	144 (24)	(2, 99) = 0.09	not significant	171 (27)	168 (26)	169 (24)	(2, 98) = 0.09	not significant
FSIQ [c]	102 (15)	97 (14)	104 (13)	(2, 99) = 2.6	not significant	101 (13)	97 (14)	106 (13)	(2, 93) = 5.3	<0.01
Motor tics, YGTSS [d]	12.1 (7.3)	0.33 (1.9)	0.0	(2, 99) = 102.1	<0.001	5.9 (5.0)	0.73 (2.6)	0.22 (0.89)	(2, 99) = 29.2	<0.001
Phonic tics, YGTSS [d]	10.2 (5.2)	0.06 (0.35)	0.0	(2, 99) = 159.6	<0.001	5.4 (5.8)	0.99 (3.0)	0.22 (0.89)	(2, 99) = 20.2	<0.001

ADHD-C, attention-deficit hyperactivity disorder, combined type; TS, Tourette's syndrome.

[a] At baseline (T1), 11 patients with TS had comorbid disorders: 1 × obsessive compulsive disorder (OCD), 1 × oppositional defiant disorder (ODD), 1 × ODD and ADHD-C, 2 × ADHD-I, 2 × ADHD-C, 3 × Asperger's syndrome, 1 × ADHD-I/Asperger's syndrome. Two received a low dose of quetiapine and two received a low dose of aripiprazole, whereas the remaining 15 participants with TS were medicine naive upon inclusion and testing. At T2, seven patients in the TS group no longer satisfied formal diagnostic criteria for a tic disorder and one fulfilled criteria for chronic motor tic disorder. At T2, the two children with TS and either OCD or ODD retained this comorbid diagnosis at T2. One child with TS and no comorbid diagnosis at T1 fulfilled criteria for a comorbid general anxiety disorder at T2.

[b] At T1, only two children with ADHD were on any medication, with low doses of risperidone and quetiapine, respectively. At T2, 11 retained the diagnosis of ADHD-C, 6 fulfilled criteria for ADHD-I, and 2 no longer fulfilled criteria for ADHD. No other cooccurring disorders were registered in this group.

[c] Full scale IQ (FSIQ). IQ estimated measures from the Wechsler Abbreviated Scale of Intelligence (WASI).

[d] Yale Global Tic Severity Scale (YGTSS). The group with TS had significantly more motor and phonic tics than the group with ADHD-C and typically developing children at T1 and T2.

A total of 19 children with TS, 33 children with ADHD-combined sub-type (ADHD-C) and 50 typically developing children were recruited for the study. The clinical sample was referred consecutively to the Child and Adolescent Mental Health Centres at Innlandet Hospital Trust (IHT) in Norway in 2009 and 2010. All participants underwent a comprehensive diagnostic assessment based on separate interviews of the participant and parent(s). Additional information about academic and social functioning was included in the assessment. A diagnosis was confirmed if DSM-IV-TR (American Psychiatric Association, 2000) criteria were met through an evaluation of K-SADS-PL, parent reports, and self-reporting together with information from teachers concerning academic and social functioning. Typically developing children were recruited from local schools and underwent the same assessment procedure as the clinical participants. Additional criteria of exclusion for the typically developing children were any history of a psychiatric disorder, dyslexia, or head injury. Exclusion criteria for all groups were prematurity (<36 weeks), IQ estimate below 70, and neurological disease. No significant difference in age, gender, or FSIQ was found for the groups at T1. At T2, the level of FSIQ was significantly lower for the ADHD-C group compared to the typically developing children, whereas no difference was registered between the two clinical groups (Table 14.1).

The results on the decision-making task at baseline and at follow-up testing 2 years later provided clues to some interesting changes taking place in the children with TS's decision-making preferences (Table 14.2). At baseline, there was no clear pattern of preference for safer or riskier choices in any of the groups as shown in the diagram to the left in Fig. 14.1; however, the diagram to the right reveals a clear pattern in that the children with TS exhibited an increasing tendency to prefer safer choices toward the end of the trial.

Examination of the overall results indicates that both the children with TS and the children with ADHD-C were subconsciously learning which doors gave overall favorable outcomes, because they were selecting doors that gave an overall benefit over time. However, the TS group clearly favored the safer choice, whereas the ADHD-C group preferred the riskier choice. One interpretation of this distinct pattern is that the children with TS developed a higher sensitivity to the risk of enduring large penalties over the course of 2 years and thus subconsciously tended to avoid large losses. Sensitivity to penalties has been shown to be related to dopamine transmission, which is believed to be dysfunctional in TS (Palminteri et al., 2009).

Another interesting observation from the results is that both children with TS and ADHD-C were more rigid in their decision-making response tendencies at T2 than the typically developing children. The typically developing children were more balanced in their selection between the two overall advantageous outcomes. The tendency in the ADHD-C group toward a riskier strategy (i.e., less sensitive to magnitude of penalty) is consistent with the findings in a cross-sectional decision-making study involving ADHD children ages

TABLE 14.2 Results on a Decision-Making Task (Raw Scores) at T1 and T2: Means and Standard Deviations Within the TS, ADHD-C, and Typically Developing Children Groups, and Results From Mixed Model ANOVA

Variable	TS (n = 19)		ADHD-C (n = 33)		Typically Developing Children (n = 50)		Group		Time		Group × Time[c]		
	T1	T2	T1	T2	T1	T2	F	P	F	P	F	P	η_p^2
Safer choices[a]	12.5 (7.9)	21.5 (16.1)	12.8 (7.9)	12.3 (4.9)	14.1 (9.5)	12.9 (8.6)	2.35 (2.94)	not significant	3.4	not significant	5.1	<0.01	0.10
Riskier choices[b]	22.7 (12.5)	15.6 (9.0)	19.4 (10.9)	18.5 (11.0)	17.6 (8.6)	19.0 (9.4)	2.943 (1.4)	not significant	2.1	not significant	2.5	not significant	

ADHD, attention-deficit hyperactivity disorder; ANOVA, analysis of variance; TS, Tourette's syndrome.
[a]The Hungry Donkey Task—Lower level of loss and gain last four blocks.
[b]The Hungry Donkey Task—Higher level of loss and gain last four blocks.
[c]Effect size is specified only for significant interactions.

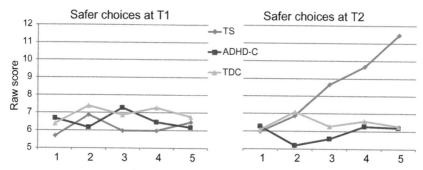

FIGURE 14.1 Rates of selecting an advantageous, less risky alternative, across five blocks of trials of the HDT at T1 and T2. The "safer" choice tendency in the TS group at T2 involves a preference for frequent, lower level losses compared to a less frequent higher level loss alternative. *ADHD-C*, attention-deficit hyperactivity disorder, combined type; HDT, Hungry Donkey Task; *TDC*, typically developing control; *TS*, Tourette's syndrome.

7–12 years compared to typically developing children (Luman, Oosterlaan, Knol, & Sergeant, 2008). This type of response tendency has not been previously studied in children with TS in a longitudinal perspective. As the brain regions responsible for rational decision-making are not fully developed until early adulthood (Smith et al., 2012), the children in the current study were presumably not consciously aware of any strategy in their responses.

Although we did not specifically question the participants about their decision-making strategy, some underlying factor seemed to have been subconsciously influencing the TS group's response preferences. The repeated suppression of tics is a subconscious process known to influence their neurobiology (Jackson et al., 2011; Mueller et al., 2006) and possibly also their decision-making. The change in response pattern in the TS group from T1 to T2 could be an indication of the emergence of a compensatory response influencing behavior (Greenberg, Callina, & Mueller, 2013; Overton, 2013). The overly inhibitory response style emerging through the constant suppression of tics in the TS group could be influencing children with TS to select the less emotionally activating and less impulsive alternative in the decision-making task. For children with TS, an overly cautious response style is particularly activated when the outcome of a response is uncertain (Jackson et al., 2007), as in the decision-making task used in the current study.

A DAUNTING DISORDER

The complex behavioral spectrum of TS is daunting (Cavanna, Servo, Monaco, & Robertson, 2009), and no single approach is sufficient to grasp the complexity of challenges faced by children with TS (Robertson, 2000). The biopsychosocial paradigm is wide reaching in scope and helpful in understanding the complexity of factors underlying and influencing the course of a complex disorder such as TS. In addition, a top-down, bottom-up view of executive control can be used to provide a simple framework in which we try to understand potential factors influencing executive control over thoughts, emotion, and behavior (Banich, 2009; Heatherton & Wagner, 2011).

A priori we know that youth diagnosed with TS suffer from persistent, disturbing tics that they can delay but cannot fully stop or control (Leckman et al., 2006). Conceptualizing TS as a difficulty inhibiting sensory urges or behavior as in the neurobiological model implies impairment in basic top-down regulatory processes (O'Connor, 2002). Some studies addressing inhibition in children with TS have reported impaired inhibitory abilities in children with TS using traditional neuropsychological tasks (Crawford et al., 2005; Muller et al., 2003); yet others have not found differences in inhibitory function in children with TS compared to typically developing children (Roessner, Albrecht, Dechent, Baudewig, & Rothenberger, 2008). Studies on behavioral inhibition in children with TS are thus equivocal. Interestingly, a number of recent studies using neuroimaging techniques have described enhanced inhibitory activity in brain regions involved in inhibiting responses in children with TS compared with typically developing children (Baym et al., 2008; Jackson et al., 2007; Mueller et al., 2006). One approach to resolving these somewhat inconsistent findings is to consider that enhanced brain activity may be activated to compensate for a deficit, i.e., a compensatory strategy to maintain task performance (Jackson et al., 2011). Enhanced activation to maintain task performance would require a greater application of cognitive resources to the brain region responsible for coordinating the task. Repeated activation in the same brain region will likely result in a strengthening of capacity, which may then have a generalizable effect to other areas. This explanation would support a hypothesis of stronger top-down executive control in children who repeatedly practice inhibiting unwanted impulses to act, which is precisely the case in children with TS.

We are not aware of any prior studies investigating the decision-making skills of youth with TS. One study examining decision-making skills in adults with TS and adults with OCD reported deficient decision-making skills in the adult subjects with TS compared with typically developing children (Watkins et al., 2005). This study used a different decision-making task that the one used in our study, however, and only reported overall proportion of choices with the most likely outcome. The study did not investigate the possibility of subjects showing a preference for cautious or riskier choices. Studies investigating the decision-making skills in children with ADHD have reported contradictory findings (DeVito et al., 2008; Skogli, Egeland, Andersen, Hovik, & Oie, 2014; Toplak, Jain, & Tannock, 2005). Because of the lack of literature for children with TS and conflicting results in studies for children with ADHD, we were not able to confidently predict the likely outcome on this task in advance of our study. We were also unsure whether any particular pattern of decision-making would emerge, as decision-making skills are not believed to reach adult levels until late adolescence (Crone & van der Molen, 2004).

Although we did not ask the subjects in a systematic way whether they had a strategy in their choices on the decision-making task (HDT), we assumed that they would subconsciously learn which doors gave favorable outcomes over time. Interestingly, we found that the rate of selecting overall advantageous choices was the same in the children with TS, the children with ADHD, and the typically developing children at both baseline and follow-up. When we examined the tendency to prefer the cautious or riskier advantageous choice, however, a distinct pattern of decision-making emerged for the children with TS. Whereas no difference in cautious or riskier decision-making was registered between the any of the groups at T1, the children with TS clearly preferred the more cautious choice compared with the children with ADHD-C at T2. In other words, the children with TS had developed after a period of 2 years a preference for the advantageous choice that involved lower but more frequent losses compared to the alternative equally advantageous choice that involved much higher but less frequent losses. This shift in decision-making bias by the children with TS suggests a developmental shift toward more cautious choices during their adolescent years. It can be argued that the preference by the children with TS for the cautious alternative in the decision-making task is consistent with the more accurate response style shown in previous studies described earlier. However, the latent tendency shown at baseline in the cold task did not manifest itself in performance on the decision-making task until 2 years later. Cautious and accurate responding versus an emphasis on speed is a process mediated in frontostriatal networks (van Maanen et al., 2011). Selecting accurately and selecting cautiously both reflect enhanced top-down executive control. The children with TS seemed to be exerting a distinct top-down control over their responses compared to the children with ADHD or the typically developing children on these widely differing tasks.

Interestingly, the results of a study involving children with ADHD with or without tics provide evidence to support the argument that having tics may boost executive control capacity. The study examined attention and inhibition in children with ADHD and found that the effect of tics in children with ADHD was to improve performance on these measures compared with the children with ADHD but without tics (Greimel, Herpertz-Dahlmann, Gunther, Vitt, & Konrad, 2008). Greimel and her colleagues proposed that the consequence of inhibiting tics over time in the children with ADHD may be the emergence of compensatory neural mechanisms that improved neuropsychological performance compared with the children without tics. A basic property of the living brain—neuroplasticity—is the ability to adjust and adapt to internal and external influences (Pascual-Leone, Amedi, Fregni, & Merabet, 2005). Based on this basic property of brain change over time due to internal or external influences, it is reasonable to consider the likelihood that having tics over time may enhance top-down control of some types of behavior.

In summary, the executive control of cognition in children with TS is characterized by more accurate responding in a cold EF task and more cautious responding in a hot EF task compared with typically developing children. These findings support a hypothesis of more top-down control over responses in children with TS compared with typically developing children during important developmental years in childhood and adolescence.

CLINICAL IMPLICATIONS

Although I was not able to conduct an intervention study involving the children with TS as part of my graduate work, the findings may have clinical implications that could be tested in future intervention studies. Symptoms of anxiety and depression are common in children with TS. An important issue is whether there might be a close relationship between changes in EF abilities over time and changes in levels of anxiety or depression symptoms over that same time period. A close association might provide evidence to suggest the possibility of training EF functions to address the emotional distress frequently associated with TS. Cognitive behavioral therapy (CBT) is a therapeutic approach in which a patient learns to self-regulate unpleasant emotions that is essential for mental health (Beauregard, 2007). The ability to regulate one's emotions has been argued to be one of the keys to a healthy and productive life (Silvers, Buhle, & Ochsner, 2013). CBT targets higher order executive cognitive functions involving the orbitofrontal cortex (OFC), the medial prefrontal cortex (mPFC), and the ventral and dorsal anterior cingulated cortex (ACC) (Ochsner & Gross, 2007). From a neurobiological perspective, the top-down regulation trained in therapeutic approaches such as CBT leads to reduced emotional response and regulation of negative emotional states (Jokic-Begic, 2010). Frontal areas such as the OFC, mPFC, and ACC are all implicated in the top-down processing of emotion (Ochsner et al., 2004; Taylor, Phan, Decker, & Liberzon, 2003; Wright et al., 2008). A review of neurobiology studies of psychotherapeutic changes concluded that CBT leads to reduced fronto-striato-thalamic activity in anxiety disorder and also possibly, but less certain, for depression (Linden, 2006). Importantly, the fronto-striato-thalamic circuit is the same feedback loop implicated in tic production. Habit reversal training (HRT) and exposure with response prevention are both recommended as first-line behavioral treatments for tics for children in the European Clinical Guidelines for TS (Verdellen, van de Griendt, Hartmann, Murphy, & Group, 2011), and studies have shown HRT to be as effective in reducing tics as antipsychotic medication and with long-lasting benefits (Piacentini et al., 2010). If this type of top-down therapy is effective in treating tics that are generated by the same frontal systems as those involved in regulating emotional distress, then the same principles underlying this treatment approach may also be effective in treating the anxiety and depression symptoms reported by children with TS.

There is considerable uncertainty regarding the underlying mechanisms affecting cognitive, emotional, and behavior change in young persons with TS, and future research should attempt to disentangle the complex web of processes contributing to positive change and development in these youth.

FUTURE RESEARCH

Factors favorably influencing the maturation of decision-making processes should be an important focus of future TS research aimed at developing more efficient treatment approaches. An important area for future research on children and adolescents with TS is how compensatory mechanisms due to the constant suppression of tics may be affecting their development. Future studies should attempt to disentangle the influence of age and other factors by narrowing the age groups investigated, ensuring better control over factors potentially influencing maturational development and including larger groups. There is also a need for longitudinal studies following development over a few years.

CONCLUSION

The interaction of genetic, environmental, and emerging factors arising from the combination of many sources of influence in disease expression in TS reflects the complexity of the disorder, which has become a model for understanding developmental psychopathology in a broad sense (Leckman et al., 2006). When facing choices involving uncertain outcomes on a decision-making task involving higher emotional salience than in cold EF tasks, the children with TS seemed to develop over a 2-year period in early adolescence a less flexible and more cautious decision-making preference than typically developing children. Based on earlier research, this tendency could be understood as a behavioral pattern developed in response to having to constantly inhibit tics. Gaining a better understanding of how cognitive, emotional, and behavioral factors can influence the development of executive control in youth with TS can provide clues to better treat youth with TS. Furthermore, gaining an insight into these processes in children with TS may shed light on factors influencing the emergence of complex behaviors in developing children in general.

REFERENCES

Abelson, J. F., Kwan, K. Y., O'Roak, B. J., Baek, D. Y., Stillman, A. A., Morgan, T. M., & State, M. W. (2005). Sequence variants in SLITRK1 are associated with Tourette's syndrome. *Science, 310*(5746), 317–320. Available from http://dx.doi.org/10.1126/science.1116502.

Albin, R. L., & Mink, J. W. (2006). Recent advances in Tourette syndrome research. *Trends in Neuroscience, 29*(3), 175–182. Available from http://dx.doi.org/10.1016/j.tins.2006.01.001.

Ali, Fizzah, Morrison, Karen, & Cavanna, Andrea (2013). *The complex genetics of Gilles de la Tourette syndrome: Implications for clinical practice* (Vol. 3, pp. 321–330). London: Future Medicine Ltd.

American Psychiatric Association (2000). *Diagnostic and statistical manual of mental disorders: DSM-IV-TR*. Washington, DC: American Psychiatric Association.

Anderson, P. (2002). Assessment and development of executive function (EF) during childhood. *Child Neuropsychology*, *8*(2), 71–82. Available from http://dx.doi.org/10.1076/chin.8.2.71.8724.

Aron, A. R. (2007). The neural basis of inhibition in cognitive control. *Neuroscientist*, *13*(3), 214–228. Available from http://dx.doi.org/10.1177/1073858407299288.

Banich, M. T. (2009). Executive function: The search for an integrated account. *Current Directions in Psychological Science*, *18*(2), 89–94. Available from http://dx.doi.org/10.1111/j.1467-8721.2009.01615.x.

Bargh, J. A., & Ferguson, M. J. (2000). Beyond behaviorism: On the automaticity of higher mental processes. *Psychological Bulletin*, *126*(6), 925–945. Available from http://dx.doi.org/10.1037/0033-2909.126.6.925.

Baym, C. L., Corbett, B. A., Wright, S. B., & Bunge, S. A. (2008). Neural correlates of tic severity and cognitive control in children with Tourette syndrome. *Brain*, *131*(Pt 1), 165–179. Available from http://dx.doi.org/10.1093/brain/awm278.

Beauregard, M. (2007). Mind does really matter: Evidence from neuroimaging studies of emotional self-regulation, psychotherapy, and placebo effect. *Progress in Neurobiology*, *81*, 218–236.

Bechara, A. (1997). Deciding advantageously before knowing the advantageous strategy. *Science*, *275*(5304), 1293–1295. Available from http://dx.doi.org/10.1126/science.275.5304.1293.

Bechara, A., Damasio, A. R., Damasio, H., & Anderson, S. W. (1994). Insensitivity to future consequences following damage to human prefrontal cortex. *Cognition*, *50*(1-3), 7–15.

Bechara, A., Damasio, H., Tranel, D., & Damasio, A. R. (2005). The Iowa Gambling task and the somatic marker hypothesis: Some questions and answers. *Trends in Cognitive Sciences*, *9*(4), 159–162. discussion 162–154. http://dx.doi.org/10.1016/j.tics.2005.02.002.

Berenbaum, S. A., & Beltz, A. M. (2011). Sexual differentiation of human behavior: Effects of prenatal and pubertal organizational hormones. *Frontiers in Neuroendocrinology*, *32*, 183–200. Available from http://dx.doi.org/10.1016/j.yfrne.2011.03.001.

Bernard, B. A., Stebbins, G. T., Siegel, S., Schultz, T. M., Hays, C., Morrissey, M. J., ... Goetz, C. G. (2009). Determinants of quality of life in children with Gilles de la Tourette syndrome. *Moving Disorders*, *24*(7), 1070–1073. Available from http://dx.doi.org/10.1002/mds.22487.

Best, J. R., & Miller, P. H. (2010). A developmental perspective on executive function. *Child Development*, *81*(6), 1641–1660. Available from http://dx.doi.org/10.1111/j.1467-8624.2010.01499.x.

Blakemore, S. J., & Choudhury, S. (2006). Development of the adolescent brain: implications for executive function and social cognition. *Journal of Child Psychology and Psychiatry*, *47*(3-4), 296–312. Available from http://dx.doi.org/10.1111/j.1469-7610.2006.01611.x.

Bloch, M. H., & Leckman, J. F. (2009). Clinical course of Tourette syndrome. *Journal of Psychosomatic Research*, *67*(6), 497–501. Available from http://dx.doi.org/10.1016/j.jpsychores.2009.09.002.

Bohlhalter, S., Goldfine, A., Matteson, S., Garraux, G., Hanakawa, T., Kansaku, K., ... Hallett, M. (2006). Neural correlates of tic generation in Tourette syndrome: An event-related functional MRI study. *Brain*, *129*(Pt 8), 2029–2037. Available from http://dx.doi.org/10.1093/brain/awl050.

Bonelli, R. M., & Cummings, J. L. (2007). Frontal-subcortical circuitry and behavior. *Dialogues in Clinical Neuroscience*, *9*(2), 141–151.

Boyer, T. W. (2006). The development of risk-taking: A multi-perspective review. *Developmental Review*, *26*(3), 291–345. Available from http://dx.doi.org/10.1016/j. dr.2006.05.002.

Brand, M., Recknor, E. C., Grabenhorst, F., & Bechara, A. (2007). Decisions under ambiguity and decisions under risk: Correlations with executive functions and comparisons of two different gambling tasks with implicit and explicit rules. *Journal of Clinical and Experimental Neuropsychology*, *29*(1), 86–99. Available from http://dx.doi.org/10.1080/13803390500507196.

Canales, J. J., & Iversen, S. D. (2000). Dynamic dopamine receptor interactions in the core and shell of nucleus accumbens differentially coordinate the expression of unconditioned motor behaviors. *Synapse*, *36*(4), 297–306.

Carter, Alice S., O'Donnell, Deborah A., Schultz, Robert T., Scahill, Lawrence, Leckman, James F., & Pauls, David L. (2000). Social and emotional adjustment in children affected with Gilles de la Tourette's syndrome: Associations with ADHD and family functioning. *Journal of Child Psychology and Psychiatry*, *41*(2), 215–223.

Casey, B. J., Jones, R. M., & Hare, T. A. (2008). The adolescent brain. *Annals of the New York Academy of Sciences*, *1124*, 111–126. Available from http://dx.doi.org/10.1196/annals.1440.010.

Casey, B. J., Tottenham, N., & Fossella, J. (2002). Clinical, imaging, lesion, and genetic approaches toward a model of cognitive control. *Developmental Psychobiology*, *40*(3), 237–254. Available from http://dx.doi.org/10.1002/dev.10030.

Castellanos, F. X., Sonuga-Barke, E. J., Milham, M. P., & Tannock, R. (2006). Characterizing cognition in ADHD: Beyond executive dysfunction. *Trends in Cognitive Sciences*, *10*(3), 117–123. Available from http://dx.doi.org/10.1016/j.tics.2006.01.011.

Cavanna, A. E., Servo, S., Monaco, F., & Robertson, M. M. (2009). The behavioral spectrum of Gilles de la Tourette syndrome. *Journal of Neuropsychiatry & Clinical Neuroscience*, *21*(1), 13–23. Available from http://dx.doi.org/10.1176/appi.neuropsych.21.1.13.

Chan, Raymond C. K., Shum, David, Toulopoulou, Timothea, & Chen, Eric Y. H. (2008). Assessment of executive functions: Review of instruments and identification of critical issues. *Archives of Clinical Neuropsychology*, *23*(2), 201–216. Available from http://dx.doi.org/10.1016/j.acn.2007.08.010.

Crawford, S., Channon, S., & Robertson, M. M. (2005). Tourette's syndrome: Performance on tests of behavioural inhibition, working memory and gambling. *Journal of Child Psychology and Psychiatry*, *46*(12), 1327–1336. Available from http://dx.doi.org/10.1111/j.1469-7610.2005.01419.x.

Crone, E. A., & van der Molen, M. W. (2004). Developmental changes in real life decision making: Performance on a gambling task previously shown to depend on the ventromedial prefrontal cortex. *Developmental Neuropsychology*, *25*(3), 251–279. Available from http://dx.doi.org/10.1207/s15326942dn2503_2.

Cunningham, W. A., Zelazo, P. D., Packer, D. J., & Van Bavel, J. J. (2007). The iterative reprocessing model: A multilevel framework for attitudes and evaluation. *Social Cognition*, *25*(5), 736–760. Available from http://dx.doi.org/10.1521/soco.2007.25.5.736.

Dale, R. C. (2003). Autoimmunity and the basal ganglia: New insights into old diseases. *QJM: An International Journal of Medicine*, *96*(3), 183–191. Available from http://dx.doi.org/10.1093/qjmed/hcg026.

Davis, L. K., Yu, D., Keenan, C. L., Gamazon, E. R., Konkashbaev, A. I., Derks, E. M., & Scharf, J. M. (2013). Partitioning the heritability of Tourette syndrome and obsessive compulsive disorder reveals differences in genetic architecture. *PLoS Genetics*, *9*(10), e1003864. Available from http://dx.doi.org/10.1371/journal.pgen.1003864.

Denckla, M. B. (2006). Attention-deficit hyperactivity disorder (ADHD) comorbidity: A case for "Pure"' Tourette syndrome? *Journal of Child Neurology*, *21*(8), 701–703. Available from http://dx.doi.org/10.1177/08830738060210080701.

DeVito, E. E., Blackwell, A. D., Kent, L., Ersche, K. D., Clark, L., Salmond, C. H., ... Sahakian, B. J. (2008). The effects of methylphenidate on decision making in attention-deficit/hyperactivity disorder. *Biological Psychiatry*, *64*(7), 636–639. Available from http://dx.doi.org/10.1016/j.biopsych.2008.04.017.

Diamond, A. (2013). Executive functions. *Annual Review of Psychology*, *64*, 135–168. Available from http://dx.doi.org/10.1146/annurev-psych-113011-143750.

Eapen, V., & Crncec, R. (2009). Tourette syndrome in children and adolescents: Special considerations. *Journal of Psychosomatic Research*, *67*(6), 525–532. Available from http://dx.doi.org/10.1016/j.jpsychores.2009.08.003.

Eddy, C. M., Rizzo, R., & Cavanna, A. E. (2009). Neuropsychological aspects of Tourette syndrome: A review. *Journal of Psychosomatic Research*, *67*(6), 503–513. Available from http://dx.doi.org/10.1016/j.jpsychores.2009.08.001.

Eisenberg, N., & Spinrad, T. L. (2004). Emotion-related regulation: Sharpening the definition. *Child Development*, *75*(2), 334–339. Available from http://dx.doi.org/10.1111/j.1467-8624.2004.00674.x.

Elliott, R. (2003). Executive functions and their disorders. *British Medical Bulletin*, *65*(1), 49–59. Available from http://dx.doi.org/10.1093/bmb/65.1.49.

Eysenck, M. W., Derakshan, N., Santos, R., & Calvo, M. G. (2007). Anxiety and cognitive performance: attentional control theory. *Emotion*, *7*(2), 336–353. Available from http://dx.doi.org/10.1037/1528-3542.7.2.336.

Felling, Ryan J., & Singer, HarveyS. (2011). Neurobiology of Tourette syndrome: Current status and need for further investigation. *The Journal of Neuroscience*, *31*(35), 12387–12395.

Freeman, R. D., Fast, D. K., Burd, L., Kerbeshian, J., Robertson, M. M., & Sandor, P. (2000). An international perspective on Tourette syndrome: selected findings from 3,500 individuals in 22 countries. *Developmental Medicine and Child Neurology*, *42*(7), 436–447.

Freeman, R. D., & Tourette Syndrome International Database, Consortium (2007). Tic disorders and ADHD: answers from a world-wide clinical dataset on Tourette syndrome. *European Child & Adolescent Psychiatry*, *16*(Suppl 1), 15–23. Available from http://dx.doi.org/10.1007/s00787-007-1003-7.

Ganos, C., Roessner, V., & Munchau, A. (2013). The functional anatomy of Gilles de la Tourette syndrome. *Neuroscience & Biobehavioral Reviews*, *37*(6), 1050–1062. Available from http://dx.doi.org/10.1016/j.neubiorev.2012.11.004.

Gomis, M., Puente, V., Pont-Sunyer, C., Oliveras, C., & Roquer, J. (2008). Adult onset simple phonic tics after caudate stroke. *Movement Disorders*, *23*, 765–766.

Grafman, J., & Krueger, F. (2006). Volition and the human prefrontal cortex. In: Sebanz, N., & Prinz, W. (Eds.), *Disorders of Volition* (pp. 347–371).

Greenberg, G. (2014). How new ideas in physics and biology influence developmental science. *Research in Human Development*, *11*(1), 5–21. Available from http://dx.doi.org/10.1080/15427609.2014.874730.

Greenberg, G., Callina, K. S., & Mueller, M. K. (2013). Emergence, self-organization and developmental science. *Advances in Child Development and Behavior*, *44*, 95–126.

Greimel, E., Herpertz-Dahlmann, B., Gunther, T., Vitt, C., & Konrad, K. (2008). Attentional functions in children and adolescents with attention-deficit/hyperactivity disorder with and without comorbid tic disorder. *Journal of Neural Transmission*, *115*(2), 191–200. Available from http://dx.doi.org/10.1007/s00702-007-0815-4.

Groen, Y., Gaastra, G. F., Lewis-Evans, B., & Tucha, O. (2013). Risky behavior in gambling tasks in individuals with ADHD—A systematic literature review. *PLoS One*, *8*(9), e74909. Available from http://dx.doi.org/10.1371/journal.pone.0074909.

Hanif, A., Ferrey, A. E., Frischen, A., Pozzobon, K., Eastwood, J. D., Smilek, D., & Fenske, M. J. (2012). Manipulations of attention enhance self-regulation. *Acta Psychologica*, *139*(1), 104–110. Available from http://dx.doi.org/10.1016/j.actpsy.2011.09.010.

Heatherton, T. F., & Wagner, D. D. (2011). Cognitive neuroscience of self-regulation failure. *Trends in Cognitive Sciences*, *15*(3), 132–139. Available from http://dx.doi.org/10.1016/j.tics.2010.12.005.

Heilman, RenataM., Crişan, Liviu G., Houser, Daniel, Miclea, Mircea, Miu, Andrei C., & Phelps, Elizabeth A. (2010). Emotion regulation and decision making under risk and uncertainty. *Emotion*, *10*(2), 257–265. Available from http://dx.doi.org/10.1037/a0018489.

Hirschtritt, M. E., Lee, P. C., Pauls, D. L., Dion, Y., Grados, M. A., Illmann, C., ... Tourette Syndrome Association International Consortium for, Genetics (2015). Lifetime prevalence, age of risk, and genetic relationships of comorbid psychiatric disorders in Tourette syndrome. *Journal of the American Medical Association Psychiatry*, *72*(4), 325–333. Available from http://dx.doi.org/10.1001/jamapsychiatry.2014.2650.

Hoekstra, P. J., Lundervold, A. J., Lie, S. A., Gillberg, C., & Plessen, K. J. (2013). Emotional development in children with tics: a longitudinal population-based study. *European Child & Adolescent Psychiatry*, *22*(3), 185–192. Available from http://dx.doi.org/10.1007/s00787-012-0337-y.

Hofmann, Wilhelm, Schmeichel, Brandon J., & Baddeley, Alan D. (2012). Executive functions and self-regulation. *Trends in Cognitive Sciences*, *16*(3), 174–180. Available from http://dx.doi.org/10.1016/j.tics.2012.01.006.

Horesh, N., Zimmerman, S., Steinberg, T., Yagan, H., & Apter, A. (2008). Is onset of Tourette syndrome influenced by life events? *Journal of Neural Transmission*, *115*(5), 787–793. Available from http://dx.doi.org/10.1007/s00702-007-0014-3.

Hovik, K. T., Egeland, J., Isquith, P. K., Gioia, G., Skogli, E. W., Andersen, P. N., & Oie, M. (2014). Distinct patterns of everyday executive function problems distinguish children with Tourette syndrome from children with ADHD or autism spectrum disorders. *Journal of Attention Disorders*, , 1–13. Available from http://dx.doi.org/10.1177/1087054714550336.

Hovik, K. T., Plessen, K. J., Cavanna, A. E., Skogli, E. W., Andersen, P. N., & Oie, M. (2015). Cognition, emotion and behavior in children with Tourette's syndrome and children with ADHD-combined subtype—A two-year follow-up study. *PLoS One*, *10*(12), e0144874. Available from http://dx.doi.org/10.1371/journal.pone.0144874.

Hovik, K. T., Plessen, K. J., Skogli, E. W., Andersen, P. N., & Oie, M. (2016). Dissociable response inhibition in children with Tourette's syndrome compared with children with ADHD. *Journal of Attention Disorders*, *20*(10), 825–835. http://dx.doi.org/10.1177/1087054713512371.

Ikemoto, S., Yang, C., & Tan, A. (2015). Basal ganglia circuit loops, dopamine and motivation: A review and enquiry. *Behavioural Brain Research*, *290*, 17–31. Available from http://dx.doi.org/10.1016/j.bbr.2015.04.018.

Jackson, G. M., Mueller, S. C., Hambleton, K., & Hollis, C. P. (2007). Enhanced cognitive control in Tourette syndrome during task uncertainty. *Experimental Brain Research*, *182*(3), 357–364. Available from http://dx.doi.org/10.1007/s00221-007-0999-8.

Jackson, S. R., Parkinson, A., Jung, J., Ryan, S. E., Morgan, P. S., Hollis, C., & Jackson, G. M. (2011). Compensatory neural reorganization in Tourette syndrome. *Current Biology*, *21*(7), 580–585. Available from http://dx.doi.org/10.1016/j.cub.2011.02.047.

Johnson, M. H., Jones, E. J., & Gliga, T. (2015). Brain adaptation and alternative developmental trajectories. *Developmental Psychopathology*, *27*(2), 425–442. Available from http://dx.doi.org/10.1017/S0954579415000073.

Jokic-Begic, N. (2010). Cognitive-behavioral therapy and neuroscience: Towards closer integration. *Psychological Topics*, *2*, 235–254.

Kelley, A. E., Lang, C. G., & Gauthier, A. M. (1988). Induction of oral stereotypy following amphetamine microinjection into a discrete subregion of the striatum. *Psychopharmacology*, *95*(4), 556–559.

Khalifa, N., & Von Knorring, A. L. (2003). Prevalence of tic disorders and Tourette syndrome in a Swedish school population. *Developmental Medicine and Child Neurology*, *45*(5), 315–319. Available from http://dx.doi.org/10.1017/S0012162203000598.

Koechlin, E., Ody, C., & Kouneiher, F. (2003). The architecture of cognitive control in the human prefrontal cortex. *Science*, *302*(5648), 1181–1185. Available from http://dx.doi.org/10.1126/science.1088545.

Leckman, J. F. (2003). Phenomenology of tics and natural history of tic disorders. *Brain & Development*, *25*(Suppl 1), S24–28.

Leckman, J. F., Bloch, M. H., Scahill, L., & King, R. A. (2006). Tourette syndrome: The self under siege. *Journal of Child Neurology*, *21*(8), 642–649.

Leckman, J. F., & Riddle, M. A. (2000). Tourette's syndrome: When habit-forming systems form habits of their own?. *Neuron*, *28*(2), 349–354 . http://dx.doi.org/10.1016/s0896-6273(00)00114-8

Lin, Haiqun, Yeh, Chin-Bin, Peterson, Bradley S., Scahill, Lawrence, Grantz, Heidi, Findley, Diane B., ... King, Robert A. (2002). Assessment of symptom exacerbations in a longitudinal study of children with Tourette's syndrome or obsessive-compulsive disorder. *Journal of the American Academy of Child & Adolescent Psychiatry*, *41*(9), 1070–1077.

Linden, D. E. (2006). How psychotherapy changes the brain—The contribution of functional neuroimaging. *Molecular Psychiatry*, *11*(6), 528–538. Available from http://dx.doi.org/10.1038/sj.mp.4001816.

Litt, A., Plassmann, H., Shiv, B., & Rangel, A. (2011). Dissociating valuation and saliency signals during decision-making. *Cerebral Cortex*, *21*(1), 95–102. Available from http://dx.doi.org/10.1093/cercor/bhq065.

Luman, M., Oosterlaan, J., Knol, D. L., & Sergeant, J. A. (2008). Decision-making in ADHD: Sensitive to frequency but blind to the magnitude of penalty? *Journal of Child Psychology and Psychiatry*, *49*(7), 712–722. Available from http://dx.doi.org/10.1111/j.1469-7610.2008.01910.x.

Luna, Beatriz, Garver, Krista E., Urban, Trinity A., Lazar, Nicole A., & Sweeney, John A. (2004). Maturation of cognitive processes from late childhood to adulthood. *Child Development*, *75*(5), 1357–1372. Available from http://dx.doi.org/10.1111/j.1467-8624.2004.00745.x.

Lyons, Ke, & Zelazo, P. D. (2011). Monitoring, metacognition, and executive function: Elucidating the role of self-reflection in the development of self-regulation. *Advances in Child Development and Behavior*, *40*, 379–412.

Maia, T. V., & McClelland, J. L. (2004). A reexamination of the evidence for the somatic marker hypothesis: What participants really know in the Iowa gambling task. *Proceedings of the National Academy of Sciences of the United States of America*, *101*(45), 16075–16080. Available from http://dx.doi.org/10.1073/pnas.0406666101.

Maier, S. F. (2015). Behavioral control blunts reactions to contemporaneous and future adverse events: Medial prefrontal cortex plasticity and a corticostriatal network. *Neurobiology Stress, 1,* 12–22. Available from http://dx.doi.org/10.1016/j.ynstr.2014.09.003.

Marsh, R., Alexander, G. M., Packard, M. G., Zhu, H., & Peterson, B. S. (2005). Perceptual-motor skill learning in Gilles de la Tourette syndrome. Evidence for multiple procedural learning and memory systems. *Neuropsychologia, 43*(10), 1456–1465. Available from http://dx.doi.org/10.1016/j.neuropsychologia.2004.12.012.

Marsh, R., Alexander, G. M., Packard, M. G., Zhu, H., Wingard, J. C., Quackenbush, G., & Peterson, B. S. (2004). Habit learning in Tourette syndrome: A translational neuroscience approach to a developmental psychopathology. *Archives of General Psychiatry, 61*(12), 1259–1268. Available from http://dx.doi.org/10.1001/archpsyc.61.12.1259.

Marsh, R., Maia, T., & Peterson, B. (2009). Functional disturbances within frontostriatal circuits across multiple childhood psychopathologies. *The American Journal of Psychiatry, 166*(6), 664–674.

Marsh, R., Zhu, H., Wang, Z., Skudlarski, P., & Peterson, B. S. (2007). A developmental fMRI study of self-regulatory control in Tourette's syndrome. *American Journal of Psychiatry, 164*(6), 955–966. Available from http://dx.doi.org/10.1176/ajp.2007.164.6.955.

Mathews, C. A., Waller, J., Glidden, D., Lowe, T. L., Herrera, L. D., Budman, C. L., & Reus, V. I. (2004). Self injurious behaviour in Tourette syndrome: correlates with impulsivity and impulse control. *Journal of Neurology, Neurosurgery & Psychiatry, 75*(8), 1149–1155. Available from http://dx.doi.org/10.1136/jnnp.2003.020693.

Miller, E. K., & Cohen, J. D. (2001). An integrative theory of prefrontal cortex function. *Annual Review of Neuroscience, 24,* 167–202. Available from http://dx.doi.org/10.1146/annurev.neuro.24.1.167.

Mink, J. W. (2001). Neurobiology of basal ganglia circuits in Tourette syndrome: Faulty inhibition of unwanted motor patterns? *Advanced Neurology, 85,* 113–122.

Mink, J. W. (2003). The basal ganglia and involuntary movements: Impaired inhibition of competing motor patterns. *Archives of Neurology, 60*(10), 1365–1368. Available from http://dx.doi.org/10.1001/archneur.60.10.1365.

Miyake, A., & Friedman, N. P. (2012). The nature and organization of individual differences in executive functions: Four general conclusions. *Current Directions in Psychological Science, 21*(1), 8–14. Available from http://dx.doi.org/10.1177/0963721411429458.

Moriguchi, Y., Chevalier, N., & Zelazo, P. D. (2016). Editorial: Development of executive function during childhood. *Frontiers in Psychology, 7,* 6. Available from http://dx.doi.org/10.3389/fpsyg.2016.00006.

Mueller, S. C., Jackson, G. M., Dhalla, R., Datsopoulos, S., & Hollis, C. P. (2006). Enhanced cognitive control in young people with Tourette's syndrome. *Current Biology, 16*(6), 570–573. Available from http://dx.doi.org/10.1016/j.cub.2006.01.064.

Muller, S. V., Johannes, S., Wieringa, B., Weber, A., Muller-Vahl, K., Matzke, M., ... Munte, T. F. (2003). Disturbed monitoring and response inhibition in patients with Gilles de la Tourette syndrome and co-morbid obsessive compulsive disorder. *Behavioral Neurology, 14*(1-2), 29–37.

Nixon, E., Glazebrook, C., Hollis, C., & Jackson, G. M. (2014). Reduced tic symptomatology in Tourette syndrome after an acute bout of exercise: An observational study. *Behavior Modification, 38*(2), 235–263. Available from http://dx.doi.org/10.1177/0145445514532127.

O'Connor, K. (2002). A cognitive-behavioral/psychophysiological model of tic disorders. *Behaviour Research Therapy, 40*(10), 1113–1142.

Ochsner, K. N., & Gross, J. J. (2007). The neural architecture of emotion regulation. In J. J. Gross (Ed.), *Handbook of emotion regulation* (pp. 87−109). New York: Guilford Press.

Ochsner, K. N., Knierim, K., Ludlow, D. H., Hanelin, J., Ramachandran, T., Glover, G., & Mackey, S. C. (2004). Reflecting upon feelings: An fMRI study of neural systems supporting the attribution of emotion to self and other. *Journal of Cognitive Neuroscience, 16*(10), 1746−1772.

Osman, M. (2004). An evaluation of dual-process theories of reasoning. *Psychonomic Bulletin & Review, 11*(6), 988−1010.

Overton, Willis F. (2013). A new paradigm for developmental science: Relationism and relational-developmental systems. *Applied Developmental Science, 17*(2), 94−107. Available from http://dx.doi.org/10.1080/10888691.2013.778717.

Palminteri, S., Lebreton, M., Worbe, Y., Grabli, D., Hartmann, A., & Pessiglione, M. (2009). Pharmacological modulation of subliminal learning in Parkinson's and Tourette's syndromes. *Proceedings of the National Academy of Sciences, 106*(45), 19179−19184. Available from http://dx.doi.org/10.1073/pnas.0904035106.

Pascual-Leone, A., Amedi, A., Fregni, F., & Merabet, L. B. (2005). The plastic human brain cortex. *Annual Review of Neuroscience, 28*, 377−401. Available from http://dx.doi.org/10.1146/annurev.neuro.27.070203.144216.

Pashler, H., Johnston, J. C., & Ruthruff, E. (2001). Attention and performance. *Annual Review of Psychology, 52*(1), 629−651. Available from http://dx.doi.org/10.1146/annurev.psych.52.1.629.

Petanjek, Z., Judas, M., Simic, G., Rasin, M. r, Uylings, Hbm, Rakic, P., & Kostovic, I. (2011). Extraordinary neoteny of synaptic spines in the human prefrontal cortex. *Proceedings of the National Academy of Sciences, 108*(32), 13281−13286. Available from http://dx.doi.org/10.1073/pnas.1105108108.

Piacentini, J., Woods, G., Scahill, L., Wilhelm, S., Peterson, A. L., Chang, S., & Walkup, J. T. (2010). Behavior therapy for children with Tourette disorder: A randomized controlled trial. *Journal of the American Medical Association, 303*(19), 1929−1937.

Plessen, K. J. (2013). Tic disorders and Tourette's syndrome. *European Child & Adolescent Psychiatry, 22*(Suppl 1), S55−S60. Available from http://dx.doi.org/10.1007/s00787-012-0362-x.

Povinelli, D. J., & Bering, J. M. (2002). The mentality of Apes revisited. *Current Directions in Psychological Science, 11*(4), 115−119.

Prencipe, A., Kesek, A., Cohen, J. D., Lamm, C., Lewis, M. D., & Zelazo, P. D. (2011). Development of hot and cool executive function during the transition to adolescence. *Journal of Experimental Child Psychology, 108*(3), 621−637. Available from http://dx.doi.org/10.1016/j.jecp.2010.09.008.

Rasmussen, C., Soleimani, M., Carroll, A., & Hodlevskyy, O. (2009). Neuropsychological functioning in children with Tourette syndrome (TS). *Journal of the Canadian Academy of Child and Adolescent Psychiatry, 18*(4), 307−315.

Redgrave, P., Prescott, T. J., & Gurney, K. (1999). The basal ganglia: A vertebrate solution to the selection problem? *Neuroscience, 89*(4), 1009−1023.

Robertson, M. M. (2000). Tourette syndrome, associated conditions and the complexities of treatment. *Brain, 123*(Pt 3), 425−462.

Robertson, M. M., Eapen, V., & Cavanna, A. E. (2009). The international prevalence, epidemiology, and clinical phenomenology of Tourette syndrome: A cross-cultural perspective. *Journal of Psychosomatic Research, 67*(6), 475−483. Available from http://dx.doi.org/10.1016/j.jpsychores.2009.07.010.

Roessner, V., Albrecht, B., Dechent, P., Baudewig, J., & Rothenberger, A. (2008). Normal response inhibition in boys with Tourette syndrome. *Behavioral and Brain Functions*, *4*, 29. Available from http://dx.doi.org/10.1186/1744-9081-4-29.

Sacks, O. (1981). Witty Ticcy Ray. *London Review of Books*, *3*(5), 3−5.

Serrien, D. J., Orth, M., Evans, A. H., Lees, A. J., & Brown, P. (2005). Motor inhibition in patients with Gilles de la Tourette syndrome: Functional activation patterns as revealed by EEG coherence. *Brain*, *128*(Pt 1), 116−125. Available from http://dx.doi.org/10.1093/brain/awh318.

Silvers, J., Buhle, J. T., & Ochsner, K. N. (2013). The neuroscience of emotion regulation: Basic mechanisms and their role in development, aging, and psychopathologyIn K. N. Ochsner, & S. Kosslyn (Eds.), *The Oxford Handbook of Cognitive Neuroscience* (Volume 2, pp. 52−78). New York: Oxford University Press, *The Cutting Edges*.

Singer, H. S. (2005). Tourette's syndrome: from behaviour to biology. *The Lancet Neurology, 4* (3), 149−159 , doi:10.1016/S1474-4422(05)01012-4

Skogli, E. W., Egeland, J., Andersen, P. N., Hovik, K. T., & Oie, M. (2014). Few differences in hot and cold executive functions in children and adolescents with combined and inattentive subtypes of ADHD. *Child Neuropsychology*, *20*(2), 162−181. Available from http://dx.doi.org/10.1080/09297049.2012.753998.

Smith, D. G., Xiao, L., & Bechara, A. (2012). Decision making in children and adolescents: Impaired Iowa Gambling task performance in early adolescence. *Developmental Psychology*, *48*(4), 1180−1187. Available from http://dx.doi.org/10.1037/a0026342.

Solanto, M. V. (2002). Dopamine dysfunction in AD/HD: Integrating clinical and basic neuroscience research. *Behavioural Brain Research*, *130*(1-2), 65−71.

Sonuga-Barke, E. J. (2003). The dual pathway model of AD/HD: An elaboration of neuro-developmental characteristics. *Neuroscience & Biobehavioral Reviews*, *27*(7), 593−604.

Spencer, T., Biederman, J., Harding, M., O'Donnell, D., Wilens, T., Faraone, S. V., & Geller, D. (1998). Disentangling the overlap between Tourette's disorder and ADHD. *Journal of Child Psychology and Psychiatry*, *39*(7), 1037−1044.

Steinberg, T., Shmuel-Baruch, S., Horesh, N., & Apter, A. (2013). Life events and Tourette syndrome. *Comprehensive Psychiatry*, *54*(5), 467−473. Available from http://dx.doi.org/10.1016/j.comppsych.2012.10.015.

Stern, E. R., Blair, C., & Peterson, B. S. (2008). Inhibitory deficits in Tourette's syndrome. *Developmental Psychobiology*, *50*(1), 9−18. Available from http://dx.doi.org/10.1002/dev.20266.

Stern, J. S., Burza, S., & Robertson, M. M. (2005). Gilles de la Tourette's syndrome and its impact in the UK. *Postgraduate Medical Journal*, *81*(951), 12−19. Available from http://dx.doi.org/10.1136/pgmj.2004.023614.

Suls, J., & Rothman, A. (2004). Evolution of the biopsychosocial model: Prospects and challenges for health psychology. *Health Psychology*, *23*(2), 119−125. Available from http://dx.doi.org/10.1037/0278-6133.23.2.119.

Swerdlow, N. R., & Young, A. B. (2001). Neuropathology in Tourette syndrome: An update. *Advanced Neurology*, *85-151*, 151−161.

Taylor, S. F., Phan, K. L., Decker, L. R., & Liberzon, I. (2003). Subjective rating of emotionally salient stimuli modulates neural activity. *NeuroImage*, *18*(3), 650−659.

Toplak, M. E., Jain, U., & Tannock, R. (2005). Executive and motivational processes in adolescents with attention-deficit-hyperactivity disorder (ADHD). *Behavioral and Brain Functions*, *1*(1), 8. Available from http://dx.doi.org/10.1186/1744-9081-1-8.

Tye, K. M., Mirzabekov, J. J., Warden, M. R., Ferenczi, E. A., Tsai, H. C., Finkelstein, J., & Deisseroth, K. (2013). Dopamine neurons modulate neural encoding and expression of depression-related behaviour. *Nature, 493*(7433), 537−541. Available from http://dx.doi.org/ 10.1038/nature11740.

van Maanen, L., Brown, S. D., Eichele, T., Wagenmakers, E. J., Ho, T., Serences, J., & Forstmann, B. U. (2011). Neural correlates of trial-to-trial fluctuations in response caution. *The Journal of Neuroscience, 31*(48), 17488−17495. Available from http://dx.doi.org/ 10.1523/JNEUROSCI.2924-11.2011.

Vendrell, P., Junque, C., Pujol, J., Jurado, M. A., Molet, J., & Grafman, J. (1995). The role of prefrontal regions in the Stroop task. *Neuropsychologia, 33*(3), 341−352.

Verdellen, C., van de Griendt, J., Hartmann, A., Murphy, T., & Group, Essts Guidelines (2011). European clinical guidelines for Tourette syndrome and other tic disorders. Part III: Behavioural and psychosocial interventions. *European Child & Adolescent Psychiatry, 20* (4), 197−207. Available from http://dx.doi.org/10.1007/s00787-011-0167-3.

Vohs, K. D., & Baumeister, R. F. (2004). Understanding self-regulation. In R. R. B. K. D. Vohs (Ed.), *Handbook of self-regulation: Research, theory and applications* (pp. 1−9). New York: Guilford Press.

Volkow, N. D., Wang, G. J., Kollins, S. H., Wigal, T. L., Newcorn, J. H., Telang, F., & Swanson, J. M. (2009). Evaluating dopamine reward pathway in ADHD: Clinical implications. *The Journal of the American Medical Association, 302*(10), 1084−1091. Available from http://dx.doi.org/10.1001/jama.2009.1308.

Wagner, S., Müller, C., Helmreic, I., Muss, M., & Tadic, A. (2015). A meta-analysis of cognitive functions in children and adolescents with major depressive disorder. *European Child & Adolescent Psychiatry, 24*(1), 5−19. Available from http://dx.doi.org/10.1007/s00787-014-0559-2.

Wand, R. R., Matazow, G. S., Shady, G. A., Furer, P., & Staley, D. (1993). Tourette syndrome: Associated symptoms and most disabling features. *Neuroscience and Biobehavioral Reviews, 17*, 271−275.

Watkins, L. H., Sahakian, B. J., Robertson, M. M., Veale, D. M., Rogers, R. D., Pickard, K. M., & Robbins, T. W. (2005). Executive function in Tourette's syndrome and obsessive-compulsive disorder. *Psychological Medicine, 35*(4), 571−582.

Wright, P., Albarracin, D., Brown, R. D., Li, H., He, G., & Liu, Y. (2008). Dissociated responses in the amygdala and orbitofrontal cortex to bottom-up and top-down components of emotional evaluation. *NeuroImage, 39*(2), 894−902. Available from http://dx.doi.org/10.1016/j. neuroimage.2007.09.014.

Zelazo, P. D., & Carlson, S. M. (2012). Hot and cool executive function in childhood and adolescence: Development and plasticity. *Child Development Perspectives, 6*(4), 354−360. Available from http://dx.doi.org/10.1111/j.1750-8606.2012.00246.x.

Zelazo, P. D., & Cunningham, W. A. (2007). *Executive function: Mechanisms underlying emotion regulation*. New York, NY: Guilford Press.

Zelazo, P. D., Qu, L., & Kesek, A. C. (2010). Hot executive function: Emotion and the development of cognitive control. In S. D. Calkins, & M. A. Bell (Eds.), *Child Development: At the Intersection of Emotion and Cognition* (pp. 97−112). Washington, D.C.: American Psychological Association.

Zinner, Samuel H. (2004). Tourette syndrome—Much more than tics. *Contemporary Pediatrics, 21*(8), 22−49.

Chapter 15

Inside the Triple-Decker: Tourette's Syndrome and Cerebral Hemispheres

Kjell Tore Hovik[1], Merete Øie[2,3] and Elkhonon Goldberg[4,5]

[1]*Division of Mental Health Care, Innlandet Hospital Trust, Sanderud, Norway,*
[2]*Research Department, Innlandet Hospital Trust, Lillehammer, Norway,* [3]*Department of Psychology, University of Oslo, Oslo, Norway,* [4]*Luria Neuroscience Institute, New York, NY, United States,* [5]*New York University School of Medicine, New York, NY, United States*

THE TRIPLE-DECKER

The prefrontal cortex (PFC), the striatum, and the dopaminergic nuclei of the ventral brain stem constitute three levels of a closely integrated functional hierarchy. At each level of this hierarchy, close integration also exists between its left- and right-hemispheric components. Schematically, this relationship can be represented as a bilateral triple-decker (Fig. 15.1).

Different disorders are linked to the dysregulation at different levels of the triple-decker: Parkinson's disease (PD) to the dysregulation at the nigro-striatal interface and TS to the dysregulation at the frontostriatal interface. The uppermost level of the triple-decker may be affected by focal prefrontal lesions of various etiologies (e.g., cerebrovascular accident (CVA), traumatic brain injury (TBI), or neoplasms). These different disorders correspond to disparate taxonomic niches and are usually regarded separately without much attempt to discern any invariant properties among them. Yet, strong vertical integration within the triple-decker makes it possible for each of these disorders to inform our understanding of, and help guide further research into, the cognitive characteristics of the others. In this chapter, we will examine how our earlier research into the effects of lateralized prefrontal lesions may guide the inquiry into the characteristics and subtypes of TS.

Lateralized differences in the cognitive consequences of prefrontal lesions have been demonstrated with the use of an agent-centered paradigm examining the subjects' response selection preference using an intentionally ambiguous, underconstrained cognitive bias task (CBT) (Goldberg, Podell, & Lovell, 1994; Goldberg, Podell, Harner, Lovell, and Riggio (1994); Goldberg

Executive Functions in Health and Disease. DOI: http://dx.doi.org/10.1016/B978-0-12-803676-1.00015-5

The Triple-Decker

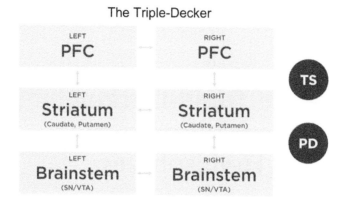

FIGURE 15.1 The Triple-Decker. Schematic representation of the three-level hierarchy involving the prefrontal cortex (*PFC*), striatum, and the dopaminergic nuclei of the brainstem—substantia nigra (*SN*) and ventral tegmental area (*VTA*). Parkinson's disease (*PD*) involves the breakdown of the SN/VTA-striatal interface. Tourette's syndrome (*TS*) involves the breakdown of the striatal—PFC interface.

& Podell, 1995; Podell, Lovell, Zimmerman, & Goldberg, 1995). The lesion effects were characterized by strong gender differences: very asymmetric in males and essentially symmetric in females (Goldberg et al., 1994a). In males, left prefrontal lesions resulted in overly context-independent perseverative response selection and right prefrontal lesions in overly context-dependent field-dependent response selection compared to healthy controls (Goldberg, Podell, & Lovell, 1994; Goldberg, Podell, Harner, Lovell, and Riggio, 1994; Goldberg & Podell, 1995; Podell et al., 1995). By contrast, in females both left and right prefrontal lesions resulted in extreme context-dependent response selection compared to healthy controls (Goldberg et al., 1994a). Double dissociation between the effects of lateralized focal prefrontal lesions in males was confirmed in a separate patient sample using a different cognitive task, The Executive Control Battery. Here left frontal lesions in males resulted in perseveration and right frontal lesions in echopraxic field-dependent behavior (Goldberg, Podell, Bilder, & Jaeger, 2000; Podell, 2009).

These findings prompted a study of cognitive impairment in hemi-Parkinsonian syndromes. Using the CBT, it was possible to demonstrate gender differences between the cognitive characteristics of males and females afflicted with PD, as well as differences between the cognitive characteristics of the left and right hemi-Parkinsonian syndromes (Varanese, Perfetti, Mason, Di Rocco, & Goldberg, 2010). The lateralized differences between the cognitive profiles of the left and right hemi-Parkinsonian (hemi-PD) syndromes closely parallel the effects of lateralized prefrontal lesions: right hemi-PD (predominantly left nigrostriatal dysfunction) is associated with relatively context-independent perseverative response selection, and left hemi-PD (predominantly right nigrostriatal dysfunction) with relatively context-dependent field-dependent response selection (Varanese et al., 2010). The differences between the cognitive profiles of left versus right hemi-Parkinsonian syndromes are likely to reflect the functional differences between the left and right striatal systems; and further exploration of these cognitive profiles may provide a window into the functional lateralization of the normal striatum.

The close parallelism between the effects of lateralized prefrontal lesions and lateralized nigrostriatal dysfunction suggests close vertical functional integration within the left and the right halves of the triple-decker and prompts the next question: Can these findings also inform our inquiry into the nature of TS and its variants?

SUBTYPING TOURETTE'S SYNDROME

TS is a disorder characterized by motor and vocal tics (DSM V, 2013). It has been suggested that these forced stereotypic behaviors are a form of perseveration not identical with, but closely related to, the perseveration caused by prefrontal dysfunction (Goldberg, 2009). Although the diagnostic criteria for TS are based exclusively on the presence of tics (DSM V, 2013), excessive and unusual exploratory behaviors are also common in TS. Whereas the primary site of abnormality in TS is unclear, dysfunctional dopaminergic signaling is a leading candidate (Felling & Singer, 2011). Changes in dopamine signaling are implicated in a range of exploratory behaviors (Costa, Tran, Turchi, & Averbeck, 2014). The commonly occurring presence of excessive exploratory behaviors in TS was originally pointed out by Sacks (1992) and further discussed by Goldberg (2009). Failure to account for excessive exploratory behaviors in the standard diagnostic criteria for TS could be a potential source of diagnostic confusion, whereby exploratory behaviors may be erroneously conflated with hyperactivity. The causes and consequences of such diagnostic confusion are discussed below.

Dysfunction of fronto-striato-thalamic connectivity involving the putamen and caudate nuclei and the breakdown of their interaction with the PFC has been implicated in TS (Makki, Govindan, Wilson, Behen, & Chugani, 2009; Stern et al., 2000; Wang et al., 2011), placing the disorder at the interface between the striatal and cortical levels of our proposed triple-decker model. Volumetric abnormalities in the sizes of striatal nuclei caudate and putamen in TS have also been reported (Bloch, Leckman, Zhu, & Peterson, 2005; Hassan & Cavanna, 2012; Roessner et al, 2011). Because perfect symmetry rarely obtains in nature, in any individual patient the pathophysiological processes responsible for the frontostriatal dysfunction in TS are likely to have an idiosyncratically asymmetric expression. The likely result is an expression affecting the frontostriatal interface in one hemisphere somewhat more than in the other in TS, in a manner similar to the one in which the nigrostriatal dysfunction is usually asymmetric in individual PD patients. Therefore, at least conceptually, it is possible to introduce the notion of "hemi-Tourette's (Hemi-TS)" by analogy with "hemi-Parkinsonian" syndromes and to ask the question about any possible cognitive differences between the left and right "hemi-" variants of TS. While conceptually intriguing, this distinction may be difficult to operationalize. Whereas hemi-Parkinsonian syndromes can be readily defined through the asymmetric resting tremor severity, no such unequivocal motor or otherwise readily observable lateralized clinical symptom exists for TS. It may be possible, however, to utilize the performance on standard neuropsychological tests of motor functions as the basis for plausible inference about the lateralized nature of frontostriatal dysfunction in individual TS cases.

This is precisely what we attempted to do. Because both the frontal lobes and the striatum are closely linked to motor functions, it may be possible to use lateralized dysfunction on a test of motor dexterity as a marker of contralateral dysfunction in the frontostriatal system. According to this scenario, particularly impaired dexterity in the right hand may reflect especially severe breakdown within the left frontostriatal system, and particularly impaired dexterity in the left hand may reflect especially severe breakdown within the right frontostriatal system. In this way, the left and right "hemi-TS" subgroups can be operationalized and putatively identified, and any cognitive or clinical differences between them examined.

METHODS

Participants

We studied a sample of 16 right-handed boys diagnosed with TS aged 9–17 years, and a typically developing control (TDC) sample consisting of 30 right-handed boys. Handedness was determined by questioning in separate interviews with parent and child and subsequently confirmed by observation during neurocognitive testing. Of the 16 children with TS, 8 received the diagnosis of TS only; 5 received the diagnosis of TS cooccurring with attention-deficit hyperactivity disorder (ADHD); and 3 of TS cooccurring with autism spectrum disorder (ASD). The participants were recruited by referral to the Centres for Child and Adolescent Mental Health in Innlandet Hospital Trust (IHT) in Norway for a child and adolescent psychiatric diagnostic assessment. The TDC subjects were recruited from local schools and received a small compensation for their participation. The participants in the TS and TDC groups did not differ significantly in age, mother's educational level, ethnic background, or estimated IQ based on results from the Wechsler Abbreviated Scale of Intelligence (WASI) (Wechsler et al., 2004). (See Table 15.1 for overview of demographic characteristics.)

TABLE 15.1 Demographic Characteristics: Means and Standard Deviations of the Comparison Groups

Variable	Right Hemi-TS[e] (n = 5)	Left Hemi-TS[e] (n = 4)	Symmetric (n = 7)	TDC[f] (n = 30)	Group Comparison F	P
Age in years (SD)	12.2 (2.9)	11.2 (2.0)	11.7 (2.1)	11.5 (1.9)	$F_{(3,42)} = 0.882$	NS
Mother's education (years)	12.2 (2.0)	12.7 (2.8)	12.3 (2.9)	14.5 (2.6)	$F_{(3,42)} = 0.094$	NS
GP dominant	70.6 (11.5)	69.7 (5.7)	77.0 (10.7)	74.6 (8.6)	$F_{(3,42)} = 0.821$	NS
GP nondominant	65.4 (10.0)	89.2 (7.3)	82.6 (8.8)	79.9 (12.5)	$F_{(3,42)} = 3.64$	<0.01 1 < 2
VIQ (WASI)[a]	106.4 (23.5)	93.0 (26.1)	93.8 (18.0)	96.8 (15.8)	$F_{(3,42)} = 0.619$	NS
PIQ (WASI)[b]	111.6 (17.9)	117.0 (8.2)	107.7 (11.3)	106.9 (16.8)	$F_{(3,42)} = 0.64$	NS
FSIQ (WASI)[c]	108.8 (18.4)	104.5 (12.2)	100.7 (12.4)	102.0 (12.9)	$F_{(3,42)} = 0.72$	NS
CBCL—Total problems[d]	68.2 (5.2)	70.7 (6.5)	62.9 (8.3)	37.9 (9.2)	$F_{(3,40)} = 38.64$	>0.01 1, 2, 3 >4

CBCL, Child Behaviour Checklist; SD, standard deviation; TDC, typically developing controls; TS, Tourette's syndrome; WASI, Wechsler Abbreviated Scale of Intelligence.
[a]WASI Verbal Scale IQ.
[b]WASI Performance Scale IQ.
[c]WASI Full Scale IQ.
[d]Child Behaviour Checklist/6–18. Higher scores denote greater pathology.
[e]Hemi-Tourette's syndrome.
[f]Typically developing children.

Ethics Statement

Parents and children (12 years and older) signed consent forms before participating in the study. The study was conducted in accordance with Helsinki Declaration of the World Medical Association Assembly. It was approved by the Regional Committee for Medical Research Ethics in Eastern Norway (REK-Øst), and by the Privacy protection ombudsman for research at Innlandet Hospital Trust (IHT).

PROCEDURE

Clinical Questionnaires and Scales

Experienced clinicians at IHT, who were trained and supervised by a specialist in child neuropsychology in the diagnostic assessment tools and the neuropsychological tests used in the study, were responsible for the assessment process. The test session lasted approximately 2.5–3.0 h, including two breaks of 10 min each. In the diagnostic process, each participant and one or both parents were interviewed separately using Kiddie Schedule for Affective Disorders and Schizophrenia (K-SADS) (Kaufman et al., 1997). Supplemental information was available in report forms completed by the same parent(s) using Yale Global Tic Severity Scale (YGTSS) (Leckman et al., 1989; Storch et al., 2005; Storch et al., 2007); ADHD Rating Scale-IV (DuPaul, Power, Anastoupolous, & Reid, 1998), Autism Spectrum Screening Questionnaire (Ehlers, Gillberg, & Wing, 1999), and Child Behaviour Checklist (CBCL) (Achenbach & Rescorla, 2001). Information from teachers about the child's school functioning (academic, social, and emotional competencies) is mandatory on referral to IHT and was used in the diagnostic evaluations. The results from the K-SADS interview and additional information were then reviewed independently by the supervising senior clinician who is a specialist in neurodevelopmental disorders (M.Ø.). Disagreements were discussed in meetings with all the clinicians present to arrive at a "Best estimate" DSM-IV consensus diagnosis (Leckman et al., 1989; American Psychiatric Association, 2000). Exclusion criteria were prematurity (<36 weeks), neurological disorder, estimated full scale IQ < 70, or previous stimulant treatment. The TDC were also screened in separate interviews of the child and the parent(s) for head injuries involving loss of consciousness, known dyslexia, or any psychiatric condition meeting K-SADS criteria.

Neurocognitive Assessment

The neuropsychological test battery administered in the project included 14 well-known standardized measures commonly used in research on children with neuropsychiatric disorders. All participants received the same test battery in the following fixed order: (1) Grooved Pegboard; (2) Hungry Donkey (children's version of the Iowa Gambling Task); (3) Vocabulary, Similarities, Block Design, and Matrix Reasoning subtests of the WASI; (4) Color-Word Interference Test—four conditions (D-KEFS); (5) Hopkins Verbal Learning Test-Revised (Norwegian version), (6) Conners' Continuous Performance Test-II (CCPT-II), (7) Tower Test (D-KEFS) (8) Brief Visuospatial Memory Test-II; (9) Letter-Number Sequencing (WISC-IV); (10) Verbal Fluency Test (D-KEFS); (11) Dichotic Listening; (12) Spatial Span (WISC-IV); (13) Design Fluency Test (D-KEFS); and (14) Trail Making Test—Conditions 2, 3, and 4 (D-KEFS). The following tests were not included in the current analyses: Hungry Donkey and Spatial Span Test.

Test of Fine Motor Dexterity

The Grooved Pegboard Test (GPT) contains 25 holes with randomly positioned slots and pegs, which have a key along one side. Pegs must be rotated to match the hole before they can be inserted (Ruff & Parker, 1993). The test measures performance speed in each hand. Higher raw scores indicated difficulties with the task.

For a more detailed description of the diagnostic instruments used in the study, see Appendix.

Data Analyses

Data analyses were conducted using the statistical package IBM SPSS Statistics for Windows (version 19.0; SPSS, Inc., Chicago, IL).

Demographic characteristics were investigated using analysis of variance (ANOVA) followed up by post hoc tests for group comparisons. We analyzed the neurocognitive and symptomology scale data with ANOVAs and post hoc analyses to compare performance by the four groups on the selected measures.

RESULTS

TS Versus TDC Sample Comparison

Several distinct differences between the TS and TDC samples were evident as summarized below:

1. Parents of children with TS reported a higher level of attention and hyperactivity/impulsivity problems compared with the TDC sample (Table 15.2).
2. More psychosocial problems were reported by parents of children in the TS sample compared with the TDC sample (Table 15.3).
3. More executive behavior regulation difficulties and behavioral problems were reported by parents of children in the TS sample compared with the TDC sample (Table 15.4).

TABLE 15.2 ADHD Rating Scale (MANOVA): Means and Standard Deviations Within the Four Groups

ADHD Symptoms							Group Comparison
Variable	Right Hemi-TS ($n=5$)	Left Hemi-TS ($n=4$)	Symmetric ($n=7$)	TDC ($n=30$)	Group Comparison		Bonferroni
					F	P	
Attention[a]	16.4 (6.5)	18.7 (9.7)	8.7 (7.8)	1.9 (2.1)	$F(3,42)=25.796$	<0.01	1, 2, 3 > 4; 2 > 3
Hyperactivity/impulsivity[b]	16.0 (8.0)	14.2 (5.3)	7.9 (3.5)	1.1 (1.3)	$F(3,42)=43.465$	<0.01	1, 2, 3 > 4; 1, 2 > 3
Total[c]	32.4 (12.6)	33.0 (12.2)	16.6 (10.5)	3.0 (3.3)	$F(3,42)=43.465$	<0.01	1, 2, 3 < 4; 1, 2 > 3
CBCL-ADHD subscale[d]	67.6. (4.0)	65.7 (7.9)	58.1 (7.9)	50.7 (1.5)	$F(3,40)=35.54$	<0.01	1, 2, 3 > 4; 1, 2 > 3

ADHD, attention-deficit hyperactivity disorder; CBCL, Child Behaviour Checklist; MANOVA, multivariate analysis of variance; TDC, typically developing controls; TS, Tourette's syndrome.
[a]ADHD rating scale – IV.
[b]ADHD rating scale – IV.
[c]Total of Inattention and Hyperactivity/Impulsivity subscales of ADHD rating scale – IV.
[d]CBCL-ADHD subscale.

TABLE 15.3 Group Differences and Interaction Effects on Symptom Ratings (MANOVA): Means and Standard Deviations

CBCL[a]	Group				Group Comparison		
	Right Hemi-TS (n = 5)	Left Hemi-TS (n = 4)	Symmetric (n = 7)	TDC (n = 30)	F	P	Bonferroni
Anxious/depressed	62.5 (3.4)	61.0 (3.4)	63.1 (2.6)	51.5 (4.2)	$F(3,37) =$	<0.01	1, 3 > 4
Withdrawn/depressed	60.5 (2.8)	64.5 (2.8)	68.4 (2.1)	51.6 (2.7)	$F(3,37) =$	<0.01	1, 2, 3 > 4
Somatic complaints	57.8 (6.5)	62.5 (4.6)	61.6 (9.5)	53.1 (4.9)	$F(3,40) = 5.856$	<0.01	2, 3 > 4
Social problems	66.6 (12.1)	73.5 (14.5)	61.3 (7.1)	50.5 (1.6)	$F(3,40) = 23.616$	<0.01	1, 2, 3 > 4; 2 > 3
Thought problems	69.8 (5.3)	72.0 (14.9)	63.9 (9.6)	50.8 (1.6)	$F(3,40) = 29.778$	<0.01	1, 2, 3 > 4
Attention problems	66.2 (5.3)	70.2 (9.8)	59.7 (8.7)	50.8 (1.5)	$F(3,40) = 31.792$	<0.01	1, 2, 3 > 4; 2 > 3
Rule-breaking	60.6 (10.8)	66.0 (8.2)	54.4 (6.5)	50.9 (2.7)	$F(3,40) = 12.583$	<0.01	1, 2 > 4; 2 > 3
Aggressive behavior	68.8 (6.6)	74.0 (14.1)	62.6 (11.7)	50.9 (1.9)	$F(3,40) = 24.347$	<0.01	1, 2, 3 > 4; 2 > 3
Affective problems	66.6 (4.6)	68.7 (9.5)	63.9 (9.9)	51.5 (3.8)	$F(3,40) = 21.995$	<0.01	1, 2, 3 > 4
Anxiety problems	65.0 (7.0)	56.7 (6.2)	60.9 (7.8)	51.1 (3.4)	$F(3,40) = 15.602$	<0.01	1, 3 > 4
Somatic problems	57.0 (7.5)	60.5 (3.3)	63.6 (8.7)	53.5 (5.1)	$F(3,40) = 6.120$	<0.01	3 > 4
Oppositional problems	65.8 (4.7)	67.5 (9.7)	59.1 (10.0)	51.4 (2.3)	$F(3,40) = 19.993$	<0.01	1, 2, 3 > 4
Conduct problems	64.4 (10.5)	70.7 (9.0)	56.9 (9.6)	51.2 (2.7)	$F(3,40) = 17.150$	<0.01	1, 2 > 4

MANOVA, multivariate analysis of variance; TDC, typically developing controls; TS, Tourette's syndrome.
[a]*Child Behaviour Checklist.*

TABLE 15.4 Group Differences and Interaction Effects on Executive Function Ratings (MANOVA): Means and Standard Deviations

BRIEF[a]	Group				Group Comparison		
	Right Hemi-TS (n = 5)	Left Hemi-TS (n = 4)	Symmetric (n = 7)	TDC (n = 30)	F	P	Bonferroni
Inhibit	71.2 (13.0)	73.2 (8.8)	62.7 (17.0)	42.5 (3.5)	F(3,42) = 33.475	<0.01	1, 2, 3 > 4
Shift	67.0 (10.4)	70.2 (24.0)	67.0 (22.3)	40.9 (5.9)	F(3,42) = 17.153	<0.01	1, 2, 3 > 4
Emotional control	67.8 (12.1)	77.5 (4.2)	68.7 (16.0)	40.8 (3.7)	F(3,42) = 51.909	<0.01	1, 2, 3 > 4
Initiate	65.2 (5.8)	65.5 (8.5)	57.7 (18.0)	41.4 (7.3)	F(3,42) = 17.021	<0.01	1, 2, 3 > 4
Working memory	69.6 (9.1)	77.0 (8.5)	58.9 (20.8)	42.0 (4.8)	F(3,42) = 26.699	<0.01	1, 2, 3 > 4; 2 > 3
Plan/organize	63.2 (9.4)	67.2 (11.9)	54.1 (17.9)	41.9 (5.1)	F(3,42) = 16.323	<0.01	1, 2, 3 > 4
Organization of materials	59.8 (13.4)	60.2 (9.2)	51.9 (26.6)	41.8 (7.8)	F(3,42) = 5.001	<0.01	1 > 4
Monitor	66.6 (10.1)	67.7 (10.43)	58.4 (16.1)	38.4 (6.)	F(3,42) = 28.641	<0.01	1, 2, 3 > 4

Note: Elevated BRIEF T-scores indicate a higher degree of impairment, with T-scores of 65 and above considered to represent clinically significant areas of concern. MANOVA, multivariate analysis of variance; TDC, typically developing controls; TS, Tourette's syndrome.
[a]Behaviour Rating Inventory of Executive Function.

TS Subtype Comparison

The children with TS (all right-handed) were subdivided into three groups: "left hemi-TS," "right hemi-TS," and "symmetric TS" subgroups based on their performance on the GPT, a test of motor speed and dexterity. "Right hemi-TS," presumably caused by predominantly left frontostriatal dysfunction, was defined as the left-hand superior to right-hand performance on GPT. "Left hemi-TS," presumably caused by predominantly right frontostriatal dysfunction, was defined as the right-hand superior to left-hand performance by more than 1.5 standard deviations. All other cases (i.e., cases characterized by a modest degree of right-hand superiority typically expected in healthy right-handers) were assigned to the "symmetric TS" category. Based on these criteria, five subjects were classified as "right hemi-TS"/presumed left frontostriatal dysfunction; four subjects were classified as "left hemi-TS"/presumed right frontostriatal dysfunction; and seven subjects as "symmetric TS"/presumably relatively bilateral frontostriatal dysfunction.

Several differences emerged between the three TS subtypes thus defined. They are described below:

1. Neurocognitive tests. Significant difference was present for several of the CPT composites. The right hemi-TS group performance was significantly more impaired on the Focus/Attention and Sustained Attention composites compared to the TDC sample. The left hemi-TS group performance was significantly more impaired on the Hyperactivity/Impulsivity composite compared to the TDC sample (Table 15.5).

   No significant differences were evident between any of the groups on the executive function measures (Table 15.6). No significant difference between any of the groups on the Dichotic Listening task was evident. A strong trend was evident, however, indicating better performance by the right hemi-TS group compared to the TDC on the forced-left left ear condition (FLLE) ($P = 0.053$) (Table 15.7). No significant difference between any of the groups was registered on the verbal or visual memory tasks (Table 15.8).

2. Child self-report scales. The right hemi-TS group reported significantly more symptoms of depression and anxiety compared to the TDC. The left hemi-TS group reported significantly more symptoms of physiological anxiety compared to the TDC (Table 15.9).

3. Parent reporting. Parents of the right and left hemi-TS groups reported almost twice as many attention and hyperactivity/impulsivity symptoms (ADHD rating scale IV) compared to the symmetric group. An item analysis of the responses to the hyperactivity/impulsivity scale did not discern different patterns in the right and left hemi-TS groups. The finding of a higher symptom load in the right and left hemi-TS groups compared to the symmetric group and the TDC is supported by a similar result in another of the parent report scales (the CBCL-ADHD subscale).

TABLE 15.5 CPT Composites (MANOVA): Means and Standard Deviations Within the Four Groups

CPT Composites							Group Comparison
					Group Comparison		Bonferroni
Variable	Right Hemi-TS ($n = 5$)	Left Hemi-TS ($n = 4$)	Symmetric ($n = 7$)	TDC ($n = 30$)	F	P	
Focus/attention[a]	62.0 (11.3)	53.7 (13.6)	45.3 (7.1)	47.3 (6.2)	$F(3,38) = 5.198$	<0.01	1 > 3 and 4
Hyperactivity/impulsivity[a]	53.0 (4.8)	58.0 (11.0)	49.1 (5.2)	47.2 (4.8)	$F(3,38) = 5.190$	<0.01	2 > 4
Sustained attention [a]	61.4 (7.1)	54.0 (10.5)	44.1 (5.7)	45.8 (9.8)	$F(3,38) = 4.117$	<0.05	1 > 4
Vigilance[a]	53.7 (1.8)	42.3 (8.9)	46.4 (5.8)	47.4 (7.0)	$F(3,38) = 1.924$	NS	

Note. Means of T-scores are reported. Higher scores denote greater pathology.
[a]*Conners' Continuous Performance Test-II.*

TABLE 15.6 Group Differences and Interaction Effects on Executive Function Measures (MANOVA): Means and Standard Deviations

	Group				Group Comparison	
	Right Hemi-TS ($n = 5$)	Left Hemi-TS ($n = 4$)	Symmetric ($n = 7$)	TDC ($n = 30$)	F	P
LN[a]	19.0 (2.9)	18.5 (2.1)	14.7 (4.8)	17.9 (2.1)	$F(3,38) = 2.960$	NS
TMT4[b]	90.6 (17.5)	99.7 (78.4)	129.0 (56.1)	103.4 (35.1)	$F(3,42) = 0.987$	NS
CW3[c]	85.4 (26.6)	77.0 (10.2)	83.0 (5.4)	77.7 (24.1)	$F(3,42) = 0.266$	NS
CW4[d]	80.8 (22.6)	93.0 (22.6)	97.4 (13.7)	80.2 (21.0)	$F(3,42) = 1.646$	NS
Tower[e]	15.2 (3.4)	15.5 (3.5)	16.5 (2.7)	17.4 (3.0)	$F(3,38) = 0.813$	NS
DF3[f]	6.2 (3.1)	8.5 (2.1)	5.0 (2.1)	7.1 (2.5)	$F(3,38) = 1.553$	NS
LF[g]	31.7 (14.8)	25.5 (3.5)	22.3 (6.5)	30.0 (11.4)	$F(3,38) = 0.950$	NS

MANOVA, multivariate analysis of variance; TDC, typically developing controls; TS, Tourette's syndrome.
[a]The Letter-Number Sequencing Test.
[b]The Trail Making Test, Condition 4.
[c]The Color-Word Interference Test, Condition 3.
[d]The Color-Word Interference Test, Condition 4.
[e]The Tower Test.
[f]The Design Fluency Test, Condition 3.
[g]The Letter Fluency Test.

TABLE 15.7 Group Differences and Interaction Effects (MANOVA): Means and Standard Deviations

Dichotic Listening	Group				Group Comparison	
	Right Hemi-TS ($n = 5$)	Left Hemi-TS ($n = 4$)	Symmetric ($n = 7$)	TDC ($n = 30$)	F	P
NFRE[a]	41.4 (15.9)	51.1 (15.4)	42.7 (7.4)	49.5 (11.0)	$F(3,38) = 1.19$	NS
NFLE[b]	33.8 (12.7)	22.2 (10.2)	33.3 (3.6)	31.3 (8.4)	$F(3,38) = 1.36$	NS
FRRE[c]	53.6 (14.7)	38.2 (20.4)	44.2 (8.1)	53.9 (12.3)	$F(3,38) = 2.152$	NS
FRLE[d]	30.5 (15.0)	25.5 (16.8)	28.3 (7.5)	27.7 (10.4)	$F(3,38) = 0.14$	NS
FLRE[e]	39.3 (8.6)	45.5 (13.5)	43.3 (7.0)	51.5 (12.3)	$F(3,38) = 2.19$	NS
FLLE[f]	48.0 (13.4)	31.1 (8.4)	39.4 (9.3)	33.4 (10.8)	$F(3,38) = 2.95$	NS

MANOVA, multivariate analysis of variance; TDC, typically developing controls; TS, Tourette's syndrome.
Note: Elevated scores indicate a higher level of performance.
[a]Non-Forced-Right Ear.
[b]Non-Forced-Left Ear.
[c]Forced Right-Right Ear.
[d]Forced Right-Left Ear.
[e]Forced Left-Right Ear.
[f]Forced Left-Left Ear.

TABLE 15.8 Memory Measures (MANOVA): Means and Standard Deviations Within the Four Groups

Variable	Right Hemi-TS ($n = 5$)	Left Hemi-TS ($n = 4$)	Symmetric ($n = 7$)	TDC ($n = 30$)	Group Comparison F	P
BVMT-R total learning[a]	25.2 (7.4)	23.5 (5.3)	22.9 (8.6)	24.2 (4.5)	$F(3,42) = 0.191$	NS
BVMT-R delayed recall[a]	10.0 (2.8)	10.0 (1.4)	9.1 (3.2)	10.5 (1.3)	$F(3,42) = 1.117$	NS
HVLT-R total learning[b]	23.2 (3.1)	23.5 (5.5)	23.7 (3.7)	25.9 (3.4)	$F(3,42) = 1.229$	NS
HVLT-R delayed recall[b]	8.0 (1.9)	8.5 (1.9)	9.1 (2.5)	9.2 (2.1)	$F(3,42) = 0.507$	NS

MANOVA, multivariate analysis of variance; TDC, typically developing controls; TS, Tourette's syndrome.
[a]Brief Visuospatial Memory Test—Revised.
[b]Hopkins Verbal Learning Test—Revised.

TABLE 15.9 Child Self-Report of Anxiety and Depression Symptoms (MANOVA): Means and Standard Deviations Within the Four Groups

Variable	Right Hemi-TS ($n = 5$)	Left Hemi-TS ($n = 4$)	Symmetric ($n = 7$)	TDC ($n = 30$)	Group Comparison F	Group Comparison P	Group Comparison Bonferroni
SMFQ[a]	7.2 (1.3)	2.0 (1.7)	3.2 (1.2)	2.3 (0.6)	$F(3,39) = 34.605$	<0.001	1 > 4
RCMAS-2[b]							
Physiological anxiety	5.4 (1.1)	**6.7 (1.5)**	4.6 (3.5)	2.6 (2.2)	$F(3,40) = 4.826$	<0.01	2 > 4
Worry	**6.6 (3.8)**	2.7 (3.8)	3.3 (4.0)	2.1 (1.9)	$F(3,40) = 4.135$	<0.05	1 > 4
Social anxiety	3.4 (1.7)	0.7 (0.6)	2.7 (4.2)	1.3 (1.7)	$F(3,40) = 1.973$	NS	
STAIC[c]							
State	34.4 (8.3)	29.7 (4.2)	32.4 (8.7)	27.6 (3.8)	$F(3,40) = 3.193$	<0.05	
Trait	**38.0 (7.8)**	25.3 (5.9)	26.7 (11.1)	27.5 (4.7)	$F(3,40) = 4.220$	<0.05	1 > 4; 1 > 3

MANOVA, multivariate analysis of variance; TDC, typically developing controls; TS, Tourette's syndrome.
Note. Higher scores denote greater pathology.
[a]The Short Mood and Feelings Questionnaire.
[b]The Revised Children's Manifest Anxiety Scale, second edition.
[c]The State-Trait Anxiety Inventory for Children: State and Trait.

A pattern of reporting a higher level of conduct problems by the parents of children in the right and left hemi-TS groups compared to the symmetric group is also apparent. Specifically, both the left and right hemi-TS groups are *above* the clinical cutoff point (*T*-score of 65) on a number of CBCL subscales (e.g., total problems, affect problems, ADHD, opposition problems, aggression, conduct problems, externalizing problems), while the symmetric group is *below* the clinical cutoff point on the same measures.

No significant differences were reported between the left hemi-TS, right hemi-TS and symmetric TS groups on any of the tic measures (Table 15.10).

Clinical Diagnosis and Left Versus Right "Hemi-TS"

A double dissociation between the left hemi-TS versus right hemi-TS groups and the clinical diagnosis emerged. Of the five "right hemi-TS"/presumed left frontostriatal dysfunction cases, four cases had the diagnosis of pure TS and one case had the diagnosis of TS + (TS comorbid with ADHD). By contrast, of the four "left hemi-TS"/presumed right frontostriatal dysfunction cases, zero cases had the diagnosis of pure TS and all four cases had the diagnosis of TS + (three of TS comorbid with ADHD and one of TS comorbid with ASD). Among the seven "symmetric TS"/presumably relatively bilateral frontostriatal dysfunction cases, the breakdown between the TS and TS + diagnoses was roughly equal (four with pure TS, two with TS comorbid with ASD, and one with TS comorbid with ADHD). These breakdowns are summarized in Table 15.11. While the samples are admittedly small, the interaction between the clinical diagnosis of TS versus TS + and the "hemi" designation is significant (Fisher exact probabilities test, $P = 0.04762$).

DISCUSSION

On the whole, children with TS exhibited more psychosocial, behavioral, and attentional difficulties than the TDC controls. These findings are consistent with earlier reports and are hardly novel or surprising. The novelty of our findings lies in the analysis of the hemi-TS groups.

TS Subtypes and Lateralized Frontostriatal Involvement

We believe that the novelty of our study is in pointing out the existence of several distinct subtypes of TS. The findings reported here suggest that TS is not a unitary syndrome and that it may be possible to identify distinct subtypes. Drawing on the earlier research into (1) the effects of lateralized prefrontal lesions and (2) hemi-Parkinsonian syndromes may be of considerable heuristic value in delineating such subtypes. The nigrostriatal involvement in PD is rarely perfectly symmetric, the asymmetries resulting in the distinct

TABLE 15.10 Group Differences and Interaction Effects on Yale Global Tic Severity Scale (YGTSS) (MANOVA): Means and Standard Deviations

YGTSS	Group				Group Comparison		Bonferroni
	Right Hemi-TS (n = 5)	Left Hemi-TS (n = 4)	Symmetric (n = 7)	TDC (n = 30)	F	P	
Motor tics—Last[a]	10.4 (2.7)	11.5 (2.7)	14.0 (4.8)	0.0 (0.0)	F(3,33) = 19.84	<0.01	1, 2, 3 > 4
Motor tics—Worst[b]	13.2 (4.4)	10.5 (7.6)	16.9 (10.3)	0.1 (0.4)	F(3,33) = 23.43	<0.01	1, 2, 3 > 4
Phonic tics—Last[c]	10.0 (3.5)	12.0 (4.2)	10.3 (6.8)	0.0 (0.0)	F(3,33) = 30.02	<0.01	1, 2, 3 > 4
Phonic tics—Worst[d]	12.0 (6.2)	11.7 (8.3)	13.9 (5.9)	0.0 (0.0)	F(3,33) = 28.91	<0.01	1, 2, 3 > 4
Total tics[e]	45.6 (16.5)	45.7 (20.1)	55.0 (32.5)	0.1 (0.4)	F(3,33) = 28.93	<0.01	1, 2, 3 > 4

MANOVA, multivariate analysis of variance; TDC, typically developing controls; TS, Tourette's syndrome.
[a]Parent report of Motor tics the past week.
[b]Parent report of Motor tics during the worst period.
[c]Parent report of Phonic tics the past week.
[d]Parent report of Phonic tics during the worst period.
[e]Derived by adding the Total Motor Tic Score and the Total Phonic Tic Score.

TABLE 15.11 The Interaction Between the Clinical Diagnosis of TS Versus TS + and the Right Versus Left "Hemi" Designation

Clinical Diagnosis	Clinical Diagnosis by TS Subtype		
	Right Hemi-TS ($n = 5$)	Left Hemi-TS ($n = 4$)	Symmetric ($n = 7$)
TS	4	0	4
TS +	1	4	3

TS, Tourette's syndrome.

left and right hemi-Parkinsonian syndromes. Similarly, the frontostriatal involvement in TS is not likely to be perfectly symmetric, the asymmetries resulting in the distinct left and right hemi-TS. Recognition and identification of the hemi-TS subtypes may result in important ramifications for the ways TS is defined, conceptualized, and diagnosed. Although the size of the sample in our study is quite small, the findings generate intriguing hypotheses that should be investigated in more comprehensive studies. Some of these ramifications are discussed below.

Several previously unreported differences emerged between the TS subtypes. The right hemi-TS subtype is characterized by a particular impairment of focus/attention, including sustained attention and significant symptoms of depression and anxiety compared to the TDC. By contrast, the left hemi-TS subtype is characterized by a greater degree of hyperactivity, impulsivity, and physiological anxiety.

Assuming that the right hemi-TS reflects particular dysregulation within the left frontostriatal system and the left hemi-TS reflects particular dysregulation within the right frontostriatal system, these findings suggest different underlying neuroanatomical substrates behind the TS subtypes. The subtypes may reflect functional differences and complementarities between the left and right frontostriatal systems, which parallel the previously reported lateralized focal-lesion effects linking left prefrontal lesions with rigid perseverative behavior and right prefrontal lesions with echopractic field-dependent behaviors (Goldberg et al., 1994; Podell, 2009).

Both left and right hemi-TS subgroups were characterized by a greater degree of inattention, impulsivity/hyperactivity, and conduct problems than the symmetric TDC subgroup. This is an unexpected finding awaiting explanation. It may suggest that not only complementarity but actual functional reciprocity exists between the left and right frontostriatal systems, so that their combined damage "cancels out" or at least attenuates the separate effects of lateralized lesions.

"Hemi-TS" and Clinical Diagnosis

A particularly intriguing aspect of our findings is the relationship between the presumed lateralization of frontostriatal dysfunction inferred on the basis of motor asymmetries and the clinical diagnosis. Four out of five children with the presumed left frontostriatal dysfunction (right hemi-TS) received the "pure TS" diagnosis (TS). By contrast, all four children with the presumed right frontostriatal dysfunction (left hemi-TS) received the diagnosis of "TS comorbid with ADHD or ASD" (TS+). The patients with the presumably symmetric frontostriatal dysfunction were essentially evenly split between the TS and TS + diagnoses. Despite the small number of subjects, the interaction between the presumed frontostriatal dysfunction laterality and the clinical diagnosis is statistically significant and thus must be regarded, at a minimum, as a suggestive preliminary finding in need of replication.

Our attempts to understand the relationship between the hemi-TS groups and clinical diagnosis may benefit from considering the findings of focal lateralized prefrontal lesions. As pointed out earlier, left prefrontal lesions may result in extremely perseverative behavior (Goldberg et al., 1994; Podell, 2009). As dictated by DSM-V and other commonly used diagnostic criteria, the diagnosis of "pure TS" requires a clinical picture dominated by tics. Tics are a form of perseveration (Goldberg, 2009); thus continuity exists between the effects of focal prefrontal lesions and the effects of frontostriatal dysfunction lateralized to the left hemisphere. In both instances, the resulting presentation appears in the form of perseverative behaviors that are similar, but not identical, because the respective underlying neuroanatomies, while closely related and similarly lateralized, are not identical.

By contrast, right prefrontal lesions result in extremely field-dependent behavior (Goldberg et al., 1994; Podell, 2009). Extreme field-dependent exploratory behavior has also been described in some individuals with TS (Goldberg, 2009; Sacks, 1992). We hypothesize that such behaviors are prominent in the TS cases with significant right frontostriatal involvement. But because exploratory behaviors are not part of the standard definition of TS, such behaviors are not typically recognized by most clinicians as an integral part of TS. Instead, the notion of a "comorbid" parallel disorder is invoked when exploratory behaviors are prominently present. In reality, however, tics and exploratory behaviors may be the manifestations of the same pathophysiological process idiosyncratically affecting in different proportions the left frontostriatal systems (this resulting in tics and triggering the TS diagnosis) or the right frontostriatal systems (this resulting in exploratory behaviors and triggering the (mis)diagnosis of "comorbid something else"). The analogy with PD, which is almost never perfectly symmetric in its clinical manifestations (resting tremor being usually more pronounced on one side or the other), is inescapable. Compounding such misdiagnosis is the failure in the neuropsychiatric literature to recognize excessive exploratory behavior as a distinct clinical phenomenon. Instead, exploratory behavior is commonly conflated with hyperactivity. This further contributing to the spurious conclusion that ADHD is that "something else" and prompting the often misguided diagnosis of "ADHD comorbid with TS."

Exploratory Behavior Versus Hyperactivity

"Excessive exploratory behavior" does not exist as a distinct diagnostic category in DSM-V or in any other commonly used diagnostic manual nor do any commonly used structured scales exist to document and quantify "exploratory behavior." In a clinical culture dominated by the imperative to fit every clinical manifestation into a discrete diagnostic category, it is therefore unavoidable that an orphaned clinical manifestation such as "excessive exploratory behavior" will be shoehorned into the closest available diagnostic pigeonhole. What in reality is exploratory behavior could easily be misdiagnosed as hyperactivity or as something else. The problem, of course, is that the closest pigeonhole may not be close enough. Therefore, it is important to clarify the difference between hyperactivity and excessive exploratory behavior.

In the classic neuropsychological and behavioral neurological literature, exploratory behavior is understood as behavior driven by incidental external stimuli. By contrast, hyperactivity is understood as an excessive amount of motor activity. Conceptually, the distinction between excessive exploratory behavior and hyperactivity is an important one, although it is not commonly made. This means that if the line of reasoning advanced in this chapter is valid, a category of patients may exist in whom excessive exploratory behaviors are present in the relative absence of tics due to a strongly lateralized right frontostriatal dysfunction. These patients will not even be recognized as representing a subtype of TS at all and will likely be diagnosed simply as ADHD cases, when in fact the underlying pathophysiology is the same as in TS, just with a slightly differently lateralized neuroanatomical expression.

Excessive exploratory behavior is well recognized in neuropsychology and behavioral neurology of frontal lobe dysfunction as a distinct clinical phenomenon under the names of "field-dependent behavior" (Goldberg, Costa 1985; Goldberg 2001, 2009) and "utilization behavior" (Lhermitte, 1983). Once the conceptual difference between the hyperactivity and excessive exploratory behavior is clearly stated, it becomes easily apparent to an experienced clinical eye and is easy to operationalize. Patients with TS report an urge to touch, sniff, or lick incidental objects in their environment even at the risk of hurting themselves (e.g., touching a hot electric bulb), and to touch strangers even at the risk of violating social proprieties. They also report an urge to imitate strangers motorically or vocally. This resulting in echopraxia or echolalia (Goldberg, 2009). These behaviors are neither tics nor hyperactivity; they are exploratory behaviors. The patients also report a peculiar morphing of exploratory behaviors into tics, whereby what starts as imitative echo behavior then becomes a tic. This is very similar to the intermingling of field-dependent behavior and perseveration commonly seen in patients with bilateral prefrontal damage (Goldberg, 2009).

Exploratory behavior is not nearly as well recognized in neuropsychiatric circles as a separate and distinct phenomenon, however, and, as pointed out earlier, it is frequently conflated with hyperactivity. To the best of our knowledge, no clinical scales of exploratory behavior exist, which further contributes to the common misclassification of such behaviors as "hyperactivity." A greater recognition of "exploratory behavior" as a distinct phenomenon may, and perhaps even should, lead to the broadening of the clinical diagnostic criteria for TS. With the availability of more nuanced diagnostic tools (e.g., clinical scales) better capable of distinguishing between hyperactivity and exploratory behavior, a subset of patients currently classified as ADHD will likely be reclassified as cases of TS. Frontostriatal dysfunction has been implicated both in TS and in ADHD. We propose that at least the subsets of these two diagnoses in fact represent the same pathophysiological mechanisms with slightly different neuroanatomical expressions: the diagnosis of TS when the left frontostriatal systems are particularly involved; ADHD when the right frontostriatal systems are particularly involved; and TS "comorbid" with ADHD when both are involved to considerable degrees.

Cutting Across Taxonomic Boundaries and Redefining TS

There is a growing recognition in clinical neurosciences that traditional rigid taxonomic boundaries often become obstacles to discerning important general shared mechanisms underlying specific conditions (Harciarek, Malaspina, Sun, & Goldberg, 2013). These rigid boundaries promote Balkanization of clinical neurosciences with woefully little interaction and sharing of data and ideas among the denizens of disparate taxonomic pigeonholes. Such Balkanization is increasingly seen as detrimental to scientific progress. In this chapter we attempted to build bridges across traditional taxonomic boundaries by considering the relationship between three types of disorders traditionally of interest to very different biomedical communities: focal-lesion neurology (CVA, TBI, or neoplasms), movement disorders, and neuropsychiatry. The clinical sample examined in our study is relatively small, and future research is required to further address the issues raised in this chapter. Nonetheless, we hope that our effort helps to clarify the mechanisms of TS, its subtypes, and their relationship to ADHD, as well as provides direction for future research. Future research should aim to characterize the clinical symptomatology of tics and exploratory behavior in conjunction with neuroimaging (both structural and functional) aiming to identify the lateralized patterns.

One outcome of such future research may be the conclusion that the traditional standard definitions and diagnostic criteria of TS in fact split the true clinical spectrum of this syndrome in half, recognize half of the spectrum (tics) as part and parcel of TS, while treating the other half (excessive exploratory behaviors) as although they represented some other, "comorbid" clinical entity. This results in an unfortunate situation whereby two neuroanatomical variants of the same disorder (predominantly left vs right frontostriatal involvement) are diagnosed as although they were distinct and separate disorders. This may be the time to consider broadening the conceptual understanding and clinical diagnostic criteria of TS by bringing them in line with the underlying neurobiological mechanisms and their diverse expressions.

ACKNOWLEDGMENTS

We thank the late Oliver Sacks, MD, as well as Orrin Devinsky, MD, for their valuable comments, Per Normann Andersen, PhD, and Erik Winther Skogli, PhD, for their indispensible contribution to the collection of data and references used in this chapter, and Fredrick Duong for technical assistance.

REFERENCES

Achenbach, & Rescorla. (2001). Manual for the Child Behavior Checklist/6–18 Profile. Burlington, VT: University of Vermont *Research Center for Children, Youth, and Families*.

American Psychiatric Association. (2000). Diagnostic and statistical manual of mental disorders (text revision). Washington, DC.

Angold, A., Costello, E. J., Messer, S. C., Pickles, A., Winder, F., & Silver, D. (1995). The development of a short questionnaire for use in epidemiological studies of depression in children and adolescents. *International Journal of Methods in Psychiatric Research, 5*, 1–12.

Benedict, Ralph H. B., Schretlen, David, Groninger, Lowell, & Brandt, Jason (1998). Hopkins verbal learning test? Revised: Normative data and analysis of inter-form and test-retest reliability. *The Clinical Neuropsychologist (Neuropsychology, Development and Cognition: Section D), 12*(1), 43–55. Available from http://dx.doi.org/10.1076/clin.12.1.43.1726.

Benedict, R. H. B., & Brandt, J. (2007). *Hopkins verbal learning test-revised/Brief visuospatial memory test-revised. Professional manual supplement*. Lutz, Fl: PAR Psychological Assessment Resources Inc.

Boehnke, K., Sillbereisen, R. K., Reynolds, C. R., & Richmond, B. O. (1986). What I think and feel: German experience with the revised form of the children's manifest anxiety scale. *Personality and Individual Differences, 7*(4), 5.

Bloch, M. H., Leckman, J. F., Zhu, H., & Peterson, B. S. (2005). Caudate volumes in childhood predict symptom severity in adults with Tourette syndrome. *Neurology, 65*(8), 1253–1258.

Conners, C. K. (2004). *Conners' Continuous Performance Test (CPT II): Version 5 for Windows: Technical Guide and Software Manual*. North Tonawanda, NY: Multi Health Systems.

Costa, V. D., Tran, V. L., Turchi, J., & Averbeck, B. B. (2014). Dopamine modulates novelty seeking behavior during decision making. *Behavioral Neuroscience, 128*(5), 556–566. Available from http://dx.doi.org/10.1037/a0037128.

Costello, E. J., & Angold, A. (1988). Scales to assess child and adolescent depression: Checklists, screens, and nets. *Journal of the American Academy of Child & Adolescent Psychiatry, 27*(6), 726–737.

Costello, E. J., Benjamin, R., Angold, A., & Silver, D. (1991). Mood variability in adolescents: A study of depressed, nondepressed and comorbid patients. *Journal of Affective Disorders, 23*(4), 199–212.

Delis, D., Kaplan, E., & Kramer, J. (2001). *Delis-Kaplan Executive Function System (D-KEFS). Norwegian version.* Stockholm: Pearson Assessment.

DuPaul, G. J., Power, T. J., Anastoupolous, A. D., & Reid, R. (1998). *ADHD rating scale—IV. Checklists, norms & clinical interpretation.* New York: Guilford.

Egeland, J., & Kovalik-Gran, I. (2010). Measuring several aspects of attention in one test: The factor structure of conners's continuous performance test. *Journal of Attention Disorders, 13* (4), 339–346. Available from http://dx.doi.org/10.1177/1087054708323019.

Ehlers, S., Gillberg, C., & Wing, L. (1999). A Screening questionnaire for asperger syndrome and other high-functioning autism spectrum disorders in school age children. *Journal of Autism and Developmental Disorders, 29*(2), 129–141.

Fallmyr, O., & Egeland, J. (2011). Psychometric properties of the Norwegian version of BRIEF—For children from 5 to 18 years old. *Journal of the Norwegian Psychological Association, 48*, 339–343.

Felling, Ryan J., & Singer, Harvey S. (2011). Neurobiology of Tourette syndrome: Current status and need for further investigation. *The Journal of Neuroscience, 31*(35), 12387–12395.

Ferrando, P. J. (1994). Factorial structure of the revised children manifest anxiety scale in a Spanish sample: Relations with Eysenck personality dimensions. *Personality and Individual Differences, 16*(5), 693–699.

Gadea, M., Marti-Bonmatj, L., Arana, E., Espert, R., Casanova, V., & Pascual, A. (2002). Dichotic listening and corpus callosum magnetic resonance imaging in relapsing-remitting multiple sclerosis with emphasis on sex differences. *Neuropsychology, 16*, 275–281.

Gioia, G. A., Isquith, P. K., Guy, S. C., & Kenworthy, L. (2000). Behavior rating inventory of executive function. *Child Neuropsychology, 6*(3), 235–238. Available from http://dx.doi.org/10.1076/chin.6.3.235.3152.

Gootjes, L., Bouma, A., Van Strien, J. W., Schijndel, R. V., Barkhof, F., & Scheltens, P. (2006). Corpus callosum size correlates with asymmetric performance on a dichotic listening task in healthy aging but not in Alzheimer's disease. *Neuropsychologia, 44*, 208–217.

Goldberg, E. (2001). *The executive brain: Frontal lobes and the civilized mind.* New York, NY: Oxford University Press.

Goldberg, E. (2009). *The new executive brain: Frontal lobes in a complex world.* New York, NY: Oxford University Press.

Goldberg, E., & Costa, L. (1985). Qualitative indices in neuropsychological assessment: An extension fo Luria's approach to executive deficit following prefrontal lesion. In I. Grant, & K. Adams (Eds.), *Neuropsychological Assessment of Neuropsychiatric Disorders* (pp. 48–64). New York, NY: Oxford University Press.

Goldberg, E., & Podell, K. (1995). Lateralization in the frontal lobes. *Advances in Neurology, 66*, 85–96.

Goldberg, E., Podell, K., Bilder, R., & Jaeger, J. (2000). *The executive control battery.* Melbourne, Australia: PsychPress.

Goldberg, E., Podell, K., Harner, R., Lovell, M., & Riggio, S. (1994). Cognitive bias, functional cortical geometry, and the frontal lobes: Laterality, sex, and handedness. *Journal of Cognitive Neuroscience, 6*, 274–294.

Goldberg, E., Podell, K., & Lovell, M. (1994). Lateralization of frontal lobe functions and cognitive novelty. *Journal of Neuropsychiatry and Clinical Neurosciences, 6,* 371−378.

Harciarek, M., Malaspina, D., Sun, T., & Goldberg, E. (2013). Schizophrenia and frontotemporal dementia: Shared causation? *International Review of Psychiatry, 25*(2), 168−177.

Hassan, N., & Cavanna, A. E. (2012). The prognosis of Tourette syndrome: Implications for clinical practice. *Functional Neurology, 27*(1), 23−27.

Hugdahl, K., Westerhausen, R., Alho, K., Medvedev, S., Laine, M., & Hamalainen, H. (2009). Attention and cognitive control: Unfolding the dichotic listening story. *Scandinavian Journal of Psychology, 50*(1), 11−22. Available from http://dx.doi.org/10.1111/j.1467-9450.2008.00676.x.

Ivanova, M. Y., Dobrean, A., Dopfner, M., Erol, N., Fombonne, E., Fonseca, A. C., & Chen, W. J. (2007). Testing the 8-syndrome structure of the child behavior checklist in 30 societies. *Journal of Clinical Child and Adolescent Psychology, 36*(3), 405−417.

Kaufman, J., Birmaher, B., Brent, D., Rao, U., Flynn, C., Moreci, P., & Ryan, N. (1997). Schedule for affective disorders and schizophrenia for school-age children-present and lifetime version (K-SADS-PL): Initial reliability and validity data. *Journal of the American Academy of Child and Adolescent Psychiatry, 36*(7), 980.

Kovacs, M. (1983). *The children's depression inventory: A self-rated depression scale for school-aged youngsters.* Pittsburgh, PA: University of Pittsburgh School of Medicine.

Leckman, J. F., Riddle, M. A., Hardin, M. T., Ort, S. I., Swartz, K. L., Stevenson, J., & Cohen, D. J. (1989). The Yale Global Tic Severity Scale: Initial testing of a clinician-rated scale of tic severity. *Journal of the American Academy of Child and Adolescent Psychiatry, 28*(4), 566−573. Available from http://dx.doi.org/10.1097/00004583-198907000-00015.

Lhermitte, F. (1983). Utilization behavior and its relationship to the lesions of the frontal lobes. *Brain, 106,* 237−255.

Makki, M. I., Govindan, R. M., Wilson, B. J., Behen, M. E., & Chugani, H. T. (2009). Altered fronto-striato-thalamic connectivity in children with Tourette syndrome assessed with diffusion tensor MRI and probabilistic fiber tracking. *Journal of Child Neurology, 24*(6), 669−678. Available from http://dx.doi.org/10.1177/0883073808327838.

Nøvik, T. S. (1999). Validity of the child behaviour checklist in a Norwegian sample. *European Child & Adolescent Psychiatry, 8*(4), 247−254.

Nøvik, T. S. (2000). Child behavior checklist item scores in Norwegian children. *European Child & Adolescent Psychiatry, 9*(1), 54−60.

Pela, O. A., & Reynolds, C. R. (1982). Cross-cultural application of the revised-Children's Manifest Anxiety Scale: Normative and reliability data for Nigerian primary school children. *Psychological Reports, 51*(3), 1135−1138.

Podell, K. (2009). When East meets West: Systematizing Luria's approach to executive control assessment. In A. L. Christensen, E. Goldberg, & D. Bougakov (Eds.), *The Legacy of Luria in the 21st Century* (pp. 122−145). New York, NY: Oxford University Press. Available from http://dx.doi.org/10.1093/acprof:oso/9780195176704.001.0001.

Podell, K., Lovell, M., Zimmerman, M., & Goldberg, E. (1995). The cognitive bias task and lateralized frontal lobe functions in males. *Journal of Neuropsychiatry and Clinical Neuroscience, 7,* 491−501.

Reynolds, C. R. (1980). Concurrent validity of "What I think and feel:" The Revised Children's Manifest Anxiety Scale. *Journal of Consulting and Clinical Psychology, 48*(6), 774−775.

Reynolds, C. R. (1981). Long-term stability of scores on the Revised-Children's Manifest Anxiety Scale. *Perceptual and Motor Skills, 53*(3), 702−702.

Reynolds, C. R. (1982). Convergent and divergent validity of the Revised Children's Manifest Anxiety Scale. *Educational and Psychological Measurement, 42*(4), 1205.

Reynolds, C. R., & Paget, K. D. (1981). Factor analysis of the Revised Children's Manifest Anxiety Scale for Blacks, Whites, males, and females with a national normative sample. *Journal of Consulting and Clinical Psychology, 49*(3), 352.

Reynolds, C. R., & Richmond, B. O. (1985). *Revised Children's Manifest Anxiety Scale (RCMAS): Manual.* Torrance, CA: Western Psychological Services.

Roessner, V., Overlack, S., Schmidt-Samoa, C., Baudewig, J., Dechent, P., Rothenberger, A., & Helms, G. (2011). Increased putamen and callosal motor subregion in treatment-naïve boys with Tourette syndrome indicates changes in the bihemispheric motor network. *Journal of Child Psychology and Psychiatry, 52*(3), 306−314. http://dx.doi.org/10.1111/j.1469-7610.2010.02324.x.

Ruff, R. M., & Parker, S. B. (1993). Gender- and age-specific changes in motor speed and eye-hand coordination in adults: Normative values for the finger tapping and grooved pegboard tests. *Perceptual and Motor Skills, 76*(3 Pt 2), 1219−1230. Available from http://dx.doi.org/10.2466/pms.1993.76.3c.1219.

Sacks, O. W. (1992). Tourette's syndrome and creativity. *British Medical Journal, 305*, 1515−1516.

Scholwinski, E., & Reynolds, C. R. (1985). Dimensions of anxiety among high IQ children. *Gifted Child Quarterly, 29*(3), 125−130.

Seligman, L. D., Ollendick, T. H., Langley, A. K., & Baldacci, H. B. (2004). The utility of measures of child and adolescent anxiety: A meta-analytic review of the Revised Children's Manifest Anxiety Scale, the State-Trait Anxiety Inventory for Children, and the Child Behavior Checklist. *Journal of Clinical Child and Adolescent Psychology, 33*(3), 557−565.

Stern, E., Silbersweig, D. A., Chee, K. Y., Holmes, A., Robertson, M. M., & Dolan, R. J. (2000). A functional neuroanatomy of tics in Tourette syndrome. *Archives of General Psychiatry, 57*, 741−748.

Storch, Eric A., Murphy, Tanya K., Fernandez, Melanie, Krishnan, Mohan, Geffken, Gary R., Kellgren, Ashley R., & Goodman, Wayne K. (2007). Factor-analytic study of the Yale global tic severity scale. *Psychiatry Research, 149*(1), 231−237.

Storch, Eric A., Murphy, Tanya K., Geffken, Gary R., Sajid, Muhammad, Allen, Pam, Roberti, Jonathan W., & Goodman, Wayne K. (2005). Reliability and validity of the Yale Global Tic severity scale. *Psychological Assessment, 17*(4), 486−490.

Tam, J. W., & Schmitter-Edgecombe, M. (2013). The role of processing speed in the Brief Visuospatial Memory Test—Revised. *Clinical Neuropsychologist, 27*(6), 962−972. Available from http://dx.doi.org/10.1080/13854046.2013.797500.

Turgeon, L., & Chartrand, É. (2003). Reliability and validity of the revised children's manifest anxiety scale in a French-Canadian sample. *Psychological Assessment, 15*(3), 378.

Varanese S., Perfetti B., Mason S., Di Rocco A., Goldberg E. (2010) Lateralized profiles of frontal lobe dysfunction in Parkinson's disease. Presented at 7th International Congress on mental dysfunctions and other non-motor features in Parkinson's disease and related disorders, Barcelona, Spain.

Wang, Z., Maia, T. V., Marsh, R., Colibazzi, T., Gerber, A., & Peterson, B. S. (2011). The neural circuits that generate tics in Tourette's syndrome. *American Journal of Psychiatry, 168* (12), 1326−1337. Available from http://dx.doi.org/10.1176/appi.ajp.2011.09111692, Epub 2011 Sep 28.

Wechsler, D., Kaplan, E., Fein, D., Kramer, J., Morris, R., Delis, D., & Maerlender, A. (2004). *Wechsler Intelligence Scale for Children Fourth Edition—Integrated: Technical and interpretative manual.* San Antonio: The Psychological Corporation.

Wechsler, D. (2004). *Wechsler Intelligence Scale for children—Fourth edition. Norwegian version.* Stockholm: The Psychological Corporation.

DISCLOSURE

The authors declare no conflict of interest with respect to authorship or publication of this article.

The data presented in this paper are from the research project "Cognitive and emotional development of children and adolescents with neuropsychiatric disorders." Professor Merete Glenne Øie has been the project leader, and Erik Winther Skogli, Per Normann Andersen, and Kjell Tore Hovik have all earned their doctorates at the University of Oslo working on sections of the data relating to children with specific developmental disorders (ADHD, ASDs, and TS, respectively). A total of 14 peer-reviewed articles have been published thus far based on data collected in the baseline and the 2-year follow-up study. Funding for the project was provided by the Research Department of Innlandet Hospital Trust and the Regional Resource Center for Autism, ADHD, Tourette's syndrome, and Narcolepsy.

APPENDIX   DESCRIPTION OF THE DIAGNOSTIC INSTRUMENTS USED IN THE STUDY

Neurocognitive Assessment

Tests of Executive Functions

Working memory: The Letter-number Sequencing Test (LN) (Wechsler, 2004) consists of 10 items. Each item contains three trials with the same number of digits and letters. The examiner reads aloud each trial and asks the child to recall the numbers in ascending order and the letters in alphabetical order. In the present study, total correct recalled trials were examined. Lower raw scores indicated difficulties with the task.

Inhibition: The Color-Word Interference Test, Condition 3 (CW3) from D-KEFS (Delis, Kaplan, & Kramer, 2001). The examinee must inhibit an overlearned verbal response when naming the dissonant ink colors in which the words are printed. For the present study, completion time in seconds was examined. Higher raw scores indicated difficulties with the task.

Cognitive flexibility: The Color-Word Interference Test, Condition 4 (CW4), is also a measure of cognitive flexibility. The examinee is asked to switch back and forth between naming the dissonant ink colors and reading the words. For the present study, completion time in seconds was examined. Higher raw scores indicated difficulties with the task.

The Trail Making Test, condition 4 (TMT 4). The examinee is asked to draw a line interchangeably between numbers and letters in the right order. For the present study, time to complete task was examined. Higher raw scores indicated difficulties with the task.

The Design Fluency Test, condition 3 (DF) (Delis et al., 2001) is also a measure of cognitive flexibility. The examinee is asked to draw as many different designs as possible using four straight lines connecting five filled and empty dots interchangeably. The examinee is given 60-s for the task. For the present study, total correct responses were examined. Lower scaled scores indicated difficulties with the task.

Planning and rule learning: The Tower Test (Delis et al., 2001). In this task, the examinee is asked to construct several target towers by moving five disks, varying in size, across three pegs in the fewest number of moves possible. While doing this, the examinee is allowed only to move one disk at a time and not to place a larger disk over a smaller disk. In the present study, move accuracy ratio was examined. Lower raw scores indicated difficulties with the task.

Verbal fluency: In the Letter Fluency Test (LF), the examinee is asked to generate words fluently in an effortful, phonemic format. The task includes three 60-s trials. For the present study, total correct responses were examined. Lower raw scores indicated difficulties with the task.

Attentional control: In the Dichotic Listening (DL) task, two different auditory stimuli (syllables) are presented simultaneously, one in each ear, without the subject being aware of the dichotic nature of the stimulus presentation (Hugdahl et al., 2009). The participants are asked to report the syllable they hear on each trial with no instruction of focus of attention (nonforced condition) or to explicitly focus attention and report either the right- or left-ear syllable (forced-right and forced-left condition, respectively). The task applies a forced-attention paradigm reflecting different cognitive processes: perception (nonforced condition), attention (forced-right condition), and cognitive (executive) control (forced-left condition) (Gadea et al., 2002; Gootjes et al., 2006; Hugdahl et al., 2009).

Tests of Focused and Sustained Attention

Accuracy and sustainability of attention: Conners' Continuous Performance Test-II (CCPT-II). In this task, the child is presented with a repetitive array of visual stimuli on a computer screen for 14 min (Conners, 2004). The child is instructed to press the space bar every time a letter other than "X" appears and to not press the space bar when "X" appears. The rate of stimulus presentation varies according to 1, 2, and 4 s intervals throughout the task. From the 12 measures available on the test, 4 composites were calculated based on findings in an earlier study applying principal component analysis to derive four salient measures of attention (Egeland & Kovalik-Gran, 2010). Focused attention is the mean *t*-score of Omissions, Perseverations, Variability, and Hit Reaction time Standard Error. Hyperactivity−Impulsivity is the mean *t*-scores of Hit Reaction Time, Commission Errors, and Response Style. Sustained attention is computed from Block Change and Block Change Standard Error, measuring the change in reaction time or increase in variability of reaction time as a function of time on task. Vigilance is computed from the Interstimulus interval (ISI) change score and the standard error of ISI change.

Memory Tests

The Norwegian version of the Hopkins Verbal Learning Test—Revised (HVLT-R) (Benedict, Schretlen, Groninger, & Brandt, 1998) was used to assess acquisition and delayed recall. The HVLT-R is a list learning test, which consists of 12 nouns within three semantic groups. The acquisition variable consists of three acquisition trials in which the administrator reads the words aloud and then asks the child to repeat as many as he/she can remember in any order. A delayed recall trial is introduced after 20−25 min, in which the child is asked to simply retrieve as many of the words listed in the acquisition trial as he/she can remember. The children are not informed about the delayed recall trial beforehand. Lower raw scores indicate difficulties with the task.

To assess visuospatial learning and memory, we applied the Brief Visuospatial Memory Test-revised (BVMT-R) (Tam & Schmitter-Edgecombe, 2013). BVMT-R measures visuospatial learning and memory. The child is shown a sheet displaying six geometric shapes for a period of 10 s and is then asked to draw figures from memory with proper form and proper positioning on the sheet. This is then repeated twice and constitutes the total acquisition measure. After a break of 20 min, the child is asked to draw the shapes from memory, which represents the free recall variable. Finally, the child is shown each of the six original figures along with six others, and answers Yes/No on whether they belong to the original group. Research using BVMT-R and studies using HVLT-R has shown good discriminant validity and test−retest reliability (Benedict & Brandt, 2007). HVLT-R and BVMT-R are compatible psychometric tests for measuring learning and memory in the auditory/verbal and visuospatial domains, respectively (Benedict & Brandt, 2007).

Clinical Questionnaires and Scales

Tic Severity Reported by Parent

The YGTSS is a commonly used index of motor and phonic tic severity in children and adolescents (Storch et al., 2007). Findings suggest that the instrument is a reliable and valid assessment of childhood TS (Storch et al., 2005). Higher scores indicate greater symptom severity.

Child Self-Report of Anxiety and Depression Symptoms

The Revised Children's Manifest Anxiety Scale, second edition (RCMAS-2) (Reynolds & Richmond, 1985) is a 49-item self-report instrument designed to measure anxiety symptoms in children 6–19 years of age. Children respond either "Yes" or "No" to all 49 items. The instrument reveals three anxiety factors: physiological anxiety, worry, and social anxiety. The three anxiety factors are summed yielding a Total Anxiety score. Elevated raw scores indicate a higher degree of anxiety symptoms. The RCMAS Total Anxiety Scale has been found to have satisfactory psychometric properties with high test–retest reliability (Pela & Reynolds, 1982; Reynolds, 1981) and consistent construct validity (Reynolds & Paget, 1981; Reynolds, 1980, 1982; Scholwinski & Reynolds, 1985). Satisfactory psychometric properties have been replicated among other cultures as well (Boehnke, Sillbereisen, Reynolds, & Richmond, 1986; Ferrando, 1994; Pela & Reynolds, 1982; Turgeon & Chartrand, 2003).

The State-Trait Anxiety Inventory for Children (STAIC) includes two 20-item self-report scales that measure both enduring tendencies (Trait) and situational variations (State) in levels of perceived anxiety (Seligman, Ollendick, Langley, & Baldacci, 2004). Children respond on a three-point scale indicating varying degree of worry, feelings of tension, and/or nervousness. Elevated raw scores indicate a higher degree of situational and temporal anxiety. In a quantitative review by Seligman et al. (2004), the authors argue that the STAIC possess satisfactory psychometric properties.

The Short Mood and Feelings Questionnaire (SMFQ) is a 13-item self-report instrument designed to measure depressive symptoms in children 8–18 years of age (Angold et al., 1995). The SMFQ is derived from the original 30-item Mood and Feelings Questionnaire (Costello & Angold, 1988) where children respond on a three-point scale ("not true," "sometimes true," and "true"). A net score was generated based on the 13 items with elevated raw scores indicating a higher degree of depression symptoms. The SMFQ have demonstrated high internal consistency (Crohnbach's alpha = 0.90) (Costello, Benjamin, Angold, & Silver, 1991), and test–retest stability in children for a 2-week period yielded an intraclass correlation of 0.66 (Costello & Angold, 1988). Angold and colleagues (1995) found SMFQ to correlate strongly with Children's Depression Inventory (Kovacs, 1983) and Diagnostic Interview Schedule for Children depression scores (Costello & Angold, 1988) (r = 0.67 and 0.51, respectively).

Clinical Symptoms Reported by Parents

ADHD Rating Scale IV (ARS-IV) (DuPaul et al., 1998). The ARS-IV is an 18-item rating scale, with each item corresponding to one of the 18 DSM-IV-TR diagnostic criteria. Inattention symptoms are designated as odd numbered items and hyperactivity/impulsivity symptoms are displayed as even numbered items. Elevated scores indicate a higher degree of ADHD-related problems.

The Child Behavior Checklist/6-18 (CBCL) (Achenbach & Rescorla, 2001) is a widely used scale containing 7 competence items and 113 specific problem items, each of which is rated on a 0−2 metric. The 120 items assess adaptive behavior and eight narrow band factors (anxious/depressed, withdrawn/depressed, somatic complaints, social problems, thought problems, attention problems, rule-breaking behavior, and aggressive behavior) and two broadband factors (externalizing and internalizing symptoms) of coexisting symptoms. The 2001 revision also includes seven DSM-oriented scales consistent with DSM diagnostic categories (affective problems, anxiety problems, somatic problems, ADHD, oppositional defiant problems, and conduct problems). Elevated T-scores indicate a higher degree of coexisting internalizing and externalizing symptoms. Cross-cultural studies have demonstrated satisfactory discriminant validity with mean factor loadings across societies at 0.62 (Ivanova et al., 2007). The official Norwegian version of the CBCL was used, which has been shown to offer acceptable reliability and validity values as reported by Nøvik (Nøvik, 1999, 2000).

The Behaviour Rating Inventory of Executive Function (BRIEF) for children and adolescents aged 5−18 years includes a parent form and a teacher form (Gioia, Isquith, Guy, & Kenworthy, 2000). In the current study, the Norwegian parent rating version was used. The BRIEF is composed of eight clinical scales (inhibition, shift, emotional control, initiate, working memory, plan/organize, organization of materials, and monitor). Fallmyr and Egeland (2011) reported high internal consistency (Chronbach's $\alpha = 0.76-0.92$) on the Norwegian parent rating version of the BRIEF. These values are at the same level as Chronbachs α reported in the BRIEF manual (0.80−0.98) (Gioia et al., 2000). Elevated BRIEF T-scores indicate a higher degree of impairment.

Chapter 16

Executive Dysfunction in Addiction

Antonio Verdejo-Garcia

School of Psychological Sciences and Monash Institute of Cognitive and Clinical Neurosciences (MICCN), Melbourne, VIC, Australia

INTRODUCTION

This chapter reviews existing evidence concerning the impact of drugs of abuse on executive functions. It focuses on the chronic (nonacute) effects of four illicit substances, namely cannabis, cocaine, methamphetamine, and opioids, which represent the most prevalent drugs of concern among treatment-seeking individuals worldwide (European Monitoring Centre for Drugs and Drug Abuse, Annual Report, 2016; Substance Abuse & Mental Health Services Administration, 2016). This chapter specifically analyzes the impact of these four substances on four well-established, relatively independent domains of executive functions: working memory, cognitive flexibility, response inhibition, and decision-making, as indicated by validated neuropsychological tests (Miyake & Friedman, 2012; Miyake et al., 2000; A. Verdejo-Garcia & Perez-Garcia, 2007). Human lesion and neuroimaging studies have linked these executive domains to separate aspects of the prefrontal cortex, namely the dorsolateral prefrontal cortex (working memory), the ventrolateral prefrontal cortex (cognitive flexibility), the inferior frontal gyrus (response inhibition), and the medial orbitofrontal cortex (decision-making), along with their anatomical and functional connections with striatal and limbic regions (Aron, Robbins, & Poldrack, 2014; Bechara, Damasio, & Damasio, 2000; Robbins, 2007; Verdejo-Garcia et al., 2015).

The literature review's approach focuses as much as possible on "hard" metaanalytic research evidence and is restricted to neuropsychological studies including individuals with substance use disorders as compared to healthy, nondrug using controls and other relevant comparison groups (i.e., nonaffected twins, recreational drug users, and individuals with behavioral addictions sparing neurotoxicity). The overarching aim is to provide a

Executive Functions in Health and Disease. DOI: http://dx.doi.org/10.1016/B978-0-12-803676-1.00016-7

clear-cut vision of the neuropsychological impact of each of the nominated drugs on the specified components of executive functions.

CANNABIS

Metaanalytic research has not found consistent associations between chronic cannabis use and executive functions (Broyd, van Hell, Beale, Yucel, & Solowij, 2016; I. Grant, Gonzalez, Carey, Natarajan, & Wolfson, 2003). However, there is coherent evidence from well-controlled case—control and twin studies indicating that cannabis use is linked to poorer performance in cognitive tests of complex planning, such as Block Design and Stockings of Cambridge (Grant, Chamberlain, Schreiber, & Odlaug, 2012; Lyons et al., 2004), and decision-making, including the Cambridge Gamble Task and the Iowa Gambling Task (Grant et al., 2012; Verdejo-Garcia, A. Benbrook, et al., 2007).

In addition, recent studies have emphasized the role of genetic makeup and age of onset in determining the detrimental effects of cannabis use on executive functions. It has been shown that cannabis users carrying the *val/val* genotype of the COMT gene and the *short/short* genotype of the SLC6A4 gene, linked to reduced availability of prefrontal dopamine and serotonin, respectively, display poorer performance in tests of sustained attention (CANTAB Rapid Visual Processing) and decision-making (Iowa Gambling Task) (Verdejo-Garcia et al., 2013). Moreover, cannabis users with age of onset before 15 years have shown decreased performance in tests of response inhibition (Stroop) and cognitive flexibility (Wisconsin Card Sorting Test and Frontal Assessment Battery) compared to later-onset users and nondrug using controls (Fontes et al., 2011).

Altogether, existing findings suggest that chronic cannabis use is (1) linked to specific deficits in complex planning and decision-making skills, sparing other executive functions and (2) associated with further executive deficits (sustained attention/response inhibition, and flexibility) and greater decision-making alterations among individuals carrying at-risk dopamine and serotonin genotypes and those starting cannabis use in early adolescence.

COCAINE

Metaanalytic research has shown that cocaine use is associated with significant deficits, of moderate-to-large effect size, in the executive function domains of working memory, response inhibition, cognitive flexibility (specifically in reward-related tasks), and decision-making (Jovanovski, Erb, & Zakzanis, 2005; Potvin, Stavro, Rizkallah, & Pelletier, 2014). These deficits manifest both during early and intermediate length abstinence (c. 12 weeks) (Potvin et al., 2014). The evidence from existing longitudinal studies suggest that these deficits can fully recover after 1 year of abstinence (Potvin et al., 2014; Vonmoos et al., 2014), although working memory and decision-making deficits can be long-lasting in individuals with early onset of cocaine use and/or polysubstance, heavy use (Verdejo-Garcia, Rivas-Perez, Vilar-Lopez, & Perez-Garcia, 2007; Vonmoos et al., 2014).

Recent studies have applied innovative experimental designs, including specific comparison groups, to better understand which of the above-described executive deficits are cocaine-induced versus premorbid. The comparison between chronic and recreational cocaine users has shown that cocaine exposure is significantly associated with greater deficits in working memory (Letter Number Sequencing, CANTAB Spatial Working Memory) (Vonmoos, Hulka, Preller, Jenni, Baumgartner, et al., 2013). Similarly, the comparison between chronic cocaine users and pathological gamblers, which shares premorbid characteristics but is spared of cocaine-related neu-roadaptive effects, has shown that cocaine use is specifically associated with deficits in working memory (n-back) and reward-related inflexibility or perseveration (Probabilistic Reversal Learning) (Albein-Urios, Martinez-Gonzalez, Lozano, Clark, & Verdejo-Garcia, 2012; Verdejo-Garcia et al., 2015). Conversely, deficits in response inhibition are similar in chronic cocaine users, recreational users, and pathological gamblers (Albein-Urios et al., 2012; Vonmoos, Hulka, Preller, Jenni, Schulz, et al., 2013), suggesting that they precede onset of cocaine use disorders (Verdejo-Garcia, Lawrence, & Clark, 2008).

Altogether, existing findings suggest that chronic cocaine use is linked to significant deficits in working memory and reward-related inflexibility (leading to perseveration). These deficits persist for at least 3 months after onset of abstinence but users can fully recover after 1 year of sobriety, particularly in less severe cases (i.e., late age of onset, limited polysubstance use). Cocaine users also display deficits in response inhibition and decision-making, which may precede cocaine use disorders, and hence being manifest even after long-term abstinence.

METHAMPHETAMINE

There is a lack of metaanalytic data on methamphetamine use and executive functions, and the systematic reviews on the topic have yielded contentious conclusions, suggesting both negative and positive findings (Dean, Groman, Morales, & London, 2013; Hart, Marvin, Silver, & Smith, 2012).

The analysis of individual case—control studies suggests that chronic methamphetamine use is associated with significant deficits in the domain of response inhibition (King, Alicata, Cloak, & Chang, 2010; Rendell, Mazur, & Henry, 2009; Simon et al., 2000; Simon, Dean, Cordova, Monterosso, & London, 2010). Furthermore, a well-controlled study using domain-specific experimental tasks showed methamphetamine-related deficits in tests of spatial working memory, flexibility, and decision-making (van der Plas, Crone, van den Wildenberg, Tranel, & Bechara, 2009). Decision-making deficits have also been consistently associated with neural alterations in the processing of risk and loss, as indicated by decreased insula, rostral anterior cingulate cortex, and dorsolateral prefrontal cortex activation during risk-taking choices involving negative feedback (Gowin et al., 2014; Kohno, Morales, Ghahremani, Hellemann, & London, 2014). It has been argued that the above-described executive deficits have not yet been reliably associated with patterns of methamphetamine use (i.e., dose-related alterations) (Hart et al., 2012), a limitation that can be addressed using detailed biological/toxicological measures.

The genetic contribution to methamphetamine-related cognitive effect has been illustrated by a pharmacogenetic study, which showed that methamphetamine users carrying cytochrome P450-2D6 (CYP2D6) genotypes linked to fast extensive metabolization of methamphetamine after drug intake display greater overall executive function impairments (Cherner et al., 2010). This finding suggests that the metabolic products derived of methamphetamine breakup in the body can negatively impact neural function and ultimately cognitive performance.

Altogether, chronic methamphetamine use has been associated with deficits in several executive domains in isolated studies although more research is required to establish the robustness of these deficits and their specific link to methamphetamine use patterns and neuropharmacological effects.

OPIOIDS

Metaanalytic research has shown that chronic opioids use is associated with significant deficits, of small-to-medium effect size, in verbal working memory, flexibility (as indicated by fluency tests), and decision-making (Baldacchino, Balfour, Passetti, Humphris, & Matthews, 2012). These deficits are mostly attributable to "street heroin use," although research has also shown detrimental effects of methadone substitution pharmacotherapy on specific executive functions, such as working memory and decision-making (Baldacchino, Balfour, & Matthews, 2015; Pirastu et al., 2006; Verdejo, Toribio, Orozco, Puente, & Perez-Garcia, 2005).

A more recent concern is related to the overconsumption and subsequent dependence of opioid prescription drugs used in the treatment of chronic pain (e.g., oxycodone). However, the one available study has not shown significant detrimental effects of pain-related opioid prescription medications on executive functions (Baldacchino et al., 2015).

Altogether, existing findings suggest that chronic heroin and methadone use are linked to significant deficits in the executive domains of working memory and decision-making. Opioid prescription drugs used in the treatment of chronic pain have not shown a noticeable impact on executive functions.

DISCUSSION AND FUTURE DIRECTIONS

Current evidence has demonstrated that chronic cocaine and heroin use are associated with significant deficits in working memory, cognitive flexibility, and decision-making. Chronic methamphetamine use has been mainly associated with response inhibition and decision-making deficits although a clear-cut dose performance association has not yet been established. Chronic cannabis users have generally spared executive functions although there is converging evidence of complex planning deficits and decision-making deficits among heavy users, and some users are at higher risk of executive deficits by virtue of genetic characteristics and early use.

An outstanding question in the substance use—executive functions literature relates to the causality of deficits: are they drug-induced or premorbid alterations? There is sufficient evidence to suggest that chronic cocaine use provokes neuropsychological deficits in the domains of working memory and flexibility, and this notion is also substantiated by animal studies (Porter et al., 2011; Stalnaker et al., 2007; Sudai et al., 2011). The same applies to chronic use of heroin and methadone although the severity of executive functions deficits among opioid-dependent users is notably milder than in cocaine-dependent users (A. Verdejo-Garcia & Perez-Garcia, 2007; A. J. Verdejo-Garcia, Perales, & Perez-Garcia, 2007). The neuropharmacological effects of these drugs on frontostriatal and frontolimbic catecholamine and serotonin systems, along with long-term induced neuroadaptations in stress systems, are plausible biological mechanisms conducive to these deficits.

The role of premorbid factors has been better illustrated among users of substances with comparatively milder neuroadaptive effects, such as cannabis. Response inhibition and decision-making deficits in cannabis users have been linked to genetic factors, such as hardwired-diminished activity of prefrontal cortex dopamine and serotonin systems (Verdejo-Garcia et al., 2013). The link between deficits in executive functions and early age of onset also emphasizes the role of late prefrontal cortex maturation in the incidence of substance use disorders (Paus, Keshavan, & Giedd, 2008). Future studies in substance users should also consider the influence of early environmental factors, such as history of trauma and/or parental neglect, which are known to significantly impact prefrontal cortex development.

A final intriguing pathway into drug-related executive function deficits relates to genetic variations involved in pharmacokinetics (i.e., what the body does to the drugs). Novel strands of evidence have shown that the genotypes that dictate individual differences in how well or bad a drug is metabolized have an ultimate impact on cognitive performance (Cherner et al., 2010; Cuyas et al., 2011). This is a new research avenue that integrates the genetic predispositions with drug-mobilized pharmacological processes in the interpretation of substance-related cognitive deficits. More broadly, the integration of these two variables (the individual and the drug) with the more complex social context, including interpersonal and environmental influences, via population neuroscience studies, may be needed to fully understand the impact of substance use on executive functions (Paus, 2010).

Altogether, it seems reasonable to conclude that executive dysfunction is a hallmark of substance addiction and thus an important pathway to guide the development of novel treatment interventions. Novel cognitive training interventions targeting executive function deficits have shown to be promising strategies to restore or compensate executive deficits and also to improve treatment outcomes (Verdejo-Garcia, 2016). More research is needed to establish the validity of this exciting new executive function–centered approach to the treatment of substance use disorders.

REFERENCES

Albein-Urios, N., Martinez-Gonzalez, J. M., Lozano, O., Clark, L., & Verdejo-Garcia, A. (2012). Comparison of impulsivity and working memory in cocaine addiction and pathological gambling: Implications for cocaine-induced neurotoxicity. *Drug and Alcohol Dependence*, *126* (1-2), 1–6. Available from http://dx.doi.org/10.1016/j.drugalcdep.2012.03.008.

Aron, A. R., Robbins, T. W., & Poldrack, R. A. (2014). Inhibition and the right inferior frontal cortex: One decade on. *Trends in Cognitive Sciences*, *18*(4), 177–185. Available from http://dx.doi.org/10.1016/j.tics.2013.12.003.

Baldacchino, A., Balfour, D. J., & Matthews, K. (2015). Impulsivity and opioid drugs: Differential effects of heroin, methadone and prescribed analgesic medication. *Psychological Medicine*, *45* (6), 1167–1179. Available from http://dx.doi.org/10.1017/S0033291714002189.

Baldacchino, A., Balfour, D. J., Passetti, F., Humphris, G., & Matthews, K. (2012). Neuropsychological consequences of chronic opioid use: A quantitative review and meta-analysis. *Neuroscience and Biobehavioral Reviews*, *36*(9), 2056–2068. Available from http://dx.doi.org/10.1016/j.neubiorev.2012.06.006.

Bechara, A., Damasio, H., & Damasio, A. R. (2000). Emotion, decision making and the orbito-frontal cortex. *Cerebral Cortex*, *10*(3), 295–307.

Broyd, S. J., van Hell, H. H., Beale, C., Yucel, M., & Solowij, N. (2016). Acute and chronic effects of cannabinoids on human cognition—A systematic review. *Biological Psychiatry*, *79*(7), 557–567. Available from http://dx.doi.org/10.1016/j.biopsych.2015.12.002.

Cherner, M., Bousman, C., Everall, I., Barron, D., Letendre, S., Vaida, F., & Grant, I. (2010). Cytochrome P450-2D6 extensive metabolizers are more vulnerable to methamphetamine-associated neurocognitive impairment: Preliminary findings. *Journal of the International Neuropsychological Society: JINS*, *16*(5), 890–901. Available from http://dx.doi.org/ 10.1017/S1355617710000779.

Cuyas, E., Verdejo-Garcia, A., Fagundo, A. B., Khymenets, O., Rodriguez, J., Cuenca, A., & de la Torre, R. (2011). The influence of genetic and environmental factors among MDMA users in cognitive performance. *PLoS One*, *6*(11), e27206. Available from http://dx.doi.org/ 10.1371/journal.pone.0027206.

Dean, A. C., Groman, S. M., Morales, A. M., & London, E. D. (2013). An evaluation of the evidence that methamphetamine abuse causes cognitive decline in humans. *Neuropsychopharmacology: Official Publication of the American College of Neuropsychopharmacology*, *38*(2), 259–274. Available from http://dx.doi.org/10.1038/npp.2012.179.

European Monitoring Centre for Drugs and Drug Addiction (2016), European drug report 2016: Trends and developments, Publications Office of the European Union, Luxembourg.

Fontes, M. A., Bolla, K. I., Cunha, P. J., Almeida, P. P., Jungerman, F., Laranjeira, R. R., & Lacerda, A. L. (2011). Cannabis use before age 15 and subsequent executive functioning. *British Journal of Psychiatry: The Journal of Mental Science, 198*(6), 442–447. Available from http://dx.doi.org/10.1192/bjp.bp.110.077479.

Gowin, J. L., Stewart, J. L., May, A. C., Ball, T. M., Wittmann, M., Tapert, S. F., & Paulus, M. P. (2014). Altered cingulate and insular cortex activation during risk-taking in methamphetamine dependence: Losses lose impact. *Addiction, 109*(2), 237–247. Available from http://dx.doi.org/10.1111/add.12354.

Grant, I., Gonzalez, R., Carey, C. L., Natarajan, L., & Wolfson, T. (2003). Non-acute (residual) neurocognitive effects of cannabis use: A meta-analytic study. *Journal of the International Neuropsychological Society: JINS, 9*(5), 679–689. Available from http://dx.doi.org/10.1017/S1355617703950016.

Grant, J. E., Chamberlain, S. R., Schreiber, L., & Odlaug, B. L. (2012). Neuropsychological deficits associated with cannabis use in young adults. *Drug and Alcohol Dependence, 121*(1-2), 159–162. Available from http://dx.doi.org/10.1016/j.drugalcdep.2011.08.015.

Hart, C. L., Marvin, C. B., Silver, R., & Smith, E. E. (2012). Is cognitive functioning impaired in methamphetamine users? A critical review. *Neuropsychopharmacology: Official Publication of the American College of Neuropsychopharmacology, 37*(3), 586–608. Available from http://dx.doi.org/10.1038/npp.2011.276.

Jovanovski, D., Erb, S., & Zakzanis, K. K. (2005). Neurocognitive deficits in cocaine users: A quantitative review of the evidence. *Journal of Clinical and Experimental Neuropsychology, 27*(2), 189–204. Available from http://dx.doi.org/10.1080/13803390490515694.

King, G., Alicata, D., Cloak, C., & Chang, L. (2010). Neuropsychological deficits in adolescent methamphetamine abusers. *Psychopharmacology, 212*(2), 243–249. Available from http://dx.doi.org/10.1007/s00213-010-1949-x.

Kohno, M., Morales, A. M., Ghahremani, D. G., Hellemann, G., & London, E. D. (2014). Risky decision making, prefrontal cortex, and mesocorticolimbic functional connectivity in methamphetamine dependence. *JAMA Psychiatry, 71*(7), 812–820. Available from http://dx.doi.org/10.1001/jamapsychiatry.2014.399.

Lyons, M. J., Bar, J. L., Panizzon, M. S., Toomey, R., Eisen, S., Xian, H., & Tsuang, M. T. (2004). Neuropsychological consequences of regular marijuana use: A twin study. *Psychological Medicine, 34*(7), 1239–1250.

Miyake, A., & Friedman, N. P. (2012). The nature and organization of individual differences in executive functions: Four general conclusions. *Current Directions in Psychological Science: A Journal of the American Psychological Society, 21*(1), 8–14. Available from http://dx.doi.org/10.1177/0963721411429458.

Miyake, A., Friedman, N. P., Emerson, M. J., Witzki, A. H., Howerter, A., & Wager, T. D. (2000). The unity and diversity of executive functions and their contributions to complex "frontal lobe" tasks: A latent variable analysis. *Cognitive Psychology, 41*(1), 49–100. Available from http://dx.doi.org/10.1006/cogp.1999.0734.

Paus, T. (2010). Population neuroscience: Why and how. *Human Brain Mapping, 31*(6), 891–903. Available from http://dx.doi.org/10.1002/hbm.21069.

Paus, T., Keshavan, M., & Giedd, J. N. (2008). Why do many psychiatric disorders emerge during adolescence? *Nature Reviews. Neuroscience, 9*(12), 947–957. Available from http://dx.doi.org/10.1038/nrn2513.

Pirastu, R., Fais, R., Messina, M., Bini, V., Spiga, S., Falconieri, D., & Diana, M. (2006). Impaired decision-making in opiate-dependent subjects: Effect of pharmacological therapies. *Drug and Alcohol Dependence, 83*(2), 163–168. Available from http://dx.doi.org/10.1016/j.drugalcdep.2005.11.008.

Porter, J. N., Olsen, A. S., Gurnsey, K., Dugan, B. P., Jedema, H. P., & Bradberry, C. W. (2011). Chronic cocaine self-administration in rhesus monkeys: Impact on associative learning, cognitive control, and working memory. *Journal of Neuroscience, 31*(13), 4926–4934. Available from http://dx.doi.org/10.1523/JNEUROSCI.5426-10.2011.

Potvin, S., Stavro, K., Rizkallah, E., & Pelletier, J. (2014). Cocaine and cognition: A systematic quantitative review. *Journal of Addiction Medicine, 8*(5), 368–376. Available from http://dx.doi.org/10.1097/ADM.0000000000000066.

Rendell, P. G., Mazur, M., & Henry, J. D. (2009). Prospective memory impairment in former users of methamphetamine. *Psychopharmacology, 203*(3), 609–616. Available from http://dx.doi.org/10.1007/s00213-008-1408-0.

Robbins, T. W. (2007). Shifting and stopping: Fronto-striatal substrates, neurochemical modulation and clinical implications. *Philosophical Transactions of the Royal Society of London. Series B, Biological Sciences, 362*(1481), 917–932. Available from http://dx.doi.org/10.1098/rstb.2007.2097.

Simon, S. L., Dean, A. C., Cordova, X., Monterosso, J. R., & London, E. D. (2010). Methamphetamine dependence and neuropsychological functioning: Evaluating change during early abstinence. *Journal of Studies on Alcohol and Drugs, 71*(3), 335–344.

Simon, S. L., Domier, C., Carnell, J., Brethen, P., Rawson, R., & Ling, W. (2000). Cognitive impairment in individuals currently using methamphetamine. *American Journal on Addictions, 9*(3), 222–231.

Stalnaker, T. A., Roesch, M. R., Calu, D. J., Burke, K. A., Singh, T., & Schoenbaum, G. (2007). Neural correlates of inflexible behavior in the orbitofrontal-amygdalar circuit after cocaine exposure. *Annals of the New York Academy of Sciences, 1121*, 598–609. Available from http://dx.doi.org/10.1196/annals.1401.014.

Substance Abuse and Mental Health Services Administration, Center for Behavioral Health Statistics and Quality. Treatment Episode Data Set (TEDS): 2004–2014. National admissions to substance abuse treatment services. BHSIS Series S-84, HHS Publication No. (SMA) 16-4986. Rockville, MD: Substance Abuse and Mental Health Services Administration, 2016.

Sudai, E., Croitoru, O., Shaldubina, A., Abraham, L., Gispan, I., Flaumenhaft, Y., & Yadid, G. (2011). High cocaine dosage decreases neurogenesis in the hippocampus and impairs working memory. *Addiction Biology, 16*(2), 251–260. Available from http://dx.doi.org/10.1111/j.1369-1600.2010.00241.x.

van der Plas, E. A., Crone, E. A., van den Wildenberg, W. P., Tranel, D., & Bechara, A. (2009). Executive control deficits in substance-dependent individuals: A comparison of alcohol, cocaine, and methamphetamine and of men and women. *Journal of Clinical and Experimental Neuropsychology, 31*(6), 706–719. Available from http://dx.doi.org/10.1080/13803390802484797.

Verdejo, A., Toribio, I., Orozco, C., Puente, K. L., & Perez-Garcia, M. (2005). Neuropsychological functioning in methadone maintenance patients versus abstinent heroin abusers. *Drug and Alcohol Dependence, 78*(3), 283–288. Available from http://dx.doi.org/10.1016/j.drugalcdep.2004.11.006.

Verdejo-Garcia, A. (2016). Cognitive training for substance use disorders: Neuroscientific mechanisms. *Neuroscience and Biobehavioral Reviews, 68*, 270–281. Available from http://dx.doi.org/10.1016/j.neubiorev.2016.05.018.

Verdejo-Garcia, A., Benbrook, A., Funderburk, F., David, P., Cadet, J. L., & Bolla, K. I. (2007). The differential relationship between cocaine use and marijuana use on decision-making performance over repeat testing with the Iowa Gambling Task. *Drug and Alcohol Dependence*, *90*(1), 2−11. Available from http://dx.doi.org/10.1016/j.drugalcdep.2007.02.004.

Verdejo-Garcia, A., Clark, L., Verdejo-Roman, J., Albein-Urios, N., Martinez-Gonzalez, J. M., Gutierrez, B., & Soriano-Mas, C. (2015). Neural substrates of cognitive flexibility in cocaine and gambling addictions. *British Journal of Psychiatry: The Journal of Mental Science*, *207*(2), 158−164. Available from http://dx.doi.org/10.1192/bjp.bp.114.152223.

Verdejo-Garcia, A., Fagundo, A. B., Cuenca, A., Rodriguez, J., Cuyas, E., Langohr, K., & de la Torre, R. (2013). COMT val158met and 5-HTTLPR genetic polymorphisms moderate executive control in cannabis users. *Neuropsychopharmacology: Official Publication of the American College of Neuropsychopharmacology*, *38*(8), 1598−1606. Available from http://dx.doi.org/10.1038/npp.2013.59.

Verdejo-Garcia, A., Lawrence, A. J., & Clark, L. (2008). Impulsivity as a vulnerability marker for substance-use disorders: Review of findings from high-risk research, problem gamblers and genetic association studies. *Neuroscience and Biobehavioral Reviews*, *32*(4), 777−810. Available from http://dx.doi.org/10.1016/j.neubiorev.2007.11.003.

Verdejo-Garcia, A., & Perez-Garcia, M. (2007). Profile of executive deficits in cocaine and heroin polysubstance users: Common and differential effects on separate executive components. *Psychopharmacology*, *190*(4), 517−530. Available from http://dx.doi.org/10.1007/s00213-006-0632-8.

Verdejo-Garcia, A., Rivas-Perez, C., Vilar-Lopez, R., & Perez-Garcia, M. (2007). Strategic self-regulation, decision-making and emotion processing in poly-substance abusers in their first year of abstinence. *Drug and Alcohol Dependence*, *86*(2-3), 139−146. Available from http://dx.doi.org/10.1016/j.drugalcdep.2006.05.024.

Verdejo-Garcia, A. J., Perales, J. C., & Perez-Garcia, M. (2007). Cognitive impulsivity in cocaine and heroin polysubstance abusers. *Addictive Behaviors*, *32*(5), 950−966. Available from http://dx.doi.org/10.1016/j.addbeh.2006.06.032.

Vonmoos, M., Hulka, L. M., Preller, K. H., Jenni, D., Baumgartner, M. R., Stohler, R., & Quednow, B. B. (2013). Cognitive dysfunctions in recreational and dependent cocaine users: Role of attention-deficit hyperactivity disorder, craving and early age at onset. *British Journal of Psychiatry: The Journal of Mental Science*, *203*(1), 35−43. Available from http://dx.doi.org/10.1192/bjp.bp.112.118091.

Vonmoos, M., Hulka, L. M., Preller, K. H., Jenni, D., Schulz, C., Baumgartner, M. R., & Quednow, B. B. (2013). Differences in self-reported and behavioral measures of impulsivity in recreational and dependent cocaine users. *Drug and Alcohol Dependence*, *133*(1), 61−70. Available from http://dx.doi.org/10.1016/j.drugalcdep.2013.05.032.

Vonmoos, M., Hulka, L. M., Preller, K. H., Minder, F., Baumgartner, M. R., & Quednow, B. B. (2014). Cognitive impairment in cocaine users is drug-induced but partially reversible: Evidence from a longitudinal study. *Neuropsychopharmacology: Official Publication of the American College of Neuropsychopharmacology*, *39*(9), 2200−2210. Available from http://dx.doi.org/10.1038/npp.2014.71.

Chapter 17

Seizures of the Frontal Lobes: Clinical Presentations and Diagnostic Considerations

Sara Wildstein[1] and Silvana Riggio[1,2,3]

[1]Department of Psychiatry, Icahn School of Medicine at Mount Sinai, New York, NY, United States, [2]Department of Neurology, Icahn School of Medicine at Mount Sinai, New York, NY, United States, [3]Psychosomatic Medicine, Consultation Liaison Psychiatry Service, James Peters Bronx Veterans Administration Hospital, Bronx, NY, United States

INTRODUCTION

The frontal lobes control motor voluntary movements, behavior, planning, and language. They are fundamental to memory, problem solving, judgment, and abstract thinking, as well as impacting personality, impulse control, mood, and affect. The frontal lobes connectivity with the rest of the brain can make localization of a seizure to the frontal lobe difficult, and the evaluation of patients with suspected frontal lobe epilepsy (FLE) is challenging even for the experienced clinician. It often requires a multidisciplinary collaboration between specialties including psychiatry and neurology. Some of the clinical manifestations of FLE are classic and easily identified, e.g., focal clonic motor activity. Other types of frontal lobe seizures are less obvious and can present a diagnostic dilemma, e.g., autonomic or behavioral presentations. Frontal lobe seizures can mimic a behavioral disorder, e.g., panic attacks or repetitive motor activity (RMA) and vice versa. Awareness of the spectrum of clinical presentations in FLE and the possible overlap with psychiatric disorders is fundamental to the evaluation of a patient with a behavioral complaint. A systematic approach to the history and physical examination can help in making the diagnosis and testing direct diagnosis. It can also avoid misdiagnoses with consequent unnecessary testing and treatments.

THE FRONTAL LOBE AND ITS ANATOMY

The frontal lobes are the largest cortical regions of the brain, comprising approximately 40% of the cerebral cortex (Fig. 17.1). They comprised the

Executive Functions in Health and Disease. DOI: http://dx.doi.org/10.1016/B978-0-12-803676-1.00017-9

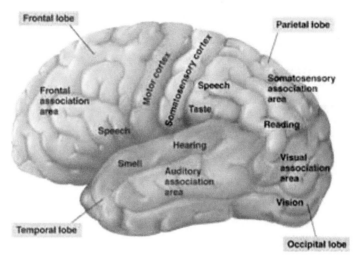

FIGURE 17.1   The frontal lobe is the largest of the four lobes of the brain.

medial frontal region, the dorsolateral region, and the frontopolar region. Each area is responsible for a specific function, e.g., motor, speech, executive function, and behavior. The extensive network of connections between the frontal lobe and other parts of the brain makes understanding frontal lobe functions and dysfunctions challenging.

The corticospinal tract, frontopontocerebellar tract, and other efferent fiber systems originate in the frontal lobe. Other connections exist between the frontal lobe, the caudate, putamen, subthalamic nucleus, red nucleus, brainstem reticular formation, substantia nigra, inferior olive, and the thalamus. Furthermore, there are connections closely linking the temporal and occipital lobes with the frontal lobe. Such complex and widespread connections, rapid propagation within the ipsilateral and contralateral hemisphere, and structures outside the frontal lobe make localizing seizures of the frontal lobe origin a challenge. This is compounded by the fact that much of its surface is inaccessible to scalp electroencephalographic (EEG) recording (Riggio and Harner, 1995).

The recognition and localization of FLE can be problematic not only because of the great overlap of clinical presentations within the frontal lobe and their constellation of symptoms but also because of its overlap with other clinical entities including psychiatric disorders. The differential diagnosis of many frontal lobe seizures including nocturnal frontal lobe epilepsy (NFLE) includes nonneurogenic seizures, panic disorder, and nonrapid eye movements (NREM) sleep parasomnia.

ETIOLOGY AND GENETICS

FLE is the second most common focal epilepsy after temporal lobe epilepsy. Causes include genetic disorders (see below), cryptogenic/nonlesional disorders, central nervous system infections, tumors, vascular malformations, vascular injuries, cortical dysplasias, posttraumatic abnormalities, and developmental abnormalities. Family history is important because it may increase the possibility of arriving at the right diagnosis especially in the case of autosomal dominant FLE (O'Muircheartaigh and Richardson, 2012).

FLE is the second most common focal epilepsy of childhood. The typical age of onset is between the ages 4 and 8 years. While the prevalence of cognitive impairment in children remains to be clarified, deficits have been associated with attention, executive function, and behavior (distractibility, aggression, and disinhibition). Attention-deficit hyperactivity disorder is a common comorbidity in children with FLE and reported in up to 67% of these patients (Braakman et al, 2011).

Advances in genetic sequencing have enabled the identification of a genetic base for some types of epilepsy. Autosomal dominant nocturnal frontal lobe epilepsy (ADNFLE) is an example of this and has been demonstrated to be inherited with 70%–80% penetrance. ADNFLE is the only partial epilepsy syndrome that follows a single gene inheritance. Sporadic, familial, idiopathic, cryptogenic, or asymptomatic forms exist. They can be characterized by different sleep-related motor events of increasing complexity and duration even in a single night.

ADNFLE typically presents during teenage years with brief, nocturnal seizures that generally respond to antiepileptic drugs (Jobst and Williamson, 2005). Different mutations have been implicated in these types of epilepsies. Studies initially showed mutations of the neuronal nicotinic acetylcholine receptor (nAChR) alpha 4 subunit. It is now known that there are other mutations within the nAChR system that are associated with ADNFLE (Derry, 2011; Nobili, 2007). Three loci have been identified in ADNFLE-2 mutant genes, coding for the alpha 4 (CHRNA4) and beta 2 (CHRNB2) subunits of the nicotinic AChR, which demonstrated the heterogeneity of this genetic disorder (Ryvlin, Rheims, and Risse, 2006). The subunit genes CHRNA4 and CHRNB2 are responsible for the clinical phenotype in approximately 12%–15% of ADNFLE cases (Steinlein, Hoda, Betrand, and Betrand, 2012). Positron emission tomographic (PET) studies in patients with ADNFLE have shown increased activation of the cholinergic pathway, starting in the brainstem, which may help explain the nocturnal predominance as cholinergic neurons help to regulate sleep and arousal at the thalamic and cortical levels, although the pathophysiologic mechanism is still unclear (Bisulli, Vignatelli, & Provini, 2011; Picard, 2005).

Further linkage analysis in ADNFLE families without known mutations have revealed three additional loci on chromosomes 15q24, 3p22–24, and

8q11.2–q21.1 (Bisulli et al., 2011; Philips, Scheffer, & Berkovic, 1995). Within these regions, the gene most likely involved in ADNFLE pathogenesis is the one for corticotropin-releasing hormone (CRH) on chromosome 8. Two nucleotide variations in the CRH promotor region have been identified in four families and two sporadic cases of ADNFLE. In vitro functional analysis suggests that there is a connection between CRH concentration and neuronal excitability, which may affect thalamocortical loop dysfunction (Combi, Ferini-Strambi, and Tenchini, 2008).

Another gene coding for the sodium-activated potassium channel subunit 1 (KCNT1) found on chromosome 9 was found to be associated with ADNFLE. Four variants were found to show a severe ADNFLE phenotype with an early age of onset, severe impairment in intellectual functioning, and psychiatric and behavioral problems (psychosis, catatonia, and aggression). Mutations in KCNT1 were found to have complete penetrance (Heron, Smith, and Bahlo, 2012). More recently, mutations in the DEPDC5 gene were found to be implicated in various focal epilepsies, including ADNFLE (Ishida, Picard, and Rudolf, 2013).

In summary, frontal lobe seizures can have either a primary or a secondary etiology. Being the largest lobe of the brain, the frontal lobe is at risk of insult from a variety of insults including trauma, infection, and tumors. Advanced genetic sequencing is providing tools that are unlocking the etiology of many frontal lobe seizures that were once simply placed in the "cryptogenic" category.

CLINICAL PRESENTATIONS OF FRONTAL LOBE EPILEPSY

Seizures of frontal lobe origin are typically brief (rarely last longer than 1 min), repetitive, and occur in clusters. Depending on the type, they often occur nocturnally, although daytime events also take place (Jobst and Williamson, 2005). FLE can have diverse clinical presentations that depend on the area of the frontal lobe involved and whether the event remains focal or spreads. They predominantly manifest with motor signs and include clonic motor activity of the contralateral extremities with potential subsequent slow spreading or quick generalization (Bancaud et al., 1992). Although focal clonic motor activity usually originates from the prerolandic gyrus, it can also be associated with diffuse hemispheric abnormalities such as seen in Rasmussen's syndrome (Rasmussen and Anderman, 1989).

Motor manifestations are common with FLE, including, but not limited to, complex motor actions, forced actions, and automatisms. Automatisms may be simple consisting of perseverative movements such as kicking or tapping, or complex and repetitive movements such as rubbing, gesturing, rearranging clothes, thrashing, picking, sexual automatisms, running, or rocking (Geier, Bancaud, & Talairach, 1976; Riggio & Harner, 1995; Williamson, Spencer, & Spencer, 1985a). RMA was found to be the single most common ictal feature in one series of 21 patients with FLE: 62% of patients in this study were found to have RMA, characterized by rubbing of hands, running, and moaning or vocalization (Williamson et al., 1985a). Vocalizations may be a major manifestation of seizures of frontal lobe origin, with as high as 50% of cases reported to have vocalization ranging from simple (grunting, moaning, or screaming) to complex in nature (intelligible words) (Chauvel, Kliemann, & Vignal, 1995; Williamson et al., 1985a; Williamson, Wieser, & Delgado Escueta, 1987). Other clinical manifestations of frontal lobe origin include speech arrest, (Penfield & Rasmussen, 1949) autonomic dysfunction (Williamson et al., 2000), and somatosensory symptoms (Williamson and Spencer, 1986).

Many patients also experience subjective sensory manifestations, such as somatosensory, visual, auditory, olfactory, and vegetative symptoms. Other objective autonomic manifestations can include visceromotor signs that can be digestive (salivation, swallowing, and chewing), cardiovascular (tachycardia, pallor, and facial flushing), respiratory (tachypnea, bradypnea, and apnea), urogenital (urination, erection, and complex sexual behavior), and ocular intrinsic muscles (mydriasis) (Bancaud et al., 1992; Chauvel et al., 1995).

Ictal panic has also been seen in patients with seizures arising from the orbitofrontal cortex in the nondominant hemisphere. Patients usually present with sudden panic-stricken shouting, nonverbal screams, or verbal vocalizations saying things such as "Oh my God!" or asking for help (Kanner, 2011).

Seizures of frontal lobe origin are challenging to categorize, resulting in significant variation in the literature. Various presentations of frontal lobe seizures may somewhat be explained by the origin of seizure onset and frontal lobe anatomy; however, this is not entirely specific. Seizures that present similarly may reflect neuronal discharge in overlapping brain circuits; however, due to propagation of discharge, it is difficult to say with certainty where the seizure origin is (O'Muircheartaigh and Richardson, 2012).

In 1989, the International League Against Epilepsy classified frontal lobe seizures in accordance with gross anatomical localization based on the functional subregions of the frontal lobe (O'Muircheartaigh and Richardson, 2012). Primary motor cortex seizures present with contralateral tonic/clonic movements, speech arrest, and frequent generalization. Supplementary motor area seizures manifest typically as simple focal tonic seizures with either vocalizations or speech arrest, "fencing" postures, and complex motor activity. Cingulate seizures are typified by complex motor activity and automatisms, and may have sexual features, vegetative signs, alterations in mood and affect, and urinary incontinence. Frontopolar seizures present with initial loss of contact, and movements of the head and eyes, axial clonic jerking, falls, and autonomic signs. Orbitofrontal seizures manifest are complex focal motor seizures that have initial automatisms or olfactory hallucinations, autonomic signs, and urinary incontinence. Dorsolateral/premotor seizures are simple focal tonic seizures with versive movements and aphasia, complex focal motor activity with initial automatisms. Opercular seizures manifest with mastication, salivation, swallowing, and speech arrest. They frequently have an epigastric aura, fear, and autonomic signs.

Tinuper, Provini, Bisulli, & Lugaresi (2005) characterized NFLE based on videopolymnographic recordings into four types:

- very brief motor seizures (also known as paroxysmal arousals),
- hypermotor seizures,
- asymmetric bilateral tonic seizures, and
- prolonged seizures (also known as epileptic wanderings).

Very brief motor seizures usually manifest as bilateral and axial movement that resembles a sudden arousal from sleep with the patient generally opening his eyes, sitting up, and appearing frightened. Hypermotor seizures occur generally out of NREM sleep with body movements generally starting in the limbs, as well as complex and frequently violent behavior, typically with a dystonic−dyskinetic component. There may be cycling, rocking, or repetitive body movements during this type of seizure. The patient may have vocalizations (screaming and swearing) and may have a fearful expression. In asymmetric bilateral tonic seizures, the patient typically has a sustained and unusual forced position; muscles of the face and mouth may be affected as well. Prolonged seizures have a similar presentation to the aforementioned seizure types but typically have an extended phase (lasting 1−2 min) with continued semipurposeful behavior or more complex motor activity, which may resemble sleepwalking.

FLE may be associated with convulsive and nonconvulsive status epilepticus (NCSE)—a condition of continuous or intermittent seizure activity without a return to baseline lasting more than 30 min. NCSE differs from convulsive status by the lack of predominant motor component. The hallmark of NCSE is a change in behavior or mental status that is associated with diagnostic EEG changes. NCSE can last for hours to months with variable levels of altered consciousness, and its diagnosis can be extremely challenging (Williamson, Spencer, and Spencer, 1985b).

DIFFERENTIATING FLE FROM PSYCHIATRIC DISORDERS AND PARASOMNIAS

Depending on the presentation, the differential diagnosis of FLE can include nonneurogenic seizures, panic attacks, parasomnias, and/or other psychiatric disorders. Early recognition and diagnosis is essential as the treatment plan can vary significantly impacting outcomes.

FLE can frequently present with bizarre behavior, including behavioral automatisms and bilateral tonic motor activity, whereas EEG and imaging studies can be unremarkable, thus potentially leading to incorrect diagnosis, specifically a psychiatric one. The most crucial alternative diagnosis to consider is nonneurogenic seizures. However, nonneurogenic seizures are usually less stereotyped, more asynchronous, and last longer than those seen in FLE. People maintain consciousness during the event and/or react to noxious stimuli or to suggestions. Nonneurogenic seizures do not occur while the patient is asleep, although recognizing if an event occurs out of sleep or after a brief arousal can at times be challenging (Jobst & Williamson, 2005; Waterman, Purves, & Kosaka, 1987). When clinical manifestations alone are not diagnostic, a more extensive evaluation using 24 h video EEG (vEEG) monitoring is warranted to correlate the clinical manifestations with EEG changes. Of note, nonneurogenic epileptic seizures are associated with a normal EEG. At times, muscle artifact can be present, but there is no association with epileptiform activity.

Differentiating a panic attack from ictal panic can also be quite challenging and of major importance to correct patient management. Panic attacks can occur in the context of an anxiety disorder and other mental disorders (e.g., depressive disorders, posttraumatic stress disorder, and substance use disorder) and some medical conditions (e.g., cardiac, respiratory, vestibular, and gastrointestinal). Recurrent unexpected panic attacks are required for a diagnosis of a panic disorder. The essential feature of a panic attack is an abrupt surge of intense fear or intense discomfort that reaches a peak within minutes and during which time 4 or more of 13 physical and cognitive symptoms occur (American Psychiatric Association, 2013; Table 17.1). Symptoms can last for half an hour to an hour.

By contrast, ictal panic is the most frequent type of simple partial seizure. They are sudden in onset and short in duration. They have been associated with partial seizure arising from the nondominant orbitofrontal cortex and the mesial temporal origin (Birabena, Taussigb, & Thomasd, 2001; Young, Chandarana, & Blume, 1995). Different than panic attacks, ictal panic is sudden in onset and short in duration. They may last seconds to minutes. A careful history of the symptoms at presentation, as well as associated symptoms, comorbid medical conditions, laboratory tests, neuroimaging, and at times prolactin level and medications generally help to reach a final diagnosis and hopefully improve outcome.

It is also difficult to differentiate between FLE and other sleep-related events. NREM sleep parasomnias are undesirable physical phenomena that

TABLE 17.1 Physical and Cognitive Symptoms of Panic Attack

Physical symptoms	<ul><li>Palpitations</li><li>Sweating</li><li>Shaking</li><li>Shortness of breath</li><li>Chest pain/discomfort</li><li>Nausea/abdominal distress</li><li>Shaking</li><li>Feeling of choking</li><li>Feeling of dizziness</li><li>Chills/heat sensation</li><li>Parasthesias</li></ul>
Cognitive symptoms	<ul><li>Fear of losing control</li><li>Fear of dying</li></ul>

occur mainly during sleep but are not dysfunctions of the processes responsible for the sleep–wake cycle. NFLE and NREM arousal parasomnias may present similarly posing a diagnostic dilemma. Similar semiological features of NFLE and parasomnias may be due to common neuronal networks ("central pattern generators") that generate stereotyped rhythmic movements. These central pattern generators are typically subcortical in the brainstem and spinal cord (Ferini-Strambi, Sansoni, and Combi, 2012).

NFLE refers to a syndromic entity whose hallmark is defined by the recurrence of hypermotor seizures during sleep. The episodes can be characterized by distinct paroxysmal related attacks of variable duration and complexity. Stero-EEG studies have shown that hyperkinetic automatisms and complex behavior are present when the ictal discharge involves the extratemporal structures such as the cingulate, frontal, and parietal regions, independent of its origin (Bisulli et al., 2011).

The usual features of NFLE are similar in both the sporadic and familial forms—sleep-related motor events with various degrees of complexity. These sleep-related motor behaviors frequently resemble physiologic movements and NREM sleep parasomnias. Features that are more consistent with NREM sleep parasomnias versus FLE are listed in Table 17.2.

Clinical history of more complex motor movements of dystonic or hypertonic posturing that occur in NFLE are more easily differentiated from parasomnias. Tinuper et al. (2005) demonstrated that there is a high prevalence of parasomnias in patients with a personal and family history of NFLE. A survey of 100 patients with NFLE demonstrated that 39% of cases had a family history of parasomnia, which included nightmares, sleep walking, sleep terror, enuresis, and buxisms (Provini, Plazzi, and Tinuper, 1999). Such comorbidity, which is present in both sporadic and familial forms of NFLE, suggests a common genetic link between parasomnias and NFLE, possibly related to an impairment in the pathway that regulates physiological arousal (Ryvlin, Bouvard, and Le Bars, 1998).

Seizures with affective symptoms and agitated behaviors are more difficult to differentiate from parasomnias occurring during NREM sleep (i.e., confusional arousals, sleepwalking, and sleep terrors). There is tremendous overlap in the dysfunction in the neuronal network that causes these complex seizures and the manifestations of various parasomnias, which leads to increased confusion in distinguishing NFLE from NREM parasomnias.

DIAGNOSTIC EVALUATION

The diagnosis of FLE is generally made based on clinical history, clinical manifestations, and EEG findings. A history of stereotyped, brief, episodes with nocturnal predominance, with minimal or no postictal confusion is suggestive of FLE. Due to the structure and depth of the frontal lobe, EEG changes—ictally and interictally—may be absent or nonspecific. Diagnosis

TABLE 17.2 Features of Nonrapid Eye Movement Sleep Parasomnias Versus Frontal Lobe Seizures

Features more consistent with parasomnias	• Duration longer than 2 min • Discrepancy between the duration and severity • Waxing and waning pattern • The recorded event changing clinical manifestations from one event to the next. • Nocturnal predominance • Verbal/physical interaction during the event • Yawning • Scratching • Nose rubbing • Rolling over in bed • Internal or external triggers (noises, coughing, and snoring) • Emotional behavior • Unable to fully arouse after the event
Features more consistent with FLE	• Abrupt onset and ending • Brief (seconds to minutes) • Stereotypic • Nocturnal predominance • Absent or minimal postictal confusion • Focal motor activity • Automatisms simple and complex (repetitive motor activity) • Head version and eye version • Speech arrest • Vocalizations • Autonomic dysfunctions • Somatosensory symptoms

is made difficult by the fact that initial outpatient, standard EEG in any type of focal epilepsy detects only interictal epileptiform activity in 29%–55% of patients (Goodin, Aminoff, and Laser, 1990). Ictal surface EEG findings can be also misleading due to areas of involvement of the frontal lobe that are inaccessible to the surface EEG. Several series have reported no ictal EEG changes in 33%–36% (Williamson and Spencer, 1986). One case series reported that focal frontal interictal spiking was present in only 14% of patients with FLE; bilateral spike and slow waves were present in 29% of patients; focal temporal spikes were present in 43% of patients; and the EEG was normal in 14% of patients (Riggio, 1995). It is believed that the presence of bilateral discharges in FLE are due to the interhemispheric propagation of discharges through the corpus callosum (Riggio, 1995).

If the seizure origin is in the orbital frontal region, mesial (interhemispheric) cortex, or cingulum, the seizure is much more difficult to detect by scalp EEG. It can be volume conducted over a wide region bifrontally, at times with a frontal maximum as in the case of discharges arising from the mesial frontal cortex. Furthermore, as FLE is typically associated with motor behaviors, motor artifact during EEG may obscure findings (Jobst, Siegel, and Thadani, 2000). Frequently, EEG can be misleading as well by showing temporal lobe changes, likely due to direct and indirect connections between the two lobes, generalization of seizures, and rapid spread of ictal discharge (Riggio, 1995).

Computed topographic EEG analysis can be useful in that it may process activity that is not recognized on typical EEG inspection. It may show broad-band abnormalities in power spectra, which would be otherwise undetected. Additionally, visual evoked responses to flash may elicit frontal lobe dysfunction, which can aid in diagnosing frontal lobe lesions (Riggio and Harner, 1995).

High-resolution magnetic resonance imaging (MRI) can be useful in detecting tumors, vascular malformations, and other such lesions, which may be the seizure focus. Imaging sequences should be specific to identify dysplasias (i.e., fluid-attenuated inversion recovery sequences), blood products, and vascular malformations. Still, MRI may appear normal in patients with frontal lobe seizures (Jobst and Williamson, 2005).

Other imaging techniques may also prove useful in diagnosis. Fluorode oxyglucose-PET and ictal single photon emission computed tomography (SPECT) are helpful when a patient has already been diagnosed with FLE and surgical intervention is a consideration (Bernasconi, 2003; Engel, Henry, & Risinger, 1990; Ryvlin et al., 1998). MRI can be helpful when there are structural lesions; however, its clinical utility is diminished when a patient has intractable frontal lobe seizures without evidence of a structural lesion as it cannot adequately help in the localization or lateralization of the epileptogenic focus. PET studies have not demonstrated much benefit in patients without space-occupying lesions already visualized by CT or MRI. While SPECT has been useful for generally evaluating seizures and particularly seizures of the frontal lobe, results are variable depending on when the study was conducted, during the ictal or interictal period (Henry, Sutherling, & Engel, 1991; Swartz, Halgren, & Delgado Escueta, 1989).

To aid in making the diagnosis, scales have been developed that are based on the clinical features of FLE and parasomnias. Tools based on these scales give considerable attention to disorders frequently confused with NFLE—particularly NREM sleep parasomnias (i.e., sleep walking and night terrors). Clinical features incorporated into the scales include age of onset, duration of event, typical number of events per night, time of night, aura, wandering, complex behaviors, dystonic posturing/tonic limb extension, cramping, stereotypy, recollection, and vocalization. Derry, Davey, and Johns (2006) found that NFLE can be reliably diagnosed using clinical history using the frontal lobe epilepsy and parasomnias (FLEP) scale and therefore may be particularly helpful for clinicians with limited experience with NFLE (Tables 17.3 and 17.4). Another study conducted by Manni, Terzaghi,

TABLE 17.3 Clinical Features Examined in the Frontal Lobe Epilepsy and Parasomnias Scale

Clinical Feature		Score
Age of onset of the first clinical event	<55 years	0
	≥55 years	−1
Duration of typical event	<2 min	+1
	2−10 min	0
	>10 min	−2
Is there clustering of events/how many occur in a single night?	1 or 2	0
	3−5	+1
	>5	+2
What time of night do events most commonly occur?	Within 30 min of sleep onset	+1
	Other times (including no clear pattern)	0
Are the events associated with a distinct aura?	Yes	+2
	No	0
Are there episodes of wandering outside the bedroom during events?	Yes	−2
	No (or uncertain)	0
Are their complex, directed behaviors during events?	Yes	−2
	No (or uncertain)	0
Is there a clear history of prominent dystonic posturing, limb extension, or cramping during events?	Yes	+1
	No (or uncertain)	0
Is there stereotypy between events?	Highly stereotyped	+1
	Some variability/uncertain	0
	Highly variable	−1
Does the patient recall the event?	Yes, lucid recall	+1
	No (or vague recollection only)	0
Does the patient speak during events/is there subsequent recollection of speech?	No	0
	Yes, sounds/single words only	0
	Yes, coherent speech with incomplete/no recall	−2
	Yes, coherent speech with recall	+2

TABLE 17.4 Interpretation of Frontal Lobe Epilepsy and Parasomnias Scale

Score	Interpretation
≤ 0	Unlikely to have epilepsy
+1 to +3	Relatively high chance of epilepsy, further investigation is required
≥ +3	Very likely to have epilepsy

and Repetto (2008) found that the FLEP scale has high positive and negative predictive values in distinguishing NFLE from other parasomnias and REM sleep behavior disorders. Nevertheless, they also found that there was a risk of misdiagnosis and was inconclusive in about one-third of cases (particularly in patients who presented with episodes of nocturnal wandering) and the FLEP scale's sensitivity and negative predictive value were determined to be lower than those found in the initial validation study. Further exploration of the utility of this scale and a consistent algorithm to guide clinicians in diagnosis is still warranted.

The gold standard for diagnosis remains vEEG monitoring in conjunction with clinical history.

CONCLUSION

FLE is the second most common type of epilepsy. Despite advances in diagnostic approaches, it often remains a diagnostic and therapeutic challenge. Some ictal presentations seem to be clearly localizing and typical of a certain anatomical area, e.g., seizures originating from the frontal mesial region with subsequent bilateral asymmetric tonic posturing. However, other ictal manifestations such as bizarre behavior as seen in seizures with RMA, dystonic−dyskinetic posturing, or autonomic seizures are difficult to localize to a specific cortical frontal area. One important consideration is that ictal cortical discharges are not merely confined to the orbitofrontal region but disinhibit other cortical (deep temporal) or subcortical structures responsible for many of the bizarre clinical presentations. To render the diagnosis even more challenging is the fact that both scalp and intracranial EEG studies can be misleading due to limitations in sampling of different regions of the frontal lobe. The limitations of neuroimaging in detecting underlying structural pathologies is yet another factor. Advances in genetic sequencing is rapidly contributing to our understanding of the frontal lobe epilepsies and hold potential for future diagnostic approaches. At the present time, diagnosis relies primarily on a careful and structured history and physical assessment combined with EEG studies.

REFERENCES

American Psychiatric Association (2013). *Diagnostic and statistical manual of mental disorders: DSM-5*. Washington, DC: American Psychiatric Association.

Bancaud, J., & Tailarach, J. (1992). Clinical semeiology of frontal lobe seizures. In P. Chauvel, A. Delgado-Escueta, et al. *Frontal lobe seizures and epilepsies* (pp. 3–58). New York, NY: Raven Press, Advances in Neurology. Vol 57.

Bernasconi, A. (2003). Advanced MRI analysis methods for detection of focal cortical dysplasia. *Epileptic Disorders: International Epilepsy Journal With Videotape, 5*(Suppl 2), S81–S84.

Birabena, A., Taussigb, D., Thomasd, P., et al. (2001). Fear as the main feature of epileptic seizures. *Journal of Neurology, Neurosurgery, and Psychiatry, 70*, 186–191.

Bisulli, F., Vignatelli, L., Provini, F., et al. (2011). Parasomnias and nocturnal frontal lobe epilepsy (NFLE): Lights and shadows—Controversial points in the differential diagnosis. *Sleep Medicine, 12*, S27–S32.

Braakman, H. M. H., Vaessen, M. J., et al. (2011). Cognitive and behavioral complications of frontal lobe epilepsy in children: A review of the literature. *Epilepsia, 52*, 849–856.

Chauvel, P., Kliemann, F., Vignal, J. P., et al. (1995). The clinical signs and symptoms of frontal lobe seizures: Phenomenology and classification. In H. H. Jasper, S. Riggio, & P. Goldman-Rakic (Eds.), *Epilepsy and the functional anatomy of the frontal lobe* (pp. 115–126). New York, NY: Raven Press, Advances in Neurology. Vol 66.

Combi, R., Ferini-Strambi, L., & Tenchini, M. L. (2008). Compound heterozygosity with dominance in the corticotropin releasing hormone (CRH) promotor in a case of nocturnal frontal lobe epilepsy. *Journal of Sleep Research, 17*, 361–362.

Derry, C. P. (2011). The sleep manifestations of frontal lobe epilepsy. *Current Neurology and Neuroscience Reports, 11*, 218–226.

Derry, C. P., Davey, M., Johns, M., et al. (2006). Distinguishing sleep disorders from seizures: Diagnosing bumps in the night. *Archives of Neurology, 63*, 705–709.

Engel, J. J., Henry, T. H., Risinger, M. W., et al. (1990). Presurgical evaluation for partial epilepsy: Relative contributions of chronic depth electrode recordings versus FDG-PET and scalp sphenoidal ictal EEG. *Neurology, 40*, 1670–1677.

Ferini-Strambi, L., Sansoni, V., & Combi, R. (2012). Nocturnal frontal lobe epilepsy and the acetylcholine receptor. *Neurologist, 18*, 343–349.

Geier, J., Bancaud, J., Talairach, J., et al. (1976). Automatisms during frontal lobe epileptic seizures. *Brain, 99*, 447–458.

Goodin, D. S., Aminoff, M. J., & Laser, K. D. (1990). Detection of epileptiform activity by different non invasive EEG methods in complex partial epilepsy. *Annals of Neurology, 27*, 330–334.

Henry, T. R., Sutherling, W. W., Engel, J., et al. (1991). Interictal cerebral metabolism in partial epilepsies of neocortical origin. *Epilepsy Research, 10*, 174–182.

Heron, S. E., Smith, K. R., Bahlo, M., et al. (2012). Missense mutations in the sodium-gated potassium channel gene KCNT1 cause severe autosomal dominant nocturnal frontal lobe epilepsy. *Nature Genetics, 44*, 1188–1190.

Ishida, S., Picard, F., Rudolf, G., et al. (2013). Mutations of DEPDC5 cause autosomal dominant focal epilepsies. *Nature Genetics, 45*, 552–555.

Jobst, B. C., Siegel, A. M., Thadani, V. M., et al. (2000). Intractable seizures of frontal origin. *Epilepsia, 41*, 1139–1152.

Jobst, B. C., & Williamson, P. D. (2005). Frontal lobe seizures. *Psychiatric Clinics of North America, 28*, 635–651.

Kanner, A. M. (2011). Ictal panic and interictal panic attacks: Diagnostic and therapeutic principles. *Neurologic Clinics, 29,* 163–175.

Manni, R., Terzaghi, M., & Repetto, A. (2008). The FLEP scale in diagnosing nocturnal frontal lobe epilepsy, NREM and REM parasomnias: Data from a tertiary sleep and epilepsy unit. *Epilepsia, 49,* 1581–1585.

Nobili, L. (2007). Nocturnal frontal lobe epilepsy and non-rapid eye movement sleep parasomnias: Differences and similarities. *Sleep Medicine Reviews, 11,* 251–254.

O'Muircheartaigh, J., & Richardson, M. P. (2012). Epilepsy and the frontal lobes. *Cortex: A Journal Devoted to the Study of the Nervous System and Behavior, 48,* 144–155.

Penfield, W., & Rasmussen, T. (1949). Vocalization and arrest of speech. *Archives of Neurology and Psychiatry, 61,* 21–27.

Philips, H. A., Scheffer, I. E., Berkovic, S. F., et al. (1995). Localization of a gene for autosomal dominant nocturnal frontal lobe epilepsy to chromosome 20q 13.2. *Nature Genetics, 10,* 117–118.

Picard, F. (2005). Alteration of the in vivo nicotinic receptor density in ADNFLE patients: A PET study. *Brain, 129,* 2047–2060.

Provini, F., Plazzi, G., Tinuper, P., et al. (1999). Nocturnal frontal lobe epilepsy. A clinical and polygraphic overview of 100 consecutive cases. *Brain, 122,* 1017–1031.

Rassmussen, T., & Anderman, F. (1989). Update on the syndrome of "chronic encephalitis" and epilepsy. *Cleveland Clinic Journal of Medicine, 56*(suppl. Part 2), S5181–S5184.

Riggio, S. (1995). Frontal lobe epilepsy: Clinical syndromes and presurgical evaluation. *Journal of Epilepsy, 8,* 178–189.

Riggio, S., & Harner, R. N. (1995). Repetitive motor activity in frontal lobe epilepsy. In H. H. Jasper, S. Riggio, & P. Goldman-Rakic (Eds.), *Epilepsy and the functional anatomy of the frontal lobe* (pp. 153–166). New York, NY: Raven Press, Advances in Neurology. Vol 66.

Ryvlin, P., Bouvard, S., Le Bars, D., et al. (1998). Clinical utility of flumazenil-PET versus [18F]fluorodeoxyglucose-PET and MRI in refractory partial epilepsy: A prospective study in 100 patients. *Brain, 121*(Pt 11), 2067–2081.

Ryvlin, P., Rheims, S., & Risse, G. (2006). Nocturnal frontal lobe epilepsy. *Epilepsia, 47*(suppl 2), 83–86.

Steinlein, O. K., Hoda, J. C., Betrand, S., & Betrand, D. (2012). Mutations in familial nocturnal frontal lobe epilepsy might be associated with distinct neurological phenotypes. *Seizure: The Journal of the British Epilepsy Association, 21,* 118–123.

Swartz, B. E., Halgren, E., Delgado Escueta, A. V., et al. (1989). Neuroimaging in patients with seizures of probable frontal lobe origin. *Epilepsia, 30,* 547–558.

Tinuper, P., Provini, F., Bisulli, F., & Lugaresi, E. (2005). Hyperkinetic manifestations in nocturnal frontal lobe epilepsy. Semeiological features and physiopathological hypothesis. *Neurological Sciences: Official Journal of the Italian Neurological Society and of the Italian Society of Clinical Neurophysiology, 26,* s210–s214.

Waterman, K., Purves, S. J., Kosaka, B., et al. (1987). An epileptic syndrome caused by mesial frontal lobe foci. *Neurology, 37,* 577–582.

Williamson, P., Wieser, H., & Delgado Escueta, A. (1987). Clinical characteristics of partial seizures. In J. Engel, T. Babb, P. Crandall, et al. *Surgical treatment of the epilepsies* (pp. 101–123). New York, NY: Raven Press.

Williamson, P. D., & Jobst, B. C. (2000). Frontal lobe epilepsy. In P. D. Williamson, et al. (Eds.), *Advances in neurology* (pp. 215–242). Philadelphia, PA: Lippincott Williams & Wilkins.

Williamson, P. D., Spencer, D. D., Spencer, S. S., et al. (1985a). Complex partial seizures of frontal origin. *Annals of Neurology, 18*, 497−504.

Williamson, P. D., Spencer, D. D., Spencer, S. S., et al. (1985b). Complex partial status epilepticus: A depth-electrode study. *Annals of Neurology, 18*, 647−654.

Williamson, P. D., & Spencer, S. S. (1986). Clinical and EEG features of complex partial seizures of extratemporal origin. *Epilepsia, 27*(suppl 2), S46−S63.

Young, G. B., Chandarana, P. C., Blume, W. T., et al. (1995). Mesial temporal lobe seizures presenting as anxiety disorders. *Journal of Neuropsychiatry and Clinical Neurosciences, 7*, 352−357.

Chapter 18

Executive Functions After Traumatic Brain Injury: From Deficit to Recovery

Irene Cristofori[1,2] and Jordan Grafman[1,2,3]

[1]*Cognitive Neuroscience Laboratory, Rehabilitation Institute of Chicago, Chicago, IL, United States,* [2]*Department of Physical Medicine and Rehabilitation, Feinberg School of Medicine, Northwestern University, Chicago, IL, United States,* [3]*Department of Neurology, Feinberg School of Medicine, Northwestern University, Chicago, IL, United States*

Before discussing the effects of traumatic brain injury (TBI) on executive functions (EF), we begin this chapter with a brief discussion of TBI. We will primarily discuss studies of the effects of closed TBI on EF but occasionally refer to some of our own EF studies with penetrating TBI (pTBI) patients.

TRAUMATIC BRAIN INJURY

TBI is the principal cause of death and disability worldwide; in the United States alone, 1.7 million new TBIs occur every year among individuals younger than 35 years (Faul, Xu, Wald, Coronado, & Dellinger, 2010). TBI is an alteration in brain structure or function caused by external forces (Menon et al., 2010) that results in vascular and axonal damage, edema, and neuronal cell death (Zetterberg, Smith, & Blennow, 2013). TBI may result in a cascade of pathological events including local neural dysfunction and/or disruption of neural networks. Moderate and severe TBI can lead to lifelong impairments. More than 3 million individuals in the United States are living with chronic disabilities because of TBI (Zaloshnja, Miller, Langlois, & Selassie, 2008). TBI-related chronic disability predicts difficulty in day-to-day life such as returning to work or reintegrating socially resulting in a decreased quality of life.

TBI is typically evaluated in the emergency department with scales such as the Glasgow Coma Scale (Teasdale & Jennett, 1974), which estimates current level of consciousness, presence of posttraumatic amnesia, response to commands, and pain. Structural neuroimaging is usually obtained at the

Executive Functions in Health and Disease. DOI: http://dx.doi.org/10.1016/B978-0-12-803676-1.00018-0

421

same time. TBI can be classified into three levels of severity: mild, moderate, and severe, as summarized in Table 18.1.

TBI can also be characterized on the basis of the physical mechanism causing the damage: closed, penetrating, blast, and concussion, as shown in Table 18.2.

TABLE 18.1 Classification of Traumatic Brain Injury Severity

	Mild	Moderate	Severe
Glasgow Coma Scale	13–15	9–12	3–8
Loss of consciousness	<30 min	>30 min <24 h	>24 h
Posttraumatic amnesia	<24 h	>24 h <7 days	≥7 days
Altered consciousness	≤24 h	>24 h	>24 h
Structural neuroimaging	Normal	Normal or abnormal	Normal or abnormal

TABLE 18.2 Classification of TBI Based on the Physical Mechanism

Closed TBI	• Rapid rotations, accelerations/decelerations, shaking of the brain within the skull, or impact to the skull itself • Results from motor vehicle accident • Severity depends on LOC
Penetrating TBI	• Focal brain lesions produced by the entrance of an external object into the brain • Results from projectiles or knife wounds (in civilians); blast-related shrapnel or missile injuries (in military) • Severity depends on location and extension of the lesion
Blast TBI	• Primary: Wave-induced changes in atmospheric pressure caused by a blast explosion • Secondary: penetrating and blunt trauma • Tertiary: body is displaced, striking a surface • Quaternary: toxic inhalation and radiation
Concussion	• High-impact sport-related trauma (including boxing, American football, ice hockey, soccer, and rugby) • Direct bump, blow, or jolt to the head, but also from a fall or a blow to the body that causes the brain to move rapidly back and forth • Repeated concussions are associated with longer clinical recovery and chronic traumatic encephalopathy

LOC, loss of consciousness; *TBI*, traumatic brain injury.

EXECUTIVE FUNCTION DEFICITS AFTER TRAUMATIC BRAIN INJURY

EF are a complex set of cognitive abilities including planning, initiating, monitoring, problem solving, inhibitory control, and metacognition (Cicerone et al., 2000; Kennedy et al., 2008). These functions manage and control other cognitive abilities (e.g., attention and memory) and enable adaptation to novel and complex scenarios (Collette, Hogge, Salmon, & Van der Linden, 2006). Growing evidence suggests that EF deficits cause short- and long-term consequences, resulting in poor goal-directed behavior (Busch, McBride, Curtiss, & Vanderploeg, 2005; Hanks, Rapport, Millis, & Deshpande, 1999). These deficits lead to lower quality and dependent social functioning (Busch et al., 2005).

Working Memory

Working memory is used to hold information online during the execution of other cognitive functions. According to the Baddeley and Hitch model (Baddeley & Hitch, 1974), working memory consists of two subsystems and a central executive. The two subsystems are the visual spatial sketchpad and the phonological loop, storing and processing, temporarily, visual and verbal information. The central executive is responsible for distributing resources between the visual spatial sketchpad and the phonological loop. The central executive system has limited capacity; therefore, tasks requiring multitasking can be challenging (Baddeley & Hitch, 1974).

Only a few studies have examined working memory after TBI. Perlstein et al. (2004) studied parametric modulation of the working memory load on the n-back task in mild, moderate, and severe TBI patients (Perlstein et al., 2004). During the n-back task, a series of stimuli is presented and subjects have to indicate if the current stimulus matches one that appeared earlier in the series. An increase in n increases working memory load, making the task more demanding. Because a decision needs to be made after each stimulus, the n-back task requires a continuous online updating of information in working memory. The findings of this study showed that compared to mild TBI patients and healthy controls, moderate and severe TBI patients made more errors when challenged with a greater working memory load (e.g., 2- and 3-back). In the same study, functional magnetic resonance imaging (fMRI) revealed that an increased working memory load corresponded to an increase in brain activity in both TBI and controls. However, moderate and severe TBI patients showed increased activity in the dorsolateral prefrontal cortex (dlPFC) and Broca's areas as an effect of increased working memory load. Their selective impairment at higher loads on the n-back task suggests that moderate and severe TBI patients have specific deficits in coding and maintaining sequential information.

More recently, Sanchez-Carrion et al. (2008) performed a longitudinal study on working memory impairments after TBI. In this study, the authors examined brain activation during an n-back task, while TBI patients underwent fMRI in two separate sessions at 6-month intervals. Over time, TBI patients exhibited changes in brain activation. During the first evaluation, both groups showed bilateral frontoparietal region activation during the n-back task. Activation in the right superior frontal gyrus was lower in the TBI group compared to controls. Remarkably, the neural and behavioral differences between the TBI and matched controls were reduced after 6 months. Indeed, at 6 months after the first evaluation, TBI patients showed increased activation in the right superior frontal cortex and improved performance on the n-back task (Sanchez-Carrion et al., 2008). More longitudinal studies are needed because they provide key evidence of progressive recovery of EF after brain injury.

Inhibition

Inhibition is an EF that interacts with working memory and cognitive control to monitor and control adaptive behaviors. Examples of inhibition-based tasks include withholding or suppressing a response which is no longer relevant (e.g., go/no-go task) or suppressing the recovery of irrelevant information from memory (e.g., directed forgetting). Even mild TBI patients may show inhibition deficits, especially during the acute (Mayer et al., 2009) phase (Bate, Mathias, & Crawford, 2001) of the recovery process. In a recent study of TBI patients, Mayer et al. (2009) found that inhibition deficits were linked to hyperactivation of several brain regions including the right posterior parietal cortex, presupplementary motor area, bilateral frontal eye fields, and right ventrolateral prefrontal cortex (PFC; Mayer et al., 2009).

Cognitive Flexibility

Shifting is an EF ability that allows us to switch from one task to another, and it is linked with inhibition and working memory. Shifting ability is frequently impaired in individuals with PFC damage. This ability has been widely investigated using the Wisconsin Card Sorting Test (WCST; Milner, 1963). Successful performance on the WCST requires more than simply shifting ability: conceptualizing the sorting criteria, making hypothesis about the criteria, monitoring the performance, and using feedback to modify the strategy once the rule has changed are necessary to adequately perform this task. Individuals with PFC damage fail to switch between criteria after a rule change and they perseverate in their behavior. Levin et al. (1993) reported that the number of correctly sorted categories to criterion on the WCST was associated with TBI severity and the volume of damage to the left PFC (Levin et al., 1993).

Planning

Planning is a higher level cognitive function that includes EF processes involved in the formulation, evaluation, and selection of actions required to attain a goal. Planning ability has been studied using various tasks, including the Tower of London (Shallice, 1982). This task requires the subject to rearrange beads on three vertical rods to match a model in as few moves as possible. The Tower of London relies on working memory to reach intermediate goals, while the final goal is maintained in memory. The capacity to recognize and use the optimal strategy to plan a set of actions to achieve a goal has been linked to dlPFC (Cabeza & Nyberg, 2000). Another common test used to measure planning and problem-solving abilities is the Tower of Hanoi puzzle. Goel and Grafman (1995) tested TBI patients with focal lesions in the PFC on the Tower of Hanoi. TBI patients showed lower performance than controls, after accounting for intelligence, memory, and lesion size. These findings suggest that both TBI and controls used the same general strategy to solve the problems and that TBI performance was best explained in terms of an inability to solve a goal−subgoal conflict. The authors' interpretation is compatible with several existing theories of frontal lobe dysfunction that postulate a failure of inhibition of dominant responses (Goel & Grafman, 1995).

Taken together, these studies show that EF impairments are a common outcome after mild, moderate, and severe TBI. Because EFs are crucial in everyday life, EF deficits limit functional independence. For this reason, remediating EF deficits represents one of the biggest challenges for researchers and clinicians involved in TBI patient rehabilitation.

LOCATION OF BRAIN LESIONS ASSOCIATED WITH EF DEFICITS

The PFC is the brain region most associated with EF. The PFC is also frequently damaged after TBI (Adams, Graham, Scott, Parker, & Doyle, 1980; Levin et al., 1987). Studies involving individuals with pTBI have documented that both the dorsolateral and orbitofrontal parts of the PFC are associated with EF impairments (Barbey et al., 2012; Barbey, Koenigs, & Grafman, 2011). Individuals with lesions to different parts of the PFC may present with the so-called *dysexecutive syndrome* (Baddeley & Wilson, 1988). This syndrome affects cognition, emotion, social behavior, and goal-oriented behavior (Brooks, Fos, Greve, & Hammond, 1999; Cicerone et al., 2000; Gansler, Covall, McGrath, & Oscar-Berman, 1996). Damage to the orbitofrontal cortex and anterior cingulate cortex leads to social behavior and motivated behavior deficits. Individuals with lesions to the dlPFC have higher order cognitive problems involving goal-directed behaviors (al-Adawi, Powell, & Greenwood, 1998), cognitive control (Larson, Perlstein, Demery, & Stigge-Kaufman, 2006), inhibition (Picton et al., 2007), planning (Cicerone & Wood, 1987; Shallice, 1982), and working memory (Serino et al., 2006). Because these deficits impair patients' everyday activities, they are considered good predictors of negative outcomes (Reid-Arndt, Nehl, & Hinkebein, 2007; Villki et al., 1994).

More recently, Cristofori et al. (2015) investigated the association between regional white and gray matter volume loss and performance on EF in patients with pTBI (Cristofori et al., 2015). This study showed that white matter integrity after brain damage had an important influence on recovery. Voxel-based lesion-symptom analysis revealed that damage to the PFC gray matter, anterior corona radiata, and superior longitudinal fasciculus was associated with a poorer functional recovery. Verbal fluency, which relies on the fronto-temporo-parietal network, was best predicted by a lesion in the superior longitudinal fasciculus. The Trail Making and Twenty Questions tasks, which are linked to more focal left frontal damage, were better predicted by PFC lesions. White matter damage may place additional burden on recovery by impairing signal transmission between cortical areas within a functional brain network. A more accurate understanding of the relative roles of gray and white matter damage for impairing functional recovery will be useful to clinicians planning and projecting individualized therapeutic interventions.

NEUROPSYCHOLOGICAL TESTING TO ASSESS EF IN TBI

Standard Tests of Executive Functions

Several neuropsychological tests assess these complex abilities, including the WCST (i.e., assessing the ability to learn and shift rules; Milner, 1963), the Trail Making part B (i.e., assessing the ability of shifting; Armitage, 1946), and the Stroop Color Word Interference Test (i.e., assessing the ability of inhibition of irrelevant information; Perret, 1974).

Ecological Tests for Evaluating Executive Functions

The challenge in evaluating EF derives not only from determining the appropriate tests to administer but also from assessing the importance of EF in ecological settings. Several measures address the need for ecological evaluations of EF, but most of them require the input of a caregiver to compare to self-report by the TBI patient. For example, the Frontal Systems Behavior Scale (FrSBe; Grace & Malloy, 2001a) evaluates apathy, disinhibition, and executive dysfunctions. In a recent study, Reid-Arndt et al. (2007) found that the FrSBe was a good predictor of TBI patient community reintegration (Reid-Arndt et al., 2007). A lower EF score predicted less community reintegration. Standard neuropsychological tests were unrelated to community reintegration after outcome. Because the FrSBe is a good predictor of functional outcomes such as social reintegration, its addition to the standard neurobehavioral could be useful.

Another questionnaire with ecological validity for evaluating EF is the Brock Adaptive Functioning Questionnaire (BAFQ) (Dywan & Segalowitz, 1996). The BAFQ evaluates the frequency of EF deficits in 12 domains: planning, initiation, flexibility, excess caution, attention, memory, arousal level, emotionality, impulsivity, aggressiveness, social monitoring, and empathy. Simpson and collaborators (2002) claimed that the BAFQ is able to distinguish between individuals with TBI who might return to their preinjury employment level from those who might require employment reassignment (Simpson & Schmitter-Edgecombe, 2002).

Ecological measures of EF can complement an objective test-based evaluation to better estimate the TBI patient's potential to resume everyday adaptive functioning. Moreover, along with standard neuropsychological assessments, an ecological evaluation can help to define more tailored interventions to improve EF.

EXECUTIVE FUNCTION NEUROPLASTICITY AND TRAUMATIC BRAIN INJURY

TBI leads to a cascade of neurochemical responses and may also cause a neural network to structurally and functionally reorganize itself (Pascual-Leone, Amedi, Fregni, & Merabet, 2005). Rewiring and reshaping neural connections can lead to unimpaired brain regions assuming the functions of a damaged region. Neuroplasticity after TBI involves processes such as the unmasking of previously latent synapses, synaptic alteration of receptor sensitivity, dendritic growth, collateral sprouting of new synaptic connections, and arborization from neighboring undamaged neural structures (Jang et al., 2005). Neuronal loss and white matter disruptions throughout the brain are common outcomes after moderate and severe TBI (Ewing-Cobbs et al., 2008; Wilde et al., 2006). As a consequence, TBI may result in posttraumatic epilepsy (Lowenstein, 2009), inappropriate neuronal rewiring (Giza & Hovda, 2014), and abnormal neuronal responses (D'Ambrosio, Maris, Grady, Winn, & Janigro, 1998). Recent studies in an animal TBI model revealed long-term impaired plasticity even in remote, noninjured cortical areas (Li et al., 2014). This was demonstrated by a decrease in the ability to induce long-term potentiation—a major cellular mechanism of plasticity—and neuronal hypoactivity. The claim of neural hypoactivity was supported by an observed decrease in evoked neuronal responses in contralateral, noninjured cortical neurons. Neuronal hypoactivity after TBI has been considered a key factor in post-injury epileptogenesis (Ping & Jin, 2016) thus contributing to persistent neurological and cognitive disability.

Attempts to Remediate EF After TBI

Even in healthy individuals, it has been difficult to demonstrate improved EF after training (Lindelov et al., 2016). Researchers often look for direct training effects versus transfer of training effects. This distinction is known as domain-specific versus domain-general or near-transfer versus far transfer. Instead, the evidence shows a prevalence of *domain-specific* effects of rehabilitation interventions. There is little evidence of transfer of the trained skill to untrained skills. More recent research efforts are aiming to promote such a transfer, especially using computer-based cognitive interventions. A key factor in fostering far transfer is adaptivity. Positive results have been found in healthy subjects (Jaeggi, Buschkuehl, Jonides, & Shah, 2011). However, adaptivity is not always found (Chooi & Thompson, 2012; Jaeggi et al., 2011). Other factors, such as training intensity, duration, and time intervals between sessions, could be influential but the results are unclear (Chein & Morrison, 2010). Working memory is considered to be domain-general because it operates on a wide range of stimuli and in diverse contexts (Kane et al., 2004). As a consequence, improved working memory performance should lead to better performances on all tasks that depend on working memory. If that improvement was brought about by training, then such an effect would be considered far transfer. In contrast, domain-specific processes apply to a narrow range of stimuli and contexts. For example, Westerberg et al. (2007) and Lundqvist, Grundström, Samuelsson, and Rönnberg (2010) administered the CogMed training program to TBI patients and observed improvements on digit span and a spatial span task, but both tasks were part of the training program (Lundqvist et al. 2010; Westerberg et al., 2007). Therefore, these results could be attributed to mere training effects specific to those tasks although the authors suggested that the training led to more generally improved working memory. Others assessed this testing–training similarity effect and found narrow transfer effects (Sturm & Willmes, 1991). In rehabilitation, the prevalence of training effects over transfer effects supports in choosing compensatory interventions over remediation of specific skills in many but not all situations.

Recently, Lindeløv et al. (2016) performed a controlled randomized trial where TBI patients and healthy controls completed training on an n-back task. The healthy group showed greater improvements compared to the TBI patients, but neither group showed transfer to untrained tasks, such as digit span. The authors claimed that computerized training improve specific skills rather than high-level cognition. The most effective use of computerized training may be to make the task resemble the targeted behaviors to exploit the stimulus-specificity of learning.

As suggested by Lindeløv et al. (2016), future studies on computerized cognitive interventions may progress along two different routes (Lindelov et al., 2016). Training on a large array of different tasks may not be the best strategy to help TBI patients as demonstrated by several null findings from those who used it (Chen et al., 1997; Middleton, Lambert, & Seggar, 1991). A true context-breaking intervention would constantly present novel problems, shift between devices, change colors, be trained at different locations, etc. We suspect that this approach would be too chaotic to be effectively used with TBI patients. An alternative approach, as mentioned above, would be to exploit context-specific effects and make the training task as similar to the transfer target as possible. For example, you might ask the TBI patient to practice reading television subtitles or doing mental arithmetic with shopping costs. Yip and Man (2013) successfully improved real-life shopping performance after training patients in a similar virtual reality environment (Yip & Man, 2013). This is a much less ambitious target than training high-level cognition, but it may be a more pragmatic approach.

RECOVERY OF EF AFTER TBI

Recovering from a TBI depends upon the severity of the level of injury (i.e., mild, moderate, or severe). Normally, individuals with a mild TBI return to their preinjury cognitive level within 3−6 months (Belanger, Curtiss, Demery, Lebowitz, & Vanderploeg, 2005; Schretlen & Shapiro, 2003), whereas individuals with moderate and severe TBI recover slower and often they are not able to return to their preinjury cognitive level (Dikmen, Machamer, Powell, & Temkin, 2003). Although the recovery process is associated with injury severity, it is important to recognize that recovery is an individualized process depending on many factors including age, health, preinjury cognitive level (Raymont et al., 2008), genetic and epigenetic predisposition, and social milieu. The combination of these factors determines the pattern of recovery from TBI (Faul, Xu, Wald, & Coronado, 2010). Generally, 85%−95% of persons who have suffered a mild TBI will make a complete recovery when compared to 60% of those who have experienced a moderate TBI and 15%−20% who have experienced a severe TBI (Faul et al., 2010). At 1-year post-injury, 47% of hospitalized TBI patients reported functional difficulties (Pickelsimer, Selassie, Gu, & Langlois, 2006) and 24% of patients with moderate-to-severe TBI failed to return to work (Whiteneck et al., 2004). Similarly, only 56% of pTBI patients were employed 15 years following their injury (Schwab, Grafman, Salazar, & Kraft, 1993).

Cognitive Rehabilitation of Executive Functions

EF are characterized by a number of subcomponents. To date, cognitive rehabilitation has aimed at improving specific subcomponents rather than the entire EF domain. Cognitive rehabilitation of EF is crucial because this cognitive domain significantly affects everyday life and social functioning.

Some EF training studies focus on awareness of EF deficits during the treatment. For example, Goverover and collaborators (2007) studied the effects of training on instrumental activities of daily living (IADL) in moderate-to-severe TBI patients. The experimental group completed the IADL along with self-awareness training, whereas the control group completed the IADL training only. Participants in the experimental group had to forecast performance before each task and assess performance after completing the task. Compared to the control group, the experimental group showed better IADL performances and self-regulation (Goverover et al., 2007). More recently, Toglia and collaborators (2010) conducted a single-subject trial design, using a multicontext approach to promote strategy use across situations and increase self-regulation, awareness, and functional performance (Toglia et al., 2010). Sessions were divided into three phases: error discovery, strategy, and reinforcement. All participants demonstrated positive changes in self-regulation and strategy use. These results provide support for the feasibility of cognitive rehabilitation therapies to enhance functional performance and awareness. However, larger controlled studies are needed to confirm or qualify these observations (Toglia et al., 2010).

Another group of EF training studies did not take deficit awareness into account. For instance, in the study from Evans and collaborators (2009), the authors assessed the efficacy of cognitive-motor dual-task training to enhance the performance of TBI patients with EF impairments. This treatment included exercises such as walking in combination with tasks of increasing cognitive load. The "treatment" group was compared to a "no treatment" group. The primary outcome measure was a task requiring participants to walk and carry out a spoken sentence. Secondary outcome measures involved performing either two motor tasks or two cognitive tasks. The findings revealed better performance on the primary outcome measure but little generalization to other measures in the treatment group (Evans et al., 2009). Similarly, Hewitt and collaborators (2006) assessed the ability of TBI patients to develop a plan to accomplish a familiar task such as planning a trip. The outcome measures were number of steps listed and effectiveness of the plan. These measures were assessed after the training by blinded raters. Both groups improved on these measures. However, the strategy training group improved more from pre- to post-training. This study indicates that combining learning and using strategies is useful in improving complex planning (Hewitt et al., 2006).

Individuals with EF impairments have relative preservation of verbal knowledge. However, they may fail to use this knowledge to guide goal-oriented behaviors. Goal Management Training (GMT) is a well-established rehabilitation technique focused on goal-directed behaviors. The aim of this training is to monitor and adjust goals during ongoing behavior (Levine et al., 2000; Robertson, 1996). This approach is based on a theory of sustained attention (Robertson & Garavan, 2000). This theory claims that the right fronto-thalamic-parietal network provides the neural support for ongoing activation of attention, and it allows for the maintenance of higher order goals in working memory. Impairments in sustained attention may determine a displacement of higher order goals (e.g., preparing a dinner or posting a letter), resulting in inadequate and distracted behaviors. The GMT consists of five steps: (1) orient awareness toward the actual state of the situation; (2) define the goal of the task; (3) list subgoals; (4) learn the subgoals; and (5) check if the result of an action corresponds to the stated goal. In the case of a discrepancy, the steps are repeated. Levine et al. (2000) assessed the effectiveness of GMT in patients with TBI. Participants were randomly assigned to GMT or motor skills training. Only participants enrolled in the GMT improved on paper-and-pencil tasks. This study provided support for the efficacy of GMT for improving EFs (Levine et al., 2000). Levine et al. (2011) replicated the effectiveness of GMT for the treatment of EF in patients with frontal lobes damage (Levine, Schweizer, O'Connor, et al., 2011). The authors compared an extended version of GMT to an alternative intervention, the Brain Health Workshop. The findings provided evidence of the beneficial effects of GMT on sustained attention and visuospatial problem solving, reflecting generalization of training (Levine, Schweizer, O'Connor, et al., 2011).

From Executive Function Rehabilitation to Social Reintegration

EF deficits reduce individuals' abilities to regain satisfactory social lives. Understanding the processes that promote social reintegration after a TBI that involve EF deficits is challenging. Libin and collaborators (2015) are attempting to address this urgent need (Libin et al., 2011). They developed the Community Participation through Self-Efficacy Skills Development program (COMPASS goal), a novel patient-centered intervention for community reintegration in veterans with mild TBI. COMPASS goals are based on the principles of goal self-management. Goal setting is a core skill in self-management training by which individuals learn to improve their abilities. Over a 3-year period, this ongoing project plans to recruit 110 participants with EF impairments at least 3 years post-injury. This program has strict inclusion criteria combining both clinical diagnosis and standardized scores that are >1 standard deviation from the normative score on the FrSBe (Grace & Malloy, 2001b). Participants will be randomized into two groups: goal management (training) and supported discharge (control). The training is administered in eight sessions. Assessments occur before training, after training, and 3 months posttraining. Goal management is the core of EF rehabilitation. However, collaborative goal setting between clinicians/case managers and patients can be delayed by the cognitive deficits that follow TBI. Training in goal management would treat deficits in EF and help individuals with TBI to regain social activities. A structured approach to goal self-management such as the COMPASS goal can foster greater independence and self-efficacy as well as help individuals with TBI to reach realistic goals.

Noninvasive Brain Stimulation: TMS and TDCS Studies in TBI

Noninvasive brain stimulation may enhance EF recovery after TBI through the causal induction of plasticity processes. Despite intensive cognitive training, a large majority of TBI fails to fully regain normal EF. Emerging research suggests that noninvasive brain stimulation tools, such as transcranial magnetic stimulation (TMS) and transcranial direct current stimulation (tDCS), in association with cognitive training may enhance cognitive recovery.

In TMS, a small coil held near the scalp generates a magnetic field that produces an electric field in the underlying brain areas. With the appropriate frequency and intensity of stimulation, TMS can be used to excite the specific brain regions. Animal TBI models have shown that a TBI results in abnormal neuronal hypoactivity even in nondamaged brain area. Reshaping abnormal post-injury neuronal activity may be an effective strategy to facilitate clinical rehabilitation effects. Lu et al. (2015) tested whether high-frequency TMS delivered twice a week over a 4-week period to rats could restore neuronal activity and improve neurophysiological and behavioral functions. The findings showed that TBI rats that underwent TMS therapy had increased evoked cortical responses (189%), evoked synaptic activity (46%), evoked neuronal firing (200%), and increased expression of cellular markers of neuroplasticity in the noninjured brain area compared to TBI rats that did not receive therapy. Notably, these rats showed less hyperactivity on behavioral tests. Recent studies have shown that enhancing bilateral dlPFC could improve EF deficits. Vanderhasselt and collaborators (2007) used high-frequency repetitive transcranial magnetic stimulation (rTMS) to excite dlPFC neurons in healthy participants during a task-switching paradigm (Vanderhasselt et al., 2007). The task-switching paradigm required switching between two conditional responses with mutually incompatible response selection rules. The results showed that reaction time on cued switching trials decreased with rTMS, when compared to noncued switch trials. No changes occurred after the sham condition where no magnetic stimulation is provided. Mood remained stable after rTMS. These findings demonstrated the importance of the right dlPFC in cued intentional set switch initiation.

TDCS uses low amplitude direct current to modify neuronal activity. Anodal or cathodal direct current polarization to induce neural firing changes has been used since the 1960s. Anodal tDCS elicits prolonged increases in neural excitability and facilitates regional brain activity, whereas cathodal tDCS elicits the opposite effects (Nitsche & Paulus, 2001). While the duration of the induced effects lasts the period of the stimulation, repeated stimulations reportedly results in effects lasting several weeks, a crucial feature regarding cortical plasticity (Boggio et al., 2007; Fregni et al., 2006).

Recently, Dockery and collaborators (2009) studied the effects of tDCS of the left dlPFC on planning functions (Dockery et al., 2009). They assessed performance on the Tower of London task during and after anodal, cathodal (1 mA, 15 minutes), and sham tDCS in 24 healthy participants. The results revealed a double dissociation of polarity and training phase. Better planning performances were found with cathodal tDCS during acquisition and early consolidation and with anodal tDCS in the later sessions. The findings indicated that both anodal and cathodal tDCS could improve planning performance. These data demonstrated training phase—specific effects of tDCS. The authors concluded that the excitability supported by decreasing cathodal tDCS mediates the early beneficial effect through noise reduction of neuronal activity, whereas the excitability supported by anodal tDCS is mediated by adaptive configurations of specific neuronal connections. The improvement in planning was maintained at 6 and 12 months after training. The specific coupling of stimulation and training phase interventions encourages its application to treating individuals suffering from TBI.

Taken together, TMS and tDCS studies suggest that noninvasive brain stimulation is a complementary tool for combating the adverse neuronal mechanisms activated following TBI.

GENETIC PREDISPOSITION, EXECUTIVE FUNCTIONS, AND TRAUMATIC BRAIN INJURY

Evidence has suggested that EF outcomes after TBI may be influenced by genetic polymorphisms.

Catechol-O-Methyltransferase

Dopamine plays a key role in the modulation of activities in the PFC during working EF tasks (Sawaguchi & Goldman-Rakic, 1991; Seamans, Floresco, & Phillips, 1998; Williams & Goldman-Rakic, 1995). These modulations have led researchers to become more interested in genes that influence dopamine levels and their role in EF. Catechol-O-methyltransferase (COMT) is an enzyme that metabolizes catecholamine neurotransmitters, such as dopamine, epinephrine, and norepinephrine. This enzyme, encoded by the COMT gene, is also an important regulator of dopamine levels in the PFC. Studies of COMT knockout mice showed that memory performance had improved (Gogos et al., 1998). Similarly, in humans, higher concentrations of catecholamine in the brain can result in better working memory performance following TBI. Specifically, the Val158Met polymorphism—a common COMT gene variation—is associated with cognitive control during working memory tasks (Goldberg et al., 2003). While the Met allele is associated with a reduction in COMT enzyme activity and subsequent increased levels of prefrontal dopamine, the Val allele is associated with high COMT enzyme activity and lower levels of prefrontal dopamine. As a consequence, individuals with the Met/Met genotype performed better on working memory tasks compared to individuals with at least one Val allele. Thus, individuals with the Met/Met genotype may respond better to working memory training compared to individuals with other polymorphisms. The Met allele may protect against the EF decline after TBI. Egan et al. (2001) found that the functional Val108/ 158 Met polymorphism in the COMT gene was associated with better EF performance on the WCST (Egan et al., 2001). In a more recent study, TBI patients with Met alleles also performed better on the WCST compared to TBI patients with Val alleles (Lipsky et al., 2005). This finding suggested that the COMT gene could influence EF recovery after TBI by modulating prefrontal dopamine availability.

Brain-derived Neurotrophic Factor

Another gene that might influence EF recovery after TBI is the brain-derived neurotrophic factor (BDNF). After TBI, the brain activates restoration mechanisms and promotes neuroregeneration, which is facilitated by a unique family of neurotrophic factors, including BDNF (Ray, Dixon, & Banik, 2002). BDNF promotes survival and synaptic plasticity in the brain (Binder & Scharfman, 2004; McAllister, Katz, & Lo, 1996). Within nucleotide 196 of the BDNF gene, there can be a G-to-A substitution, which results in a Val to Met (Val66Met) substitution at codon 66 (Chen et al., 2004). The Val66Met BDNF polymorphism has been associated with cognitive functioning and clinical pathology (Bath & Lee, 2006). In healthy populations, the Met allele has been linked to impaired working memory (Egan et al., 2003; Hariri et al., 2003). However, Met alleles carriers have a functional advantage over Val allele carriers in response inhibition tasks (Beste et al., 2010). Krueger and collaborators (2011) investigated the way in which the Val66Met BDNF polymorphism affects EF recovery after pTBI. Compared to healthy controls with the Val allele, TBI patients with the Val allele performed worse on EF tests measured with the Delis–Kaplan Executive Function System battery. No differences in EF performance were found between TBI patients with damage to the PFC and healthy controls that had the Met allele (Krueger et al., 2011). This study suggests that having the BDNF met allele is a good predictor of better EF recovery after PFC brain damage.

Apolipoprotein E

Another gene that has a crucial role in cognitive function is the apolipoprotein E (APOE), specifically the e4 allele. APOE transports, recycles, and clears lipids in the brain (Mahley & Rall, 2000). Lipids play a key role in maintaining neurological integrity and in assisting neural repair after TBI (Adibhatla & Hatcher, 2007). In addition, it has been observed that APOE has antioxidant properties, potentially associated with the integrity of the blood–brain barrier following TBI (Horsburgh, McColl, White, & McCulloch, 2003). Thus, APOE has a pivotal role in early neurological responses to TBI. A recent study from Padgett, Summers, Vickers, McCormack, and Skilbeck (2016) examined the effect of the APOE gene on EF, working memory tasks, and processing speed during the early period of recovery after TBI. In addition, researchers wanted to understand whether the APOEe4—associated with neurological disorders such Alzheimer disease—had a potential post-injury protective role (particularly the APOEe2 allele) after moderate or severe TBI. Stepwise multiple regression analyses compared APOEe4 carriers to APOEe3 homozygotes and included injury severity, age, and estimated premorbid functioning in the first step. This model significantly predicted performance on all tasks (EF, working memory, and processing speed) accounting for around 20% of the variance. The effect of APOEe4 in moderate and severe TBI revealed no significant effects. Thus, it is unlikely that APOE genotypes have an effect on EF in the early recovery period following TBI, notwithstanding the severity of the injury.

Overall, genetic studies have started to identify individual differences in polymorphisms that could affect recovery following TBI. Examining the influence of polymorphisms on TBI outcome has the potential to contribute to an understanding of variations in TBI outcome, aid in the triaging and treatment of TBI patients, and lead to interventions based on individualized profiles.

FUTURE DIRECTIONS

Impairments in EFs reduce individuals' ability to return to work or school and to regain satisfactory social activities. Understanding the consequences of a TBI on EF is crucial for an accurate diagnosis and a tailored rehabilitation program to help individuals recover independent lives. It is evident that there are still gaps in our understanding of TBI-related impairments and prognosis. However, further research in cognitive neuroscience, brain imaging, and genetics can mitigate this problem. Longitudinal studies investigating the effect of EF impairments following TBI are crucial because they provide information about the recovery and return to premorbid level of EF and social functioning. Ecologically valid studies can also be invaluable in determining the extent to which deficits measured in laboratory settings can be generalized to real-world functioning. Cognitive neuroscience research can provide a better understanding about the relationship between TBI and EF impairments at different stages of severity and recovery. Moreover, genetics can provide important information concerning premorbid influences on the rehabilitation of EF. Studies that include different disciplines can best promote a holistic approach for the understanding and treatment of EF deficits after TBI.

REFERENCES

Adams, J. H., Graham, D. I., Scott, G., Parker, L. S., & Doyle, D. (1980). Brain damage in fatal non-missile head injury. *Journal of Clinical Pathology*, *33*(12), 1132−1145.

Adibhatla, R. M., & Hatcher, J. F. (2007). Role of lipids in brain injury and diseases. *Future Lipidology*, *2*(4), 403−422. Available from http://dx.doi.org/10.2217/17460875.2.4.403.

al-Adawi, S., Powell, J. H., & Greenwood, R. J. (1998). Motivational deficits after brain injury: A neuropsychological approach using new assessment techniques. *Neuropsychology*, *12*(1), 115−124.

Armitage, S. (1946). Analysis of certain psychological tests used for the evaluation of brain damage. *Psychological Monographs*, *60*(1), 1−277.

Baddeley, A., & Wilson, B. (1988). Frontal amnesia and the dysexecutive syndrome. *Brain and Cognition*, *7*(2), 212−230.

Baddeley, A. D., & Hitch, G. J. (1974). Working memory. In G. A. Bowler (Ed.), *The psychology of learning and motivation: Advances in research and theory* (Vol. 8, pp. 47−89). New York, NY: Academic Press.

Barbey, A. K., Colom, R., Solomon, J., Krueger, F., Forbes, C., & Grafman, J. (2012). An integrative architecture for general intelligence and executive function revealed by lesion mapping. *Brain*, *135*(Pt 4), 1154−1164. Available from http://dx.doi.org/10.1093/brain/aws021.

Barbey, A. K., Koenigs, M., & Grafman, J. (2011). Orbitofrontal contributions to human working memory. *Cerebral Cortex*, *21*(4), 789−795. Available from http://dx.doi.org/10.1093/cercor/bhq153.

Bate, A. J., Mathias, J. L., & Crawford, J. R. (2001). The covert orienting of visual attention following severe traumatic brain injury. *Journal of Clinical and Experimental Neuropsychology*, *23*(3), 386−398. Available from http://dx.doi.org/10.1076/jcen.23.3.386.1190.

Bath, K. G., & Lee, F. S. (2006). Variant BDNF (Val66Met) impact on brain structures and function. *Cognitive, Affective & Behavioral Neuroscience*, *6*, 79−85.

Belanger, H. G., Curtiss, G., Demery, J. A., Lebowitz, B. K., & Vanderploeg, R. D. (2005). Factors moderating neuropsychological outcomes following mild traumatic brain injury: A meta-analysis. *Journal of the International Neuropsychological Society: JINS*, *11*(3), 215−227. Available from http://dx.doi.org/10.1017/S1355617705050277.

Beste, C., Kolev, V., Yordanova, J., Domschke, K., Falkenstein, M., Baune, B. T., & Konrad, C. (2010). The role of the BDNF Val66Met polymorphism for the synchronization of error-specific neural networks. *Journal of Neuroscience*, *30*(32), 10727−10733. Available from http://dx.doi.org/10.1523/JNEUROSCI.2493-10.2010.

Binder, D. K., & Scharfman, H. E. (2004). Brain-derived neurotrophic factor. *Growth Factors*, *22*(3), 123−131.

Boggio, P. S., Nunes, A., Rigonatti, S. P., Nitsche, M. A., Pascual-Leone, A., & Fregni, F. (2007). Repeated sessions of noninvasive brain DC stimulation is associated with motor function improvement in stroke patients. *Restorative Neurology and Neuroscience*, *25*(2), 123−129.

Brooks, J., Fos, L. A., Greve, K. W., & Hammond, J. S. (1999). Assessment of executive function in patients with mild traumatic brain injury. *Journal of Trauma*, *46*(1), 159−163.

Busch, R. M., McBride, A., Curtiss, G., & Vanderploeg, R. D. (2005). The components of executive functioning in traumatic brain injury. *Journal of Clinical and Experimental Neuropsychology*, 27(8), 1022–1032. Available from http://dx.doi.org/10.1080/13803390490919263.

Cabeza, R., & Nyberg, L. (2000). Imaging cognition II: An empirical review of 275 PET and fMRI studies. *Journal of Cognitive Neuroscience*, 12(1), 1–47.

Chein, J. M., & Morrison, A. B. (2010). Expanding the mind's workspace: Training and transfer effects with a complex working memory span task. *Psychonomic Bulletin & Review*, 17(2), 193–199. Available from http://dx.doi.org/10.3758/PBR.17.2.193.

Chen, R., Classen, J., Gerloff, C., Celnik, P., Wassermann, E. M., Hallett, M., & Cohen, L. G. (1997). Depression of motor cortex excitability by low-frequency transcranial magnetic stimulation. *Neurology*, 48(5), 1398–1403.

Chen, Z. Y., Patel, P. D., Sant, G., Meng, C. X., Teng, K. K., Hempstead, B. L., & Lee, F. S. (2004). Variant brain-derived neurotrophic factor (BDNF) (Met66) alters the intracellular trafficking and activity-dependent secretion of wild-type BDNF in neurosecretory cells and cortical neurons. *Journal of Neuroscience*, 24(18), 4401–4411. Available from http://dx.doi.org/10.1523/JNEUROSCI.0348-04.2004.

Chooi, W.-T., & Thompson, L. A. (2012). Working memory training does not improve intelligence in healthy young adults. *Intelligence*, 40(6), 531–542.

Cicerone, K. D., Dahlberg, C., Kalmar, K., Langenbahn, D. M., Malec, J. F., Bergquist, T. F., & Morse, P. A. (2000). Evidence-based cognitive rehabilitation: Recommendations for clinical practice. *Archives of Physical Medicine and Rehabilitation*, 81(12), 1596–1615. Available from http://dx.doi.org/10.1053/apmr.2000.19240.

Cicerone, K. D., & Wood, J. C. (1987). Planning disorder after closed head injury: A case study. *Archives of Physical Medicine and Rehabilitation*, 68(2), 111–115.

Collette, F., Hogge, M., Salmon, E., & Van der Linden, M. (2006). Exploration of the neural substrates of executive functioning by functional neuroimaging. *Neuroscience*, 139(1), 209–221. Available from http://dx.doi.org/10.1016/j.neuroscience.2005.05.035.

Cristofori, I., Zhong, W., Chau, A., Solomon, J., Krueger, F., & Grafman, J. (2015). White and gray matter contributions to executive function recovery after traumatic brain injury. *Neurology*, 84 (14), 1394–1401. Available from http://dx.doi.org/10.1212/WNL.0000000000001446.

D'Ambrosio, R., Maris, D. O., Grady, M. S., Winn, H. R., & Janigro, D. (1998). Selective loss of hippocampal long-term potentiation, but not depression, following fluid percussion injury. *Brain Research*, 786(1–2), 64–79.

Dikmen, S. S., Machamer, J. E., Powell, J. M., & Temkin, N. R. (2003). Outcome 3 to 5 years after moderate to severe traumatic brain injury. *Archives of Physical Medicine and Rehabilitation*, 84(10), 1449–1457.

Dockery, C. A., Hueckel-Weng, R., Birbaumer, N., & Plewnia, C. (2009). Enhancement of planning ability by transcranial direct current stimulation. *Journal of Neuroscience*, 29(22), 7271–7277. Available from http://dx.doi.org/10.1523/JNEUROSCI.0065-09.2009.

Dywan, J., & Segalowitz, S. (1996). Self and family ratings of adaptive behavior after traumatic brain injury: Psychometric scores and frontally generated ERPs. *Journal of Head Trauma Rehabilitation*, 11, 79–95.

Egan, M. F., Goldberg, T. E., Kolachana, B. S., Callicott, J. H., Mazzanti, C. M., Straub, R. E., & Weinberger, D. R. (2001). Effect of COMT Val108/158 Met genotype on frontal lobe function and risk for schizophrenia. *Proceedings of the National Academy of Sciences of the United States of America*, 98(12), 6917–6922. Available from http://dx.doi.org/10.1073/pnas.111134598.

Egan, M. F., Kojima, M., Callicott, J. H., Goldberg, T. E., Kolachana, B. S., Bertolino, A., & Weinberger, D. R. (2003). The BDNF val66met polymorphism affects activity-dependent secretion of BDNF and human memory and hippocampal function. *Cell, 112*(2), 257–269.

Evans, J. J., Greenfield, E., Wilson, B. A., & Bateman, A. (2009). Walking and talking therapy: Improving cognitive motor dual-tasking in neurological illness. *Journal of the International Neuropsychological Society: JINS, 15,* 112–120.

Ewing-Cobbs, L., Prasad, M. R., Swank, P., Kramer, L., Cox, C. S., Jr., Fletcher, J. M., & Hasan, K. M. (2008). Arrested development and disrupted callosal microstructure following pediatric traumatic brain injury: Relation to neurobehavioral outcomes. *NeuroImage, 42*(4), 1305–1315. Available from http://dx.doi.org/10.1016/j.neuroimage.2008.06.031.

Faul, M., Xu, L., Wald, M. M., Coronado, V., & Dellinger, A. M. (2010). Traumatic brain injury in the United States: National estimates of prevalence and incidence, 2002–2006. . *Injury Prevention, 16*(1), A268.

Faul, M., Xu, L., Wald, M. M., & Coronado, V. G. (2010). *Traumatic brain injury in the United States: Emergency department visits, hospitalizations and deaths 2002–2006.* Atlanta, GA: Centers for Disease Control and Prevention, National Center for Injury Prevention and Control.

Fregni, F., Boggio, P. S., Santos, M. C., Lima, M., Vieira, A. L., Rigonatti, S. P., & Pascual-Leone, A. (2006). Noninvasive cortical stimulation with transcranial direct current stimulation in Parkinson's disease. *Movement Disorders: Official Journal of the Movement Disorder Society, 21*(10), 1693–1702. Available from http://dx.doi.org/10.1002/mds.21012.

Gansler, D. A., Covall, S., McGrath, N., & Oscar-Berman, M. (1996). Measures of prefrontal dysfunction after closed head injury. *Brain and Cognition, 30*(2), 194–204. Available from http://dx.doi.org/10.1006/brcg.1996.0012.

Giza, C. C., & Hovda, D. A. (2014). The new neurometabolic cascade of concussion. *Neurosurgery, 75*(Suppl 4), S24–S33. Available from http://dx.doi.org/10.1227/NEU.0000000000000505.

Goel, V., & Grafman, J. (1995). Are the frontal lobes implicated in "planning" functions? Interpreting data from the Tower of Hanoi. *Neuropsychologia, 33*(5), 623–642.

Gogos, J. A., Morgan, M., Luine, V., Santha, M., Ogawa, S., Pfaff, D., & Karayiorgou, M. (1998). Catechol-O-methyltransferase-deficient mice exhibit sexually dimorphic changes in catecholamine levels and behavior. *Proceedings of the National Academy of Sciences of the United States of America, 95*(17), 9991–9996.

Goldberg, T. E., Egan, M. F., Gscheidle, T., Coppola, R., Weickert, T., Kolachana, B. S., & Weinberger, D. R. (2003). Executive subprocesses in working memory: Relationship to catechol-O-methyltransferase Val158Met genotype and schizophrenia. *Archives of General Psychiatry, 60*(9), 889–896. Available from http://dx.doi.org/10.1001/archpsyc.60.9.889.

Goverover, Y., Johnston, M. V., Toglia, J., & Deluca, J. (2007). Treatment to improve self-awareness in persons with acquired brain injury. *Brain Injury, 21*(9), 913–923. Available from http://dx.doi.org/10.1080/02699050701553205.

Grace, J., & Malloy, P. (2001a). *The Frontal Systems Behavior Scale manual.* Odessa, FL: Psychological Assessment Resources.

Grace, J., & Malloy, P. F. (2001b). *FrSBe: Frontal Systems Behavior Scale professional manual.* Lutz, FL: Psychological Assessment Resources.

Hanks, R. A., Rapport, L. J., Millis, S. R., & Deshpande, S. A. (1999). Measures of executive functioning as predictors of functional ability and social integration in a rehabilitation sample. *Archives of Physical Medicine and Rehabilitation, 80*(9), 1030–1037.

Hariri, A. R., Goldberg, T. E., Mattay, V. S., Kolachana, B. S., Callicott, J. H., Egan, M. F., & Weinberger, D. R. (2003). Brain-derived neurotrophic factor Val66met polymorphism affects human memory-related hippocampal activity and predicts memory performance. *Journal of Neuroscience, 23*(17), 6690–6694.

Hewitt, J., Evans, J. J., & Dritschel, B. (2006). Theory driven rehabilitation of executive functioning: Improving planning skills in people with traumatic brain injury through the use of an autobiographical episodic memory cueing procedure. *Neuropsychologia, 44*(8), 1468–1474. Available from http://dx.doi.org/10.1016/j.neuropsychologia.2005.11.016.

Horsburgh, K., McColl, W., White, F., & McCulloch, J. (2003). Apolipoprotein E influences neuronal death and repair. *International Congress Series, 1252*, 171–178.

Jaeggi, S. M., Buschkuehl, M., Jonides, J., & Shah, P. (2011). Short- and long-term benefits of cognitive training. *Proceedings of the National Academy of Sciences of the United States of America, 108*(25), 10081–10086. Available from http://dx.doi.org/10.1073/pnas.1103228108.

Jang, S. H., You, S. H., Hallett, M., Cho, Y. W., Park, C. M., Cho, S. H., & Kim, T. H. (2005). Cortical reorganization and associated functional motor recovery after virtual reality in patients with chronic stroke: An experimenter-blind preliminary study. *Archives of Physical Medicine and Rehabilitation, 86*(11), 2218–2223. Available from http://dx.doi.org/10.1016/j.apmr.2005.04.015.

Kane, M. J., Hambrick, D. Z., Tuholski, S. W., Wilhelm, O., Payne, T. W., & Engle, R. W. (2004). The generality of working memory capacity: A latent-variable approach to verbal and visuospatial memory span and reasoning. *Journal of Experimental Psychology. General, 133*(2), 189–217. Available from http://dx.doi.org/10.1037/0096-3445.133.2.189.

Kennedy, M. R., Coelho, C., Turkstra, L., Ylvisaker, M., Moore Sohlberg, M., Yorkston, K., & Kan, P. F. (2008). Intervention for executive functions after traumatic brain injury: A systematic review, meta-analysis and clinical recommendations. *Neuropsychological Rehabilitation, 18*(3), 257–299. Available from http://dx.doi.org/10.1080/09602010701748644.

Krueger, F., Pardini, M., Huey, E. D., Raymont, V., Solomon, J., Lipsky, R. H., & Grafman, J. (2011). The role of the Met66 brain-derived neurotrophic factor allele in the recovery of executive functioning after combat-related traumatic brain injury. *Journal of Neuroscience, 31*(2), 598–606. Available from http://dx.doi.org/10.1523/JNEUROSCI.1399-10.2011.

Larson, M. J., Perlstein, W. M., Demery, J. A., & Stigge-Kaufman, D. A. (2006). Cognitive control impairments in traumatic brain injury. *Journal of Clinical and Experimental Neuropsychology, 28*(6), 968–986. Available from http://dx.doi.org/10.1080/13803390600646860.

Levin, H. S., Culhane, K. A., Mendelsohn, D., Lilly, M. A., Bruce, D., Fletcher, J. M., & Eisenberg, H. M. (1993). Cognition in relation to magnetic resonance imaging in head-injured children and adolescents. *Archives of Neurology, 50*(9), 897–905.

Levin, H. S., Mattis, S., Ruff, R. M., Eisenberg, H. M., Marshall, L. F., Tabaddor, K., & Frankowski, R. F. (1987). Neurobehavioral outcome following minor head injury: A three-center study. *Journal of Neurosurgery, 66*(2), 234–243. Available from http://dx.doi.org/10.3171/jns.1987.66.2.0234.

Levine, B., Robertson, I. H., Clare, L., Carter, G., Hong, J., Wilson, B. A., & Stuss, D. T. (2000). Rehabilitation of executive functioning: An experimental-clinical validation of goal management training. *Journal of the International Neuropsychological Society: JINS, 6*(3), 299–312.

Levine, B., Schweizer, T. A., O'Connor, C., Turner, G., Gillingham, S., Stuss, D. T., & Robertson, I. H. (2011). Rehabilitation of executive functioning in patients with frontal lobe brain damage with goal management training. *Frontiers in Human Neuroscience, 5*, 9. Available from http://dx.doi.org/10.3389/fnhum.2011.00009.

Levine, B., Schweizer, T. A., O'Connor, C., Turner, G., Gillingham, S., Stuss, D. T., & Robertson, I. H. (2011). Rehabilitation of executive functioning in patient with frontal lobe brain damage with goal management training. *Frontiers in Human Neuroscience, 17*, 5–9.

Li, K., Nicaise, C., Sannie, D., Hala, T. J., Javed, E., Parker, J. L., & Lepore, A. C. (2014). Overexpression of the astrocyte glutamate transporter GLT1 exacerbates phrenic motor neuron degeneration, diaphragm compromise, and forelimb motor dysfunction following cervical contusion spinal cord injury. *Journal of Neuroscience, 34*(22), 7622–7638. Available from http://dx.doi.org/10.1523/JNEUROSCI.4690-13.2014.

Libin, A. V., Scholten, J., Schladen, M. M., Danford, E., Shara, N., Penk, W., & Dromerick, A. (2015). Executive functioning in TBI from rehabilitation to social reintegration: COMPASS (goal,) a randomized controlled trial (grant: 1I01RX000637-01A3 by the VA ORD RR&D, 2013-2016). *Military Medical Research, 2*, 32. Available from http://dx.doi.org/10.1186/s40779-015-0061-2.

Lindelov, J. K., Dall, J. O., Kristensen, C. D., Aagesen, M. H., Olsen, S. A., Snuggerud, T. R., & Sikorska, A. (2016). Training and transfer effects of N-back training for brain-injured and healthy subjects. *Neuropsychological Rehabilitation, 26*(5–6), 895–909. Available from http://dx.doi.org/10.1080/09602011.2016.1141692.

Lipsky, R. H., Sparling, M. B., Ryan, L. M., Xu, K., Salazar, A. M., Goldman, D., & Warden, D. L. (2005). Association of COMT Val158Met genotype with executive functioning following traumatic brain injury. *Journal of Neuropsychiatry and Clinical Neurosciences, 17*(4), 465–471. Available from http://dx.doi.org/10.1176/appi.neuropsych.17.4.465.

Lowenstein, D. H. (2009). Epilepsy after head injury: An overview. *Epilepsia, 50*(Suppl 2), 4–9. Available from http://dx.doi.org/10.1111/j.1528-1167.2008.02004.x.

Lu, H., Kobilo, T., Robertson, C., Tong, S., Celnik, P., & Pelled, G. (2015). Transcranial magnetic stimulation facilitates neurorehabilitation after pediatric traumatic brain injury. *Scientific Reports, 5*, 14769. Available from http://dx.doi.org/10.1038/srep14769.

Lundqvist, A., Grundstrom, K., Samuelsson, K., & Ronnberg, J. (2010). Computerized training of working memory in a group of patients suffering from acquired brain injury. *Brain Injury, 24* (10), 1173–1183. Available from http://dx.doi.org/10.3109/02699052.2010.498007.

Mahley, R. W., & Rall, S. C., Jr. (2000). Apolipoprotein E: Far more than a lipid transport protein. *Annual Review of Genomics and Human Genetics, 1*, 507–537. Available from http://dx.doi.org/10.1146/annurev.genom.1.1.507.

Mayer, A. R., Mannell, M. V., Ling, J., Elgie, R., Gasparovic, C., Phillips, J. P., & Yeo, R. A. (2009). Auditory orienting and inhibition of return in mild traumatic brain injury: A FMRI study. *Human Brain Mapping, 30*(12), 4152–4166. Available from http://dx.doi.org/10.1002/hbm.20836.

McAllister, A. K., Katz, L. C., & Lo, D. C. (1996). Neurotrophin regulation of cortical dendritic growth requires activity. *Neuron, 17*(6), 1057–1064.

Menon, D. K., Schwab, K., Wright, D. W., Maas, A. I., & Demographics and Clinical Assessment Working Group of the International and Interagency Initiative toward Common Data Elements for Research on Traumatic Brain Injury and Psychological Health (2010). Position statement: Definition of traumatic brain injury. *Archives of Physical Medicine and Rehabilitation, 91*(11), 1637–1640. Available from http://dx.doi.org/10.1016/j.apmr.2010.05.017.

Middleton, D. K., Lambert, M. J., & Seggar, L. B. (1991). Neuropsychological rehabilitation: Microcomputer-assisted treatment of brain-injured adults. *Perceptual and Motor Skills, 72* (2), 527–530. Available from http://dx.doi.org/10.2466/pms.1991.72.2.527.

Milner, B. (1963). Effects of different brain lesions on card sorting: The role of the frontal lobes. *Archives of Neurology, 9*(1), 90.

Nitsche, M. A., & Paulus, W. (2001). Sustained excitability elevations induced by transcranial DC motor cortex stimulation in humans. *Neurology, 57*(10), 1899–1901.

Padgett, C. R., Summers, M. J., Vickers, J. C., McCormack, G. H., & Skilbeck, C. E. (2016). Exploring the effect of the apolipoprotein E (APOE) gene on executive function, working memory, and processing speed during the early recovery period following traumatic brain injury. *Journal of Clinical and Experimental Neuropsychology, 38*(5), 551–560. Available from http://dx.doi.org/10.1080/13803395.2015.1137557.

Pascual-Leone, A., Amedi, A., Fregni, F., & Merabet, L. B. (2005). The plastic human brain cortex. *Annual Review of Neuroscience, 28*, 377–401. Available from http://dx.doi.org/10.1146/annurev.neuro.27.070203.144216.

Perlstein, W. M., Cole, M. A., Demery, J. A., Seignourel, P. J., Dixit, N. K., Larson, M. J., & Briggs, R. W. (2004). Parametric manipulation of working memory load in traumatic brain injury: Behavioral and neural correlates. *Journal of the International Neuropsychological Society: JINS, 10*(5), 724–741. Available from http://dx.doi.org/10.1017/S1355617704105110.

Perret, E. (1974). The left frontal lobe of man and the suppression of habitual responses in verbal categorical behaviour. *Neuropsychologia, 12*(3), 323–330.

Pickelsimer, E. E., Selassie, A. W., Gu, J. K., & Langlois, J. A. (2006). A population-based outcomes study of persons hospitalized with traumatic brain injury: Operations of the South Carolina Traumatic Brain Injury Follow-up Registry. *Journal of Head Trauma Rehabilitation, 21*(6), 491–504.

Picton, T. W., Stuss, D. T., Alexander, M. P., Shallice, T., Binns, M. A., & Gillingham, S. (2007). Effects of focal frontal lesions on response inhibition. *Cerebral Cortex, 17*(4), 826–838. Available from http://dx.doi.org/10.1093/cercor/bhk031.

Ping, X., & Jin, X. (2016). Transition from initial hypoactivity to hyperactivity in cortical layer v pyramidal neurons after traumatic brain injury in vivo. *Journal of Neurotrauma, 33*(4), 354–361. Available from http://dx.doi.org/10.1089/neu.2015.3913.

Ray, S. K., Dixon, C. E., & Banik, N. L. (2002). Molecular mechanisms in the pathogenesis of traumatic brain injury. *Histology and Histopathology, 17*(4), 1137–1152.

Raymont, V., Greathouse, A., Reding, K., Lipsky, R., Salazar, A., & Grafman, J. (2008). Demographic, structural and genetic predictors of late cognitive decline after penetrating head injury. *Brain, 131*(Pt 2), 543–558. Available from http://dx.doi.org/10.1093/brain/awm300.

Reid-Arndt, S. A., Nehl, C., & Hinkebein, J. (2007). The Frontal Systems Behaviour Scale (FrSBe) as a predictor of community integration following a traumatic brain injury. *Brain injury, 21*(13-14), 1361–1369. Available from http://dx.doi.org/10.1080/02699050701785062.

Robertson, I. A. (1996). *Goal management training: A clinical manual*. Cambridge, UK: PsyConsult.

Robertson, I. H., & Garavan, H. (2000). Vigilant attention. In M. Gazzaniga (Ed.), *The cognitive neurosciences* (3rd ed.). Cambridge, MA: MIT Press.

Sanchez-Carrion, R., Fernandez-Espejo, D., Junque, C., Falcon, C., Bargallo, N., Roig, T., & Vendrell, P. (2008). A longitudinal fMRI study of working memory in severe TBI patients with diffuse axonal injury. *NeuroImage, 43*(3), 421–429. Available from http://dx.doi.org/10.1016/j.neuroimage.2008.08.003.

Sawaguchi, T., & Goldman-Rakic, P. S. (1991). D1 dopamine receptors in prefrontal cortex: Involvement in working memory. *Science, 251*(4996), 947–950.

Schretlen, D. J., & Shapiro, A. M. (2003). A quantitative review of the effects of traumatic brain injury on cognitive functioning. *International Review of Psychiatry*, *15*(4), 341–349. Available from http://dx.doi.org/10.1080/09540260310001606728.

Schwab, K., Grafman, J., Salazar, A. M., & Kraft, J. (1993). Residual impairments and work status 15 years after penetrating head injury: Report from the Vietnam Head Injury Study. *Neurology*, *43*(1), 95–103.

Seamans, J. K., Floresco, S. B., & Phillips, A. G. (1998). D1 receptor modulation of hippocampal-prefrontal cortical circuits integrating spatial memory with executive functions in the rat. *Journal of Neuroscience*, *18*(4), 1613–1621.

Serino, A., Ciaramelli, E., Di Santantonio, A., Malagu, S., Servadei, F., & Ladavas, E. (2006). Central executive system impairment in traumatic brain injury. *Brain Injury*, *20*(1), 23–32. Available from http://dx.doi.org/10.1080/02699050500309627.

Shallice, T. (1982). Specific impairments of planning. *Philosophical Transactions of the Royal Society of London. Series B, Biological Sciences*, *298*(1089), 199–209.

Simpson, A., & Schmitter-Edgecombe, M. (2002). Prediction of employment status following traumatic brain injury using a behavioural measure of frontal lobe functioning. *Brain injury*, *16*(12), 1075–1091. Available from http://dx.doi.org/10.1080/02699050210155249.

Sturm, W., & Willmes, K. (1991). Efficacy of a reaction training on various attentional and cognitive functions in stroke patients. *Neuropsychological Rehabilitation*, *1*(4), 259–280.

Teasdale, G., & Jennett, B. (1974). Assessment of coma and impaired consciousness. A practical scale. *Lancet*, *2*(7872), 81–84.

Toglia, J., Johnston, M. V., Goverover, Y., & Dain, B. (2010). A multicontext approach to promoting transfer of strategy use and self regulation after brain injury: An exploratory study. *Brain injury*, *24*(4), 664–677. Available from http://dx.doi.org/10.3109/02699051003610474.

Vanderhasselt, M. A., De Raedt, R., Baeken, C., Leyman, L., Clerinx, P., & D'Haenen, H. (2007). The influence of rTMS over the right dorsolateral prefrontal cortex on top-down attentional processes. *Brain Research*, *1137*(1), 111–116. Available from http://dx.doi.org/10.1016/j.brainres.2006.12.050.

Villki, J., Ahola, K., Holst, P., Ohman, J., Servo, A., & Heiskanen, O. (1994). Prediction of psychosocial recovery after head injury with cognitive test and neurobehavioral ratings. *Journal of Clinical and Experimental Neuropsychology*, *16*, 325–338.

Westerberg, H., Jacobaeus, H., Hirvikoski, T., Clevberger, P., Ostensson, M. L., Bartfai, A., & Klingberg, T. (2007). Computerized working memory training after stroke—A pilot study. *Brain injury*, *21*(1), 21–29. Available from http://dx.doi.org/10.1080/02699050601148726.

Whiteneck, G., Brooks, C. A., Mellick, D., Harrison-Felix, C., Terrill, M. S., & Noble, K. (2004). Population-based estimates of outcomes after hospitalization for traumatic brain injury in Colorado. *Archives of Physical Medicine and Rehabilitation*, *85*(4 Suppl 2), S73–S81.

Wilde, E. A., Chu, Z., Bigler, E. D., Hunter, J. V., Fearing, M. A., Hanten, G., & Levin, H. S. (2006). Diffusion tensor imaging in the corpus callosum in children after moderate to severe traumatic brain injury. *Journal of Neurotrauma*, *23*(10), 1412–1426. Available from http://dx.doi.org/10.1089/neu.2006.23.1412.

Williams, G. V., & Goldman-Rakic, P. S. (1995). Modulation of memory fields by dopamine D1 receptors in prefrontal cortex. *Nature*, *376*(6541), 572–575. Available from http://dx.doi.org/10.1038/376572a0.

Yip, B. C., & Man, D. W. (2013). Virtual reality-based prospective memory training program for people with acquired brain injury. *NeuroRehabilitation*, *32*(1), 103–115. Available from http://dx.doi.org/10.3233/NRE-130827.

Zaloshnja, E., Miller, T., Langlois, J. A., & Selassie, A. W. (2008). Prevalence of long-term disability from traumatic brain injury in the civilian population of the United States, 2005. *Journal of Head Trauma Rehabilitation*, 23(6), 394–400. Available from http://dx.doi.org/10.1097/01.HTR.0000341435.52004.ac.

Zetterberg, H., Smith, D. H., & Blennow, K. (2013). Biomarkers of mild traumatic brain injury in cerebrospinal fluid and blood. *Nature Reviews. Neurology*, 9(4), 201–210. Available from http://dx.doi.org/10.1038/nrneurol.2013.9.

Chapter 19

Dementias and the Frontal Lobes

Michał Harciarek[1], Emilia J. Sitek[2,3] and Anna Barczak[4]

[1]*Department of Clinical Psychology and Neuropsychology, Institute of Psychology, University of Gdańsk, Gdańsk, Poland,* [2]*Department of Neurology, St. Adalbert Hospital, Gdańsk, Poland,* [3]*Department of Neurological and Psychiatric Nursing, Medical University of Gdańsk, Gdańsk, Poland,* [4]*Neurodegenerative Department, Neurology Clinic, MSW Hospital, Warsaw, Poland*

INTRODUCTION

Frontal lobes are basically affected in all dementia syndromes, earlier or later in the disease course. Furthermore, the extent of frontal or frontostriatal involvement implies the severity of executive and behavioral symptoms in the clinical presentation of each dementia syndrome. Depending on the dementia type, the patient's functional decline may be primarily due to memory, language, visuospatial function, praxis, and executive or behavioral abnormalities. Dementia literature has been initially dominated by studies of memory and language decline, with significantly less research aiming to characterize what we now define as executive function, i.e., "cognitive abilities necessary for complex goal-oriented behavior and adaptation to a range of environmental changes and demands" (Loring, 1999). Also, although some neurologists like Arnold Pick made a clear assumption that a dementing disease of the frontal cortex may lead to progressive changes in behavior, including goal-oriented behavior and defective adaptation, it was not until the last 25 years of the 20th century when the interest in frontal lobe dysfunction as a result of a neurodegenerative process was revived. Consequently, many disease-related cognitive symptoms (e.g., executive problems) have been often misinterpreted as memory loss and called Alzheimer's disease (AD), especially by the general public. Of note, the research underlying the importance of frontal lobes in dementia symptomatology stems mainly from two concepts: subcortical dementia, as defined by Albert, Feldman, and Willis (1974, 2005), and frontal lobe dementia, as defined by Neary & Snowden (1988, 2013). The clinical descriptions of these neurological conditions showed that executive and behavioral

Executive Functions in Health and Disease. DOI: http://dx.doi.org/10.1016/B978-0-12-803676-1.00019-2

symptoms may be crucial in the dementia presentation. Currently, the importance of executive and behavioral symptoms in various dementia types is widely acknowledged.

One of the possible ways to classify dementias is according to the broad neuroanatomical distinction between anterior and posterior brain areas (Snowden et al., 2011). Although, in general, all dementias tend to affect frontal lobe function (Mendez & Cummings, 2003), it is typically agreed that conditions affecting more anterior parts of the brain (i.e., frontal lobe) (e.g., frontotemporal dementia—FTD, early-onset Alzheimer's disease—eoAD, or vascular dementia—VaD) are frequently characterized by greater executive and behavioral problems. In comparison, neurodegenerative diseases affecting more posterior brain areas (predominantly parietal, temporal, and occipital lobes) (e.g., late-onset Alzheimer's disease—loAD) are often associated with more pronounced visuospatial or memory dysfunctions, although in some of these conditions prominent executive problems may also appear early (e.g., in dementia with Lewy bodies—DLB). In neurodegenerative disorders with primary frontostriatal involvement (progressive supranuclear palsy—PSP, corticobasal degeneration—CBD, Huntington's disease—HD, and some VaD subtypes), executive dysfunction usually accompanies predominant motor presentation.

In this chapter, frontal lobe pathology and associated executive dysfunction has been reviewed in most commonly encountered dementias (AD, VaD, FTD, DLB, PD with dementia [PDD], and dementia in the course of HD). Also, because executive deficits typically imply the presence of neuropsychiatric symptoms even in mild cognitive impairment (Rosenberg et al., 2011), behavior and affect has been also discussed. As most traditional executive measures, applicable in focal brain damage, are not feasible in the context of even mild dementia (Enright, Oconnell, Mackinnon, & Morgan, 2015), the presentation of executive and behavioral profile of each disorder has additionally been accompanied by practical methodological considerations focusing on both the quantitative and qualitative aspects of the patient's performance.

ALZHEIMER'S DISEASE

AD has been repeatedly shown to be the most common cause of progressive dementia, especially among elderly (Prince et al., 2013). However, AD is rather a type of dementia with predominant memory impairment, where dysexecutive features, although present, are typically not considered a hallmark of AD. Thus, it is not rare to find spared executive functions early in the course of the disease, in particular, in the amnestic (typical) variant of AD, although some reports suggest that that executive abilities may be disturbed to the same extent as memory or other cognitive domains (Karantzoulis & Galvin, 2011). As the disease progresses, however, executive dysfunction tends to become more apparent and behavioral problems increase. Thus, executive functioning may eventually be disrupted in all AD patients, with the extension of impairment being commonly related to the severity and duration of the disease as well as the age of onset. Importantly, the extent of executive problems in AD is also dependent on the parts of the brain being affected first, which determines the clinical variant of this devastating disease (e.g., frontal/executive/behavioral vs amnestic variant) (Sitek, Barczak, & Harciarek, 2015). The phenotypical differences between AD patients (predominant executive dysfunction vs severe episodic memory problems) are due to the disproportionate amyloid plaque and neurofibrillary tangle burden in the frontal and temporoparietal lobes. As a result, even in the preclinical phases of AD a greater dysexecutive phenomenon may be found in patients with predominant frontoparietal cortical thinning (Mez et al., 2013).

Because the frontal lobe involvement in AD has been more often seen in patients with early onset AD and therefore some of these patients have also been described as having the frontal variant of AD (fvAD), the neuropsychological characteristics of the fvAD is presented in the following section. Subsequently, changes in frontal lobe function (i.e., executive function, behavior, and affect) in relation to different stages of a more typical presentation of AD have been described.

Frontal Variant of Alzheimer's Disease

About two-thirds of individuals with an eoAD exhibit nonamnestic clinical manifestation (Mendez, Lee, Joshi, & Shapira, 2012). These patients are often reported to present with a more pronounced dysexecutive impairment and behavioral dysfunction compared to those with the loAD (Balasa et al., 2011; Kaiser et al., 2012; Suribhatla et al., 2004). In this younger AD population, these nonamnestic abnormalities (e.g., executive dysfunction) have been directly related to the greater frontal pathology (Cho et al., 2013) that contributes to the loss of functional connectivity in dorsolateral areas of the frontal lobes (Gour et al., 2014). Some of these less typical nonamnestic eoAD cases have a familial history of AD. This familial AD manifestation, often caused by mutations in presenilin 1 located on chromosome 14 in humans (together with less common amyloid precursor protein and presenilin 2 mutation), has been repeatedly shown to be associated with frontal lobe degeneration (Portet et al., 2003; Raux et al., 2000; Ringman et al., 2005) along with executive dysfunctions (MacPherson, Parra, Moreno, Lopera, & Della Sala, 2012), poor fluency (Lleó et al., 2001), and behavioral disturbances (Żekanowski et al., 2003).

Importantly, a subset of AD patients with disproportionate and early frontal deficits (often referred to as patients with the fvAD) may have a similar age of onset, disease duration, and survival as those with the amnestic AD (Johnson, Head, Kim, Starr, & Cotman, 1999; Ossenkoppele et al., 2015;

Taylor, Probst, Miserez, Monsch, & Tolnay, 2008). Their tests performance is, however, characterized by predominant executive dysfunction, mainly poor verbal fluency, problems with mental set-shifting, and perseverations and confabulations (Johnson, Brun, & Head, 2007; Warren, Fletcher, & Golden, 2012). Also, these patients' social, behavioral, and personality changes (disinhibition, apathy, or inertia) (Alladi et al., 2007; Ossenkoppele et al., 2015) often lead to a more pronounced disturbance in daily living in comparison with typical AD patients (Warren et al., 2012).

In comparison to an amnestic AD, the prevalence of fvAD is rare (Snowden et al., 2007). Despite new diagnostic criteria for AD (McKhann et al., 2011), the correct clinical diagnosis of eoAD/fvAD remains difficult and the condition itself is still often misdiagnosed for FTD (Warren et al., 2012). Neuroimaging, indicating the atrophy of the frontal (particularly prefrontal) cortex (Wong et al., 2016) and frontal hypoperfusion (Taylor et al., 2008) along with medial and orbital frontal hypometabolism (Woodward, Rowe, Jones, Villemagne, & Varos, 2015), is often neither specific nor sufficient to better differentiate this less common variant of AD from FTD. However, in fvAD an unusually high degree of frontal tangle pathology can be seen at autopsy (Johnson et al., 1999).

Executive Function

In the early stages of AD, executive dysfunction manifests in attentional and working memory disturbances, impairment of abstract reasoning, difficulties in multitasking and calculation, lack of mental flexibility, and planning problems leading to a failure to perform more complex tasks requiring problem solving or decision making (Duke & Kaszniak, 2000; Harciarek & Jodzio, 2005; Tarawneh & Holtzman, 2012). Patients with AD seem to be particularly impaired on dual tasks (regardless of the difficulty of the task), verbal fluency, delayed alternation, Self-Ordered Pointing Test, and Wisconsin Card Sorting Tests, together with Logical Matrices and Trail Making Test (TMT) (Baudic et al., 2006). As the disease progresses, executive problems encompass also difficulties initiating and completing a task, poor judgment, and defective logical reasoning (Mendez & Cummings, 2003). Until late stages of dementia, awareness of cognitive and social deficits may be intact, although some patients may have anosognosia relatively early, particularly those who initially present with impaired "frontal lobe-related" neuropsychological measures (Morris & Hannesdottir, 2004).

Behavior and Affect

Apathy is the most common affective disorder in AD patients (Duke & Kaszniak, 2000; Harciarek & Jodzio, 2005). Severe behavioral problems are typical for later stages of AD, and their presence in the early stages should alert clinicians to examine the environmental factors that could provoke those symptoms. Along with the disease progression, agitation, anxiety, irritability, dysphoria, and aberrant motor behavior together with disinhibition and psychotic features may develop (Mega, Cummings, Fiorello, & Gornbein, 1996). Personality changes are also reported. However, in contrast to patients with FTD, in AD these abnormalities are less severe. Nonetheless, some individuals with AD, especially those with eoAD and fvAD, may exhibit withdrawal, increased irritability, self-centered behavior, and diminished empathy. In a typical amnestic AD, most behavioral and affective changes occur in the later stages of the disease (Torralva, Dorrego, Sabe, Chemerinski, & Starkstein, 2000) and are much less apparent than cognitive symptoms (Bozeat et al., 2000). Also, these changes have been typically linked to the spreading of neuropathological changes to the medial- and orbitofrontal areas of the brain. Hyperorality, inappropriate affect, and social disruption are barely seen in this population (Duke & Kaszniak, 2000; Harciarek & Jodzio, 2005). Moreover, in AD social impairment, including deficits in moral judgments and decision-making as well as deficient reasoning regarding psychological versus physical causation (Verdon et al., 2007), are generally accounted for by global cognitive decline (Shany-Ur & Rankin, 2011).

VASCULAR DEMENTIA

VaD, a condition characterized by a cumulative decline in cognitive functioning due to multiple or locally placed infarctions, ischemia, or hemorrhagic lesions, is, next to AD, the most common form of dementing disease in the elderly. Furthermore, the overall incidence of VaD worldwide is probably underestimated because it does not include less severe forms of cognitive impairment due to cerebrovascular disease (e.g., milder forms of vascular cognitive impairment).

The first attempts to codify VaD comes from the end of 19th century when Otto Binswanger examined eight patients with "encephalitis subcorticalis chronica progressiva" who at autopsy turned to have a profound atrophy of the white matter and pronounced arteriosclerosis of cerebral arteries (Román, 1999). Subsequently, Emil Kraepelin described "arteriosclerotic dementia," Alois Alzheimer introduced "dementia post apoplexiam," and, in 1909, Marie proposed a concept of cognitive impairment due to multiple lacunar strokes. More recently, the infarct concept of VaD and the role of vascular risk factors in diagnosis of VaD have been emphasized by Hachinski et al. (2006) and Hachinski (2008). In addition, the development of neuroimaging techniques has significantly contributed to the accuracy of defining VaD.

Currently, a majority of criteria for the clinical diagnosis of VaD relies on the diagnosis of dementia, cerebrovascular disease, and their probable relationship with each other. Unfortunately, the presence of cerebrovascular disease in a patient with dementia is not sufficient to determine a causal relationship between the two. Thus, VaD is often used as an umbrella term because it has a heterogeneous presentation and a variety of conditions fall under the label of VaD (Kling, Trojanowski, Wolk, Lee, & Arnold, 2013).

Subtypes of Vascular Dementia and Their Relationship to Frontal Lobe Function

Executive Functions

Cerebrovascular disease may impair frontal lobe function and lead to the emergence of executive dysfunctions in a number of ways. Thus, it is well established that the specificity of executive problems in patients with VaD typically vary as a function of differences in the underlying pathology of VaD as and depends on the location and size of lesions, often producing a relatively heterogeneous profile of executive dysfunction in this population (Pantoni, Poggesi, & Inzitari, 2009). For example, although a relatively massive infarct encompassing frontal lobes or its reciprocal connections with other brain regions often result in severe executive problems, a majority of patients with VaD have multiple subcortical ischemic strokes and white matter lesions (Menon & Kelley, 2009) and, thus, they have been found to predominantly present with cognitive deficits resulting from a disruption of subcortical–frontal circuits, motor and executive problems in particular (Kramer & Wetzel, 2009; Mendez & Cummings, 2003). Moreover, because hypometabolic changes in patients with VaD appear not only where the infarct took place but also in more remote brain regions, diminished activity has been frequently seen in areas receiving projections from the affected structures (Mori et al., 1999), with frontal regions being particularly susceptible to such effects (Tullberg et al., 2004). Hence, most patients with VaD are markedly impaired on cognitive measures assessing psychomotor speed, sustained and divided attention, self-regulation and planning, response inhibition, and shifting of mental set, as well as they have a high number of perseverations (Almkvist, 1994; Babikian, Wolfe, Linn, Knoefel, & Albert, 1990; Bennett, Gilley, Lee, & Cochran, 1994; Buffon et al., 2006; Desmond, 1996; Kertesz & Clydesdale, 1994; Looi & Sachdev, 1999; Wolfe, Linn, Babikian, Knoefel, & Albert, 1990). In addition, subcortical–frontal deficits seen in VaD have been shown to significantly contribute to patients' defective working memory, retrieval and procedural memory (Cummings, 1994; Libon et al., 1998; Tierney et al., 2001). Despite poor free recall, encoding of new information in VaD seems to be relatively preserved, as indicated by relatively good recognition memory (Cummings, 1994). Thus, the neuropsychological profile of patients with VaD is often consistent with that of frontosubcortical dementia (e.g., HD, Parkinson's disease (PD), PSP, or even FTD) rather than to that of cortical amnesic dementia (e.g., AD) (Bonelli & Cummings, 2008; Wolfe et al.,

1990). Of note, similar cognitive profile, with pronounced psychomotor slowing and executive dysfunction, is also often observed in cerebral autosomal-dominant arteriopathy with subcortical infarcts and leukoencephalopathy (Buffon et al., 2006), a genetic variant of subcortical VaD characterized by extensive white matter lesions and/or lacunes in frontal white matter, basal ganglia, corpus callosum, and brainstem (Chabriat, Joutel, Dichgans, Tournier-Lasserve, & Bousser, 2009; Davous, 1998; Scott, Metz, Hu, & Hudon, 1999; see also Mendez & Cummings, 2003).

The executive problems in VaD are also seen in patients with strategically placed lacunar strokes, particularly in the thalamus, frontal white mater, basal ganglia, angular gyrus, basal forebrain, or genu of the internal capsule (Makin, Turpin, Dennis, & Wardlaw, 2013; Vermeer et al., 2003). For instance, Bogousslavsky and coworkers (1988) demonstrated that occlusion of the paramedial artery that supplies anteromedial thalamic regions will typically lead to bilateral infarction of the dorsomedial nucleus and the mammillothalamic tracts. This will result in disconnecting the prefrontal executive from diencephalic memory systems. Also, dorsal midbrain lesions often lead to abulia from disconnection of thalamofrontal tracts (Meador et al., 1996). Moreover, because the caudate nucleus mediates frontal functions through frontal—subcortical circuits, damage to the dorsolateral portion of this nucleus may produce apathy and hypokinesia, whereas infarcts to the right ventromedial caudate typically result in disinhibition and impulsiveness (Mendez, Adams, & Lewandowski, 1989). Additionally, difficulties in set-shifting have been noted in individuals with bilateral globus pallidus infarction (McPherson & Cummings, 1996).

Behavior and Affect

Similar to executive deficits, behavioral and emotional impairment in VaD is often heterogeneous. Patients with VaD are typically less spontaneous as well as apathetic and emotionally blunted (Mendez & Cummings, 2003), specifically when vascular lesions predominantly encompass the medial frontal cortex (Kertesz, Nadkarni, Davidson, & Thomas, 2000). Other psychiatric symptoms that may in part be related to these patients' frontal lobe lesions include depression, impulsivity, irritability, and motor agitation (Ballard et al., 2000; Dian, Cummings, Petry, & Hill, 1990; Stewart, 2007). For example, Korczyn and Halperin (2009) have also posited that depression in VaD, although sometimes a reactive phenomenon, may be strongly related to white matter vascular changes, thus, advancing the concept of "vascular depression" (for a critical review, see Jellinger, 2013). Additionally, according to Robinson (1998) and in line with other investigators (Heilman, Blonder, Bowers, & Valenstein, 2003), more severe depression in VaD may be predominantly observed in subjects with more advanced pathology of the left frontal lobe.

FRONTOTEMPORAL DEMENTIA

FTD, a term introduced by Brun et al. (1994), is a new umbrella name for clinical Pick's disease described for the first time over a century ago by Arnold Pick (1892). It represents a spectrum of non-Alzheimer's young onset (usually younger than 65 years) degenerative conditions associated with focal atrophy of the frontal lobes and/or temporal lobes (Sitek, Barczak, & Harciarek, 2015; Harciarek & Cosentino, 2013; Hodges, 2007; Kertesz, Blair, Davidson, McMonagle, & Munoz, 2005). Nowadays, FTD has been considered the second most common cause of dementia after AD (Ratnavalli, Brayne, Dawson, & Hodges, 2002; Rosso et al., 2003). Clinically, FTD can be divided into two variants: behavioral variant (bvFTD) and the language variant (lvFTD), the latter also known as primary progressive aphasia (PPA) (Hodges, 2007; see also Mesulam, 1987). The bvFTD is characterized by pronounced personality changes and decrease in social conduct, both associated with progressive atrophy of the frontal lobes, mesial frontal surface in particular (Rascovsky et al., 2011). By comparison, the lvFTD is characterized by a gradual and relatively selective language speech and/or semantic impairment resulting from degenerative changes in the left frontotemporal regions (Gorno-Tempini et al., 2011; Harciarek & Kertesz, 2011; Mesulam et al., 2009). Based on the constellation of specific language symptoms, PPA associated with FTD is typically classified into a nonfluent/agrammatic (nfvPPA) and semantic (svPPA) variant, the latter also known as semantic dementia. Of note, there is also a third variant PPA, so called logopenic PPA (Gorno-Tempini et al., 2011; Harciarek, Sitek, & Kertesz, 2014). However, its inclusion under the umbrella of the FTD syndromes is somewhat problematic. For example, although a subset of these cases has been shown to have frontotemporal lobar degeneration − a pathology typically associated with FTD—the majority of patients with logopenic variant PPA have in fact AD (Grossman, 2010). Also, most of the cases with logopenic PPA have atrophy extending beyond the frontotemporal regions (e.g., parietal lobule) (Gorno-Tempini et al., 2004). Thus, the executive and behavioral changes in logopenic PPA have not been described below.

Importantly, FTD syndromes have been shown to overlap clinically, pathologically, and biologically with other conditions, such as motor neuron disease (MND; including amyotrophic lateral sclerosis—ALS), CBD, and PSP (Hodges, 2011; Kertesz et al., 2000, 2005; Kertesz, Blair, McMonagle, & Munoz, 2007; McMonagle, Deering, Berliner, & Kertesz, 2006; Neary et al., 1998; Seelaar, Rohrer, Pijnenburg, Fox, & van Swieten, 2011; Snowden et al., 2006; Snowden et al., 2007). Thus, although FTD remains the most widely applied term to denote both clinical and pathological changes associated with progressive frontal and/or temporal atrophy, the overlap with MND, CBD, and PSP leads to the introduction of an umbrella term of Pick Complex (Kertesz, McMonagle, & Jesso, 2011), encompassing all the related entities both clinically and pathologically. Others have used "frontotemporal lobar degeneration" (FTLD) (Snowden, Neary, & Mann, 1996).

Behavioral Variant Frontotemporal Dementia

Executive Functions

Given the well established and pronounced association between executive functions and frontal lobe integrity (Gazzaley, Sheridan, Cooney, & D'Esposito, 2007; Royall et al., 2002), executive problems are often believed to be a hallmark feature of bvFTD that may even be detected as early features in "presymptomatic" tau mutation carriers (Alberici et al., 2004; Ferman et al., 2003). Thus, the initial syndrome of bvFTD is sometimes only a deficit of executive function, such as the inability to plan or carry out complex tasks. Furthermore, impaired performance on, e.g., Stroop Test, Tower of London, phonemic verbal fluency or subtests of the Delis–Kaplan Executive Function Systems (D-KEFS) battery, has been described in both clinically defined (Carlin et al., 2000; Cosentino, Chute, Libon, Moore, & Grossman, 2006; Huey et al., 2009; Johns et al., 2009; Krueger, Rostami, Huey, Snyder, & Grafman, 2007; Libon et al., 2007; Strenziok et al., 2011; Walker, Meares, Sachdev, & Brodaty, 2005) and pathologically confirmed cases of bvFTD (Grossman et al., 2007; Rascovsky et al., 2002; Rascovsky, Salmon, Hansen, & Galasko, 2008). Additionally, a longitudinal study by Hornberger, Piguet, Kipps, & Hodges (2008) has indicated that, in comparison to patients whose clinical symptoms remained stable (the so-called "phenocopy group"), individuals with bvFTD who progressed over time typically demonstrated executive deficits on tests including Digit Span, Verbal Fluency, Trail Making, and the Hayling Test of Inhibitory Control. Also, research applying experimental tasks to isolate specific elements of executive functioning including planning and decision-making has also indicated that these functions seem particularly defective in bvFTD (Harciarek & Cosentino, 2013). Importantly, in bvFTD executive dysfunction has been reported not just for total score but also for time to completion, number of moves, repetitions, and total rule violations (e.g., on Tower of London). This seems in line with findings by Possin and colleagues (2009, 2012) showing that the integrity of bilateral prefrontal regions contributes to the frequency of rule violations as well as repetitions/perseverations, and thus, while performing design fluency test, bvFTD patients tend to make more design repetitions than other dementia groups despite similar scores for overall number of correct designs. Similarly, Carey et al. (2008) found that, while AD and FTD groups were comparably impaired for the overall accuracy score, the FTD group was more likely to violate task rules either by moving two disks at once or by placing a large disk on top of a small disk. Hence, in assessing executive problems in individuals with bvFTD, a qualitative error analysis may often be more critical than the total score, especially when the differential diagnosis is concerned (Sitek et al., 2015).

However, in early stage of the disease, the executive dysfunctions are not mandatory, and some bvFTD patients may perform well on "frontal" tests, especially if they are seen early (Gleichgerrcht, Torralva, Roca, & Manes, 2010; Lough, Gregory, & Hodges, 2001; Rahman, Robbins, & Sahakian, 1999; Torralva, Roca, Gleichgerrcht, Bekinschtein, & Manes, 2009). Also, the kind and severity of executive dysfunctions, as determined by neuropsychological assessment, tend to vary, depending on location of neurodegeneration within the frontal lobes, the tests being used (Elfgren et al., 1994; Harciarek & Jodzio, 2005; Hodges et al., 1999; Miller et al., 1991), and the fact that more complex executive tasks strongly rely on working memory capacity in part supported by posterior regions of the brain (Stopford, Thompson, Neary, Richardson, & Snowden, 2012). For example, instead of severe atrophy encompassing the dorsolateral prefrontal cortex typically associated with executive function (Fuster, 2003), the majority of bvFTD cases initially present with neurodegenerative changes within orbitofrontal, ventromedial prefrontal, and anterior temporal lobe areas (Hornberger et al., 2014; Lam, Halliday, Irish, Hodges, & Piguet, 2014; Seeley et al., 2008), helping to explain why, in the context of impaired behavior and social cognition as well as loss of insight, some individuals with bvFTD have executive abilities relatively preserved. The executive tasks performance in bvFTD is not consistently related to frontal white matter integrity measures, albeit cingulum is particularly implicated in the performance of executive measures in this group (Tartaglia et al., 2012). Also, in comparison to AD, more atrophy is detected in ventral frontostriatal regions in bvFTD (Bertoux, O'Callaghan, Flanagan, Hodges, & Hornberger, 2015), which seems to correspond to the prominent inhibitory control deficit seen in this FTD variant (O'Callaghan, Naismith, Hodges, Lewis, & Hornberger, 2013).

Behavior and Affect

The behavioral and personality changes, primarily associated with progressive atrophy of orbitofrontal, ventromedial prefrontal, and anterior temporal lobe areas (Seeley et al., 2008), represent a true hallmark of bvFTD. In most bvFTD cases the behavioral abnormalities often begin with apathy, disinterest, and abulia, which may be mistaken for depression (Blass & Rabins, 2009). Additionally, in many patients with bvFTD the symptoms of disinhibition appear early, suggesting a manic psychosis or an obsessive compulsive or a sociopathic personality disorder as a differential diagnosis (Gregory & Hodges, 1996). The patient may be also inattentive, impulsive, and distractible.

When the striking disinhibition and asocial behavior appear, the diagnosis is unmistakable, but neuroimaging is essential to exclude neoplasm. Childish behavior, rudeness, inappropriate sexual remarks, impatient, careless driving, excessive spending or hoarding of certain items, inappropriate joking, perseverative routines, compulsive roaming, insistence of certain foods, excessive food intake, neglect of personal hygiene, disinterest in the immediate family, or others are the most characteristic features (e.g. Marczinski, Davidson, & Kertesz, 2004; Rascovsky et al., 2011; see also Harciarek & Jodzio, 2005). The personality change often prompts the family members to remark that the patient is not the same person any more. Pilfering, shoplifting, swearing, undressing in public, or unexpected urinary and fecal incontinence rapidly bring the patient to the physician, sometimes after the police is involved. Of note, the personality changes in bvFTD often mirror those seen in a famous case of Phineas Gage, whereas some advanced behavioral changes may resemble the so-called Klüver–Bucy syndrome (Cummings & Duchen, 1981), a syndrome produced in monkeys by bilateral ablation of the temporal lobes as well as seen in humans after encephalitis. The syndrome consists of hyperorality (first a sweet tooth, then excessively eating anything), hypersexuality (mostly words and gestures), compulsive touching (also called utilization behavior), and disinhibited exploration of the environment.

Other social conduct deficits, strongly associated with progressive atrophy of the orbitofrontal cortex, ventromedial prefrontal cortex, and anterior temporal lobes and thus also frequently seen in bvFTD (Seeley et al., 2008), include impaired ability to process facial emotions, detect socially inappropriate speech, adopt the perspective of another person, solve social dilemmas, or perceive sarcasm (for review, see Harciarek & Cosentino, 2013). Of note, although in most cases deficits in social cognition precede executive dysfunction (Eslinger et al., 2007; Libon, et al., 2007), some of these social problems may reflect executive dysfunction. For example, Eslinger, Moore, Anderson, and Grossman (2011) found that the ability to solve social dilemmas was best predicted by cognitive flexibility.

History provided by the caregiver and responses to a questionnaire, such as the "Frontal Behavioral Inventory" (Kertesz, Davidson, & Fox, 1997, 2000), at the initial interview, are the most useful diagnostic tools. The inventory was designed as a series of structured questions scripted so that both the normal and abnormal aspects of the behaviors were included. Each item was scored on a scale of 4, where 0 = none, 1 = mild or occasional, 2 = moderate, 3 = severe or most of the time. The first group of items contained negative behaviors such as apathy, aspontaneity, indifference, inflexibility, concreteness, personal neglect, distractibility, inattention, loss of insight, logopenia, verbal apraxia, and alien hand. These last three items were included to capture specific motor and speech behaviors, which may be associated with FTD. The second group of items contained disinhibited behaviors such as perseveration, irritability, jocularity, irresponsibility, inappropriateness, impulsivity, restlessness, aggression, and hyperorality. A score above 27 is cutoff for bvFTD. It has been demonstrated that using cognitive tests alone was only 75% with distinguishing bvFTD from AD patients, while adding FBI to the discriminant function achieved 100% discrimination (Kertesz et al., 2000).

Language Variant Frontotemporal Dementia (Primary Progressive Aphasia)

Executive Functions

The initial presentation of PPA is often word finding difficulty or anomia (Harciarek et al., 2014). The relatively isolated language disturbance in the first 2 years of the illness was suggested by Mesulam (2003) as the operational definition of PPA, which has been also included in the most recent PPA classification (Gorno-Tempini et al., 2011). Thus, executive deficits, despite some left frontal involvement, are rarely seen early in PPA, and the impaired performance on tests measuring executive functions may simply reflect these patients' language impairment (Zakzanis, 1999; for review, see Sitek et al., 2015). For example, the integrity of nonverbal executive abilities (i.e., sorting and shifting) was supported in the first relatively large study of PPA (primarily nfvPPA) (Wicklund, Johnson, & Weintraub, 2004). At more advanced stages of the disease, however, many PPA cases, especially with svPPA, may also present with executive problems (Gorno-Tempini et al., 2004; Hsiung et al., 2012; Knibb, Woollams, Hodges, & Patterson, 2009; Wicklund, Rademaker, Johnson, Weitner, & Weintraub, 2007), being sometimes as prominent as in bvFTD (Heidler-Gary et al., 2007).

Behavior and Affect

Although most PPA cases are characterized by a relative preservation of nonverbal cognition in the first 2 years of the illness, some of these patients develop early behavioral features of bvFTD. For example, Marczinski et al. (2004) found that, in addition to early apathy symptoms quite often seen in nfvPPA (see also Rohrer & Warren, 2010), there was a significant increase in disorganization, inattention, poor judgment, inappropriateness, aggression, and hyperorality. Moreover, by the third year of testing, FBI scores of patients with nfvPPA were approaching scores of patients with bvFTD, further supporting the clinical overlap with bvFTD (Kertesz et al., 2007).

The behavioral and personality changes as well as impaired social cognition, often indicating impaired functions of limbic-associated frontotemporal networks, are particularly frequently seen in patients with svPPA (Bozeat et al., 2000; Kertesz et al., 2007, 2010; Kumfor & Piguet, 2012; Rankin, Kramer, Mychack, & Miller, 2003; Rosen et al., 2006; Seeley et al., 2005; Snowden, Goulding, & Neary, 1989, 2001). These abnormalities often encompass increased social seeking, profound pragmatic disturbances with stereotypic thematic perseverations, irritability, disinhibition, and food fads such as the development of a sweet tooth. Many svPPA cases also present with pronounced coldness with loss of social affiliation and nurturance seen in svPPA (Rankin et al., 2003). Furthermore, many subjects develop a strong interest in new religious movements and start to dress in a very eccentric fashion (Edwards-Lee et al., 1997). Loss of empathy and insight, utilization behaviors, mental inflexibility, and compulsions are also noted, particularly at the later stages of svPPA (Seeley et al., 2005). Severely impaired recognition of emotions based on facial expression and voices has been also demonstrated (Perry et al., 2001). Of note, whereas depressive symptoms in PPA are most often seen in patients with predominant left-sided atrophy, impaired social conduct is the most common behavioral symptom following the right-sided atrophy (Harciarek & Cosentino, 2013) (Table 19.1).

PROGRESSIVE SUPRANUCLEAR PALSY AND CORTICOBASAL SYNDROME

PSP and CBD were initially regarded either as two atypical Parkinsonian syndromes with the underlying tau pathology (in contrast to alpha-synuclein pathology in PD, DLB, and multiple system atrophy) or as disorders falling under the FTLD spectrum due to a strong frontal involvement early in the disease course (Kertesz et al., 2005). Nowadays, however, PSP itself is seen as a spectrum of different clinical presentations: (1) the typical one of Richardson syndrome (PSP-RS), (2) the one with PNFA, (3) with pure akinesia with gait freezing, (4) with predominant Parkinsonism, and (5) with a phenotype of combined PSP with features of the corticobasal syndrome (CBS) (PSP-CBS). Here, we will focus on PSP-RS as this syndrome is the most common one and is well defined in the neuropsychological literature. Similarly, there are several CBS phenotypes: (1) the typical one attributable to CBD (CBS-CBD), (2) the one with overlapping nonfluent aphasia and apraxia of speech (CBS-PNFA), (3) the frontal behavioral spatial syndrome, (4) progressive supranuclear palsy-like syndrome, and (5) a cognitive phenotype attributable to AD pathology (Lopez, Bayulkem, & Hallett, 2016). Again, we will focus on CBS-CBD, as this phenotype has the most extensive coverage in the literature.

Executive Functions

Both PSP and CBS share various clinical and neuroanatomical frontal characteristics with FTD (Kertesz et al., 2005; Kertesz et al., 2007; Lang, Bergeron, Pollanen, & Ashby, 1992; Lippa, Smith, & Fontneau, 1990; Tovar-Moll et al., 2014); the main pathological difference is the prominent midbrain atrophy in PSP and marked frontal−parietal asymmetry in CBS. As a result of this overlap, executive dysfunction is the most salient

TABLE 19.1 Specificity of Executive Impairment in Selected Neurodegenerative Diseases

	Early/Late	Severity	Executive/Behavioral Dysfunction as Core/Secondary Deficit	Profile of Executive Performance	Behavioral Characteristics
Late-onset AD	Late	Mild/moderate	Secondary deficit	Difficulty in solving complex problems, multi-tasking; executive tasks failed due to attentional problems	Apathy
Early-onset AD	Early	Moderate/severe	Sometimes core deficit	Attentional problems/set-shifting deficit	Apathy disinhibition
PD	Early	Mild/moderate	Sometimes core deficit	Difficulty in initiation, planning, and set-shifting	Apathy, depression impulse control disorder
DLB	Early	Moderate/severe	Sometimes core deficit	Difficulty in initiation and set-shifting, visuoconstructive tasks are failed due to perceptual problems	Apathy
BvFTD	Early	Severe	Core deficit	Three possible profiles: – no executive impairment on traditional tasks – pure executive problems – failure on all cognitive tasks due to poor cooperation and economy of effort	Apathy disinhibition loss of empathy

SvPPA/ SD	Early	Mild	Secondary deficit	Good performance if semantic knowledge is not needed to solve a given problem	Rigid behavior impatience food fads impaired pragmatics
nfvPPA	Late	Mild/ moderate	Secondary deficit	Poor sequencing	Apathy, depression
FTD-MND	Early	Moderate	Sometimes core deficit	Low verbal fluency	Apathy disinhibition
PSP-RS	Early	Severe	Core deficit	Deficient inhibitory control frequent rule violations, perseverations	Apathy, aspontaneity disinhibition
CBD	Early	Moderate/ severe	Sometimes core deficit	Deficient inhibitory control	Apathy, aspontaneity irritability, disinhibition (however, less frequently than in PSP)
HD	Early	Moderate/ severe	Core deficit	Decline in all aspects of executive functions	Apathy irritability

AD, Alzheimer's disease; *PD*, Parkinson's disease; *DLB*, dementia with Lewy bodies; *bvFTD*, behavioral variant frontotemporal dementia; *svPPA*, semantic variant primary progressive aphasia; *SD*, semantic dementia; *nfvPPA*, nonfluent variant primary progressive aphasia; *FTD-MND*, frontotemporal dementia with motor neuron disease; *PSP-RS*, progressive supranuclear palsy−Richardson syndrome; *CBD*, corticobasal degeneration; *HD*, Huntington's disease.

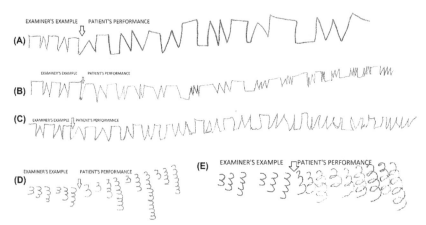

FIGURE 19.1 Luria's alternate designs' and multiple loop drawings' performance in patients with progressive supranuclear palsy (*PSP*) and corticobasal syndrome (*CBS*). (A) Impaired set-shifting evidenced by Luria's alternate design drawing in a 61-year-old patient with Richardson syndrome of PSP, symptoms lasting for about 1 year, Mini-Mental State Examination score 27/30, Frontal Assessment Battery score 14/18, Addenbrooke's Cognitive Examination-III 83/100. (B) Impaired set-shifting evidenced by Luria's alternate design drawing in 71-year-old patient with Richardson syndrome of PSP, symptoms lasting for about 2 years, Mini-Mental State Examination score 25/30. (C) Impaired set-shifting evidenced by Luria's alternate design drawing in 66-year-old patient with pure akinesia with gait freezing, symptoms lasting for about 5 years, Mini-Mental State Examination score 25/30. (D) Inhibition problems evidenced by multiple loop drawing in a 59-year-old patient with CBS phenotype, symptoms lasting for about 3 years, Mini-Mental State Examination score 29/30, Frontal Assessment Battery score 16/18. (E) Inhibition problems evidenced by multiple loop drawing in a 71-year-old patient with a mixed PSP-CBS phenotype, symptoms lasting for about 3 years, Mini-Mental State Examination score 22/30, Frontal Assessment Battery score 5/18.

neuropsychological feature of PSP-RS (Gerstenecker, Mast, Duff, Ferman, & Litvan, 2013) (Fig. 19.1). Due to severe motor impairment, verbal fluency tasks remain the most popular executive measure in PSP. In CBS, executive impairment is accompanied by more widespread cognitive dysfunction, with predominent apraxia and language/visuospatial deficits, depending on the asymmetry of atrophy in a given case. Also, in CBS, dorsal frontal, parietal, and temporal—parietal cortex is associated with executive task performance. While both patients with CBS and FTD exhibit impairment on D-KEFS, Twenty Questions and Tower test can well help in differentiating CBS from FTD, with FTD patients typically obtaining lower scores than those with CBS (Huey et al., 2009).

Behavior and Affect

Patients with PSP often share behavioral abnormalities with other atypical Parkinsonian syndromes (e.g., depression and sleeping problems). Some behavioral changes seen in PSP are however more typical for bvFTD (disinhibition and eating problems), and some symptoms are those commonly seen in both Parkinsonian syndromes and FTLD (e.g., apathy) (Gerstenecker, Duff, Mast, & Litvan, 2013).

In PSP behavioral changes, as revealed by the Frontal Behavior Inventory scores, are correlated with the degree of frontal atrophy (Cordato et al., 2002). For example, severity of withdrawal and apathy has been related to atrophy of the corpus callosum, right superior longitudinal, and uncinate fasciculi (Agosta et al., 2014). Additionally, PSP patients with dysexecutive symptoms, apathy, and personality change also exhibit changes in the inferior frontooccipital fasciculus (Kvickström et al., 2011). In fact, early apathy and perseverative behavior are the most common FTD features seen in PSP patients (Kobylecki et al., 2015). As a result, about 20% of all PSP cases present with frontal features at onset (Donker Kaat et al., 2007) and around 30% of PSP cases fulfill the cognitive and behavioral criteria of possible FTD (*op. cit.*). Both in PSP and CBS, aspontaneity is the most common behavioral feature, while irritability is slightly more common in CBS, as assessed with FBI (Borroni, Alberici, Agosti, Cosseddu, & Padovani, 2009).

MOTOR NEURON DISEASE

The association of MND and clinical, radiological, and pathological FTD features has been frequently described (Neary et al., 1990). For example, it is now well established that cases of dementia with MND have ubiquitin positive, tau negative inclusions in the cortex, previously described in the motor neurons in ALS (Okamoto, Hirai, Yamazaki, Sun, & Nakazato, 1991), and subsequently named MND inclusion dementia (Jackson, Lennox, & Lowe, 1996). Many of the individuals with MND, particularly those with ALS, also have the atrophy encompassing frontal cortex, thus, the high prevalence of below-described executive and behavioral impairment (Lomen-Hoerth, Anderson, & Miller, 2002; Strong, Lomen-Hoerth, Caselli, Bigio, & Yang, 2003).

Executive Functions

In ALS, distinct executive deficits are related to the atrophy of the selective white matter prefrontal tracts (Pettit et al., 2013). When examining executive function in patients with ALS, the impact of motor deficits need to be controlled for. For instance, Abrahams et al. (2000) devised a special verbal fluency assessment procedure, in which verbal fluency may be administered both orally or in a written format, together with a control task (reading words or writing them to dictation), allowing to disentangle motor and executive/language aspects of the performance (Abrahams et al., 2000).

Behavior and Affect

To meet the criteria for MND with FTD, at least two characteristic features of bvFTD need to be present (Burrell et al., 2016). Patients with MND-FTD who also have the C9orf72 mutation more often present with psychosis, apathy, disinhibition, and the loss of empathy than those without this repeat expansion (Snowden et al., 2013). In ALS, behavioral abnormalities are typically related to white matter changes, notably in the left superior longitudinal fasciculus (Trojsi et al., 2013). Importantly, decline in behavior of MND-FTD patients is not linked to motor dysfunction (de Silva et al., 2016), while the presence of apathy is negatively related to survival (Caga et al., 2016).

PARKINSON'S DISEASE

PD is an extrapyramidal movement disorder accompanied by slowly progressive neuropsychological deficits that often result in dementia. The etiology of this predominantly sporadic disorder remains unknown. The onset of PD is typically between 50 and 65 years of age, and PD may be somewhat more frequently seen in men than females (de Rijk et al., 2000). The prevalence of PD has been estimated at 0.3% of the population, with the incidence that increases with advancing age (Nussbaum & Ellis, 2003).

At onset, patients with PD may exhibit no or very mild and selective neuropsychological deficits. As the disease progresses, up to 60% of these individuals seem to develop full-blown dementia syndrome (PDD) (Robottom & Weiner, 2009). The diagnosis of dementia in the course of PD requires the presence of significant deficits in at least two of the following domains: attention, executive functions, visuospatial functions, and memory (Emre et al., 2007). As the dysexecutive profile on neuropsychological testing and its association with dopaminergic dysfunction are well established in PD, it was believed that the conversion to dementia corresponds to the further deterioration of executive function. However, dementia in PD may be driven by cholinergic dysfunction itself, as it is associated with decline in semantic fluency, visuospatial functions, visual and verbal memory (Kehagia, Barker, & Robbins, 2010). Dementia develops earlier (even <7 years since onset) in the context of predominantly akinetic-rigid motor phenotype (Selikhova et al., 2009), but after 20 years of the disease, more than 80% of patients fulfill the criteria of dementia (Hely, Reid, Adena, Halliday, & Morris, 2008).

Executive Functions

Slowed responses as well as defective attention and executive dysfunctions are among the earliest and most frequently observed cognitive deficits in PD (Claus & Mohr, 1996; Peavy et al., 2001; Sawamoto, Honda, Hanakawa,

Fukuyama, & Shibasaki, 2002). Due to progressive bradykinesia, patients with PD are predominantly impaired on timed measures (e.g., Digit Symbol, TMT). The performance on some of these cognitive tasks may be further compromised by decreased initiation, defective planning, and difficulties in set-shifting (Cools, Barker, Sahakian, & Robbins, 2001a,b; Falchook et al., 2011; Hozumi, Hirata, Tanaka, & Yamazaki, 2000). Furthermore, it has been recently suggested that planning in PD patients may be particularly affected when the information provided is ambiguous in terms of the sequential order of subgoals (McKinlay et al., 2008). Additionally, individuals with PD often present with difficulties in abstract thinking, concept formation, and problem solving (Beauchamp, Dagher, Panisset, & Doyon, 2008; Kuzis, Sabe, Tiberti, Leiguarda, & Starkstein, 1997; Muslimović, Post, Speelman, De Haan, & Schmand, 2009). In PD, dysexecutive symptoms due to a defective functioning of the frontal−subcortical circuits may also sometimes account for the visuospatial and visuoconstructive disturbances as well as memory retrieval deficit and impaired procedural memory (Zgaljardic et al., 2006). As in other disorders affecting frontal−basal ganglia circuits (e.g., CBD and PSP), subjects with PD significantly benefit from cuing (Hsieh & Lee, 1999; Pillon et al., 1994).

Behavior and Affect

Among the most common neuropsychiatric features of PD are apathy, depression, anxiety, and sleep disorders. For example, apathy and depression may be present in more than a half of all patients with PD, having important consequences for their quality of life and daily functioning (Aarsland, Marsh, & Schrag, 2009). Additionally, patients with PD also frequently have impaired processing of emotional faces and prosody, with marked deficits in both perception and expression of affective stimuli (Heilman et al., 2003; Skodda, Rinsche, & Schlegel, 2009). Recent interest in obsessive behaviors, gambling, hypersexuality, punding (obsessive roaming and touching) expanded the study of nonmotor symptoms of PD, in addition to hallucinations and psychosis, which are often related to the side effects of medications (Friedman, 2010). In fact, impulse control disorders, such as gambling, compulsive sexual behavior, compulsive buying, and binge eating, occur in about 14% of PD patients. They are more often seen in younger patients treated with dopamine agonists. Additional risk factors include being unmarried, current cigarette smoking, and a family history of gambling problems (Weintraub et al., 2010). Risk taking has been related to the dysfunction of ventral striatum (Rao et al., 2010). Of note, PD patients treated with dopaminergic medication are prone to impulsive reactions only in the ON phase, which confirms that the syndrome is dopaminergically driven (Leroi et al., 2013).

DEMENTIA WITH LEWY BODIES

DLB is a form of Parkinsonian dementia (McKeith et al., 2005). Similarly to AD, the onset of DLB is typically after 65 years of age but the survival is somewhat shorter, averaging 7.7 ± 3.0 years from the onset of cognitive deficits (Olichney et al., 1998).

In addition to meeting criteria for dementia, the clinical picture of DLB typically include Parkinsonism, fluctuations of cognitive functioning, and visual hallucinations (McKeith et al., 2005). Parkinsonian signs are similar to those described in individuals with PD although usually symmetrical and less severe. Also, most of the patients with DLB do not present with a PD characteristic tremor (Aarsland, Ballard, McKeith, Perry, & Larsen, 2001).

The neuroimaging profile of patients with DLB is characterized by diffuse atrophy, particularly in temporal lobes (McKeith et al., 2005). However, decreased frontal metabolism has also been described (Defebvre et al., 1999).

Executive Functions

Similarly to patients with PD, subjects with DLB may also present with prominent dysexecutive syndrome that includes defective attention, poor monitoring, and cognitive rigidity (Aarsland et al., 2001). What is more, the degree of executive dysfunctions in DLB may be similar to that in FTD, although patients with DLB are typically slower (Johns et al., 2009), likely due to an overall decrease in dopaminergic-related processing speed and other nonexecutive problems. Also, the presence of mental set-shifting difficulties, perseverations, and especially intrusions arising from the visual environment occur in DLB much more often than in AD patients (Doubleday, Snowden, Varma, & Neary, 2002). Despite DLB is not characterized by aphasia, most of these patients have decreased verbal fluency, predominantly resulting from executive problems due to impaired functioning of frontal–basal ganglia circuits (Salmon et al., 1996).

Overall, similarly to posture and gait impairment, executive problems in DLB are correlated with dopamine transporter loss (Siepel et al., 2016). Resting state functional connectivity (Lowther, O'Brien, Firbank, & Blamire, 2014) and synchronization (Peraza, Taylor, & Kaiser, 2015) are more affected in DLB in comparison to AD, and white matter deterioration starts earlier in the course of DLB than AD (Firbank, Watson et al., 2016). Also, DLB patients show heightened task-related deactivations of the default mode network than AD patients (Firbank, Kobeleva et al., 2016), all of which correspond to the severe attentional problems in DLB.

Behavior and Affect

In general, behavioral and affective symptoms of DLB are similar to those described in other Parkinsonian disorders, but the presence of elaborate visual hallucinations early in the course of the disease favors the diagnosis of DLB. Also, the presence of well-formed visual hallucinations best discriminate patients with DLB from those with AD and bvFTD (Shea & Chu, 2015). The core psychiatric features of DLB encompass anxiety, followed by depression, apathy, agitation, and rapid eye movement sleep disorder as well as psychosis (Borroni, Agosti, & Padovani, 2008). Importantly, the severity of these symptoms is not typically associated with the degree of motor disability. The severity of apathy in DLB is comparable to bvFTD, albeit it is not accompanied by disinhibition typical for bvFTD (Perri, Monaco, Fadda, Caltagirone, & Carlesimo, 2014). Interestingly, a recent study has shown that neurobehavioral disturbances in DLB may not be related to dopamine transporter loss (Siepel et al., 2016).

HUNTINGTON'S DISEASE

HD is an autosomal dominant neurological disease that was initially described by George Huntington in 1872, who recognized the exclusively penetrant dominant inheritance. Choreoathetosis, dementia, psychiatric features, and caudate atrophy, resulting from a gene mutation involving an excessive number of trinucleotide repeats, characterize the disease. Of note, choreic movements add to the initial oculomotor deficits present few years before HD formal diagnosis, at the conversion time. Later in the disease course, dystonic movements, bradykinesia, posture and gait impairment, dysarthria, and dysphagia become more prominent. Although the severity of motor, cognitive, and behavioral signs is variable, functional decline is inevitable. Furthermore, in HD observable cognitive or behavioral manifestations often precede the occurrence of motor symptomatology by at least few years and are detectible on sensitive tasks every 10 years before formal clinical diagnosis (Papoutsi, Labuschagne, Tabrizi, & Stout, 2014). Whereas an estimated disease course ranges from 10 to 20 years, HD progresses at a faster rate in patients with earlier disease onset and greater genetic burden (Andresen et al., 2007; Mahant, McCusker, Byth, Graham, & the Huntington Study Group, 2003).

However, in HD, which used to be initially regarded as subcortical dementia, early striatal atrophy (mainly in the caudate) is not an isolated sign of neurodegeneration. Already at the preclinical stage, the atrophy frequently occurs also within the anterior insula, lateral prefrontal, premotor, supplementary motor, and parietal areas as well as cingulate cortex (Aylward et al., 2000; Dogan et al., 2015; Grafton et al., 1990; Paulsen et al., 2004; Reading et al., 2004). Deep gray matter atrophy, especially in putamen, precedes detectible abnormalities in white matter (Faria et al., 2016). For years, it was hypothesized that HD cognitive and motor deficits are mainly due to the involvement of corticostriatal loops: motor, spatial, visual, and affective (Lawrence, Sahakian, & Robbins, 1998). More recent white matter imaging studies consistently support the involvement of those previously hypothe-sized tracts in HD (Douaud et al., 2009).

Executive Functions

Cognitive problem characteristics of subcortical dementia with frontal lobe involvement (e.g., PD or small vessels ischemic disease) are typical for HD. These primarily encompass early deficits of attention, executive dysfunc-tions, and psychomotor slowing, typically associated with frontostriatal white matter volume (Brandt, Folstein, & Folstein, 1988, 1990; Jason et al., 1997; Matsui et al., 2015; Novak et al., 2015; Papp et al., 2013; Thompson et al., 2010; Ward et al., 2006). These deficits are also often seen in asymp-tomatic carriers of abnormal HD gene (Papp et al., 2013; Paulsen et al., 2001). For example, Muller et al. (2002) have shown that subjects with HD display pronounced impairment of selective attention as well as intensity and supervisory control. As the disease progresses, other aspects of abnor-mal functioning of frontal−subcortical networks appear. Among the most prominent executive problems, patients with HD often experience are impaired judgment, planning, organizing, sequencing, and difficulties in abstract thinking (Snowden et al., 2001). In contrast to patients with PD or cervical dystonia, subjects with HD seem to have limited insight into their executive problems (Sitek et al., 2013). Severe executive dysfunctions also contribute to deficits in memory retrieval (Lawrence et al., 1996). Additionally, there is evidence to suggest that impaired performance on tests assessing visuospatial memory is, similarly to the defective performance on measures of verbal learning, only secondary to patients' attentional execu-tive problems.

Because HD affects basal ganglia that projects to and receives input from the motor and premotor regions of the frontal lobes (Alexander, DeLong, & Strick, 1986), motor learning /atomicity and other forms of nondeclarative memory in HD are also often impaired (Thompson et al., 2010). For exam-ple, individuals with HD have been found to be impaired in learning differ-ent types of categorization rules and in learning the pursuit rotor task (Filoteo, Maddox, & Davis, 2001; Heindel, Butters, & Salmon, 1988), most likely related to the attentional deficits. Also, individuals with HD typically experience difficulties generating lists of words (Henry, Crawford, & Phillips, 2005), a deficit primary linked to progressive dysarthria and the impaired function of the subcortical−frontal circuits involved in initiating, maintaining, and monitoring the cognitive activity.

Patients with HD usually fail social cognition tasks, both cartoon and stories. However, they tend to provide misconstrued explanations to social vignettes rather concrete answers, such as patients with FTD (Snowden et al., 2003).

Behavior and Affect

In addition to the movement disorder and decline in frontosubcortical executive functions, affective and behavioral features are an integral part of HD (Rosenblatt, 2007). Individuals with HD may, thus, present with apathy, depression and anxiety, suicidal ideation, perseverative behavior, obsessive compulsive disorder symptoms, irritability, and aggression as well as psychotic symptoms (de Marchi, Morris, Mennella, La Pia, & Nestadt, 1998; Mendez & Cummings, 2003; Rosenblatt, 2007). However, among these symptoms, only apathy increases steadily throughout the disease course, while irritability after the initial slight increases tends to decrease over time (Thompson et al., 2012). Apathy correlates positively with the severity of motor symptoms (Thompson, Snowden, Craufurd, & Neary, 2002) and negatively with the fractional anisotropy of the gyrus rectus bilaterally in the early HD, whereas such associations do not apply to depression (Delmaire et al., 2013). Also, depressive symptoms in HD do not tend to progress gradually, neither at the preclinical stage (Kim et al., 2015) nor at the symptomatic phase of the disease (Thompson et al., 2012).

Similarly to impaired insight into cognitive impairment, individuals with HD may be unaware either of the presence or of the severity of different symptoms, such as chorea, cognitive impairment, or behavioral manifestations. The unawareness of HD signs is a much more complex phenomenon than impaired insight in bvFTD (Rascovsky et al., 2011) or PSP (O'Keeffe et al. 2007), as in HD physiological mechanisms (for poor awareness of chorea) and coping mechanisms (due to familial nature of the disorder, the affected individuals know the trajectory of the disease and may deny the presence or intensity of unequivocal signs) also play a role (Sitek, Thompson, Craufurd, & Snowden, 2014).

ASSESSMENT OF EXECUTIVE FUNCTION IN DEMENTIA

More than 60% of patients with dementia cannot complete standard executive measures such as Stroop test or TMT-B (Enright et al., 2015). The choice of executive tasks to be used in a dementia clinic is made based on their simplicity and their minimal reliance upon the basic cognitive processes, such as language, visuospatial, and memory functions. The task instruction should be short, straightforward, and easy to remember, and the test material needs to be easily handled. In patients with movement disorders accuracy scores should not be time-dependent. The examples of tests/tasks of executive processes feasible in a dementia clinic are provided in Table 19.2. Of note, whereas most traditional executive tasks engage mostly dorsolateral frontal pathways, the presence of environmental dependency syndrome, frequently seen in both bvFTD (Ghosh, Dutt, Bhargava, &

TABLE 19.2 Assessment of Executive Function in Dementia

Observed/Assessed Aspect of Executive Function	Observable Sign/Psychometric Test/Clinical Task
Inhibition	Observation — Environmental dependency behavior — Manual groping behavior (magnetic apraxia) — Incidental imitation behavior — Incidental utilization behavior — Echolalia/palilalia — Compulsive attraction of the gaze — Compulsory reading aloud
	Neurological examination — The presence of frontal release signs, especially: — Grasp reflex (forced grasping, compulsory grasping) — Palmomental reflex — Snout reflex — Clapping task (to elicit applause sign)
	Neuropsychological examination — Hayling test — Tasks with conflicting instructions — Go/no-go task — Drawing multiple loops — Stroop task (applicable only in patients without language impairment and in mild dementia)
Initiation and generation	Observation — Possible mutism — Possible akinesia
	Neuropsychological examination — Verbal fluency tasks (phonemic vs semantic; broad vs narrow semantic categories, alternating fluency) — Design fluency
Mental set-shifting	Observation — Possible perseverative responses
	Neuropsychological examination — Alternating sequences (motor, drawing) — Weigl block sorting test — Sorting test from D-KEFS — The Brixton Spatial Anticipation Test

(Continued)

TABLE 19.2 (Continued)

Observed/Assessed Aspect of Executive Function	Observable Sign/Psychometric Test/Clinical Task
	— The Modified WCST (applicable only in mild dementia without significant working memory impairment) — TMT
Planning and sequencing	Observation — Improper order of steps when executing complex activities of daily living Neuropsychological examination — Modified Tower of London and other simplified tower tasks — Picture sequencing—pictures that are easy to distinguish perceptually — Motor sequencing tasks
Executive screening tasks	Frontal Assessment Battery (FAB) INECO Frontal Screening Frontier Executive Screen Executive Interview-25 (EXIT-25) CLOX—an executive clock drawing test
Proxy report of executive/behavioral symptoms in daily life	Interview format (I) or paper version (P) General, with various behavioral items — NPI-(I): designed especially for dementia clinics — CBI-(P): designed especially for dementia clinics Frontally focused — FBI-(I): designed especially for dementia clinics — BRIEF-2-(P): general measure, sensitive to mild problems — FrSBe-(P): general measure, sensitive to mild problems — IRSPC-(P): general measure, sensitive to mild problems — DEX-(P): general measure, sensitive to mild problems

BRIEF-2, Behavior Rating Inventory of Executive Function-2; *CBI*, Cambridge Behavioural Inventory; *DEX*, Dysexecutive Questionnaire; *D-KEFS*, Delis–Kaplan Executive Function System; *FBI*, Frontal Behavioral Inventory; *FrSBe*, The Frontal Systems Behavior Scale; *INECO*, The Institute of Cognitive Neurology; *IRSPC*, Iowa Rating Scale for Personality Change; *NPI*, Neuropsychiatric Inventory; *TMT*, Trail Making Test; *WCST*, Wisconsin Card Sorting Test.

Snowden, 2013) and PSP (Ghika, Tennis, Growdon, Hoffman, & Johnson, 1995), may alert the clinician to the potential involvement of other frontal areas (i.e., mesial, orbitofrontal, frontostriatal, or frontothalamic tracts) (Archibald, Mateer, & Kerns, 2001). Importantly, both EDS and disinhibition may be examples of environmentally driven rather than internally generated patterns of behavior.

Motor impersistence assessment can also be sometimes useful for the differential diagnosis. For instance, inability to sustain tongue protrusion (>10 s) is one of the typical signs of HD. In the context of predominant psychiatric symptoms and lack of family history, the presence of this sign should alert the clinician to look out for other HD symptoms.

SUMMARY

This chapter attempts to characterize the most common dementing diseases that may affect frontal lobe function. In particular, behavioral changes, affect disturbances, and executive dysfunction known to be a result of frontal lobe damage or impaired functioning have been described. It has been presented that the functioning of the frontal lobes may not only be compromised in neurodegenerative conditions with predominant frontal involvement (such as FTD) but is also frequently seen in patients with early onset AD or dementias associated with movement disorders. Moreover, because the assessment of executive deficits in patients with dementia is challenging, especially in the context of more general decline, some implications for assessment of frontal lobe function have been also discussed. Specifically, it has been posited that scores on tasks assessing executive function need to be interpreted only in light of a full cognitive and language profile as well as qualitative observations.

REFERENCES

Aarsland, D., Ballard, C., McKeith, I., Perry, R. H., & Larsen, J. P. (2001). Comparison of extrapyramidal signs in dementia with Lewy bodies and Parkinson's disease. *Journal of Neuropsychiatry and Clinical Neurosciences, 13*, 374–379.

Aarsland, D., Marsh, L., & Schrag, A. (2009). Neuropsychiatric symptoms in Parkinson's disease. *Movement Disorders, 24*, 2175–2186.

Abrahams, S., Leigh, P. N., Harvey, A., Vythelingum, G. N., Grisé, D., & Goldstein, L. H. (2000). Verbal fluency and executive dysfunction in amyotrophic lateral sclerosis (ALS). *Neuropsychologica, 38*, 734–747.

Agosta, F., Galantucci, S., Svetel, M., Lukić, M. J., Copetti, M., Davidovic, K., & Filippi, M. (2014). Clinical, cognitive, and behavioural correlates of white matter damage in progressive supranuclear palsy. *Journal of Neurology, 261*, 913–924.

Alberici, A., Gobbo, C., Panzacchi, A., Nicosia, F., Ghidoni, R., Benussi, L., & Binnetti, G. (2004). Frontotemporal dementia: Impact of P301L tau mutation on a healthy carrier. *Journal of Neurology, Neurosurgery, and Psychiatry, 75*, 1607–1610.

Albert, M. L. (2005). Subcortical dementia: Historical review and personal view. *Neurocase, 11,* 243–245.

Albert, M. L., Feldman, R. G., & Willis, A. L. (1974). The 'subcortical dementia' of progressive supranuclear palsy. *Journal of Neurology, Neurosurgery, and Psychiatry, 37,* 121–130.

Alexander, G. E., DeLong, M. R., & Strick, P. L. (1986). Parallel organization of functionally segregated circuits linking basal ganglia and cortex. *Annual Review of Neuroscience, 9,* 357–381.

Alladi, S., Xuereb, J., Bak, T., Nestor, P., Knibb, J., Patterson, K., & Hodges, J. R. (2007). Focal cortical presentations of Alzheimer's disease. *Brain, 130,* 2636–2645.

Almkvist, O. (1994). Neuropsychological deficits in vascular dementia in relation to Alzheimer's disease: Reviewing evidence for functional similarity or divergence. *Dementia, 5,* 203–209.

Andresen, J. M., Gayán, J., Djoussé, L., Roberts, S., Brocklebank, D., Cherny, S. S., & Wexler, N. S. (2007). The relationship between CAG repeat length and age of onset differs for Huntington's disease patients with juvenile onset or adult onset. *Annals of Human Genetics, 71,* 295–301.

Archibald, S. J., Mateer, C. A., & Kerns, K. A. (2001). Utilization behavior: Clinical manifestations and neurological mechanisms. *Neuropsychology Review, 11,* 117–130.

Aylward, E. H., Codori, A. M., Rosenblatt, A., Sherr, M., Brandt, J., Stine, O. C., & Ross, C. A. (2000). Rate of caudate atrophy in presymptomatic and symptomatic stages of Huntington's disease. *Movement Disorders, 15,* 552–560.

Babikian, V. L., Wolfe, N., Linn, R., Knoefel, J. E., & Albert, M. L. (1990). Cognitive changes in patients with multiple cerebral infarcts. *Stroke, 21,* 1013–1018.

Balasa, M., Gelpi, E., Antonell, A., Rey, M. J., Sánchez-Valle, R., Molinuevo, J. L., & Lladó, A. (2011). Clinical features and APOE genotype of pathologically proven early-onset Alzheimer disease. *Neurology, 76,* 1720–1725.

Ballard, C., Neill, D., O'Brien, J., McKeith, I. G., Ince, P., & Perry, R. (2000). Anxiety, depression and psychosis in vascular dementia: Prevalence and associations. *Journal of Affective Disorders, 59,* 97–106.

Baudic, S., Dalla Barba, G., Thibaudet, M. C., Smagghe, A., Remy, F., & Traykov, L. (2006). Executive function deficits in early Alzheimer's disease and their relations with episodic memory. *Archives of Clinical Neuropsychology, 21,* 15–21.

Beauchamp, M. H., Dagher, A., Panisset, M., & Doyon, J. (2008). Neural substrates of cognitive skill learning in Parkinson's disease. *Brain and Cognition, 68,* 134–143.

Bennett, D. A., Gilley, D. W., Lee, S., & Cochran, E. J. (1994). White matter changes: Neurobehavioral manifestations of Binswanger's disease and clinical correlates in Alzheimer's disease. *Dementia, 5,* 148–152.

Bertoux, M., O'Callaghan, C., Flanagan, E., Hodges, J. R., & Hornberger, M. (2015). Fronto-striatal atrophy in behavioral variant frontotemporal dementia and Alzheimer's disease. *Frontiers in Neurology, 6,* 147.

Blass, D. M., & Rabins, P. V. (2009). Depression in frontotemporal dementia. *Psychosomatics, 50,* 239–247.

Bogousslavsky, J., Regli, F., & Uske, A. (1988). Thalamic infarcts: Clinical syndromes, etiology, and prognosis. *Neurology, 38,* 837–848.

Bonelli, R. M., & Cummings, J. L. (2008). Frontal-subcortical dementias. *Neurologist, 14,* 100–107.

Borroni, B., Agosti, C., & Padovani, A. (2008). Behavioral and psychological symptoms in dementia with Lewy-bodies (DLB): Frequency and relationship with disease severity and motor impairment. *Archives of Gerontology and Geriatrics, 46,* 101–106.

Borroni, B., Alberici, A., Agosti, C., Cosseddu, M., & Padovani, A. (2009). Pattern of behavioral disturbances in corticobasal degeneration syndrome and progressive supranuclear palsy. *International Psychogeriatrics, 21*, 463–468.

Bozeat, S., Gregory, C. A., Ralph, M. A., & Hodges, J. R. (2000). Which neuropsychiatric and behavioural features distinguish frontal and temporal variants of frontotemporal dementia from Alzheimer's disease? *Journal of Neurology, Neurosurgery, and Psychiatry, 69*, 178–186.

Brandt, J., Folstein, S. E., & Folstein, M. F. (1988). Differential cognitive impairment in Alzheimer's disease and Huntington's disease. *Annals of Neurology, 23*, 555–561.

Brandt, J., Folstein, S. E., Wong, D. F., Links, J., Dannals, R. F., McDonnell-Sill, A., & Tune, L. E. (1990). D2 receptors in Huntington's disease: Positron emission tomography findings and clinical correlates. *Journal of Neuropsychiatry and Clinical Neurosciences, 2*, 20–27.

Brun, A., Englund, B., Gustafson, L., Passant, U., Mann, D. M. A., Neary, D., & Snowden, J. S. (1994). Clinical and neuropathological criteria for frontotemporal dementia. *Journal of Neurology, Neurosurgery, and Psychiatry, 57*, 416–418.

Buffon, F., Porcher, R., Hernandez, K., Kurtz, A., Pointeau, S., Vahedi, K., & Chabriat, H. (2006). Cognitive profile in CADASIL. *Journal of Neurology, Neurosurgery, and Psychiatry, 77*, 175–180.

Burrell, J. R., Halliday, G. M., Kril, J. J., Ittner, L. M., Götz, J., Kiernan, M. C., & Hodges, J. R. (2016). The frontotemporal dementia-motor neuron disease continuum. *Lancet, 388*(10047), 919–931.

Caga, J., Turner, M. R., Hsieh, S., Ahmed, R. M., Devenney, E., Ramsey, E., & Kiernan, M. C. (2016). Apathy is associated with poor prognosis in amyotrophic lateral sclerosis. *European Journal of Neurology, 23*, 891–897.

Carey, C. L., Woods, S. P., Damon, J., Halabi, C., Dean, D., Delis, D. C., & Kramer, J. H. (2008). Discriminant validity and neuroanatomical correlates of rule monitoring in frontotemporal dementia and Alzheimer's disease. *Neuropsychologia, 46*, 1081–1087.

Carlin, D., Bonerba, J., Phipps, M., Alexander, G., Shapiro, M., & Grafman, J. (2000). Planning impairments in frontal lobe dementia and frontal lobe lesion patients. *Neuropsychologia, 38*, 655–665.

Chabriat, H., Joutel, A., Dichgans, M., Tournier-Lasserve, E., & Bousser, M. G. (2009). CADASIL. *Lancet Neurology, 8*, 643–653.

Cho, H., Seo, S. W., Kim, J. H., Suh, M. K., Lee, J. H., Choe, Y. S., & Na, D. L. (2013). Amyloid deposition in early onset versus late onset Alzheimer's disease. *Journal of Alzheimer's Disease: JAD, 35*, 813–821.

Claus, J. J., & Mohr, E. (1996). Attentional deficits in Alzheimer's, Parkinson's, and Huntington's diseases. *Acta Neurologica Scandinavica, 93*, 346–351.

Cools, R., Barker, R. A., Sahakian, B. J., & Robbins, T. W. (2001a). Enhanced or impaired cognitive function in Parkinson's disease as a function of dopaminergic medication and task demands. *Cerebral Cortex, 11*, 1136–1143.

Cools, R., Barker, R. A., Sahakian, B. J., & Robbins, T. W. (2001b). Mechanisms of cognitive set flexibility in Parkinson's disease. *Brain, 124*, 2503–2512.

Cordato, N. J., Pantelis, C., Halliday, G. M., Velakoulis, D., Wood, S. J., Stuart, G. W., ... Morris, J. G. L. (2002). Frontal atrophy correlates with behavioural changes in progressive supranuclear palsy. *Brain, 125*, 789–800.

Cosentino, S., Chute, D., Libon, D., Moore, P., & Grossman, M. (2006). How does the brain support script comprehension? A study of executive processes and semantic knowledge in dementia. *Neuropsychology, 20*, 307–318.

Cummings, J. L. (1994). Vascular subcortical dementias: Clinical aspects. *Dementia, 5,* 177−180.

Cummings, J. L., & Duchen, L. W. (1981). Kluver-Bucy syndrome in Pick disease: Clinical and pathologic correlations. *Neurology, 31,* 1415−1422.

Davous, P. (1998). CADASIL: A review with proposed diagnostic criteria. *European Journal of Neurology, 5,* 219−233.

Defebvre, L. J., Leduc, V., Duhamel, A., Lecouffe, P., Pasquier, F., Lamy-Lhullier, C., & Destée, A. (1999). Technetium HMPAO SPECT study in dementia with Lewy bodies, Alzheimer's disease and idiopathic Parkinson's disease. *Journal of Nuclear Medicine, 40,* 956−962.

Delmaire, C., Dumas, E. M., Sharman, M. A., van den Bogaard, S. J. A., Valabregue, R., Jauffret, C., & Lehéricy, S. (2013). The structural correlates of functional deficits in early Huntington's disease. *Human Brain Mapping, 34,* 2141−2153.

de Marchi, N., Morris, M., Mennella, R., La Pia, S., & Nestadt, G. (1998). Association of obsessive-compulsive disorder and pathological gambling with Huntington's disease in an Italian pedigree: Possible association with Huntington's disease mutation. *Acta Psychiatrica Scandinavica, 97,* 62−65.

de Rijk, M. C., Launer, L. J., Berger, K., Breteler, M. M., Dartigues, J. F., Baldereschi, M., . . . Hofman, A. (2000). Prevalence of Parkinson's disease in Europe: A collaborative study of population-based cohorts. Neurologic diseases in the Elderly Research Group. *Neurology, 58* (11 Suppl 5), S21−S23.

de Silva, D., Hsieh, S., Caga, J., Leslie, F. V. C., Kiernan, M. C., Hodges, J. R., . . . Burrell, J. R. (2016). Motor function and behaviour across the ALS-FTD spectrum. *Acta Neurologica Scandinavica, 133,* 367−372.

Desmond, D. W. (1996). Vascular dementia: A construct in evolution. *Cerebrovascular and Brain Metabolism Reviews, 8,* 296−325.

Dian, L., Cummings, J. L., Petry, S., & Hill, M. A. (1990). Personality alterations in multi-infarct dementia. *Psychosomatics, 31,* 415−419.

Dogan, I., Eickhoff, C. R., Fox, P. T., Laird, A. R., Schulz, J. B., Eickhoff, S. B., & Reetz, K. (2015). Functional connectivity modeling of consistent cortico-striatal degeneration in Huntington's disease. *NeuroImage. Clinical, 7,* 640−652.

Donker Kaat, L., Boon, A. J., Kamphorst, W., Ravid, R., Duivenvoorden, H. J., & van Swieten, J. C. (2007). Frontal presentation in progressive supranuclear palsy. *Neurology, 69,* 723−729.

Douaud, G., Behrens, T. E., Poupon, C., Cointepas, Y., Jbabdi, S., Gaura, V., & yRemy, P. (2009). In vivo evidence for the selective subcortical degeneration in Huntington's disease. *NeuroImage, 46,* 958−966.

Doubleday, E. K., Snowden, J. S., Varma, A. R., & Neary, D. (2002). Qualitative performance characteristics differentiate dementia with Lewy bodies and Alzheimer's disease. *Journal of Neurology, Neurosurgery, and Psychiatry, 72,* 602−607.

Duke, L. M., & Kaszniak, A. (2000). Executive control functions in degenerative dementias: A comparative review. *Neuropsychology Review, 10,* 75−99.

Edwards-Lee, T., Miller, B. L., Benson, D. F., Cummings, J. L., Russell, G. L., Boone, K., & Mena, I. (1997). The temporal variant of frontotemporal dementia. *Brain, 120,* 1027−1040.

Elfgren, C., Brun, A., Gustafson, L., Johanson, A., Minthon, L., Passant, U., & Risberg, J. (1994). Neuropsychological tests as discriminators between dementia of Alzheimer type and frontotemporal dementia. *International Journal of Geriatric Psychiatry, 9,* 635−642.

Emre, M., Aarsland, D., Brown, R., Burn, D. J., Duyckaerts, C., Mizuno, Y., & Dubois, B. (2007). Clinical diagnostic criteria for dementia associated with Parkinson's disease. *Movement Disorders, 22,* 1689−1707.

Enright, J., Oconnell, M. E., Mackinnon, S., & Morgan, D. G. (2015). Predictors of completion of executive-functioning tasks in a memory clinic dementia sample. *Applied Neuropsychology. Adult, 22,* 459−464.

Eslinger, P. J., Moore, P., Anderson, C., & Grossman, M. (2011). Social cognition, executive functioning, and neuroimaging correlates of empathic deficits in frontotemporal dementia. *Journal of Neuropsychiatry and Clinical Neuroscience, 23,* 74−82.

Eslinger, P. J., Moore, P., Troiani, V., Antani, S., Cross, K., Kwok, S., & Grossman, M. (2007). Oops! Resolving social dilemmas in frontotemporal dementia. *Journal of Neurology, Neurosurgery, and Psychiatry, 78,* 457−460.

Falchook, A. D., Decio, D., Williamson, J. B., Okun, M. S., Malaty, I. A., Rodriguez, R. L., & Heilman, K. M. (2011). Alternate but do not swim: A test for executive motor dysfunction in Parkinson disease. *Journal of the International Neuropsychological Society: JINS, 17,* 702−708.

Ferman, T. J., McRae, C. A., Arvanitakis, Z., Tsuboi, Y., Vo, A., & Wszolek, Z. K. (2003). Early and pre-symptomatic neuropsychological dysfunction in the PPND family with the N279K tau mutation. *Parkinsonism & Related Disorders, 9,* 265−270.

Faria, A. V., Ratnanather, J. T., Tward, D. J., Lee, D. S., van den Noort, F., Wu, D., et al. (2016). Linking white matter and deep gray matter alterations in premanifest Huntington disease. *Neuroimage Clinical, 11,* 450−460. http://dx.doi.org/10.1016/j.nicl.2016.02.014

Filoteo, J. V., Maddox, W. T., & Davis, J. D. (2001). A possible role of the striatum in linear and nonlinear category learning: Evidence from patients with Huntington's disease. *Behavioral Neuroscience, 115,* 786−798.

Firbank, M., Kobeleva, X., Cherry, G., Killen, A., Gallagher, P., Burn, D. J., & Taylor, J.-P. (2016). Neural correlates of attention-executive dysfunction in Lewy body dementia and Alzheimer's disease. *Human Brain Mapping, 37,* 1254−1270.

Firbank, M. J., Watson, R., Mak, E., Aribisala, B., Barber, R., Colloby, S. J., & O'Brien, J. T. (2016). Longitudinal diffusion tensor imaging in dementia with Lewy bodies and Alzheimer's disease. *Parkinsonism & Related Disorders, 24,* 76−80.

Friedman, J. H. (2010). Parkinson's disease psychosis 2010: A review article. *Parkinsonism & Related Disorders, 16,* 553−560.

Fuster, J. M. (2003). *Cortex and mind.* New York, NY: Oxford University Press.

Gazzaley, A., Sheridan, M. A., Cooney, J. W., & D'Esposito, M. (2007). Age-related deficits in component processes of working memory. *Neuropsychology, 21,* 532−539.

Gerstenecker, A., Duff, K., Mast, B., & Litvan, I. (2013). Behavioral abnormalities in progressive supranuclear palsy. *Psychiatry Research, 210,* 1205−1210.

Gerstenecker, A., Mast, B., Duff, K., Ferman, T. J., & Litvan, I. (2013). Executive dysfunction is the primary cognitive impairment in progressive supranuclear palsy. *Archives of Clinical Neuropsychology, 28,* 104−113.

Ghika, J., Tennis, M., Growdon, J., Hoffman, E., & Johnson, K. (1995). Environment-driven responses in progressive supranuclear palsy. *Journal of the Neurological Sciences, 130,* 104−111.

Ghosh, A., Dutt, A., Bhargava, P., & Snowden, J. (2013). Environmental dependency behaviours in frontotemporal dementia: Have we been underrating them? *Journal of Neurology, 260,* 861−868.

Gleichgerrcht, E., Torralva, T., Roca, M., & Manes, F. (2010). Utility of an abbreviated version of the executive and social cognition battery in the detection of executive deficits in early behavioral variant frontotemporal dementia patients. *Journal of the International Neuropsychological Society: JINS, 16*, 687−694.

Gorno-Tempini, M. L., Dronkers, N. F., Rankin, K. P., Ogar, J. M., Phengrasamy, L., Rosen, H. J., & Miller, B. L. (2004). Cognition and anatomy in three variants of primary progressive aphasia. *Annals of Neurology, 55*, 335−346.

Gorno-Tempini, M. L., Hillis, A. E., Weintraub, S., Kertesz, A., Mendez, M., Cappa, S. F., & Grossman, M. (2011). Classification of primary progressive aphasia and its variants. *Neurology, 76*, 1006−10014.

Gour, N., Felician, O., Didic, M., Koric, L., Gueriot, C., Chanoine, V., & Ranjeva, J. P. (2014). Functional connectivity changes differ in early and late-onset Alzheimer's disease. *Human Brain Mapping, 35*, 2978−2994.

Grafton, S. T., Mazziotta, J. C., Pahl, J. J., St, George-Hyslop, P., Haines, J. L., Gusella, J., & Phelps, M. E. (1990). A comparison of neurological, metabolic, structural, and genetic evaluations in persons at risk for Huntington's disease. *Annals of Neurology, 28*, 614−621.

Gregory, C. A., & Hodges, J. R. (1996). Frontotemporal dementia: Use of consensus criteria and prevalence of psychiatric features. *Neuropsychiatry, Neuropsychology, and Behavioral Neurology, 9*, 145−153.

Grossman, M. (2010). Primary progressive aphasia: Clinicopathological correlations. *Nature Review. Neurology, 6*, 88−97.

Grossman, M., Libon, D. J., Forman, M. S., Massimo, L., Wood, E., Moore, P., & Trojanowski, J. Q. (2007). Distinct antemortem profiles in patients with pathologically defined frontotemporal dementia. *Archives of Neurology, 64*, 1601−1609.

Hachinski, V. (2008). World stroke day 2008: "Little strokes, big trouble". *Stroke, 39*, 2407−2420.

Hachinski, V., Iadecola, C., Petersen, R. C., Breteler, M. M., Nyenhuis, D. L., Black, S. E., & Leblanc, G. G. (2006). National Institute of Neurological Disorders and Stroke-Canadian Stroke Network vascular cognitive impairment harmonization standards. *Stroke, 37*, 2220−2241.

Harciarek, M., & Cosentino, S. (2013). Language, executive function and social cognition in the diagnosis of frontotemporal dementia syndromes. *International Review of Psychiatry, 25*, 178−196.

Harciarek, M., & Jodzio, K. (2005). Neuropsychological differences between frontotemporal dementia and Alzheimer's disease. *Neuropsychology Review, 3*, 131−145.

Harciarek, M., & Kertesz, A. (2011). Primary progressive aphasias and their contribution to the contemporary knowledge about the brain-language relationship. *Neuropsychology Review, 21*, 271−287.

Harciarek, M., Sitek, E. J., & Kertesz, A. (2014). The patterns of progression in primary progressive aphasia—Implications for assessment and management. *Aphasiology, 28*, 964−980.

Heidler-Gary, J., Gottesman, R., Newhart, M., Chang, S., Ken, L., & Hillis, A. E. (2007). Utility of behavioral versus cognitive measures in differentiating between subtypes of frontotemporal lobar degeneration and Alzheimer's disease. *Dementia and Geriatric Cognitive Disorders, 23*, 184−193.

Heilman, K. M., Blonder, L. X., Bowers, D., & Valenstein, E. (2003). Emotional disorders associated with neurological diseases. In K. M. Heilman, & E. Valenstein (Eds.), *Clinical neuropsychology* (pp. 447−478). New York, NY: Oxford University Press.

Heindel, W. C., Butters, N., & Salmon, D. P. (1988). Impaired learning of a motor skill in patients with Huntington's disease. *Behavioral Neuroscience, 102*, 141–147.

Hely, M. A., Reid, W. G. J., Adena, M. A., Halliday, G. M., & Morris, J. G. L. (2008). The Sydney Multicenter Study of Parkinson's disease: The inevitability of dementia at 20 years. *Movement Disorders, 23*, 837–844.

Henry, J. D., Crawford, J. R., & Phillips, L. H. (2005). A meta-analytic review of verbal fluency deficits in Huntington's disease. *Neuropsychology, 19*, 243–252.

Hodges, J. R. (2007). *Frontotemporal dementia syndromes*. New York, NY: Cambridge University Press.

Hodges, J. R. (2011). Clinico-pathological correlations in frontotemporal dementia: An update on the Cambridge series and review of the literature. *Acta Neuropsychologica, 9*, 177–192.

Hodges, J. R., Patterson, K., Ward, R., Garrard, P., Bak, T., Perry, R., & Gregory, C. (1999). The differentiation of semantic dementia and frontal lobe dementia (temporal and frontal variants of frontotemporal dementia) from early Alzheimer's disease: A comparative neuropsychological study. *Neuropsychology, 13*, 31–40.

Hornberger, M., Piguet, O., Kipps, C., & Hodges, J. R. (2008). Executive function in progressive and nonprogressive behavioral variant frontotemporal dementia. *Neurology, 71*, 1481–1488.

Hornberger, M., Yew, B., Gilardoni, S., Mioshi, E., Gleichgerrcht, E., Manes, F., & Hodges, J. R. (2014). Ventromedial-frontopolar prefrontal cortex atrophy correlates with insight loss in frontotemporal dementia and Alzheimer's disease. *Human Brain Mapping, 35*, 616–626.

Hozumi, A., Hirata, K., Tanaka, H., & Yamazaki, K. (2000). Perseveration for novel stimuli in Parkinson's disease: An evaluation based on event-related potentials topography. *Movement Disorders, 15*, 835–842.

Hsieh, S., & Lee, C. Y. (1999). Source memory in Parkinson's disease. *Perceptual and Motor Skills, 89*, 355–367.

Hsiung, G. Y., DeJesus-Hernandez, M., Feldman, H. H., Sengdy, P., Bouchard-Kerr, P., Dwosh, E., & Mackenzie, I. R. (2012). Clinical and pathological features of familial frontotemporal dementia caused by C9ORF72 mutation on chromosome 9p. *Brain, 135*, 709–722.

Huey, E. D., Goveia, E. N., Paviol, S., Pardini, M., Krueger, F., Zamboni, G., & Grafman, J. (2009). Executive dysfunction in frontotemporal dementia and corticobasal syndrome. *Neurology, 72*, 453–459.

Jackson, M., Lennox, G., & Lowe, J. (1996). Motor neurone disease-inclusion dementia. *Neurodegeneration, 5*, 339–350.

Jason, G. W., Suchowersky, O., Pajurkova, E. M., Graham, L., Klimek, M. L., Garber, A. T., & Poirier-Heine, D. (1997). Cognitive manifestations of Huntington disease in relation to genetic structure and clinical onset. *Archives of Neurology, 54*, 1081–1088.

Jellinger, K. A. (2013). Organic bases of late-life depression: A critical update. *Journal of Neural Transmission, 120*, 1109–1125.

Johns, E. K., Phillips, N. A., Belleville, S., Goupil, D., Babins, L., Kelner, N., & Chertkow, H. (2009). Executive functions in frontotemporal dementia and Lewy body dementia. *Neuropsychology, 23*, 765–777.

Johnson, J. K., Brun, A., & Head, E. (2007). Frontal variant of Alzheimer's disease. In B. L. Miller, & J. L. Cummings (Eds.), *The human frontal lobes: functions and disorders* (pp. 429–444). New York, NY: The Guilford Press.

Johnson, J. K., Head, E., Kim, R., Starr, A., & Cotman, C. W. (1999). Clinical and pathological evidence for a frontal variant of Alzheimer disease. *Archives of Neurology, 56*, 1233–1239.

Kaiser, N. C., Melrose, R. J., Liu, C., Sultzer, D. L., Jimenez, E., Su, M., & Mendez, M. F. (2012). Neuropsychological and neuroimaging markers in early versus late-onset Alzheimer's disease. *American Journal of Alzheimer's Disease and Other Dementias, 27*, 520−529.

Karantzoulis, S., & Galvin, J. E. (2011). Distinguishing Alzheimer's disease from other major forms of dementia. *Expert Review of Neurotherapeutics, 11*, 1579−1591.

Kehagia, A. A., Barker, R. A., & Robbins, T. W. (2010). Neuropsychological and clinical heterogeneity of cognitive impairment and dementia in patients with Parkinson's disease. *Lancet Neurology, 9*, 1200−1213.

Kertesz, A., Blair, M., Davidson, W., McMonagle, P., & Munoz, D. G. (2005). The evolution and pathology of frontotemporal dementia. *Brain, 128*, 1996−2005.

Kertesz, A., Blair, M., McMonagle, P., & Munoz, D. G. (2007). The diagnosis and course of frontotemporal dementia. *Alzheimer Disease and Associated Disorders, 21*, 155−163.

Kertesz, A., & Clydesdale, S. (1994). Neuropsychological deficits in vascular dementia vs. Alzheimer's disease. Frontal lobe deficits prominent in vascular dementia. *Archives of Neurology, 51*, 1226−1231.

Kertesz, A., Davidson, W., & Fox, H. (1997). Frontal behavioral inventory: Diagnostic criteria for frontal lobe dementia. *Canadian Journal of Neurological Sciences, 24*, 29−36.

Kertesz, A., Jesso, S., Harciarek, M., Blair, M., & McMonagle, P. (2010). What is semantic dementia? A cohort study of diagnostic features and clinical boundaries. *Archives of Neurology, 67*, 483−489.

Kertesz, A., Martinez-Lage, P., Davidson, W., & Munoz, D. G. (2000). The corticobasal degeneration syndrome overlaps progressive aphasia and frontotemporal dementia. *Neurology, 55*, 1368−1375.

Kertesz, A., McMonagle, P., & Jesso, S. (2011). Extrapyramidal syndromes in frontotemporal degeneration. *Journal of Molecular Neuroscience, 45*, 336−342.

Kertesz, A., Nadkarni, N., Davidson, W., & Thomas, A. W. (2000a). The frontal behavioral inventory in the differential diagnosis of frontotemporal dementia. *Journal of the International Neuropsychological Society: JINS, 6*, 460−468.

Kim, J.-I., Long, J. D., Mills, J. A., McCusker, E., Paulsen, J. S., & De Soriano, . . . Zschiegner, R. (2015). Multivariate clustering of progression profiles reveals different depression patterns in prodromal Huntington disease. *Neuropsychology, 29*, 949−960.

Kling, M. A., Trojanowski, J. Q., Wolk, D. A., Lee, V. M., & Arnold, S. E. (2013). Vascular disease and dementias: Paradigm shifts to drive research in new directions. *Alzheimer's & Dementia: The Journal of the Alzheimer's Association, 9*, 76−92.

Knibb, J. A., Woollams, A. M., Hodges, J. R., & Patterson, K. (2009). Making sense of progressive non-fluent aphasia: An analysis of conversational speech. *Brain, 132*, 2734−2746.

Kobylecki, C., Jones, M., Thompson, J. C., Richardson, A. M., Neary, D., Mann, D. M. A., & Gerhard, A. (2015). Cognitive−behavioural features of progressive supranuclear palsy syndrome overlap with frontotemporal dementia. *Journal of Neurology, 262*, 916−922.

Korczyn, A. D., & Halperin, I. (2009). Depression and dementia. *Journal of the Neurological Sciences, 283*, 139−142.

Kramer, J. H., & Wetzel, M. E. (2009). Vascular dementia. In J. R. Festa, & R. M. Lazar (Eds.), *Neurovascular neuropsychology* (pp. 87−102). New York, NY: Springer Science.

Krueger, F., Rostami, E., Huey, E. D., Snyder, A., & Grafman, J. (2007). Evidence of an inferior total-order planning strategy in patients with frontotemporal dementia. *Neurocase, 13*, 426−437.

Kumfor, F., & Piguet, O. (2012). Disturbance of emotion processing in frontotemporal dementia: A synthesis of cognitive and neuroimaging findings. *Neuropsychology Review*, 22, 280–297.

Kuzis, G., Sabe, L., Tiberti, C., Leiguarda, R., & Starkstein, S. E. (1997). Cognitive functions in major depression and Parkinson disease. *Archives of Neurology*, 54, 982–986.

Kvickström, P., Eriksson, B., van Westen, D., Lätt, J., Elfgren, C., & Nilsson, C. (2011). Selective frontal neurodegeneration of the inferior fronto-occipital fasciculus in progressive supranuclear palsy (PSP) demonstrated by diffusion tensor tractography. *BMC Neurology*, 11, 13.

Lam, B. Y. K., Halliday, G. M., Irish, M., Hodges, J. R., & Piguet, O. (2014). Longitudinal white matter changes in frontotemporal dementia subtypes. *Human Brain Mapping*, 35, 3547–3557.

Lang, A. E., Bergeron, C., Pollanen, M. S., & Ashby, P. (1992). Parietal Pick's disease mimicking cortical-basal degeneration. *Neurology*, 44, 1436–1440.

Lawrence, A. D., Sahakian, B. J., Hodges, J. R., Rosser, A. E., Lange, K. W., & Robbins, T. W. (1996). Executive and mnemonic functions in early Huntington's disease. *Brain*, 119, 1633–1645.

Lawrence, A. D., Sahakian, B. J., & Robbins, T. W. (1998). Cognitive functions and corticostriatal circuits: Insights from Huntington's disease. *Trends in Cognitive Sciences*, 2, 379–388.

Leroi, I., Barraclough, M., McKie, S., Hinvest, N., Evans, J., Elliott, R., & McDonald, K. (2013). Dopaminergic influences on executive function and impulsive behaviour in impulse control disorders in Parkinson's disease. *Journal of Neuropsychology*, 7, 306–325.

Libon, D. J., Bogdanoff, B., Cloud, B. S., Skalina, S., Giovannetti, T., Gitlin, H. L., & Bonavita, J. (1998). Declarative and procedural learning, quantitative measures of the hippocampus, and subcortical white alterations in Alzheimer's disease and ischaemic vascular dementia. *Journal of Clinical and Experimental Neuropsychology*, 20, 30–41.

Libon, D. J., Xie, S. X., Moore, P., Farmer, J., Antani, S., McCawley, G., & Grossman, M. (2007). Patterns of neuropsychological impairment in frontotemporal dementia. *Neurology*, 68, 369–375.

Lippa, C. F., Smith, T. W., & Fontneau, N. (1990). Corticonigral degeneration with neuronal achromasia. A clinicopathological study of two cases. *Journal of the Neurological Sciences*, 98, 301–310.

Lleó, A., Blesa, R., Gendre, J., Castellví, M., Pastor, P., Queralt, R., & Oliva, R. (2001). A novel presenilin 2 gene mutation (D439A) in a patient with early-onset Alzheimer's disease. *Neurology*, 57, 1926–1928.

Looi, J. C., & Sachdev, P. S. (1999). Differentiation of vascular dementia from AD on neuropsychological tests. *Neurology*, 53, 670–678.

Lomen-Hoerth, C., Anderson, T., & Miller, B. (2002). The overlap of amyotrophic lateral sclerosis and frontotemporal dementia. *Neurology*, 59, 1077–1079.

Lopez, G., Bayulkem, K., & Hallett, M. (2016). Progressive supranuclear palsy (PSP): Richardson syndrome and other PSP variants. *Acta Neurologica Scandinavistica*, 134(4), 242–249. http://dx.doi.org/10.1111/ane.12546 [Epub ahead of print].

Loring, D. W. (1999). *INS dictionary of neuropsychology*. New York, NY: Oxford University Press.

Lough, S., Gregory, C., & Hodges, J. R. (2001). Dissociation of social cognition and executive function in frontal variant frontotemporal dementia. *Neurocase*, 7, 123–130.

Lowther, E. R., O'Brien, J. T., Firbank, M. J., & Blamire, A. M. (2014). Lewy body compared with Alzheimer dementia is associated with decreased functional connectivity in resting state networks. *Psychiatry Research*, 223, 192–201.

MacPherson, S. E., Parra, M. A., Moreno, S., Lopera, F., & Della Sala, S. (2012). Dual task abilities as a possible preclinical marker of Alzheimer's disease in carriers of the E280A presenilin-1 mutation. *Journal of the International Neuropsychological Society: JINS, 18,* 234–241.

Mahant, N., McCusker, E. A., Byth, K., Graham, S., & the Huntington Study Group (2003). Huntington's disease: Clinical correlates of disability and progression. *Neurology, 61,* 1085–1092.

Makin, S. D., Turpin, S., Dennis, M. S., & Wardlaw, J. M. (2013). Cognitive impairment after lacunar stroke: Systematic review and meta-analysis of incidence, prevalence and comparison with other stroke subtypes. *Journal of Neurology, Neurosurgery, and Psychiatry, 84,* 893–900.

Marczinski, C. A., Davidson, W., & Kertesz, A. (2004). A longitudinal study of behavior in frontotemporal dementia and primary progressive aphasia. *Cognitive and Behavioral Neurology: Official Journal of the Society for Behavioral and Cognitive Neurology, 17,* 185–190.

Matsui, J. T., Vaidya, J. G., Wassermann, D., Kim, R. E., Magnotta, V. A., Johnson, H. J., Paulsen, J. S., & PREDICT-HD Investigators and Coordinators of the Huntington Study Group (2015). Prefrontal cortex white matter tracts in prodromal Huntington disease. *Human Brain Mapping, 36,* 3717–3732.

McKeith, I. G., Dickson, D. W., Lowe, J., Emre, M., O'Brien, J. T., Feldman, H., & Consortium on DLB (2005). Diagnosis and management of dementia with Lewy bodies: Third report of the DLB Consortium. *Neurology, 65,* 1863–1872.

McKhann, G. M., Knopman, D. S., Chertkow, H., Hyman, B. T., Jack, C. R., Jr, Kawas, C. H., & Phelps, C. H. (2011). The diagnosis of dementia due to Alzheimer's disease: Recommendations from the National Institute on Aging Alzheimer's Association workgroups on diagnostic guidelines for Alzheimer's disease. *Alzheimers Dementia, 7,* 263–269.

McKinlay, A., Kaller, C. P., Grace, R. C., Dalrymple-Alford, J. C., Anderson, T. J., Fink, J., & Roger, D. (2008). Planning in Parkinson's disease: A matter of problem structure? *Neuropsychologia, 46,* 384–389.

McMonagle, P., Deering, F., Berliner, Y., & Kertesz, A. (2006). The cognitive profile of posterior cortical atrophy. *Neurology, 66,* 331–338.

McPherson, S. E., & Cummings, J. L. (1996). Neuropsychological aspects of vascular dementia. *Brain and Cognition, 31,* 269–282.

Meador, K. J., Loring, D. W., Sethi, K. D., Yaghmai, F., Styren, S. D., & DeKosky, S. T. (1996). Dementia associated with dorsal midbrain lesion. *Journal of the International Neuropsychological Society: JINS, 2,* 359–367.

Mega, M. S., Cummings, J. L., Fiorello, T., & Gornbein, J. (1996). The spectrum of behavioral changes in Alzheimer's disease. *Neurology, 46,* 130–135.

Mendez, M. F., Adams, N. L., & Lewandowski, K. S. (1989). Neurobehavioral changes associated with caudate lesions. *Neurology, 39,* 349–354.

Mendez, M. F., & Cummings, J. L. (2003). *Dementia—A clinical approach* (3rd ed). Philadelphia, PA: Butterworth-Heinemann (Elsevier).

Mendez, M. F., Lee, A. S., Joshi, A., & Shapira, J. S. (2012). Nonamnestic presentations of early-onset Alzheimer's disease. *American Journal of Alzheimer's Disease and Other Dementias, 27,* 413–420. Available from http://dx.doi.org/10.1177/1533317512454711.

Menon, U., & Kelley, R. E. (2009). Subcortical ischemic cerebrovascular dementia. *International Review of Neurobiology, 84,* 21–33.

Mesulam, M. M. (1987). Primary progressive aphasia—Differentiation from Alzheimer's disease. *Annals of Neurology, 22,* 533–534.

Mesulam, M. M. (2003). Primary progressive aphasia—A language-based dementia. *New England Journal of Medicine, 349,* 1535–1542.

Mesulam, M., Weineke, C., Rogalski, E., Cobia, D., Thompson, C., & Weintraub, S. (2009). Quantitative template for subtyping primary progressive aphasia. *Archives of Neurology, 66,* 1545−1551.

Mez, J., Cosentino, S., Brickman, A. M., Huey, E. D., Manly, J. J., & Mayeux, R. (2013). Dysexecutive versus amnestic Alzheimer disease subgroups: Analysis of demographic, genetic, and vascular factors. *Alzheimer's Disease and Associated Disorders, 27,* 218−225.

Miller, B. L., Cummings, J. L., Villanueva-Meyer, J., Boone, K., Mehringer, C. M., Lesser, I. M., & Mena, I. (1991). Frontal lobe degeneration: Clinical, neuropsychological, and SPECT characteristics. *Neurology, 41,* 1374−1382.

Mori, E., Ishii, K., Hashimoto, M., Imamura, T., Hirono, N., & Kitagaki, H. (1999). Role of functional brain imaging in the evaluation of vascular dementia. *Alzheimer Disease and Associated Disorders, 13,* 91−101.

Morris, R. G., & Hannesdottir, K. (2004). Loss of 'awareness' in Alzheimer's disease. In R. G. Morris, & J. Becker (Eds.), *Cognitive neuropsychology of Alzheimer's disease* (pp. 275−296). New York, NY: Oxford University Press.

Muller, S. V., Jung, A., Preinfalk, J., Kolbe, H., Ridao-Alonso, M., Dengler, R., & Munte, T. F. (2002). Disturbance of "extrinsic alertness" in Huntington's disease. *Journal of Clinical and Experimental Neuropsychology, 24,* 517−526.

Muslimović, D., Post, B., Speelman, J. D., De Haan, R. J., & Schmand, B. (2009). Cognitive decline in Parkinson's disease: A prospective longitudinal study. *Journal of the International Neuropsychological Society: JINS, 15,* 426−437.

Neary, D., & Snowden, J. (2013). A modern perspective on some of the most highly cited JNNP papers of all time: Frontal lobe dementia, motor neuron disease, and clinical and neuropathological criteria. *Journal of Neurology, Neurosurgery, and Psychiatry, 84,* 713−714.

Neary, D., Snowden, J. S., Gustafson, L., Passant, U., Stuss, D., Black, S., & Benson, D. F. (1998). Frontotemporal lobar degeneration: A consensus on clinical diagnostic criteria. *Neurology, 51,* 1546−1554.

Neary, D., Snowden, J. S., Mann, D. M. A., Northen, B., Goulding, P. J., & Macdermott, N. (1990). Frontal lobe dementia and motor neuron disease. *Journal of Neurology, Neurosurgery, and Psychiatry, 53,* 23−32.

Novak, M. J. U., Seunarine, K. K., Gibbard, C. R., Mccolgan, P., Draganski, B., Friston, K., & Tabrizi, S. J. (2015). Basal ganglia-cortical structural connectivity in Huntington's disease. *Human Brain Mapping, 36,* 1728−1740.

Nussbaum, R. L., & Ellis, C. E. (2003). Alzheimer's disease and Parkinson's disease. *New England Journal of Medicine, 348,* 1356−1364.

O'Callaghan, C., Naismith, S. L., Hodges, J. R., Lewis, S. J. G., & Hornberger, M. (2013). Fronto-striatal atrophy correlates of inhibitory dysfunction in Parkinson's disease versus behavioural variant frontotemporal dementia. *Cortex, 49,* 1833−1843.

Okamoto, K., Hirai, S., Yamazaki, T., Sun, X., & Nakazato, Y. (1991). New ubiquitin-positive intraneuronal inclusions in the extra-motor cortices in patients with amyotrophic lateral sclerosis. *Neuroscience Letters, 129,* 233−236.

O'Keeffe, F. M., Murray, B., Coen, R. F., Dockree, P. M., Bellgrove, M. A., Garavan, H., & Robertson, I. H. (2007). Loss of insight in frontotemporal dementia, corticobasal degeneration and progressive supranuclear palsy. *Brain, 130,* 753−764.

Olichney, J. M., Galasko, D., Salmon, D. P., Hofstetter, C. R., Hansen, L. A., Katzman, R., & Thal, L. J. (1998). Cognitive decline is faster in Lewy body variant than in Alzheimer's disease. *Neurology, 51,* 351−357.

Ossenkoppele, R., Pijnenburg, Y. A. L., Perry, D. C., Cohn-Sheehy, B. I., Scheltens, N. M. E., Vogel, J. W., & Rabinovici, G. D. (2015). The behavioural/dysexecutive variant of Alzheimer's disease: Clinical, neuroimaging and pathological features. *Brain, 138*, 2732–2749.

Pantoni, L., Poggesi, A., & Inzitari, D. (2009). Cognitive decline and dementia related to cerebrovascular diseases: Some evidence and concepts. *Cerebrovascular Diseases, 27*, 191–196.

Papoutsi, M., Labuschagne, I., Tabrizi, S. J., & Stout, J. C. (2014). The cognitive burden in Huntington's disease: Pathology, phenotype, and mechanisms of compensation. *Movement Disorders, 29*, 673–683.

Papp, K. V., Snyder, P. J., Mills, J. A., Duff, K., Westervelt, H. J., Long, J. D., & Paulsen, J. S. (2013). Measuring executive dysfunction longitudinally and in relation to genetic burden, brain volumetrics, and depression in prodromal Huntington disease. *Archives of Clinical Neuropsychology, 28*, 156–168.

Paulsen, J. S., Zhao, H., Stout, J. C., Brinkman, R. R., Guttman, M., Ross, C. A., & Shoulson, I. (2001). Clinical markers of early disease in persons near onset of Huntington's disease. *Neurology, 57*, 658–662.

Paulsen, J. S., Zimbelman, J. L., Hinton, S. C., Langbehn, D. R., Leveroni, C. L., Benjamin, M. L., & Rao, S. M. (2004). fMRI biomarker of early neuronal dysfunction in presymptomatic Huntington's Disease. *American Journal of Neuroradiology, 25*, 1715–1721.

Peavy, G. M., Salmon, D., Bear, P. I., Paulsen, J. S., Cahn, D. A., Hofstetter, C. R., & Shult, C. W. (2001). Detection of mild cognitive deficits in Parkinson's disease patients with the WAIS-R NI. *Journal of the International Neuropsychological Society: JINS, 7*, 535–543.

Peraza, L. R., Taylor, J.-P., & Kaiser, M. (2015). Divergent brain functional network alterations in dementia with Lewy bodies and Alzheimer's disease. *Neurobiology of Aging, 36*, 2458–2467.

Perri, R., Monaco, M., Fadda, L., Caltagirone, C., & Carlesimo, G. A. (2014). Neuropsychological correlates of behavioral symptoms in Alzheimer's disease, frontal variant of frontotemporal, subcortical vascular, and Lewy body dementias: A comparative study. *Journal of Alzheimer's Disease: JADS, 39*, 669–677.

Perry, R. J., Rosen, H. R., Kramer, J. H., Beer, J. S., Levenson, R. L., & Miller, B. L. (2001). Hemispheric dominance for emotions, empathy and social behaviour: Evidence from right and left handers with frontotemporal dementia. *Neurocase, 7*, 145–160.

Pettit, L. D., Bastin, M. E., Smith, C., Bak, T. H., Gillingwater, T. H., & Abrahams, S. (2013). Executive deficits, not processing speed relates to abnormalities in distinct prefrontal tracts in amyotrophic lateral sclerosis. *Brain, 136*, 3290–3304.

Pick, A. (1892). Über die Beziehungen der senilen Hirnatrophie zur Aphasie. *Prager Medizinische Wochenschrift, 17*, 165–167.

Pillon, B., Deweer, B., Michon, A., Malapani, C., Agid, Y., & Dubois, B. (1994). Are explicit memory disorders of progressive supranuclear palsy related to damage to striatofrontal circuits? Comparison with Alzheimer's, Parkinson's, and Huntington's diseases. *Neurology, 44*, 1264–1270.

Portet, F., Dauvilliers, Y., Campion, D., Raux, G., Hauw, J. J., Lyon-Caen, O., & Touchon, J. (2003). Very early onset AD with a de novo mutation in the presenilin 1 gene (Met 233 Leu). *Neurology, 61*, 1136–1137.

Possin, K., Brambati, S. M., Rosen, H., Johnson, J. K., Pa, J., Weiner, M. W., & Kramer, J. K. (2009). Rule violation errors are associated with right lateral prefrontal cortex atrophy in neurodegenerative disease. *Journal of the International Neuropsychological Society: JINS, 15*, 354–364.

Possin, K., Chester, S. K., Laluz, V., Bostrom, A., Rosen, H., Miller, B. L., & Kramer, J. K. (2012). The frontal-anatomic specificity of design fluency repetitions and their diagnostic relevance for behavioral variant frontotemporal dementia. *Journal of the International Neuropsychological Society: JINS, 18,* 834–844.

Prince, M., Bryce, R., Albanese, E., Wimo, A., Ribeiro, W., & Ferri, C. P. (2013). The global prevalence of dementia: A systematic review and metaanalysis. *Alzheimer's & Dementia: The Journal of the Alzheimer's Association, 9,* 63–75, e2.

Rahman, S., Robbins, T. W., & Sahakian, B. J. (1999). Comparative cognitive neuropsychological studies of frontal lobe function: Implications for therapeutic strategies in frontal variant frontotemporal dementia. *Dementia and Geriatric Cognitive Disorders, 10,* 15–28.

Rankin, K. P., Kramer, J. H., Mychack, P., & Miller, B. L. (2003). Double dissociation of social functioning in frontotemporal dementia. *Neurology, 60,* 266–271.

Rao, H., Mamikonyan, E., Detre, J. A., Siderowf, A. D., Stern, M. B., Potenza, M. N., & Weintraub, D. (2010). Decreased ventral striatal activity with impulse control disorders in Parkinson's disease. *Movement Disorders, 25,* 1660–1669.

Rascovsky, K., Hodges, J. R., Knopman, D., Mendez, M. F., Kramer, J. H., Neuhaus, J., ... Miller, B. L. (2011). Sensitivity of revised diagnostic criteria for the behavioural variant of frontotemporal dementia. *Brain, 134,* 2456–2477.

Rascovsky, K., Salmon, D. P., Hansen, L. A., & Galasko, D. (2008). Distinct cognitive profiles and rates of decline on the Mattis Dementia Rating Scale in autopsy-confirmed frontotemporal dementia and Alzheimer's disease. *Journal of the International Neuropsychological Society: JINS, 14,* 373–383.

Rascovsky, K., Salmon, D. P., Ho, G. J., Galasko, D., Peavy, G. M., Hansen, L. A., & Thal, L. J. (2002). Cognitive profiles differ in autopsy-confirmed frontotemporal dementia and AD. *Neurology, 58,* 1801–1808.

Ratnavalli, E., Brayne, C., Dawson, K., & Hodges, J. R. (2002). The prevalence of frontotemporal dementia. *Neurology, 58,* 1615–1621.

Raux, G., Gantier, R., Thomas-Anterion, C., Boulliat, J., Verpillat, P., Hannequin, D., & Campion, D. (2000). Dementia with prominent frontotemporal features associated with L113P presenilin 1 mutation. *Neurology, 55,* 1577–1578.

Reading, S. A., Dziorny, A. C., Peroutka, L. A., Schreiber, M., Gourley, L. M., Yallapragada, V., & Ross, C. A. (2004). Functional brain changes in presymptomatic Huntington's disease. *Annals of Neurology, 55,* 879–883.

Ringman, J. M., Diaz-Olavarrieta, C., Rodriguez, Y., Chavez, M., Fairbanks, L., Paz, F., & Kawas, C. (2005). Neuropsychological function in nondemented carriers of presenilin-1 mutations. *Neurology, 65,* 552–558.

Robinson, R. (1998). *The clinical neuropsychiatry of stroke—Cognitive, behavioral and emotional disorders following vascular brain injury.* New York, NY: Cambridge University Press.

Robottom, B. J., & Weiner, W. J. (2009). Dementia in Parkinson's disease. *International Review of Neurobiology, 84,* 229–244.

Rohrer, J. D., & Warren, J. D. (2010). Phenomenology and anatomy of abnormal behaviours in primary progressive aphasia. *Journal of the Neurological Sciences, 293,* 35–38.

Román, G. C. (1999). A historical review of the concept of vascular dementia: Lessons from the past for the future. *Alzheimer Disease and Associated Disorders, 13*(Suppl 3), S4–S8.

Rosen, H. J., Allison, S. C., Ogar, J. M., Amici, S., Rose, K., Dronkers, N., & Gorno-Tempini (2006). Behavioral features in semantic dementia vs other forms of progressive aphasias. *Neurology, 67*(10), 1752–1756.

Rosenberg, P. B., Mielke, M. M., Appleby, B., Oh, E., Leoutsakos, J.-M., & Lyketsos, C. G. (2011). Neuropsychiatric symptoms in MCI subtypes: The importance of executive dysfunction. *International Journal of Geriatric Psychiatry*, *26*, 364–372.

Rosenblatt, A. (2007). Neuropsychiatry of Huntington's disease. *Dialogues in Clinical Neuroscience*, *9*, 191–197.

Rosso, S. M., Donker Kaat, L., Baks, T., Joosse, M., de Koning, I., Pijnenburg, Y., & van Swieten, J. C. (2003). Frontotemporal dementia in the Netherlands: Patient characteristics and prevalence estimates from a population-based study. *Brain*, *126*, 2016–2022.

Royall, D. R., Lauterbach, E. C., Cummings, J. L., Reeve, A., Rummans, T. A., Kaufer, D. I., & Coffey, C. E. (2002). Executive control function: A review of its promise and challenges for clinical research. A report from the Committee on Research of the American Neuropsychiatric Association. *Journal of Neuropsychiatry and Clinical Neurosciences*, *14*, 377–405.

Salmon, D. P., Galasko, D., Hansen, L. A., Masliah, E., Butters, N., Thal, L. J., & Katzman, R. (1996). Neuropsychological deficits associated with diffuse Lewy body disease. *Brain and Cognition*, *31*, 148–165.

Sawamoto, N., Honda, M., Hanakawa, T., Fukuyama, H., & Shibasaki, H. (2002). Cognitive slowing in Parkinson's disease: A behavioral evaluation independent of motor slowing. *Journal of Neuroscience*, *22*, 5198–5203.

Scott, J. N., Metz, L., Hu, W. Y., & Hudon, M. (1999). Cerebral autosomal dominant arteriopathy with subcortical infarcts and leukoencephalopathy (CADASIL). *Canadian Journal of Neurological Sciences*, *26*, 311–312.

Seelaar, H., Rohrer, J. D., Pijnenburg, Y. A., Fox, N. C., & van Swieten, J. C. (2011). Clinical, genetic and pathological heterogeneity of frontotemporal dementia: A review. *Journal of Neurology, Neurosurgery, and Psychiatry*, *82*, 476–486.

Seeley, W. W., Bauer, A. M., Miller, B. L., Gorno-Tempini, M. L., Kramer, J. H., Weiner, M., & Rosen, H. J. (2005). The natural history of temporal variant frontotemporal dementia. *Neurology*, *64*, 1384–1390.

Seeley, W. W., Crawford, R., Rascovsky, K., Kramer, J. H., Weiner, M., Miller, B. L., & Gorno-Tempini, M. L. (2008). Frontal paralimbic network atrophy in very mild behavioral variant frontotemporal dementia. *Archives of Neurology*, *65*, 249–255.

Selikhova, M., Williams, D. R., Kempster, P. A., Holton, J. L., Revesz, T., & Lees, A. J. (2009). A clinico-pathological study of subtypes in Parkinson's disease. *Brain*, *132*, 2947–2957.

Shany-Ur, T., & Rankin, K. P. (2011). Personality and social cognition in neurodegenerative disease. *Current Opinion in Neurology*, *24*, 550–555.

Shea, Y. F., Ha, J., & Chu, L.-W. (2015). Comparisons of clinical symptoms in biomarker-confirmed Alzheimer's disease, dementia with Lewy bodies, and frontotemporal dementia patients in a local memory clinic. *Psychogeriatrics*, *15*, 235–241.

Siepel, F. J., Dalen, I., Grüner, R., Booij, J., Brønnick, K. S., Buter, T. C., & Aarsland, D. (2016). Loss of dopamine transporter binding and clinical symptoms in dementia with Lewy bodies. *Movement Disorders*, *31*, 118–125.

Sitek, E. J., Barczak, A., & Harciarek, M. (2015). Neuropsychological assessment and differential diagnosis in young-onset dementias. *Psychiatry Clinics of North America*, *38*, 265–279.

Sitek, E. J., Sołtan, W., Wieczorek, D., Schinwelski, M., Robowski, P., Harciarek, M., Guzińska, K., & Sławek, J. (2013). Self-awareness of executive dysfunction in Huntington's disease: Comparison with Parkinson's disease and cervical dystonia. *Psychiatry and Clinical Neurosciences*, *67*, 59–62.

Sitek, E. J., Thompson, J. C., Craufurd, D., & Snowden, J. S. (2014). Unawareness of deficits in Huntington's disease. *Journal of Huntington's Disease, 3*, 125−135.

Skodda, S., Rinsche, H., & Schlegel, U. (2009). Progression of dysprosody in Parkinson's disease over time—A longitudinal study. *Movement Disorders, 24*, 716−722.

Snowden, J., Craufurd, D., Griffiths, H., Thompson, J., & Neary, D. (2001). Longitudinal evaluation of cognitive disorder in Huntington's disease. *Journal of the International Neuropsychological Society: JINS, 7*, 33−44.

Snowden, J. S., Goulding, P. J., & Neary, D. (1989). Semantic dementia: A form of circumscribed cerebral atrophy. *Behavioral Neurology, 2*, 167−182.

Snowden, J. S., Gibbons, Z. C., Blackshaw, A., Doubleday, E., Thompson, J., Craufurd, D., & Neary, D. (2003). Social cognition in frontotemporal dementia and Huntington's disease. *Neuropsychologia, 41*, 688−701.

Snowden, J. S., Harris, J., Richardson, A., Rollinson, S., Thompson, J. C., Neary, D., & Pickering-Brown, S. (2013). Frontotemporal dementia with amyotrophic lateral sclerosis: A clinical comparison of patients with and without repeat expansions in C9orf72. *Amyotrophic Lateral Sclerosis & Frontotemporal Degeneration, 14*, 172−176.

Snowden, J. S., Neary, D., & Mann, D. M. A. (1996). *Fronto-temporal lobar degeneration: Fronto-temporal dementia, progressive aphasia, semantic dementia*. London, United Kingdom: Churchill Livingstone.

Snowden, J. S., Pickering-Brown, S. M., Mackenzie, I. R., Richardson, A. M., Varma, A., Neary, D., & Mann, D. M. (2006). Progranulin gene mutations associated with frontotemporal dementia and progressive non-fluent aphasia. *Brain, 129*, 3091−3102.

Snowden, J. S., Stopford, C. L., Julien, C. L., Thompson, J. C., Davidson, Y., Gibbons, L., & Mann, D. (2007). Cognitive phenotypes in Alzheimer's disease and genetic risk. *Cortex, 43*, 835−845.

Snowden, J. S., Thompson, J. C., Stopford, C. L., Richardson, A. M. T., Gerhard, A., Neary, D., & Mann, D. M. A. (2011). The clinical diagnosis of early-onset dementias: Diagnostic accuracy and clinicopathological relationships. *Brain, 134*, 2478−2492.

Stewart, J. T. (2007). Psychiatric and behavioral manifestations of vascular dementia. *American Journal of Geriatric Cardiology, 16*, 165−170.

Stopford, C. L., Thompson, J. C., Neary, D., Richardson, A. M., & Snowden, J. S. (2012). Working memory, attention, and executive function in Alzheimer's disease and frontotemporal dementia. *Cortex, 48*, 429−446.

Strenziok, M., Pulaski, S., Krueger, F., Zamboni, G., Clawson, D., & Grafman, J. (2011). Regional brain atrophy and impaired decision making on the balloon analog risk task in behavioral variant frontotemporal dementia. *Cognitive and Behavioural Neurology, 24*, 59−67.

Strong, M. J., Lomen-Hoerth, C., Caselli, R. J., Bigio, E. H., & Yang, W. (2003). Cognitive impairment, frontotemporal dementia, and the motor neuron diseases. *Annals of Neurology, 54*, S20−S23.

Suribhatla, S., Baillon, S., Dennis, M., Marudkar, M., Muhammad, S., Munro, D., & Lindesay, J. (2004). Neuropsychological performance in early and late onset Alzheimer's disease: Comparisons in a memory clinic population. *International Journal of Geriatric Psychiatry, 19*, 1140−1147.

Tarawneh, R., & Holtzman, D. M. (2012). The clinical problem of symptomatic Alzheimer disease and mild cognitive impairment. *Cold Spring Harbor Perspectives in Medicine, 2*, a006148.

Tartaglia, M. C., Zhang, Y., Racine, C., Laluz, V., Neuhaus, J., Chao, L., & Weiner, M. (2012). Executive dysfunction in frontotemporal dementia is related to abnormalities in frontal white matter tracts. *Journal of Neurology, 259,* 1071–1080.

Taylor, K. I., Probst, A., Miserez, A. R., Monsch, A. U., & Tolnay, M. (2008). Clinical course of neuropathologically confirmed frontal-variant Alzheimer's disease. *Nature Clinical Practice. Neurology, 4,* 226–232.

Thompson, J. C., Harris, J., Sollom, A. C., Stopford, C. L., Howard, E., Snowden, J. S., & Craufurd, D. (2012). Longitudinal evaluation of neuropsychiatric symptoms in Huntington's disease. *Journal of Neuropsychiatry and Clinical Neurosciences, 24,* 53–60.

Thompson, J. C., Poliakoff, E., Sollom, A. C., Howard, E., Craufurd, D., & Snowden, J. S. (2010). Automaticity and attention in Huntington's disease: When two hands are not better than one. *Neuropsychologia, 48,* 171–178.

Thompson, J. C., Snowden, J. S., Craufurd, D., & Neary, D. (2002). Behavior in Huntington's disease: Dissociating cognition-based and mood-based changes. *Journal of Neuropsychiatry and Clinical Neurosciences, 14,* 37–43.

Tierney, M. C., Black, S. E., Szalai, J. P., Snow, W. G., Fisher, R. H., Nadon, G., & Chui, H. C. (2001). Recognition memory and verbal fluency differentiate probable Alzheimer disease from subcortical ischemic vascular dementia. *Archives of Neurology, 58,* 1654–1659.

Torralva, T., Dorrego, F., Sabe, L., Chemerinski, E., & Starkstein, S. E. (2000). Impairments of social cognition and decision making in Alzheimer's disease. *International Psychogeriatrics, 12,* 359–368.

Torralva, T., Roca, M., Gleichgerrcht, E., Bekinschtein, T., & Manes, F. (2009). A neuropsychological battery to detect specific executive and social cognitive impairments in early frontotemporal dementia. *Brain, 132,* 1299–1309.

Tovar-Moll, F., De Oliveira-Souza, R., Bramati, I. E., Zahn, R., Cavanagh, A., Tierney, M., & Grafman, J. (2014). White matter tract damage in the behavioral variant of frontotemporal and corticobasal dementia syndromes. *PLoS One, 9,* e102656.

Trojsi, F., Corbo, D., Caiazzo, G., Piccirillo, G., Monsurrò, M. R., Cirillo, S., & Tedeschi, G. (2013). Motor and extramotor neurodegeneration in amyotrophic lateral sclerosis: A 3T high angular resolution diffusion imaging (HARDI) study. *Amyotrophic Lateral Sclerosis and Frontotemporal Degeneration, 14,* 553–561.

Tullberg, M., Fletcher, E., DeCarli, C., Mungas, D., Reed, B. R., Harvey, D. J., & Jagust, W. J. (2004). White matter lesions impair frontal lobe function regardless of their location. *Neurology, 63,* 246–253.

Verdon, C. M., Fossati, P., Verny, M., Dieudonne, B., Teillet, L., & Nadel, J. (2007). Social cognition: An early impairment in dementia of the Alzheimer type. *Alzheimer Disease and Associated Disorders, 21,* 25–30.

Vermeer, S. E., Prins, N. D., den Heijer, T., Hofman, A., Koudstaal, P. J., & Breteler, M. M. (2003). Silent brain infarcts and the risk of dementia and cognitive decline. *New England Journal of Medicine, 348,* 1215–1222.

Walker, A. J., Meares, S., Sachdev, P. S., & Brodaty, H. (2005). The differentiation of mild frontotemporal dementia from Alzheimer's disease and healthy aging by neuropsychological tests. *International Psychogeriatrics, 17,* 57–68.

Ward, J., Sheppard, J. M., Shpritz, B., Margolis, R. L., Rosenblatt, A., & Brandt, J. (2006). A four-year prospective study of cognitive functioning in Huntington's disease. *Journal of the International Neuropsychological Society: JINS, 12,* 445–454.

Warren, J. D., Fletcher, P. D., & Golden, H. L. (2012). The paradox of syndromic diversity in Alzheimer disease. *Nature Reviews in Neurology, 8,* 451–464.

Weintraub, D., Koester, J., Potenza, M. N., Siderowf, A. D., Stacy, M., Voon, V., & Lang, A. E. (2010). Impulse control disorders in Parkinson disease: A cross-sectional study of 3090 patients. *Archives of Neurology, 67,* 589–595.

Wicklund, A. H., Johnson, N., & Weintraub, S. (2004). Preservation of reasoning in primary progressive aphasia: Further differentiation from Alzheimer's disease and the behavioral presentation of frontotemporal dementia. *Journal of Clinical and Experimental Neuropsychology, 26,* 347–355.

Wicklund, A. H., Rademaker, A., Johnson, N., Weitner, B. B., & Weintraub, S. (2007). Rate of cognitive change measured by neuropsychologic test performance in 3 distinct dementia syndromes. *Alzheimer Disease and Associated Disorders, 21,* S70–S78.

Wolfe, N., Linn, R., Babikian, V. L., Knoefel, J. E., & Albert, M. L. (1990). Frontal systems impairment following multiple lacunar infarcts. *Archives of Neurology, 47,* 129–132.

Wong, S., Bertoux, M., Savage, G., Hodges, J. R., Piguet, O., & Hornberger, M. (2016). Comparison of prefrontal atrophy and episodic memory performance in dysexecutive Alzheimer's disease and behavioral-variant frontotemporal dementia. *Journal of Alzheimer's Disease: JADS, 51,* 889–903.

Woodward, M. C., Rowe, C. C., Jones, G., Villemagne, V. L., & Varos, T. A. (2015). Differentiating the frontal presentation of Alzheimer's disease with FDG-PET. *Journal of Alzheimer's Disease: JADS, 44,* 233–242.

Zakzanis, K. K. (1999). The neuropsychological signature of primary progressive aphasia. *Brain and Language, 70,* 70–85.

Żekanowski, C., Styczyńska, M., Pepłońska, B., Gabryelewicz, T., Religa, D., Ilkowski, J., & Barcikowska, M. (2003). Mutations in presenilin 1, presenilin 2 and amyloid precursor protein genes in patients with early-onset Alzheimer's disease in Poland. *Experimental Neurology, 184,* 991–996.

Zgaljardic, D. J., Borod, J. C., Foldi, N. S., Mattis, P. J., Gordon, M. F., Feigin, A., & Eidelberg, D. (2006). An examination of executive dysfunction associated with frontostriatal circuitry in Parkinson's disease. *Journal of Clinical and Experimental Neuropsychology, 28,* 1127–1144.

Chapter 20

Executive Function in Posttraumatic Stress Disorder

Jennifer Newman and Charles Marmar

Department of Psychiatry, New York University Langone Medical Center, New York, NY, United States

CHAPTER OVERVIEW

Exposure to trauma is a common experience, and for those who develop posttraumatic stress disorder (PTSD), it can be debilitating (Davidson, 2000; Kessler, 2006; Kessler, Sonnega, Bromet, Hughes, & Nelson, 1995). Executive functions are important in PTSD, as they impact symptom presentation, functional abilities, and quality of life and may negatively impact treatment response (Polak, Witteveen, Reitsma, & Olff, 2012; Vasterling & Verfaellie, 2009; Wrocklage et al., 2016). Executive functions are abilities that allow the brain to monitor, self-regulate/inhibit, plan, create strategies, switch tasks, and have mental flexibility, especially during complex and/or goal-directed tasks (Miyake, Friedman, Emerson, Witzki, & Howerter, 2000; Vasterling, Verfaellie, & Sullivan, 2009). They help to regulate impulsive behavior and mood. Impairments in executive function in PTSD have been widely noted; however, these deficits are often subtle and findings have been inconsistent (DeGutis et al., 2015; Falconer et al., 2008; Leskin & White, 2007; Pineles, Shipherd, Mostoufi, Abramovitz, & Yovel, 2009; Polak et al., 2012; Samuelson et al., 2006; Twamley, Hami, & Stein, 2004).

In this chapter we will start by reviewing the current diagnostic criteria, prevalence, and impact of PTSD. Next we will explain the findings related to general cognitive impairments in PTSD, then focus on executive function, attention, inhibition, flexibility, planning, set-shifting, and working memory. It is a complex area of research with many contradictory findings. We will review both sides of the literature, showing evidence for and against particular impairments. The scientific community is in the early phases of using imaging technology to explore how the structure and functions of the brain are uniquely impacted by trauma and cognitive impairments. We will present the current findings from imaging research.

Executive Functions in Health and Disease. DOI: http://dx.doi.org/10.1016/B978-0-12-803676-1.00020-9

Next, the complex factors involved in understanding PTSD and neurocognitive functioning will be explored. Many of these factors likely contribute to the divergent findings. These include the role of premorbid functioning and developmental factors (i.e., childhood onset and aging). There also are several key comorbidities that are considered in detail, including traumatic brain injury (TBI), depression, substance use, attention-deficit hyperactivity disorder (ADHD), health behaviors, and medical concerns. These comorbidities are prevalent for people presenting with PTSD, have shared symptoms with either PTSD or neurocognitive deficits, and further compromise functioning.

At the end of this chapter, treatments for PTSD will be reviewed. Findings about the relationship between neurocognitive functioning and treatment outcomes are limited. Further knowledge in this area would improve the ability to tailor future PTSD care. Limitations of the literature will be presented and future strategies offered. It is our hope that future work will continue to advance our scientific understanding of PTSD, neurocognitive impairments, and related conditions, with the goal of improving outcomes for those encountering trauma.

DIAGNOSIS AND PREVALENCE OF POSTTRAUMATIC STRESS DISORDER

The diagnosis of PTSD was first included in the third edition of the *Diagnostic and Statistical Manual of Mental Disorder* (DSM-III, American Psychiatric Association, 1980). At the time of introduction into the vernacular of mental health disorders, this diagnosis was meant to capture persistent and impairing fear-based reactions to stressors. In the newest edition of the *Diagnostic and Statistical Manual of Mental Disorders, fifth edition* (DSM-5; American Psychiatric Association, 2013), trauma and stressor-related disorders were separated into a distinct category of diagnostic disorders to best capture the variety of emotional, cognitive, and behavioral responses that occur after exposure to a traumatic event. To meet criteria for a diagnosis of PTSD, a person must have experienced, witnessed, or have been confronted with an event that involved actual or threatened death or serious injury, or a threat to the physical integrity of self or others. Examples of these types of events include experiencing a major disaster, serious accidents, or fire, being physically or sexually assaulted, seeing another person badly injured or killed, or experiencing war zone traumas.

Following trauma exposure, symptoms must be present within four clusters, with the minimum number of symptoms, as follows: at least one intrusive symptom (i.e., unwanted memories of the event, distress with reminders of the event, nightmares, or flashbacks), at least one avoidance symptom (i.e., avoiding situations, conversations, people, memories, or feelings related to the trauma), at least two symptoms of negative alterations in cognitions and mood (i.e., exaggerated negative beliefs, distorted blame, persistent negative emotional state, diminished interest in activities, feelings of detachment, or difficulty experiencing positive feelings), and at least two symptoms of marked alterations in arousal and reactivity associated with the traumatic event (i.e., irritable behavior, recklessness, hypervigilance, startle, concentration, or sleep difficulties). To meet criteria, symptoms must develop and persist for more than 1 month and cause clinically significant distress or impairment in social, occupational, or other important areas of functioning.

According to the National Comorbidity Survey the lifetime prevalence of PTSD in the United States is estimated to be nearly 8% of the general population (Kessler et al., 1995). Women are twice as likely as men to have lifetime PTSD although men are more likely to be exposed to at least one traumatic event (approximately 61% of men reported one or more trauma exposures compared with 51% for females). The prevalence rate of PTSD is significantly higher among veteran populations. For current service members who served in Operation Iraqi Freedom and Operation Enduring Freedom, PTSD estimates range from 13% to 20% (Hoge et al., 2004; Seal, Bertenthal, Minder, Sen, & Marmar, 2007; Tanielian & Jaycox, 2008). Deployment itself has been shown to be a risk factor for neurocognitive dysfunction (Vasterling et al., 2006). Furthermore, the prevalence of PTSD increases among service members with repeated combat exposures (Hoge et al., 2004). Given that combat veterans often are exposed to multiple traumas and are more likely to develop PTSD in their lifetime, many studies related to trauma use this population. A substantial amount of the research presented in this chapter is based on veteran samples.

Chronic PTSD is a debilitating condition, resulting in impairments across areas of social, emotional, and occupational functioning. Despite the burden, people living with PTSD are not likely to seek treatment, and when they do, they tend to drop out (Kessler et al., 1999). PTSD has been associated with elevated rates of hospitalization, increased rates of suicide attempts, and higher rates of other psychiatric conditions including substance use disorders, depression, and anxiety disorders (Davidson, 2000; Kessler et al., 1995; Kessler, 2006).

COGNITIVE FUNCTIONING IN POSTTRAUMATIC STRESS DISORDER

Research on cognitive functioning in PTSD has increased over the past several decades. The definition of these is skills are very broad and involve mental operations, such as perception, memory, thinking, awareness, and judgment (McGraw-Hill Concise Dictionary of Modern Medicine, 2002). Cognitive functioning is recognized as one of the key mediating factors in psychopathology and affects daily living. Impairments in this area impact a person's ability to successfully manage stressors, maintain healthy relationships, and actively engage in important areas of life such as work or school (Kessler & Frank, 1997; Lezak, Howieson, & Loring, 2004; Wood, Allen, & Pantelis, 2009; Zen, Whooley, Zhao, & Cohen, 2012).

There are many measures used to assess cognitive functioning. Commonly used tests include the California Verbal Learning Test (CVLT; Delis, Kramer, Kaplan, & Ober, 1987). This task measures episodic verbal learning and memory. There are several different forms of continuous performance tasks (Conners, 1994; Loong, 1988), which measure sustained attention to auditory or visual stimuli. Digit span tasks, included in the Wechsler Adult Intelligence Scale, fourth edition (Wechsler, 2008), measure attention and working memory. The go/no-go task measures behavioral inhibition and has many different variations (Costantini & Hoving, 1973; Reynolds & Jeeves, 1978). The Rey–Osterrieth complex figure test (Osterrieth, 1944; Rey, 1941) targets visual organization and planning. The Stroop color and word test (Stroop, 1935) is a measure of attentional inhibition. The trail making test (Partington & Leiter, 1949) measures divided attention. The Wisconsin Card Sorting Test (Heaton, 1981) or Delis–Kaplan Executive Function Scale (Delis, Kaplan, & Kramer, 2001) measures set-shifting or cognitive flexibility. This list represents only a sample of the many tests available for neurocognitive assessment. Each particular cognitive skill has a variety of different tasks that can be used to assess functioning. The use of diverse assessment tools complicates integrating findings across studies.

Cognitive difficulties related to PTSD have been found across a variety of these domains, including intellectual functioning, processing speed, attention, working memory, learning, and executive functions (Bremner et al., 1993; Horner & Hamner, 2002; Leskin & White, 2007; Samuelson et al., 2009; Stein, Kennedy, & Twamley, 2002; Vasterling et al., 2002). Two recent metaanalytic studies summarized findings across these broad cognitive domains. Scott and colleagues (2015) reviewed 60 studies that included 4,108 participants, of which 1,779 were with PTSD. They found an overall medium effect size for cognitive outcomes in PTSD. Significant deficits were found in verbal learning (i.e., immediate memory), delayed memory, complex information processing speed, attention, working memory, and executive functions. These domains had medium effects. Smaller, but significant, effects also were found for language, visuospatial functioning, visual learning, and memory. These differences were relatively consistent across the various samples, with different trauma types, and a variety of methodological approaches. Results also were similar across studies that had control groups with or without trauma exposure.

A review of 21 articles by Qureshi and colleagues (2011) looked at studies with samples of PTSD participants and included as the comparison group participants who had trauma exposure without PTSD. Most studies included in this review found significant cognitive impairments in PTSD, with many studies finding a correlation of these impairments to severity of PTSD symptoms. The most consistent finding across studies was related to deficits in attention for PTSD. Although memory was one of the most frequently assessed cognitive areas, results were inconsistent across studies. Results also varied for tasks of executive function and learning. Most studies did not find performance deficits in visuospatial abilities.

Executive Function

Executive functions are cognitive skills used to monitor, regulate mood and behavior, plan, and have mental flexibility, especially during complex and/or goal-directed tasks (Miyake et al., 2000; Vasterling et al., 2009). Executive functions are especially important with PTSD, as they impact symptom presentations, functional abilities, and quality of life and may negatively impact treatment response (Polak et al., 2012; Vasterling & Verfaellie, 2009; Wrocklage et al., 2016). Impairments in executive function in PTSD have been widely noted; however, these deficits are often subtle, and findings have been inconsistent (DeGutis et al., 2015; Falconer et al., 2008; Leskin & White, 2007; Pineles et al., 2009; Polak et al., 2012; Samuelson et al., 2006; Twamley et al., 2004). Polak and colleagues (2012) reviewed executive function performance across 18 studies, which included more than 1000 participants. They found that there was an association between PTSD and general deficits in executive function. The participants with PTSD demonstrated significant impairments on several measures when compared with trauma-exposed controls.

Several studies have explored particular issues of attention and inhibition in PTSD, as these skills impact a person's ability to plan and complete tasks. Impairments in auditory and visual sustained attention have been found (Gilbertson, Gurvits, Lasko, Orr, & Pitman, 2001; Jenkins, Langlais, Delis, & Cohen, 2000; Lagarde, Doyon, & Brunet, 2010; Vasterling et al., 2002; Wu et al., 2010). These impairments are across trauma types and are inversely related to PTSD symptom severity (Burriss, Ayers, Ginsberg, & Powell, 2008; Vasterling et al., 2002). However, not all studies have found deficits in sustained attention (Leskin & White, 2007; Neylan et al., 2004; Samuelson et al., 2006; Sullivan et al. 2003).

A particular finding involving attention and PTSD has been noted for trauma or threat-related stimuli. With PTSD, attention is diverted towards a threat, reducing the capacity to attend to other stimuli (Constans, 2005; Kimble, Fleming, Bandy, Kim, & Zambetti, 2010; Mueller-Pfeiffer et al., 2010). It has also been suggested that impairments in disengagement and inhibition may factor into attention deficits in the presence of a perceived threat (Pineles, Shipherd, Welch, & Yovel, 2007). Interestingly, there have been relatively consistent findings of overall deficits in inhibition with PTSD (Aupperle, Melrose, Stein, & Paulus, 2012; DeGutis et al., 2015; Falconer et al., 2008; Jenkins et al., 2000; Leskin & White, 2007; Wu et al., 2010).

Inhibition involves the capacity to stop or change automatic responses (i.e., inhibit) and sustain one's attention away from internal or external distractions. Deficits in inhibition may contribute to the neuropsychological and emotional impairments observed in PTSD (Aupperle, Melrose et al., 2012; Vasterling, Brailey, Constans, & Sutker, 1998). Additionally PTSD symptom severity has been shown to correlate with impairments in inhibition (Falconer et al., 2008; Leskin & White, 2007).

There are also errors of commission in PTSD (Vasterling et al., 1998; Wu et al., 2010). Errors of commission are the number of times a participant responds but the target was not presented, indicating issues with attention and impulsivity. Errors of commission have been found across performance on several neurocognitive tasks (i.e., inhibition, attention, and working memory) and have been shown to relate to severity of reexperiencing and hyperarousal symptoms in PTSD (Aupperle, Melrose et al., 2012; Vasterling et al., 1998).

Aupperle, Melrose, and colleagues (2012) suggested the possibility that inhibitory deficits may predate PTSD and increase the likelihood of developing trauma-related symptoms, such as intrusive trauma memories, hypervigilance, and problems with concentration. They also noted that the symptoms of PTSD, such as reexperiencing and hyperarousal, may impact one's ability to sustain attention and inhibit response. Impairments in disengagement and inhibition of threat-related stimuli may play a central role in understanding deficits in executive function in PTSD, as this creates additional burden upon inhibition and attention regulation systems (Constans, 2005; Kimble et al., 2010; Mueller-Pfeiffer et al., 2010).

Research findings related to cognitive flexibility, planning, and set-shifting vary (Beckham, Crawford, & Feldman, 1998; Jenkins et al., 2000; Lagarde et al., 2010; Stein et al., 2002; Vasterling et al., 1998). These tasks involve higher cognitive skills to create strategies to complete tasks and have the flexibility to switch strategies in response to changes in test conditions. When examining individual components of these tasks, evidence suggests that PTSD is associated with a greater number of trials for learning (Kanagaratnam & Asbørnsen, 2007). This conveys that there are impairments in initial learning, problem solving, or strategy development. In their 2015 review, DeGutis and colleagues did not find significant impairments on measures of switching. Additional studies are needed to determine the components of flexibility, planning, and set-shifting in PTSD.

Working Memory

Executive function relies on working memory, which provides a buffer zone to learn or take in new information, hold onto it, and manipulate it, which is important for reasoning and decision-making (Gilbertson et al., 2001; Vasterling et al., 1998). Extensive research has been conducted on working memory. Two metaanalyses have shown a relationship between PTSD and verbal memory deficits (Brewin, Kleiner, Vasterling, & Field, 2007; Johnsen & Asbjørnsen, 2008). Effect sizes were small to medium. Findings were similar for both immediate and delayed recall (Brewin et al., 2007). Deficits also were found in visual–spatial learning tasks; however, these effects were smaller (Brewin et al., 2007). When studies compared control samples of trauma-exposed participants without PTSD versus nontrauma exposed controls, the strength of the results weakened. This suggests that trauma exposure, in the absence of PTSD, may lead to subtle impairments in memory. Although these findings have been found in both military and civilian samples, the effects have been noted to be stronger in veterans (Johnsen & Asbjørnsen, 2008).

The majority of studies have found no deficits in visual memory related to PTSD symptoms (Stein et al., 2002; Vasterling et al., 1998) or memory retention and recognition (for review, see Golier & Yehuda, 2002). Additional research found no working memory impairments in PTSD (DeGutis et al., 2015; Jenkins et al., 2000; Samuelson et al., 2006).

BRAIN IMAGING RESEARCH

Advances in imaging technology have allowed for new avenues of research to explore structural and functional brain abnormalities. Tools such as functional magnetic resonance imaging, computerized axial tomography, positron emission tomography, and electroencephalography have been used to detect neural activity, structure, and size of the brain. Studies have combined these sensitive imaging tools with various pencil-and-paper or computerized neurocognitive tasks to evaluate differences that may underlie impairments. Functional and molecular imaging has been used to evaluate responses to trauma stimuli, emotionally salient stimuli, or triggering symptoms (Aupperle, Melrose et al., 2012). These methods may help to explain the mechanisms of PTSD and neurocognitive functioning, and in the future may provide ways to objectively identify, prevent, and treat disease.

Functional Neuroimaging

Functional neuroimaging studies have evaluated differences in neural activity and brain connectivity between PTSD and non-PTSD participants. Findings show *hyperactivation*, or exaggerated responsiveness, within limbic regions (especially amygdala and insula) and *hypoactivation*, or a diminished response, of prefrontal regions (including the anterior cingulate cortex (ACC) both rostral and dorsal and ventromedial prefrontal cortex) and the hippocampus (Aupperle, Allard et al., 2012; Etkin & Wager, 2007; Falconer et al., 2008; Hayes, Hayes, & Mikedis, 2012; Shin & Liberzon, 2010). The limbic regions of the brain are primarily involved with processing emotion, whereas the prefrontal brain regions and the hippocampus are involved in complex behaviors, including planning and regulation of emotions. The primary function of the hippocampus is context-dependent memory formation and storage. Neurocognitive deficits in PTSD may be related to this imbalance in brain connectivity, where affective, emotion, or sensory processing is enhanced, and control, inhibition, or the ability to disengage from stimuli is reduced (Aupperle, Melrose et al., 2012; Falconer et al., 2008). Devoting more resources towards emotion processing may lead to problems in using other cognitive skills, such as processing speed (Aupperle, Melrose et al., 2012).

Impairments in executive control become more apparent with increased severity of PTSD (Falconer et al., 2008). Results have been found across different trauma types, for example, research specific to veterans has demonstrated impaired functional connectivity in the frontal lobes (Morey, Petty, Cooper, LaBar, & McCarthy, 2008; Schuff et al., 2011). There also is preliminary evidence regarding lowered motivation and deficits in reward activation as possible impairing factors in PTSD. This is consistent with studies that link functional neuroimaging findings with deficits in cognitive tasks and increased PTSD symptom severity (Falconer et al., 2008).

Results pointing to PTSD as impairing executive control have been shown with tasks requiring inhibition and attentional switching (Falconer et al., 2008) in reaction to symptom provocation (Bremner, Narayan et al., 1999; Liberzon, Britton, & Phan, 2003; Shin et al., 2004), and during processing of threat-related stimuli (Rauch, Shin, & Phelps, 2006; Shin et al., 2005). While the research on decision-making is limited, Sailer et al. (2008) showed that PTSD patients were slower in learning best responses during decision-making and had less activation of the nucleus accumbens, a critical component of the reward system.

Structural Neuroimaging

Structural brain imaging allows for the evaluation of differences in anatomical structure in PTSD. The best established finding from structural imaging studies is reduced hippocampus volume in chronic PTSD (Bremner et al., 1995; Bremner, 2006; Dolan et al., 2012; Gilbertson et al., 2002; Hull, 2002; Karl et al., 2006; Woon, Sood, & Hedges, 2010). The hippocampus plays an important role in memory functioning. Decreased volume may explain the memory deficits that are observed in PTSD (Brewin et al., 2007; Squire, Stark, & Clark, 2004).

Additional findings related to anatomical structure of the brain in PTSD show reduced volume in the frontal cortex (Carrion et al., 2001; De Bellis et al., 1999), medial prefrontal cortex structures (Kasai et al., 2008; Milad & Rauch, 2007; Shin et al., 2005) amygdala (Karl et al., 2006), and lower ACC (Karl et al. 2006). These brain structures are involved in a variety of higher level functions, including executive function tasks (i.e., attention and planning), memory emotional expression, reward systems, and motivation. The ACC also is implicated in autonomic functions, such as regulating heart rate and blood pressure. In a sample of veterans with PTSD, Schuff and colleagues (2011) also discovered a reduced fractional anisotropy in white matter in the prefrontal lobe near the ACC, in the prefrontal cortex, and posterior angular gyrus.

Taken as a whole, these abnormalities may show the structural underpinnings of the affective, cognitive, and physical symptoms of PTSD. However, anatomical findings are not consistent, and even if present do not always relate to neurocognitive performance (Carrion et al., 2001; Neylan et al., 2004). Clarity is needed to determine whether the observed structural difference is indicative of preexisting risk factors (Gilbertson et al., 2001; Kimble, 2008). Some evidence suggests that volume reductions in limbic and paralimbic structures, including the hippocampus, ACC, and the left and right insulae, are acquired with PTSD, whereas others point to preexisting vulnerabilities (Kasai et al., 2008; Kremen, Koenen, Afari, & Lyons, 2012). More research is needed to explain structural findings in PTSD and how they correlate with specific clinical, neurocognitive, and functional outcomes.

DEVELOPMENTAL FACTORS

In making sense of these various findings, it is useful to consider the developmental course of PTSD and neurocognitive impairments. Longitudinal studies are especially sparse; however, two growing areas of interest include the impact of childhood trauma on development and the progression of these symptoms in aging or later life. Studying children also may be especially helpful, as they may not present with the level of complexity that comes in older age groups. These two topics will be fully considered in the next sections.

Childhood Trauma and Executive Function

Children are exposed to trauma at alarmingly high rates. The National Survey of Children's Exposure to Violence contains data from a large sample of youth ($n = 4503$, age 1 month to 17 years old) regarding trauma exposure rates for children (Finkelhor, Turner, Shattuck, & Hamby, 2013). According to this study, lifetime rates of different types of abuse are as follows: physical assault: 54.5%, sexual victimization: 9.5%, maltreatment by a caregiver: 25.6%, property victimization including robbery: 40.2%, indirect victimization: 39.2%, and indirect exposure to violence: 10.1%. Additionally, exposure to one trauma increases the likelihood of exposure to other types of trauma.

Evidence indicates that cognitive impairments are present in children exposed to trauma, with some findings similar to what is found with adults.

Impairments have been found across almost all cognitive domains, including learning and memory (De Bellis, Woolley, & Hooper, 2013; Samuelson, Krueger, Burnett, & Wilson, 2010), language (De Bellis et al., 2013; Noll et al., 2010), attention and concentration (Beers & De Bellis, 2002; De Bellis et al., 2013; Porter, Lawson, & Bigler, 2005), and executive functions (Barrera, Calderon, & Bell, 2013; Beers & De Bellis; 2002; De Bellis et al., 2013; Navalta, Polcari, Webster, Boghossian, & Teicher's, 2006). Maltreatment also has been connected to lower IQ and achievement (Carrey, Butter, Persinger, & Bialik, 1995; De Bellis et al., 2013).

Researchers have shown that some of these impairments may be independent of PTSD diagnosis (Barrera et al., 2013; De Bellis et al., 2013; Samuelson et al., 2010). This is consistent with other findings that show lower IQ performance, lower academic performance, and neurocognitive impairments do not specifically relate to the presence or absence of clinical symptomatology (Hedges & Woon, 2011; Samuelson et al., 2010). Additionally, very few studies have examined the longitudinal course for children, but evidence shows that children with documented cases of maltreatment have lower IQ scores and lower reading abilities in later adolescent and adulthood (Mills et al., 2011).

It has been noted that the functional and behavioral consequences of childhood chronic or extreme stress persist long after exposure (Johnson & Blum, 2012). Several areas of the brain, including those involved in learning, memory, and emotion regulation, have been found to be vulnerable to the impact of such stress (Johnson & Blum, 2012). Brain imaging in children with PTSD demonstrates functional abnormalities similar to adults, with hyperactivation of the affective emotional circuits and hypoactivation of inhibitory controls (Carrion & Wong, 2012; Carrion, Garrett, Menon, Weems, & Reiss, 2008; De Bellis & Hooper, 2012; Mueller et al., 2010). Impairments in memory functioning also have been noted and may underlie learning problems and processing of trauma memories (Carrion & Wong, 2012). Structural findings for children with PTSD show smaller cerebral and cerebellar brain volumes (Carrion et al., 2001; De Bellis & Kuchibhatla, 2006; De Bellis et al., 2002). This is especially true with younger age of onset and longer length of trauma (De Bellis et al., 1999). Although findings have shown specific reductions in hippocampal volume for adults, this is not always found for children or in younger veterans (Carrion et al., 2001; De Bellis et al., 2002). However, a longitudinal study by Carrion and Wong (2012) found that persistently elevated cortisol levels in children, due to stress and chronic PTSD symptoms, led to reductions over time in hippocampal volumes. This provides evidence that this abnormality may develop over the course of time. More longitudinal data are needed to explore the association of early PTSD or trauma exposure and structural brain abnormalities.

Based on these findings, it is observed that children who have experienced trauma should receive comprehensive evaluations. These should include neuropsychological assessments to further understand, identify, and address possible impairments. Additionally, assessments should be repeated periodically to measure changes in functioning and brain structures over time. Beginning assessments in childhood and continuing through adulthood and older age also offers the opportunity to measure the effects of trauma and its sequelae on executive functions over the life span.

Aging

The impact of PTSD on cognitive functioning and aging is not fully understood and is difficult to distinguish from the impact of normal aging (Hannay & Lezak, 2004; Lapp, Agbokou, & Ferreri, 2011). The older population is increasing, and life spans continue to grow (U.S. Census Bureau, 2010). Research in this area is complex because multiple factors may contribute to cognitive changes in older adults, such as age-related medical issues and medications for those conditions, and neurological changes that may or may not relate to age or psychiatric presentations. Research generally shows that cognitive decline occurs in the normal aging process, even in the absence of any specific neurological or psychiatric conditions (Craik & Bialystok, 2006; Lindeboom & Weinstein, 2004).

A review by Polak and colleagues (2012) found that older age significantly related to decreased executive function in PTSD, specifically in divided attention and working memory. Similarly, most studies have concluded that there are cognitive declines in PTSD across measures of neuropsychological functioning, especially with memory and learning, processing speed, and executive functions (Schuitevoerder et al., 2013; Yehuda, Golier, Harvey et al., 2005; Yehuda, Golier, Tischler, Stravitsky, & Harvey, 2005), but these findings are not definitive (Jelinek, Wittekind, Moritz, Kellner, & Muhtz, 2013). In a study of 53,155 veterans with PTSD and 174,806 age- and gender-matched controls, in their late 60s at baseline, Yaffe et al. (2010) found that PTSD doubles the 7-year onset of dementia. Age-related cognitive declines also have been suggested to increase symptoms of PTSD, as these skills may have prevented or been used to manage such symptoms (Floyd, Rice, & Black, 2002; Mittal, Torres, Abashidze, & Jimerson, 2001).

A 5-year longitudinal study, conducted by Yehuda, Tischler, Golier et al. (2006) evaluated memory with Holocaust survivors. Overall findings indicated that aging impacted explicit memory significantly for the PSTD group. Additionally, the PTSD-positive group displayed worse performance than the PTSD-negative group across measures; however, trauma exposure also was a risk factor for age-related cognitive decline. Both the PTSD-positive and PTSD-negative trauma-exposed groups performed worse on memory tasks when compared to nontrauma-exposed controls. Survivors with PTSD showed greater decline in paired associates learning, and this impairment increased as age increased, even when PTSD symptoms improved. Contrary findings for learning were noted, with initial deficits in word list learning on the CVLT no longer appearing at the follow-up assessment comparing survivors with or without PTSD. It was noted, however, that improvements in PTSD symptoms led to better attention and were correlated with improved CVLT performance at the time of the follow-up assessment. The authors suggested that when examining the longitudinal trajectory of PTSD, some cognitive deficits may remain, become exaggerated, or resolve. The course and presentation over time could give important information about the relation of these deficits to PTSD symptoms and/or aging.

Samuelson and colleagues (2009) conducted a longitudinal study assessing memory with Vietnam veterans with and without PTSD. The primary aims were to see if aging would impact neurocognitive functioning in similar ways as found with Holocaust survivors (Yehuda et al., 2006) and to follow changes in PTSD symptom levels over time to determine whether they subsequently impacted memory. Measures of visual, verbal, and working memory were included in the study. The study tested veterans twice at 2- to 5-year intervals. Over time PTSD symptoms did not significantly change or improve. When comparing veterans with and without PTSD, the PTSD group showed a greater decline in delayed visual recognition and recall and delayed facial recognition; however, this was very subtle. The other measured areas of memory were not significantly different between groups of PTSD versus non-PTSD Vietnam veterans. These findings were similar to a previous study that showed no differences in measures of attention and memory with a sample of Vietnam veterans with and without PTSD (Neylan et al., 2004).

It has been suggested that age may not be the key factor related to cognitive impairments, rather the total number of years living with symptoms of PTSD that may lead to cognitive declines (Gilbertson et al., 2001). However, as noted in the above studies, some symptoms may improve, stay stable, or worsen. Because research has relied mostly on cross-sectional methods, the progression of cognitive impairments over time is not well understood. It should also be noted that much of the research to date about aging, PTSD, and cognitive functioning have been based on work with survivors of the Holocaust or veterans, so caution is warranted in generalizing these findings to other trauma survivors. Further research with varying types of trauma, different ages of exposure to trauma and length of symptoms, consideration of comorbidities related to aging and psychiatric conditions, and assessment of these symptoms over longer periods of time is needed to more fully understand the relationships between PTSD and cognitive impairments.

POSSIBLE CONFOUNDING FACTORS

There are many factors that likely contribute to the large number of inconsistent findings in PTSD and cognitive functioning research. The next section will review several of these areas that may confound results. First, we will discuss how premorbid functioning may relate to later symptoms and deficits. Next, we will touch on several key comorbidities, including TBI, depression, substance use, ADHD, health behaviors, and medical concerns. These are especially relevant as they complicate understanding the unique or combined effects of each condition on neurocognitive functioning. The comorbidities selected are highly comorbid and have shared symptom profiles with PTSD and neurocognitive deficits (Gilbertson et al., 2006; Kessler et al., 1995; Scherrer et al., 2008). Some studies find that neurocognitive impairments persist when controlling for these comorbidities. Wrocklage and colleagues (2016) found that after covarying for depression, head injuries, and substance use disorders, the observed deficits in information processing speed and executive function persisted. Other studies maintain that neurocognitive deficits are only present in PTSD when there are comorbidities. For example, Barrett, Green, Morris, Giles, and Croft (1996) found that veterans with PTSD alone did not display neurocognitive impairments; however, when a diagnosis of depression, anxiety, or substance abuse was cooccurring with PTSD, deficits emerged. Some researchers have suggested that neurocognitive deficits in PTSD actually may be accounted for by these comorbidities (Golier & Yehuda, 2002; Horner & Hamner, 2002). Although it is not yet clear what role these comorbidities play, they are important to consider as we try to understand the relationship between PTSD and cognitive functioning.

Premorbid Functioning

Different hypotheses about lower premorbid neurocognitive abilities and later cognitive deficits in PTSD have been suggested. Premorbid abilities may account for some of the later impairments; the premorbid deficits may become exacerbated by trauma creating additional impairments, or these deficits may not be related to later symptoms (Bustamante, Mellman, David, & Fins, 2001; Gilbertson et al., 2006; Marx, Doron-Lamarca, Proctor, & Vasterling, 2009; Vasterling & Brailey, 2005; Vasterling & Verfaellie, 2009). However, it is plausible that pretrauma differences can serve as either a risk or a protective factor for development of symptoms following trauma exposure (Kessler et al., 1995; Kulka et al., 1990).

One of the most widely used tools for assessing premorbid intellectual functioning in PTSD research is intelligence quotient (IQ) scores. Studies repeatedly show that individuals with above average IQ scores have lower likelihood of developing PTSD when compared to those with average IQ scores (Breslau, Lucia, & Alvarado, 2006; Gilbertson et al., 2006; Gilbertson et al., 2001). Also, above average IQ scores are related to less trauma exposure (Breslau et al., 2006). In veteran samples, the relationship between IQ and PTSD is consistently found even when controlling for levels of combat exposure (Macklin et al., 1998; Vasterling et al., 2002). Studies have also indicated that lower verbal intelligence is an especially consistent indicator of higher risk for PTSD (Vasterling, Brailey, Constans, Borges, & Sutker, 1997).

IQ scores alone are not the only premorbid variable shown to relate to later symptom development. In a monozygotic twin study, conducted by Gilbertson and colleagues (2006), where one pair of an identical male twin set was combat exposed (with or without PTSD) and the other was unexposed, several cognitive impairments appeared to predate trauma. These differences included IQ, verbal memory, attention, and executive functions for the twin pairs in which one later developed PTSD following combat. This points to a preexisting familial component for cognitive impairments in PTSD.

Several studies have shown that lower premorbid executive function predicts higher levels of PTSD symptoms. These findings have been across several domains, including impairments in immediate visual memory (Marx et al., 2009), verbal memory performance (Bustamante et al., 2001; Gilbertson et al., 2006), response inhibition, and attentional regulation (Aupperle, Melrose et al., 2012; Vasterling et al., 1998). Additionally, school difficulties, education level, and performance on military aptitude tests for veteran samples have been reported as vulnerability factors for PTSD (Breslau et al., 2006; Gilbertson et al., 2006; Macklin et al., 1998; McNally & Shin, 1995; Pitman, Orr, Lowenhagen, Macklin, & Altman, 1991; Vasterling et al., 2002).

To note, for most neurocognitive deficits found, the differences were subtle and overall level of performance was still considered to be within normal range. However, these preexisting deficits likely contribute to the course of PTSD symptoms. They may impair coping skills, impact the ability to engage fully in treatments designed to alleviate PTSD, and therefore render treatment dependent on cognitive processing, including CBT, less effective, ultimately contributing to the maintenance and possibly worsening of symptoms overtime.

Traumatic Brain Injury

Traumatic brain injuries are common, with approximately 10 million cases reported globally every year (Hyder, Wunderlich, Puvanachandra, Gururaj, & Kobusingye, 2007). PTSD rates related to injury range from 20% to 40% (Kessler, Chiu, Demler, & Walters, 2005). The relationship between neurocognitive functioning, TBI, and PTSD is complex and difficult to untangle. Understanding the unique contributions of TBI to cognitive functioning is challenging as PTSD and TBI have many shared symptoms, including problems with cognition, memory, mood, substance use, physical energy, and sleep (Dolan et al., 2012; Stein &McAllister, 2009; Tanev, Pentel, Kredlow, & Charney, 2014).

The impact of TBI itself is difficult to measure because deficits, especially in more mild cases, are subtle and often based on self-report (Carlson et al., 2011; Elder, 2015; Hill, Mobo, & Cullen, 2009). Relying on self-report can be problematic when assessing injuries that by definition involve changes in mental status and/or involve loss of consciousness (LOC). Additional challenges that may impact a person's ability to report details regarding TBI include traumatic or stressful events occurring at the time of the head injury (i.e., physical assault, serious car accident, and combat), substance use involvement, varying reasons for reporting or denying injury (i.e., possible financial gain in disability or legal cause, negative impact of reporting on employment), and the impact of length of time since the event on memory (Bigler et al., 2013; Carlson et al., 2011; Dolan et al., 2012). Finally, the definition of what is considered mild, moderate, and severe TBI, as well as the tools used to measure this, are not consistent (Carlson et al., 2011; Ruff, Iverson, Barth, Bush, & Broshek, 2009). According to the definition by the Department of Veterans Affairs and Department of Defense, mild TBIs (mTBI) are head injuries that involve an altered mental state (e.g., dizziness, confusion, and post-injury amnesia less than 24 h) with no LOC, or, if there was LOC, the length of time was relatively brief, usually no more than 30 min (O'Neal et al., 2013). If assessments, such as the Glasgow Coma Scale, are done around the time of the injury, they are also in the mild range, showing minimal/mild impairments in eye, verbal, or motor functioning (O'Neal et al., 2013).

Approximately 80% of all head injuries are considered to be mild, and a majority of research focuses on this group (Carlson et al., 2011; CDC, 2003). Warren and colleagues (2015) studied mTBI in a hospital setting and showed that when an injury involves mTBI, the rate of comorbid PTSD increased over time, compared to those who were injured but did not have a head injury. After a 6-month period, the rate of PTSD nearly doubled for those with mTBI (26% compared to 15%, respectively). These rates of PTSD in mTBI are also more than triple the lifetime of PTSD prevalence rates found in the general US population (26% compared to 8%, respectively; Kessler et al., 1995).

Studies evaluating cooccurring TBI and PTSD have been done with a variety of incident traumas, such as motor vehicle accidents, sports injuries, or assaults. However, more recently, TBI and PTSD literature often involve veteran samples most likely because of the high rates of head injury in veterans with PTSD. Head injury is considered the "signature injury" in current wars, mostly as a result of blast exposures in combat (Okie, 2005; Owens et al., 2008; Warden, 2006). Approximately 15% to 20% of post-9/11 war zone veterans reported the occurrence of a probable TBI during deployment, with a majority of these injuries classified as mild (Hoge et al., 2008; Tanielian & Jaycox; 2008; Vasterling et al., 2006). Repeated blast exposure is common, with an average of 14 exposures, and ranges from 0 to 511 (Fortier et al., 2014). This accumulation of injury increases a variety of subsequent symptoms and impairments, including changes in mood, personality, memory, and executive function (Elder, 2015). There is an increased risk for long-term progression of neurocognitive impairment, even for people with one TBI, including development of dementia, Alzheimer's disease, and chronic traumatic encephalopathy (Barnes et al., 2014; Elder, 2015; Vincent, Roebuck-Spencer, & Cernich, 2014). According to Hoge and colleagues (2008), the overall rate of veterans with comorbid PTSD and TBI is approximately 5%. When a veteran does have a TBI, the rate of also having PTSD has been estimated between 27% and 44% (Hoge et al., 2008; Tanielian & Jaycox, 2008). TBI is especially important to consider as a large amount of the data for executive function, and PTSD is based on veteran samples. Cognitive findings for veterans with mTBI are usually nominal; however, as the severity or number of injuries increases, the impairments do as well (Bigler et al., 2013; Elder, 2015; Vasterling et al., 2012).

It is commonly found that the impact of mTBI on cognitive functioning is subtle, but chronic, in domains of executive function, complex attention, learning, memory, and processing speed (Bogdanova & Verfaellie, 2012; Boyle et al., 2014; Karr, Areshenkoff, Duggan, & Garcia-Barrera, 2014; Vanderploeg, Curtiss, & Belanger, 2005). Findings also indicate that abnormalities in executive function and delayed verbal memory have a particularly strong relationship with mTBI when due to explosions (Belanger, Spiegel, & Vanderploeg, 2010; Karr et al., 2014). Imaging and postmortem studies reveal that there are persistent brain abnormalities in veterans, and civilians, with TBI, including lesions, cerebral atrophy, and white matter abnormalities (Bigler et al., 2013; Fitzgerald & Crosson, 2011; MacDonald et al., 2011; Sponheim et al., 2011; Wilde, Bigler, Pedroza, & Ryser, 2006). Taken together, these impairments compromise higher order processes and are likely to further diminish the ability to manage PTSD (Vasterling et al., 2009).

For mTBIs cases, initial cognitive symptoms tend to resolve within several months (Belanger, Curtiss, Demery, Lebowitz, & Vanderploeg, 2005; Binder, Rohling, & Larrabee, 1997; Elder, 2015; Frenchman, Fox, & Maybery, 2005; Lange, Brickell, Ivins, Vanderploeg, & French, 2013). Several researchers have observed that there are a subset of patients with mTBI for whom symptoms, especially attention and memory, will persist or worsen (Dikmen, Machamer, Fann, & Temkin, 2010; Pertab, James, & Bigler, 2009; Vanderploeg, Belanger, & Curtiss, 2009). It is possible that the impairments for this smaller group do not get captured when only considering overall group performance for larger samples (Bigler et al., 2013). However, not all agree with this, arguing that in mTBI cognitive impairments do not persist after the brief initial recovery period and there is complete resolution in all mild cases (Rohling, Larrabee, & Millis, 2012). For those with moderate to severe head injuries, any improvements in symptoms typically cease around 2 years, approximately half remain chronically symptomatic (Brickell, Lange, French, 2014; Elder, 2015).

When considering the combined effects of PTSD and TBI on cognitive functioning, some studies report that the impairment domains are similar, but the level of deficits are increased, and some distinct symptoms are found that are likely due to the interactive effects (Dolan et al., 2012). For example, impairments have been found on Stroop word reading (Brenner et al., 2010) and set-shifting (Barrett et al., 1996) when patients have both PTSD and TBI. Interestingly, certain cognitive impairments that have been found with PTSD or TBI alone are not always found when the conditions are cooccurring (Campbell et al., 2009).

There are many limitations in TBI research including varied use of diagnostic criteria and operationalization of variables, differences in length of time after injury, and severity of injury, potential confounds or comorbidities in samples, and differences in availability of objective assessments by medical professions (Bigler et al., 2013; Dolan et al., 2012). Additional research is needed to further explore these issues to better understand the complex relationship between TBI, PTSD, and cognitive functioning.

Depression

Depression and PTSD commonly cooccur; however the estimated range of cooccurrence varies widely from 28% to 84% (Keane & Kaloupek, 1997). There are many overlapping symptoms of PTSD and depression, including problems with concentration, motivation, or interest in activities and depressed mood (American Psychiatric Association, 2013). Impairments in working memory and executive function have been found in studies of depression alone (Austin, Mitchell, & Goodwin, 2001; Baune et al., 2010; Gohier et al., 2009). As these impairments are also noted in PTSD, understanding the individual and combined effects of these diagnoses are important.

In a review across many studies, Polak and colleagues (2012) found that almost all instruments evaluating executive function showed worse performance for participants that presented with comorbid severe depression and PTSD. It was unclear whether this comorbidity with depression was a mediating factor for the observed results. More recently, Olff, Polak, Witteveen, and Denys (2014) studied executive function in a group of PTSD participants with a matched group of trauma-exposed controls and evaluated the impact of symptoms of depression. They found that across all domains assessed, including response inhibition, flexibility, set-shifting, planning, working memory, and spatial working memory, PTSD patients performed more poorly. According to this study, depressive symptoms mediated this relationship between PTSD and executive function on some, but not all, measures. This relationship was found with flexibility, set-shifting errors and longer latency for planning, and working memory. The results are consistent with a study by

Dretsch et al. (2012) that found depressive symptoms mediated the relationship between PTSD and working memory deficits.

Some studies have discovered that depression relates to the cognitive findings observed in PTSD. For example, Johnsen, Kanagaratnam, and Asbjørnsen (2008) studied refugee groups with and without PTSD and found that memory performance in PTSD related to depressive symptoms. This is similar to findings by Burriss and colleagues (2008), in which impairments in memory performance were related to self-reported depression. Another study by Barrett and colleagues (1996) found neurocognitive impairments in participants with PTSD and comorbid depression, anxiety, or substance abuse. Impairments appeared specifically in concept formation, problem solving, decision-making, verbal memory, and visual organization. When examining veterans with PTSD only, deficits were no longer apparent. The observed cognitive impairments therefore were suggested to be related to the impact of these additional diagnoses.

However, contrary to these findings, in their 2015 metaanalysis, Scott and colleagues did not find that depression significantly impacted cognitive impairments in comorbid PTSD and depression. Wrocklage and colleagues (2016) also found that neurocognitive impairments observed in PTSD, specifically in processing speed and executive functioning, persisted after covarying for depression. Given the high prevalence rate of cooccurring PTSD and depression, and overlapping symptoms, continuing to clarify this relationship is essential.

Substance Use

There is a high prevalence of comorbid PTSD and substance use disorders, with nearly half of patients presenting with cooccurring diagnoses (Gilbertson et al., 2006; Kessler et al., 1995; Scherrer et al., 2008). Research indicates that substances create further impairments in PTSD, relates to worsened course and symptoms, and likely has a negative impact on treatment outcomes (for review, see Tipps, Raybuck, Lattal, 2014). Chronic alcohol and other substances use, such as amphetamine, cocaine, and marijuana, have been shown to relate to impairments in neurocognitive functioning (Cournety & Ray, 2016; Dahlgren, Sagar, Racine, Dreman, & Gruber, 2016; Jovanovski, Erb, & Zakzanis, 2005; Oscar-Berman & Marinkovic, 2007; Stavro, Pelletier, & Potvin, 2013). Benzodiazepines, which are used to treat PTSD, anxiety, panic, agitation, and sleep, also have a risk of addiction and have been associated with neurocognitive deficits even after discontinuation of use (Barker, Greenwood, Jackson, & Crowe, 2004; Gorenstein, Bernik, & Pompeia, 1994; Tata, Rollings, Collins, Pickering, & Jacobson, 1994). Prescription medication use has been shown to impact neurocognitive findings, even if being used as prescribed (Beckham et al., 1998).

Despite the high prevalence rate, substance use disorders are not always assessed or, when assessed, may be excluded from studies of neurocognitive performance in PTSD (Horner & Hamner, 2002; Neylan et al., 2004; Scott et al., 2015). In their 2015 metaanalysis, Scott and colleagues noted that only half of the studies included in the review had information reported about substance use disorders, and 40% did not provide information about current psychotropic medication use. Several studies that have controlled for alcohol and substance use find that PTSD-related neurocognitive deficits persist (Bremner et al., 1993; Bremner, Randall et al., 1995; Gilbertson et al., 2001; Wrocklage et al., 2016). The effect sizes for neurocognitive deficits in PTSD are not shown to be significantly impacted by alcohol or substance use disorders (Scott et al., 2015).

Among different substances, alcohol use is especially common in PTSD and has been considered in cognitive research. Samuelson and colleagues (2006) conducted a study in Vietnam veterans with and without PTSD presenting with and without alcohol abuse or dependence. They controlled for alcohol use disorders and for depression. When controlling for these comorbidities, an effect was found for PTSD on specific tasks, rather than global overall deficits in neurocognitive performance, specifically with worsened performance on verbal memory, working memory, attention, and processing speed performance. The effect of alcohol was nominal, only showing an effect on immediate visual memory performance but not the other neurocognitive measures. The Gilbertson Twin study (2006) also found that only performance in delayed nonverbal memory was affected by history of alcohol abuse. This is consistent with the review by Tipps and colleagues (2014), which suggested that substances, such as alcohol, nicotine, and cocaine can interact with learning and memory in PTSD.

It is possible that specific memory abilities, and other deficits, are impacted by alcohol and other substance use. Given the high rate of prevalence of substance use in PTSD, the impact of this use upon neurocognitive performance should be considered. Future studies should fully assess for the presence of comorbid substance use problems, including details such as chronicity of use and severity of substance-related symptoms, when interpreting neurocognitive findings. Additionally, use of prescription medications, which are commonly used to treat PTSD, should also be evaluated in future research.

Other Comorbidities

Some additional comorbidities that have been considered in PTSD and neurocognitive research include ADHD, medical conditions, and health-related behaviors (Cohen et al., 2013; Scott et al., 2015). The hallmark symptoms of ADHD include persistent difficulty in sustaining attention and managing impulses (American Psychiatric Association, 2013). Research of neurocognitive deficits in ADHD demonstrates impairments in sustained attention, learning, and executive functions, as well as structural and functional brain abnormalities (for reviews, see Hervey, Epstein, & Curry, 2004; Seidman, 2006). Studies have shown that the diagnoses of PTSD and ADHD are significantly associated with each other (Antshel et al., 2013; Harrington et al., 2012). PTSD has been shown to be more prevalent in ADHD than control participants, and this comorbidity relates to the presence of additional diagnoses and worse psychosocial functioning (Antshel et al., 2013). Additionally, ADHD has been considered as a risk factor for development of PTSD (Adams, Adams, Stauffacher, Mandel, & Wang, 2015; Biederman et al., 2014). However, despite these findings, it is infrequently considered in studies of neurocognitive performance of PTSD.

In their 2015 metaanalysis, Scott and colleagues found that only 13% of studies included information about ADHD. When ADHD is identified and excluded in PTSD studies, there is a significant impact on cognitive deficits, such that overall effect sizes are decreased (Scott et al., 2015). Antshel, Biederman, Spencer, and Farone (2014) were the first to publish findings in adults with comorbid ADHD and PTSD, where they controlled for ADHD diagnosis. They found that when controlling for ADHD, PTSD was associated with deficits in spatial/perceptual performance. The combined impact of ADHD and PTSD related to greater impairments in working memory, processing speed, and visuospatial processing. Additional studies are needed to further tease this relationship apart, but given these findings, ADHD may partially account for increased neurocognitive impairments in some participants with PTSD.

In PTSD there is also a higher rate of cooccurring medical conditions, such as heart disease, high blood pressure, musculoskeletal disease, digestive system disease, and diabetes, as well as declines in health-related behaviors such as physical activity and quality sleep (Andersen, Wade, Possemato, & Ouimette, 2010; Boscarino, 2006; Boscarino, 2008; Cohen et al, 2013). A study by Cohen and colleagues (2013) found that worse performance in processing speed, learning, and executive function were significantly accounted for by health behaviors and medical factors. Wrocklage and colleagues (2016) found that deficit performance in processing speed and executive function is related to poorer physical health-related quality of life. It is important to consider these additional comorbidities when trying to understand neurocognitive performance in PTSD. Each are potential confounds to pinpointing the unique deficits attributable to PTSD. Also, because they are commonly cooccurring, when a patient presents with PTSD, it is important to evaluate the presence of these other conditions, as each likely would benefit from specific targeted treatment and/or impact the ability for a patient to fully benefit from PTSD-specific approaches.

EXECUTIVE FUNCTION AND TREATMENT FOR POSTTRAUMATIC STRESS DISORDER

Evidence-based treatments for patients with PTSD are a key topic among the community of researchers and clinicians studying and treating this condition. It is plausible that particular executive function deficits impact the ability of patients to fully benefit from treatments designed to address symptoms of PTSD, or the impairments themselves would benefit from targeted treatments. Treatment often includes psychotropic medications and/or psychotherapy approaches. Longitudinal studies show evidence for medications to address both PTSD symptoms and executive function deficits, with selective serotonin reuptake inhibitors, such as paroxetine, being the most efficacious (Fani et al., 2009; Stein, Ipser, & Seedat, 2006; Vermetten, Vythilingam, Southwick, Charney, & Bremnet, 2003). However, in a review of all randomized controlled medication trials, Stein and colleagues (2006) found 41% of patients do not respond to medication interventions. Additional biological based treatments, such as brain stimulation, have been used for PTSD but have limited findings (Novakovic et al., 2011). Cognitive behavioral therapy (CBT) approaches are considered to be the most effective and widely recommended psychotherapeutic treatment approaches for PTSD (Bisson et al., 2007; Harvey, Bryant, & Tarrier, 2003). The two most widely accepted trauma-focused therapies are cognitive processing therapy (CPT; Resick & Schnicke, 1996) and prolonged exposure (PE; Foa & Kozak, 1986; Foa & Rothbaum, 1998).

The initial phase of CPT involves providing psychoeducation about trauma, PTSD, thoughts, and emotions. Patients learn about the "just world" hypothesis that explains that we are raised to believe that the world is a "just" place where good things happen to good people. When something bad happens, such as trauma, we have to figure out a way to integrate that information by changing our beliefs about ourselves, other people, or the world or we have to modify details about the trauma narrative to make sense of it. These changes in our beliefs, or in the narrative, become a focus of our treatment. Patients create a personal impact statement about their trauma experience. They learn how trauma has impacted their own beliefs or narratives. In the next phase of treatment, patients learn to identify their "stuck points" and learn cognitive techniques to question and modify them. The goal is to reduce avoidance related to trauma and increase flexibility of these thought patterns. The final phase of treatment addresses several other key themes that are typically impacted by trauma exposure, including safety, trust, power, control, esteem, and intimacy.

In PE, similar to CPT, patients are provided with psychoeducation about trauma and PTSD. They are taught how to monitor their levels of distress and learn skills to manage anxiety. They are then guided to repeatedly expose themselves to the memories and reminders of their traumatic experiences through imaginal and in vivo (also known as real-life) exposure techniques. Imaginal exposure techniques involve recalling details of the trauma and create a narrative of that experience over several sessions. These narratives are often written and/or read aloud. Audiotaping is used and patients listen to their narratives for homework. In vivo exposure involves in identifying stimuli in the current environment associated with their trauma and creating a hierarchy from the least to the most distressing. Exposure exercises are designed for each, and patients work up their individually developed hierarchy towards the situations identified as the most distressing. The goal of PE is to habituate overtime to the trauma-related stimuli (both memories and current reminders) and learn alternative coping strategies to reduce avoidance. Both CPT and PE address avoidance, which is commonly thought to maintain PTSD, and provide skills to manage thoughts, feelings, and behaviors in effective ways.

Few studies look at neurological changes posttreatment; however, recent findings demonstrated functional brain changes after medication and/or CBT treatments for PTSD (Aupperle, Melrose et al., 2012; Carrion & Wong, 2012). However, not everyone benefits from CBT approaches, as approximately 30%–50% are nonresponders (Bradley, Greene, Russ, Dutra, & Westen, 2005). Additionally, approximately two-thirds (60%–72%) of treatment responders continue to meet diagnostic criteria for PTSD at the end of treatment studies (Bomyea & Lang, 2012; Cukor, Olden, Lee, & Difede, 2010; Steenkamp, Litz, Hoge, & Marmar, 2015). Interventions such as CPT or PE rely on being able to learn and apply new skills, and process memories, thoughts, and emotions (Polak et al., 2012; Schuitevoerder et al., 2013). The role of executive functions has not been extensively explored in relation to CBT treatments. There is some evidence that impairments in verbal memory relate to worse treatment outcomes for PTSD patients receiving CBT (Nijdam, de Vries, Gersons, & Olff, 2015; Wild & Gur, 2008). These differences persist when controlling for IQ, attention, baseline PTSD severity, depression, length of time since the traumatic event, and substance use (Wild & Gur, 2008).

Implementing treatments specifically to target cognitive skills, such as employing cognitive remediation (i.e., attention or executive function training) has been suggested for PTSD (Aupperle, Melrose et al., 2012; Schuitevoerder et al., 2013). For example, attentional training involves training patients to respond quicker to probes that are shown away from negative stimuli (MacLeod, Rutherford, Campbell, Ebsworthy, & Holker, 2002). The goal of attentional training is to help patients to refocus attention away from threatening stimuli. This would make sense given impairments in attention and inhibition, which have been noted in PTSD, such as overattending to threat-related stimuli (Falconer et al., 2008; Fani et al., 2009; Pineles et al., 2007) and the imbalance between emotional overprocessing and under control in PTSD (Aupperle, Allard et al., 2012). Attention training has been beneficial for a variety of anxiety disorders, including social anxiety, general anxiety disorder, and obsessive compulsive disorder (Amir, Beard, Burns, & Bomyea, 2009; Amir, Weber, Beard, Bomyea, & Taylor, 2008; Najmi & Amir, 2010; Schmidt, Richey, Buckner, & Timpano, 2009; Tata, Leibowitz, Prunty, Cameron, & Pickering, 1996).

Compensatory cognitive training approaches also are potentially beneficial. These approaches introduce strategies to manage memory, attention, and executive function impairments. For example, this could include teaching patients to effectively use organizational tools such as calendars, reminder alarms, and notes. Addressing these impairments has been shown to help to manage the cognitive deficit being targeted and reduce cognitive symptoms, mood symptoms, and improve overall quality of life (Twamley et al., 2015; Twamley, Vella, Burton, Heaton, & Jeste, 2012).

Studies to date have reported some promising findings for addressing executive function, and other cognitive deficits, in PTSD; however, there are very few, and among those available, several factors limited the ability to generalize findings including: diversity of samples, small sample sizes, different treatment methods including psychotherapy and/or medication approaches, and varied outcome measures (Fani et al., 2009; Vermetten et al., 2003; Walter, Palmieri, & Gunstad, 2010). Future research should continue to develop and identify the most effective approaches for treating both PTSD and the neurocognitive deficits observed.

CONCLUSIONS

Exposure to trauma is a common experience, and for those who develop PTSD, the effects can be debilitating (Davidson, 2000; Kessler et al., 1995; Kessler, 2006). PTSD has been associated with elevated rates of hospitalization, increased rates of suicide attempts, and higher rates of other psychiatric conditions including substance use disorders, depression, and anxiety disorders (Davidson, 2000; Kessler et al., 1995; Kessler, 2006). Impairments in executive function are particularly important in PTSD as they are related to worsened psychological symptoms, functioning, and quality of life, and negatively impact treatment (Polak et al., 2012; Vasterling & Verfaellie, 2009; Wrocklage et al., 2016). These deficits are subtle and often inconsistent (DeGutis et al., 2015; Falconer et al., 2008; Leskin & White, 2007; Neylan et al., 2004; Pineles et al., 2009; Polak et al., 2012; Qureshi et al., 2011; Samuelson et al., 2006; Twamley et al., 2004). Imaging studies have demonstrated functional and structural abnormalities in PTSD. However, even when found, the observed abnormalities do not always relate to neurocognitive performance (Carrion et al., 2001; Neylan et al., 2004).

In children exposed to trauma, some findings are consistent with cognitive outcomes found in adults (Barrera et al., 2013; De Bellis et al., 2013; Finkelhor et al., 2013; Noll et al., 2010; Porter et al., 2005; Samuelson et al.,

2010). Also, persistent functional and behavioral consequences well after trauma exposure has occurred have been reported and also found independent of PTSD (Barrera et al., 2013; Carrion & Wong, 2012; De Bellis et al., 2013; Johnson & Blum, 2012; Samuelson et al., 2010). In aging populations, findings show declines in cognitive functioning for PTSD beyond what would be explainable by normal aging (Polak et al., 2012; Schuitevoerder et al., 2013; Yehuda Golier, Tischler et al., 2005; Yehuda, Golier, Harvey et al., 2005). But, cognitive impairments are not consistently found in aging research, and improvements in some cognitive abilities have been noted (Jelinek et al., 2013; Yehuda et al., 2006).

The discrepancies highlighted throughout this chapter may relate to a variety of issues, including inconsistent operationalization and measurement of psychological and neurocognitive variables, small sample sizes, divergent methodologies, and differences in participant variables, such as differences in trauma (i.e., type of trauma, length of time since event, age at exposure, severity of symptoms, and number of trauma exposures), differences in demographics (i.e., age, gender, ethnicity, and education), comorbidities, and premorbid functioning (Polak et al., 2012; Schuitevoerder et al., 2013). Some deficits may be explained by PTSD-related symptoms, which complicate the interpretation of lower scores (Samuelson et al., 2006). Comorbidities, which were highlighted in this chapter, are especially difficult to tease apart from PTSD and neurocognitive deficits due to high frequency of cooccurrence and shared symptom profiles (Gilbertson et al., 2006; Kessler et al., 1995; Scherrer et al., 2008). In research they are challenging to control for statistically, as they may be associated with levels of PTSD. If these comorbidities are removed, this may take out part of the unique outcome for more severe symptom presentations (Gilbertson et al., 2006; Miller & Chapman, 2001).

Future studies should continue to work toward uncovering the role of executive function in PTSD. Longitudinal studies would be helpful to track progression of symptoms over time, evaluate the impact of age upon functioning, and determine how the severity and length of symptoms impact neurocognitive deficits. It also would be useful to evaluate the relationships between PTSD and neurocognitive symptoms pre- and post-trauma exposure. Military samples may be especially relevant in this regard. Service members can be assessed before deployment, are likely to experience repeated trauma exposures during their service, and are more likely to develop PTSD than civilians. However, given that a large amount of research is conducted with veteran samples, including other types of trauma-exposed samples, would benefit future studies as well. Technological approaches should continue to explore the relationship among clinical symptoms, neurocognitive deficits, and biological differences in PTSD. The use of technology is a critical component to understanding the relationship between executive function and PTSD and likely will be useful in identification and treatment of such conditions (Dolan et al., 2012; MacDonald et al., 2011).

The role of executive function impairments on treatment outcomes in PTSD is especially important. We know that those suffering with PTSD are not likely to seek out treatment and when they often do drop out or experience limited benefits (Bomyea & Lang, 2012; Bradley et al., 2005; Cukor et al., 2010; Kessler et al., 1999; Steenkamp et al., 2015; Stein et al., 2006). It is plausible that impairments in executive function interfere with the benefits of treatment. There is some, but limited, evidence that these cognitive impairments can be successfully treated (Fani et al., 2009; Vermetten et al., 2003; Walter et al., 2010). Specific neurocognitive impairments may also provide insight to who would best respond to particular types of treatments (Nijdam et al., 2015; Wild & Gur, 2008). Future work should focus on developing better methods of identifying, preventing, and treating PTSD and comorbid neurocognitive impairments as a way to improve symptoms, daily functioning, and the quality of life of people living with these conditions. It is our hope that advancements will lead to better outcomes for those encountering trauma.

ACKNOWLEDGMENTS

This material is based on work at NYU Langone Medical Center supported by the Cohen Foundation with a grant entitled, "The Steven and Alexandra Cohen Veterans Center for PTSD and TBI." A special thanks to Rohini Bagrodia, MA, Laura Price, PhD, and Nadia Rahman, BA, for helping with preparation of this chapter. Also, a special acknowledgment to the army of project managers, clinicians, and research associates at the Steven and Alexandra Cohen Veterans Center for PTSD and TBI. They demonstrate endless dedication in moving forward the scientific understanding of PTSD, TBI, and related conditions with our veteran population. Finally, the authors would like to acknowledge the people who have volunteered their time, and shared their own personal experiences with trauma, to contribute to the many studies presented in this chapter.

REFERENCES

Adams, Z., Adams, T., Stauffacher, K., Mandel, H., & Wang, Z. (2015). The effects of inattentiveness and hyperactivity on posttraumatic stress symptoms: Does a diagnosis of posttraumatic stress disorder matter? *Journal of Attention Disorders*, ePub.

American Psychiatric Association (1980). *Diagnostic and statistical manual of mental disorders* (3rd ed.). Washington, DC: American Psychiatric Association.

American Psychiatric Association (2013). *Diagnostic and statistical manual of mental disorders* (5th ed.). Washington, DC: American Psychiatric Association.

Amir, N., Beard, C., Burns, M., & Bomyea, J. (2009). Attention modification program in individuals with Generalized Anxiety Disorder. *Journal of Abnormal Psychology*, *118*(1), 28−33.

Amir, N., Weber, G., Beard, C., Bomyea, J., & Taylor, C. T. (2008). The effect of a single session attention modification program on response to a public speaking challenge in socially anxious individuals. *Journal of Abnormal Psychology*, *117*(4), 860−868.

Andersen, J., Wade, M., Possemato, K., & Ouimette, P. (2010). Association between posttraumatic stress disorder and primary care provider-diagnosed disease among Iraq and Afghanistan veterans. *Psychosomatic Medicine, 72*(5), 498−504.

Antshel, K. M., Biederman, J., Spencer, T. J., & Farone, S. V. (2014). The neuropsychological profile of comorbid post-traumatic stress disorder in adult ADHD. *The Journal of Attention Disorders, 20*(12), 1047−1055.

Antshel, K. M., Kaul, P., Biederman, J., Spencer, T. J., Hier, B. O., Hendricks, J., et al. (2013). Posttraumatic stress disorder in adult attention-deficit/hyperactivity disorder: Clinical features and familial transmission. *The Journal of Clinical Psychiatry, 74*(3), e197−e204.

Aupperle, R. L., Allard, C. B., Grimes, E. M., Simmons, A. N., Flagan, T., Behroozni, M., et al. (2012). Dorsolateral prefrontal cortex activation during emotional anticipation and neuropsychological performance in posttraumatic stress disorder. *Archives of General Psychiatry, 69*(4), 360−371.

Aupperle, R. L., Melrose, A. J., Stein, M. B., & Paulus, M. P. (2012). Executive function and PTSD: Disengaging from trauma. *Neuropharmacology, 62*(2), 686−694.

Austin, M. P., Mitchell, P., & Goodwin, G. M. (2001). Cognitive deficits in depression: Possible implications for functional neuropathology. *British Journal of Psychiatry, 178*(3), 200−206.

Barker, M. J., Geenwood, K. M., Jackson, M., & Crowe, S. F. (2004). Cognitive effects of long-term benzodiazepine use: A meta-analysis. *CNS Drugs, 18*(1), 37−48.

Barnes, D. E., Kaup, A., Kirby, K. A., Byers, A. L., Diaz-Arrastia, R., & Yaffe, K. (2014). Traumatic brain injury and risk of dementia in older veterans. *Neurology, 83*(4), 312−319.

Barrera, M., Calderón, L., & Bell, V. (2013). The cognitive impact of sexual abuse and PTSD in children: A neuropsychological study. *Journal of Child Sexual Abuse, 22*(6), 625−638.

Barrett, D. H., Green, M. L., Morris, R., Giles, W. H., & Croft, J. B. (1996). Cognitive functioning and posttraumatic stress disorder. *The American Journal of Psychiatry, 153*(11), 1492−1494.

Baune, B. T., Miller, R., McAfoose, J., Johnson, M., Quirk, F., & Mitchell, D. (2010). The role of cognitive impairment in general functioning in major depression. *Psychiatry Research, 176*(2−3), 183−189.

Beckham, J. C., Crawford, A. L., & Feldman, M. E. (1998). Trail Making Test performance in Vietnam combat veterans with and without posttraumatic stress disorder. *Journal of Traumatic Stress, 11*(4), 811−819.

Beers, S. R., & De Bellis, M. D. (2002). Neuropsychological function in children with maltreatment-related posttraumatic stress disorder. *The American Journal of Psychiatry, 159*(3), 483−486.

Belanger, H. G., Curtiss, G., Demery, J. A., Lebowitz, B. K., & Vanderploeg, R. D. (2005). Factors moderating neuropsychological outcomes following mild traumatic brain injury: A meta-analysis. *Journal of the International Neuropsychological Society, 11*(3), 215−227.

Belanger, H. G., Spiegel, E., & Vanderploeg, R. D. (2010). Neuropsychological performance following a history of multiple self-reported concussions: A meta-analysis. *Journal of the International Neuropsychological Society, 16*(2), 262−267.

Biederman, J., Petty, C., Spencer, T. J., Woodworth, K. Y., Bhide, P., Zhu, J., et al. (2014). Is ADHD a risk for posttraumatic stress disorder (PTSD)? Results from a large longitudinal study of referred children with and without ADHD. *The World Journal of Biological Psychiatry, 15*(1), 49−55.

Bigler, E. D., Farrer, T. J., Pertab, J. L., James, K., Petrie, J. A., & Hedges, D. W. (2013). Reaffirmed limitations of meta-analytic methods in the study of mild traumatic brain injury: A response to Rohling et al. *The Clinical Neuropsychologist, 27*(2), 176−214.

Binder, L. M., Rohling, M. L., & Larrabee, G. J. (1997). A review of mild head trauma: I. Meta-analytic review of neuropsychological studies. *Journal of Clinical and Experimental Neuropsychology, 19*(3), 421–431.

Bisson, J., Ehlers, A., Matthews, R., Pilling, S., Richards, D., & Turner, S. (2007). Psychological treatments for chronic post-traumatic stress disorder. *Systematic Review and Meta-analysis. The British Journal of Psychiatry, 190*(2), 97–104.

Bogdanova, Y., & Verfaellie, M. (2012). Cognitive sequelae of blast-induced traumatic brain injury: Recovery and rehabilitation. *Neuropsychological Review, 22*(1), 4–20.

Bomyea, J., & Lang, A. J. (2012). Emerging interventions for PTSD: Future directions for clinical care and research. *Neuropharmacology, 62*(2), 607–616.

Boscarino, J. A. (2006). Posttraumatic stress disorder and mortality among U.S. Army veterans 30 years after military service. *Annals of Epidemiology, 16*(4), 248–256.

Boscarino, J. A. (2008). A prospective study of PTSD and early-age heart disease mortality among Vietnam veterans: Implications for surveillance and prevention. *Psychosomatic Medicine, 70*(6), 668–676.

Boyle, E., Cancelliere, C., Hartvigsen, J., Carroll, L. J., Holm, L. W., & Cassidy, D. (2014). Systematic review of prognosis after mild traumatic brain injury in the military: Results of the international collaboration on mild traumatic brain injury prognosis. *Archives of Physical Medicine and Rehabilitation, 95*(3 S2), S230–S237.

Bradley, R., Greene, J., Russ, E., Dutra, L., & Westen, D. (2005). A multidimensional meta-analysis of psychotherapy for PTSD. *The American Journal of Psychiatry, 162*(2), 214–227.

Bremner, J. D. (2006). Traumatic stress: Effects on the brain. *Dialogues in Clinical Neuroscience, 8*(4), 445–461.

Bremner, J. D., Narayan, M., Staib, L. H., Southwick, S. M., McGlashan, T., & Charney, D. S. (1999). Neural correlates of memories of childhood sexual abuse in women with and without posttraumatic stress disorder. *American Journal of Psychiatry, 156*(11), 1787–1795.

Bremner, J. D., Randall, P., Scott, T. M., Bronen, R. A., Seibyl, J. P., Southwick, S. M., et al. (1995). MRI-based measurement of hippocampal volume in patients with combat-related posttraumatic stress disorder. *American Journal of Psychiatry, 152*(7), 973–981.

Bremner, J. D., Scott, T. M., Delaney, R. C., Southwick, S. M., Mason, J. W., Johnson, D. R., et al. (1993). Deficits in short-term memory in posttraumatic stress disorder. *American Journal of Psychiatry, 150*(7), 1015–1019.

Brenner, L. A., Terrio, H., Homaifar, B. Y., Gutierrez, P. M., Staves, P. J., Harwood, J. E., et al. (2010). Neuropsychological test performance in soldiers with blast-related mild TBI. *Neuropsychology, 24*(2), 160–167.

Breslau, N., Lucia, V. C., & Alvarado, G. F. (2006). Intelligence and other predisposing factors in exposure to trauma and posttraumatic stress disorder: A follow-up study at age 17 years. *Archives of General Psychiatry, 63*(11), 1238–1245.

Brewin, C. R., Kleiner, J. S., Vasterling, J. J., & Field, A. P. (2007). Memory for emotionally neutral information in posttraumatic stress disorder: A meta-analytic investigation. *Journal of Abnormal Psychology, 116*(3), 448–463.

Brickell, T. A., Lange, R. T., & French, L. M. (2014). Three-year outcome following moderate-to-severe TBI in U.S. military service members: A descriptive cross-sectional study. *Military Medicine, 179*(8), 839–848.

Burriss, L., Ayers, E., Ginsberg, J., & Powell, D. A. (2008). Learning and memory impairment in PTSD: Relationship to depression. *Depression and Anxiety, 25*(2), 149–157.

Bustamante, V., Mellman, T. A., David, D., & Fins, A. I. (2001). Cognitive functioning and the early development of PTSD. *Journal of Traumatic Stress, 14*(4), 791–797.

Campbell, T. A., Nelson, L. A., Lumpkin, R., Yoash-Gantz, R. E., Pickett, T. C., & McCornick, C. L. (2009). Neuropsychological measures of processing speed and executive functioning in combat Veterans with PTSD, TBI, and comorbid TBI/PTSD. *Psychiatric Annals*, *39*(8), 796–803.

Carlson, K. F., Kehle, S. M., Meis, L. A., Greer, N., MacDonald, R., Rutks, I., & Wilt, T. J. (2011). Prevalence, assessment, and treatment of mild traumatic brain injury and posttraumatic stress disorder: A systematic review of the evidence. *The Journal of Head Trauma Rehabilitation*, *26*(2), 103–115.

Carrey, N. J., Butter, H. J., Persinger, M. A., & Bialik, R. J. (1995). Physiological and cognitive correlates of child abuse. *Journal of the American Academy of Child & Adolescent Psychiatry*, *34*(8), 1067–1075.

Carrion, V. G., Garrett, A., Menon, V., Weems, C. F., & Reiss, A. L. (2008). Posttraumatic stress symptoms and brain function during a response-inhibition task: An fMRI study in youth. *Depression and Anxiety*, *25*(6), 514–526.

Carrion, V. G., Weems, C. F., Eliez, S., Patwardhan, A., Brown, W., Ray, R. D., et al. (2001). Attenuation of frontal asymmetry in pediatric posttraumatic stress disorder. *Biological Psychiatry*, *50*(12), 943–951.

Carrion, V. G., & Wong, S. S. (2012). Can traumatic stress alter the brain? Understanding the implications of early trauma on brain development and learning. *The Journal of Adolescent Health*, *51*(2S), S23–S28.

Centers for Disease Control and Prevention (CDC); National Center for Injury and Control (2003). *Report to Congress on mild traumatic brain injury in the United States: Steps to prevent a serious public health problem*. Atlanta, GA: Centers for Disease Control and Prevention.

Cohen, B. E., Neylan, T. C., Yaffe, K., Samuelson, K. W., Li, Y., & Barnes, D. E. (2013). Posttraumatic stress disorder and cognitive function: Findings from the mind your heart study. *The Journal of Clinical Psychiatry*, *74*(11), 1063–1070.

Conners, K. (1994). *The Conner's continuous performance test*. Toronto, Ontario, Canada: Multi-Health Systems.

Constans, J. I. (2005). Information-processing biases in PTSD. In J. J. Vasterling, & C. R. Brewin (Eds.), *Neuropsychology of PTSD: Biological, cognitive, and clinical perspectives* (pp. 105–130). New York: Guildford Press.

Costantini, A. F., & Hoving, K. L. (1973). The relationship of cognitive and motor response inhibition to age and IQ. *Journal of Genetic Psychology*, *123*(2), 309–319.

Courtney, K. E., & Ray, L. A. (2016). Clinical neuroscience of amphetamine-type stimulants: From basic science to treatment development. In H. Ekhtiari, & M. Paulus (Eds.), *Progress in brain research, neuroscience for addiction medicine: From prevention to rehabilitation—Constructs and drugs* (Volume 223, pp. 295–310). Elsevier Science.

Craik, F. M., & Bialystok, E. (2006). Cognition through the lifespan: Mechanisms of change. *Trends in Cognitive Sciences*, *10*(3), 131–138.

Cukor, J., Olden, M., Lee, F., & Difede, J. (2010). Evidence-based treatments for PTSD, new directions, and special challenges. *Annals of the New York Academy of Sciences*, *1208*, 82–89.

Dahlgren, M. K., Sagar, K. A., Racine, M. T., Dreman, M. W., & Gruber, S. A. (2016). Marijuana use predicts cognitive performance on tasks of executive function. *Journal of Studies on Alcohol and Drugs*, *77*(2), 298–308.

Davidson, J. R. (2000). Trauma: The impact of posttraumatic stress disorder. *Journal of Psychopharmacology*, *14*(2 suppl 1), S5–S12.

De Bellis, M. D., & Hooper, S. R. (2012). Neural substrates for processing task-irrelevant emotional distracters in maltreated adolescents with depressive disorders: A pilot study. *Journal of Traumatic Stress*, *25*(2), 198−202.

De Bellis, M. D., Keshavan, M. S., Clark, D. B., Casey, B. J., Giedd, J. N., Boring, A. M., et al. (1999). Developmental traumatology part II: Brain development. *Biological Psychiatry*, *45*(10), 1271−1284.

De Bellis, M. D., Keshavan, M. S., Shifflett, H., Iyengar, S., Beers, S. R., Hall, J., et al. (2002). Brain structures in pediatric maltreatment-related posttraumatic stress disorder: A sociodemographically matched study. *Biological Psychiatry*, *52*(11), 1066−1078.

De Bellis, M. D., & Kuchibhatla, M. (2006). Cerebellar volumes in pediatric maltreatment-related posttraumatic stress disorder. *Biological Psychiatry*, *60*(7), 697−703.

De Bellis, M. D., Woolley, D. P., & Hooper, S. T. (2013). Neuropsychological findings in pediatric maltreatment: Relationship of PTSD, dissociative symptoms, and abuse/ neglect indices to neurocognitive outcomes. *Child Maltreatment*, *18*(3), 171−183.

DeGutis, J., Esterman, M., McCulloch, B., Rosenblatt, A., Milberg, W., & McGlinchey, R. (2015). Posttraumatic psychological symptoms are associated with reduced inhibitory control, not general executive dysfunction. *Journal of the International Neuropsychological Society*, *21*(5), 342−352.

Delis, D. C., Kaplan, E., & Kramer, J. H. (2001). *Delis−Kaplan executive function system*. San Antonio, TX: The Psychological Corporation.

Delis, D. C., Kramer, J. H., Kaplan, E., & Ober, B. A. (1987). *California verbal learning test: Adult version*. San Antonio, TX: The Psychological Corporation.

Dikmen, S., Machamer, J., Fann, J. R., & Temkin, N. R. (2010). Rates of symptom reporting following traumatic brain injury. *Journal of the International Neuropsychological Society*, *16*(3), 401−411.

Dolan, S., Martindale, S., Robinson, J., Kimbrel, N. A., Meyer, E. C., Kruse, M. I., et al. (2012). Neuropsychological sequelae of PTSD and TBI following war deployment among OEF/OIF veterans. *Neuropsychology Review*, *22*(1), 21−34.

Dretsch, M. N., Thiel, K. J., Athy, J. R., Irvin, C. R., Sirmon-Fjordbak, B., & Salvatore, A. (2012). Mood symptoms contribute to working memory decrement in active-duty soldiers being treated for posttraumatic stress disorder. *Brain and Behavior*, *2*(4), 357−364.

Elder, G. A. (2015). Update on TBI and cognitive impairment in military veterans. *Current Neurology and Neuroscience Reports*, *15*(10), 68.

Etkin, A., & Wager, T. D. (2007). Functional neuroimaging of anxiety: A meta-analysis of emotional processing in PTSD, social anxiety disorder, and specific phobia. *The American Journal of Psychiatry*, *164*(10), 1476−1488.

Falconer, E., Bryant, R., Felmingham, K. L., Kemp, A. H., Gordon, E., Peduto, A., et al. (2008). The neural networks of inhibitory control in posttraumatic stress disorder. *Journal of Psychiatry and Neuroscience*, *33*(3), 413−422.

Fani, N., Kitayama, N., Ashraf, A., Reed, L., Afzal, N., Jawed, F., & Bremner, J. D. (2009). Neuropsychological functioning in patients with posttraumatic stress disorder following short-term paroxetine treatment. *Psychopharmacology Bulletin*, *42*(1), 53−68.

Finkelhor, D., Turner, H., Shattuck, A., & Hamby, S. (2013). Violence, crime, and abuse exposure in a national sample of children and youth: An update. *JAMA Pediatrics*, *167*(7), 614−621.

FitzGerald, D. B., & Crosson, B. A. (2011). Diffusion weighted imaging and neuropsychological correlates in adults with mild traumatic brain injury. *International Journal of Psychophysiology*, *82*(1), 79−85.

Floyd, M., Rice, J., & Black, S. R. (2002). Recurrence of posttraumatic stress disorder in late life: A cognitive aging perspective. *Journal of Clinical Geropsychology*, *8*(4), 303–311.

Foa, E. B., & Kozak, M. J. (1986). Emotional processing of fear: Exposure to corrective information. *Psychological Bulletin*, *99*(1), 20–35.

Foa, E. B., & Rothbaum, B. O. (1998). *Treating the trauma of rape: A cognitive behavioral therapy for PTSD*. New York: The Guildford Press.

Fortier, C. B., Amick, M. M., Grande, L., McGlynn, S., Kenna, A., Morra, L., et al. (2014). The Boston Assessment of Traumatic Brain Injury-Lifetime (BAT-L) semistructured interview: Evidence of research utility and validity. *The Journal of Head Trauma and Rehabilitation*, *29*(1), 89–98.

Frenchman, K. A., Fox, A. M., & Mayberry, M. T. (2005). Neuropsychological studies of mild traumatic brain injury: A meta-analytic review of research since 1995. *Journal of Clinical and Experimental Neuropsychology*, *27*(3), 334–351.

Gilbertson, M. W., Gurvits, T. V., Lasko, N. B., Orr, S. P., & Pitman, R. K. (2001). Multivariate assessment of explicit memory function in combat veterans with posttraumatic stress disorder. *Journal of Traumatic Stress*, *14*(2), 413–432.

Gilbertson, M. W., Paulus, L. A., Williston, S. K., Gurvits, T. V., Lasko, N. B., Pitman, R. K., et al. (2006). Neurocognitive function in monozygotic twins discordant for combat exposure: Relationship to posttraumatic stress disorder. *Journal of Abnormal Psychology*, *115*(3), 484–495.

Gilbertson, M. W., Shenton, M. E., Ciszewski, A., Kasai, K., Lasko, N. B., Orr, S. P., et al. (2002). Smaller hippocampal volume predicts pathologic vulnerability to psychological trauma. *Nature Neuroscience*, *5*(11), 1242–1247.

Gohier, B., Ferracci, L., Surguladze, S. A., Lawrence, E., El, H. W., Kefi, M. Z., et al. (2009). Cognitive inhibition and working memory in unipolar depression. *Journal of Affective Disorders*, *116*(1-2), 100–105.

Golier, J., & Yehuda, R. (2002). Neuropsychological processes in post-traumatic stress disorder. *The Psychiatry Clinics of North America*, *25*(2), 295–315.

Gorenstein, C., Bernik, M. A., & Pompéia, S. (1994). Differential acute psychomotor and cognitive effects of diazepam on long-term benzodiazepine users. *International Clinical Psychopharmacology*, *9*(3), 145–153.

Hannay, J. H., & Lezak, M. D. (2004). The neuropsychological examination: Interpretation. In M. D. Lezak, D. B. Howieson, & D. W. Loring (Eds.), *Neuropsychological Assessment* (4th ed., pp. 133–155). New York, NY: Oxford University Press.

Harrington, K. M., Miller, M. W., Wolf, E. J., Reardon, A. F., Ryabchenko, K. A., & Ofrat, S. (2012). Attention-deficit/ hyperactivity disorder comorbidity in a sample of veterans with posttraumatic stress disorder. *Comprehensive Psychiatry*, *53*(6), 679–690.

Harvey, A. G., Bryant, R., & Tarrier, N. (2003). Cognitive behaviour therapy for posttraumatic stress disorder. *Clinical Psychology Review*, *23*(3), 501–522.

Hayes, J. P., Hayes, S. M., & Mikedis, A. M. (2012). Quantiative meta-analysis of neural activity in posttraumatic stress disorder. *Biology of Mood & Anxiety Disorders*, *2*(9), 1–13.

Heaton, R. K. (1981). *A manual for the Wisconsin Card Sorting Test*. Odessa, FL: Psychological Assessment Services.

Hedges, D. W., & Woon, F. L. (2011). Early-life stress and cognitive outcome. *Psychopharmacology*, *214*(1), 121–130.

Hervey, A. S., Epstein, J., & Curry, J. F. (2004). The neuropsychology of adults with attention deficit hyperactivity disorder: A meta-analytic review. *Neuropsychology*, *18*(3), 485–503.

Hill, J. J., Mobo, B. H., & Cullen, M. R. (2009). Separating deployment-related traumatic brain injury and posttraumatic stress disorder in veterans: Preliminary findings from the Veterans Affairs traumatic brain injury screening program. *American Journal of Physical Medicine & Rehabilitation, 88*(8), 605−614.

Hoge, C. W., Castor, C. A., Messer, S. C., McGurk, D., Cotting, D., & Koffman, M. D. (2004). Combat duty in Iraq and Afghanistan, mental health problems, and barriers to care. *The New England Journal of Medicine, 351*(1), 13−22.

Hoge, C. W., McGurk, D., Thomas, J. L., Cox, A. L., Engel, C. C., & Castro, C. A. (2008). Mild traumatic brain injury in U.S. soldiers returning from Iraq. *The New England Journal of Medicine, 358*(5), 453−463.

Horner, M. D., & Hamner, M. B. (2002). Neurocognitive functioning in posttraumatic stress disorder. *Neuropsychology Review, 12*(1), 15−30.

Hull, A. M. (2002). Neuroimaging findings in post-traumatic stress disorder: Systematic review. *The British Journal of Psychiatry, 181*(2), 102−110.

Hyder, A. A., Wunderlich, C. A., Puvanachandra, P., Gururaj, G., & Kobusingye, O. C. (2007). The impact of traumatic brain injuries: A global perspective. *NeuroRehabilitation, 22*(5), 341−353.

Jelinek, L., Wittekind, C. E., Moritz, S., Kellner, M., & Muhtz, C. (2013). Neuropsychological functioning in posttraumatic stress disorder following forced displacement in older adults and their offspring. *Psychiatry Research, 210*(2), 584−589.

Jenkins, M. A., Langlais, P. J., Delis, D., & Cohen, R. A. (2000). Attentional dysfunction associated with posttraumatic stress disorder among rape survivors. *The Clinical Neuropsychologist, 14*(1), 7−12.

Johnsen, G. E., & Asbjørnsen, A. E. (2008). Consistent impaired verbal memory in PTSD: A meta-analysis. *Journal of Affective Disorders, 111*(1), 74−82.

Johnsen, G. E., Kanagaratnam, P., & Asbjørnsen, A. E. (2008). Memory impairments in post-traumatic stress disorder are related to depression. *Journal of Anxiety Disorders, 22*(3), 464−474.

Johnson, S. B., & Blum, R. W. (2012). Stress and the brain: How experiences and exposures across the life span shape health, development, and learning in adolescence. *Journal of Adolescent Health, 51*(2), S1−S2.

Jovanovski, D., Erb, S., & Zakzanis, K. K. (2005). Neurocognitive deficits in cocaine users: A quantitative review of the evidence. *Journal of Clinical and Experimental Neuropsychology, 27*(2), 189−204.

Kanagaratnam, P., & Asbornsen, A. E. (2007). Executive deficits in chronic PTSD related to political violence. *Journal of Anxiety Disorders, 21*(4), 510−525.

Karl, A., Schaefer, M., Malta, S., Dorfel, D., Rohleder, N., & Werner, A. (2006). A meta-analysis of structural brain abnormalities in PTSD. *Neuroscience and Biobehavioral Reviews, 30*(7), 1004−1031.

Karr, J. E., Areshenkoff, C. N., Duggan, E. C., & Garcia-Barrera, M. A. (2014). Blast-related mild traumatic brain injury: A Bayesian random effects meta-analysis on the cognitive outcomes of concussion among military personnel. *Neuropsychology Review, 24*(4), 428−444.

Kasai, K., Yamasue, H., Gilbertson, M. W., Shenton, M. E., Rauch, S. L., & Pitman, R. K. (2008). Evidence for acquired pregenual anterior cingulate gray matter loss from a twin study of combat-related posttraumatic stress disorder. *Biological Psychiatry, 63*(6), 550−556.

Keane, T. M., & Kaloupek, D. G. (1997). Comorbid psychiatric disorders in PTSD. Implications for research. *Annals of the New York Academy of Sciences, 821*, 24−34.

Kessler, R. C. (2006). Posttraumatic stress disorder: The burden to the individual and to society. *Journal of Clinical Psychiatry*, *61*(suppl 5), 4–12.

Kessler, R. C., Chiu, W. T., Demler, O., & Walters, E. E. (2005). Prevalence, severity, and comorbidity of 12-Month DSM-IV disorders in the national comorbidity survey replication. *Archives of General Psychiatry*, *62*(6), 617–627.

Kessler, R. C., & Frank, R. G. (1997). The impact of psychiatric disorders on work loss days. *Psychological Medicine*, *27*(4), 861–873.

Kessler, R. C., Sonnega, A., Bromet, E., Hughes, M., & Nelson, C. (1995). Posttraumatic stress disorder in the national comorbidity survey. *Archives of General Psychiatry*, *52*(12), 1048–1060.

Kessler, R. C., Zhao, S., Katz, S. J., Kouzis, A. C., Frank, R. G., Edlund, M., et al. (1999). Past-year use of outpatient services for psychiatric problems in the national comorbidity survey. *The American Journal of Psychiatry*, *156*(1), 115–123.

Kimble, M. (2008). Neurobiological models in posttraumatic stress disorder: Effects on public perception and patient care. *Journal of Psychological Trauma*, *6*(4), 57–78.

Kimble, M. O., Fleming, K., Bandy, C., Kim, J., & Zambetti, A. (2010). Eye tracking and visual attention to threating stimuli in veterans of the Iraq war. *Journal of Anxiety Disorders*, *24*(3), 293–299.

Kremen, W. S., Koenen, K. C., Afari, N., & Lyons, M. J. (2012). Twin studies in posttraumatic stress disorder: Differentiating vulnerability factors from sequelae. *Neuropharmacology*, *62*(2), 647–653.

Kulka, R. A., Schlenger, W. E., Fairbank, J. A., Hough, R. L., Jordan, B. K., Marmar, C. R., et al. (1990). *Trauma and the Vietnam War generation: Report of findings from the National Vietnam Veterans Readjustment study*. New York: Brunner/Mazel.

Lagarde, G., Doyon, J., & Brunet, A. (2010). Memory and executive dysfunctions associated with acute posttraumatic stress disorder. *Psychiatry Research*, *177*(1-2), 144–149.

Lange, R. T., Brickell, T. A., Ivins, B., Vanderploeg, R. D., & French, L. M. (2013). Variable, not always persistent, postconcussion symptoms after mild TBI in U.S. military service members: A five-year cross-sectional outcome study. *Journal of Neurotrauma*, *30*(11), 958–969.

Lapp, L. K., Agbokou, C., & Ferreri, F. (2011). PTSD in the elderly: The interaction between trauma and aging. *International Psychogeriatrics*, *23*(6), 858–868.

Leskin, L. P., & White, P. M. (2007). Attentional networks reveal executive function deficits in posttraumatic stress disorder. *Neuropsychology*, *21*(3), 275–284.

Lezak, M. D., Howieson, D. B., & Loring, D. W. (2004). *Neuropsychological assessment* (4th ed). New York, NY: Oxford University Press.

Liberzon, I., Britton, J. C., & Phan, K. L. (2003). Neural correlates of traumatic recall in post-traumatic stress disorder. *Stress*, *6*(3), 151–156.

Lindeboom, J., & Weinstein, H. (2004). Neuropsychology of cognitive ageing, minimal cognitive impairment, Alzheimer's disease, and vascular cognitive impairment. *European Journal of Pharmacology*, *490*(1-3), 83–86.

Loong, J. (1988). *The Continuous Performance Test*. San Luis Obispo, CA: Wang Neuropsychological Laboratory.

Mac Donald, C. L., Johnson, A. M., Cooper, D., Nelson, E. C., Werner, N. J., Shimony, J. S., et al. (2011). Detection of blast-related traumatic brain injury in U.S. military personnel. *The New England Journal of Medicine*, *364*(22), 2091–2100.

Macklin, M. L., Metzger, L. J., Litz, B. T., McNally, R. J., Lasko, N. B., Orr, S. P., et al. (1998). Lower precombat intelligence is a risk factor for posttraumatic stress disorder. *Journal of Consulting and Clinical Psychology*, *66*(2), 323–326.

MacLeod, C., Rutherford, E., Campbell, L., Ebsworthy, G., & Holker, L. (2002). Selective attention and emotional vulnerability: Assessing the causal basis of their association through the experimental manipulation of attentional bias. *Journal of Abnormal Psychology, 111*(1), 107–123.

Marx, B. P., Doron-Lamarca, S., Proctor, S. P., & Vasterling, J. J. (2009). The influence of pre-deployment neurocognitive functioning on post-deployment PTSD symptom outcomes among Iraq deployed Army soldiers. *Journal of the International Neuropsychological Society, 15*(6), 840–852.

McNally, R. J., & Shin, L. M. (1995). Association of intelligence with severity of posttraumatic stress disorder symptoms in Vietnam combat veterans. *American Journal of Psychiatry, 152* (6), 936–938.

Milad, M. R., & Rauch, S. L. (2007). The role of the orbitofrontal cortex in anxiety disorders. *Annals of the New York Academy of Sciences, 1121,* 546–561.

Miller, G. A., & Chapman, J. P. (2001). Misunderstanding analysis of covariance. *Journal of Abnormal Psychology, 110*(1), 40–48.

Mills, R., Alati, R., O'Callaghan, M., Najman, J. M., Williams, G. M., Bor, W., et al. (2011). Child abuse and neglect and cognitive function at 14 years of age: Findings from a birth cohort. *Pediatrics, 127*(1), 4–10.

Mittal, D., Torres, R., Abashidze, A., & Jimerson, N. (2001). Worsening of post-traumatic stress disorder with cognitive decline: Case series. *Journal of Geriatric Psychiatry and Neurology, 14*(1), 17–20.

Miyake, A., Friedman, N. P., Emerson, M. J., Witzki, A. H., & Howerter, A. (2000). The unity and diversity of executive functions and their contributions to complex "frontal lobe" tasks: A latent variable analysis. *Cognitive Psychology, 41*(1), 49–100.

Morey, R. A., Petty, C. M., Cooper, D. A., LaBar, K. S., & McCarthy, G. (2008). Neural systems for executive and emotional processing are modulated by symptoms of posttraumatic stress disorder in Iraq War veterans. *Psychiatry Research: Neuroimaging, 162*(1), 59–72.

Mueller, S., Maheu, F. S., Dozier, M., Peloso, E., Mandell, D., Leibenluft, E., et al. (2010). Early-life stress is associated with impairment in cognitive control in adolescence: An fMRI study. *Neuropsychologia, 48*(10), 3037–3044.

Mueller-Pfeiffer, C., Martin-Soelch, C., Blair, J. R., Carnier, A., Kaiser, N., Rufer, M., et al. (2010). Impact of emotion on cognition in trauma survivors: What is the role of posttraumatic stress disorder? *Journal of Affective Disorders, 126*(1-2), 287–292.

Najmi, S., & Amir, N. (2010). The effect of attention training on a behavioral test of contamination fears in individuals with subclinical obsessive-compulsive symptoms. *Journal of Abnormal Psychology, 119*(1), 136–142.

Navalta, C. P., Polcari, A., Webster, D. M., Boghossian, A., & Teicher, M. H. (2006). Effects of childhood sexual abuse on neuropsychological and cognitive function in college women. *The Journal of Neuropsychiatry and Clinical Neurosciences, 18*(1), 45–53.

Neylan, T. C., Lenoci, M., Rothlind, J., Metzler, T. J., Schuff, N., Du, A. T., et al. (2004). Attention, learning, and memory in posttraumatic stress disorder. *Journal of Traumatic Stress, 17*(1), 41–46.

Nijdam, M. J., de Vries, G. J., Gersons, B. P. R., & Olff, M. (2015). Response to psychotherapy for posttraumatic stress disorder: The role of pretreatment verbal memory performance. *The Journal of Clinical Psychiatry, 76*(8), e1023–1028.

Noll, J. G., Shenk, C. E., Yeh, M. T., Ji, J., Putnam, F. W., & Tickett, P. K. (2010). Receptive language and educational attainment for sexually abused females. *Pediatrics, 126*(3), e615–e622.

Novakovic, V., Sher, L., Lapidus, K. A. B., Mindes, J., Golier, J. A., & Yehuda, R. (2011). Brain stimulation in posttraumatic stress disorder. *European Journal of Psychotraumatology*, *2*, 5609.

Okie, S. (2005). Traumatic brain injury in the war zone. *The New England Journal of Medicine*, *352*(20), 2043–2047.

Olff, M., Polak, A. R., Witteveen, A. B., & Denys, D. (2014). Executive function in posttraumatic stress disorder (PTSD) and the influence of comorbid depression. *Neurobiology of Learning and Memory*, *112*, 114–121.

O'Neal, M. E., Carlson, K., Storzbach, D., Brenner, L., Freeman, M., Quinones, A., et al. (2013). *Complications of mild traumatic brain injury in veterans and military personnel: A systematic review*. Washington, DC: Department of Veterans Affairs.

Oscar-Berman, M., & Marinkovic, K. (2007). Alcohol: Effects on neurobehavioral functions and the brain. *Neuropsychology Review*, *17*(3), 239–257.

Osterrieth, P. A. (1944). Le test de copie d'une figure complex: Contribution a l'etude de la perception et de la memoire. *Archives de Psychologie*, *30*, 286–356.

Owens, B. D., Kragh, J. F., Jr., Wenke, J. C., Macaitis, J., Wade, C. E., & Holcomb, J. B. (2008). Combat wounds in Operation Iraqi Freedom and Operation Enduring Freedom. *The Journal of Trauma: Injury, Infection, and Critical Care*, *64*(2), 295–299.

Partington, J. E., & Leiter, R. G. (1949). Partington's pathways test. *Psychological Service Center Bulletin*, *1*, 9–20.

Pertab, J. L., James, J. M., & Bigler, E. D. (2009). Limitations of mild traumatic brain injury meta-analyses. *Brain Injury*, *23*(6), 498–508.

Pineles, S. L., Shipherd, J. C., Mostoufi, S. M., Abramovitz, S. M., & Yovel, I. (2009). Attentional biases in PTSD: More evidence for interference. *Behaviour Research and Therapy*, *47*(12), 1050–1057.

Pineles, S. L., Shipherd, J. C., Welch, L. P., & Yovel, I. (2007). The role of attentional biases in PTSD: Is it interference or facilitation? *Behaviour Research and Therapy*, *45*(8), 1903–1913.

Pitman, R. K., Orr, S. P., Lowenhagen, M. J., Macklin, M. L., & Altman, B. (1991). Pre-Vietnam contents of posttraumatic stress disorder veterans' service medical and personnel records. *Comprehensive Psychiatry*, *32*(5), 416–422.

Polak, A. R., Witteveen, A. B., Reitsma, J. B., & Olff, M. (2012). The role of executive function in posttraumatic stress disorder: A systematic review. *Journal of Affective Disorders*, *141*(1), 11–21.

Porter, C., Lawson, J. S., & Bigler, E. D. (2005). Neurobehavioral sequelae of child sexual abuse. *Journal of Child Neuropsychology*, *11*(2), 203–220.

Qureshi, S. U., Long, M. E., Bradshaw, M. R., Pyne, J. M., Magruder, K. M., Kimbrell, T., et al. (2011). Does PTSD impair cognition beyond the effect of trauma? *The Journal of Neuropsychiatry and Clinical Neurosciences*, *23*(1), 16–28.

Rauch, S. L., Shin, L. M., & Phelps, E. A. (2006). Neurocircuitry models of posttraumatic stress disorder and extinction: Human neuroimaging research – past, present, and future. *Biological Psychiatry*, *60*(4), 376–382.

Resick, P. A., & Schnicke, M. K. (1996). *Cognitive processing therapy for rape victims: a treatment manual*. Newbury Park, CA: Sage Publications.

Rey, A. (1941). L'examen psychologique dans les cas d'encephalopathie traumatique. *Archives de Psychologie*, *28*, 286–340.

Reynolds, D. M., & Jeeves, M. A. (1978). A developmental study of hemisphere specialization for recognition of faces in normal subjects. *Cortex*, *14*(4), 511–520.

Rohling, M. L., Larrabee, G. J., & Millis, S. R. (2012). The "miserable minority" following mild traumatic brain injury: Who are they and do met-analyses hide them? *The Clinical Neuropsychologist, 26*(2), 197−213.

Ruff, R. M., Iverson, G. L., Barth, J. T., Bush, S. S., & Broshek, D. K. (2009). Recommendations for diagnosing a mild traumatic brain injury: A national academy of neuropsychology education paper. *Archives of Clinical Neuropsychology, 24*(1), 3−10.

Sailer, U., Robinson, S., Fischmeister, F. P., Konig, D., Oppenauer, C., Lueger- Schuster, B., et al. (2008). Altered reward processing in the nucleus accumbens and mesial prefrontal cortex of patients with posttraumatic stress disorder. *Neuropsychologia 46*(11), 2836−2844.

Samuelson, K. W., Krueger, C. E., Burnett, C., & Wilson, C. K. (2010). Neuropsychological functioning in children with posttraumatic stress disorder. *Child Neuropsychology, 16*(2), 119−133.

Samuelson, K. W., Neylan, T. C., Metzler, T. J., Lenoci, M., Rothlind, J., Henn-Haase, C., et al. (2006). Neuropsychological functioning in posttraumatic stress disorder and alcohol abuse. *Neuropsychology, 20*(6), 716−726.

Samuelson, K. W., Neylan, T. C., Lenoci, M., Metzler, T. J., Cardenas, V., Weiner, M. W., et al. (2009). Longitudinal effects of PTSD on memory functioning. *Journal of the International Neuropsychological Society, 15*, 853−861.

Scherrer, J. F., Xian, H., Lyons, M. J., Goldberg, J., Eisen, S. A., True, W. R., et al. (2008). Posttraumatic stress disorder; combat exposure; and nicotine dependence, alcohol dependence, and major depression in male twins. *Comprehensive Psychiatry, 49*(3), 297−304.

Schmidt, N. B., Richey, J. A., Buckner, J. D., & Timpano, K. R. (2009). Attention training for generalized social anxiety disorder. *Journal of Abnormal Psychology, 118*(1), 5−14.

Schuff, N., Zhang, Y., Zhan, W., Lenoci, M., Ching, C., Boreta, L., et al. (2011). Patterns of altered cortical perfusion and diminished subcortical integrity in posttraumatic stress disorder: An MRI study. *NeuroImage, 54*(suppl 1), S62−S68.

Schuitevoerder, S., Rosen, J. W., Twamley, E. W., Ayers, C. R., Sones, H., Lohr, J. B., et al. (2013). A meta-analysis of cognitive functioning in older adults with PTSD. *Journal of Anxiety Disorders, 27*(6), 550−558.

Scott, J. C., Matt, G. E., Wrocklage, K. M., Crnich, C., Jordan, J., Southwick, S. M., et al. (2015). A quantitative meta-analysis of neurocognitive functioning in posttraumatic stress disorder. *Psychological Bulletin, 141*(1), 105−140.

Seal, K. H., Bertenthal, D., Miner, C. R., Sen, S., & Marmar, C. (2007). Bringing the war back home: Mental health disorders among 103,788 US veterans returning from Iraq and Afghanistan seen at Department of Veterans Affairs facilities. *Archives of Internal Medicine, 167*(5), 476−482.

Segen, J. C. (2002). *Concise Dictionary of Modern Medicine*. New York: McGraw-Hill Companies, Inc. Retrieved August 2, 2016 from: http://medicaldictionary.thefreedictionary. com/cogntive+function.

Seidman, L. J. (2006). Neuropsychological functioning in people with ADHD across the lifespan. *Clinical Psychology Review, 26*(4), 466−485.

Shin, L. M., & Liberzon, I. (2010). The neurocircuitry of fear, stress, and anxiety disorders. *Neuropsychopharmacology, 35*(1), 169−191.

Shin, L. M., Orr, S. P., Carson, M. A., Rauch, S. L., Macklin, M. L., Lasko, N. B., et al. (2004). Regional cerebral blood flow in the amygdala and medial prefrontal cortex during traumatic imagery in male and female Vietnam veterans with PTSD. *Archives of General Psychiatry, 61*(2), 168−176.

Shin, L. M., Wright, C. I., Cannistraro, P. A., Wedig, M. M., McMullin, K., Matis, B., et al. (2005). A functional magnetic resonance imaging study of amygdala and medial prefrontal cortex responses to overtly presented fearful faces in posttraumatic stress disorders. *Archives of General Psychiatry*, *62*(3), 273–281.

Sponheim, S. R., McGuire, K. A., Kang, S. S., Davenport, N. D., Aviyente, S., Bernat, E. M., et al. (2011). Evidence of disrupted functional connectivity in the brain after combat-related blast injury. *NeuroImage*, *53*(S1), S21–S29.

Squire, L. R., Stark, C. E., & Clark, R. E. (2004). The medial temporal lobe. *Annual Review of Neuroscience*, *27*, 279–306.

Stavro, K., Pelletier, J., & Potvin, S. (2013). Widespread and sustained cognitive deficits in alcoholism: A meta-analysis. *Addiction Biology*, *18*(2), 203–213.

Steenkamp, M. M., Litz, B. T., Hoge, C. W., & Marmar, C. M. (2015). Psychotherapy for military-related PTSD: A review of randomized clinical trials. *The Journal of the American Medical Association*, *314*(5), 489–500.

Stein, D. J., Ipser, J. C., & Seedat, S. (2006). Pharmacotherapy for post traumatic stress disorder (PTSD). *The Cochrane Database of Systematic Reviews*, *25*, 1.

Stein, M. B., Kennedy, C. M., & Twamley, E. W. (2002). Neuropsychological function in female victims of intimate partner violence with and without posttraumatic stress disorder. *Biological Psychiatry*, *52*(11), 1079–1088.

Stein, M. B., & McAllister, T. W. (2009). Exploring the convergence of posttraumatic stress disorder and mild traumatic brain injury. *American Journal of Psychiatry*, *166*(7), 768–776.

Stroop, J. R. (1935). Studies of interference in serial verbal reactions. *Journal of Experimental Psychology*, *18*(6), 643–662.

Sullivan, K., Krengel, M., Proctor, S. P., Devine, S., Heeren, T., & White, R. F. (2003). Cognitive functioning in treatment-seeking Gulf War veterans: Pyridostigmine bromide use and PTSD. *Journal of Psychopathology and Behavioral Assessment*, *25*(2), 95–103.

Tanev, K. S., Pentel, K. Z., Kredlow, M. A., & Charney, M. E. (2014). PTSD and TBI comorbidity: Scope, clinical presentation and treatment options. *Brain Injury*, *28*(3), 261–270.

Tanielian, T. L., & Jaycox, L. H. (Eds.), (2008). *Invisible wounds of war: Psychological and cognitive injuries, their consequences, and services to assist recovery* Santa Monica, CA: Rand Corporation.

Tata, P., Leibowitz, J., Prunty, M. J., Cameron, M., & Pickering, A. D. (1996). Attentional bias in obsessional disorder. *Behaviour Research and Therapy*, *34*(1), 53–60.

Tata, P. R., Rollings, J., Collins, M., Pickering, A., & Jacobson, R. R. (1994). Lack of cognitive recovery following withdrawal from long-term benzodiazepine use. *Psychological Medicine*, *24*(1), 203–213.

Tipps, M. E., Raybuck, J. D., & Lattal, K. M. (2014). Substance abuse, memory, and posttraumatic stress disorder. *Neurobiology of Learning and Memory*, *112*, 87–100.

Twamley, E. W., Hami, S., & Stein, M. B. (2004). Neuropsychological function in college students with and without posttraumatic stress disorder. *Psychiatry Research*, *126*(3), 265–274.

Twamley, E. W., Thomas, K. R., Gregory, A. M., Jak, A. J., Bondi, M. W., Delis, D. C., et al. (2015). CogSMART compensatory cognitive training for traumatic brain injury: Effects over 1 year. *The Journal of Head Trauma Rehabilitation*, *30*(6), 391–401.

Twamley, E. W., Vella, L., Burton, C. Z., Heaton, R. K., & Jeste, D. V. (2012). Compensatory training for psychosis: Effects in a randomly controlled trial. *Journal of Clinical Psychiatry*, *27*(9), 1212–1219.

U.S. Census Bureau (2010). *The next four decades: the older population in the United States: 2010 to 2050, current population reports* (pp. 25−1138). Washington, DC: Author. Retrieved from: http://www.census.gov.

Vanderploeg, R. D., Belanger, H. G., & Curtiss, G. (2009). Mild traumatic brain injury and post-traumatic stress disorder and their associations with health symptoms. *Archives of Physical and Medical Rehabilitation, 90*(7), 1084−1093.

Vanderploeg, R. D., Curtiss, G., & Belanger, H. G. (2005). Long-term neuropsychological outcomes following mild traumatic brain injury. *Journal of the International Neuropsychological Society, 11*(3), 228−236.

Vasterling, J. J., & Brailey, K. (2005). Neuropsychological findings in adults with PTSD. In J. J. Vasterling, & C. R. Brewin (Eds.), *Neuropsychology of PTSD: Biological, cognitive, and clinical perspectives* (pp. 178−207). New York: Guilford Press.

Vasterling, J. J., Brailey, K., Constans, J. I., Borges, A., & Sutker, P. B. (1997). Assessment of intellectual resources in Gulf War veterans: Relationship to PTSD. *Assessment, 4*(1), 51−59.

Vasterling, J. J., Brailey, K., Constans, J. I., & Sutker, P. B. (1998). Attention and memory dysfunction in posttraumatic stress disorder. *Neuropsychology, 12*(1), 125−133.

Vasterling, J. J., Brailey, K., Proctor, S. P., Kane, R., Heeren, T., & Franz, M. (2012). Neuropsychological outcomes of mild traumatic brain injury, post-traumatic stress disorder and depression in Iraq-deployed US Army soldiers. *British Journal of Psychiatry, 201*(3), 186−192.

Vasterling, J. J., Duke, L. M., Brailey, K., Constans, J. I., Allain, A. N., & Sutker, P. B. (2002). Attention, learning and memory performance and intellectual resources in Vietnam veterans: PTSD and no disorder comparisons. *Neuropsychology, 16*(1), 5−14.

Vasterling, J. J., Proctor, S. P., Amoroso, P., Kane, R., Heeren, T., & White, R. F. (2006). Neuropsychological outcomes of Army personnel following deployment to the Iraq War. *The Journal of the American Medical Association, 296*(5), 519−529.

Vasterling, J. J., & Verfaellie, M. (2009). Introduction-posttraumatic stress disorder: A neurocognitive perspective. *Journal of the International Neuropsychological Society, 15*(6), 826−829.

Vasterling, J. J., Verfaellie, M., & Sullivan, K. D. (2009). Mild traumatic brain injury and post-traumatic stress disorder in returning veterans: Perspectives from cognitive neuroscience. *Clinical Psychology Review, 29*(8), 674−684.

Vermetten, E., Vythilingam, M., Southwick, S. M., Charney, D. S., & Bremnet, J. D. (2003). Long-term treatment with paroxetine increases verbal declarative memory and hippocampal volume in posttraumatic stress disorder. *Biological Psychiatry, 54*(7), 693−702.

Vincent, A. S., Roebuck-Spencer, T. M., & Cernich, A. (2014). Cognitive changes and dementia risk after traumatic brain injury: Implications for aging military personnel. *Alzheimer's & Dementia, 10*(3), S174−S187.

Walter, K. H., Palmieri, P. A., & Gunstad, J. (2010). More than symptom reduction: Changes in executive function over the course of PTSD treatment. *Journal of Traumatic Stress, 23*(2), 292−295.

Warden, D. (2006). Military TBI during the Iraq and Afghanistan wars. *The Journal of Head Trauma and Rehabilitation, 21*(5), 398−402.

Warren, A. M., Boals, A., Elliot, T. R., Reynolds, M., Weddle, R. J., Holtz, P., et al. (2015). Mild traumatic brain injury increases risk for the development of posttraumatic stress disorder. *Journal of Trauma and Acute Care Surgery, 79*(6), 1062−1066.

Wechsler, D. (2008). *Wechsler Adult Intelligence Scale. Technical manual* (Fourth Edition). San Antonio, TX: The Psychological Corporation.

Wild, J., & Gur, R. C. (2008). Verbal memory and treatment response in posttraumatic stress disorder. *The British Journal of Psychiatry, 193*(3), 254–255.

Wilde, E. A., Bigler, E. D., Pedroza, C., & Ryser, D. K. (2006). Post-traumatic amnesia predicts long-term cerebral atrophy in traumatic brain injury. *Brain Injury, 20*(7), 695–699.

Wood, S. J., Allen, N. H., & Pantelis, C. (2009). *The Neuropsychology of Mental Illness.* Cambridge, United Kingdom: Cambridge University Press.

Woon, F. L., Sood, S., & Hedges, D. W. (2010). Hippocampal volume deficits associated with exposure to psychological trauma and posttraumatic stress disorder in adults: A meta-analysis. *Progress in Neuro-Psychopharmacology and Biological Psychiatry, 34*(7), 1181–1188.

Wrocklage, K. M., Schweinsburg, B. C., Krystal, J. H., Trejo, M., Roy, A., Weisser, V., et al. (2016). Neuropsychological functioning in veterans with posttraumatic stress disorder: Associations with performance validity, comorbidities, and functional outcomes. *Journal of the International Neuropsychological Society, 22*(4), 399–411.

Wu, J., Ge, Y., Shi, Z., Duan, X., Wang, L., Sun, X., & Zhang, K. (2010). Response inhibition in adolescent earthquake survivors with and without posttraumatic stress disorder: A combined behavioral and ERP study. *Neuroscience Letters, 486*(3), 117–121.

Yaffe, K., Vittinghoff, E., Lindquist, K., Barnes, D., Covinsky, K. E., Neylan, T., et al. (2010). Posttraumatic stress disorder and risk of dementia among U.S. veterans. *Archives of General Psychiatry, 67*(6), 608–613.

Yehuda, R., Golier, J. A., Harvey, P. D., Stavitsky, K., Kaufman, S., Grossman, R. A., et al. (2005). Relationship between cortisol and age-related memory impairments in Holocaust survivors with PTSD. *Psychoneuroendocrinology, 30*(7), 678–687.

Yehuda, R., Golier, J. A., Tischler, L., Stravitsky, K., & Harvey, P. D. (2005). Learning and memory in aging combat veterans with PTSD. *Journal of Clinical and Experimental Neuropsychology, 27*(4), 504–515.

Yehuda, R., Tischler, L., Golier, J. A., Grossman, R., Brand, S. R., Kaufman, S., et al. (2006). Longitudinal assessment of cognitive performance in Holocaust survivors with and without PTSD. *Biological Psychiatry, 60*(7), 714–721.

Zen, A. L., Whooley, M. A., Zhao, S., & Cohen, B. E. (2012). Post-traumatic stress disorder is associated with poor health behaviors: Findings from the heart and soul study. *Health Psychology, 31*(2), 194–201.

Chapter 21

Executive Dysfunction in Medical Conditions

Michał Harciarek and Aleksandra Wojtowicz
Department of Social Sciences, University of Gdańsk, Gdańsk, Poland

INTRODUCTION

Medical neuropsychology is a relatively new but dynamically evolving branch of clinical neuropsychology. In contrast to characterizing cognitive disorders in patients with brain damage, as it has systematically been done since the middle of the 19th century (Benton, 2000), medical neuropsychology predominantly aims to investigate how diseases of organs or systems, together with their treatment, can affect brain functioning and, as a result, lead to cognitive impairment. Thus, medical neuropsychology has been recognized as a multidisciplinary field of science, combining the theories and methods of neuropsychology with knowledge derived from internal medicine, neurology, and neuropsychiatry.

Due to the advances in molecular and genetic research as well as the development of new technologies, the last three decades have been associated with a substantial progress in understanding the relationship between the severity of some chronic nonneurological somatic diseases (such as kidney disease, thyroid disease, diabetes mellitus, or rheumatoid arthritis) and cognitive abilities. As a result, it has been shown that many of these diseases may affect the central nervous system, predominantly frontosubcortical networks. Thus, many of individuals with these primary nonneurological diseases present with some degree of attention and executive dysfunction. Also, although in most of these conditions an appropriate disease-directed treatment has a beneficial effect on cognition, some treatment methods may amplify or produce new neuropsychological symptoms. Moreover, the effects of somatic diseases and their treatment on frontal—subcortical networks and executive function can additionally interact with patient's age and other comorbid conditions, further impoverishing these patients' activities of daily living and increasing the risk for developing dementia.

Executive Functions in Health and Disease. DOI: http://dx.doi.org/10.1016/B978-0-12-803676-1.00021-0

In this chapter we have attempted to characterize attention and executive function of individuals suffering from somatic diseases that have been relatively frequently encountered in clinical practice (i.e., hypertension, diabetes mellitus, chronic kidney disease (CKD), human immunodeficiency virus (HIV)/acquired immune deficiency syndrome (AIDS), hepatic encephalopathy (HE), thyroid disease, and rheumatoid arthritis). Additionally, some adverse treatment effects and possible mechanisms that could account for these cognitive problems have been discussed.

HYPERTENSION

Hypertension is a common vascular condition characterized by higher levels of baseline blood pressure. It is a significant risk factor for stroke and is the greatest risk factor for small-vessel disease frequently leading to lacunar infarction and intracerebral hemorrhage (see Chapter 17: Seizures of the Frontal Lobes: Clinical Presentations and Diagnostic Considerations). Additionally, hypertension has been repeatedly shown to be associated with cognitive impairment that further increases the risk of vascular dementia (Tzourio, 2007). Nevertheless, the results of multiple neuropsychological studies on neurocognitive function in patients with hypertension are not always consistent, likely due to the differences in patients' selection and cognitive tests employed. Thus, the pattern of neuropsychological changes in this population remains controversial and largely debated. In this section we have attempted to summarize the results of the studies presenting the contemporary view on executive and other frontal/subcortical—related cognitive abnormalities in persons with hypertension.

Most studies assessing cognitive functioning of hypertensive patients, in comparison to normotensive ones, indicate that adult patients with higher levels of blood pressure (BP) tend to obtain poorer results on a variety of tests aimed at measuring attention and executive functions (Waldstein, Manuck, Ryan, & Muldoon, 1991). More recent findings have also shown that these cognitive problems decline over time, both in children (Kupferman, Lande, Adams, & Pavlakis, 2013) and adults (Hajjar, Goldstein, Martin, & Quyyumi, 2016). Furthermore, these deficits in elderly hypertensive patients are often accompanied by decrements in psychomotor and visuospatial functions (Bucur & Madden, 2010; Hamada, Chikamori, Nishinaga, & Doi, 2003; Harrington, Saxby, McKeith, Wesnes, & Ford, 2000).

The disruption of white matter tracts, both within the frontal lobe and between frontal cortex and other (more posterior) brain regions has been consistently linked with impairment of attention, executive functions, and speed processing seen in patients with hypertension (Prins, van Dijk, & den Heijer, 2005; see also Tullberg et al., 2004). Such disruption has been most often a result of widespread small ischemic lesions as well as the coexisting degenerative pathologies (Ganguli et al., 2014). Also, hypertension has been associated with total and regional brain atrophy (Beauchet et al., 2013). Furthermore, in comparison to normotensives individuals, adults with hypertension have been shown to present with a progressive decrease in cerebral blood flow mainly in the hippocampus, anterior cingulate gyrus, and prefrontal cortex (Beason-Held, Moghekar, & Zonderman, 2007). Additionally, although hypertension itself has been often associated with increased risk for cognitive decline and for developing Alzheimer's disease (AD) (Bermejo-Pareja et al., 2010), decreased cortical thickness in subjects with hypertension further increases the risk for AD (Querbes et al., 2009).

Of note, the relation between hypertension and dementia remains controversial. For example, although large body of evidence indicates that older adult with hypertension may be more vulnerable to BP-related cognitive decline than younger hypertensive individuals (Oveisgharan & Hachinski, 2010), some results suggest that young adults are as susceptible to BP-related longitudinal decline in cognitive performance as are older adults (Elias, Elias, Robbins, &Budge, 2004). Importantly, the Canadian Study of Health and Aging has shown that the presence of hypertension predicted progression to dementia in older persons with executive dysfunction but no memory impairment (Oveisgharan et al., 2010). However, other factors (e.g., history of diabetes or obesity, Ganguli et al., 2014) may also moderate the relationship between hypertension and cognitive decline, including executive function.

Recently, Spinelli et al. (2014) have examined the effect of treatment of hypertension on cognition. They found that poor controlled hypertension results in decreased executive capacities, particularly in the domain of selective attention, working memory, and verbal fluency. Hence, the results of this study provide further support for the notion that high BP values have an early negative and rather selective effect on cognitive function that predominantly rely on frontal–subcortical networks. Furthermore, it has subsequently been demonstrated that the association between hypertension and executive dysfunction could be primarily accounted for by the increased arterial stiffness (Hajjar et al., 2016), and a good pharmacological control of hypertension can prevent progression to dementia in one-third of the subjects with cognitive impairment (Kohler et al., 2014). However, because the relationship between the antihypertensive treatment and cerebral perfusion is complex (Alosco et al., 2014), future research is needed to better understand the effects of hypertension treatment on attention and executive function.

DIABETES MELLITUS

Diabetes mellitus is a common metabolic disease characterized by hyperglycemia due to impaired insulin secretion, resistance to insulin, or both. Type 1 diabetes mellitus (DM1) is caused by an autoimmune destruction of pancreatic β cells, resulting in nearly complete deficiency of insulin secretion.

Thus, to sustain control of plasma glucose levels, patients with DM1 must take exogenous insulin, either by subcutaneous injection or by a continuous infusion pump. However, the most common form of diabetes is type 2 diabetes (DM2), characterized not only by the resistance to insulin but also by an inadequate compensation in the secretion of insulin. Importantly, both types of diabetes are associated with reduced performance in numerous cognitive domains, including attention and executive function (Bolo et al., 2015; Graveling, Deary, & Frier, 2013; Kálcza-Jánosi, Lukács, Barkai, & Szamosközi, 2013). As in all metabolic conditions, the exact mechanism(s) of the cognitive problems of patients with diabetes is relatively complex. However, cognitive changes in these individuals seem to be associated with deleterious effects of diabetes mellitus (e.g., dysregulation of blood glucose levels) on the renal, retina, and cardiovascular systems as well as directly on the nervous system (Brands, Biessels, de Haan, Kappelle, & Kessels, 2005).

The pattern of neurocognitive impairment among patients with DM1 appears to be heterogeneous. Some studies report predominant deficits in attention and executive functions, whereas other research indicates more general cognitive dysfunctions (i.e., vocabulary and general intelligence) (for review, see Lezak, Howieson, Bigler, & Tranel, 2012). Nonetheless, the most frequent cognitive deficits are slowed speed of information processing (Kodl & Seaquist, 2008) and worsening psychomotor efficiency (Brands et al., 2005). Also, it has been posited that individuals with diabetes mainly have difficulty with effortful tasks due to a limited attentional capacity (Brands & Kessels, 2009), and this seems characteristic for both hypoglycemia and hyperglycemia. Moreover, these cognitive problems tend to be accompanied by functional and structural changes on neuroimaging (e.g., abnormalities in cerebral blood flow), predominantly in the frontal lobes and basal ganglia (Bolo et al., 2015). Additionally, Musen et al. (2006) have demonstrated that executive dysfunction (e.g., defective planning) may also be associated with cerebellar gray matter density. Interestingly, however, Weinger et al. (2008) did not find an association between the clinical characteristics of DM1 and white matter hyperintensities.

It has been shown that individuals who developed DM1 at less than 4 years of age had impaired executive skills, attention, and processing speed when compared to patients diagnosed after 4 years of age (Northam et al., 2001). Thus, apart from episodes of severe hypoglycemia and chronic hyperglycemia, age of diabetes onset seems to be another significant factor influencing executive functioning in DM1 (Tonoli et al., 2014).

Similarly to DM1, patients with DM2 also present with a lowered performance on a wide range of neuropsychological tests although the severity of cognitive impairment and the cognitive profile of individuals with DM2 may not be exactly the same as that seen in DM1 (Brands et al., 2005). For example, although the performance on tests aimed at measuring executive function may not differentiate between DM1 and DM2, it has been suggested that cognitive impairment may be more pronounced in DM2 than in DM1, (Brands et al., 2007). Also, whereas in patients with DM1 deficits in information processing speed, psychomotor efficiency, attention, mental flexibility, and visual perception belong to the most frequently reported cognitive problems, in individuals with DM2 these abnormalities are often accompanied by memory deficits (Kodl & Seaquist, 2008). To better understand cognitive profile of individuals with DM2, Yeung, Fischer, and Dixon (2009) applied a set of comprehensive, multidimensional neuropsychological tests to a large cohort of adults with DM2 and controls. The results of this study confirmed previous research (Manschot et al., 2006) and showed that, in comparison to nondiabetic individuals, patients with diabetes obtained lowered scores only on measures of mental processing speed and executive function. What is more, the deleterious effect of DM2 on the performance on these tests remained significant even when participants were divided into two groups: young−old (53−70 years) and old−old (71−90 years). Also, a cohort study of DM2 showed that, whereas both the presence of diabetes and the duration of disease are associated with slower processing speed, executive dysfunction seem to be only related to the duration of disease (executive problems were found in individuals with a history of diabetes lasting 15 years or longer) (Saczynski et al., 2008). Nonetheless, Ruis et al. (2009) reported that, when IQ of the study participants is controlled, statistically significant differences in executive functions between individuals with DM2 and controls may no longer be present. However, although the association between the functional abilities of patients with DM2 and executive dysfunctions remains unclear (Rucker, McDowd, & Kluding, 2012), in comparison to DM1, patients with DM2 tend to experience more difficulties with self-management (e.g., medication adherence, self-care, and self-management), and self-management has been recognized as a good indicator of dysexecutive syndrome (Thabit et al., 2009).

Although cognitive problems have frequently been reported among individuals with DM2, the exact neuroanatomical effects of DM2 on cognitive performance, including the performance on tests of executive function, remain relatively obscure. A recent report on MRI abnormalities and cognitive changes found that patients with DM2 exhibited as much as 23% more cortical atrophy, 12% more subcortical atrophy, and significantly more deep white matter lesions and infarcts than those without DM2 (Manschot et al., 2006). Also, in contrast to individuals with DM1 with more than 30 years of diabetes, demographically matched DM2 patients with only 7 years of the disease duration present with significantly more deep white matter lesions and cortical atrophy on MRI (Brands et al., 2007). Additionally, the study by Manschot et al. (2006) showed that deep white matter lesions and cortical atrophy predicted information processing speed, whereas subcortical atrophy was associated with attention and executive function. Furthermore, the same authors suggested that patients with DM2 present with an accelerated rate of age-related structural changes, similarly to other comorbid conditions (e.g., hypertension, cardiovascular, and cerebrovascular disease) that exacerbate neurocognitive sequelae of diabetes patients (Ruis et al., 2009).

CHRONIC KIDNEY DISEASE

CKD is a multifactorial condition characterized by a progressive loss in kidney function that has been associated with encephalopathy and cognitive decline. In particular, individuals with end-stage renal disease (ESRD), being the fifth and the last stage of CKD that require dialysis or kidney transplant, have repeatedly been shown to develop cognitive impairment (Griva et al., 2003; Harciarek, Biedunkiewicz, Lichodziejewska-Niemierko, Dębska-Ślizień, & Rutkowski, 2009, 2011; for review, see Pliskin, Kiolbasa, Hart, & Umans, 2001). Furthermore, these cognitive abnormalities, predominantly psychomotor slowing and attention/executive dysfunction (Dixit, Dhawan, Raizada, Yadav, Vaney, & Kalra, 2013; Drew et al., 2015; Harciarek, Williamson, Biedunkiewicz, Lichodziejewska-Niemierko, Dębska-Ślizień, & Rutkowski, 2012), are often accompanied by functional and structural brain abnormalities, particularly within the frontal and frontosubcortical areas (Chen, Zhang, & Lu, 2015). Whereas the exact mechanism accounting for these neurobehavioral disorders is not entirely known, the cognitive impairment in patients with CKD seems to predominantly result from a significantly reduced glomerular filtration rate that leads to the accumulation of uremic toxins, which impair brain functioning. Also, because cardiovascular problems (e.g., hypertension and coronary artery disease) and diabetes are frequently associated with CKD and independently predict cognitive impairment, these comorbid conditions and their treatment (e.g., coronary artery bypass grafting) (Harciarek et al., 2010) may additionally contribute to cognitive dysfunction in patients with CKD. Moreover, whereas adequate dialysis reduces some of the CKD-associated cognitive deficits, the hemodialysis itself may induce dialysis disequilibrium, cerebral ischemia, or cerebral edema. Thus, hemodialysis may produce new or amplify already existing cognitive deficits (Kurella-Tamura et al., 2009), further increasing the risk of both dementia and death (Fig. 21.1).

Executive Function in Patients With End-stage Renal Disease Treated With Dialysis

Although memory problems have also been described in relation to CKD and dialysis (Kurella-Tamura et al., 2009; Murray, 2008) and the neuropsychological functioning of patients with CKD is often heterogeneous (e.g., depending on the severity of the disease, age, and c-morbid conditions; see Harciarek, 2009), cognitive problems in adequately dialyzed patients with ESRD seem relatively selective, primarily encompassing psychomotor

Factors that contribute to the development of chronic kidney disease / co-morbidities

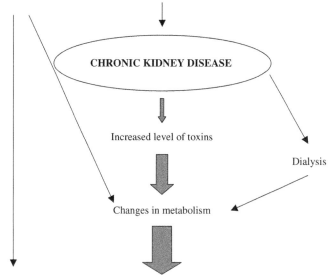

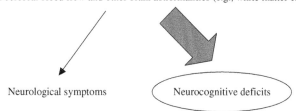

FIGURE 21.1   A model of cognitive impairment in patients with chronic kidney disease.

slowing and executive functions /executive functions (Harciarek et al., 2012; Harciarek et al., 2016). For example, it has been demonstrated that in contrast to well-preserved semantic fluency strongly relying on the temporal lobe, the dialyzed patients have selectively impaired phonemic fluency, preferentially depending on functions of frontal−subcortical systems (Stuss et al., 1998). Furthermore, their performance on the phonemic fluency task declined over time, whereas there was no change in semantic fluency. Thus, it has been suggested that the brain regions/networks involved in the attentional/executive processes, predominantly frontal−subcortical regions, are more susceptible to the effects of CKD and dialysis than others. This hypothesis seems to be in line with the neuroimaging observations indicating that individuals with CKD often present with structural and/or functional abnormalities in these areas (Pereira et al., 2005). As a result, the cognitive profile of well-dialyzed patients with CKD often resembles that of persons with diseases affecting frontal−basal ganglia circuits (e.g., HIV-AIDS and Parkinson's disease).

Attention and executive functions encompass a variety of supervisory processes (e.g., vigilance and monitoring) and these processes are mediated, at least in part, by different neuronal networks. For example, Stuss et al. (2005) showed that when compared to other frontal and nonfrontal regions, the superior medial parts of the frontal lobe (particularly in the right hemisphere) appear to produce a selective deficit in so called "energizing," resulting in psychomotor slowing and impaired sustained attention. This cerebral activation−arousal deficit has been also defined as a decreased facilitation of the neural systems or a disturbance in phasic alertness, with akinetic mutism being the most dramatic example of deficient energizing (Alexander, 2001). Because patients with ESRD present with psychomotor slowing but do not seem to have impaired inhibition or monitoring (Dixit et al., 2013), we have recently tested the hypothesis that adequately dialyzed individuals with ESRD may primarily present with defective performance on tasks highly dependent on superior medial region of the frontal lobe (Harciarek et al., 2016). Indeed, the results demonstrated that the performance of dialyzed individuals mirrors that of patients with lesions to superior medial parts of the frontal lobes. Hence, we have not only provided further evidence for the selectivity of cognitive dysfunction in subjects with ESRD but also indicated that the main cognitive problem that impairs these individuals may be a disturbance of a phasic alertness (energizing). Of note, these results are in line with research using electroencephalography (EEG), which demonstrate that uremic encephalopathy is primarily associated with generalized slowing of the normal background, and this slowing indicates a reduction of cerebral activation and arousal (Röhl, Harms, & Pommer, 2007). Also, in a recent event-related potentials study (Michałowski et al., in press), we have shown that the primary problem of dialyzed patients with ESRD may be an impaired ability to sustain action preparation (action-intentional persistence), possibly resulting from a defective function of the medial frontal−subcortical networks.

Executive Function in Patients With End-stage Renal Disease Following a Successful Kidney Transplant

Kidney transplant is so far the most effective method of ESRD treatment (Miller, Levine, D'Elia & Bistrian, 1986) that has been additionally shown to contribute to the improvement of neuropsychological functions, including executive processes (Griva et al., 2006; Harciarek et al., 2009, 2011; Koushik, McArthur, & Baird, 2010; Kramer et al., 1996; Pereira et al., 2005; see also Pliskin et al., 2001). For example, a well-controlled longitudinal study aimed at assessing the effects of kidney transplantation on cognition in dialyzed patients has demonstrated that a successful kidney transplantation predominantly leads to a significant, relatively early and long-lasting improvement of performance on tests of psychomotor speed, planning, abstract reasoning, and retrieval of learned material (Harciarek et al., 2011). The finding that the cognitive recovery was predominantly observed on tests relying on psychomotor speed and executive processes is consistent with the observation of posttransplant improvement in P300 latency, a motor-free event-related potential that appears to be a sensitive EEG index of mental processing speed (Kramer et al., 1996). Furthermore, because the improvement of psychomotor speed and executive function tend to emerge shortly after transplantation, it is likely that the preoperative accumulation of toxins in the brain, resulting in defective energization/action—intention, may significantly (although not mutually exclusively) contribute to cognitive changes seen in dialyzed patients.

HUMAN IMMUNODEFICIENCY VIRUS

HIV is a lentivirus responsible for the HIV infection that progressively transforms into AIDS. Shortly after it had been discovered, it was demonstrated that infected individuals commonly present with neurocognitive abnormalities (i.e., HIV-associated neurocognitive disorders—HAND) (Diederich et al., 1988; Reger, Welsh, Razani, Martin, & Boone, 2002). Since 1987, when the first effective therapy against HIV (the nucleoside reverse transcriptase inhibitor) was approved in the United States, both the neuropsychological pattern and the severity of HAND have changed, resulting in a significant decrease in cognitive problems among infected patients. The reduction in HAND was especially robust following the use of the highly active antiretroviral therapy and combine antiretroviral therapy (CART).

However, despite the initiation of antiretroviral therapy and the fact that seropositive patients are often able to stay in good general health without clinically detectable dementia, attention/executive dysfunction and psychomotor slowing remain highly prevalent in this population (Heaton et al., 2011). In fact, even in an asymptomatic stage, patients with HIV tend to experience subtle but increasing attentional/executive problems that may eventually result in dementia, typically more common in AIDS stage (Heaton et al., 2011; Maruff et al., 1995; Reger et al., 2002; White, Heaton, & Monsch, 1995). For example, Heaton and coworkers (2011) demonstrated that HIV-infected individuals treated with CART still present with executive impairment that increases with successive disease stages.

Among the most frequently seen executive dysfunction in HIV population are impaired abstract thinking (Heaton et al., 1995), deficient inhibition (Tozzi et al., 1999), impaired cognitive flexibility (Carter, Rourke, Murji, Shore, & Rourke, 2003), and defective decision-making and planning (Cattie, Doyle, Weber, Grant, & Woods, 2012; Martin et al., 2007; Maruff et al., 1994). Importantly, these executive problems have often been a direct result of the infection, neurotoxicity of antiretro virals, and a consequence of the accelerated aging seen in this population (Lakatos, Szabó, Bozzai, Bánhegyi, & Gazdag, 2014). Moreover, there is evidence to suggest that significantly decreased information processing speed is the core neuropsychological disorder among HIV-infected individuals that contribute to the above-mentioned executive processes and memory (Fellows, Byrd, & Morgello, 2014; Jiang, Barasky, Olsen, Riesenhuber, & Magnus, 2016).

Psychomotor slowing and executive problems in patients with HIV/AIDS have typically been associated with brain abnormalities seen in this group of individuals. For example, HIV-associated neuropathologies commonly affect the integrity of frontostratial circuits (Becker, Sanders, & Madsen, 2011; Everall et al., 1994) that mediate motor and executive functions (Tekin & Cummings, 2002). Additionally, it has been demonstrated that in the HIV population, several brain regions supporting higher order cognition and integration of functions show acceleration of the normal aging trajectory. For example, the accelerated loss of cortical tissue has been observed in the frontal and temporal poles as well as parietal lobe and the thalamus (Pfefferbaum et al., 2014).

The consequences of executive impairment seen in HIV-infected individuals are salient and have a significant impact on a wide range of everyday activities (Heaton et al., 2004). Most studies suggest that impaired executive function, working memory, and the ability to learn new information are among the strongest predictors of medication management (Heaton et al., 2004; Hinkin et al., 2004), unsafe driving (Marcotte et al., 2004; Marcotte et al., 2006), and vocational status (Van Gorp, Baerwald, Ferrando, McElhiney, & Rabkin, 1999).

HEPATIC ENCEPHALOPATHY

HE represents a heterogeneous spectrum of neuropsychiatric and neuropsychological abnormalities seen in patients with liver dysfunction, after the exclusion of other causes of brain disease. The most frequent cause of liver cirrhosis and HE are viral hepatitis B or C, excessive alcohol intake, as well as other forms of liver toxicity that leads to fibrosis (Blei & Cordoba, 2001). Clinically, HE is typically characterized by impaired attention, functional disability, and changes in personality. The severity of HE symptoms can range from mildly altered cognition and disorders of consciousness to coma, depending on the duration and stages of the illness (from stage 0 till stage 4) (Blei & Cordoba, 2001; Ferenci et al., 2002; Mullen, 2007). Also, HE can be primarily classified into two main groups: minimal (stage 0) and overt (stages 1–4), with minimal HE being considered a preclinical stage of overt HE (Bajaj, Wade, & Sanyal, 2009).

Unfortunately, the diagnostic approach to the assessment of HE is not uniform. Various combinations of psychometric tests with or without neurophysiologic measures (e.g., EEG) have been considered for their use in the diagnosis of minimal encephalopathy. Nowadays, the West Haven criteria and the Glasgow Coma Scale are recommended to stratify patients by severity. These criteria have been applied not only for clinical but also for research purposes (e.g., to assess outcomes after intervention). However, the heterogeneity and variability of the manifestations of HE make the condition difficult to diagnose and to categorize with respect to severity. A comprehensive neurologic examination and neuropsychological investigation typically reveal some degree of disorders, which are almost always related to frontal lobe abnormalities, especially when alcoholic history occurs. For example, most patients with HE primarily present with impaired psychomotor speed as well as executive and attentional problems (Meyer, Eshelman, & Abouljoud, 2006) that, particularly in individuals with overt HE, are often accompanied by structural brain damage as revealed by neuroimaging (Mullen, 2007).

In comparison to overt HE, in which neuropsychological and psychiatric abnormalities may be relatively severe, minimal HE is typically characterized only by a degree of cognitive problems. However, these often include executive and motor dysfunctions, slowed information processing speed, and attention deficits (Singhal et al., 2010; Sarma et al., 2011; Weissenborn, Hecker, & Rückert, 2015). In fact, impaired attention seems to be a major cognitive problem of individuals with minimal HE, encompassing both vigilance and orienting. Furthermore, it has also been demonstrated that attention deficits may account not only for executive and working memory impairment seen in HE but also for these patients' impoverished learning. Moreover, difficulties in visuomotor coordination and construction have been described. These abnormalities can be easily detected during neuropsychological assessment that includes the application of such measures as the Digit Symbol Test and the Trail Making Test (Chen et al., 2012). In this regard, the Working Party on Hepatic Encephalopathy recommends the use of at least two of the following instruments: Trail Making Test (version A and B), Block Design Test, or Digit Symbol Test. However, to best tap the neuropsychological changes associated with HE, extended neuropsychological evaluation is needed. This should predominantly include the assessment of attention, working memory, and the following executive functions: planning, decision-making, mental flexibility, abstract reasoning, and judgment skills. Thus, while assessing cognition in individuals with HE, it is often recommended to apply one of the following instruments: the Portal-Systemic Encephalopathy Syndrome Test or the Repeatable Battery for the Assessment of Neuropsychological Status (Iduru & Mullen, 2008; Weissenborn, Ennen, Rückert, & Hecker, 2001).

As mentioned, in many patients with HE, particularly those with overt HE, the attention deficits, executive dysfunction, and psychomotor slowing are accompanied by structural and/or functional changes on neuroimaging. For example, a recent magnetic resonance imaging study found that individuals with a history of overt HE have decreased brain tissue density

(Guevara et al., 2011). Furthermore, Catafau et al. (2000) has also demonstrated that cirrhotic patients with minimal HE present with a SPECT pattern of impaired prefrontal perfusion. However, these prefrontal changes did not seem to account for these patients' neuropsychologic deficits. By comparison, there was a relationship between the perfusion in some parts of the limbic system and limbic-connected brain regions (e.g., the striatum and mesial temporal regions) and the neuropsychologic impairment seen in these individuals.

One of the main causes of HE is the excessive consumption of alcohol. It has been repeatedly shown, however, that increased alcohol intake itself leads to neuronal loss, particularly in the frontal lobe and related subcortical areas, as well as to attention/executive problems (Harper, 2009). Thus, because both the neurocognitive and neuroanatomical consequences overlap with those associated with alcohol intake, it is problematic to conclude what kind of neuropsychological deficits (and to what extent) are specific for HE only. To answer that question, Lee and coworkers (2016) have recently hypothesized that patients with liver cirrhosis due to alcoholism may present with different cognitive deficits when compared to those with viral liver cirrhosis. A comprehensive neuropsychological battery including attention, language, visuospatial, verbal memory, visual memory, and frontal/executive function was applied to both of patients and to age-matched normal controls. In the comparison to controls, both cirrhotic groups presented with impaired memory and executive dysfunction. However, these abnormalities and early development of overt HE were more common among patients with alcoholic cirrhosis (Lee et al., 2016). Thus, it could be posited that whereas both liver dysfunction and excessive alcohol intake lead to executive problems, these abnormalities are more pronounced in individuals with HE due to increased alcohol consumption.

Similar to other disorders characterized by frontosubcortical changes and related attention/executive dysfunction, executive and attentional impairment seen in HE have a major impact on the patients' everyday functioning. For example, in their study aimed at evaluating the ability to drive a vehicle, Schomerus et al. (1981) comprehensively examined 40 cirrhotic patients with minimal HE and a control group of 12 patients with alcoholic pancreatitis. As a result, whereas only 15% of all HE patients were considered to be able to drive, 60% of cirrhotic patients were found unfit to drive, and in another 25% driving capacity was questionable. In contrast, 75% of the patients with alcoholic pancreatitis were considered fit to drive.

THYROID DISEASE

Due to an important role of thyroid hormone in regulating metabolism, thyroid diseases have an adverse effect on brain function. Overall, thyroid disease can be divided into two main groups: (1) when thyroid gland does not produce enough thyroid hormone (hypothyroidism) and (2) when there is an excessive production of thyroid hormone (hyperthyroidism). Importantly, both overt hypothyroidism and overt hyperthyroidism are associated with psychiatric (e.g., anxiety and depression) and cognitive complaints and symptoms. However, the cognitive symptoms in patients with thyroid disease, including attention and executive function, tend to be rather mild and treatable (Samuels, 2014).

Recent neuropsychological studies confirm that overt hypothyroidism is associated with cognitive decrements. Among the most typical consequences of overt hypothyroidism, in addition to problems with verbal and visual recall, are executive dysfunction, working memory impairment, and attention deficits (Beydoun et al., 2015; Joffe, Pearce, Hennessey, Ryan, & Stern, 2013). However, cognitive dysfunction seen in individuals with hypothyroidism seems to be largely reversible with treatment. For example, Del Ser Quijano, Delgado, Martínez Espinosa, & Vázquez (2000) have demonstrated that hormonal treatment resulted in a significant improvement of cognition and normalization of test performance in almost all cognitive domains that had previously been affected.

Similarly, also individuals with hyperthyroidism frequently present with cognitive impairment that includes executive dysfunctions and problems with attention, in particular difficulties with concentration and impoverished memory (Jabłkowska-Górecka et al., 2008; see also Yudiarto, Muliadi, Moeljanto, & Hartono, 2006). Furthermore, although the exact mechanism underlying these cognitive abnormalities has not be fully elucidated, it has been posited that cognitive impairment in individuals with hyperthyroidism may primarily result from the long-term central effects of the elevated concentration of thyroid hormones that adversely affects brain function. Also, Yuan et al. (2015) have shown that patients with hyperthyroidism perform abnormally in tasks aimed at measuring decision-making under ambiguous conditions and suggested that this impaired performance may result from metabolic abnormalities (e.g., dopamine dysregulation) within the frontal limbic networks. This postulate is supported by neuroimaging studies that revealed decreased gray matter volume and abnormal cerebral metabolism in regions subserving these networks (e.g., frontal lobe) (Miao et al., 2011; Schreckenberger et al., 2006; Zhang et al., 2014). Additionally, Constant and coworkers (2005) have demonstrated that in comparison to less anxious patients, more anxious individuals with hypothyroidism have decreased phasic alertness, as evidenced by greater slowing of reaction time, as well as higher interference, as evidenced by the Stroop test. Hence, these results further suggest a link between symptoms of dysregulated limbic system and attention/executive function in hypothyroid patients.

In contrast to patients with overt hyper- or hypothyroidism, conclusions regarding frontal/executive function in subclinical thyroid disease, characterized by elevated or lowered plasma thyroid-stimulating hormone concentration with a normal free triiodothyronine and thyroxine levels (Rugge, Balshem, Sehgal, Relevo, Gorman, & Helfand, 2011), remain inconsistent. Most recent cross-sectional and longitudinal natural history studies were unsuccessful in finding significant effects of subclinical hyper- or hypothyroidism on cognition (including executive and attention processes), both at baseline and over time (Biondi, Bartalena, Cooper, Hegedüs, Laurberg, & Kahaly, 2015; Ceresini et al., 2009; Hogervorst, Huppert, Matthews, & Brayne, 2008). Nonetheless, Zhu et al. (2006) conducted a longitudinal functional MRI experiment in which individuals with euthyroidism, patients with hypo- and hyperthyroidism, and patients with subclinical hypothyroidism were asked to perform the n-back working memory task. The follow-up testing took place approximately 6 months after patients with subclinical hypothyroidism had been treated with L-thyroxine. The results of this study showed that patients with subclinical hypothyroidism have more working memory problems than euthyroid individuals, and that these patients' working memory performance may be fully normalized following treatment. Moreover, the neuroimaging data revealed that whereas in the euthyroid and hyperthyroid subjects, the load effect of blood oxygen level-dependent (BOLD) response appeared in bilateral middle/inferior frontal gyri, bilateral dorsolateral prefrontal cortex, bilateral premotor areas, the supplementary motor area/anterior cingulate cortex, and bilateral parietal areas, in the pretreatment patients with subclinical hypothyroidism, the load effect of BOLD response was only found in the parietal and premotor areas but not in other areas of the frontal cortex. Thus, although more research is needed to better understand the effects of subclinical thyroid disease on frontal lobe and related executive processes, the results of this study suggest that the functioning of the common frontoparietal working memory network may be affected also in individuals with subclinical thyroid disease. Of note, the relationship between subclinical hypothyroidism and cognitive function may be mediated by age at the disease onset. For example, it has been proposed that subclinical thyroid disease may more frequently result in cognitive impairment, including attention deficits and executive dysfunction, in the elderly (Biondi et al., 2015).

RHEUMATOID ARTHRITIS

Rheumatoid arthritis (RA) is a chronic autoimmune and inflammatory disease that affects the joints (Sierakowski & Cutolo, 2011). It has systemic and progressive manifestations. In the initial state, patients with RA predominantly experience morning stiffness, edema, and pain. However, the involvement of other organs, i.e., pachymeningitis, vasculitis, or interstitial pneumonia, with spinal cord compression and the involvement of the peripheral nervous system tend to reduce these individuals' life expectancy by 5–10 years. As the disease progresses, patients with RA often develop affective disorders (e.g., depression) as well as memory, attention, and executive deficits that significantly compromise these patients' ability to normally perform their activities of daily living (Hanly, Fisk, McCurdy, Fougere, & Douglas, 2005).

In patients with RA, cognitive problems (including executive dysfunction) are due to the disease itself, their comorbidities, or an interaction of these factors as well as treatment. Simos et al. (2016) have demonstrated that about 20% of individuals with RA can be classified as cognitively impaired within the first 3 years from the diagnosis. Although, according to these authors, early cognitive deficits in this population predominantly encompass memory problems, the performance on tests such as phonemic fluency is typically also impaired. Thus, the results of this study suggest that some executive dysfunction, together with memory impairment, may belong to the early cognitive symptoms in RA.

To investigate cognitive problems in the RA population, Bartolini et al. (2002) used a comprehensive neuropsychological test battery to evaluate cognitive performance of a well-characterized cohort of patients with RA. The analyses revealed that only 2 out of 30 subjects had no impairment. Overall, cognitive dysfunctions were primarily detected in memory and executive domain. Specifically, over 70% of individuals with RA had impaired planning and almost 40% had difficulties in mental flexibility. Additionally, almost half of all patients had other executive problems, as evidenced the Wisconsin Sorting Cart Test. Furthermore, these cognitive disorders were associated with neuroimaging findings: hypoperfusion of the frontal and parietal lobes on brain single photon—emission computed tomography and increased white matter alterations on magnetic resonance imaging. Other investigators have also found executive deficits in patients with RA (Abeare et al., 2010), further confirming that executive impairment is common in this population. However, when Melo and Da-Silva (2012) compared patterns of cognitive decline in three chronic pain diseases: RA, fibromyalgia, and systemic lupus, although individuals with RA presented with impaired phonemic fluency and executive deficits where rather characteristic for patients with fibromyalgia.

There is some evidence that both memory decline and/or executive impairment seen in individuals with RA may occur as an adverse effect of the commonly used medications, such as the disease modifying antirheumatic drugs (e.g., methotrexate) and corticosteroids (Filipowicz-Sosnowska, 2006). For example, although Appenzeller, Bertolo, and Costallat (2004) did not find a significant relationship between cognitive function of patients with RA and the use of corticotherapy or disability, Brown et al. (2004, 2008) showed that in comparison to demographically and medically matched controls, patients treated with chronic corticosteroid therapy have smaller hippocampal and amygdala volumes and often present with declarative memory deficits and executive deficits, as evidenced by the performance on the

Stroop Color Word Test. Also, because individuals with RA are more likely to develop cardiovascular problems that predominantly tend to affect frontal—subcortical networks and related executive function (Chui, 2001; see Chapter 17: Seizures of the Frontal Lobes: Clinical Presentations and Diagnostic Considerations), executive abnormalities in the RA population might represent a direct effect of these comorbid conditions. The executive dysfunction in RA can also be induced or amplified by chronic pain or depression. For example, Brown, Glass, and Park (2002) demonstrated that individuals with RA who performed poorly on cognitive tasks reported more pain and depression symptoms than patients who performed well on such tasks. Similarly, Abeare and coworkers (2010) also showed that higher pain level in individuals with RA is associated with these patients' poorer performance on tests of executive function. Other factors that found in RA to increase the risk for cognitive decline including executive deficits encompass low education and low socioeconomic status (Shin, Katz, Wallhagen, & Julian, 2012). Due to methodological limitation of previous research (e.g., small sample size, variable duration of the disease, and differences in comorbidities and patients' demographics), further studies with carefully matched comparison groups are still needed to provide a better understanding of the relationships between RA, treatment, psychiatric comorbidities, and executive function.

CONCLUSIONS

The aim of this chapter was to characterize executive/attention disorders in individuals with somatic and chronic disease that may indirectly affect brain function. It has been shown that in most of these primary nonneurological conditions frontal networks (e.g., frontobasal gangliathalamic, and frontotemporal networks) that mediate executive functions are particularly sensitive to metabolic and endocrine disorders such as HE hypothyroidism, HIV, or CKD, and especially in ESRD. Additionally, although in most of these conditions an appropriate treatment often reveres some of the disease-specific symptoms (including cognitive impairment), in some cases chronic treatment such as hemodialysis may also contribute to decline in attention and executive function.

The reason why most of these long-lasting medical disorders predominantly impact the function of the frontal—subcortical networks is not entirely clear. However, a gradual decrease in executive function and speed of processing has been observed in aging that also seems to predominantly affect networks mediating arousal/energization intention. Additionally, with aging there is a significant reduction in cellular functions that contribute to, e.g., decrease in glomerular filtration rate and cardiovascular problems. Thus, it could be posited that a rather nonspecific, arousal/energization-based cognitive decline in most of these multifactorial primary nonneurological conditions (e.g., diabetes and CKD) may represent the accelerated aging of the central nervous system (Brands & Kessel, 2009; Harciarek et al., 2016).

Many previous studies on cognition in medical/somatic disorders have been confounded by methodological problems; only some of them controlled for demographics or comorbid conditions. Also, most of the previous research has not directly addressed the issue of executive problems that, if investigated, were rather assessed using a standard neuropsychological tests and not experimental paradigms. Therefore, to better understand the impact of nonneurological diseases on frontosubcortical networks and executive function, more studies that take into account the limitations of previously conducted research are needed. Determining the nature and the course of the cognitive decline in subjects with such diseases as hypertension, ESRD, diabetes, liver disease, endocrinological diseases, or HIV/AIDS will not only enrich our knowledge about the organ systems—brain relationship but will also enable us to help our patients by providing them with specific and more comprehensive health services.

ACKNOWLEDGMENTS

This study was funded by the National Science Centre, Poland (grant Opus No. 2015/17/B/HS6/03951), PI: Michał Harciarek.

REFERENCES

Abeare, C. A., Cohen, J. L., Axelrod, B. N., Leisen, J. C. C., Mosley-Williams, A., & Lumley, M. A. (2010). Pain, executive functioning, and affect in patients with rheumatoid arthritis. *Clinical Journal of Pain, 26*(8), 683−689.

Alexander, M. P. (2001). Chronic akinetic mutism after mesencephalic diencephalic infarction: Remediated with dopaminergic medications. *Neurorehabilitation and Neural Repair, 15,* 151−156.

Alosco, M. L., Gunstad, J., Xu, X., Clark, U. S., Labbe, D. R., Riskin-Jones, H. H., & Sweet, L. H. (2014). The impact of hypertension on cerebral perfusion and cortical thickness in older adults. *Journal of the American Society of Hypertension: JASH, 8,* 561−570. Available from http://dx.doi.org/10.1016/j.jash.2014.04.002.

Appenzeller, S., Bertolo, M. B., & Costallat, L. T. (2004). Cognitive impairment in rheumatoid arthritis. *Methods and Findings in Experimental and Clinical Pharmacology, 26,* 339−343.

Bajaj, J. S., Wade, J. B., & Sanyal, A. J. (2009). Spectrum of neurocognitive impairment in cirrhosis: Implications for the assessment of hepatic encephalopathy. *Hepatology, 50,* 2014−2021.

Bartolini, M., Candela, M., Brugni, M., Mari, F., Pomponio, G., Provinciali, L., & Danieli, G. (2002). Are behaviour and motor performances of rheumatoid arthritis patients influenced by subclinical cognitive impairments? A clinical and neuroimaging study. *Clinical and Experimental Rheumatology, 20,* 491−497.

Beason-Held, L. L., Moghekar, A., & Zonderman, A. B. (2007). Longitudinal changes in cerebral blood flow in the older hypertensive brain. *Stroke; A Journal of Cerebral Circulation, 38,* 1766−1773.

Beauchet, O., Celle, S., Roche, F., Bartha, R., Montero-Odasso, M., Allali, G., & Annweiler, C. (2013). Blood pressure levels and brain volume reduction: A systematic review and meta-analysis. *Journal of Hypertension*, *31*, 1502−1516.

Becker, J. T., Sanders, J., & Madsen, S. K. (2011). Subcortical brain atrophy persists even in HAART-regulated HIV disease. *Brain Imaging and Behavior*, *5*, 77−85.

Benton, A. L. (2000). *Exploring the* history of neuropsychology. Selected papers. New York: Oxford University Press.

Bermejo-Pareja, F., Benito-Leon, J., Louis, E., Trincado, R., Carro, E., Villarejo, A., et al. (2010). Risk of incident dementia in drug-untreated arterial hypertension: A population based study. *Journal of Alzheimer's Disease*, *22*(3), 949−958.

Beydoun, M. A., Beydoun, H. A., Rostant, O. S., Dore, G. A., Fanelli-Kuczmarski, M. T., Evans, M. K., & Zonderman, A. B. (2015). Thyroid hormones are associated with longitudinal cognitive change in an urban adult population. *Neurobiology of Aging*, *36*, 3056−3066. Available from http://dx.doi.org/10.1016/j.neurobiolaging.2015.08.002.

Biondi, B., Bartalena, L., Cooper, D. S., Hegedüs, L., Laurberg, P., & Kahaly, G. J. (2015). The 2015 European Thyroid Association Guidelines on Diagnosis and Treatment of Endogenous Subclinical Hyperthyroidism. *European Thyroid Journal*, *4*, 149−163. Available from http://dx.doi.org/10.1159/000438750.

Blei, A. T., & Cordoba, J. (2001). Hepatic encephalopathy. *American Journal of Gastroenterology*, *96*, 1968−1976.

Bolo, N. R., Musen, G., Simonson, D. C., Nickerson, L. D., Flores, V. L., Siracusa, T., & Jacobson, A. M. (2015). Functional connectivity of insula, basal ganglia, and prefrontal executive control networks during hypoglycemia in type 1 diabetes. *Journal of Neuroscience*, *35*, 11012−11023.

Brands, A. M. A., Biessels, G. J., de Haan, E. H. F., Kappelle, L. J., & Kessels, R. P. C. (2005). The effects of type 1 diabetes on cognitive performance: A meta-analysis. *Diabetes Care*, *28*, 726−735.

Brands, A. M. A., Biessels, G. J., Kappelle, L. J., de Haan, E. H., de Valk, H. W., Algra, A., Kessels, R. P., & Utrecht Diabetic Encephalopathy Study Group (2007). Cognitive functioning and brain MRI in patients with type 1 and type 2 diabetes mellitus: A comparative study. *Dementia and Geriatric Cognitive Disorders*, *23*, 343−350.

Brands, A. M. A., & Kessels, R. P. C. (2009). Diabetes and the brain: Cognitive performance in type 1 and type 2 diabetes. In I. Grant, & K. M. Adams (Eds.), *Neuropsychological assessment of neuropsychiatric and neuromedical disorders* (3rd ed.). New York: Oxford University Press.

Brown, E. S., Woolston, D., Frol, A., Bobadilla, L., Khan, D. A., Hanczyc, M., Rush, A. J., Fleckenstein, J., Babcock, E., & Cullum, C. M. (2004). Hippocampal volume, spectroscopy, cognition, and mood in patients receiving corticosteroid therapy. *Biological Psychiatry*, *55* (5), 538−545.

Brown, E. S., Woolston, D. J., & Frol, A. B. (2008). Amygdala volume in patients receiving chronic corticosteroid therapy. *Biological Psychiatry*, *63*(7), 705−709. Available from http://dx.doi.org/10.1016/j.biopsych.2007.09.014.

Brown, S. C., Glass, J. M., & Park, D. C. (2002). The relationship of pain and depression to cognitive function in rheumatoid arthritis patients. *Pain*, *96*(3), 279−284.

Bucur, B., & Madden, D. J. (2010). Effects of adult age and blood pressure on executive function and speed of processing. *Experimental Aging Research*, *36*(2), 153−168. Available from http://dx.doi.org/10.1080/03610731003613482.

Carter, S. L., Rourke, S. B., Murji, S., Shore, D., & Rourke, B. P. (2003). Cognitive complaints, depression, medical symptoms, and their association with neuropsychological functioning in HIV infection: A structural equation model analysis. *Neuropsychology*, *17*, 410−419. Available from http://dx.doi.org/10.1037/0894-4105.17.3.410.

Catafau, A. M., Kulisevsky, J., Berna, L., Pujol, J., Martin, J. C., Otermin, P., Balanza, J., & Carria, I. (2000). Relationship between cerebral perfusion in frontal limbic-basal ganglia circuits and neuropsychologic impairment in patients with subclinical hepatic encephalopathy. *Journal of Nuclear Medicine*, *3*, 405−410.

Cattie, J. E., Doyle, K., Weber, E., Grant, I., & Woods, S. P. (2012). Planning deficits in HIV-associated neurocognitive disorders: Component processes, cognitive correlates, and implications for everyday functioning. *Journal of Clinical and Experimental Neuropsychology*, *34*, 906−918.

Ceresini, G., Lauretani, F., Maggio, M., Ceda, G. P., Morganti, S., Usberti, E., Chezzi, C., Valcavi, R., Bandinelli, S., Guralnik, J. M., Cappola, A. R., Valenti, G., & Ferrucci, L. (2009). Thyroid function abnormalities and cognitive impairment in elderly people: Results of the Invecchiare in Chianti Study. *Journal of the American Geriatrics Society*, *57*, 89−93.

Chen, H. J., Zhu, X. Q., Shu, H., Yang, M., Zhang, Y., Ding, J., Wang, Y., & Teng, G. J. (2012). Structural and functional cerebral impairments in cirrhotic patients with a history of overt hepatic encephalopathy. *European Journal of Radiology*, *81*, 2463−2469.

Chen, H. J., Zhang, L. J., & Lu, G. M. (2015). Multimodality MRI findings in patients with end-stage renal disease. *BioMed Research International*, 12 pp. Available from http://dx.doi.org/10.1155/2015/697402.

Chui, H. (2001). Dementia due to subcortical ischemic vascular disease. *Clinical Cornerstone*, *3*, 40−51.

Constant, E. L., Adam, S., Seron, X., Bruyer, R., Seghers, A., & Daumerie, C. (2005). Anxiety and depression, attention, and executive functions in hypothyroidism. *Journal of the International Neuropsychological Society*, *11*, 535−544.

Del Ser Quijano, T., Delgado, C., Martínez Espinosa, S., & Vázquez, C. (2000). Cognitive deficiency in mild hypothyroidism. *Neurologia*, *15*(5), 193−198.

Diederich, N., Ackermann, R., Jürgens, R., Ortseifen, M., Thun, F., Schneider, M., & Vukadinovic, I. (1988). Early involvement of the nervous system by human immune deficiency virus (HIV). A study of 79 patients. *European Neurology*, *28*, 93−103.

Dixit, A., Dhawan, S., Raizada, A., Yadav, A., Vaney, N., & Kalra, O. P. (2013). Attention and information processing in end stage renal disease and effect of hemodialysis: A bedside study. *Renal Failure*, *35*, 1246−1250. Available from http://dx.doi.org/10.3109/0886022X.2013.819768.

Drew, D. A., Weiner, D. E., Tighiouart, H., Scott, T., Lou, K., Kantor, A., ... Sarnak, M. J. (2015). Cognitive function and all-cause mortality in maintenance hemodialysis patients. *American Journal of Kidney Diseases*, *65*, 303−311. Available from http://dx.doi.org/10.1053/j.ajkd.2014.07.009.

Elias, P. K., Elias, M. F., Robbins, M. A., & Budge, M. M. (2004). Blood pressure-related cognitive decline: Does age make a difference?. *Hypertension*, *44*, 631−636.

Everall, I. P., Glass, J. D., McArthur, J., Spargo, E., & Lantos, P. (1994). Neuronal density in the superior frontal and temporal gyri does not correlate with the degree of human immunodeficiency virus-associated dementia. *Acta Neuropathologica*, *88*, 538−544.

Fellows, R. P., Byrd, D. A., & Morgello, S. (2014). Effects of information processing speed on learning, memory, and executive functioning in people living with HIV/AIDS. *Journal of Clinical and Experimental Neuropsychology*, *36*(8), 806−817. Available from http://dx.doi.org/10.1080/13803395.2014.943696.

Ferenci, P., Lockwood, A., Mullen, K., Tarter, R., Weissenborn, K., & Blei, A. T. (2002). Hepatic encephalopathy: Definition, nomenclature, diagnosis, and quantification—Final report of the working party at the 11th World Congresses of Gastroenterology, Vienna, 1998. *Hepatology*, *35*, 716−721.

Filipowicz-Sosnowska, A. (2006). Reumatoidalne zapalenie stawów. In A. Szczeklik (Ed.), Choroby wewnętrzne. *Tom II* (pp. 1645−1657). Kraków: Medycyna Praktyczna.

Ganguli, M., Fu, B., Snitz, B. E., Unverzagt, F. W., Loewenstein, D. A., Hughes, T. F., & Chang, C. C. H. (2014). Vascular risk factors and cognitive decline in a population sample. *Alzheimer Disease and Associated Disorders*, *28*(1), 9−15. Available from http://dx.doi.org/10.1097/WAD.0000000000000004.

Graveling, A. J., Deary, I. J., & Frier, B. M. (2013). Acute hypoglycemia impairs executive cognitive function in adults with and without type 1 diabetes. *Diabetes Care*, *36*(10), 3240−3246. Available from http://dx.doi.org/10.2337/dc13-0194.

Griva, K., Newman, S. P., Harrison, M. J., Hankins, M., Davenport, A., Hansraj, S., & Thompson, D. (2003). Acute neuropsychological changes in hemodialysis and peritoneal dialysis patients. *Health Psychology*, *22*, 570−578.

Griva, K., Thompson, D., Jayasena, D., Davenport, A., Harrison, M., & Newman, S. P. (2006). Cognitive functioning pre- to post-kidney transplantation—A prospective study. *Nephrology, Dialysis, Transplantation: Official Publication of the European Dialysis and Transplant Association—European Renal Association*, *21*, 3275−3282.

Guevara, M., Baccaro, M. E., Gomez-Anson, B., Frisoni, G., Testa, C., Torre, A., Molinuevo, J. L., Rami, L., Pereira, G., Sotil, E. U., Córdoba, J., Arroyo, V., & Ginès, P. (2011). Cerebral magnetic resonance imaging reveals marked abnormalities of brain tissue density in patients with cirrhosis without overt hepatic encephalopathy. *Journal of Hepatology*, *55*, 564−573.

Hajjar, I., Goldstein, F. C., Martin, G. S., & Quyyumi, A. A. (2016). Roles of arterial stiffness and blood pressure in hypertension-associated cognitive decline in healthy adults. *Hypertension*, *67*(1), 171−175. Available from http://dx.doi.org/10.1161/HYPERTENSIONAHA.

Hamada, T., Chikamori, T., Nishinaga, M., & Doi, Y. (2003). Long-term effect of hypertension on neurobehavioral and cardiac function in the apparently healthy community-dwelling elderly: A 5-year follow-up study. *Nihon Ronen Igakkai Zasshi*, *40*(4), 375−380.

Hanly, J., Fisk, J., McCurdy, G., Fougere, L., & Douglas, J. A. (2005). Neuropsychiatric syndromes in patients with systemic lupus erythematosus and rheumatoid arthritis. *Journal of Rheumatology*, *32*(8), 1459−1466.

Harciarek, M. (2009). Heterogeneity of cognitive deficits in patients with end-stage renal disease receiving dialysis. *Psychological Studies*, *47*, 21−32.

Harciarek, M., Biedunkiewicz, B., Lichodziejewska-Niemierko, M., Dębska-Ślizień, A., & Rutkowski, B. (2011). Continuous cognitive improvement 1 year following successful kidney transplant. *Kidney International*, *79*, 1353−1360.

Harciarek, M., Michałowski, J., Williamson, J., Biedunkiewicz, B., Dębska-Ślizień, A., Rutkowski, B., & Heilman, K. M. (2016). Disorders of the anterior attentional-intentional system in patients with end stage renal disease: Evidence from reaction time studies. *Brain and Cognition*, *107*, 1−9.

Harciarek, M., Williamson, J. B., Biedunkiewicz, B., Lichodziejewska-Niemierko, M., Dębska-Ślizień, A., & Rutkowski, B. (2010). Memory performance in adequately dialyzed patients with end-stage renal disease: Is there an association with coronary artery bypass grafting?. *Journal of Clinical and Experimental Neuropsychology*, *32*, 881−889.

Harciarek, M., Williamson, J. B., Biedunkiewicz, B., Lichodziejewska-Niemierko, M., Dębska-Ślizień, A., & Rutkowski, B. (2012). Risk factors for selective cognitive decline in dialyzed patients with end-stage renal disease: Evidence from verbal fluency analysis. *Journal of the International Neuropsychological Society*, *18*, 162−167. Available from http://dx.doi.org/10.1017/S1355617711001445.

Harper, C. (2009). The neuropathology of alcohol-related brain damage. *Alcohol*, *44*, 136−140.

Harrington, F., Saxby, B. K., McKeith, I. G., Wesnes, K., & Ford, G. A. (2000). Cognitive performance in hypertensive and normotensive older subjects. *Hypertension*, *36*, 1079−1082.

Heaton, R. K., Franklin, D. R., Ellis, R. J., McCutchan, J. A., Letendre, S. L., LeBlanc, S., & for the CHARTER and HNRC Groups (2011). HIV-associated neurocognitive disorders before and during the era of combination antiretroviral therapy: Differences in rates, nature, and predictors. *Journal of Neurovirology*, *17*(1), 3−16. Available from http://dx.doi.org/10.1007/s13365-010-0006-1.

Heaton, R. K., Grant, I., Butters, N., White, D. A., Kirson, D., Atkinson, J. H., McCutchan, J. A., Taylor, M. J., Kelly, M. D., & Ellis, R. J. (1995). The HNRC 500—Neuropsychology of HIV infection at different disease stages. HIV Neurobehavioral Research Center. *Journal of the International Neuropsychological Society*, *1*, 231−251.

Heaton, R. K., Marcotte, T. D., Mindt, M. R., Sadek, J., Moore, D. J., Bentley, H., McCutchan, J. A., Reicks, C., Grant, I., & The HIV Neurobehavioral Research Program (HNRP) Group (2004). The impact of HIV-associated neuropsychological impairment on everyday functioning. *Journal of the International Neuropsychological Society: JINS*, *10*, 317−331.

Hinkin, C. H., Hardy, D. J., Mason, K. I., Castellon, S. A., Durvasula, R. S., Lam, M. N., & Stefaniak, M. (2004). Medication adherence in HIV-infected adults: Effect of patient age, cognitive status, and substance abuse. *AIDS*, *18*, 19−25.

Hogervorst, E., Huppert, F., Matthews, F. E., & Brayne, C. (2008). Thyroid function and cognitive decline in the MRC cognitive function and ageing study. *Psychoneuroendocrinology*, *33* (7), 1013−1022. Available from http://dx.doi.org/10.1016/j.psyneuen.2008.05.008.

Iduru, S., & Mullen, K. D. (2008). The demise of the pencil? New computer-assisted tests for minimal hepatic encephalopathy. *Gastroenterology*, *135*, 1455−1456. Available from http://dx.doi.org/10.1053/j.gastro.2008.09.040.

Jabłkowska-Górecka, K., Karbownik-Lewinska, M., Nowakowska, K., Junik, R., Lewinski, A., & Borkowska, A. (2008). Working memory and executive functions in hyperthyroid patients with Graves' disease. *Psychiatria Polska*, *42*, 249−259.

Jiang, X., Barasky, R., Olsen, H., Riesenhuber, M., & Magnus, M. (2016). Behavioral and neuroimaging evidence for impaired executive function in "cognitively normal" older HIV-infected adults. *AIDS Care*, *28*, 436−440. Available from http://dx.doi.org/10.1080/09540121.2015.1112347.

Joffe, R. T., Pearce, E. N., Hennessey, J. V., Ryan, J. J., & Stern, R. A. (2013). Subclinical hypothyroidism, mood, and cognition in the elderly: A review. *International Journal of Geriatric Psychiatry*, *28*(2), 111−118.

Kálcza-Jánosi, K., Lukács, A., Barkai, L., & Szamosközi, I. (2013). Cognitive functions in type 1 and type 2 diabetes. Meta-analysis. *Orvosi Hetilap*, *5*, 694−699. Available from http://dx.doi.org/10.1556/OH.2013.29602.

Kodl, C. T., & Seaquist, E. R. (2008). Cognitive dysfunction and diabetes mellitus. *Endocrine Reviews*, *29*(4), 494−511. Available from http://dx.doi.org/10.1210/er.2007-0034.

Köhler, S., Baars, M. A. E., Spauwen, P., Schievink, S., Verhey, F. R. J., & van Boxtel, M. J. P. (2014). Temporal evolution of cognitive changes in incident hypertension prospective cohort study across the adult age span. *Hypertension*, *63*, 245−251.

Koushik, N. S., McArthur, S. F., & Baird, A. D. (2010). Adult chronic kidney disease: Neurocognition in chronic renal failure. *Neuropsychology Review, 20*, 33–51. Available from http://dx.doi.org/10.1007/s11065-009-9110-5.

Kramer, L., Madl, C., Stockenhuber, F., Yeganehfar, W., Eisenhuber, E., Derfler, K., Lenz, K., Schneider, B., & Grimm, G. (1996). Beneficial effect of renal transplantation on cognitive brain function. *Kidney International, 49*, 833–838.

Kupferman, J. C., Lande, M. B., Adams, H. R., & Pavlakis, S. G. (2013). Primary hypertension and neurocognitive & executive functioning in school-aged children. *Pediatric Nephrology, 28*(3), 401–408. Available from http://dx.doi.org/10.1007/s00467-012-2215-8.

Kurella-Tamura, M., Covinsky, K. E., Chertow, G. M., Yaffe, K., Landefeld, C. S., & McCulloch, C. E. (2009). Functional status of elderly adults before and after initiation of dialysis. *New England Journal of Medicine, 361*, 1539–1547.

Lakatos, B., Szabó, Z., Bozzai, B., Bánhegyi, D., & Gazdag, G. (2014). Neurocognitive impairments of HIV infected individuals—Preliminary results of a national prevalence study in Hungary. *Ideggyógyászati Szemle, 30*, 11–12.

Lee, Y., Kim, C., Suk, K. T., Choi, H. C., Bang, C. S., Yoon, J. H., Baik, G. H., Kim, D. J., Jang, M. U., & Sohn, J. H. (2016). Differences in cognitive function between patients with viral and alcoholic compensated liver cirrhosis. *Metabolic Brain Disease, 31*(2), 369–376. Available from http://dx.doi.org/10.1007/s11011-015-9761-2.

Lezak, M. D., Howieson, D. B., Bigler, E. D., & Tranel, D. (2012). *Neuropsychological assessment* (5th ed.). New York: Oxford University Press.

Manschot, S. M., Brands, A. M., van der Grond, J., Kessels, R. P., Algra, A., Kappelle, L. J., Biessels, G. J., & Utrecht Diabetic Encephalopathy Study Group (2006). Brain magnetic resonance imaging correlates of impaired cognition in patients with type 2 diabetes. *Diabetes, 55*, 1106–1113.

Marcotte, T. D., Lazzaretto, D., Scott, J. C., Roberts, E., Woods, S. P., Letendre, S., & HIV Neurobehavioral Research Center Group (2006). Visual attention deficits are associated with driving accidents in cognitively-impaired HIVinfected individuals. *Journal of Clinical and Experimental Neuropsychology, 28*, 13–28.

Marcotte, T. D., Wolfson, T., Rosenthal, T. J., Heaton, R. K., Gonzalez, R., Ellis, R. J., Grant, I., & HIV Neurobehavioral Research Center Group (2004). A multimodal assessment of driving performance in HIV infection. *Neurology, 63*, 1417–1422.

Martin, E. M., Nixon, H., Pitrack, D. L., Weddington, W., Rains, N. A., Nunnally, G., & Bechara, A. (2007). Characteristics of prospective memory deficits in HIV-seropositive substance-dependent individuals: Preliminary observations. *Journal of Clinical and Experimental Neuropsychology, 29*, 496–504.

Maruff, P., Currie, J., Malone, V., McArthur-Jackson, C., Mulhall, B., & Benson, E. (1994). Neuropsychological characterization of the AIDS dementia complex and rationalization of a test battery. *Archives of Neurology & Psychiatry, 51*(7), 689–695 , PubMed PMID: 8018042

Maruff, P., Malone, V., McArthur-Jackson, C., Mulhall, B., Benson, E., & Currie, J. (1995). Abnormalities of visual spatial attention in HIV infection and the HIV-associated dementia complex. *Journal of Neuropsychiatry and Clinical Neurosciences, 7*, 325–333.

Melo, L. F., & Da-Silva, S. L. (2012). Neuropsychological assessment of cognitive disorders in patients with fibromyalgia, rheumatoid arthritis, and systemic lupus erythematosus. *Revista Brasileira de Reumatologia, 52*(2), 181–188. Available from http://dx.doi.org/10.1590/S0482-50042012000200003.

Meyer, T., Eshelman, A., & Abouljoud, M. (2006). Neuropsychological changes in a large sample of liver transplant candidates. *Transplantation Proceedings*, *38*(10), 3559−3560.

Miao, Q., Zhang, S., Guan, Y. H., Ye, H. Y., Zhang, Z. Y., Zhang, Q. Y., Xue, R. D., Zeng, M. F., Zuo, C. T., & Li, Y. M. (2011). Reversible changes in brain glucose metabolism following thyroid function normalization in hyperthyroidism. *American Journal of Neuroradiology*, *32*, 1034−1042. http://dx.doi.org/10.3174/ajnr.A2449. pmid:21596814.

Michałowski, J. M., Harciarek, M., Williamson, J., Biedunkiewicz, B., Dębska-Ślizień, A., Rutkowski, B., & Heilman, K. M. (2016). Slowing with end-stage renal disease: Attentive but unprepared to act. *International Journal of Psychophysiology*, *106*, 30−38.

Miller, D. G., Levine, S. E., D'Elia, J. A., & Bistrian, B. R. (1986). Nutritional status of diabetic and nondiabetic patients after renal transplantation. *American Journal of Clinical Nutrition*, *44*, 66−69.

Mullen, K. D. (2007). Review of the final report of the 1998 Working Party on definition, nomenclature and diagnosis of hepatic encephalopathy. *Alimentary Pharmacology & Therapeutics*, *25*, 11−16.

Murray, A. M. (2008). Cognitive impairment in the aging dialysis and chronic kidney disease populations: An occult burden. *Advances in Chronic Kidney Disease*, *15*, 123−132.

Musen, G., Lyoo, I. K., Sparks, C. R., Weinger, K., Hwang, J., Ryan, C. M., Jimerson, D. C., Hennen, J., Renshaw, P. F., & Jacobson, A. M. (2006). Effects of type 1 diabetes on gray matter density as measured by voxel-based morphometry. *Diabetes*, *55*(2), 326−333 . PubMed PMID: 16443764

Northam, E. A., Anderson, P. J., Jacobs, R., Hughes, M., Warne, G. L., & Werther, G. A. (2001). Neuropsychological profiles of children with type 1 diabetes 6 years after disease onset. *Diabetes Care*, *24*, 1541−1546.

Oveisgharan, S., Hachinski, V., & Hypertension, executive dysfunction, and progression to dementia (2010). The Canadian Study of health and aging. *Archives of Neurology*, *67*, 187−192.

Pereira, A. A., Weiner, D. E., Scott, T., & Sarnak, M. J. (2005). Cognitive function in dialysis patients. *American Journal of Kidney Diseases*, *45*, 448−462.

Pfefferbaum, A., Rogosa, D. A., Rosenbloom, M. J., Chu, W., Sassoon, S. A., Kemper, C. A., & Sullivan, E. V. (2014). Accelerated aging of selective brain structures in HIV infection: A controlled, longitudinal MRI study. *Neurobiology of Aging*, *35*(7), 1755−1768.

Pliskin, N. H., Kiolbasa, T. A., Hart, R. P., & Umans, J. G. (2001). Neuropsychological function in renal disease and its treatment. In R. E. Tarter, M. Butters, & S. R. Beers (Eds.), Medical neuropsychology (2nd ed.) (pp. 107−126). New York: Kluwer Academic/Plenum Publishers.

Prins, N. D., van Dijk, E. J., & den Heijer, T. (2005). Cerebral small-vessel disease and decline in information processing speed, executive function and memory. *Brain*, *128*, 2034−2041.

Querbes, O., Aubry, F., Pariente, J., Lotterie, J. A., Démonet, J. F., Duret, V., Puel, M., Berry, I., Fort, J. C., Celsis, P., & Alzheimer's Disease Neuroimaging Initiative (2009). Early diagnosis of Alzheimer's disease using cortical thickness: Impact of cognitive reserve. *Brain*, *132*, 2036−2047.

Reger, M., Welsh, R., Razani, J., Martin, D. J., & Boone, K. B. (2002). A meta-analysis of the neuropsychological sequelae of HIV infection. *Journal of the International Neuropsychological Society: JINS*, *8*, 410−424.

Röhl, J. E., Harms, L., & Pommer, W. (2007). Quantitative EEG findings in patients with chronic renal failure. *European Journal of Medical Research*, *12*, 173−178.

Rucker, J. L., McDowd, J. M., & Kluding, P. M. (2012). Executive function and type 2 diabetes: Putting the pieces together. *Physical Therapy, 92*(3), 454–462.

Rugge, B., Balshem, H., Sehgal, R., Relevo, R., Gorman, P., & Helfand, M. (2011). *Screening and treatment of subclinical hypothyroidism or hyperthyroidism [Internet]*. Rockville (MD): Agency for Healthcare Research and Quality (US), Report No.: 11(12)-EHC033-EF.

Ruis, C., Biessels, G. J., Gorter, K. J., van den Donk, M., Kappelle, L. J., & Rutten, G. E. H. M. (2009). Cognition in the early stage of type 2 diabetes. *Diabetes Care, 32*(7), 1261–1265.

Saczynski, J. S., Jónsdóttir, M. K., Garcia, M. E., Jonsson, P. V., Peila, R., Eiriksdottir, G., & Launer, L. J. (2008). Cognitive impairment: An increasingly important complication of type 2 diabetes: The Age, Gene/Environment Susceptibility–Reykjavik Study. *American Journal of Epidemiology, 168*, 1132–1139.

Samuels, M. H. (2014). Psychiatric and cognitive manifestations of hypothyroidism. *Current Opinion in Endocrinology, Diabetes and Obesity, 21*(5), 377–383. Available from http://dx. doi.org/10.1097/MED.0000000000000089.

Sarma, M. K., Huda, A., Nagarajan, R., Hinkin, C. H., Wilson, N., Gupta, R. K., & Thomas, M. A. (2011). Multi-dimensional MR spectroscopy: Towards a better understanding of hepatic encephalopathy. *Metabolic Brain Disease, 26*(3), 173–184.

Schomerus, H., Hamster, W., Blunck, H., Reinhard, K., Mayer, K., & DoÉlle, W. (1981). Latent portasystemic encephalopathy. Nature of cerebral functional defects and their effect on fitness to drive. *Digestive Diseases and Science, 26*, 622–630.

Schreckenberger, M. F., Egle, U. T., Drecker, S., Buchholz, H. G., Weber, M. M., Bartenstein, P., & Kahaly, G. J. (2006). Positron emission tomography reveals correlations between brain metabolism and mood changes in hyperthyroidism. *Journal of Clinical Endocrinology and Metabolism, 91*, 4786–4791. Available from http://dx.doi.org/10.1210/jc.2006-0573.

Shin, S. Y., Katz, P., Wallhagen, M., & Julian, L. (2012). Cognitive impairment in persons with rheumatoid arthritis. *Arthritis Care & Research, 64*(8), 1144–1150.

Sierakowski, S., & Cutolo, M. (2011). Morning symptoms in rheumatoid arthritis: A defining characteristic and marker of active disease. *Scandinavian Journal of Rheumatology, 125*, 1–5. Available from http://dx.doi.org/10.3109/03009742.2011.566433.

Simos, P., Ktistaki, G., Dimitraki, G., Papastefanakis, E., Kougkas, N., Fanouriakis, A., Gergianaki, I., Bertsias, G., Sidiropoulos, P., & Karademas, E. C. (2016). Cognitive deficits early in the course of rheumatoid arthritis. *Journal of Clinical and Experimental Neuropsychology, 38*(7), 820–829. Available from http://dx.doi.org/10.1080/13803395.2016.1167173.

Singhal, A., Nagarajan, R., Hinkin, C. H., Kumar, R., Sayre, J., Elderkin-Thompson, V., Huda, A., Gupta, R. K., Han, S. H., & Thomas, M. A. (2010). Two-dimensional MR spectroscopy of minimal hepatic encephalopathy and neuropsychological correlates in vivo. *Journal of Magnetic Resonance Imaging, 32*, 35–43.

Spinelli, C., De Caro, M. F., Schirosi, G., Mezzapesa, D., De Benedittis, L., Chiapparino, C., & Nazzaro, P. (2014). Impaired cognitive executive dysfunction in adult treated hypertensives with a confirmed diagnosis of poorly controlled blood pressure. *International Journal of Medical Sciences, 11*(8), 771–778.

Stuss, D. T., Alexander, M. P., Hamer, L., Palumbo, C., Dempster, R., Binns, M., . . . Izukawa, D. (1998). The effects of focal anterior and posterior brain lesions on verbal fluency. *Journal of the International Neuropsychological Society, 4*, 265–278.

Stuss, D. T., Alexander, M. P., Shallice, T., Picton, T. W., Binns, M. A., Macdonald, R., Borowiec, A., & Katz, D. (2005). Multiple frontal systems controlling response speed. *Neuropsychologia, 43*, 396–417.

Tekin, S., & Cummings, J. L. (2002). Frontal-subcortical neuronal circuits and clinical neuropsychiatry: An update. *Journal of Psychosomatic Research, 53*, 647–654.

Thabit, H., Kennelly, S. M., Bhagarva, A., Ogunlewe, M., McCormack, P. M., McDermott, J. H., & Sreenan, S. (2009). Utilization of Frontal Assessment Battery and Executive Interview 25 in assessing for dysexecutive syndrome and its association with diabetes self-care in elderly patients with type 2 diabetes mellitus. *Diabetes Research and Clinical Practice, 86*, 208–212.

Tonoli, C., Heyman, E., Roelands, B., Pattyn, N., Buyse, L., Piacentini, M. F., Berthoin, S., & Meeusen, R. (2014). Type 1 diabetes-associated cognitive decline: A meta-analysis and update of the current literature. *Journal of Diabetes, 6*, 499–513. Available from http://dx.doi.org/10.1111/1753-0407.12193.

Tozzi, V., Balestra, P., Galgani, S., Narciso, P., Ferri, F., Sebastiani, G., D'Amato, C., Affricano, C., Pigorini, F., Pau, F. M., De Felici, A., & Benedetto, A. (1999). Positive and sustained effects of highly active antiretroviral therapy on HIV-1-associated neurocognitive impairment. *AIDS, 13*(14), 1889–1897.

Tullberg, M., Fletcher, E., DeCarli, C., Mungas, D., Reed, B. R., Harvey, D. J., ... Jagust, W. J. (2004). White matter lesions impair frontal lobe function regardless of their location. *Neurology, 63*, 246–253.

Tzourio, C. (2007). Hypertension, cognitive decline, and dementia: An epidemiological perspective. *Dialogues in Clinical Neuroscience, 9*(1), 61–70.

Van Gorp, W. G., Baerwald, J. P., Ferrando, S. J., McElhiney, M. C., & Rabkin, J. G. (1999). The relationship between employment and neuropsychological impairment in HIV infection. *Journal of the International Neuropsychological Society; JINS, 5*, 534–539.

Waldstein, S. R., Manuck, S. B., Ryan, C. M., & Muldoon, M. F. (1991). Neuropsychological correlates of hypertension: Review and methodologic considerations. *Psychological Bulletin, 110*, 451–468.

Weinger, K., Jacobson, A. M., Musen, G., Lyoo, I. K., Ryan, C. M., Jimerson, D. C., & Renshaw, P. F. (2008). The effects of type 1 diabetes on cerebral white matter. *Diabetologia, 51*, 417–425.

Weissenborn, K., Ennen, J. C., Rückert, N., & Hecker, H. (2001). Neuropsychological characterization of hepatic encephalopathy. *Journal of Hepatology, 34*, 768–773.

Weissenborn, K., Hecker, H., & Rückert, N. (2015). Pitfalls in psychometric testing. *Gastroenterology, 148*(3), 664–665.

White, D. A., Heaton, R. K., & Monsch, A. U. (1995). Neuropsychological studies of asymptomatic human immunodeficiency virus-type-1 infected individuals. The HNRC Group. HIV Neurobehavioral Research Center. *Journal of the International Neuropsychological Society: JINS, 1*, 304–315. Available from http://dx.doi.org/10.1017/S1355617700000308.

Yeung, S. E., Fischer, A. L., & Dixon, R. A. (2009). Exploring effects of type 2 diabetes on cognitive functioning in older adults. *Neuropsychology, 23*(1), 1–9.

Yuan, L., Tian, Y., Zhang, F., Ma, H., Chen, X., Dai, F., & Wang, K. (2015). Decision-making in patients with hyperthyroidism: A neuropsychological study. *PLoS One, 10*(6), e0129773. Available from http://dx.doi.org/10.1371/journal.pone.0129773.

Yudiarto, F. L., Muliadi, L., Moeljanto, D., & Hartono, B. (2006). Neuropsychological findings in hyperthyroid patients. *Acta Medica Indonesiana, 38*, 6–10.

Zhang, W., Song, L., Yin, X., Zhang, J., Liu, C., Wang, J., Zhoua, D., Chend, B., & Lii, H. (2014). Grey matter abnormalities in untreated hyperthyroidism: A voxel-based morphometry study using the DARTEL approach. *European Journal of Radiology, 83*, 43–48. Available from http://dx.doi.org/10.1016/j.ejrad.2013.09.019.

Zhu, D. F., Wang, Z. X., Zhang, D. R., Pan, Z. L., He, S., Hu, X. P., Chen, X. C., & Zhou, J. N. (2006). fMRI revealed neural substrate for reversible working memory dysfunction in subclinical hypothyroidism. *Brain*, *11*, 2923–2930.

FURTHER READING

Köhler, S., Baars, M.A.E., Spauwen, P., Schievink, S., Verhey, F.R.J., van Boxtel, M.J.P. (2004). Temporal evolution of cognitive changes in incident hypertension prospective cohort study across the adult age span, Hypertension, 44, 631-636.

Chapter 22

Assessment of Executive Functions in Clinical Settings

Yana Suchy, Rosemary E. Ziemnik and Madison A. Niermeyer
Department of Psychology, University of Utah, Salt Lake City, UT, United States

ASSESSMENT OF EXECUTIVE FUNCTIONS IN CLINICAL SETTINGS

Clinically Useful Definition of Executive Functioning

Many neuropsychological texts define executive functioning (EF) as a complex, multifaceted construct that comprised those abilities that allow one to plan, organize, and successfully execute purposeful, goal-directed, and future-oriented actions (Cummings & Miller, 2007; Lezak, Howieson, Bigler, & Tranel, 2012; Suchy, 2009). Despite the relative agreement on what EF can *do*, there continues to be little convergence as to what it actually *is*. Just for illustration purposes, consider that Norman and Shallice (1986) proposed that EF consists of two components, including the supervisory attentional system and contention scheduling; Lezak and colleagues (2012) proposed a model that consists of four components, including volition, planning, purposive action, and effective performance; and Stuss proposed a model comprised five components, including energization, monitoring, task setting, behavioral and emotional self-regulation, and metamonitoring (Stuss, 2011). In her recent book on EF, Suchy (2015) also proposed a five-component model; however, the subdomains of EF she described differed from those of Stuss (2011) and included *Executive Cognitive Functions, Initiation/Maintenance, Response Selection, Meta-tasking, and Social Cognition*. Due to the lack of convergence on the components of EF and the associated terminology, we feel it is important that a basic theoretical framework and associated assumptions be laid out up front in any discussion of EF. In this chapter, we will rely on the Suchy (2015) model. According to

Executive Functions in Health and Disease. DOI: http://dx.doi.org/10.1016/B978-0-12-803676-1.00022-2

this model, the ability to successfully plan and execute actions relies on the following five executive subdomains:

Executive Cognitive Functions

Executive Cognitive Functions are the prerequisite to any purposeful and goal-directed action. They allow one to generate plans, solutions to problems, or organizing structures that guide future action. They rely on working memory, mental flexibility, and retrieval of relevant information from semantic and epi-sodic memory stores. Importantly, intact Executive Cognitive Functions do not, in and of themselves, assure that behaviors will be effectively executed. In other words, it is possible for a person to generate exquisitely detailed and well-reasoned plans but never be able to realize them.

Initiation/Maintenance

Once plans are generated, one needs to initiate and maintain behaviors that allow completion of those plans. While initiation refers to efficient "chunk-ing" of motor programs just prior to the release of an action, maintenance refers to the internal "refresh" cycle that continuously, in approximately 10-s intervals, refreshes the mental set. In addition to the elemental processes of initiation and maintenance, this subdomain also relies on effort mobilization; this is the driving force behind any behavior and relies at least in part on suf-ficient sympathetic activation and sufficient sensitivity to rewards.

Response Selection

Even if action is appropriately initiated and maintained, multitude of stimuli continuously bombard one's attentional and perceptual systems, triggering a variety of prepotent behavioral urges, whether they be based on inherent stimulus-response impulses or on associations learned from previous reward-ing or punishing outcomes. Thus, every step of the way, one response must be selected from among many other behavioral options. Response Selection relies on a number of elemental processes, including the ability to update con-tingencies based on a context, the ability to inhibit less desired actions from taking place, and adequate sensitivity to threats, discrepancies, or errors.

Meta-Tasking

Although the above-described subdomains of EF will allow one to succeed on many discrete executively demanding tasks, they are not sufficient for effective coordination of multiple goals across extended periods of time. Specifically, it is often the case in the course of the day that one must inter-leave completion of subgoals for one task with subgoals for another task. For effective management of multiple tasks in daily life, one relies on prospec-tive memory and on the ability to monitor, in an effortful, top-down fashion, whether all subgoals for all tasks are on track. In other words, one needs to self-cue appropriately to, for example, pick up the dry cleaning while driving home from work and check off items on an explicit to-do list to ascertain that all subgoals for all tasks are on track.

Social Cognition

Although Social Cognition is rarely explicitly subsumed under the EF umbrella, its importance for successful execution of future-oriented actions is sometimes implied. For example, Lezak and colleagues (2012) actually included the phrase "appropriate, and socially responsible" in their definition of EF (p. 666). Additionally, much research supports both phylogenetic and ontogenetic associations between EF and Social Cognition. In particular, species that are social are also more advanced with respect to EF (Reader & Laland, 2002), and EF and Social Cognition evolve in tandem in childhood (Hensler et al., 2014; Zelazo, Chandler, & Crone, 2010) and remain associated in adulthood (Eslinger, Moore, Anderson, & Grossman, 2011; Santorelli & Ready, 2015; Wingbermühle, Theunissen, Verhoeven, Kessels, & Egger, 2012). Social Cognition relies on one's ability to understand implied socially relevant verbal communication, paralinguistic messages (e.g., facial expressions, posture, and gestures), and social situations. Additionally, it also relies on adequate insight about one's own emotions. In the absence of these abilities, the best laid plans, initiated and maintained action, and inhibition of inappropriate or irrelevant responses will not lead to ultimate success, as social interactions are virtually ever present, and actions that ignore social cues will likely thwart goal attainment.

Importantly, the above subdomains of EF correspond to previously described syndromes that are characterized by unique groupings of executive deficits. In particular, deficiencies in Executive Cognitive Functions, Initiation/Maintenance, and Response Selection have been described as the dysexecutive, apathetic, and impulsive syndromes, respectively (Duffy, Campbell III, Salloway, & Malloy, 2001). In addition, "strategy application disorder" (Shallice & Burgess, 1991) or the "disorganized syndrome" (Suchy, 2015) characterized by deficits in Meta-Tasking has also been reported in the literature. Lastly, clinicians often assume that behaviors that are grossly socially inappropriate reflect EF dysfunction; in line with this clinical thinking, Suchy (2015) has proposed that deficiencies in Social Cognition be termed the "inappropriate syndrome," falling under the umbrella of syndromes associated with EF deficiencies.

Assessment Considerations and Challenges in Relation to Assessment Purposes

Prior to discussing specific assessment methods, it is important to consider the purpose of assessment or the questions that the clinician wants to answer. This is because different assessment purposes warrant fundamentally different assessment approaches. While a full review of all potential goals of neuropsychological assessment is beyond the scope of this chapter, one important distinction will be considered here: (1) is the assessment conducted for the purpose of arriving at a diagnosis versus (2) is it conducted for the purpose of characterizing the patient's daily functioning.

Diagnosis

In clinical neuropsychology, two main types of diagnoses are considered: psychiatric and neurologic. Although many psychiatric conditions are associated with deficiencies in EF (Snyder, Miyake, & Hankin, 2015), the cognitive profiles that are seen in such conditions are relatively nonspecific; thus, cognitive profiles are typically not the deciding factor when differentiating between, say, depression versus obsessive compulsive disorder. In contrast, cognitive profiles (in conjunction with other background information, such as interview, medical records, and behavioral observations, discussed in more detail later in this chapter) represent an important factor in diagnostic decision-making when differentiating between psychiatric versus neurologic etiology or when differentiating among several potential neurologic conditions.

To effectively utilize cognitive data for the purpose of diagnostic decision-making, clinicians need to ask the following questions: First, does the patient exhibit a decline in cognition? If so, what is the course of such a decline (i.e., sudden, gradual, and rapid) and what is the severity of impairment? And second, is this decline characterized by a particular cognitive profile? If so, what brain systems are implicated by this profile? The answers to these questions then need to be integrated with the clinician's knowledge of the natural history and pathophysiology of different disorders, as well as thorough understanding of brain—behavior relationships, so as to align the patient's cognitive profile with corresponding neuroanatomic substrates that may implicate a given disorder.

When it comes to answering the first set of questions, that is, has there been a decline, the clinician needs to compare current test performance to the estimated premorbid level of functioning. To accomplish this, cognitive results need to be compared to norms that consider demographic factors, such as age, educational background, gender, and ethnicity, as all these factors have been shown to relate to cognition more generally and to EF specifically (Arentoft et al., 2015; Constantinidou, Christodoulou, & Prokopiou, 2012; Dorbath, Hasselhorn, & Titz, 2013; Martins, Maruta, Freitas, & Mares, 2013; Neguţ, Matu, Sava, & David, 2016; Tripathi, Kumar, Bharath, Marimuthu, & Varghese, 2014). Importantly, these factors alone do not provide a foolproof premorbid estimate, as even within relatively narrow demographic categories individual difference still exist. For example, there are individual differences in the quality of obtained education or learning opportunities afforded (or not afforded) due to the patient's socioeconomic status or acculturation (Manly, 2005). Thus, thoughtful adjustments based on background information need to be made.

In addition, increasing evidence points to the importance of personality as a contributor to individual differences in EF, beyond demographics. First, the personality trait known as Neuroticism (as assessed via the NEO Personality Inventory-Revised; Costa & McCrae, 1992) has been consistently shown to be associated with EF, such that individuals with higher neuroticism exhibit poorer EF (Murdock, Oddi, & Bridgett, 2013; Williams, Suchy, & Kraybill, 2010). In contrast to neuroticism, higher Openness to Experience is associated with better EF (Franchow, Suchy, Thorgusen, & Williams, 2013; Murdock et al., 2013; Williams et al., 2010). Importantly, Openness to Experience contributes to cognition beyond education, especially at lower ends of educational attainment (Franchow et al., 2013). In other words, individuals who may have not had the benefit of formal higher education, but who are high on the Openness trait, are likely to be characterized by higher premorbid EF abilities than demographically corrected norms would suggest. Thus, once again, careful consideration of personality traits may help a clinician to hone in on a more accurate estimate of premorbid functioning.

In addition to determining the appropriate premorbid estimate of EF, diagnostic decision-making also relies on judgments about which neuroanatomic networks are compromised. Answering this question may be more complex for EF than for other neurocognitive domains because EF networks are widely distributed (for a review, see Suchy, 2015). Consequently, deficiencies in EF may stem from a variety of lesion locations explaining why EF dysfunction is a relatively common finding in a variety of disorders. Many tests presumed to measure EF have actually been originally validated purely based on their sensitivity to lesions in the frontal lobes (Baldo, Shimamura, Delis, Kramer, & Kaplan, 2001; Demakis, 2003; Reitan & Wolfson, 1995). Thus, frontal lobe dysfunction can generally be suspected if consistent with other diagnostic indicators, especially if occurring in the context of relatively preserved functions in other neurocognitive domains.

Daily Functioning and Ecological Validity of Executive Functioning Tests

Often, instead of (or in addition to) diagnostic decision-making, clinicians are called upon to make judgments about a patient's functioning in daily life. Such questions may occur in the context of a formal capacity evaluation, treatment planning, or simple recommendations to physicians and family members. In group studies, EF has consistently emerged as the best predictor of daily functioning (often operationalized as the ability to perform instrumental activities of daily living—IADLs; Grigsby, Kaye, Kowalsky, & Kramer, 2002; Iampietro, Giovannetti, Drabick, & Kessler, 2012; Kraybill & Suchy, 2011; Kraybill, Thorgusen, & Suchy, 2013; MacDougall & Mansbach, 2013; Manning et al., 2012; Martyr & Clare, 2012; Puente, Lindbergh, & Miller, 2015; Rog et al., 2014; Vordenberg, Barrett, Doninger, Contardo, & Ozoude, 2014).

However, clinicians are well aware that judgments about a specific patient's functionality are fraught with much uncertainty. This difficulty, along with the potentially devastating consequences of misclassifying patients along the functional capacity dimension, has led to some considerable criticism of EF tests as lacking *ecological validity* (Burgess, Alderman, Evans, Emslie, & Wilson, 1998; Cripe, 1996; Goldberg & Podell, 2000).

A number of reasons for poor ecological validity of EF tests have been extensively discussed in the literature, including low correspondence with real-world tasks, narrow definition of the EF construct, and the inherently structured environment of the assessment contexts that does not allow functional difficulties to emerge (Burgess et al., 2006). The latter issue in particular has received considerable attention in the literature (Jurado & Rosselli, 2007; Lezak et al., 2012). The principal presumed reason for the disconnect between performance on standardized tests of EF and daily functioning is that the clinician is actively working to minimize the presence of factors that could negatively affect EF performance (e.g., reassuring the patient if he or she seems emotionally overwhelmed or providing cues or prompts if a patient loses mental set). Additionally, due to the structure of each test, there is little to no goal-directed planning or decision-making required from the patient. In other words, the structured testing environment is a far cry from the real-world scenarios in which EF is needed.

In support of the criticism of the structured testing environment, recent research has shown that EF fluctuates in response to certain common daily stressors or events. These include exposure to novel contexts (Euler, Niermeyer, & Suchy, 2015; Suchy, Euler, & Eastvold, 2014), lack of sleep (Benitez & Gunstad, 2012; Bernier, Beauchamp, Bouvette-Turcot, Carlson, & Carrier, 2013; Guoping, Kan, Danmin, & Fuen, 2008; Harrison & Horne, 2000), pain (Berryman et al., 2014; Karp et al., 2006), or even simple daily engagement in emotion regulation (Baumeister & Alquist, 2009; Franchow & Suchy, 2015; Niermeyer, Franchow, & Suchy, 2016). Importantly, some of these fluctuations appear to be of a sufficient magnitude so as to be clinically significant (Franchow & Suchy, 2015) and appear to be fairly unique to EF— in order words, EF is disproportionately affected, as compared to other neurocognitive domains. These findings support the notion that EF is a limited resource that is both depletable and renewable (Baumeister & Alquist, 2009; Baumeister, Vohs, & Tice, 2007; Hagger, Wood, Stiff, & Chatzisarantis, 2010), and help to elucidate why a patient may perform well on tests of EF on one day but may exhibit lapses in functioning the next day. One potential solution for this problem is for the field to expand its mindset from, on the one hand, eliciting the best possible EF performance (which is helpful when assessing a change from a premorbid baseline) to also examining the *resiliency* of a patient's EF under conditions of stress. In other words, future work in EF assessment should evaluate the utility of an EF "stress test," analogous to a cardiac stress test used to help predict outcomes for heart disease patients.

In addition to EF lapses that occur due to exposure to certain depleting stressors, lapses may also signal a mild impairment in EF. Specifically, while severe EF impairment presents as a stable inability to perform executively demanding tasks, mild impairment often presents as *intermittent functional lapses* interspersed in between apparently normal functionality. The notion that lapses are themselves a sign of EF weakness is supported by research showing that older age (which is associated with poorer EF) is also associated with greater variability on EF tasks (West, Murphy, Armilio, Craik, & Stuss, 2002).

Unfortunately, during neuropsychological assessment, performance on EF tests is often similarly characterized by lapses that are intermittent. Thus, performances may be well within normal limits on most tests, with only one or two impaired performances. In general, clinicians are discouraged from overinterpreting singular poor performance as impairment in a corresponding neurocognitive domain. This is well warranted when interpreting such singular impairments within neuroanatomic and diagnostic frameworks. However, when functionality in daily life is the question of interest, clinicians should instead consider the possibility that a patient who exhibits lapses or variability in performance even in the context of a structured and supportive environment will likely exhibit lapses in the context of a busy or stressful daily life. In fact, research shows that intraindividual variability in EF within a single testing session predicts performance variability across time (West et al., 2002).

Last but not least, the current assessment approaches are limited by the fact that norms are designed to detect deviations in performance relative to other individuals of similar age (i.e., population-based norms) or relative to estimated premorbid baseline (i.e., demographically corrected norms). In either case, such norms are not useful for determining whether a patient will have functional difficulties in daily life. For example, a 90-year-old patient with 8 years of education may produce EF performance that is well within normal limits relative to demographically corrected norms, suggesting that he is *neurocognitively healthy*. However, such a patient may still have considerable functional difficulties in daily life, which may well be normative for his age. In fact, functional lapses among apparently cognitively healthy community-dwelling older adults are common (Burton, Strauss, Hultsch, & Hunter, 2006; Plehn, Marcopulos, & McLain, 2004), with about 35% of older adults making mistakes on tasks of IADLs (Suchy, Kraybill, & Franchow, 2011). To address this limitation, criterion-based norms would be preferable. Such norms could provide the base rates of IADL errors associated with a given cognitive score or increases in risk for lapses relative to better-scoring individuals. Clinicians need to be aware that in the absence of such criterion-based norms, they are essentially shooting from the hip when making judgments about functionality. Until such norms are developed, in the very least, population-based, rather than demographically corrected, norms should be used when answering questions about the patient's daily functioning, so as to compare a patient's functioning relative to broader population, rather than relative to his or her own estimated premorbid baseline.

In sum, the purpose of assessment has important ramifications for the types of normative comparisons one makes: For diagnostic decision-making, comparison of current performance to a presumed premorbid baseline is key, as it allows detection of decline. Thus, demographically corrected norms should be used for this purpose, supplemented with other relevant information, such as the patient's personality traits, acculturation, or quality of education. Additionally, consistent patterns of scores across a test battery should be carefully considered so as to make judgments about the integrity of relevant neuroanatomic substrates—overinterpretation of one or two isolated impaired scores should be avoided. In contrast, for functional determinations, population-based norms should be used, so as to determine how the patient is functioning relative to others of similar age. Given that virtually all available norms are age-corrected, clinicians should recognize that, with increasing age, the potential for lapses increases, and that this potential increase is not reflected in the age-corrected normative comparisons. Lastly, few isolated impaired scores, while not necessarily signaling brain dysfunction, may signal the potential for intermittent lapses in daily life, and should not be ignored.

Assessment Methods: Gathering Background Information

In the next section, we focus on concrete methods for gathering background information from patient records and clinical interviews, which play a key role in helping to determine (1) the highest premorbid level of EF ability, (2) the time course of EF decline/change, and (3) the type, frequency, and severity of EF difficulties in daily life.

Records Review

It has become a standard of practice that a comprehensive neuropsychological evaluation should include a review of the patient's records (Heilbronner, Sweet, Morgan, Larrabee, & Millis, 2009). School and/or work records, medical records, and legal/criminal records are usually among the most informative.

As mentioned earlier, a good estimate of premorbid level of functioning is necessary to determine whether obtained test scores indicate a decline in EF. To that end, records should be reviewed with an eye toward determining the highest premorbid level of EF. School and work records are particularly useful in this regard, as they may allow clinicians to glean the complexity of the patient's scholastic demands or employment, as well as their capacity to handle such demands. An important caveat is that school and job records can only assuredly provide the *lowest necessary* level of ability. Thus, while individuals in highly demanding jobs likely had high EF premorbidly, those in lower level jobs may have had EF capacity that well surpassed their job demands. Consequently, although low scores on tests of EF likely represent a decline for a former high-level professional, they may or may not indicate a decline in an unskilled laborer.

In addition to helping with the determination of the premorbid level of functioning, records often shed light on the time course of the patient's presenting concerns or the time of onset. This is particularly important when the time course is critical for diagnostic decision-making. Medical and legal records are particularly useful in this regard. For example, such records may provide objective evidence of an increase in emergency room visits due to injuries stemming from EF lapses or psychiatric hospitalization due to episodes of psychosis, gross social inappropriateness, or profound personality changes. Similarly, legal records may provide objective evidence of an increase in motor vehicle accidents due to lapses in attention or behavioral control, or even sudden onset of criminal behavior (e.g., theft or sexual harassment) secondary to deficits in Social Cognition or Response Selection. School and work records may also provide a time frame for the patient's decline, with indications of sudden onset of absences, tardiness, decline in grades, or disciplinary actions. However, unlike medical and legal records, school and work records may sometimes exhibit a delayed timeline of such transgressions, especially if school or work personnel responsible for recording such incidences are leniently inclined toward the patient due to an unblemished previous record.

Clinical Interview With Patient and Collateral Sources

Ideally, an interview involves not only the patient but also at least one collateral source and is conducted after the patient's records have been reviewed. An interview can be seen as the opportunity to extend upon, or clarify, the information gained through the records, fill gaps about aspects of life that are not covered in records, and observe the patient's behavior. While a thorough clinical interview covers many domains, here we only provide some examples of the types of information that will aid in the assessment of EF.

With respect to the estimation of premorbid level of EF, it is useful to find out if the patient's occupational or educational success was self-driven or whether it was a result of scaffolding from parents or a spouse. It is also helpful to find out about the specific responsibilities involved in a given job, as sometimes the same job title may involve very different levels of responsibility. For those who do not have an occupational history outside a home, it is useful to inquire about their premorbid abilities to pay bills on time, plan and cook meals, organize birthday parties, or handle emergencies or other unexpected challenges.

Regarding the type, frequency, and severity of EF difficulties in daily life, it is important to cover the nature of symptoms, the course, and the broader context in which symptoms began to emerge (e.g., in the context of major stressful life events). Regarding specific symptoms, it is generally best to start the interview with open-ended questions about daily functioning and then follow up with clarification questions. For example, if a patient reports forgetfulness, it is important to determine whether the difficulty is with encoding, retrieving, and retaining information, or whether the forgetfulness reflects poor prospective memory. For patients with poor insight, such as those with difficulties in Social Cognition, the ability to speak to collateral sources is critical, as such patients may have no awareness of their deficits or have no understanding that some of their behaviors are socially inappropriate.

Assessment Methods: Patient's Presentation During Assessment

Behavioral Observations and Pathognomonic Signs

Behavioral signs of EF deficits may or may not be evident during interview and testing, although if they are, they should be noted and carefully documented for a later integration with background information and testing data. Some behavioral signs may at times be quite dramatic, and in those cases they represent pathognomonic indications of a particular syndrome. For example, a patient who is severely perseverative or echolalic, or who is extremely stimulus-bound, is likely suffering from an extreme case of the disinhibited syndrome. A patient who is extremely amotivational, stopping a task within a few seconds after starting, or perhaps even presenting with symptoms of akinetic mutism, undoubtedly falls under the rubric of the apathetic syndrome. And a patient who attempts to grope the examiner is undoubtedly afflicted with the inappropriate syndrome.

However, such clear pathognomonic signs, while relatively common among inpatients, are rarely encountered on an outpatient basis. Rather, an outpatient evaluation is more likely to be characterized by "soft" signs of EF dysfunction. For example, patients with disorganized syndrome are prone to arriving late and missing appointments, as well as forgetting to bring requested items such as reading glasses or hearing aids. Patients with disinhibited syndrome might begin to work on a task before the instructions are completely given, may repeatedly rummage through their pockets for their cell phone, or may reach across the table for the examiner's pen or a stopwatch. Patients with apathetic syndrome often need additional prompting to continue with the task at hand, speeding up after prompts, only to slow down again a few seconds later. In the case of the inappropriate syndrome, presentation may include inappropriately forward remarks, insensitive jokes, or awkward and uncomfortable social interactions.

Challenges in the Use of Standardized Tests

Clinicians have many choices when deciding how to assess EF using standardized neuropsychological measures. When making this decision, there are a number of important considerations to take into account. First, it is well accepted in neuropsychology that cognition is hierarchically structured, such that more complex (i.e., higher order) processes, such as EF, rely on more basic (i.e., lower order) processes. Some of the lower order processes that contribute to EF performance include, but are not are not limited to, arousal, sensory perception, processing speed, and basic motor functioning (Stuss, Picton, & Alexander, 2001). Limitations in lower order processes can produce deficits on tasks that purport to measure higher order processes. Thus, when assessing EF, it is critical that lower order processes be accounted for.

Conveniently, there are some tasks that are designed explicitly to account for component lower order processes that contribute to a specific measure of EF. For example, most commonly used versions of the Stroop task require that patients complete a trial of color naming and word reading to account for those component processes, before completing the executively taxing color–word interference trial. If performance is equally impaired across all three conditions, then the clinician can infer that a lower order process or set of processes (e.g., slow verbal output) is the cause of the apparent EF deficit on the color–word interference trial. In contrast, a large discrepancy across conditions, with the color–word interference trial being most impaired, suggests a bona fide executive dysfunction.

However, control conditions that allow for this subtraction of lower order processes are not available for all measures of EF, nor do they represent the only means by which the clinician can address this issue. A typical neuropsychological battery includes measures that tap into all major neurocognitive domains, including many of the relevant lower order processes such as perception, language, and speed of processing. Thus, the patient's cognitive profile across multiple neurocognitive domains allows the clinician to determine whether impaired performance on EF measures can be explained by a deficit elsewhere.

Processing speed is a particularly important lower order process for the clinician to consider. Many commonly used EF measures are timed, and completion time often represents the primary outcome score. This is an especially relevant consideration for populations with known processing speed difficulties. For example, a recent study using both neuropsychological measures and brain imaging suggests that deficits on common EF measures can be completely accounted for by processing speed limitations in patients with multiple sclerosis (Leavitt et al., 2014). This concern is also particularly salient for older adult populations, as some literature suggests that the majority of age-related variance in EF can be accounted for by slowed processing speed (Salthouse, 2005). It is important to note, however, that other research has shown a relationship between reduced EF and aging above and beyond speed (Keys & White, 2000). A thorough review of whether speed represents the primary cause of EF deficits seen in these (and other) populations on the group level is beyond the scope of this chapter. However, the presence of these debates serves as a reminder of the importance, and difficulty, of disentangling these influences for any given patient.

One factor that complicates clinician's ability to differentiate between deficits in EF and deficits in processing speed is the fact that processing speed measures themselves are not particularly pure. It has been shown that many of the most commonly used processing speed measures in neuropsychology (e.g., the Digit Symbols Modalities Test) require goal maintenance and working memory manipulation and are therefore somewhat confounded with EF (Albinet, Boucard, Bouquet, & Audiffren, 2012; Cepeda, Blackwell, & Munakata, 2013). Therefore, instead of simply relying on subtraction logic for assessing the potential effect of lower order component processes, clinicians should include various measures of EF that rely on a diverse set of processes (e.g., verbal and visually based measures, not all of which are timed) and look for consistency and patterns across their entire battery.

In addition to the impurity of EF tests with respect to contributions from various lower order component processes, EF tests are also impure with respect to various EF subdomains. For example, letter fluency almost certainly requires the abilities to retrieve words, hold information in working memory so as to avoid repetition, monitor the retrieved words for errors or discrepancies with task rules, flexibly generate new strategies when getting stuck, and inhibit "foils," such as words that begin with the correct sound but the wrong letter. A similarly rich list of EF processes can be generated for any EF test (for a detailed discussion, see Suchy, 2015). Of course more research is needed to demonstrate empirically which aspects of EF are tapped by commonly used measures, but existing evidence does support the notion that the end score achieved on most measures (e.g., completion time or total correct responses) is the product of multiple EF processes (Jurado & Rosselli, 2007). For example, research shows design (also known as "figural") fluency measures rely on initiation, mental flexibility, and generation of strategies (Gardner, Vik, & Dasher, 2013; Kraybill & Suchy, 2008; Suchy, Kraybill, & Gidley Larson, 2010).

Unfortunately, in research involving EF, it is not uncommon to see statements that perpetuate the belief that individual tasks are pure measures of specific elemental processes (e.g., Trails B is a pure measure of mental flexibility or the Stroop only relies on inhibition). While this is an oversimplification and should be avoided, it is also the case that no one test taps into all EF processes or subdomains. Thus, it is important to ensure that any assessment battery contains a variety of EF tests, so as to cover as many different subdomains (and elemental processes) of EF as possible. Furthermore, clinicians should seek out new instruments that assess aspects of EF that are known to be missed by traditional EF measures. Specifically, the EF measures typically used in neuropsychology generally rely heavily on Executive Cognitive Functions, Response Selection, and Initiation/Maintenance, while the subdomains of Social Cognition and Meta-Tasking are often neglected. There are available measures that can help to fill these gaps, such as the WAIS-IV Advanced Clinical Solutions Social Cognition Battery (Pearson, 2009) and the Memory for Intentions Test (Raskin, Buckheit, & Sherrod, 2010).

In addition to difficulty capturing the entire EF construct, EF tests are also limited by lower reliabilities as compared to tests of other neuropsychological domains (Calamia, Markon, & Tranel, 2013). Thus, there is likely to be more variability across different EF tasks administered in a single session, as well as variability on a single EF test across time. In particular, it is not uncommon for clinicians to encounter a profile that is characterized by, for example, impaired Trail Making but normal Stroop during baseline, and the opposite pattern during reassessment. Rather than attempting to interpret these changes for each individual test, clinicians are advised to average across EF performances on each testing occasion and then examine the changes (or a lack thereof) on the composite score over time. Such practice not only facilitates interpretation but also improves test–retest reliability for the composite score relative to single tests (Suchy, 2015, p. 130).

In summary, when assessing EF using standardized testing, clinicians should ensure that they can account for the effect of lower order processes by using tasks specifically designed as controls for EF measures, integrating information about impairment in other cognitive domains, and selecting the EF measures that rely on a diverse set of lower order processes. Clinicians are also advised to give more measures of EF than they might for other cognitive domains to ensure they are adequately capturing the multifaceted construct of EF and to improve reliability. Relatedly, clinicians should avoid the trap of interpreting a single impaired measure of EF as evidence for impairment in a single EF subdomain; instead, they are advised to interpret the degree of variability across EF measures given. As discussed earlier in this chapter, variability across EF measures can itself be an indication of mild EF impairment and is likely to better predict lapses in daily life than a single impaired EF score.

CONCLUSIONS

EF is a complex, multifaceted construct. In this chapter, we relied on the Suchy (2015) model of EF that consists of five subdomains: Executive Cognitive Functions, Response Selection, Initiation/Maintenance, Meta-tasking, and Social Cognition. When assessing EF, clinicians need to carefully consider the purpose of their assessment: For diagnostic decision-making, determination of whether there has been a decline in EF from a premorbid baseline is key. Convergence of multiple methods should be used for this purpose, including review of records, interviews, behavioral observations, and comparisons of test results to demographically corrected norms. However, because EF tests tend to have lower reliabilities and because EF is vulnerable to fluctuation due to various situational factors, clinicians should avoid overinterpreting isolated impaired scores.

For decisions about functionality in daily life, clinicians need to exercise care, as criterion-based norms that could facilitate determination of functionality generally do not exist. However, some tentative conclusions can be drawn: First, if EF is moderately to severely impaired relative to population-based norms, then functional limitations can be assumed. Second, if a patient exhibits much variability on tests within a single session or exhibits even one or two severely impaired performances in the context of an otherwise normal profile, it is likely that risk for intermittent functional lapses in daily life exists.

Lastly, the chapter reviewed a number of challenges associated with standardized tests of EF, including somewhat low reliabilities, test impurity with respect to lower order component processes and with respect to other tests of EF, and a failure of any one test of EF to capture the entire EF construct. To address these limitations, we recommend that clinicians (1) use multiple tests of EF in a given battery, (2) use tests that rely on different sets of component processes, (3) average across multiple tests of EF to improve reliability (especially in serial assessments), and (4) enrich their assessment batteries with newer instruments that tap into EF subdomains that are not traditionally assessed (i.e., Meta-tasking and Social Cognition).

REFERENCES

Albinet, C. T., Boucard, G., Bouquet, C. A., & Audiffren, M. (2012). Processing speed and executive functions in cognitive aging: How to disentangle their mutual relationship? *Brain and Cognition, 79,* 1−11. Available from http://dx.doi.org/10.1016/j.bandc.2012.02.001.

Arentoft, A., Byrd, D., Monzones, J., Coulehan, K., Fuentes, A., Rosario, A., & Rivera Mindt, M. (2015). Socioeconomic status and neuropsychological functioning: Associations in an ethnically diverse HIV + cohort. *Clinical Neuropsychologist, 29*(2), 232−254. Available from http://dx.doi.org/10.1080/13854046.2015.1029974.

Baldo, J. V., Shimamura, A. P., Delis, D. C., Kramer, J., & Kaplan, E. (2001). Verbal and design fluency in patients with frontal lobe lesions. *Journal of the International Neuropsychological Society: JINS, 7,* 586−596. Available from http://dx.doi.org/10.1017/S1355617701755063.

Baumeister, R. F., & Alquist, J. L. (2009). Is there a downside to good self-control? *Self and Identity, 8,* 115−130.

Baumeister, R. F., Vohs, K. D., & Tice, D. M. (2007). The strength model of self-control. *Current Directions in Psychological Science, 16,* 351−355. Available from http://dx.doi.org/10.1111/j.1467-8721.2007.00534.x.

Benitez, A., & Gunstad, J. (2012). Poor sleep quality diminishes cognitive functioning independent of depression and anxiety in healthy young adults. *Clinical Neuropsychologist, 26*(2), 214−223.

Bernier, A., Beauchamp, M. H., Bouvette-Turcot, A. A., Carlson, S. M., & Carrier, J. (2013). Sleep and cognition in preschool years: Specific links to executive functioning. *Child Development*, *84*, 1542–1553. Available from http://dx.doi.org/10.1111/cdev.12063.

Berryman, C., Stanton, T. R., Bowering, K. J., Tabor, A., McFarlane, A., & Moseley, G. L. (2014). Do people with chronic pain have impaired executive function? A meta-analytical review. *Clinical Psychology Review*. Available from http://dx.doi.org/10.1016/j.cpr.2014.08.003.

Burgess, P. W., Alderman, N., Evans, J., Emslie, H., & Wilson, B. A. (1998). The ecological validity of tests of executive function. *Journal of the International Neuropsychological Society: JINS*, *4*, 547–558.

Burgess, P. W., Alderman, N., Forbes, C., Costello, A., Coates, L. M.-A., Dawson, D. R., & Channon, S. (2006). The case for the development and use of "ecologically valid" measures of executive function in experimental and clinical neuropsychology. *Journal of the International Neuropsychological Society: JINS*, *12*, 194–209. Available from http://dx.doi.org/10.1017/S1355617706060310.

Burton, C. L., Strauss, E., Hultsch, D. F., & Hunter, M. A. (2006). Cognitive functioning and everyday problem solving in older adults. *Clinical Neuropsychologist*, *20*, 432–452.

Calamia, M., Markon, K., & Tranel, D. (2013). The robust reliability of neuropsychological measures: Meta-analyses of test-retest correlations. *Clinical Neuropsychologist*, *27*, 1077–1105. Available from http://dx.doi.org/10.1080/13854046.2013.809795.

Cepeda, N. J., Blackwell, K. A., & Munakata, Y. (2013). Speed isn't everything: Complex processing speed measures mask individual differences and developmental changes in executive control. *Developmental Science*, *16*, 269–286. Available from http://dx.doi.org/10.1111/desc.12024.

Constantinidou, F., Christodoulou, M., & Prokopiou, J. (2012). The effects of age and education on executive functioning and oral naming performance in Greek Cypriot adults: The neurocognitive study for the aging. *Folia Phoniatrica et Logopaedica*, *64*, 187–198. Available from http://dx.doi.org/10.1159/000340015.

Costa, P. T., & McCrae, R. R. (1992). *Manual for the Revised NEO Personality Inventory (NEO-PI-R) and the NEO Five-Factor Inventory (NEO-PI)*. Odessa, FL: Psychological Assessment Resources.

Cripe, L. I. (1996). *The ecological validity of executive function testing. Ecological validity of neuropsychological testing* (pp. 171–202). Delray Beach, FL: Gr Press/St Lucie Press, Inc.

Cummings, J. L., & Miller, B. L. (2007). *Conceptual and clinical aspects of the frontal lobes. The human frontal lobes: Functions and disorders* (2nd ed. New York, NY: Guilford Press.

Demakis, G. J. (2003). A meta-analytic review of the sensitivity of the Wisconsin Card Sorting Test to frontal and lateralized frontal brain damage. *Neuropsychology*, *17*, 255–264. Available from http://dx.doi.org/10.1037/0894-4105.17.2.255.

Dorbath, L., Hasselhorn, M., & Titz, C. (2013). Effects of education on executive functioning and its trainability. *Educational Gerontology*, *39*, 314–325. Available from http://dx.doi.org/10.1080/03601277.2012.700820.

Duffy, J. D., Campbell, J. J., III, Salloway, S. P., & Malloy, P. F. (2001). *Regional prefrontal syndromes: A theoretical and clinical overview. The frontal lobes and neuropsychiatric illness* (pp. 113–123). Arlington, VA: American Psychiatric Publishing, Inc.

Eslinger, P. J., Moore, P., Anderson, C., & Grossman, M. (2011). Social cognition, executive functioning, and neuroimaging correlates of empathic deficits in frontotemporal dementia. *Journal of Neuropsychiatry and Clinical Neurosciences*, *23*(1), 74–82. Available from http://dx.doi.org/10.1176/appi.neuropsych.23.1.74.

Euler, M., Niermeyer, M., & Suchy, Y. (2016). Neurocognitive and neurophysiological correlates of motor planning during familiar and novel contexts. *Neuropsychology, 30*(1), 109–119.

Franchow, E. I., & Suchy, Y. (2015). Naturally-occurring expressive suppression in daily life depletes executive functioning. *Emotion, 15*, 78–89.

Franchow, E. I., Suchy, Y., Thorgusen, S. R., & Williams, P. G. (2013). More than education: Openness to experience contributes to cognitive reserve in older adulthood. *Journal of Aging Science, 1*, 109. Available from http://dx.doi.org/10.4172/2329-8847.1000109.

Gardner, E., Vik, P., & Dasher, N. (2013). Strategy use on the Ruff Figural Fluency Test. *Clinical Neuropsychologist, 27*, 37–41. Available from http://dx.doi.org/10.1080/13854046.2013.771216.

Goldberg, E., & Podell, K. (2000). Adaptive decision making, ecological validity, and the frontal lobes. *Journal of Clinical and Experimental Neuropsychology, 22*, 56–68.

Grigsby, J., Kaye, K., Kowalsky, J., & Kramer, A. M. (2002). Association of behavioral self-regulation with concurrent functional capacity among stroke rehabilitation patients. *Journal of Clinical Geropsychology, 8*, 25–33.

Guoping, S., Kan, Z., Danmin, M., & Fuen, H. (2008). Effects of sleep deprivation on executive function. *Psychological Science, 31*, 32–34.

Hagger, M. S., Wood, C., Stiff, C., & Chatzisarantis, N. L. D. (2010). Ego depletion and the strength model of self-control: A meta-analysis. *Psychological Bulletin, 136*, 495–525. Available from http://dx.doi.org/10.1037/a0019486.

Harrison, Y., & Horne, J. A. (2000). The impact of sleep deprivation on decision making: A review. *Journal of Experimental Psychology. Applied, 6*, 236–249. Available from http://dx.doi.org/10.1037/1076-898X.6.3.236.

Heilbronner, R. L., Sweet, J. J., Morgan, J. E., Larrabee, G. J., & Millis, S. R. (2009). American Academy of Clinical Neuropsychology Consensus Conference Statement on the neuropsychological assessment of effort, response bias, and malingering. *Clinical Neuropsychologist, 23*, 1093–1129.

Hensler, M., Wolfe, K., Lebensburger, J., Nieman, J., Barnes, M., Nolan, W., & Madan-Swain, A. (2014). Social skills and executive function among youth with sickle cell disease: A preliminary investigation. *Journal of Pediatric Psychology, 39*, 493–500.

Iampietro, M., Giovannetti, T., Drabick, D. A. G., & Kessler, R. K. (2012). Empirically defined patterns of executive function deficits in schizophrenia and their relation to everyday functioning: A person-centered approach. *Clinical Neuropsychologist, 26*(7), 1166–1185.

Jurado, M. B., & Rosselli, M. (2007). The elusive nature of executive functions: A review of our current understanding. *Neuropsychology Review, 17*(3), 213–233. Available from http://dx.doi.org/10.1007/s11065-007-9040-z.

Karp, J. F., Reynolds, C. F., III, Butters, M. A., Dew, M. A., Mazumdar, S., Begley, A. E., & Weiner, D. K. (2006). The relationship between pain and mental flexibility in older adult pain clinic patients. *Pain Medicine, 7*, 444–452.

Keys, B. A., & White, D. A. (2000). Exploring the relationship between age, executive abilities, and psychomotor speed. *Journal of the International Neuropsychological Society: JINS, 6*(1), 76–82. Available from http://dx.doi.org/10.1017/S1355617700611098.

Kraybill, M. L., & Suchy, Y. (2008). Evaluating the role of motor regulation in figural fluency: Partialing variance in the Ruff Figural Fluency Test. *Journal of Clinical and Experimental Neuropsychology, 30*, 903–912. Available from http://dx.doi.org/10.1080/13803390701874361.

Kraybill, M. L., & Suchy, Y. (2011). Executive functioning, motor programming, and functional independence: Accounting for variance, people, and time. *Clinical Neuropsychologist, 25*, 210–223.

Kraybill, M. L., Thorgusen, S. R., & Suchy, Y. (2013). The Push-Turn-Taptap task outperforms measures of executive functioning in predicting declines in functionality: Evidence-based approach to test validation. *Clinical Neuropsychologist, 27*, 238–255.

Leavitt, V. M., Wylie, G., Krch, D., Chiaravalloti, N., DeLuca, J., & Sumowski, J. F. (2014). Does slowed processing speed account for executive deficits in multiple sclerosis? Evidence from neuropsychological performance and structural neuroimaging. *Rehabilitation Psychology, 59*, 422–428. Available from http://dx.doi.org/10.1037/a0037517.

Lezak, M. D., Howieson, D. B., Bigler, E. D., & Tranel, D. (2012). *Neuropsychological assessment* (5th Ed). New York, NY: Oxford University Press.

MacDougall, E. E., & Mansbach, W. E. (2013). The Judgment Test of the Neuropsychological Assessment Battery (NAB): Psychometric considerations in an assisted-living sample. *Clinical Neuropsychologist, 27*(5), 827–839. Available from http://dx.doi.org/10.1080/13854046.2013.786759.

Manly, J. J. (2005). Advantages and disadvantages of separate norms for African Americans. *Clinical Neuropsychologist, 19*, 270–275. Available from http://dx.doi.org/10.1080/13854040590945346.

Manning, K. J., Clarke, C., Lorry, A., Weintraub, D., Wilkinson, J. R., Duda, J. E., & Moberg, P. J. (2012). Medication management and neuropsychological performance in Parkinson's disease. *Clinical Neuropsychologist, 26*(1), 45–58. Available from http://dx.doi.org/10.1080/13854046.2011.639312.

Martins, I. P., Maruta, C., Freitas, V., & Mares, I. (2013). Executive performance in older Portuguese adults with low education. *Clinical Neuropsychologist, 27*, 410–425. Available from http://dx.doi.org/10.1080/13854046.2012.748094.

Martyr, A., & Clare, L. (2012). Executive function and activities of daily living in Alzheimer's disease: A correlational meta-analysis. *Dementia and Geriatric Cognitive Disorders, 33*, 189–203. Available from http://dx.doi.org/10.1159/000338233.

Murdock, K. W., Oddi, K. B., & Bridgett, D. J. (2013). Cognitive correlates of personality: Links between executive functioning and the big five personality traits. *Journal of Individual Differences, 34*, 97–104.

Neguţ, A., Matu, S.-A., Sava, F. A., & David, D. (2016). Virtual reality measures in neuropsychological assessment: A meta-analytic review. *Clinical Neuropsychologist, 30*(2), 165–184. Available from http://dx.doi.org/10.1080/13854046.2016.1144793.

Niermeyer, M. A., Franchow, E. I., & Suchy, Y. (2016). Reported expressive suppression in daily life is associated with slower action planning. *Journal of the International Neuropsychological Society: JINS, 22*, 671–681. Available from http://dx.doi.org/10.1017/S1355617716000473.

Norman, D. A., & Shallice, T. (1986). Attention to action: Willed and automatic control of behavior. In D. L. Shapiro, & G. Schwartz (Eds.), *Consciousness and self-regulation in research: Advances in research*. New York, NY: Plenum Press SP.

Pearson (2009). *Advanced clinical solutions for WAIS-IV and WMS-IV*. San Antonio, TX: Pearson.

Plehn, K., Marcopulos, B. A., & McLain, C. A. (2004). The relationship between neuropsychological test performance, social functioning, and instrumental activities of daily living in a sample of rural older adults. *Clinical Neuropsychologist, 18*, 101–113.

Puente, A. N., Lindbergh, C. A., & Miller, L. S. (2015). The relationship between cognitive reserve and functional ability is mediated by executive functioning in older adults. *Clinical Neuropsychologist, 29*(1), 67–81. Available from http://dx.doi.org/10.1080/13854046.2015.1005676.

Raskin, S., Buckheit, C., & Sherrod, C. (2010). *MIST Memory for Intentions Test professional manual.* Lutz, FL: Psychological Assessment Resources.

Reader, S. M., & Laland, K. N. (2002). Social intelligence, innovation, and enhanced brain size in primates. *Proceedings of the National Academy of Sciences of the United States of America, 99,* 4436−4441.

Reitan, R. M., & Wolfson, D. (1995). Category test and trail making test as measures of frontal lobe functions. *Clinical Neuropsychologist, 9,* 50−56. Available from http://dx.doi.org/10.1080/13854049508402057.

Rog, L. A., Park, L. Q., Harvey, D. J., Huang, C.-J., Mackin, S., & Farias, S. T. (2014). The independent contributions of cognitive impairment and neuropsychiatric symptoms to everyday function in older adults. *Clinical Neuropsychologist, 28*(2), 215−236. Available from http://dx.doi.org/10.1080/13854046.2013.876101.

Salthouse, T. A. (2005). Relations between cognitive abilities and measures of executive functioning. *Neuropsychology, 19,* 532−545. Available from http://dx.doi.org/10.1037/0894-4105.19.4.532.

Santorelli, G. D., & Ready, R. E. (2015). Alexithymia and executive function in younger and older adults. *Clinical Neuropsychologist, 29*(7), 938−955. Available from http://dx.doi.org/10.1080/13854046.2015.1123296.

Shallice, T., & Burgess, P. W. (1991). Deficits in strategy application following frontal lobe damage in man. *Brain, 114,* 727−741.

Snyder, H. R., Miyake, A., & Hankin, B. L. (2015). Advancing understanding of executive function impairments and psychopathology: Bridging the gap between clinical and cognitive approaches. *Frontiers in Psychology, 6,* 328. Available from http://dx.doi.org/10.3389/fpsyg.2015.00328.

Stuss, D. T. (2011). Functions of the frontal lobes: Relation to executive functions. *Journal of the International Neuropsychological Society, 17,* 759−765. Available from http://dx.doi.org/10.1017/S1355617711000695.

Stuss, D. T., Picton, T. W., & Alexander, M. P. (2001). Consciousness, self-awareness, and the frontal lobes. In S. P. Salloway, P. F. Malloy, & J. D. Duffy (Eds.), *The frontal lobes and neuropsychiatric illness* (pp. 101−109). Arlington, VA: American Psychiatric Publishing, Inc.

Suchy, Y. (2009). Executive functioning: Overview, assessment, and research issues for nonneuropsychologists. *Annals of Behavioral Medicine, 37,* 106−116. Available from http://dx.doi.org/10.1007/s12160-009-9097-4.

Suchy, Y. (2015). *Executive functioning: A comprehensive guide for clinical practice.* New York, NY: Oxford University Press.

Suchy, Y., Euler, M., & Eastvold, A. (2014). Exaggerated reaction to novelty as a subclinical consequence of mild traumatic brain injury. *Brain Injury, 28,* 972−979. Available from http://dx.doi.org/10.3109/02699052.2014.888766.

Suchy, Y., Kraybill, M. L., & Franchow, E. (2011). Instrumental activities of daily living among community-dwelling older adults: Discrepancies between self-report and performance are mediated by cognitive reserve. *Journal of Clinical and Experimental Neuropsychology, 33,* 92−100. Available from http://dx.doi.org/10.1080/13803395.2010.493148.

Suchy, Y., Kraybill, M. L., & Gidley Larson, J. C. (2010). Understanding design fluency: Motor and executive contributions. *Journal of the International Neuropsychological Society: JINS, 16,* 26−37. Available from http://dx.doi.org/10.1017/S1355617709990804.

Tripathi, R., Kumar, K., Bharath, S., Marimuthu, P., & Varghese, M. (2014). Age, education and gender effects on neuropsychological functions in healthy Indian older adults. *Dementia & Neuropsychologia, 8,* 148−154.

Vordenberg, J. A., Barrett, J. J., Doninger, N. A., Contardo, C. P., & Ozoude, K. A. (2014). Application of the Brixton spatial anticipation test in stroke: Ecological validity and performance characteristics. *Clinical Neuropsychologist*, *28*(2), 300–316. Available from http://dx.doi.org/10.1080/13854046.2014.881555.

West, R., Murphy, K. J., Armilio, M. L., Craik, F. I. M., & Stuss, D. T. (2002). Lapses of intention and performance variability reveal age-related increases in fluctuations of executive control. *Brain and Cognition*, *49*, 402–419. Available from http://dx.doi.org/10.1006/brcg.2001.1507.

Williams, P. G., Suchy, Y., & Kraybill, M. L. (2010). Five-factor model personality traits and executive functioning among older adults. *Journal of Research in Personality*, *44*, 485–491.

Wingbermühle, E., Theunissen, H., Verhoeven, W. M. A., Kessels, R. P. C., & Egger, J. I. M. (2012). The neurocognition of alexithymia: Evidence from neuropsychological and neuroimaging studies. *Acta Neuropsychiatrica*, *24*(2), 67–80.

Zelazo, P. D., Chandler, M., & Crone, E. (2010). *Developmental social cognitive neuroscience. The Jean Piaget symposium series*. New York, NY: Psychology Press.

Index

A

ACC. *See* Anterior cingulate cortex (ACC)
Acquired immune deficiency syndrome
  (AIDS), 525–526
"Action organ", 4
Activation likelihood estimation (ALE),
  173–177, 254, 256*t*, 259*f*
  creation of ALE maps, 173–177
AD. *See* Alzheimer's disease (AD)
Adaptive control hypothesis, 154
Adaptive gating mechanism, 120
Adaptive resonance theory, 111, 117
Addiction, 231–232
  executive dysfunction in
    cannabis, 396
    cocaine, 396–397
    methamphetamine, 397–398
    opioids, 398
ADHD. *See* Attention-deficit hyperactivity
  disorder (ADHD)
ADHD Rating Scale IV (ARS-IV), 392–393
ADHD-combined subtype (ADHD-C),
  346–348
ADNFLE. *See* Autosomal dominant nocturnal
  frontal lobe epilepsy (ADNFLE)
Adolescence, 148, 335, 339
  early, 155–156
  skills of, 150–151
Adolescents, 150–151, 328, 337
  developmental factor in, 337
  with TS, 336, 339–340, 343
Adult six-layered cerebral neocortex, 42
Adulthood, 336
  brain networks and executive functions in
    older, 182–187
    goal-directed perceptual processing,
      182–183

Adults, 340–341
  older, 180–182
  younger, 177–179
Aging, 170, 187–189, 497–498. *See also*
  Neurocognitive—aging
Agrammatic PPA. *See* Nonfluent variant PPA
  (nfvPPA)
AI. *See* Anterior insula (AI)
AIDS. *See* Acquired immune deficiency
  syndrome (AIDS)
AIFO. *See* Anterior insula/inferior frontal
  operculum (AIFO)
Alcohol, 231
  effect of, 505
  chronic, 504
  intake, 536
ALE. *See* Activation likelihood estimation
  (ALE)
Alerting attention, 151–152
Alpha-2A noradrenergic influence, 33–34
α-amino-3-hydroxy-5-methyl-4-
  isoxazolepropionic acid receptor
  (AMPAR), 28–29, 28*f*
α2A-adrenoreceptors (α2A-AR), 33
ALS. *See* Amyotrophic lateral sclerosis (ALS)
Alzheimer's disease (AD), 23–24, 434–435,
  445–449, 526–527
  fvAD, 447–449
American Psychological Association, 200
American Society of Addiction Medicine, 231
Amos's model, 118–119
AMPAR. *See* α-amino-3-hydroxy-5-methyl-4-
  isoxazolepropionic acid receptor
  (AMPAR)
Amygdala, 225–226, 235, 301–302
Amyotrophic lateral sclerosis (ALS),
  452–453, 461

Analysis of variance (ANOVA), 369
Anterior cingulate cortex (ACC), 72–74, 110,
    220–222, 249–250, 351–352,
    493–494
Anterior insula (AI), 253
Anterior insula/inferior frontal operculum
    (AIFO), 75
  network, 86–88
  subregions, 92
Anxiety
  child self-report of, 378t, 392
  cognitive perseveration in disorders of
    mood and, 234–240
  disorders, 278–279
  emotional and cognitive perseveration in
    disorders, 234–240
Apathy, 448–449, 455–456, 461, 463
Apolipoprotein E (APOE), 434–435
ARS-IV. See ADHD Rating Scale IV (ARS-
    IV)
ASD. See Autism spectrum disorder (ASD)
Asian Disease Problem, 108
Assessment methods, EF, 558–560
  clinical interview with patient and collateral
    sources, 559–560
  considerations and challenges, 553–558
    daily functioning, 555–558
    ecological validity, 555–558
  in dementia, 467–470, 468t
  patient's presentation during assessment,
    560–563
    behavioral observations, 560
    challenges in standardized tests,
      561–563
    pathognomonic signs, 560
  records review, 558–559
Asymmetric
  bilateral tonic seizures, 410
  neural development, 339
  resting tremor severity, 365–366
Attention, 508–509, 526–528, 530. See also
    Executive functions (EF)
  skills, 149–150
  training, 508–509
Attention Network Test, 149–150
Attention-deficit hyperactivity disorder
    (ADHD), 25, 76–77, 144–145, 319,
    321, 334, 338–339, 343–344,
    349–350, 366, 488, 505–506
  children with, 350
  differences between ADHD and controls,
    322–323

  hallmark symptoms of, 505–506
  rating scale, 370t
"Attentive set", 8
Attraction effect, 109
Auditory–visual memory cells, 10
Autism, 144–145
Autism spectrum disorder (ASD), 42, 47–48,
    255–262, 366
  ALE metaanalysis, 259f
    of neuroimaging studies of cognitive
      control, 260t
Autonomic response, 321, 323
Autosomal dominant nocturnal frontal lobe
    epilepsy (ADNFLE), 407
  linkage analysis in, 407–408
  phenotype, 408

B

Back propagation network, 119–120
BAFQ. See Brock Adaptive Functioning
    Questionnaire (BAFQ)
Balkanization of clinical neuroscience, 384
Basal ganglia, 301–302, 335
  basal ganglia–thalamocortical loops, 109,
    116, 118
  HD affecting, 466
  hyperactivation of, 271
  models of PFC–basal ganglia interactions,
    115, 121
  performing gating function, 121
Bayesian model selection process, 95–96
BDNF. See Brain-derived neurotrophic factor
    (BDNF)
Behavior Rating Inventory of Executive
    Function (BRIEF), 146–147,
    201–202, 393
Behavioral
  flexibility, 219–220, 303
  neurological literature, 382–383
  observations, EF, 560
  policies, 144–145
  process, 122
  systems, 337
Behavioral variant FTD (bvFTD), 452–456
  behavior and affect, 454–456
  executive functions, 453–454
Benzodiazepines, 504
Bias nodes, 117
"Biased competition", 9–10
Bigrams, 114
Bilingual brain, 148

Bilingualism, 148, 154
Biopsychosocial
    approach, 340
    paradigm, 348–349
Blindsight, 134–135
Block Design Test, 535
Blood oxygen level-dependent (BOLD),
    537–538
Blood pressure (BP), 526
BOLD. *See* Blood oxygen level-dependent
    (BOLD)
Bottom-up influences, 335–336, 339–340
Botvinick–Plaut model, 114
BP. *See* Blood pressure (BP)
Brain, 350
    adaptation, 342–343
    brain-based model of decision data, 111
    brain's sensitive period, 153–154
    development, 337
    function, 187–189, 339–340
    lesions associated with EF deficits,
        425–426
    networks in older adulthood, 182–187
        goal-directed perceptual processing,
        182–183
    processes, 334–335
    regions, 346–348
    science, 169
    structure, 169–170
    systems, 554
Brain activity, 170, 349
    EF, aging and, 172–182
        metaanalysis methods, 172–173
        metaanalysis results, 177–182
Brain imaging
    in children, 496
    research, 493–495
        functional neuroimaging, 493–494
        structural neuroimaging, 494–495
    techniques, 105
Brain-derived neurotrophic factor (BDNF),
    434
BrainMap, 173–177
    GingerALE software, 279
BRIEF. *See* Behavior Rating Inventory of
    Executive Function (BRIEF); Brief
    Rating Scale of Executive Function
    (BRIEF)
Brief Rating Scale of Executive Function
    (BRIEF), 144–145
Brief Visuospatial Memory Test-revised
    (BVMT-R), 391

Brock Adaptive Functioning Questionnaire
    (BAFQ), 201–202, 427
bvFTD. *See* Behavioral variant FTD (bvFTD)
BVMT-R. *See* Brief Visuospatial Memory
    Test-revised (BVMT-R)

C

California Verbal Learning Test (CVLT), 490
Cambridge Neuropsychological Test Automated
    Battery (CANTAB), 144–145
    Rapid Visual Processing, 396
    Spatial Working Memory, 397
cAMP. *See* Cyclic AMP (cAMP)
Cannabis, 395–396
CANTAB. *See* Cambridge
    Neuropsychological Test Automated
    Battery (CANTAB)
"Capacity to propositionise", 3
Card sorting data, 117
Caret software, 177
CART. *See* Combine antiretroviral therapy
    (CART)
Catechol-O-Methyl-Transferase (COMT), 303,
    433–434
Catecholamine modulation of mechanisms,
    32–33
CBCL. *See* Child Behaviour Checklist (CBCL)
CBD. *See* Corticobasal degeneration (CBD)
CBS. *See* Corticobasal syndrome (CBS)
CBT. *See* Cognitive behavioral therapy
    (CBT); Cognitive bias task (CBT)
CCN. *See* Cognitive control network (CCN)
CCPT-II. *See* Conners' Continuous
    Performance Test-II (CCPT-II)
Ceiling effect, 173, 203–204
Cerebral activation–arousal deficit, 532
Cerebral cortex, 4–6
    of human brain, gene expression in, 50–61
        global gene expression patterns in
        cerebral cortex, 50–52
        noncoding RNAs as posttranscriptional
        regulators of gene expression, 58–59
        sex-biased gene expression patterns and
        laterality, 57–58
        specificities of human brain
        transcriptome during postnatal period,
        55–57
        specificities of human neocortical
        transcriptome during prenatal period,
        52–54
        transcriptomic studies, 59–61

Cerebral neocortex
  and circuitry in human fetal brain,
    development of, 42–48
  cortical pathway development in human
    fetal brain, 45*f*
  transient patterns of lamination in
    neocortical cerebral wall, 44*f*
Cerebrovascular disease, 449–451
ChE. *See* Cholinesterase (ChE)
Child Behaviour Checklist (CBCL), 368, 393
Child self-report
  of anxiety, 392
  scales, 373
Childhood, 154–155, 336–337, 339
  childhood-onset disorder, 334
  early, 151–152
  executive functions, 152–153
  FLE, 407
  trauma, 495–497
Children, 154, 495
  ADHD, 322–323
  with ADHD-C, 346
  brain imaging in, 496
  with impaired top-down control, 339–340
  with TS, 336–338, 340–341, 348
  voluntary control of saccades in, 321
Cholinesterase (ChE), 46
CHRNA4. *See* Coding for alpha 4 (CHRNA4)
CHRNB2. *See* Coding for beta 2 (CHRNB2)
Chronic
  alcohol, 504
  cannabis, 396
  cocaine, 397
  heroin, 398
  methamphetamine, 397–398
  pain, 398
  PTSD, 489
  stress
    executive dysfunction in, 309–312
    exposure, 302–303
  tic disorder, 341
Chronic kidney disease (CKD), 525–526,
    530–533
  cognitive impairment in patients with, 531*f*
  executive function in patients with ESRD
    with dialysis, 530–532
    kidney transplant, 532–533
Cingulate
  gyrus, 253–254
  seizures, 409
CKD. *See* Chronic kidney disease (CKD)
Clinical models, 198–199

Clinical neuropsychology, 207–208
  clinical models in, 198–199
  diagnoses types, 554
CNS. *See* Conserved noncoding sequences
    (CNS)
Cocaine, 231, 395–397
Coding for alpha 4 (CHRNA4), 407
Coding for beta 2 (CHRNB2), 407
Cognitive behavioral therapy (CBT),
    351–352, 507
Cognitive bias task (CBT), 321, 326,
    363–365
Cognitive control, 6, 249–250, 335, 424
  ALE metaanalysis of pooled data, 274*t*
  ASD, 255–262
  CCN, 252–254
    brain regions, 255*f*
    deficits in patient populations, 254–255
  depression, 267–272, 268*f*
  information theory approach to cognitive
    control, 250–252
  models, 120–122
  processes, 184
  supplemental method, 279
  SZ, 262–267, 263*f*
Cognitive control network (CCN), 252–254
  brain regions, 255*f*
  deficits in CCN deficits across three
    disorders, 272
  deficits in patient populations, 254–255
Cognitive processing therapy (CPT), 507
Cognitive/cognition(s), 85, 223, 228–229
  aging, 169
  cognitive-process model, 119
  cognitive–experiential theory, 112
  constructs
    network-oriented cognitive constructing,
      88–91
    VOODOO neuroimaging validations of,
      82–84
  disorders, 525
  domains, 34
  dysfunctions, 539
  executive control, 351
  flexibility, 219–220, 227, 303, 395–397,
    424–425
  functions, 41, 302–303
    executive function, 491–492
    in PTSD, 489–493
    working memory, 492–493
  metacognition, 134
  models, 198–199

neuroscience, 105
perseveration in disorders of mood and anxiety, 234–240
processes, 94, 106, 122, 319, 343
profiles, 554
psychophysiological model, 341
reasoning, 327–328, 328*f*
recognition and identification of hemi-TS subtypes, 379–381
rehabilitation of EF, 429–431
role for RIFG in, 78–81
selection mechanisms, 326
social, 560–561
theory, 321
Cold EF task, 338–340, 351
Collins–Frank model, 121
Color-Word Interference Test, Condition 3 (CW3), 389
Color-Word Interference Test, Condition 4 (CW4), 389
Combine antiretroviral therapy (CART), 533
Community Participation through Self-Efficacy Skills Development program goal (COMPASS goal), 431–432
Comorbid PTSD, 504
"Comorbid" clinical entity, 385
"Comorbid" parallel disorder, 382–383
Comorbidities, 505–506
COMPASS goal. *See* Community Participation through Self-Efficacy Skills Development program goal (COMPASS goal)
Compensatory behavior, 342–343
Competitive queuing, 114
Compulsive touching, 454–455
Computational decision theories, 108
Computational models, 106, 122
Computer-based HDT. *See* Computer-based Hungry Donkey Task (Computer-based HDT)
Computer-based Hungry Donkey Task (Computer-based HDT), 344
COMT. *See* Catechol-O-Methyl-Transferase (COMT)
Conditioned stimulus (CS), 235–236
Conners' Continuous Performance Test-II (CCPT-II), 390–391
Conscious perception, 129
argument based on lesion studies, 133–134
implications for consciousness theories, 138–139

"no-report" argument against PFC's, 129–132
paradigms, 134–135
PFC in, 129
PFC lesions, 136–138
responses to "lesion" argument, 134–136
responses to no-report argument, 132–133
Consciousness
implications for theories, 138–139
"no-report" argument against PFC's in, 129–132
Conserved noncoding sequences (CNS), 54
Context-dependent response, 326–327
Context-independent reasoning, 326
"Contingency negative variation", 8
Continuous performance tasks (CPT), 119–120, 490
Corollary discharge, 26–27
Correlation analyses, 202
Cortical circuitry, prolonged maturation of, 47–48
Cortical plate (CP), 42–44
Cortical-striatal-thalamocortical circuits (CSTC circuits), 337–338
Corticobasal degeneration (CBD), 446
Corticobasal syndrome (CBS), 457
Corticocortical reentry, 12
Corticospinal tract, 406
Corticotropin-releasing hormone (CRH), 407–408
CP. *See* Cortical plate (CP)
CPT. *See* Cognitive processing therapy (CPT); Continuous performance tasks (CPT)
CRH. *See* Corticotropin-releasing hormone (CRH)
Cross-modal memory cells, 10
Cross-sectional decision-making study, 346–348
CS. *See* Conditioned stimulus (CS)
CSTC circuits. *See* Cortical-striatal-thalamocortical circuits (CSTC circuits)
CVLT. *See* California Verbal Learning Test (CVLT)
CW3. *See* Color-Word Interference Test, Condition 3 (CW3)
Cyclic AMP (cAMP), 29–30
Cytochrome P450-2D6 genotypes (CYP2D6 genotypes), 398

D

D1 receptors (D1R), 29–30
DA. *See* Dopamine (DA)
dACC. *See* Dorsal anterior cingulate cortex (dACC)
DAN. *See* Dorsal attention network (DAN)
Daunting disorder, 348–351
Day/Night task, 146–147
DECHA. *See* Default-Executive Coupling Hypothesis of Aging (DECHA)
Decision field theory, 109
Decision-making, 12–15, 302–303, 319–321, 323–326, 333, 338–339, 395, 397–398
  deficits, 396–398
  differences between frontal lesion group and controls, 325–326, 325*f*
  models, 107–113
    IGT models, 109–111
    models of other decision data and phenomena, 111–113
  processes, 352
  skills, 349, 396
  subjects and methods, 323–325, 324*f*, 325*f*
  task, 346, 350
  test, 306–307
Default mode network (DMN), 8, 184, 259–262
Default-Executive Coupling Hypothesis of Aging (DECHA), 185–187
Dehaene and Changeux's model, 118
Delis–Kaplan Executive Function Scale, 490
Delis–Kaplan Executive Function System (D-KEFS), 146–147, 199, 453–454
Dementia with Lewy bodies (DLB), 446, 464–465
Dementia(s), 445–446
  Alzheimer's disease, 446–449
  assessment of executive function in, 467–470, 468*t*
  DLB, 464–465
  FTD, 452–457
  HD, 465–467
  MND, 461–462
  PD, 462–463
  PSP-CBS, 457–461
  VaD, 449–451
Demographic characteristics, 344, 367*t*, 369
Demographically corrected norms, 557–558
"Dense" coding scheme, 137
Depression, 267–272, 503–504

ALE metaanalysis, 268*f*
  of neuroimaging studies, 269*t*
  rumination in, 237–240
Depression symptoms, child self-report of, 392
Design Fluency Test, condition 3 (DF), 390
DEU. *See* Differential exon usage (DEU)
Developmental factors, PTSD, 495–498
  aging, 497–498
  childhood trauma, 495–497
  executive function, 495–497
DEX. *See* Differentially expressed gene (DEX); Dysexecutive Questionnaire (DEX)
DF. *See* Design Fluency Test, condition 3 (DF)
Diabetes mellitus, 527–530
Diagnostic and Statistical Manual of Mental Disorder (DSM), 231
  DSM-5, 231, 488
  DSM-III, 488
  DSM-IV-TR criteria, 346
Diagnostic instruments for TS
  clinical questionnaires and scales
    child self-report of anxiety and depression symptoms, 392
    clinical symptoms reporting by parents, 392–393
    tic severity, 391
  neurocognitive assessment, 389–391
Dialysis, end-stage renal disease with, 530–532
Dichoptic visual masking process, 130–131
Dichotic Listening task (DL task), 390
Differential exon usage (DEU), 53
Differentially expressed gene (DEX), 50–51
Digit Symbol Test, 535
Digit Symbols Modalities Test, 562
Dimensional Change Card Sort, 146–147
Dipole field, 117
"Disorganized syndrome", 553, 560
D-KEFS. *See* Delis–Kaplan Executive Function System (D-KEFS)
DL task. *See* Dichotic Listening task (DL task)
DLB. *See* Dementia with Lewy bodies (DLB)
DLPFC. *See* Dorsolateral prefrontal cortex (DLPFC)
DM1. *See* Type 1 diabetes mellitus (DM1)
DMN. *See* Default mode network (DMN)
Domain-specific effects, 428

Dopamine (DA), 28–29, 183, 340–341, 433–434
Dopaminergic
    dysfunction, 341
    dysfunctional dopaminergic signaling, 365
    nuclei of ventral brain stem, 363
    system, 334–335
Dorsal anterior cingulate cortex (dACC), 181
Dorsal attention network (DAN), 184
Dorsal frontoparietal attention network, 220–222
Dorsal striatum, 308
Dorsolateral prefrontal cortex (DLPFC), 23–26, 111, 129, 225–226, 249–250, 306–307, 319–321, 395, 397–398, 423–424
    network connections
        strengthening mechanisms, 31–32
        weakening mechanisms, 29–31
    neural circuits in, 27f
    neurons, 118
    representational circuits, molecular regulation of, 28–29, 28f
Dorsolateral striatal circuit, 230
Dorsolateral/premotor seizures, 409
Dorsomedial striatal circuit, 230
Dramatic cognitive development, 337
Drugs impact, 395
DSM. See Diagnostic and Statistical Manual of Mental Disorder (DSM)
Dual-process approach, 341–342
Dual-process model, 342
Dynamic network connectivity, 30f, 31f
Dysexecutive Questionnaire (DEX), 201–202
Dysexecutive syndrome, 425–426
Dysfunctional emotional response, 231

E
Early adolescence, 339
Early-onset Alzheimer's disease (eoAD), 446
ECoG. See Electrocorticogram (ECoG)
Ecological tests for evaluating EF, 426–427
Ecological validity of EF tests, 555–558
EEG. See Electroencephalography (EEG)
EF. See Executive functions (EF)
Electrocorticogram (ECoG), 132–133
Electroencephalography (EEG), 406, 532
Electrophysiological signals, 8
Emotion(al)
    dysregulation, 236–237
    perception, 151

perseveration in disorders of mood and anxiety, 234–240
End-stage renal disease (ESRD), 530–532
    with dialysis, 530–532
"Endogenous heuristic" map, 155–156
"Energizing", 532
Entropy in information theory, 251
eoAD. See Early-onset Alzheimer's disease (eoAD)
Epinephrine, 433–434
Errors of commission, 492
ESRD. See End-stage renal disease (ESRD)
Excessive exploratory behaviors, 382–383
Executive attention, 7–10
Executive cognition, 99
Executive Cognitive Functions, 552
Executive control, 187–189, 250, 334–335. See also Tourette syndrome (TS)
    of cognition, 351
    processes, 170
Executive dysfunctions, 426–427, 446–447, 454
    in addiction
        cannabis, 396
        cocaine, 396–397
        methamphetamine, 397–398
        opioids, 398
    in medical conditions
        CKD, 530–533
        diabetes mellitus, 527–530
        HE, 534–536
        HIV, 533–534
        hypertension, 526–527
        medical neuropsychology, 525
        RA, 538–540
        thyroid disease, 536–538
Executive functions (EF), 21, 106–107, 119, 121–122, 143, 169, 197, 209, 219–220, 249, 319–321, 334, 421, 433–435, 487, 491–492, 503–504, 551–553
    aging, brain function, and executive control, 187–189
    APOE, 434–435
    assessment considerations and challenges, 553–558
        daily functioning, 555–558
        ecological validity, 555–558
    assessment methods, 558–563
        behavioral observations, 560
        challenges in standardized tests, 561–563

Executive functions (EF) (*Continued*)
clinical interview with patient and
collateral sources, 559–560
pathognomonic signs, 560
records review, 558–559
attempts to remediate EF after TBI,
428–429
BDNF, 434
brain activity, aging and, 172–182
brain lesions associated with EF deficits,
425–426
challenges and considerations in test
selection, 202–206
appropriateness of test norms,
204–205
measures of component processes and
intelligence, 205–206
method to population(s) and research
question(s), 202–204
test reliability, 205
childhood trauma and, 495–497
COMT, 433–434
deficits after TBI, 423–425
cognitive flexibility, 424–425
inhibition, 424
planning, 425
working memory, 423–424
defining and locating, 144–147
domains, 395
Executive Cognitive Functions, 552
Executive Function Index, 201–202
functional brain changes and, 170–172
fvAD, 448
gray matter, white matter, and, 147–149
influence and interplay of internal and
exterior environmental factors,
149–151
initiation/maintenance, 552
interpretive considerations, 206–210
meta-tasking, 552–553
neurocognitive aging, 169
neurodevelopment, 146–147
neuroplasticity, 427–429
neuropsychological testing to assess EF in
TBI, 426–427
in older adulthood, 182–187
in patients with ESRD
with dialysis, 530–532
kidney transplant, 532–533
for PTSD, 507–509
recovery of EF after TBI, 429–433
cognitive rehabilitation of, 429–431

EF rehabilitation to social reintegration,
431–432
noninvasive brain stimulation, 432–433
research context, 197–199
research project investigating EF and
cognitive control, 343–348, 345t,
347t, 348f
Response Selection, 552
Social Cognition, 553
subtypes of VaD, 450–451
tools available for EF assessment, 199–202
clinical measures of EF, 199–200
experimental measures of EF, 200–201
self-and informant-reports, 201–202
training, 151–156, 508–509
in TS, 335–336
Executive functions, tests of, 389–390
Executive immaturities, 144–145
"Expectancy wave", 8
Expected utility theory, 107
Exploratory behavior, 382–384
Exposure to trauma, 487
Extrastriate cortex, 129
Extreme field-dependent exploratory behavior,
382–383
Eye movements, 321–322

F

Factor analytic methods, 170–171
Fast automatic evaluations, 342
Faulty dopamine regulation, 340–341
FEF. *See* Frontal eye fields (FEF)
"Figural" design, 562
Fine motor dexterity test, 369
Fixation point (FP), 321–322
FLE. *See* Frontal lobe epilepsy (FLE)
FLEP. *See* Frontal lobe epilepsy and
parasomnias (FLEP)
Flexibility, 397–398
Floor effect, 203–204
Fluorode oxyglucose-PET, 414
fMRI. *See* Functional magnetic resonance
imaging (fMRI)
Focal PFC lesions, 136
Focal-lesion neurology, 384
Focused attention test, 390–391
Forced stereotypic behaviors, 365
Formal learning, 151–152
FP. *See* Fixation point (FP)
FPCN. *See* Frontoparietal control network
(FPCN)

Fractionation model, 170–171
Framing effects, 111–112
Frontal Behavioral Inventory, 455–456
  scores, 461
Frontal cortices, intelligence system within,
  84–85
Frontal eye fields (FEF), 253, 322–323
Frontal lesions, 363–364
  differences between frontal lesion group
    and controls, 325–326, 325*f*
Frontal lobe epilepsy (FLE), 405, 407–410
  differentiation from psychiatric disorders
    and parasomnias, 410–412
  recognition and localization of, 406
Frontal lobe epilepsy and parasomnias
  (FLEP), 414–416, 415*t*, 416*t*
Frontal lobe(s), 365–366, 406*f*, 445–446.
  See also Dementia(s)
  and anatomy, 405–406
  clinical presentations of frontal lobe
    epilepsy, 408–410
  cognitive, emotional, memory, and
    frontostriatal circuit connectivity, 320*f*
  decision-making, 323–326
  diagnostic evaluation, 412–416
  differentiating FLE from psychiatric
    disorders and parasomnias, 410–412
  etiology and genetics, 407–408
  features of nonrapid eye movement sleep
    parasomnias *vs.* frontal lobe seizures,
    413*t*
  function, 71, 197
  gene expression
    development of cerebral neocortex and
      circuitry in human fetal brain, 42–48
    gene expression in cerebral cortex of
      human brain, 50–61
    methodological limitations of human
      transcriptomic studies, 48–50
    transcriptome, 61–62
  impairment
    frontal lobe lesions, 223–224
    schizophrenia, 225–229
  lesions, 199, 223–224
  response/behavior inhibition, 321–323,
    322*f*
  seizure to, 405
Frontal Systems Behavior Scale (FrSBe),
  201–202, 426–427
Frontal variant of AD (fvAD), 447–449
  behavior and affect, 448–449
  executive function, 448

Frontal–subcortical
  dysfunction, 229–234
  addiction, 231–232
  OCD and TS, 232–234
  networks, 525, 527, 530–532
Fronto-striato-thalamic connectivity, 365–366
Frontolimbic dysfunction, 234–240
Frontoparietal control network (FPCN), 184
Frontopolar cortex, 92
Frontopontocerebellar tract, 406
Frontostriatal
  brain circuit, 340–341
  dysfunction, 382, 384
  involvement in TS, 379–381
Frontosubcortical executive functions, 467
Frontotemporal dementia (FTD), 446, 452.
  See also Vascular dementia (VaD)
  bvFTD, 453–456
  lvFTD, 456–457
Frontotemporal lobar degeneration (FTLD),
  452–453
FrSBe. *See* Frontal Systems Behavior Scale
  (FrSBe)
FSIQ. *See* Full scale intelligence quotient
  (FSIQ)
FTD. *See* Frontotemporal dementia (FTD)
FTLD. *See* Frontotemporal lobar degeneration
  (FTLD)
FTT. *See* Fuzzy trace theory (FTT)
Full scale intelligence quotient (FSIQ), 346
Functional "hypofrontality", 262
Functional brain
  changes and EF, 170–172
  circuits, 337
Functional connectivity, 95, 170
Functional heterogeneity of human PFC,
  probing, 72–75
Functional imaging, 12
Functional lapses, 557–558
Functional magnetic resonance imaging
  (fMRI), 47, 71, 172–173, 230–231,
    338–339, 423–424
  BOLD signals, 133
  data, 120, 123
  experiment, 150–151
  IDED switching paradigm, 72–75, 73*f*, 74*f*
  studies, 129
Functional network markers of
  neuropathology, 96–97, 98*f*
Functional network perspective
  classic approach to functional brain
    mapping, 71–72

Functional network perspective (*Continued*)
combining modular and network
perspectives, 94–96
functional network markers of
neuropathology, 96–97, 98*f*
inferior frontal gyrus, 76–78
intelligence system within frontal and
parietal cortices, 84–85
limitations of modular perspectives, 75–76
network dynamics during relational
integration, 91–94, 93*f*
network-based fractionation of human
intelligence, 85–88
network-oriented cognitive constructs,
88–91
probing functional heterogeneity of human
PFC, 72–75
response inhibition, 76–78
role for RIFG in cognition, 78–81
VOODOO neuroimaging validations of
cognitive constructs, 82–84
Functional neuroimaging, 493–494
studies, 170
Functional–anatomical mappings, 91
Fuzzy trace theory (FTT), 111–112
fvAD. *See* Frontal variant of AD (fvAD)

G
GABA. *See* γ-aminobutyric acid (GABA)
GAD. *See* Generalized anxiety disorder
(GAD)
GAGE model, 110
γ-aminobutyric acid (GABA), 301–302
Gated dipole, 108
Gaussian distributions, 177
Gene expression, 342
in cerebral cortex of human brain,
50–61
in frontal lobe
development of cerebral neocortex and
circuitry, 42–48
limitations of human transcriptomic
studies, 48–50
transcriptome, 61–62
noncoding RNAs as posttranscriptional
regulators, 58–59
profile of human brain, 48–49
sex-biased, 57–58
Generalized anxiety disorder (GAD),
236–237
Genetic makeup, 396

Genetic predisposition, 429, 433–435
APOE, 434–435
BDNF, 434
COMT, 433–434
Gilbertson Twin study, 505
GingerALE v1.1 software, 173–177
Gist processing, 112
Gist traces, 111
Glasgow Coma Scale, 421–422, 534–535
Global workspace theory, 138–139
GMT. *See* Goal Management Training (GMT)
Go/no-go task, 490
Goal Management Training (GMT), 430–431
Goal setting, 431–432
Goal-directed perceptual processing, 182–183
DECHA, 185–187
modulation of network dynamics, 183–185
GPi. *See* Internal globus pallidus (GPi)
GPT. *See* Grooved Pegboard Test (GPT)
"Graceful degradation", 137
"Graveyard of neuropathologists", 225
Gray matter, 147–149
Grooved Pegboard Test (GPT), 369
Grossberg–Pearson model, 114
Group differences, 206–207
Guanfacine, 33–34

H
Habit reversal training (HRT), 351–352
Habits, 311
habit-based behavior, 230
nodes, 117
Habitual behavior, 229–234
addiction, 231–232
OCD and TS, 232–234
Habitual responses, 116–120
Stroop test models, 119–120
WCST model, 116–119
Hallucinations, 225
HAND. *See* HIV-associated neurocognitive
disorders (HAND)
Handedness, 366
HC. *See* Healthy controls (HC)
HD. *See* Huntington's disease (HD)
HE. *See* Hepatic encephalopathy (HE)
Healthy controls (HC), 254
Hemi-Parkinsonian syndromes (Hemi-PD
syndromes), 364–366, 379–381
Hemi-Tourette's syndromes (Hemi-TS),
365–366
and clinical diagnosis, 382–383

Hepatic encephalopathy (HE), 525–526, 534–536
Heroin, 231
High-functioning autism, 144–145
Higher order theories of consciousness, 138–139
Hippocampus, 225–226, 494
HIV. *See* Human immunodeficiency virus (HIV)
HIV-associated neurocognitive disorders (HAND), 533
Hopkins Verbal Learning Test—Revised (HVLT-R), 391
Hot EF tasks, 338–340, 351
HRT. *See* Habit reversal training (HRT)
"Hub-genes", 51–52
Human immunodeficiency virus (HIV), 525–526, 533–534
Human(s), 337
  behavior, 229, 335–336
  brain imaging studies, 122
  brain transcriptome, 48–49, 51–52
    sex-biased gene expression patterns and laterality of, 57–58
    specificities during postnatal period, 55–57
  brain
    frontal lobe, 41
    gene expression in cerebral cortex, 50–61
    gene expression profile, 48–49
  fetal brain
    cortical pathway development,

    45*f*
    development of cerebral neocortex and circuitry, 42–48
    transient patterns of lamination in neocortical cerebral wall, 44*f*
  frontal cortex, 61–62
  lesion, 395
  methodological limitations of human transcriptomic studies, 48–50
  neocortical transcriptome specificities, 52–54
  network-based fractionation of human intelligence, 85–88
  probing functional heterogeneity of human PFC, 72–75
  transcriptomic studies for human cerebral cortex evolution, 59–61

Huntington, George, 465
Huntington's disease (HD), 302–303, 446, 465–467. *See also* Parkinson's disease (PD)
  behavior and affect, 467
  executive dysfunction in, 308–309
  executive functions, 466
HVLT-R. *See* Hopkins Verbal Learning Test—Revised (HVLT-R)
Hyperactivation, 272, 493–494
Hyperactivity, 383–384
Hyperactivity–impulsivity, 390–391
Hypermotor seizures, 410
Hypertension, 526–527
Hyperthyroidism, 536–538
Hypo-activation, 272, 493–494
Hypothalamus, 220–222
Hypothyroidism, 536–538

I

IADL. *See* Instrumental activities of daily living (IADL)
Ictal automatisms, 223–224
Ictal electroencephalography/single photon emission computed tomography, 326
Ictal panic, 409, 411
IDED. *See* Intradimensional–extradimensional (IDED)
IFC. *See* Inferior frontal cortex (IFC)
IFS. *See* Inferior frontal sulcus (IFS)
IGT. *See* Iowa Gambling Task (IGT)
IHT. *See* Innlandet Hospital Trust (IHT)
Imitation behavior, 223–224
Immediate memory, 490
ImmunoEM studies in monkeys, 32–33
Impairments, 206–207
Impulse dysregulation, 338–339
Impulsive responses, 344
"Inappropriate syndrome", 553, 560
Indirect striatum pathways, 110
Inferior frontal cortex (IFC), 220–222
Inferior frontal gyrus, 76–78, 395
Inferior frontal sulcus (IFS), 75
  network, 86, 92
Inferior parietal cortex (IPC), 84–85
Informant-reports, 201–202
Information
  entropy, 251
  theory approach to cognitive control, 250–252

Inhibition, 143, 171, 180, 424
Inhibitory control, 143–147, 154–156, 305
Inhibitory mechanisms, 343
Inhibitory response style, 348
Innlandet Hospital Trust (IHT), 346, 366, 368
Instrumental activities of daily living (IADL), 430, 555–556
Intelligence quotient scores (IQ scores), 207, 499–500
Intelligence system within frontal and parietal cortices, 84–85
Interference control from disruption, 321
Intermittent functional lapses, 557, 564
Internal feedback "reafference", 6–7
Internal globus pallidus (GPi), 110
International Affective Picture System, 323–325
International League Against Epilepsy, 409
Interpretive considerations, 206–210
    impairments *vs.* group differences, 206–207
    interpretation of repeat assessments, 207–208
    limitations in interpreting factor structures, 208–209
    recognizing difference between self-report and performance-based measures, 209–210
Interstimulus interval (ISI), 390–391
"Intolerance of uncertainty", 237
Intradimensional–extradimensional (IDED), 72, 73*f*, 74*f*
Intraparietal sulcus (IPS), 253
Iowa Gambling Task (IGT), 109, 344
IPC. *See* Inferior parietal cortex (IPC)
IPS. *See* Intraparietal sulcus (IPS)
IQ scores. *See* Intelligence quotient scores (IQ scores)
ISI. *See* Interstimulus interval (ISI)
Item-context binding process, 145–146
Iterative Reprocessing Model, 342

J
"Jumping to conclusions" bias, 227
"Just world" hypothesis, 507

K
KCNT1. *See* Sodium-activated potassium channel subunit 1 (KCNT1)
Kiddie Schedule for Affective Disorders and Schizophrenia (K-SADS), 368

Kidney transplant, executive function in patients with ESRD, 532–533
Klüver–Bucy syndrome, 454–455

L
Lancaster transformation, 177
Language variant FTD (lvFTD), 452, 456–457
Late-onset Alzheimer's disease (loAD), 446
Lateral PFC, 323–325
Lateralization
    of frontostriatal dysfunction, 382
    lateralized focal-lesion effects, 381
    lateralized nigrostriatal dysfunction, 365
    lateralized prefrontal lesions, 379–381
Learning disorder (LD), 145–146, 319
Left "hemi-TS", 379, 381*t*
    group, 373–379
    "left hemi-TS"/presumed right frontostriatal dysfunction, 373
    subtype, 381
Left frontostriatal system, 381
Left-sided lesions/epileptic foci (LLF), 328–329
Lesion effects, 363–364
Lesion studies, 133–134
Lesion study, 328–329
    argument based on, 133–134
"Lesion" argument, responses to, 134–136
Letter Fluency test (LF test), 390
Letter Number Sequencing Test (LN Sequencing Test), 389, 397
LF test. *See* Letter Fluency test (LF test)
LFPC network, 92, 95–97
"Limbic" frontal areas, 302
Lipids, 434–435
LIST PARSE network, 114–115
LLF. *See* Left-sided lesions/epileptic foci (LLF)
LN Sequencing Test. *See* Letter Number Sequencing Test (LN Sequencing Test)
loAD. *See* Late-onset Alzheimer's disease (loAD)
LOC. *See* Loss of consciousness (LOC)
Local neural dysfunction, 421
Logopenic PPA, 452
Longitudinal studies, 495, 507
Loss of consciousness (LOC), 500–501
Lower order processes, 208
Luria's tapping test, 146–147
lvFTD. *See* Language variant FTD (lvFTD)

M

Magnetic resonance imaging (MRI), 106, 323–325, 414
Major depressive disorder (MDD), 236, 267, 269t
Marginal zone (MZ), 42–44
"Mark organ", 4
mCBT. *See* Modified CBT (mCBT)
MD cortex. *See* Multiple demand cortex (MD cortex)
MD nuclei. *See* Mediodorsal nuclei (MD nuclei)
MDD. *See* Major depressive disorder (MDD)
Medial orbitofrontal cortex, 395
Medial prefrontal cortex (mPFC), 225–226, 351–352
Medical neuropsychology, 525
Mediodorsal nuclei (MD nuclei), 46
Meditation, 152–153
Medline, 172–173
Memory
    cells, 10
    short-term, 145–146
    tests, 391
Memory-guided saccade task (MGST), 321–322, 322f
Mental disorders
    alpha-2A noradrenergic influence, 33–34
    catecholamine modulation of mechanisms, 32–33
    cortical connections within ventral and medial prefrontal cortex, 24f
    dlPFC, 25–26
    dlPFC network connections, 29–32
    molecular regulation of dlPFC representational circuits, 28–29, 28f
    PFC, 21
    physiology and microcircuitry of working memory, 26–28
    topography of PFC and its relevance to neuropsychiatric pathology, 22–25, 22f
    visual and auditory processing streams in PFC, 23f
Mental processes, 335, 343
Mental representations, 21
Mesolimbic projection, 302
Mesolimbic/mesocortical pathways, 304–305
Met allele, 434
Meta-tasking, 552–553
Metaanalysis, 82–83
    analysis, 171

metaanalytic research, 396–398
methods
    creation of ALE maps, 173–177
    selection of studies, 172–173, 174t
    of neuroimaging studies, 254
results
    older adults, 180–182
    younger adults, 177–179
Metabolic products, 398
Metacognition, 134
Metacognitive abilities, 336
Methadone, 398
Methamphetamine, 395, 397–398
MGST. *See* Memory-guided saccade task (MGST)
Microcircuitry of working memory, 26–28
MicroRNAs (miRNA), 58–61
Midbrain basal ganglia, 302
Mild TBIs (mTBI), 500–502
miRNA. *See* MicroRNAs (miRNA)
Mischel's marshmallow test, 146–147
MND. *See* Motor neuron disease (MND)
MNI. *See* Montreal Neurological Institute (MNI)
MoCA. *See* Montreal Cognitive Assessment (MoCA)
"Model-free learning", 229–230
Modern neuroscience, 143–145
Modified CBT (mCBT), 326–327
    converted mCBT score, 327
Modular perspectives, 83, 85
    limitations of, 75–76
"Modules", 51–52
Molecular regulation of dlPFC representational circuits, 28–29, 28f
Monoptic visual masking process, 130–131
Montreal Cognitive Assessment (MoCA), 204
Montreal Neurological Institute (MNI), 279
Mood
    emotional and cognitive perseveration in disorders of, 234–240
    perseveration, 237–240
Motor manifestations, 408–409
Motor neuron disease (MND), 452–453, 461–462
Motor response inhibition, 76
mPFC. *See* Medial prefrontal cortex (mPFC)
MRI. *See* Magnetic resonance imaging (MRI)
msPFC. *See* Superior medial PFC (msPFC)
mTBI. *See* Mild TBIs (mTBI)
Multilingual learning, 153–154

Multiple demand cortex (MD cortex), 84–85, 84f
  distinct functional networks within, 87f
  subnetworks of, 86
Multivoxel pattern analysis (MVPA), 133
Musical training, 154–155
MVPA. *See* Multivoxel pattern analysis (MVPA)
Myelination, 148–149
MZ. *See* Marginal zone (MZ)

N

N-Methyl-D-aspartate receptor (NMDAR), 23–24, 28–29
NAcc. *See* Nucleus accumbens (NAcc)
nAChR. *See* nicotinic acetylcholine receptor (nAChR)
NAP. *See* Negative affect priming (NAP)
National Comorbidity Survey, 489
NCSE. *See* Nonconvulsive status epilepticus (NCSE)
Negative affect priming (NAP), 238
Network dynamics during relational integration, 91–94, 93f
Network-based fractionation of human intelligence, 85–88
Network-oriented cognitive constructs, 88–91
Neural mechanism, 337–338
Neural networks, 106, 220–222, 221f, 322–323
  models, 105
    cognitive control models, 120–122
    decision making models, 107–113
    executive functions, 106
    habitual responses, 116–120
    high-level cognitive functions, 122
    neuro-computational modeling, 123
    sequence learning and working memory, models of, 113–116
Neural systems, 150, 337
Neuro-computational modeling, 123
Neuroanatomy, 319
  expressions, 384
Neurobiological/neurobiology, 348
  dysfunction, 340
  model, 340, 349
  perspective, 351–352
Neurocognitive
  aging, 169. *See also* Executive functions (EF)
  assessment, 368–369

  focused attention test, 390–391
  memory tests, 391
  sustained attention test, 390–391
  tests of executive functions, 389–390
  deficits in PTSD, 493–494
  domains, 197
  healthy norms, 557–558
  impairment, 528
  tests, 338, 373
Neurodegeneration, 454, 465–466
  executive impairment in neurodegenerative diseases, 458t
  neurodegenerative disorders, 446
  neurodegenerative process, 445–446
Neurodevelopment(al)
  disorders, 342–344
    cognitive, emotional, memory, and frontostriatal circuit connectivity, 320f
    decision-making, 323–326, 324f, 325f
    response/behavior inhibition, 321–323, 322f
    temporal integration, 326–329, 327f
  of EFs, 146–147
    defining and locating, 144–147
    executive function training, 151–156
    gray matter, white matter, and, 147–149
    influence and interplay of internal and exterior environmental factors, 149–151
Neuroimaging, 8, 395
  signals, 8
  studies, 335
  tools, 169
Neuronal circuitry, 42
Neuropathology, functional network markers of, 96–97, 98f
Neuroplasticity, 350, 427–429
Neuropsychiatric
  circles, 384
  disorders, 229
  illness
    emotional and cognitive perseveration in disorders of mood and anxiety, 234–240
    environmental factors, 219–220
    habitual behavior and frontal–subcortical dysfunction, 229–234
    perseveration as manifestation of frontal lobe impairment, 223–229
    pathology, 22–25, 22f

Neuropsychological/neuropsychology,
    205–206, 554
  assessment, 557
  basis, 227–228
  literature, 382–383, 457
  performance, 350
  studies, 395, 537
  tasks, 349
  tests, 368–369
    ecological tests for evaluating EF,
      426–427
    standard tests of EF, 426
Neuroregeneration, 434
Neuroscience, 154–155
  balkanization of clinical, 384
Neuroticism, 555
Neurotransmitters, 340–341
Next-generation sequencing, 61–62
NFL. See Nocturnal frontal lobe (NFL)
NFLE. See Nocturnal frontal lobe epilepsy
    (NFLE)
nfvPPA. See Nonfluent variant PPA (nfvPPA)
nic-α7R. See Nicotinic alpha-7 receptors (nic-
    α7R)
nicotinic acetylcholine receptor (nAChR), 407
Nicotinic alpha-7 receptors (nic-α7R), 28–29
Nigrostriatal
  dysfunction, 365–366
  interface, 363
  involvement in PD, 379–381
  pathway, 302
NMDAR. See N-Methyl-D-aspartate receptor
    (NMDAR)
No-report binocular rivalry paradigm,
    131–132
"No-report" argument
  against PFC's in consciousness, 129–132
  responses to, 132–133
Nocturnal frontal lobe (NFL), 88–89
  functional network markers of
    neuropathology, 96–97, 98f
Nocturnal frontal lobe epilepsy (NFLE), 406,
    410, 412
Noncoding RNAs, 58–59
Nonconvulsive status epilepticus (NCSE), 410
Nonfluent variant PPA (nfvPPA), 452
Noninvasive brain stimulation, 432–433
Nonneural cognitive model of decisions, 112
Nonneurogenic seizures, 410–411
Nonrapid eye movements (NREM), 406
Nonverbal reasoning, 85
Norepinephrine, 29, 433–434

Norms, test, 204–205
NREM. See Nonrapid eye movements
    (NREM)
Nucleus accumbens (NAcc), 301–302
  core, 311–312

O
Obsessive compulsive disorder (OCD), 25,
    223, 232–234, 302–303, 334
Oculomotor delayed response (ODR), 26
OFC. See Orbitofrontal cortex (OFC)
Older adults
  brain networks and EF in, 182–187
  metaanalysis result, 180–182
Olfactory tubercle, 301–302
Oligonucleotide microarrays, 48–49, 61–62
Opioids, 395, 398
Optokinetic nystagmus, 130–131
Orbitofrontal cortex (OFC), 109–110,
    222–223, 319–321, 351–352
Orbitofrontal seizures, 409
Orienting attention, 151–152
Overconsumption, 398

P
PA cycle. See Perception–action cycle (PA
    cycle)
Page–Norris model, 114
PANDAS. See Pediatric autoimmune
    neuropsychiatric disorder associated
    with Streptococcus (PANDAS)
Panic attack, 411, 411t
Parahippocampal gyrus function, 225–226
Parallel distributed processing networks (PDP
    networks), 106, 137
Paranoid delusions, 227–228
Parasomnias, differentiating FLE from,
    410–412
Parent reporting, 373–379
Parietal cortices, intelligence system within,
    84–85
Parietal–temporal–occipital cortex (PTO
    cortex), 4–6, 8
Parkinson's disease (PD), 118, 302–303, 363,
    450–451, 462–463. See also
    Huntington's disease (HD)
  behavior and affect, 463
  executive dysfunction in, 303–308
  executive functions, 462–463
  nigrostriatal in, 379–381

Paroxysmal arousals. *See* Very brief motor
  seizures
Pathognomonic signs, EF, 560
Pavlovian conditioning, 122
PCS. *See* Precentral sulcus (PCS)
PCW. *See* Postconceptional weeks (PCW)
PD. *See* Parkinson's disease (PD)
PD with dementia (PDD), 446
PDE4A. *See* Phosphodiesterase 4A (PDE4A)
PDP networks. *See* Parallel distributed
  processing networks (PDP networks)
PE. *See* Prolonged exposure (PE)
Pediatric autoimmune neuropsychiatric
  disorder associated with *Streptococcus*
  (PANDAS), 232–233
Penetrating TBI (pTBI), 421
Perception–action cycle (PA cycle), 4–7, 6f
Performance-based measures, 209–210
PET. *See* Positron emission tomography
  (PET)
PFC. *See* Prefrontal cortex (PFC)
Pharmacogenetic study, 398
Pharmacotherapy, 398
"Phenocopy group", 453–454
Phonological loop systems, 115
Phosphodiesterase 4A (PDE4A), 31–32
"Phyletic memory", 3
PKA. *See* Protein Kinase A (PKA)
PKC. *See* Protein kinase C (PKC)
Plasticity, 6–7, 143
Population(s)
  method, 202–204
  population-based norms, 557–558
Portal-Systemic Encephalopathy Syndrome
  Test, 535
Positron emission tomography (PET),
  172–173, 407
Postconceptional weeks (PCW), 42–44
"Posterior cortical" pattern, 303
Posttranscriptional regulators of gene
  expression, noncoding RNAs as,
  58–59
Posttraumatic stress disorder (PTSD),
  234–235, 487
  brain imaging research, 493–495
  cognitive functioning in, 489–493
    executive function, 491–492
    working memory, 492–493
  confounding factors, 498–506
    depression, 503–504
    other comorbidities, 505–506
    premorbid functioning, 499–500
    substance use, 504–505
    traumatic brain injury, 500–503

developmental factors, 495–498
  diagnosis and prevalence of, 488–489
  executive function and treatment for,
    507–509
  impaired fear extinction in, 234–236
Practice effect(s), 207–208
Prazosin, 33
Precentral sulcus (PCS), 136
Prefrontal cortex (PFC), 21, 42, 46, 110, 120,
  129, 151, 171, 223–224, 249–250,
  319, 335, 337, 343, 363, 395, 424.
  See also Dorsolateral prefrontal cortex
  (DLPFC)
  argument based on lesion studies, 133–134
  early neuroimaging evidence, 129
  executive functions, 4
  implications for consciousness theories,
    138–139
  layering, 115
  lesions, 136–138
  "no-report" argument against PFC's,
    129–132
  PFC–basal ganglia interactions, 115, 121
    catecholamine modulation of
      mechanisms, 32–33
    topography and relevance to
      neuropsychiatric pathology, 22–25,
      22f
  responses to "lesion" argument, 134–136
  responses to no-report argument, 132–133
Prefrontal dopamine, 396, 433–434
Prefrontal executive function, 116
  decision-making, 12–15
  executive attention, 7–10
  PA cycle, 4–7
  working memory, 10–12
Prefrontal functions, 319
Prefrontal lesions, 341–342, 363–364
Premorbid functioning, 499–500
Prenatal period, human neocortical
  transcriptome specificities during,
  52–54
Presupplementary motor area (preSMA),
  84–85
Primary progressive aphasia (PPA).
  See Language variant FTD (lvFTD)
Principal component analyses, 89, 90f
Production system, 118
Progressive supranuclear palsy (PSP),
  446
Progressive supranuclear palsy and
  corticobasal syndrome (PSP-CBS),
  457–461
  behavior and affect, 460–461

executive functions, 457–460
  Luria's alternate designs and multiple loop
    drawings, 460*f*
Prolonged exposure (PE), 507–508
Prolonged seizures, 410
Prospect theory, 108, 111
Protein Kinase A (PKA), 29–30
Protein kinase C (PKC), 29–30
PSP. *See* Progressive supranuclear palsy (PSP)
PSP-CBS. *See* Progressive supranuclear palsy
    and corticobasal syndrome (PSP-CBS)
PSP-Richardson syndrome (PSP-RS), 457
Psychiatric disorders, 234
  differentiating FLE from, 410–412
Psychomotor, 532
Psychosis, 228–229
PsycINFO, 172–173
pTBI. *See* Penetrating TBI (pTBI)
PTO cortex. *See* Parietal–temporal–occipital
    cortex (PTO cortex)
PTSD. *See* Posttraumatic stress disorder (PTSD)

Q
Quantitative theory, 105, 107

R
R-O. *See* Response-outcome (R-O)
RA. *See* Rheumatoid arthritis (RA)
rCBF. *See* Regional cerebral blood flow
    (rCBF)
RCMAS-2. *See* Revised Children's Manifest
    Anxiety Scale, second edition
    (RCMAS-2)
"Readiness potential", 8
Reasoning, 86, 448
  nonverbal, 85
  relational, 92, 99
  skill, 144–147, 154–155
  temporal integration, 326–329
  in young children, 144–145
Regional cerebral blood flow (rCBF), 226
Regional Committee for Medical Research
    Ethics in Eastern Norway (REK-Øst),
    368
Regions of interest (ROIs), 86
Regression analyses, 202
Regulator of G protein signaling 4 (RGS4), 32
Rehabilitation studies, 188
Reinforcement learning, 144–145
REK-Øst. *See* Regional Committee for
    Medical Research Ethics in Eastern
    Norway (REK-Øst)
Relational integration, network dynamics
    during, 91–94, 93*f*

Relational reasoning, 92, 99
Reliability, test, 205
Repeat assessments, interpretation of, 207–208
Repetitive motor activity (RMA), 405
Repetitive transcranial magnetic stimulation
    (rTMS), 135, 432
Research question(s) method, 202–204
Response inhibition, 76–78, 395–398
Response Selection, 552
Response-outcome (R-O), 222–223
Response/behavior inhibition, 321–323
  differences between ADHD and controls,
    322–323
  subjects and methods, 321–322, 322*f*
Revised Children's Manifest Anxiety Scale,
    second edition (RCMAS-2), 392
Reward-based behaviors, 149
Rey–Osterrieth complex figure test, 490
RGS4. *See* Regulator of G protein signaling 4
    (RGS4)
Rheumatoid arthritis (RA), 538–540
Rhodes's competitive queuing model,
    114
RIFG. *See* Right inferior frontal gyrus (RIFG)
Right "hemi-TS", 373, 379, 381*t*
  group, 373–379
  subtype, 381
Right inferior frontal gyrus (RIFG), 77
  in cognition, 78–81
Right-sided lesions/epileptic foci (RLF),
    328–329
RMA. *See* Repetitive motor activity (RMA)
RNA, 49
RNA sequencing (RNA-seq), 41, 48–49
*ROBO*1 gene, 53
Robust executive function skills, 155–156
ROIs. *See* Regions of interest (ROIs)
Rostrolateral cortex, 92
rTMS. *See* Repetitive transcranial magnetic
    stimulation (rTMS)
Rumination
  in depression, 237–240
  in GAD, 236–237

S
Saccade, 26, 136, 321–322
Salience, 150–151
  network, 80, 220–222
  system, 112–113
Schizophrenia (SZ), 23–25, 42, 55, 118–119,
    225–229, 262–267
  ALE metaanalysis, 263*f*
  of neuroimaging studies, 264*t*

Science Citation Index, 172–173
SD. *See* Standard deviations (SD)
SDMT. *See* Symbol digit modalities test (SDMT)
Seizures of frontal lobe, 408–409
"Self-control", 21, 143, 198–199, 335–336
Self-regulation, 151–152, 198–199, 430, 450–451
Self-report(s), 201–202, 209–210
Semantic dementia. *See* Semantic variant PPA (svPPA)
Semantic variant PPA (svPPA), 452
Sensory stimuli, 121
Sequence learning, neural network models of, 113–116
Serotonin, 396
Sex-biased gene expression patterns and laterality
   of human brain transcriptome, 57–58
Sexual hormones, 337
Short Mood and Feelings Questionnaire (SMFQ), 392
Short-term memory, 145–146
Short/short genotype, 396
Signature injury, 501–502
Silver bullet, 197–198
Similarity effect, 109
Single photon emission computed tomography (SPECT), 414
SMA. *See* Supplementary motor area (SMA)
SMFQ. *See* Short Mood and Feelings Questionnaire (SMFQ)
SMH. *See* Somatic marker hypothesis (SMH)
SN. *See* Substantia nigra (SN)
S-O. *See* Stimulus-outcome (S-O)
Social cognition, 148, 553
Social reintegration, EF rehabilitation to, 431–432
Sodium-activated potassium channel subunit 1 (KCNT1), 408
Somatic marker hypothesis (SMH), 323
Somatic markers, 110
Spatial ICA, 86, 87*f*, 92
SPECT. *See* Single photon emission computed tomography (SPECT)
SPL. *See* Superior parietal lobule (SPL)
SSR. *See* Sympathetic skin responses (SSR)
SSRT. *See* Stop signal response time (SSRT)
SST. *See* Stop Signal Task (SST)
STAIC. *See* State-Trait Anxiety Inventory for Children (STAIC)
Standard deviations (SD), 207
Standard tests of EF, 426
Standardized tests, challenges in, 561–563

State-Trait Anxiety Inventory for Children (STAIC), 392
Stero-EEG studies, 412
STG. *See* Superior temporal gyrus (STG)
Stimulus-outcome (S-O), 222–223
Stokes, 133
Stop signal response time (SSRT), 76–77
Stop Signal Task (SST), 76, 77*f*, 78, 81*f*
Store–ignore–recall task, 116
Strategy application disorder, 553
Stress
   catecholamine modulation of mechanisms, 32–33
   stress-induced brain dysfunction, 309–310
   test, 556
Striatal cells, 302
Striatal disorders, EF in
   anatomical and functional organization of striatum, 301–303
   executive dysfunction
      in chronic stress, 309–312
      in HD, 308–309
      in PD, 303–308
Striatal medium spiny neurons, 302
Striatum, 110, 363, 365–366
   anatomical and functional organization of, 301–303
Stroop Color Word Test, 539–540
Stroop test, 116, 118, 467–470
   models, 119–120
Structural equation modeling, 145–146
Structural neuroimaging, 149, 494–495
Substance use, 504–505
Substantia nigra (SN), 301–302
Subthalamic nucleus, 343
Subtyping TS, 365–366
   clinical diagnosis and left *vs.* right "hemi-TS", 379, 381*t*
   clinical questionnaires and scales, 368
   comparison, 373–379, 374*t*, 375*t*, 376*t*, 377*t*, 378*t*, 380*t*
   cutting across taxonomic boundaries and redefining TS, 384–385
   data analyses, 369
   ethics statement, 368
   exploratory behavior *vs.* hyperactivity, 383–384
   "hemi-TS" and clinical diagnosis, 382–383
   and lateralized frontostriatal involvement, 379–381
   neurocognitive assessment, 368–369
   participants, 366–367, 367*t*

test of fine motor dexterity, 369
TS *vs.* TDC sample comparison, 369–372,
    370*t*, 371*t*, 372*t*
Subventricular zone, 42–44
Superior medial PFC (msPFC), 181
Superior parietal lobule (SPL), 263
Superior temporal gyrus (STG), 258–259
Supervisory processes, 532
Supplemental method, 279
Supplementary motor area (SMA), 220–222,
    258–259
Surprise in information theory, 251
Sustained attention test, 390–391
svPPA. *See* Semantic variant PPA (svPPA)
Switching cost, 201
Symbol digit modalities test (SDMT),
    308
Sympathetic skin responses (SSR), 323,
    325–326
Synaptic function, 342
SZ. *See* Schizophrenia (SZ)

T

Target detection, 75–76, 78, 79*f*, 84–85
Task switching, 121, 170–173, 174*t*, 177,
    179*t*, 180, 187–188
Taylor–Taylor sequence model, 116
TBI. *See* Traumatic brain injury (TBI)
TD individuals. *See* Typically developing
    individuals (TD individuals)
TDC. *See* Typically developing control (TDC)
tDCS. *See* Transcranial direct current
    stimulation (tDCS)
Telencephalon, patterning of, 54
Temper control, 336
Temporal integration, 319–321, 326–329
    developmental changes in cognitive
        reasoning, 327–328, 328*f*
    lesion study, 328–329
    subjects and methods, 326–327, 327*f*
Temporolimbic hyperactivity, 227–228
Test norms, 204–205
Test reliability, 205
Theoretical cognitive neuroscience,
    122
Theory of evolution, 3
3D Gaussian functions, 177
Thyroid disease, 536–538
"Tic(s)", 333–334, 336–338
    chronic tic disorder, 341
    expression, factors influence,
        340–342
    severity, 391

TMS. *See* Transcranial magnetic stimulation
    (TMS)
TMT. *See* Trail Making Test (TMT)
TMT 4. *See* Trail Making Test, condition 4
    (TMT 4)
Top-down cognitive processing, 138
Top-down therapy, 351–352
Top-down/bottom-up framework, 335–336
Tourette syndrome (TS), 232–234, 333–335
    brain adaptation and compensatory
        behavior, 342–343
    clinical implications, 351–352
    critical period of development, 336–340
    daunting disorder, 348–351
    diagnostic instruments, 389–393
    executive functions, 335–336
    factors influence tic expression, 340–342
    frontostriatal in, 379–381
    future research, 352
    research project investigating EF and
        cognitive control, 343–348, 345*t*,
        347*t*, 348*f*
    subtyping, 365–366
Tower Test, 390
Trail Making Test (TMT), 303–304, 448,
    490, 535
Trail Making Test, condition 4 (TMT 4),
    389–390
Transcranial direct current stimulation (tDCS),
    432
    studies in TBI, 432–433
Transcranial magnetic stimulation (TMS),
    134, 182–183, 432
    to DLPFC, 135
    studies in TBI, 432–433
Transcriptome, 61–62
    analyses on pyramidal cells, 23–24
    human brain, 49–52, 55–58
    human neocortical, 52–54
    transcriptomic studies, 59–61
Trauma. *See also* Posttraumatic stress disorder
    (PTSD)
    childhood, 495–497
    exposure, 487–489
    trauma-related symptoms, 492
Traumatic brain injury (TBI), 363, 421–422,
    488, 500–503
    attempts to remediate EF after, 428–429
    classification of, 422*t*
    EF deficits after, 423–425
    EF neuroplasticity and, 427–429
    genetic predisposition, EF, and, 433–435
    location of brain lesions associated with EF
        deficits, 425–426

Traumatic brain injury (TBI) (*Continued*)
  neuropsychological testing to assess EF,
    426–427
  recovery of EF after, 429–433
Triple-Decker, 363–365, 364*f*
TS. *See* Tourette syndrome (TS)
Turing machine, 137
Type 1 diabetes mellitus (DM1), 527–530
Type 2 diabetes mellitus (DM2), 527–530
Typically developing control (TDC), 366,
    369–372, 370*t*, 371*t*, 372*t*
Typically developing individuals (TD
    individuals), 254–255

U

Unconditioned stimulus (US), 235–236
Uncontrollable emotional outbursts, 338
Utility theory, 108
Utilization behavior, 223–224, 454–455

V

VAC. *See* Visual association cortex (VAC)
VaD. *See* Vascular dementia (VaD)
val/val genotype, 396
Val158Met polymorphism, 433–434
Vascular dementia (VaD), 446, 449–451.
    See also Frontotemporal dementia
    (FTD)
  executive impairment in neurodegenerative
    diseases, 458*t*
  subtypes and relationship to frontal lobe
    function
    behavior and affect, 451
    executive functions, 450–451
vEEG. *See* Video EEG (vEEG)
Ventral brain stem, dopaminergic nuclei of,
    363
Ventral striatal regions, 302–303
Ventral tegmental area (VTA), 301–302
Ventricular zone, 42–44
Ventrolateral prefrontal cortex (VLPFC),
    225–226, 266–267, 395
Ventromedial cortex, pathology of, 25
Ventromedial prefrontal cortex (VMPFC),
    110, 222–223, 323
Verbal fluency, 390, 426
Verbatim traces, 111
Very brief motor seizures, 410
Video EEG (vEEG), 410–411
"Virtual lesion" of DLPFC, 134
Visual association cortex (VAC), 182–183
Visual matrix reasoning task, 152–153

Visual spatial sketchpad, 423
Visual–haptic memory cells, 10
Visuospatial sketchpad systems, 115
Visuospatial working memory, cellular basis
    of, 26
VLPFC. *See* Ventrolateral prefrontal cortex
    (VLPFC)
VMPFC. *See* Ventromedial prefrontal cortex
    (VMPFC)
VOODOO neuroimaging validations of
    cognitive constructs, 82–84
Voxel-based metaanalytic technique,
    173–177
VTA. *See* Ventral tegmental area (VTA)

W

WASI. *See* Wechsler Abbreviated Scale of
    Intelligence (WASI)
WCST. *See* Wisconsin Card Sorting Test
    (WCST)
Wechsler Abbreviated Scale of Intelligence
    (WASI), 366, 367*t*
White matter, 147–149, 526–527
Wisconsin Card Sorting Test (WCST), 72,
    116–119, 203, 220–222, 303–304,
    424–425, 490, 539
Witty Ticcy Ray, 333
Working memory, 10–12, 86, 143, 145–146,
    149, 180, 302–303, 310, 395–398,
    423–424, 492–493
  CANTAB Spatial Working Memory,
    397
  neural network models of, 113–116
  physiology and microcircuitry of, 26–28
  visuospatial working memory, cellular basis
    of, 26
Working memory, 389

Y

Yale Global Tic Severity Scale (YGTSS),
    368, 380*t*, 391
Younger adults
  brain function in, 181
  DN engagement, 186–187
  metaanalysis result, 177–179
  older *vs.*, 75, 170
  regions of activation, 179*t*
  reliable patterns of brain activity, 178*f*

Z

Zelazo's card sort task, 146–147